MYERS-BRIGGS TYPE INDICATOR®
ATLAS of TYPE TABLES™

GERALD P. MACDAID ▪ MARY H. MCCAULLEY ▪ RICHARD I. KAINZ

C A P T®

Center for Applications of Psychological Type, Inc.

Atlas of Type Tables™

Sixth Printing 2007

Published by the
Center for Applications of Psychological Type, Inc.
2815 N.W. 13th Street, Suite 401
Gainesville, FL 32609
(352) 375-0160
www.capt.org

Library of Congress Cataloging-in-Publication Data

Macdaid, Gerald P., date-
     Myers-Briggs type indicator atlas of type tables
     1. Myers-Briggs Type Indicator—Tables.
     2. Typology (Psychology)—Tables.
I. McCaulley, Mary H., date-
II. Kainz, Richard I., date-
III. Title.
BF698.8.M94M33 1986 155.2'64'0212 86-32635

ISBN 0-935652-13-2
ISBN 13 978-0-935652-13-0

Manufactured in the United States of America.

CONTENTS

INTRODUCTION

The publication of the Atlas of Type Tables is an important step in a major goal of the Center for Applications of Psychological Type (CAPT)-- to make information about MBTI types readily available to MBTI users. The Atlas is designed for career counselors, therapists, and researchers who use the MBTI in their work.

Career counselors will find information about the kinds of careers which do and do not attract each of the sixteen types, or groups of the types. This information is not meant to be used to tell a person to enter or to stay out of any occupation. It is useful to give a perspective on the kinds of occupations that are more likely to be a match or mismatch with a person's type preferences. The use of the MBTI in career counseling is discussed in Chapter 7 of the MBTI Manual.

Counselors working with individuals will find the data useful in helping the rare types in an occupation to see why they sometimes have trouble finding kindred spirits, and where they may find more people like themselves. All types are interested in how many other people are like them and where they are likely to find them.

MBTI users working with organizations will find the tables useful in understanding the "personality" of organizations--why different groups are like they are. Judiciously chosen type tables can help a group see why their way of working together is different from that of another group with a different mix of types. Tables lead to questions such as "What does it mean that we have 45% TJ types?" "What does it mean that we have no SF types?"

Researchers find the data useful in two ways. First, type tables are part of the data which provide construct validity of type theory. Second, the tables, particularly the normative tables, provide base populations with which research populations can be compared. These comparisons are an important part of MBTI research; if, for example, your sample of elementary school teachers is similar to the existing data on elementary school teachers, you will feel more comfortable generalizing from your results than if your population is very different from the known populations. Guidelines for using type tables in counseling and in research are given in Chapter 7 of the Manual.

Each set of tables is preceded by a brief comment section designed to remind readers of theoretical expectations, or to alert readers to noticeable trends. The reader is assumed to be familiar with information in this preface, with the Manual, especially Chapters 4 and 7, and with other basic readings about the MBTI. We do not attempt to provide the background in understanding type tables which is readily available in those sources.

Sources of Data for the MBTI Atlas

There are three sources of data in the Atlas:

1. The CAPT MBTI Data Bank, generated from the CAPT scoring service which began in 1971 and includes more than 250,000 records.

2. Data shared with CAPT by MBTI users as part of the Type Table Project. These data are presented as separate tables, each attributed to the contributor.

3. Tables discovered in the published literature and used with the authors' permission.

All users of this Atlas owe appreciation to those who took the time to assemble and share their data.

Format of the Atlas

The First Edition contains data primarily from the MBTI Data Bank, and a few contributed or research samples. It provides an overview of all the areas. New editions will be published annually. These will bring composite samples up to date and will add new tables contributed by MBTI users. The second edition will also include samples of students in different fields of study.

The Atlas is published in notebook format. This first edition has tables of general interest in a number of areas. Tables are in the following groups:

Normative Samples of Different Populations

Samples from Specific Populations Including
Art and Communication
Business and Management
Counseling and Mental Health
Education
Engineering, Science and Technology
Government, Justice and Military
Health
Industry, Service and Trade
Religion
Students

Dividers separate each section. These sections are somewhat arbitrary. They are a result of incorporating the original groupings from the CAPT occupation coding scheme, clusters of career areas often discussed in CAPT workshops, and the number of the various kinds of occupation samples available for this edition of the Atlas.

Reference Lists of Tables

An index to tables in each group appears at the beginning of each section, and an overall alphabetical index appears in the front of the Atlas.

Entries in lower case are samples as they were coded, with at least 50 persons in the sample. Entries in upper case are composite samples of relevant groups listed in lower case, plus relevant groups of less than 50 which are not included as individual tables.

DESCRIPTION OF THE MBTI DATA BANK

The MBTI data bank was established by Isabel Myers and Mary McCaulley in 1970 when the Typology Laboratory which preceded CAPT began scoring the MBTI. It has been maintained by CAPT to provide a data base for large-scale psychometric and normative analyses of MBTI data. When Form F and Form G answer sheets are received for scoring, the staff of CAPT Scoring Services check each answer sheet to see if the person has filled in an occupation. If so, they code the occupations following a system modified from the Dictionary of Occupational Titles. Over the years CAPT has added codes or sub-categories for occupations which have been of special interest to MBTI users. Coding requires judgment, especially if the occupation given on the answer sheet is not listed or is so general that it is hard to tell precisely which category. The coders try to assign as precise a code as the answer sheet information permits. Users of this Atlas should be constantly alert to the fact that there has been slippage in the coding as coders puzzled out the best assignment of unclear occupational titles to an imperfect classification system. Despite these limitations, the MBTI Data Bank is the largest sample of MBTI data available in English.

The initial Data Bank using the 1962 item weights contains 117,743 Form F cases scored between 1971 and March, 1978. The current Data Bank, using the current scoring weights, began in March, 1978 and continues to the present. At the time of analysis it contained 81,858 Form F and 32,956 Form G cases. Since Form F and G are almost identical in the items scored for type, both were used in creating occupation samples. Only cases with less than 35 items omitted on Form F and less than 25 on Form G were considered for analysis.

Subsets of the current Data Bank have different cutoff dates. When the Data Bank was sorted for the Manual. there were 55,971 Form F cases and 32,671 Form G cases. Those tables were reported in this Atlas for reference. New subsets will be added in the future. At the time the Data Bank was sorted for the Atlas, there were 232,557 records of which 59,784 had usable occupation codes; of these, 5,473 included occupations where there were so few people that these were included only in composite samples.

The Data Bank samples depend on cases sent to CAPT for scoring. Most of these cases were collected by professionals in counseling, education, student personnel, or organizational consulting. Therefore, the samples have the bias of the types these professions work with. The samples also have the bias toward types interested in psychology (mainly the N's) and probably under-represents the types (especially ST types) who often report little value in psychology or psychological instruments. Specifically:

The ages reported in the Data Bank are approximately: 11% under 18, 29% 18 to 20, 12% 21 to 24, 10% 25 to 29, 16% 30 to 39, 10% 40 to 49, 5% 50 to 59, 2% 60 plus, and 5% unknown.

From one half to two thirds of subjects in the Data Bank report at least one year of college. Introverts and intuitives in high school are relatively more likely to go on to college than are extraverts and sensing types. Therefore, the MBTI Data Bank almost certainly includes relatively more introverts and intuitive types than would be found in the general population. The MBTI Data Bank does appear to provide reasonable estimates of the frequencies of MBTI types in the populations who interest most MBTI users. As predicted in theory, males more frequently express a preference for thinking and females for feeling. The STJ types are the most frequent among males, and the SFJ among females. The proportion of the more academically-oriented IN types rises gradually with samples at higher levels of education.

Other data from the answer sheets are also stored in the MBTI Data Bank and are used for tables on age, sex, and education differences.

Contributed Samples

Contributed samples are usually, but not always, more representative of the populations they attempt to represent than Data Bank samples. The footnotes under the tables describe these samples with the detail given by their authors.

Sizes of Samples Reported

We had long discussions about the minimum size of samples in _Atlas_ tables. When a sample is divided into the 16 types, the numbers in any one type can be small, even for a very large sample. We finally decided that we would set the minimum size at fifty in this first edition. As we receive more contributions we plan to increase this minimum. In the meantime, please be _very_ _tentative_ in any uses you make of the smaller samples--use them as "straws in the wind" which _may_ show the way the wind blows.

Strategies and Cautions in Interpreting Atlas Data

Keep in mind the under-representation of extraverts and sensing types.

As we collect more data, type distributions in smaller samples are less likely to hold up than patterns in larger samples.

Type theory assumes people differ in the ways they like to use their minds, _and_ that these differences influence the ways people like to work, what motivates them, and what satisfies them. The MBTI is most useful in helping a person find a match between these cognitive/motivational styles and opportunities offered by occupations and work settings.

In most occupations all sixteen types are found. For each occupation, some types are more frequent and others are less frequent. In theory, the frequent types are those who would like the work of that occupation.

There are almost no studies yet to answer the question so important to career counselors: Are the frequent types in the occupation more competent than the rare types? Are the frequent types more satisfied? We think it extremely unlikely that there will be data to say that any given type will fail in any given occupation. Type should never be used to tell people they should stay out of an occupation. Type can be helpful in alerting people to occupations less chosen by their type, so that they can investigate reasons for their interest, and can make sure the reality of the occupation is still appealing.

The best course for using the _Atlas_ is to help people consider what characteristics of occupations might have attracted people of their types. "Which of these characteristics are important to you personally?" "Are there any occupations here which might be worth investigating?" "Are there other occupations which provide the characteristics you are looking for, even though they are not on this list?"

READING THE TABLES

<u>Titles</u> appear at top center in bold. Titles are designed to be precise and concise. Composite groups may have longer titles to describe the components. Under the title appears the total number in the table.

<u>The Sixteen Types</u> appear in the standard type table order. The name of the type is at the top with the dominant process in bold letters.

N — the number of persons in that type.

% — the percentage of the total sample falling in that type.

■ makes it possible to see the table visually. Each symbol accounts for 1% of the sample, rounded to the nearest whole number (5.63% will yield 6 symbols.)

<u>The Type Groupings.</u> The number and percent of cases in each type grouping are listed in the right-hand column.

The MBTI type table reports groupings of the types so that the reader will readily have at hand the data on any special subgroup of interest. We have found that systematic inspection of trends for groups of types highlights patterns we would have missed if these data were not reported in this standard fashion. The type groups are in the same format as the CAPT standard tables up to and including the group IN EN IS ES. For the <u>Atlas</u> eight more groups were listed. See Chapter Four of the <u>Manual</u> pages 30-38 for brief descriptions of the groups. The <u>Atlas</u> groups are:

<u>The Basic Preferences</u>

E   Extraversion
I   Introversion

S   Sensing Perception
N   Intuitive Perception

T   Thinking Judgment
F   Feeling Judgment

J   Judgment
P   Perception

Subgroups of the Preferences

IJ The decisive introverts
IP The adaptable introverts
EP The adaptable extraverts
EJ The decisive extraverts

ST The practical and matter-of-fact types
SF The sympathetic and friendly types
NF The enthusiastic and insightful types
NT The logical and ingenious types

SJ The realistic decision-makers
SP The adaptable realists
NP The adaptable innovators
NJ The visionary decision-makers

TJ The logical decision-makers
TP The adaptable thinkers
FP The gentle types
FJ The benevolent administrators

IN The thoughtful innovators
EN The action-oriented innovators
IS The thoughtful realists
ES The action-oriented realists

ET The action-oriented thinkers
EF The action-oriented cooperators
IF The reflective harmonizers
IT The reflective reasoners

Sdom The types with sensing dominant (ISTJ, ISFJ, ESTP, ESFP)
Ndom The types with intuition dominant (INFJ, INTJ, ENFP, ENTP)
Tdom The types with thinking dominant (ISTP, INTP, ESTJ, ENTJ)
Fdom The types with feeling dominant (ISFP, INFP, ESFJ, ENFJ)

Source of data. Notes appear directly under the sixteen types. The first note always describes the meaning of the symbol ■. Notes then describe the source of the sample, and often give more precise information about the sample. Composite samples include data from more than one source. Contributed samples show the author of the data. Any use of the tables should of course credit these author-contributors for their work.

Table Identification Number. Tables are numbered consecutively as they are prepared. The identification number for the table appears directly under the cell for ENTJ and above the notes giving the source of data. Each table has a unique number, any new generations of a table will be assigned a new number.

The first two digits represent the last numbers of the calendar year; the next three numbers represent the day of the year using the Julian calendar (which numbers the days of the year consecutively); the last two numbers represent the position among tables entered into the Atlas data system.

8602511 is read:
In 1986 on January 25 this table was the 11th table added.

Copyright Notices appear at the bottom of each table. The Atlas is copyrighted and should not be copied without express written permission. If you wish such permission, contact the CAPT Permissions Editor.

Listing of Type Groupings Follow the Tables. The tables listed in each section are followed by lists of samples in that section for preferences EI, SN, TF, JP and for the four groupings most important for understanding career choices-- ST, SF, NF and NT.

Contacting Contributors. Any readers wishing to contact Contributors may write or call CAPT to get addresses or phone numbers. Most of our contributors are willing and even eager to discuss their work further. Some who shared their data are no longer practicing professionally while others change jobs or move frequently. Therefore we choose to act as a clearinghouse rather than include addresses and phone numbers on each table.

ACKNOWLEDGEMENTS

This first edition of the Atlas is a major event in CAPT's Cornerstone Year of 1986. It would not have been possible without the willingness of MBTI users to share their data, both through the use of the CAPT scoring service and also through their participation in the Type Table Project. Sharing is a characteristic of MBTI users--we all benefit from the knowledge we collect, and saving type tables is an easy and valuable way to participate in MBTI research.

There were two sources of financial support which helped this project. Paul Westbrook generously donated a series of five cassette tapes about type, which he had personally produced. The sales of these tapes provided substantial support to the research staff during this project. The Association of Psychological Type also gave a grant to CAPT which was important support during the early development stage of the Atlas project.

The scoring staff at CAPT who have carefully coded MBTI answer sheets for occupations over the years to create the data for the Atlas have earned our gratitude.

Gerald Macdaid (ENFP) directed the project at CAPT, collecting contributed data, writing descriptions of all the data, obtaining permissions, supervising student helpers, and most of all organizing the data. He and Glenn Granade (INTP) wrote a series of programs to sort the Data Bank, select cases, clean up problems, and catalogue tables, merge tables, design the Atlas type table forms, and print the final tables. As a result of their careful and thorough work, the system to catalog, merge, retrieve and print is now in place so that future editions of the Atlas will be infinitely easier.

Mary McCaulley (INFP) wrote the introduction and the comment sections.

Richard Kainz (INFP) was the research design consultant.

Editing, design and production assistants were Jamelyn DeLong (ISTJ), Mary Bogart Crenshaw (ISFP), Duane Engel (ESTP), and Andrea Sorkin (INFJ) who designed the cover.

Students helping Gerald Macdaid were Roy Forest (INFP), Jennifer Friedman (INTP), Jon Mazzoli (INTP), Curt M. Schoeneman (ENTJ), and Lori Stirrat (ESFJ).

The Atlas is truly a project that in one way or another has engaged everyone at CAPT. We are happy to send you this First Edition and look forward to sharing new future editions.

Composition of Composite Databank Samples

Almost all of the composite samples in this edition of the _Atlas_ were made from the CAPT databank. The following tables show exactly which occupations make up each composite. Some composite tables have a good sampling of the diverse occupations found within that particular grouping. Other composites are biased, shaped mostly by one or two certain occupations. It is important to keep these facts in mind before interpreting the composite tables.

The teacher composite group, one of the largest in the databank, was also broken into smaller composites by grade level and subject matter. Separate lists of the tables composing those groups are not included here. However, they can be easily constructed from the teacher composite list which is included.

This list illustrates how much sexist language existed in the _Dictionary of Occupational Titles_ at the time the CAPT occupation codes were created. Every attempt was made to modernize and "neuter" these titles. The corrected titles appear on each table. The title foreman, is an example of a title, which creates a vivid image of the job it describes and defied translation. We welcome feedback from any users with better ideas for any titles we chose. We wish to thank the National Organization of Women in Washington, D.C. for their assistance on some titles.

Note: n.e.c. means not elsewhere classified.

WRITERS AND JOURNALISTS   530

4	playwrights
16	authors
113	editors and reporters
52	journalists
4	editorial assistant
1	tv news-anchor,commentator,etc
89	public relations men and publicity writers
40	radio and television announcers
208	writers, artists, entertainers, & agents, misc.
3	technical writers

ARTISTS AND ENTERTAINERS   378

62	actors
6	directors & producers (movies & t.v.)
1	production assistants (movies & t.v.)
6	dancers
4	dancing teachers (private)
55	designers
136	musicians and composers
3	music teachers (private)

Composition of Composite Databank Samples

4	singers
26	commercial artist-graphics
16	painters and sculptors
59	photographers

SECRETARIES   1604

77	secretaries, legal
68	secretaries, medical
1126	secretaries, not specified
333	executive secretaries, administrative assistants

CLERICAL AND KINDRED WORKERS   3339

41	bank tellers
20	data processing clerk, computer technician
15	billing clerks
150	bookkeepers
274	cashiers
6	clerical assistants, social welfare
56	clerical supervisors, misc.
7	collectors, bill and account
16	counter clerks, except food
13	dispatchers and starters, vehicle
10	communications consultant
23	enumerators and interviewers
16	estimators and investigators, misc.
23	expediters and production controllers
18	file clerks
25	insurance adjusters, examiners and investigators
3	museum worker
84	library attendants and assistants
13	mail carriers, post office
13	mail handlers, except post office
6	messengers and office boys
8	meter readers, utilities
1852	clerical workers, misc.
647	clerical workers, not specified

MANAGERS AND ADMINISTRATORS   7463

29	local public administration
756	bank officers and financial managers
172	coordinator (not specified)
24	building contractor
2	funeral directors
202	health administrators
34	managers and superintendents, building
12	management consultant
102	office managers
5	officers, pilots, and pursers; ship

46	officials and administrators; public administration
3	officials of lodges, societies, and unions
5	postmasters and mail superintendents
312	restaurant, cafeteria, bar & food service supervisors
21	sales managers and department heads, retail trade
4	sales managers, except retail trade
83	sales managers, not specified
341	school administrators, college & technical institutes
1024	school administrators, elementary and secondary
89	mgt. analysts & consultants
370	school administrators, level unspecified
122	educationally related administrators
26	organizational dev. specialist
3678	managers, administrators, and supervisors, misc.
1	security director

OFFICE MACHINE OPERATORS   4905

5	bookkeeping and billing machine operators
297	computer and peripheral equipment operators
31	keypunch operators
3	tabulating machine operators
15	office machine operators, misc.
4	data entry operator, misc.
10	payroll and timekeeping clerks
22	postal clerks
5	proofreaders
100	receptionists
77	secretaries, legal
68	secretaries, medical
6	medical transcriber
1126	secretaries, not specified
333	executive secretaries, administrative assistants
16	shipping and receiving clerks
3	statistical clerks
10	stenographers
7	word processor
67	stock clerks and storekeepers
3	telegraph operators
26	telephone operators
48	communications worker
4	ticket, station, and express agents
107	typists
3	weighers
10	ward clerk
1852	clerical workers, misc.
647	clerical workers, not specified

SALES WORKERS   1750

29	advertising agents and salesmen

Composition of Composite Databank Samples

2	advertising copywriter
1	copywriter-general
18	auctioneers
4	demonstrators
7	hucksters, peddlers, antique dealers
101	insurance agents, brokers, and underwriters
30	newsboys
1	publishers
166	real estate agents and brokers
2	real estate developer
11	stock and bond salesmen
9	travel agents
179	sales representatives, unspecified
8	sales representatives, manufacturing industries
6	sales representatives, wholesale trade
108	sales clerks, retail trade
67	salesmen, retail trade
45	salesman-unspecified
6	salesmen, services and construction
44	sales clerks, services
126	sales clerks, not specified
752	sales workers, misc.
10	service rep
18	customer service/relations

TEACHERS   16676

39	agriculture teachers unspecified
2	agriculture teachers university
7	atmospheric, earth, marine & space teachers unspec
1	atmospheric, earth, marine & space teachers univer
8	biology unspecified
5	biology university
2	biology high school
8	chemistry unspecified
6	chemistry university
1	chemistry junior college
1	chemistry high school
29	science, general unspecified
2	science, general university
10	science, general high school
5	science, general middle school or junior high school
1	science, general pre-school
12	social studies unspecified
5	social studies high school
1	physics unspecified
4	physics university
26	engineering university
50	mathematics unspecified
8	mathematics university
7	mathematics high school

13

Composition of Composite Databank Samples

6	mathematics middle school or junior high school
143	health specialties & health educators unspecified
52	health specialties & health educators university
27	health specialties & health educators junior college
1	health specialties & health educators high school
2	psychology unspecified
11	psychology university
2	psychology junior college
28	business and commerce unspecified
17	business and commerce university
2	business and commerce junior college
2	business and commerce high school
5	economics unspecified
2	economics university
4	history unspecified
6	history university
1	history high school
1	history middle school or junior high school
1	sociology high school
6	social sciences unspecified
3	social sciences university
2	social sciences middle school or junior high school
167	art, drama, and music unspecified
16	art, drama, and music university
18	art, drama, and music high school
6	art, drama, and music middle school or jrhs
6	art, drama, and music elementary school
152	coaches and physical education unspecified
4	coaches and physical education university
5	coaches and physical education high school
3	coaches and physical education middle school or jrhs
4	education teachers unspecified
4	education teachers university
132	english unspecified
19	english university
1	english junior college
20	english high school
6	english middle school or junior high school
1	english elementary school
93	media specialists unspecified
4	media specialists high school
2	media specialists middle school or junior high school
4	media specialists elementary school
92	reading teachers unspecified
1	reading teachers university
1	reading teachers high school
2	reading teachers middle school or junior high school
30	foreign language unspecified
2	foreign language university
2	foreign language high school
3	foreign language middle school or junior high school

Composition of Composite Databank Samples

1	foreign language elementary school
24	home economics unspecified
4	home economics high school
2	home economics middle school or junior high school
1	law unspecified
11	theology unspecified
1	theology university
1	theology high school
112	trade, industrial & technical teachers unspecified
5	trade, industrial & technical teachers university
1	trade, industrial & technical teachers junior coll
1	trade, industrial & technical teachers high school
20	miscellaneous teachers unspecified
1	miscellaneous teachers university
1	miscellaneous teachers junior college
1	miscellaneous teachers pre-school
139	speech pathology and therapy teachers unspecified
14	speech pathology and therapy teachers university
1	speech pathology and therapy teachers high school
1	speech pathology and therapy teachers middle school
2	speech pathology and therapy teachers elementary
1	audiology teachers unspecified
2	audiology teachers university
66	research assistant (general) unspecified
1	research assistant (general) university
6	education researcher unspecified
5	education researcher university
8580	teachers, subject not specified unspecified
2033	teachers, subject not specified university
494	teachers, subject not specified junior college
558	teachers, subject not specified high school
1084	teachers, subject not specified middle school or jrhs
782	teachers, subject not specified elementary school
98	teachers, subject not specified pre-school
189	adult education teachers unspecified
3	adult education teachers university
32	adult education teachers junior college
3	adult education teachers high school
1	adult education teachers elementary school
80	employment development specialists
36	education specialist
169	teaching assistant - not teacher aide
3	teaching assistant - not teacher aide
160	special education teachers - unspecified
1	special education teachers - university
1	special education teachers - high school
5	special education teachers - middle or jrhs
6	special education teachers - elementary
52	education consultant unspecified
1	education consultant university
1	education consultant elementary school

Composition of Composite Databank Samples

28	medical education (not md's) consultant unspecified
12	medical education (not md's) consultant university
6	humanities
432	teacher aides, except school monitors
26	tutor
11	substitute teacher

ADMINISTRATORS   1857

341	school administrators, college & technical institutes
1024	school administrators, elementary and secondary
370	school administrators, level unspecified
122	educationally related administrators

DOCTORS OF MEDICINE   1603

1179	physicians, medical & osteopathic-no specialty stated
1	anatomists
13	anesthesiology
5	cardiovascular
6	child psychiatry
3	dermatology
139	family practice, general practice
2	immunology
6	internal medicine
6	neurology
11	obstetrics and gynecology
5	ophthalmology
61	pathologists
38	pediatrics
68	psychiatry
1	pulmonary diseases
7	radiology
12	surgery - general
1	surgery - neurological
11	surgery - orthopedic
2	surgery - plastic
1	medical research (m.d.'s only)
21	medical faculty (not med. education - m.d.'s only)
1	orthodontists
1	acupuncturists
2	podiatrists

ALLIED HEALTH AND HEALTH PRACTIONERS, N.E.C.   469

11	audiologists
12	chiropractors
85	dentists
1	periodontist
70	optometrists
191	pharmacists

Composition of Composite Databank Samples

1	pharmacognosist
4	pharmacologists
27	veterinarians
65	health practitioners, n.e.c.
2	health researcher

HEALTH SERVICE WORKERS   900

35	laboratory assistants
72	dental assistants
42	health aides, except nursing
1	health trainees
4	lay midwives
314	nursing aides, orderlies, and attendants
260	practical nurses, lpn
79	medical assistants
13	pharmacy assistants
35	physicians assistants
5	chiropractic assistant
2	optometry assistant
2	occupational therapy assistant
36	health service workers, misc.

HEALTH TECHNOLOGISTS AND TECHNICIANS   1291

223	clinical laboratory technologists and technicians
15	health record technologists and technicians
19	ekg technologists and technicians
126	radiologic technologists and technicians
4	therapy assistants
40	psychology technician
41	health technologists and technicians, misc.
49	medical technicians
638	medical technologists (4 year)
28	mental health technicians (2 year)
16	occupational therapy, rehabilitation technicians
4	pharmacy technicians
12	veterinary assistants
60	dental hygienist
3	psychiatric technicians
13	paramedical (emergency medical tech.)

NURSES   3103

1880	registered nurses (rn) - no specialty stated
1	nurse anesthetists
146	nursing consultants
3	emergency room nurse
7	intensive care nurse
3	maternity nurse
42	medical surgery nurse

13	pediatric nurse
35	nurse practitioner
24	psychiatric nurse
83	public health nurse
9	nurse researcher
9	school nurse
305	nursing educator
94	nursing administrator
449	nursing, n.e.c. - level & specialty unknown

HEALTH CARE THERAPISTS   765

106	speech pathologists
30	therapist
245	occupational therapist
148	physical therapist
195	respiratory therapist
5	recreational, music and art therapists
3	rehabilitation therapist & specialist
29	speech therapist & specialist
4	psychiatric therapist

LAWYERS AND JUDGES   519

128	judges
271	lawyers
32	paralegal, legal aide
84	attorneys - administrators, non-practicing
4	law clerks and interns

MILITARY PERSONNEL   264

115	military, not specified
73	air force personnel
42	army
29	navy
2	marines
3	coastguard

PROTECTIVE SERVICE WORKERS   608

3	crossing guards and bridge tenders
12	firemen, fire protection
86	guards and watchmen
2	marshalls and constables
155	policemen and detectives
68	corrections officer, probation officer
15	parole officer
105	police supervisor
91	police trainee
22	sheriffs and bailiffs

Composition of Composite Databank Samples

49	park rangers, forester

COUNSELORS   1803

673	vocational and educational counselors
177	rehabilitation counselors
932	counselors, general
21	pastoral counselors

PSYCHOLOGISTS   402

311	psychologists
31	clinical psychologists
18	psychotherapist
33	school psychologist
9	psychometrist

SOCIAL SCIENTISTS   490

24	economists
5	political scientists
311	psychologists
31	clinical psychologists
18	psychotherapist
33	school psychologist
9	psychometrist
4	child development specialist
15	sociologists
8	urban and regional planners
6	social scientists, misc.
3	criminologists
3	anthropologists
5	historians
7	linguists
8	philosophers

RELIGIOUS WORKERS -ALL DENOMINATIONS-   2010

534	clergymen
28	military chaplin
219	priests, monks
79	religion educator
3	religious consultant
1147	religious workers, misc.(nuns)

COMPUTER SPECIALISTS   338

200	computer programmers
86	computer systems analysts, support representative
52	computer specialists, n.e.c.

Composition of Composite Databank Samples

ENGINEERING AND SCIENCE TECHNICIANS   175

11	agriculture and biological technicians,
7	agriculture extension worker & home ec. agent
3	chemical technicians
41	draftsmen
57	electrical and electronic engineering technicians
1	industrial engineering technicians
3	mechanical engineering technicians
3	mathematical technicians
8	surveyors
37	engineering and science technicians, misc.
4	computer technicians, system installers

ENGINEERS   986

54	aeronautical engineers
17	astronautical engineers
9	marine engineers
19	nuclear engineers
52	chemical engineers
19	civil engineers
54	electrical and electronic engineers
16	industrial engineers
77	mechanical engineers
1	metallurgical and materials engineers
4	environmental engineers
190	mining engineers
4	petroleum engineers
5	sales engineers
465	engineers, n.e.c.

SCIENTISTS: LIFE AND PHYSICAL   226

8	ecologists, environmentalists
36	agricultural scientists/animal scientists
1	atmospheric and space scientists
57	biologists,botanists,zoologists,cytogeneticists
61	chemists
5	nuclear scientists
5	meteorologists
5	geologists
1	marine scientists
22	physicists and astronomers
25	life and physical scientists, n.e.c.

CLEANING SERVICES   67

12	chambermaids and maids, except private household
17	cleaners and charwomen
38	janitors and sextons

Composition of Composite Databank Samples

CRAFT WORKERS   559

5	automobile accessories installers
11	bakers
1	blacksmiths and farriers
2	bookbinders
6	brickmasons and stonemasons
15	cabinetmakers
109	carpenters
7	carpenter apprentices
11	carpet installers
2	cement and concrete finishers
8	compositors and typesetters
12	printing trades apprentices, except pressmen
3	printer
3	decorators and window dressers
3	dental laboratory technicians
70	electricians
16	electrician apprentices
25	electric power linemen and cablemen
1	excavating, grading and road machine operators
52	foremen, misc.
1	forgemen and hammermen
105	steelworkers, misc.
1	furniture and wood finishers
1	furriers
1	glaziers
6	horticulturalists
7	inspectors, scalers, and graders; log and lumber
22	inspectors, misc.
2	jewelers and watchmakers
2	locksmith
48	machinists
1	machinists apprentices

FARMERS   72

16	farmers (owners and tenants)
4	farm managers
1	farm foremen
28	farm laborers, wage workers
2	farm laborers, unpaid family workers
1	farm service laborers, self-employed
17	ranch worker
2	rancher (owner)
1	horse farm-breeding, etc.

FOOD SERVICE WORKERS   1082

5	caterer
32	host, hostess

Composition of Composite Databank Samples

48	bartenders
51	busboys
180	cooks, except private household
19	dishwashers
61	food counter, fountain workers, & food service aid
540	waiters, waitresses
112	food service workers, misc, except private household
34	bagboy (grocery)

LABORERS   782

3	groom
15	horse trainer - riding instructor
9	carpenters helpers
139	construction laborer, except carpenters helpers
3	construction apprentice
2	fishermen and oystermen
38	freight and material handlers
1	garbage collectors
33	gardeners and groundskeepers, except farm
6	longshoremen and stevedores
3	lumbermen, raftsmen, and woodchoppers
15	stock handlers
2	vehicle washers and equipment cleaners
41	warehousemen, misc.
235	miscellaneous laborers
237	not specified laborers

MECHANICS   669

1	locomotive engineers
45	maintenance men, general
4	air conditioning, heating ,and refrigeration
10	aircraft
4	automobile body repairmen
15	automobile mechanics
1	automobile mechanic apprentices
1	data processing machine repairmen
2	heavy equipment mechanics, including diesel
1	household appliance, accessory installers & mechanics
1	loom fixers
2	office machine repairmen
1	mechanic, except auto, apprentices
30	miscellaneous mechanics and repairmen
127	not specified mechanics and repairmen
1	millwrights
1	molders, metal
1	motion picture projectionists
4	opticians, and lens grinders and polishers
42	painters, construction and maintenance
2	painter apprentices

1	photoengravers and lithographers
3	plasterers
1	plasterer apprentices
16	plumbers and pipe fitters
3	plumber and pipe fitter apprentices
4	power station operators
12	pressmen and plate printers, printing
6	roofers and slaters
5	sheetmetal workers and tinsmiths
1	sheetmetal apprentices
1	shoe repairmen
1	sign painters and letterers
2	tailors
4	telephone installers and repairmen
5	telephone linemen and splicers
3	tile setters
2	tool and die makers
1	tool and die makers apprentices
2	upholsterers
3	wood craftsmen
33	craftsmen and kindred workers, misc.
115	military, not specified
73	air force personnel
42	army
29	navy
2	marines
3	coastguard

OPERATIVES: NON-SPECIALIZED AND FACTORY WORKERS   97

41	miscellaneous operatives
56	not specified operatives - factory workers

OPERATIVES: SPECIALIZED   206

25	assemblers
2	blasters and powdermen
54	chainmen, rodmen and axmen; surveying
5	checkers, examiners and inspectors; manufacturing
1	cutting operatives, misc.
1	dressmakers and seamstresses, except factory
1	dry wall installers and lathers
1	dyers
1	furnacemen, smeltermen, and pourers
38	garage workers and gas station attendants
2	produce graders and packers, except factory and farm
5	laundry and dry cleaning operatives
12	meat cutters and butchers, except manufacturing
2	meat cutter apprentice
1	meat wrappers, retail trade
11	metal worker, not specified

Composition of Composite Databank Samples

1	milliners
22	mine operatives, misc.
8	packers and wrappers, except meat and produce
4	painters, manufactured articles
9	photographic process workers

PERSONAL SERVICE WORKERS   783

3	interpreter
2	translator of books
2	psychic
1	interpretor for deaf
16	airline stewardesses, flight attendants
137	attendants, recreation and amusement
3	attendants, personal service, misc.
2	tour director
4	baggage porters and bellhops
177	resident housing assistant
2	boarding and lodging house keepers
55	child care workers, except private household
1	elevator operators
96	hairdressers and cosmetologists, manicurists
18	housekeepers, except private household
6	ushers, recreation and amusement
11	welfare service aides
238	public service aide and community health workers
6	community workers, misc.
3	public safety officer

OPERATIVES: TRANSPORTATION   144

3	boatmen and canalmen
16	busdrivers
21	deliverymen and routemen
5	fork lift and tow motor operatives
17	heavy equipment operatives, misc.
2	motormen; mine, factory, logging camp, etc.
2	railroad brakemen
2	railroad switchmen
4	taxicab drivers and chauffeurs
35	truck drivers
5	transport equipment operatives, misc.
31	drivers - type unknown
1	ambulance driver

Table Index

Table Index

Table Index

Table Index

Table Index

Table Index

Table Index

Table Index

An Invitation

The *Atlas of Type Tables* is designed to whet your appetite for more knowledge about types. Even more, it is designed to inspire you to contribute data to the *Atlas*. You will look at some tables and say "I have many more of category X than that!" Or, "I know who has lots more than that!"

Please take the next step and share what you know. Alert others to share as well. Reporting type tables is the easiest of all ways to contribute to MBTI® research. We earnestly invite you to share what you have discovered.

On page 35 of this book is a form for submitting data to the Type Table Project. You will find instructions on page 34. Please make photocopies of the form for your own use in submitting type table data to CAPT.

If we use your samples in their entirety, you will be credited on the *Atlas* table. If your data are not reported separately but are included in a composite type table with other samples, a master copy of your data as you submitted it will be on file in the Isabel Briggs Myers Memorial Library.

Please send CAPT your tables so that we may all improve our applications of the MBTI.

If you have questions, write or call us and ask for the Research Services Department (352) 375-0160.

How to Contribute Data to the CAPT *Atlas of Type Tables*™

CAPT encourages users of the MBTI® instrument to contribute samples they have collected for inclusion in the *Atlas*. On the following page, you will find a form for reporting and describing data. Please photocopy the form (so that you have the original for future submissions) and complete it carefully using the following guidelines.

On the form, CAPT requests a clear and detailed description of the composition of your sample. There are two important reasons for this description. First, the samples in the *Atlas* are an attempt to get a picture of the larger population from which they were drawn. When demographic characteristics are reported one can determine more clearly whether the sample is an appropriate model of the larger population. Second, the samples may be composited. In order for a composite to be useful in applications and research, it is necessary to know the component parts. Vague descriptions make it risky or inappropriate to combine samples. So a poorly described sample is often only marginally useful.

Here is an illustration of how poorly described data may create problems. For example, a contributed type table of 100 teachers without any other description is a problem. Nothing is reported about gender, age, race, subject taught, or grade level taught. All these variables can interact with type and could be influencing the frequency distribution of the types.

Here is an example of how commingling samples results in unusable data: a type table with 67 practicing female architects, in practice for more than 5 years, between the ages of 30 and 50; and 7 secretaries. Since there is no way to determine which people in the group were secretaries and which were architects, the data are confounded and virtually unusable.

The following pointers are included to minimize such problems:

1) Report samples as distinct groups; do not mix "apples and oranges." If in doubt, report data on separate sheets (it is easy for CAPT to merge them).

2) Describe the subject thoroughly.

   a) Be clear about the description of the group. Define role, occupation, or other defining characteristics in clear, definite terms.

   b) Describe how respondents were selected. Be specific about sampling methods. Was it a random sample or volunteers? State the percentage of the larger population represented by your sample (if known).

   c) Include the major demographic characteristics: age, gender, race, education level, geographic location, and any other identifying characteristics.

   d) If you wish to report a sample but maintain confidentiality, use a global generic description. For example, the Space Needle Power and Light Company in Seattle can be described as "an urban public utility company in the northwestern United States."

3) Who owns the data? List the names of all people who participated in collecting the data and the institution they represented at the time of collecting that data. If the authors should be listed as anonymous, to protect confidentiality, please state so.

CAPT Type Table Project

Data submitted by: Give name, title, address, phone number, and project name (if any) as you wish them to be used in referring to your data. If more than one person, use additional pages as needed.

☐ YES, I wish my name, address and phone number to be given to people inquiring about my data.

Permission: I herby give CAPT permission to:

☐ Publish these data in the *Atlas of Type Tables*™

☐ Publish these data in the composite samples.

☐ Include in confidential archives only.

_____   _____
Signature   Date

Description of Data: _____ Males _____ Females

Form Used: ☐ F   ☐ G   ☐ G Self-Scorable   ☐ J   ☐ K   ☐ M   ☐ M Self-Scorable   ☐ Q

Were these cases previously scored by CAPT's computer scoring service?   ☐ Yes   ☐ No

When collected? _____   Where collected? _____

CAPT plans to report some tables separately and make composites of others. To make a composite, it is important to include only groups that truly share the same characteristics. Please describe your sample as specifically as you can (e.g. age, grade, major, occupation, specialty, ethnic origin, religious group, counseling clients, medical patients, athletic team, retirees, families, etc.)

If these data have been published, directly or indirectly, please cite reference below.

Do you have other measures on this group? (For example: Strong, Campbell, grades, job satisfaction, etc.) If so, please list them below or on an attached page.

Send Completed Table to:

Research Department: Type Table Project
Center for Applications of Psychological Type, Inc.
2815 NW 13th Street, Suite 401
Gainesville, FL 32609

Enter number of males, females and the total for each type.

ISTJ	ISFJ	INFJ	INTJ
M	M	M	M.
F	F	F	F
T	T	T	T

ISTP	ISFP	INFP	INTP
M	M	M	M
F	F	F	F
T	T	T	T

ESTP	ESFP	ENFP	ENTP
M	M	M	M
F	F	F	F
T	T	T	T

ESTJ	ESFJ	ENFJ	ENTJ
M	M	M	M
F	F	F	F
T	T	T	T

When sending in more than one table, save your time by filling in the information at the left before making copies of this form. Thank you for sharing your data.

Atlas of Type Tables is a trademark of the Center for Applications of Psychological Type, Inc., Gainesville, FL.

NORMS

Section I

NORMATIVE SAMPLES

Samples in Section I

Name of Sample	Number in Sample
High School Students from Pennsylvania	9320
Females: High School Students from Pennsylvania	4387
Males: High School Students from Pennsylvania	4933
Total SRI Sample	1105
Females: SRI Sample	659
Males: SRI Sample	446
CAPT Databank Total Population	232557
Females: Form F Databank	32731
Males: Form F Databank	23240
Females: Form G Databank	16880
Males: Form G Databank	15791
Females: Adult High School Dropouts	636
Females: Adult High School Graduates, Without College	2277
Females: Traditional Age College Students	14519
Females: Non-Traditional Age College Students	3551
Females: Adult College Graduates	7952
Females: Traditional Age High School Students	1607
Females: Traditional Age Junior High School Students	321
Males: Adult High School Dropouts	343
Males: Adult High School Graduates Without College	926
Males: Traditional Age College Students	12637
Males: Adult Non-Traditional Age College Students	1501
Males: Adult College Graduates	6814
Males: Traditional Age High School Students	1204
Males: Traditional Age Junior High School Students	256
Females: Age Group 15 To 17	4973
Females: Age Group 18 To 20	13716
Females: Age Group 21 To 24	5738
Females: Age Group 25 To 29	5178
Females: Age Group 30 To 39	8711
Females: Age Group 40 To 49	4811
Females: Age Group 50 To 59	2470
Females: Age Group 60 Plus	846
Males: Age Group 15 To 17	3979
Males: Age Group 18 To 20	11897
Males: Age Group 21 To 24	5320
Males: Age Group 25 To 29	3814
Males: Age Group 30 To 39	5601
Males: Age Group 40 To 49	3812
Males: Age Group 50 To 59	1795
Males: Age Group 60 Plus	495

Comments

The tables in this section are useful in answering questions about the distribution of the types in the general population. There exists no stratified random sample of the MBTI types in the population. However, the tables are useful in showing which types are frequent across groups, or rare across groups. All tables show males and females separately.

Tables by educational level appear here also. Both researchers and counselors are interested in comparisons with college students, high school students, graduate students, and the like. Other tables for comparisons with specific fields, such as engineering, appear in the sections for those fields.

Theoretical Expectations

1. The proportion of introverts will increase at higher levels of education. The rationale is that higher education is more concerned with concepts and ideas, and therefore is more attractive to introverts.

2. The proportion of intuitive types will increase at higher levels of education. The rationale is that higher education is more concerned with theory, abstraction, and symbols and therefore will be more interesting to intuitive types.

3. Male samples will have more thinking types and female samples more feeling types at all levels of education. The rational stems from the greater number of thinking males and feeling females in the general population.

4. The proportion of judging types will increase at higher levels of education. The rationale is that the judging types will be relatively more persistent, organized and goal-directed, and therefore will be more likely to succeed academically and will be less likely to drop out once they begin a program.

The samples are based on answer sheets where the respondent answered "yes" to "I am a student" and whose ages were reasonable for that level of education. College students are divided into undergraduates of the traditional ages, considered liberally, i.e. those answering the MBTI while they were between ages 18-24. The second group are undergraduates at non-traditional ages (25 and older). Some points to note are:

1. In most comparable tables, females have more extraverts than males.

2. Introverts and intuitive types are more frequent at higher levels of education. Higher education is usually concerned with understanding and using concepts and ideas--attractive to introverts--and with abstraction, symbols, and theory-- attractive to intuitive types.

3. Sensing types and judging types are the most frequent types in most groups. All our data of younger students bear out the prediction that sensing types are in the majority. In general, sensing types are also more likely to prefer judg- ment, and intuitive types are more likely to prefer percep- tion. In most tables, you will find more SJ than SP types, and more NP than NJ types. When you do not find these rela- tionships, look for a special selection factor affecting the data (for example, persistence in completing graduate stu- dies).

4. In many groups, the persistence of judging types in achiev- ing their goals is reflected in higher proportions of judg- ing than perceptive types.

5. The proportion of SP types is almost certainly the most underestimated in the CAPT data bank as these four types are likely to drop out of school.

Summary listings of tables for EI, SN, TF, JP, ST, SF, NF and NT will be found after the last type table.

High School Students from Pennsylvania

	SENSING		INTUITION	
	THINKING	FEELING	FEELING	THINKING

ISTJ	ISFJ	INFJ	INTJ
N= 645	N= 636	N= 167	N= 244
%= 6.92	%= 6.82	%= 1.79	%= 2.62
■■■■■■■	■■■■■■■	■■	■■■

ISTP	ISFP	INFP	INTP
N= 388	N= 503	N= 363	N= 330
%= 4.16	%= 5.40	%= 3.89	%= 3.54
■■■■	■■■■■	■■■■	■■■■

ESTP	ESFP	ENFP	ENTP
N= 608	N= 873	N= 708	N= 456
%= 6.52	%= 9.37	%= 7.60	%= 4.89
■■■■■■■	■■■■■■■■■	■■■■■■■■	■■■■■

ESTJ	ESFJ	ENFJ	ENTJ
N= 1395	N= 1302	N= 336	N= 366
%= 14.97	%= 13.97	%= 3.61	%= 3.93
■■■■■■■■■■	■■■■■■■■■■	■■■■	■■■■
■■■■■	■■■■		

Right-side labels (vertical): JUDGMENT · INTROVERSION · PERCEPTION · PERCEPTION · EXTRAVERSION · JUDGMENT

	N	%
E	6044	64.85
I	3276	35.15
S	6350	68.13
N	2970	31.87
T	4432	47.55
F	4888	52.45
J	5091	54.62
P	4229	45.38
I J	1692	18.15
I P	1584	17.00
E P	2645	28.38
E J	3399	36.47
S T	3036	32.58
S F	3314	35.56
N F	1574	16.89
N T	1396	14.98
S J	3978	42.68
S P	2372	25.45
N P	1857	19.92
N J	1113	11.94
T J	2650	28.43
T P	1782	19.12
F P	2447	26.26
F J	2441	26.19
I N	1104	11.85
E N	1866	20.02
I S	2172	23.30
E S	4178	44.83
E T	2825	30.31
E F	3219	34.54
I F	1669	17.91
I T	1607	17.24
S dom	2762	29.64
N dom	1575	16.90
T dom	2479	26.60
F dom	2504	26.87

Note: ■ = 1% of sample   8631300

Data collected by Isabel Myers during the spring of 1957 using Forms D0, D1 and primarily D2. Subjects were 47% female and 53% male high school students in 11th and 12th grades in Philadelphia area high schools. Students were primarily from 27 schools in the suburbs around Philadelphia; 64% were in college preparations curricula. These data are used with permission and were cited in:

Myers, I. B. & McCaulley, M. H. (1985). Manual: A Guide to the Development and Use of the Myers-Briggs Type Indicator. Palo Alto, CA: Consulting Psychologists Press.

Females: High School Students from Pennsylvania

N = 4387

SENSING		INTUITION	
THINKING	FEELING	FEELING	THINKING

ISTJ	ISFJ	INFJ	INTJ
N= 213	N= 415	N= 88	N= 62
%= 4.86	%= 9.46	%= 2.01	%= 1.41
■■■■■	■■■■■■■■■	■■	■

ISTP	ISFP	INFP	INTP
N= 86	N= 248	N= 191	N= 94
%= 1.96	%= 5.65	%= 4.35	%= 2.14
■■	■■■■■■	■■■■	■■

ESTP	ESFP	ENFP	ENTP
N= 169	N= 519	N= 413	N= 140
%= 3.85	%= 11.83	%= 9.41	%= 3.19
■■■■	■■■■■■■■■■■ ■■	■■■■■■■■■	■■■

ESTJ	ESFJ	ENFJ	ENTJ
N= 553	N= 897	N= 196	N= 103
%= 12.61	%= 20.45	%= 4.47	%= 2.35
■■■■■■■■■■■■ ■■■	■■■■■■■■■■■ ■■■■■■■■■	■■■■	■■

JUDGMENT / INTROVERSION
PERCEPTION
PERCEPTION / EXTRAVERSION
JUDGMENT

	N	%
E	2990	68.16
I	1397	31.84
S	3100	70.66
N	1287	29.34
T	1420	32.37
F	2967	67.63
J	2527	57.60
P	1860	42.40
I J	778	17.73
I P	619	14.11
E P	1241	28.29
E J	1749	39.87
S T	1021	23.27
S F	2079	47.39
N F	888	20.24
N T	399	9.10
S J	2078	47.37
S P	1022	23.30
N P	838	19.10
N J	449	10.23
T J	931	21.22
T P	489	11.15
F P	1371	31.25
F J	1596	36.38
I N	435	9.92
E N	852	19.42
I S	962	21.93
E S	2138	48.73
E T	965	22.00
E F	2025	46.16
I F	942	21.47
I T	455	10.37
S dom	1316	30.00
N dom	703	16.02
T dom	836	19.06
F dom	1532	34.92

Note: ■ = 1% of sample   8631301

Data collected by Isabel Myers during the spring of 1957 using Forms D0, D1 and primarily D2. Subjects were female high school students in 11th and 12th grades in Philadelphia area high schools. Students were primarily from 27 schools in the suburbs around Philadelphia with 57% in college preparations curricula. These data are used with permission and were cited in:
Myers, I. B. & McCaulley, M. H. (1985). Manual: A Guide to the Development and Use of the Myers-Briggs Type Indicator.
    Palo Alto, CA: Consulting Psychologists Press.

Males: High School Students from Pennsylvania

N = 4933

| | SENSING | | INTUITION | |
| | THINKING | FEELING | FEELING | THINKING |

ISTJ	ISFJ	INFJ	INTJ
N= 432	N= 221	N= 79	N= 182
%= 8.76	%= 4.48	%= 1.60	%= 3.69
■■■■■■■■	■■■■	■■	■■■■

ISTP	ISFP	INFP	INTP
N= 302	N= 255	N= 172	N= 236
%= 6.12	%= 5.17	%= 3.49	%= 4.78
■■■■■■	■■■■■	■■■	■■■■■

ESTP	ESFP	ENFP	ENTP
N= 439	N= 354	N= 295	N= 316
%= 8.90	%= 7.18	%= 5.98	%= 6.41
■■■■■■■■■	■■■■■■■	■■■■■■	■■■■■■

ESTJ	ESFJ	ENFJ	ENTJ
N= 842	N= 405	N= 140	N= 263
%= 17.07	%= 8.21	%= 2.84	%= 5.33
■■■■■■■■■■	■■■■■■■■	■■■	■■■■■
■■■■■■■			

JUDGMENT — INTROVERSION — PERCEPTION

PERCEPTION — EXTRAVERSION — JUDGMENT

	N	%
E	3054	61.91
I	1879	38.09
S	3250	65.88
N	1683	34.12
T	3012	61.06
F	1921	38.94
J	2564	51.98
P	2369	48.02
I J	914	18.53
I P	965	19.56
E P	1404	28.46
E J	1650	33.45
S T	2015	40.85
S F	1235	25.04
N F	686	13.91
N T	997	20.21
S J	1900	38.52
S P	1350	27.37
N P	1019	20.66
N J	664	13.46
T J	1719	34.85
T P	1293	26.21
F P	1076	21.81
F J	845	17.13
I N	669	13.56
E N	1014	20.56
I S	1210	24.53
E S	2040	41.35
E T	1860	37.71
E F	1194	24.20
I F	727	14.74
I T	1152	23.35
S dom	1446	29.31
N dom	872	17.68
T dom	1643	33.31
F dom	972	19.70

Note: ■ = 1% of sample   8631302

Data collected by Isabel Myers during the spring of 1957 using Forms D0, D1 and primarily D2. Subjects were male high school students in 11th and 12th grades in Philadelphia area high schools. Students were primarily from 27 schools in the suburbs around Philadelphia with 71% in college preparations curricula. These data are used with permission and were cited in:

Myers, I. B. & McCaulley, M. H. (1985). Manual: A Guide to the Development and Use of the Myers-Briggs Type Indicator. Palo Alto, CA: Consulting Psychologists Press.

Total SRI Sample

N = 1105

	SENSING			INTUITION				N	%
	THINKING	FEELING	FEELING	THINKING					

ISTJ	ISFJ	INFJ	INTJ
N= 211	N= 172	N= 33	N= 36
%= 19.10	%= 15.57	%= 2.99	%= 3.26
■■■■■■■■■■	■■■■■■■■■■	■■■	■■■
■■■■■■■■■	■■■■■■		

ISTP	ISFP	INFP	INTP
N= 67	N= 74	N= 42	N= 23
%= 6.06	%= 6.70	%= 3.80	%= 2.08
■■■■■■	■■■■■■■	■■■■	■■

ESTP	ESFP	ENFP	ENTP
N= 44	N= 60	N= 41	N= 23
%= 3.98	%= 5.43	%= 3.71	%= 2.08
■■■■	■■■■■	■■■■	■■

ESTJ	ESFJ	ENFJ	ENTJ
N= 110	N= 101	N= 25	N= 43
%= 9.95	%= 9.14	%= 2.26	%= 3.89
■■■■■■■■■■	■■■■■■■■■	■■	■■■■

JUDGMENT — INTROVERSION — PERCEPTION — PERCEPTION — EXTRAVERSION — JUDGMENT

	N	%
E	447	40.45
I	658	59.55
S	839	75.93
N	266	24.07
T	557	50.41
F	548	49.59
J	731	66.15
P	374	33.85
I J	452	40.90
I P	206	18.64
E P	168	15.20
E J	279	25.25
S T	432	39.10
S F	407	36.83
N F	141	12.76
N T	125	11.31
S J	594	53.76
S P	245	22.17
N P	129	11.67
N J	137	12.40
T J	400	36.20
T P	157	14.21
F P	217	19.64
F J	331	29.95
I N	134	12.13
E N	132	11.95
I S	524	47.42
E S	315	28.51
E T	220	19.91
E F	227	20.54
I F	321	29.05
I T	337	30.50
S dom	487	44.07
N dom	133	12.04
T dom	243	21.99
F dom	242	21.90

Note: ■ = 1% of sample   8631305

Data collected by Brooke Warrick of SRI International during the summer of 1983. The subjects were 60% female and 40% male and represented 55% of 2,000 people in a random national sample of households with telephones in 300 counties across the United States. Half the sample was drawn from ten metropolitan areas. These data are used with permission and were cited in: Myers, I. B. & McCaulley, M. H. (1985). Manual: A Guide to the Development and Use of the Myers-Briggs Type Indicator. Palo Alto, CA: Consulting Psychologists Press.

Females: SRI Sample

N = 659

	SENSING		INTUITION	
	THINKING	FEELING	FEELING	THINKING

ISTJ	ISFJ	INFJ	INTJ
N= 74	N= 138	N= 25	N= 14
%= 11.23	%= 20.94	%= 3.79	%= 2.12
■■■■■■■■■■■ ■	■■■■■■■■■■■ ■■■■■■■■■ ■	■■■■	■■

ISTP	ISFP	INFP	INTP
N= 30	N= 61	N= 26	N= 6
%= 4.55	%= 9.26	%= 3.95	%= .91
■■■■■	■■■■■■■■■	■■■■	■

ESTP	ESFP	ENFP	ENTP
N= 22	N= 52	N= 33	N= 9
%= 3.34	%= 7.89	%= 5.01	%= 1.37
■■■	■■■■■■■■	■■■■■	■

ESTJ	ESFJ	ENFJ	ENTJ
N= 55	N= 82	N= 18	N= 14
%= 8.35	%= 12.44	%= 2.73	%= 2.12
■■■■■■■■	■■■■■■■■■■■■ ■■	■■■	■■

JUDGMENT — INTROVERSION — PERCEPTION

PERCEPTION — EXTRAVERSION — JUDGMENT

	N	%
E	285	43.25
I	374	56.75
S	514	78.00
N	145	22.00
T	224	33.99
F	435	66.01
J	420	63.73
P	239	36.27
I J	251	38.09
I P	123	18.66
E P	116	17.60
E J	169	25.64
S T	181	27.47
S F	333	50.53
N F	102	15.48
N T	43	6.53
S J	349	52.96
S P	165	25.04
N P	74	11.23
N J	71	10.77
T J	157	23.82
T P	67	10.17
F P	172	26.10
F J	263	39.91
I N	71	10.77
E N	74	11.23
I S	303	45.98
E S	211	32.02
E T	100	15.17
E F	185	28.07
I F	250	37.94
I T	124	18.82
S dom	286	43.40
N dom	81	12.29
T dom	105	15.93
F dom	187	28.38

Note: ■ = 1% of sample   8631304

Data collected by Brooke Warrick of SRI International during the summer of 1983. Subjects were the females from 55% of 2,000 in a random national sample of households with telephones in 300 counties across the United States. Half the sample was drawn from ten metropolitan areas. These data are used with permission and were cited in:

Myers, I. B. & McCaulley, M. H. (1985). Manual: A Guide to the Development and Use of the Myers-Briggs Type Indicator. Palo Alto, CA: Consulting Psychologists Press.

Males: SRI Sample

N = 446

	SENSING		INTUITION	
	THINKING	FEELING	FEELING	THINKING

ISTJ	ISFJ	INFJ	INTJ
N= 137	N= 34	N= 8	N= 22
%= 30.72	%= 7.62	%= 1.79	%= 4.93
■■■■■■■■	■■■■■■■	■■	■■■■■
■■■■■■■■			
■■■■■■■■			
■			

ISTP	ISFP	INFP	INTP
N= 37	N= 13	N= 16	N= 17
%= 8.30	%= 2.91	%= 3.59	%= 3.81
■■■■■■■■	■■■	■■■■	■■■■

ESTP	ESFP	ENFP	ENTP
N= 22	N= 8	N= 8	N= 14
%= 4.93	%= 1.79	%= 1.79	%= 3.14
■■■■■	■■	■■	■■■

ESTJ	ESFJ	ENFJ	ENTJ
N= 55	N= 19	N= 7	N= 29
%= 12.33	%= 4.26	%= 1.57	%= 6.50
■■■■■■■■■	■■■■	■■	■■■■■■■
■■			

JUDGMENT — INTROVERSION — PERCEPTION — PERCEPTION — EXTRAVERSION — JUDGMENT

	N	%
E	162	36.32
I	284	63.68
S	325	72.87
N	121	27.13
T	333	74.66
F	113	25.34
J	311	69.73
P	135	30.27
I J	201	45.07
I P	83	18.61
E P	52	11.66
E J	110	24.66
S T	251	56.28
S F	74	16.59
N F	39	8.74
N T	82	18.39
S J	245	54.93
S P	80	17.94
N P	55	12.33
N J	66	14.80
T J	243	54.48
T P	90	20.18
F P	45	10.09
F J	68	15.25
I N	63	14.13
E N	58	13.00
I S	221	49.55
E S	104	23.32
E T	120	26.91
E F	42	9.42
I F	71	15.92
I T	213	47.76
S dom	201	45.07
N dom	52	11.66
T dom	138	30.94
F dom	55	12.33

Note: ■ = 1% of sample   8631303

Data collected by Brooke Warrick of SRI International during the summer of 1983. Subjects were the males from 55% of 2,000 in a random national sample of households with telephones in 300 counties across the United States. Half the sample was drawn from ten metropolitan areas. These data are used with permission and were cited in:

Myers, I. B. & McCaulley, M. H. (1985). Manual: A Guide to the Development and Use of the Myers-Briggs Type Indicator. Palo Alto, CA: Consulting Psychologists Press.

CAPT Databank Total Population

N = 232557

	SENSING		INTUITION				N	%
	THINKING	FEELING	FEELING	THINKING				

<table>
<tr><td colspan="2">

ISTJ

N=21755
%= 9.35

■■■■■■■■■

</td><td>

ISFJ

N=21581
%= 9.28

■■■■■■■■■

</td><td>

INFJ

N= 9990
%= 4.30

■■■■

</td><td>

INTJ

N= 9868
%= 4.24

■■■■

</td></tr>
</table>

Judgment → Introversion

ISTP N= 7419 %= 3.19 ■■■
ISFP N=11266 %= 4.84 ■■■■■
INFP N=17684 %= 7.60 ■■■■■■■■
INTP N= 9223 %= 3.97 ■■■■

Perception

ESTP N= 7154 %= 3.08 ■■■
ESFP N=12718 %= 5.47 ■■■■■
ENFP N=24472 %= 10.52 ■■■■■■■■■■■ ■
ENTP N=10100 %= 4.34 ■■■■

Perception → Extraversion

ESTJ N=21298 %= 9.16 ■■■■■■■■■
ESFJ N=22668 %= 9.75 ■■■■■■■■■■
ENFJ N=13711 %= 5.90 ■■■■■■
ENTJ N=11650 %= 5.01 ■■■■■

Judgment

	N	%
E	123771	53.22
I	108786	46.78
S	125859	54.12
N	106698	45.88
T	98467	42.34
F	134090	57.66
J	132521	56.98
P	100036	43.02
I J	63194	27.17
I P	45592	19.60
E P	54444	23.41
E J	69327	29.81
S T	57626	24.78
S F	68233	29.34
N F	65857	28.32
N T	40841	17.56
S J	87302	37.54
S P	38557	16.58
N P	61479	26.44
N J	45219	19.44
T J	64571	27.77
T P	33896	14.58
F P	66140	28.44
F J	67950	29.22
I N	46765	20.11
E N	59933	25.77
I S	62021	26.67
E S	63838	27.45
E T	50202	21.59
E F	73569	31.63
I F	60521	26.02
I T	48265	20.75
S dom	63208	27.18
N dom	54430	23.41
T dom	49590	21.32
F dom	65329	28.09

Note: ■ = 1% of sample   8631500

This table is one of a series of tables from the CAPT-MBTI Data Bank of MBTI records submitted to CAPT for computer scoring between 1971 and December 1982. This was the entire databank population from which the 59,784 records with usable occupational codes were drawn. This databank has 51% Form F cases from 1971 to 1978, 35% Form F cases from 1978 to 1983 and 14% Form G cases from 1978 to 1982. Analysis of an earilier databank subset showed Form F and G databanks were comprised of 56% females and 44% males; education level completed: 6% some grade school, 30% high school diploma, 25% some college, 18% bachelor degrees, 11% masters degrees, 3% doctoral or post doctoral work, and 6% unknown. Age group percentages were: 11% under 18, 29% 18 to 20, 12% 21 to 24, 10% 25 to 29, 16% 30 to 39, 10% 40 to 49, 5% 50 to 59, 2% 60 plus, and 5% unknown.

Females: Form F Databank

N = 32731

	SENSING THINKING	SENSING FEELING	INTUITION FEELING	INTUITION THINKING	
INTROVERSION	**ISTJ** N= 2554 %= 7.80 ■■■■■■■■	**ISFJ** N= 3829 %= 11.70 ■■■■■■■■■■■■	**INFJ** N= 1525 %= 4.66 ■■■■■	**INTJ** N= 1126 %= 3.44 ■■■	JUDGMENT
INTROVERSION	**ISTP** N= 674 %= 2.06 ■■	**ISFP** N= 1741 %= 5.32 ■■■■■	**INFP** N= 2157 %= 6.59 ■■■■■■■	**INTP** N= 889 %= 2.72 ■■■	PERCEPTION
EXTRAVERSION	**ESTP** N= 735 %= 2.25 ■■	**ESFP** N= 2173 %= 6.64 ■■■■■■■	**ENFP** N= 3692 %= 11.28 ■■■■■■■■■■■	**ENTP** N= 1205 %= 3.68 ■■■■	PERCEPTION
EXTRAVERSION	**ESTJ** N= 2660 %= 8.13 ■■■■■■■■	**ESFJ** N= 4087 %= 12.49 ■■■■■■■■■■■■	**ENFJ** N= 2201 %= 6.72 ■■■■■■■	**ENTJ** N= 1483 %= 4.53 ■■■■■	JUDGMENT

Note: ■ = 1% of sample

8631502

	N	%
E	18236	55.71
I	14495	44.29
S	18453	56.38
N	14278	43.62
T	11326	34.60
F	21405	65.40
J	19465	59.47
P	13266	40.53
I J	9034	27.60
I P	5461	16.68
E P	7805	23.85
E J	10431	31.87
S T	6623	20.23
S F	11830	36.14
N F	9575	29.25
N T	4703	14.37
S J	13130	40.11
S P	5323	16.26
N P	7943	24.27
N J	6335	19.35
T J	7823	23.90
T P	3503	10.70
F P	9763	29.83
F J	11642	35.57
I N	5697	17.41
E N	8581	26.22
I S	8798	26.88
E S	9655	29.50
E T	6083	18.58
E F	12153	37.13
I F	9252	28.27
I T	5243	16.02
S dom	9291	28.39
N dom	7548	23.06
T dom	5706	17.43
F dom	10186	31.12

This table is one of a series of tables from the CAPT-MBTI Data Bank of MBTI records submitted to CAPT for computer scoring between March, 1978 and June, 1984. This sample was a subset of the Form F databank of 81,858 used in the occupation analyses. Education level completed in this databank was 7% some grade school, 26% high school diploma, 29% some college, 18% bachelor degrees, 10% masters degrees, 2% doctoral or post doctoral work, and 8% unknown. Age group percentages were: 10% under 18, 28% 18 to 20, 14% 21 to 24, 11% 25 to 29, 17% 30 to 39, 9% 40 to 49, 5% 50 to 59, 1% 60 plus, and 5% unknown.

Males: Form F Databank

N = 23240

<table>
<tr><th colspan="2">SENSING</th><th colspan="2">INTUITION</th></tr>
<tr><th>THINKING</th><th>FEELING</th><th>FEELING</th><th>THINKING</th></tr>
<tr>
<td>ISTJ
N= 3237
%= 13.93
■■■■■■■■■
■■■■</td>
<td>ISFJ
N= 1242
%= 5.34
■■■■■</td>
<td>INFJ
N= 731
%= 3.15
■■■</td>
<td>INTJ
N= 1521
%= 6.54
■■■■■■■</td>
</tr>
<tr>
<td>ISTP
N= 1171
%= 5.04
■■■■■</td>
<td>ISFP
N= 772
%= 3.32
■■■</td>
<td>INFP
N= 1281
%= 5.51
■■■■■■</td>
<td>INTP
N= 1341
%= 5.77
■■■■■■</td>
</tr>
<tr>
<td>ESTP
N= 1108
%= 4.77
■■■■■</td>
<td>ESFP
N= 816
%= 3.51
■■■■</td>
<td>ENFP
N= 1570
%= 6.76
■■■■■■■</td>
<td>ENTP
N= 1395
%= 6.00
■■■■■■</td>
</tr>
<tr>
<td>ESTJ
N= 3199
%= 13.77
■■■■■■■■■
■■■■</td>
<td>ESFJ
N= 1184
%= 5.09
■■■■■</td>
<td>ENFJ
N= 874
%= 3.76
■■■■</td>
<td>ENTJ
N= 1798
%= 7.74
■■■■■■■■</td>
</tr>
</table>

JUDGMENT — INTROVERSION — PERCEPTION — PERCEPTION — EXTRAVERSION — JUDGMENT

	N	%
E	11944	51.39
I	11296	48.61
S	12729	54.77
N	10511	45.23
T	14770	63.55
F	8470	36.45
J	13786	59.32
P	9454	40.68
I J	6731	28.96
I P	4565	19.64
E P	4889	21.04
E J	7055	30.36
S T	8715	37.50
S F	4014	17.27
N F	4456	19.17
N T	6055	26.05
S J	8862	38.13
S P	3867	16.64
N P	5587	24.04
N J	4924	21.19
T J	9755	41.98
T P	5015	21.58
F P	4439	19.10
F J	4031	17.35
I N	4874	20.97
E N	5637	24.26
I S	6422	27.63
E S	6307	27.14
E T	7500	32.27
E F	4444	19.12
I F	4026	17.32
I T	7270	31.28
S dom	6403	27.55
N dom	5217	22.45
T dom	7509	32.31
F dom	4111	17.69

Note: ■ = 1% of sample   8631501

This table is one of a series of tables from the CAPT-MBTI Data Bank of MBTI records submitted to CAPT for computer scoring between March, 1978 and June, 1984. This sample was a subset of the Form F databank of 81,858 used in the occupation analyses. Education level completed in this databank was 7% some grade school, 23% high school diploma, 21% some college, 21% bachelor degrees, 14% masters degrees, 7% doctoral or post doctoral work, and 7% unknown. Age group percentages were: 10% under 18, 23% 18 to 20, 16% 21 to 24, 12% 25 to 29, 17% 30 to 39, 11% 40 to 49, 5% 50 to 59, 1% 60 plus, and 5% unknown.

Females: Form G Databank

N = 16880

	SENSING		INTUITION			N	%
	THINKING	FEELING	FEELING	THINKING			

ISTJ	ISFJ	INFJ	INTJ
N= 1649	N= 1738	N= 805	N= 676
%= 9.77	%= 10.30	%= 4.77	%= 4.00
■■■■■■■■■	■■■■■■■■■	■■■■■	■■■■

ISTP	ISFP	INFP	INTP
N= 451	N= 721	N= 1067	N= 541
%= 2.67	%= 4.27	%= 6.32	%= 3.20
■■■	■■■■	■■■■■■	■■■

ESTP	ESFP	ENFP	ENTP
N= 469	N= 967	N= 1655	N= 693
%= 2.78	%= 5.73	%= 9.80	%= 4.11
■■■	■■■■■■	■■■■■■■■■■	■■■■

ESTJ	ESFJ	ENFJ	ENTJ
N= 1699	N= 1800	N= 1077	N= 872
%= 10.07	%= 10.66	%= 6.38	%= 5.17
■■■■■■■■■■	■■■■■■■■■■■	■■■■■■	■■■■■
	■		

Side labels: JUDGMENT · INTROVERSION · PERCEPTION · PERCEPTION · EXTRAVERSION · JUDGMENT

	N	%
E	9232	54.69
I	7648	45.31
S	9494	56.24
N	7386	43.76
T	7050	41.77
F	9830	58.23
J	10316	61.11
P	6564	38.89
I J	4868	28.84
I P	2780	16.47
E P	3784	22.42
E J	5448	32.27
S T	4268	25.28
S F	5226	30.96
N F	4604	27.27
N T	2782	16.48
S J	6886	40.79
S P	2608	15.45
N P	3956	23.44
N J	3430	20.32
T J	4896	29.00
T P	2154	12.76
F P	4410	26.13
F J	5420	32.11
I N	3089	18.30
E N	4297	25.46
I S	4559	27.01
E S	4935	29.24
E T	3733	22.11
E F	5499	32.58
I F	4331	25.66
I T	3317	19.65
S dom	4823	28.57
N dom	3829	22.68
T dom	3563	21.11
F dom	4665	27.64

Note: ■ = 1% of sample   8631503

This table is one of a series of tables from the CAPT-MBTI Data Bank of MBTI records submitted to CAPT for computer scoring between March, 1978 and December, 1982. This sample was a subset of the Form G databank of 32,956 used in the occupation analyses. Education level completed in this databank was 6% some grade school, 35% high school diploma, 24% some college, 17% bachelor degrees, 11% masters degrees, 2% doctoral or post doctoral work, and 5% unknown. Age group percentages were: 13% under 18, 27% 18 to 20, 8% 21 to 24, 9% 25 to 29, 18% 30 to 39, 10% 40 to 49, 6% 50 to 59, 2% 60 plus, and 7% unknown.

Males: Form G Databank

	SENSING		INTUITION	
	THINKING	FEELING	FEELING	THINKING

ISTJ	ISFJ	INFJ	INTJ
N= 2440	N= 698	N= 416	N= 1149
%= 15.45	%= 4.42	%= 2.63	%= 7.28
■■■■■■■■■■ ■■■■■	■■■■	■■■	■■■■■■■

ISTP	ISFP	INFP	INTP
N= 959	N= 474	N= 752	N= 1114
%= 6.07	%= 3.00	%= 4.76	%= 7.05
■■■■■■	■■■	■■■■■	■■■■■■■

ESTP	ESFP	ENFP	ENTP
N= 931	N= 492	N= 850	N= 1083
%= 5.90	%= 3.12	%= 5.38	%= 6.86
■■■■■■	■■■	■■■■■	■■■■■■■

ESTJ	ESFJ	ENFJ	ENTJ
N= 2213	N= 693	N= 432	N= 1095
%= 14.01	%= 4.39	%= 2.74	%= 6.93
■■■■■■■■■■■■ ■■■■	■■■■	■■■	■■■■■■■

JUDGMENT — INTROVERSION — PERCEPTION — PERCEPTION — EXTRAVERSION — JUDGMENT

	N	%
E	7789	49.33
I	8002	50.67
S	8900	56.36
N	6891	43.64
T	10984	69.56
F	4807	30.44
J	9136	57.86
P	6655	42.14
I J	4703	29.78
I P	3299	20.89
E P	3356	21.25
E J	4433	28.07
S T	6543	41.43
S F	2357	14.93
N F	2450	15.52
N T	4441	28.12
S J	6044	38.27
S P	2856	18.09
N P	3799	24.06
N J	3092	19.58
T J	6897	43.68
T P	4087	25.88
F P	2568	16.26
F J	2239	14.18
I N	3431	21.73
E N	3460	21.91
I S	4571	28.95
E S	4329	27.41
E T	5322	33.70
E F	2467	15.62
I F	2340	14.82
I T	5662	35.86
S dom	4561	28.88
N dom	3498	22.15
T dom	5381	34.08
F dom	2351	14.89

Note: ■ = 1% of sample   8631504

This table is one of a series of tables from the CAPT-MBTI Data Bank of MBTI records submitted to CAPT for computer scoring between March, 1978 and December, 1982. This sample was a subset of the Form G databank of 32,956 used in the occupation analyses. Education level completed in this databank was 6% some grade school, 42% high school diploma, 25% some college, 12% bachelor degrees, 8% masters degrees, 4% doctoral or post doctoral work, and 3% unknown. Age group percentages were: 14% under 18, 40% 18 to 20, 11% 21 to 24, 7% 25 to 29, 11% 30 to 39, 7% 40 to 49, 4% 50 to 59, 1% 60 plus, and 5% unknown.

Females: Adult High School Dropouts

N = 636

	SENSING		INTUITION	
	THINKING	FEELING	FEELING	THINKING

ISTJ	ISFJ	INFJ	INTJ
N= 83	N= 116	N= 20	N= 20
%= 13.05	%= 18.24	%= 3.14	%= 3.14
∎∎∎∎∎∎∎∎∎∎ ∎∎∎	∎∎∎∎∎∎∎∎∎ ∎∎∎∎∎∎∎	∎∎∎	∎∎∎

ISTP	ISFP	INFP	INTP
N= 24	N= 41	N= 29	N= 13
%= 3.77	%= 6.45	%= 4.56	%= 2.04
∎∎∎∎	∎∎∎∎∎∎	∎∎∎∎∎	∎∎

ESTP	ESFP	ENFP	ENTP
N= 17	N= 33	N= 36	N= 12
%= 2.67	%= 5.19	%= 5.66	%= 1.89
∎∎∎	∎∎∎∎∎	∎∎∎∎∎∎	∎∎

ESTJ	ESFJ	ENFJ	ENTJ
N= 74	N= 70	N= 24	N= 24
%= 11.64	%= 11.01	%= 3.77	%= 3.77
∎∎∎∎∎∎∎∎∎∎∎ ∎∎	∎∎∎∎∎∎∎∎∎∎∎ ∎	∎∎∎∎	∎∎∎∎

JUDGMENT — INTROVERSION — PERCEPTION — PERCEPTION — EXTRAVERSION — JUDGMENT

	N	%
E	290	45.60
I	346	54.40
S	458	72.01
N	178	27.99
T	267	41.98
F	369	58.02
J	431	67.77
P	205	32.23
I J	239	37.58
I P	107	16.82
E P	98	15.41
E J	192	30.19
S T	198	31.13
S F	260	40.88
N F	109	17.14
N T	69	10.85
S J	343	53.93
S P	115	18.08
N P	90	14.15
N J	88	13.84
T J	201	31.60
T P	66	10.38
F P	139	21.86
F J	230	36.16
I N	82	12.89
E N	96	15.09
I S	264	41.51
E S	194	30.50
E T	127	19.97
E F	163	25.63
I F	206	32.39
I T	140	22.01
S dom	249	39.15
N dom	88	13.84
T dom	135	21.23
F dom	164	25.79

Note: ∎ = 1% of sample   8631512

This table is one of a series of tables from the CAPT-MBTI Data Bank of MBTI records submitted to CAPT for computer scoring between 1971 and December 1982. The subjects were females who, at time of testing, were 19 years of age or older, not enrolled in school, and had not completed high school. This sample was drawn from 55,971 Form F records and 32,671 Form G records, which represent an earlier subset of the total databank of 232,557. The Form F cases are from March, 1978 to June, 1983 and the G cases from March, 1978 to December, 1982. These two data banks were comprised of 56% females and 44% males; education level completed: 6% some grade school, 30% high school diploma, 25% some college, 18% bachelor degrees, 11% masters degrees, 3% doctoral or post doctoral work, and 6% unknown. Age group percentages were: 11% under 18, 29% 18 to 20, 12% 21 to 24, 10% 25 to 29, 16% 30 to 39, 10% 40 to 49, 5% 50 to 59, 2% 60 plus, and 5% unknown.

Females: Adult High School Graduates, Without College

N = 2277

	SENSING		INTUITION	
	THINKING	FEELING	FEELING	THINKING

ISTJ	ISFJ	INFJ	INTJ
N= 264	N= 424	N= 78	N= 51
%= 11.59	%= 18.62	%= 3.43	%= 2.24
■■■■■■■■■■■	■■■■■■■■■	■■■	■■
■■	■■■■■■■■		

ISTP	ISFP	INFP	INTP
N= 70	N= 180	N= 112	N= 35
%= 3.07	%= 7.91	%= 4.92	%= 1.54
■■■	■■■■■■■■	■■■■■	■■

ESTP	ESFP	ENFP	ENTP
N= 58	N= 161	N= 133	N= 42
%= 2.55	%= 7.07	%= 5.84	%= 1.84
■■■	■■■■■■■	■■■■■	■■

ESTJ	ESFJ	ENFJ	ENTJ
N= 235	N= 293	N= 78	N= 63
%= 10.32	%= 12.87	%= 3.43	%= 2.77
■■■■■■■■■■	■■■■■■■■■■■	■■■	■■■
	■■■		

JUDGMENT — INTROVERSION — PERCEPTION
PERCEPTION — EXTRAVERSION — JUDGMENT

	N	%
E	1063	46.68
I	1214	53.32
S	1685	74.00
N	592	26.00
T	818	35.92
F	1459	64.08
J	1486	65.26
P	791	34.74
I J	817	35.88
I P	397	17.44
E P	394	17.30
E J	669	29.38
S T	627	27.54
S F	1058	46.46
N F	401	17.61
N T	191	8.39
S J	1216	53.40
S P	469	20.60
N P	322	14.14
N J	270	11.86
T J	613	26.92
T P	205	9.00
F P	586	25.74
F J	873	38.34
I N	276	12.12
E N	316	13.88
I S	938	41.19
E S	747	32.81
E T	398	17.48
E F	665	29.21
I F	794	34.87
I T	420	18.45
S dom	907	39.83
N dom	304	13.35
T dom	403	17.70
F dom	663	29.12

Note: ■ = 1% of sample   8631513

This table is one of a series of tables from the CAPT-MBTI Data Bank of MBTI records submitted to CAPT for computer scoring between 1971 and December 1982. The subjects were females who, at time of testing, were 25 years of age or older, not enrolled in school, had completed high school and had not attended college. This sample was drawn from 55,971 Form F records and 32,671 Form G records. These two data banks were comprised of 56% females and 44% males; education level completed: 6% some grade school, 30% high school diploma, 25% some college, 18% bachelor degrees, 11% masters degrees, 3% doctoral or post doctoral work, and 6% unknown. Age group percentages were: 11% under 18, 29% 18 to 20, 12% 21 to 24, 10% 25 to 29, 16% 30 to 39, 10% 40 to 49, 5% 50 to 59, 2% 60 plus, and 5% unknown.

Females: Traditional Age College Students

N = 14519

	SENSING		INTUITION			N	%
	THINKING	FEELING	FEELING	THINKING			

ISTJ N= 996 %= 6.86 ■■■■■■■	**ISFJ** N= 1665 %= 11.47 ■■■■■■■■■■■ ■	**INFJ** N= 550 %= 3.79 ■■■■	**INTJ** N= 314 %= 2.16 ■■
ISTP N= 356 %= 2.45 ■■	**ISFP** N= 834 %= 5.74 ■■■■■■	**INFP** N= 823 %= 5.67 ■■■■■■	**INTP** N= 304 %= 2.09 ■■
ESTP N= 408 %= 2.81 ■■■	**ESFP** N= 1210 %= 8.33 ■■■■■■■■	**ENFP** N= 1705 %= 11.74 ■■■■■■■■■■■ ■■	**ENTP** N= 508 %= 3.50 ■■■
ESTJ N= 1260 %= 8.68 ■■■■■■■■	**ESFJ** N= 2185 %= 15.05 ■■■■■■■■■■■■ ■■■■■	**ENFJ** N= 932 %= 6.42 ■■■■■■	**ENTJ** N= 469 %= 3.23 ■■■

JUDGMENT · INTROVERSION · PERCEPTION · PERCEPTION · EXTRAVERSION · JUDGMENT

	N	%
E	8677	59.76
I	5842	40.24
S	8914	61.40
N	5605	38.60
T	4615	31.79
F	9904	68.21
J	8371	57.66
P	6148	42.34
I J	3525	24.28
I P	2317	15.96
E P	3831	26.39
E J	4846	33.38
S T	3020	20.80
S F	5894	40.60
N F	4010	27.62
N T	1595	10.99
S J	6106	42.06
S P	2808	19.34
N P	3340	23.00
N J	2265	15.60
T J	3039	20.93
T P	1576	10.85
F P	4572	31.49
F J	5332	36.72
I N	1991	13.71
E N	3614	24.89
I S	3851	26.52
E S	5063	34.87
E T	2645	18.22
E F	6032	41.55
I F	3872	26.67
I T	1970	13.57
S dom	4279	29.47
N dom	3077	21.19
T dom	2389	16.45
F dom	4774	32.88

Note: ■ = 1% of sample   8631514

This table is one of a series of tables from the CAPT-MBTI Data Bank of MBTI records submitted to CAPT for computer scoring between 1971 and December 1982. The subjects were females who, at time of testing, were between 18 and 25 years of age inclusive, enrolled in school and attending college. This sample was drawn from 55,971 Form F records and 32,671 Form G records. These two data banks were comprised of 56% females and 44% males; education level completed: 6% some grade school, 30% high school diploma, 25% some college, 18% bachelor degrees, 11% masters degrees, 3% doctoral or post doctoral work, and 6% unknown. Age group percentages were: 11% under 18, 29% 18 to 20, 12% 21 to 24, 10% 25 to 29, 16% 30 to 39, 10% 40 to 49, 5% 50 to 59, 2% 60 plus, and 5% unknown.

Females: Non-Traditional Age College Students

N = 3551

	SENSING		INTUITION	
	THINKING	FEELING	FEELING	THINKING

ISTJ	ISFJ	INFJ	INTJ
N= 379	N= 460	N= 173	N= 126
%= 10.67	%= 12.95	%= 4.87	%= 3.55
■■■■■■■■■■	■■■■■■■■■■	■■■■■	■■■■
■	■■■		

ISTP	ISFP	INFP	INTP
N= 111	N= 218	N= 197	N= 105
%= 3.13	%= 6.14	%= 5.55	%= 2.96
■■■	■■■■■■	■■■■■■	■■■

ESTP	ESFP	ENFP	ENTP
N= 80	N= 158	N= 309	N= 118
%= 2.25	%= 4.45	%= 8.70	%= 3.32
■■	■■■■	■■■■■■■■■	■■■

ESTJ	ESFJ	ENFJ	ENTJ
N= 359	N= 415	N= 195	N= 148
%= 10.11	%= 11.69	%= 5.49	%= 4.17
■■■■■■■■■■	■■■■■■■■■■	■■■■■	■■■■
	■■		

JUDGMENT — INTROVERSION — PERCEPTION — PERCEPTION — EXTRAVERSION — JUDGMENT

	N	%
E	1782	50.18
I	1769	49.82
S	2180	61.39
N	1371	38.61
T	1426	40.16
F	2125	59.84
J	2255	63.50
P	1296	36.50
I J	1138	32.05
I P	631	17.77
E P	665	18.73
E J	1117	31.46
S T	929	26.16
S F	1251	35.23
N F	874	24.61
N T	497	14.00
S J	1613	45.42
S P	567	15.97
N P	729	20.53
N J	642	18.08
T J	1012	28.50
T P	414	11.66
F P	882	24.84
F J	1243	35.00
I N	601	16.92
E N	770	21.68
I S	1168	32.89
E S	1012	28.50
E T	705	19.85
E F	1077	30.33
I F	1048	29.51
I T	721	20.30
S dom	1077	30.33
N dom	726	20.44
T dom	723	20.36
F dom	1025	28.87

Note: ■ = 1% of sample   8631515

This table is one of a series of tables from the CAPT-MBTI Data Bank of MBTI records submitted to CAPT for computer scoring between 1971 and December 1982. The subjects were females who, at time of testing, were 25 years of age and older, enrolled in school and attending college. This sample was drawn from 55,971 Form F records and 32,671 Form G records. These two data banks were comprised of 56% females and 44% males; education level completed: 6% some grade school, 30% high school diploma, 25% some college, 18% bachelor degrees, 11% masters degrees, 3% doctoral or post doctoral work, and 6% unknown. Age group percentages were: 11% under 18, 29% 18 to 20, 12% 21 to 24, 10% 25 to 29, 16% 30 to 39, 10% 40 to 49, 5% 50 to 59, 2% 60 plus, and 5% unknown.

Females: Adult College Graduates

N = 7952

	SENSING		INTUITION				N	%
	THINKING	FEELING	FEELING	THINKING				

ISTJ	ISFJ	INFJ	INTJ
N= 855	N= 869	N= 562	N= 486
%= 10.75	%= 10.93	%= 7.07	%= 6.11
■■■■■■■■■■	■■■■■■■■■■	■■■■■■■	■■■■■■
■	■		

ISTP	ISFP	INFP	INTP
N= 128	N= 214	N= 608	N= 295
%= 1.61	%= 2.69	%= 7.65	%= 3.71
■■	■■■	■■■■■■■■	■■■■

ESTP	ESFP	ENFP	ENTP
N= 84	N= 208	N= 729	N= 315
%= 1.06	%= 2.62	%= 9.17	%= 3.96
■	■■■	■■■■■■■■■	■■■■

ESTJ	ESFJ	ENFJ	ENTJ
N= 681	N= 682	N= 664	N= 572
%= 8.56	%= 8.58	%= 8.35	%= 7.19
■■■■■■■■	■■■■■■■■	■■■■■■■■	■■■■■■■

	N	%
E	3935	49.48
I	4017	50.52
S	3721	46.79
N	4231	53.21
T	3416	42.96
F	4536	57.04
J	5371	67.54
P	2581	32.46
I J	2772	34.86
I P	1245	15.66
E P	1336	16.80
E J	2599	32.68
S T	1748	21.98
S F	1973	24.81
N F	2563	32.23
N T	1668	20.98
S J	3087	38.82
S P	634	7.97
N P	1947	24.48
N J	2284	28.72
T J	2594	32.62
T P	822	10.34
F P	1759	22.12
F J	2777	34.92
I N	1951	24.53
E N	2280	28.67
I S	2066	25.98
E S	1655	20.81
E T	1652	20.77
E F	2283	28.71
I F	2253	28.33
I T	1764	22.18
S dom	2016	25.35
N dom	2092	26.31
T dom	1676	21.08
F dom	2168	27.26

Note: ■ = 1% of sample   8631516

This table is one of a series of tables from the CAPT-MBTI Data Bank of MBTI records submitted to CAPT for computer scoring between 1971 and December 1982. The subjects were females who, at time of testing, were 25 years of age and older, not enrolled in school and had completed four years of college. This sample was drawn from 55,971 Form F records and 32,671 Form G records. These two data banks were comprised of 56% females and 44% males; education level completed: 6% some grade school, 30% high school diploma, 25% some college, 18% bachelor degrees, 11% masters degrees, 3% doctoral or post doctoral work, and 6% unknown. Age group percentages were: 11% under 18, 29% 18 to 20, 12% 21 to 24, 10% 25 to 29, 16% 30 to 39, 10% 40 to 49, 5% 50 to 59, 2% 60 plus, and 5% unknown.

56

Females: Traditional Age High School Students

	SENSING		INTUITION	
	THINKING	FEELING	FEELING	THINKING

ISTJ	ISFJ	INFJ	INTJ
N= 81	N= 137	N= 51	N= 21
%= 5.04	%= 8.53	%= 3.17	%= 1.31
■■■■■	■■■■■■■■■	■■■	■

ISTP	ISFP	INFP	INTP
N= 35	N= 110	N= 148	N= 52
%= 2.18	%= 6.85	%= 9.21	%= 3.24
■■	■■■■■■■	■■■■■■■■■	■■■

ESTP	ESFP	ENFP	ENTP
N= 44	N= 182	N= 302	N= 78
%= 2.74	%= 11.33	%= 18.79	%= 4.85
■■■	■■■■■■■■■■■ ■	■■■■■■■■■■■ ■■■■■■■■	■■■■■

ESTJ	ESFJ	ENFJ	ENTJ
N= 93	N= 150	N= 85	N= 38
%= 5.79	%= 9.33	%= 5.29	%= 2.36
■■■■■■	■■■■■■■■■	■■■■■	■■

JUDGMENT — INTROVERSION — PERCEPTION — PERCEPTION — EXTRAVERSION — JUDGMENT

	N	%
E	972	60.49
I	635	39.51
S	832	51.77
N	775	48.23
T	442	27.50
F	1165	72.50
J	656	40.82
P	951	59.18
I J	290	18.05
I P	345	21.47
E P	606	37.71
E J	366	22.78
S T	253	15.74
S F	579	36.03
N F	586	36.47
N T	189	11.76
S J	461	28.69
S P	371	23.09
N P	580	36.09
N J	195	12.13
T J	233	14.50
T P	209	13.01
F P	742	46.17
F J	423	26.32
I N	272	16.93
E N	503	31.30
I S	363	22.59
E S	469	29.18
E T	253	15.74
E F	719	44.74
I F	446	27.75
I T	189	11.76
S dom	444	27.63
N dom	452	28.13
T dom	218	13.57
F dom	493	30.68

Note: ■ = 1% of sample   8631517

This table is one of a series of tables from the CAPT-MBTI Data Bank of MBTI records submitted to CAPT for computer scoring between 1971 and December 1982. The subjects were females who, at time of testing, were between 15 and 18 years of age inclusive, enrolled in school and had completed more than 9 but less than 12 years of school. This sample was drawn from 55,971 Form F records and 32,671 Form G records. These two data banks were comprised of 56% females and 44% males; education level completed: 6% some grade school, 30% high school diploma, 25% some college, 18% bachelor degrees, 11% masters degrees, 3% doctoral or post doctoral work, and 6% unknown. Age group percentages were: 11% under 18, 29% 18 to 20, 12% 21 to 24, 10% 25 to 29, 16% 30 to 39, 10% 40 to 49, 5% 50 to 59, 2% 60 plus, and 5% unknown.

Females: Traditional Age Junior High School Students

	SENSING		INTUITION					N	%
	THINKING	FEELING	FEELING	THINKING					

ISTJ	ISFJ	INFJ	INTJ
N= 12	N= 15	N= 13	N= 8
%= 3.74	%= 4.67	%= 4.05	%= 2.49
■■■■	■■■■■	■■■■	■■

ISTP	ISFP	INFP	INTP
N= 11	N= 15	N= 21	N= 14
%= 3.43	%= 4.67	%= 6.54	%= 4.36
■■■	■■■■■	■■■■■■■	■■■■

ESTP	ESFP	ENFP	ENTP
N= 20	N= 34	N= 48	N= 14
%= 6.23	%= 10.59	%= 14.95	%= 4.36
■■■■■■	■■■■■■■■■■ ■	■■■■■■■■■■ ■■■■■	■■■■

ESTJ	ESFJ	ENFJ	ENTJ
N= 30	N= 35	N= 17	N= 14
%= 9.35	%= 10.90	%= 5.30	%= 4.36
■■■■■■■■■	■■■■■■■■■■ ■	■■■■■	■■■■

	N	%
E	212	66.04
I	109	33.96
S	172	53.58
N	149	46.42
T	123	38.32
F	198	61.68
J	144	44.86
P	177	55.14
I J	48	14.95
I P	61	19.00
E P	116	36.14
E J	96	29.91
S T	73	22.74
S F	99	30.84
N F	99	30.84
N T	50	15.58
S J	92	28.66
S P	80	24.92
N P	97	30.22
N J	52	16.20
T J	64	19.94
T P	59	18.38
F P	118	36.76
F J	80	24.92
I N	56	17.45
E N	93	28.97
I S	53	16.51
E S	119	37.07
E T	78	24.30
E F	134	41.74
I F	64	19.94
I T	45	14.02
S dom	81	25.23
N dom	83	25.86
T dom	69	21.50
F dom	88	27.41

Note: ■ = 1% of sample

8631518

This table is one of a series of tables from the CAPT-MBTI Data Bank of MBTI records submitted to CAPT for computer scoring between 1971 and December 1982. The subjects were females who, at time of testing, were between 11 and 15 years of age inclusive, enrolled in school and had completed more than 6 but less than 9 years of school. This sample was drawn from 55,971 Form F records and 32,671 Form G records. These two data banks were comprised of 56% females and 44% males; education level completed: 6% some grade school, 30% high school diploma, 25% some college, 18% bachelor degrees, 11% masters degrees, 3% doctoral or post doctoral work, and 6% unknown. Age group percentages were: 11% under 18, 29% 18 to 20, 12% 21 to 24, 10% 25 to 29, 16% 30 to 39, 10% 40 to 49, 5% 50 to 59, 2% 60 plus, and 5% unknown.

Males: Adult High School Dropouts

N = 343

	SENSING		INTUITION	
	THINKING	FEELING	FEELING	THINKING

ISTJ	ISFJ	INFJ	INTJ
N= 65	N= 26	N= 10	N= 15
%= 18.95	%= 7.58	%= 2.92	%= 4.37
ISTP	ISFP	INFP	INTP
N= 28	N= 16	N= 11	N= 10
%= 8.16	%= 4.66	%= 3.21	%= 2.92
ESTP	ESFP	ENFP	ENTP
N= 18	N= 8	N= 10	N= 10
%= 5.25	%= 2.33	%= 2.92	%= 2.92
ESTJ	ESFJ	ENFJ	ENTJ
N= 60	N= 17	N= 6	N= 33
%= 17.49	%= 4.96	%= 1.75	%= 9.62

JUDGMENT — INTROVERSION — PERCEPTION — PERCEPTION — EXTRAVERSION — JUDGMENT

	N	%
E	162	47.23
I	181	52.77
S	238	69.39
N	105	30.61
T	239	69.68
F	104	30.32
J	232	67.64
P	111	32.36
I J	116	33.82
I P	65	18.95
E P	46	13.41
E J	116	33.82
S T	171	49.85
S F	67	19.53
N F	37	10.79
N T	68	19.83
S J	168	48.98
S P	70	20.41
N P	41	11.95
N J	64	18.66
T J	173	50.44
T P	66	19.24
F P	45	13.12
F J	59	17.20
I N	46	13.41
E N	59	17.20
I S	135	39.36
E S	103	30.03
E T	121	35.28
E F	41	11.95
I F	63	18.37
I T	118	34.40
S dom	117	34.11
N dom	45	13.12
T dom	131	38.19
F dom	50	14.58

Note: ■ = 1% of sample   8631505

This table is one of a series of tables from the CAPT-MBTI Data Bank of MBTI records submitted to CAPT for computer scoring between 1971 and December 1982. The subjects were males who, at time of testing, were 19 years of age or older, not enrolled in school, and had not completed high school. This sample was drawn from 55,971 Form F records and 32,671 Form G records, which represent an earlier subset of the total databank of 232,557. The Form F cases are from March, 1978 to June, 1983 and the G cases from March, 1978 to December, 1982. These two data banks were comprised of 56% females and 44% males; education level completed: 6% some grade school, 30% high school diploma, 25% some college, 18% bachelor degrees, 11% masters degrees, 3% doctoral or post doctoral work, and 6% unknown. Age group percentages were: 11% under 18, 29% 18 to 20, 12% 21 to 24, 10% 25 to 29, 16% 30 to 39, 10% 40 to 49, 5% 50 to 59, 2% 60 plus, and 5% unknown.

Males: Adult High School Graduates Without College

N = 926

	SENSING		INTUITION	
	THINKING	FEELING	FEELING	THINKING

ISTJ	ISFJ	INFJ	INTJ
N= 211	N= 70	N= 10	N= 25
%= 22.79	%= 7.56	%= 1.08	%= 2.70
■■■■■■■■■■	■■■■■■■■	■	■■■
■■■■■■■■■■			
■■■			

ISTP	ISFP	INFP	INTP
N= 64	N= 28	N= 10	N= 36
%= 6.91	%= 3.02	%= 1.08	%= 3.89
■■■■■■■	■■■	■	■■■■

ESTP	ESFP	ENFP	ENTP
N= 49	N= 22	N= 20	N= 28
%= 5.29	%= 2.38	%= 2.16	%= 3.02
■■■■■	■■	■■	■■■

ESTJ	ESFJ	ENFJ	ENTJ
N= 258	N= 51	N= 10	N= 34
%= 27.86	%= 5.51	%= 1.08	%= 3.67
■■■■■■■■■■	■■■■■■■	■	■■■■
■■■■■■■■■■			
■■■■■■■■			

JUDGMENT — INTROVERSION
PERCEPTION
PERCEPTION — EXTRAVERSION
JUDGMENT

	N	%
E	472	50.97
I	454	49.03
S	753	81.32
N	173	18.68
T	705	76.13
F	221	23.87
J	669	72.25
P	257	27.75
I J	316	34.13
I P	138	14.90
E P	119	12.85
E J	353	38.12
S T	582	62.85
S F	171	18.47
N F	50	5.40
N T	123	13.28
S J	590	63.71
S P	163	17.60
N P	94	10.15
N J	79	8.53
T J	528	57.02
T P	177	19.11
F P	80	8.64
F J	141	15.23
I N	81	8.75
E N	92	9.94
I S	373	40.28
E S	380	41.04
E T	369	39.85
E F	103	11.12
I F	118	12.74
I T	336	36.29
S dom	352	38.01
N dom	83	8.96
T dom	392	42.33
F dom	99	10.69

Note: ■ = 1% of sample   8631506

This table is one of a series of tables from the CAPT-MBTI Data Bank of MBTI records submitted to CAPT for computer scoring between 1971 and December 1982. The subjects were males who, at time of testing, were 25 years of age or older, not enrolled in school, had completed high school and had not attended college. This sample was drawn from 55,971 Form F records and 32,671 Form G records. These two data banks were comprised of 56% females and 44% males; education level completed: 6% some grade school, 30% high school diploma, 25% some college, 18% bachelor degrees, 11% masters degrees, 3% doctoral or post doctoral work, and 6% unknown. Age group percentages were: 11% under 18, 29% 18 to 20, 12% 21 to 24, 10% 25 to 29, 16% 30 to 39, 10% 40 to 49, 5% 50 to 59, 2% 60 plus, and 5% unknown.

Males: Traditional Age College Students

N = 12637

	SENSING		INTUITION				N	%
	THINKING	FEELING	FEELING	THINKING				

ISTJ	ISFJ	INFJ	INTJ
N= 1577	N= 687	N= 335	N= 683
%= 12.48	%= 5.44	%= 2.65	%= 5.40
■■■■■■■■■■■■ ■■	■■■■■	■■■	■■■■■

ISTP	ISFP	INFP	INTP
N= 860	N= 517	N= 672	N= 838
%= 6.81	%= 4.09	%= 5.32	%= 6.63
■■■■■■■	■■■■	■■■■■	■■■■■■■

ESTP	ESFP	ENFP	ENTP
N= 849	N= 557	N= 791	N= 855
%= 6.72	%= 4.41	%= 6.26	%= 6.77
■■■■■■■	■■■■	■■■■■■	■■■■■■■

ESTJ	ESFJ	ENFJ	ENTJ
N= 1619	N= 690	N= 377	N= 730
%= 12.81	%= 5.46	%= 2.98	%= 5.78
■■■■■■■■■■■■ ■■■	■■■■■	■■■	■■■■■■

JUDGMENT — INTROVERSION
PERCEPTION

PERCEPTION — EXTRAVERSION
JUDGMENT

	N	%
E	6468	51.18
I	6169	48.82
S	7356	58.21
N	5281	41.79
T	8011	63.39
F	4626	36.61
J	6698	53.00
P	5939	47.00
I J	3282	25.97
I P	2887	22.85
E P	3052	24.15
E J	3416	27.03
S T	4905	38.81
S F	2451	19.40
N F	2175	17.21
N T	3106	24.58
S J	4573	36.19
S P	2783	22.02
N P	3156	24.97
N J	2125	16.82
T J	4609	36.47
T P	3402	26.92
F P	2537	20.08
F J	2089	16.53
I N	2528	20.00
E N	2753	21.79
I S	3641	28.81
E S	3715	29.40
E T	4053	32.07
E F	2415	19.11
I F	2211	17.50
I T	3958	31.32
S dom	3670	29.04
N dom	2664	21.08
T dom	4047	32.03
F dom	2256	17.85

Note: ■ = 1% of sample   8631507

This table is one of a series of tables from the CAPT-MBTI Data Bank of MBTI records submitted to CAPT for computer scoring between 1971 and December 1982. The subjects were males who, at time of testing, were between 18 and 25 years of age inclusive, enrolled in school and attending college. This sample was drawn from 55,971 Form F records and 32,671 Form G records. These two data banks were comprised of 56% females and 44% males; education level completed: 6% some grade school, 30% high school diploma, 25% some college, 18% bachelor degrees, 11% masters degrees, 3% doctoral or post doctoral work, and 6% unknown. Age group percentages were: 11% under 18, 29% 18 to 20, 12% 21 to 24, 10% 25 to 29, 16% 30 to 39, 10% 40 to 49, 5% 50 to 59, 2% 60 plus, and 5% unknown.

Males: Adult Non-Traditional Age College Students

N = 1501

	SENSING		INTUITION				N	%
	THINKING	FEELING	FEELING	THINKING				

ISTJ	ISFJ	INFJ	INTJ
N= 275	N= 70	N= 36	N= 126
%= 18.32	%= 4.66	%= 2.40	%= 8.39
■■■■■■■■■■	■■■■■	■■	■■■■■■■■
■■■■■■■■			

ISTP	ISFP	INFP	INTP
N= 100	N= 41	N= 74	N= 115
%= 6.66	%= 2.73	%= 4.93	%= 7.66
■■■■■■■	■■■	■■■■■	■■■■■■■■

ESTP	ESFP	ENFP	ENTP
N= 43	N= 30	N= 63	N= 83
%= 2.86	%= 2.00	%= 4.20	%= 5.53
■■■	■■	■■■■	■■■■■■

ESTJ	ESFJ	ENFJ	ENTJ
N= 219	N= 80	N= 43	N= 103
%= 14.59	%= 5.33	%= 2.86	%= 6.86
■■■■■■■■■■■■	■■■■■	■■■	■■■■■■■
■■■■■			

JUDGMENT — INTROVERSION — PERCEPTION

PERCEPTION — EXTRAVERSION — JUDGMENT

	N	%
E	664	44.24
I	837	55.76
S	858	57.16
N	643	42.84
T	1064	70.89
F	437	29.11
J	952	63.42
P	549	36.58
I J	507	33.78
I P	330	21.99
E P	219	14.59
E J	445	29.65
S T	637	42.44
S F	221	14.72
N F	216	14.39
N T	427	28.45
S J	644	42.90
S P	214	14.26
N P	335	22.32
N J	308	20.52
T J	723	48.17
T P	341	22.72
F P	208	13.86
F J	229	15.26
I N	351	23.38
E N	292	19.45
I S	486	32.38
E S	372	24.78
E T	448	29.85
E F	216	14.39
I F	221	14.72
I T	616	41.04
S dom	418	27.85
N dom	308	20.52
T dom	537	35.78
F dom	238	15.86

Note: ■ = 1% of sample   8631508

This table is one of a series of tables from the CAPT-MBTI Data Bank of MBTI records submitted to CAPT for computer scoring between 1971 and December 1982. The subjects were males who, at time of testing, were 25 years of age and older, enrolled in school and attending college. This sample was drawn from 55,971 Form F records and 32,671 Form G records. These two data banks were comprised of 56% females and 44% males; education level completed: 6% some grade school, 30% high school diploma, 25% some college, 18% bachelor degrees, 11% masters degrees, 3% doctoral or post doctoral work, and 6% unknown. Age group percentages were: 11% under 18, 29% 18 to 20, 12% 21 to 24, 10% 25 to 29, 16% 30 to 39, 10% 40 to 49, 5% 50 to 59, 2% 60 plus, and 5% unknown.

Males: Adult College Graduates

N = 6814

	SENSING			INTUITION	
	THINKING	FEELING	FEELING	THINKING	

ISTJ	ISFJ	INFJ	INTJ
N= 1210	N= 293	N= 238	N= 671
%= 17.76	%= 4.30	%= 3.49	%= 9.85
■■■■■■■■■■ ■■■■■■■	■■■■	■■■	■■■■■■■■■
ISTP	ISFP	INFP	INTP
N= 217	N= 115	N= 337	N= 418
%= 3.18	%= 1.69	%= 4.95	%= 6.13
■■■	■■	■■■■■	■■■■■■
ESTP	ESFP	ENFP	ENTP
N= 183	N= 99	N= 391	N= 357
%= 2.69	%= 1.45	%= 5.74	%= 5.24
■■■	■	■■■■■■	■■■■■
ESTJ	ESFJ	ENFJ	ENTJ
N= 1025	N= 239	N= 272	N= 749
%= 15.04	%= 3.51	%= 3.99	%= 10.99
■■■■■■■■■■ ■■■■■	■■■■	■■■■	■■■■■■■■■■ ■

JUDGMENT — PERCEPTION — PERCEPTION — JUDGMENT
INTROVERSION — EXTRAVERSION

	N	%
E	3315	48.65
I	3499	51.35
S	3381	49.62
N	3433	50.38
T	4830	70.88
F	1984	29.12
J	4697	68.93
P	2117	31.07
I J	2412	35.40
I P	1087	15.95
E P	1030	15.12
E J	2285	33.53
S T	2635	38.67
S F	746	10.95
N F	1238	18.17
N T	2195	32.21
S J	2767	40.61
S P	614	9.01
N P	1503	22.06
N J	1930	28.32
T J	3655	53.64
T P	1175	17.24
F P	942	13.82
F J	1042	15.29
I N	1664	24.42
E N	1769	25.96
I S	1835	26.93
E S	1546	22.69
E T	2314	33.96
E F	1001	14.69
I F	983	14.43
I T	2516	36.92
S dom	1785	26.20
N dom	1657	24.32
T dom	2409	35.35
F dom	963	14.13

Note: ■ = 1% of sample   8631509

This table is one of a series of tables from the CAPT-MBTI Data Bank of MBTI records submitted to CAPT for computer scoring between 1971 and December 1982. The subjects were males who, at time of testing, were 25 years of age and older, not enrolled in school and had completed four years of college. This sample was drawn from 55,971 Form F records and 32,671 Form G records. These two data banks were comprised of 56% females and 44% males; education level completed: 6% some grade school, 30% high school diploma, 25% some college, 18% bachelor degrees, 11% masters degrees, 3% doctoral or post doctoral work, and 6% unknown. Age group percentages were: 11% under 18, 29% 18 to 20, 12% 21 to 24, 10% 25 to 29, 16% 30 to 39, 10% 40 to 49, 5% 50 to 59, 2% 60 plus, and 5% unknown.

Males: Traditional Age High School Students

N = 1204

	SENSING		INTUITION				N	%
	THINKING	FEELING	FEELING	THINKING				

<table>
<tr><td colspan="2">

ISTJ

N= 113
%= 9.39

■■■■■■■■■
</td><td colspan="2">

ISFJ

N= 46
%= 3.82

■■■■
</td><td colspan="2">

INFJ

N= 29
%= 2.41

■■
</td><td colspan="2">

INTJ

N= 71
%= 5.90

■■■■■■
</td></tr>
</table>

		N	%
E		630	52.33
I		574	47.67
S		619	51.41
N		585	48.59
T		718	59.63
F		486	40.37
J		473	39.29
P		731	60.71
I J		259	21.51
I P		315	26.16
E P		416	34.55
E J		214	17.77
S T		387	32.14
S F		232	19.27
N F		254	21.10
N T		331	27.49
S J		306	25.42
S P		313	26.00
N P		418	34.72
N J		167	13.87
T J		323	26.83
T P		395	32.81
F P		336	27.91
F J		150	12.46
I N		283	23.50
E N		302	25.08
I S		291	24.17
E S		328	27.24
E T		359	29.82
E F		271	22.51
I F		215	17.86
I T		359	29.82
S dom		340	28.24
N dom		335	27.82
T dom		314	26.08
F dom		215	17.86

ISTP

N= 79
%= 6.56

■■■■■■■

ISFP

N= 53
%= 4.40

■■■■

INFP

N= 87
%= 7.23

■■■■■■■

INTP

N= 96
%= 7.97

■■■■■■■■

ESTP

N= 102
%= 8.47

■■■■■■■■

ESFP

N= 79
%= 6.56

■■■■■■■

ENFP

N= 117
%= 9.72

■■■■■■■■■■

ENTP

N= 118
%= 9.80

■■■■■■■■■■

ESTJ

N= 93
%= 7.72

■■■■■■■■

ESFJ

N= 54
%= 4.49

■■■■

ENFJ

N= 21
%= 1.74

■■

ENTJ

N= 46
%= 3.82

■■■■

Note: ■ = 1% of sample   8631510

This table is one of a series of tables from the CAPT-MBTI Data Bank of MBTI records submitted to CAPT for computer scoring between 1971 and December 1982. The subjects were males who, at time of testing, were between 15 and 18 years of age inclusive, enrolled in school and had completed more than 9 but less than 12 years of school. This sample was drawn from 55,971 Form F records and 32,671 Form G records. These two data banks were comprised of 56% females and 44% males; education level completed: 6% some grade school, 30% high school diploma, 25% some college, 18% bachelor degrees, 11% masters degrees, 3% doctoral or post doctoral work, and 6% unknown. Age group percentages were: 11% under 18, 29% 18 to 20, 12% 21 to 24, 10% 25 to 29, 16% 30 to 39, 10% 40 to 49, 5% 50 to 59, 2% 60 plus, and 5% unknown.

Males: Traditional Age Junior High School Students

N = 256

	SENSING		INTUITION	
	THINKING	FEELING	FEELING	THINKING

ISTJ	ISFJ	INFJ	INTJ
N= 21	N= 7	N= 4	N= 7
%= 8.20	%= 2.73	%= 1.56	%= 2.73
■■■■■■■■	■■■	■■	■■■

ISTP	ISFP	INFP	INTP
N= 33	N= 7	N= 11	N= 19
%= 12.89	%= 2.73	%= 4.30	%= 7.42
■■■■■■■■■■■■■	■■■	■■■■	■■■■■■■

ESTP	ESFP	ENFP	ENTP
N= 31	N= 15	N= 32	N= 28
%= 12.11	%= 5.86	%= 12.50	%= 10.94
■■■■■■■■■■■■	■■■■■■	■■■■■■■■■■■■■	■■■■■■■■■■■

ESTJ	ESFJ	ENFJ	ENTJ
N= 21	N= 6	N= 6	N= 8
%= 8.20	%= 2.34	%= 2.34	%= 3.12
■■■■■■■■	■■	■■	■■■

JUDGMENT — INTROVERSION — PERCEPTION — PERCEPTION — EXTRAVERSION — JUDGMENT

	N	%
E	147	57.42
I	109	42.58
S	141	55.08
N	115	44.92
T	168	65.62
F	88	34.38
J	80	31.25
P	176	68.75
I J	39	15.23
I P	70	27.34
E P	106	41.41
E J	41	16.02
ST	106	41.41
SF	35	13.67
NF	53	20.70
NT	62	24.22
S J	55	21.48
S P	86	33.59
N P	90	35.16
N J	25	9.77
T J	57	22.27
T P	111	43.36
F P	65	25.39
F J	23	8.98
I N	41	16.02
E N	74	28.91
I S	68	26.56
E S	73	28.52
E T	88	34.38
E F	59	23.05
I F	29	11.33
I T	80	31.25
S dom	74	28.91
N dom	71	27.73
T dom	81	31.64
F dom	30	11.72

Note: ■ = 1% of sample   8631511

This table is one of a series of tables from the CAPT-MBTI Data Bank of MBTI records submitted to CAPT for computer scoring between 1971 and December 1982. The subjects were males who, at time of testing, were between 11 and 15 years of age inclusive, enrolled in school and had completed more than 6 but less than 9 years of school. This sample was drawn from 55,971 Form F records and 32,671 Form G records. These two data banks were comprised of 56% females and 44% males; education level completed: 6% some grade school, 30% high school diploma, 25% some college, 18% bachelor degrees, 11% masters degrees, 3% doctoral or post doctoral work, and 6% unknown. Age group percentages were: 11% under 18, 29% 18 to 20, 12% 21 to 24, 10% 25 to 29, 16% 30 to 39, 10% 40 to 49, 5% 50 to 59, 2% 60 plus, and 5% unknown.

N = 4973

	SENSING		INTUITION	
	THINKING	FEELING	FEELING	THINKING

ISTJ	ISFJ	INFJ	INTJ
N= 302	N= 455	N= 154	N= 98
%= 6.07	%= 9.15	%= 3.10	%= 1.97
■■■■■■	■■■■■■■■■	■■■	■■

ISTP	ISFP	INFP	INTP
N= 127	N= 301	N= 335	N= 137
%= 2.55	%= 6.05	%= 6.74	%= 2.75
■■■	■■■■■■	■■■■■■■	■■■

ESTP	ESFP	ENFP	ENTP
N= 192	N= 524	N= 749	N= 217
%= 3.86	%= 10.54	%= 15.06	%= 4.36
■■■■	■■■■■■■■■■ ■	■■■■■■■■■■ ■■■■■	■■■■

ESTJ	ESFJ	ENFJ	ENTJ
N= 366	N= 590	N= 260	N= 166
%= 7.36	%= 11.86	%= 5.23	%= 3.34
■■■■■■■	■■■■■■■■■■■ ■■	■■■■■	■■■

JUDGMENT — INTROVERSION — PERCEPTION
PERCEPTION — EXTRAVERSION — JUDGMENT

	N	%
E	3064	61.61
I	1909	38.39
S	2857	57.45
N	2116	42.55
T	1605	32.27
F	3368	67.73
J	2391	48.08
P	2582	51.92
I J	1009	20.29
I P	900	18.10
E P	1682	33.82
E J	1382	27.79
S T	987	19.85
S F	1870	37.60
N F	1498	30.12
N T	618	12.43
S J	1713	34.45
S P	1144	23.00
N P	1438	28.92
N J	678	13.63
T J	932	18.74
T P	673	13.53
F P	1909	38.39
F J	1459	29.34
I N	724	14.56
E N	1392	27.99
I S	1185	23.83
E S	1672	33.62
E T	941	18.92
E F	2123	42.69
I F	1245	25.04
I T	664	13.35
S dom	1473	29.62
N dom	1218	24.49
T dom	796	16.01
F dom	1486	29.88

Note: ■ = 1% of sample   8631527

This table is one of a series of tables from the CAPT-MBTI Data Bank of MBTI records submitted to CAPT for computer scoring between 1971 and December 1982. This sample was drawn from 55,971 Form F records and 32,671 Form G records. These two data banks were comprised of 56% females and 44% males; education level completed: 6% some grade school, 30% high school diploma, 25% some college, 18% bachelor degrees, 11% masters degrees, 3% doctoral or post doctoral work, and 6% unknown. Age group percentages were: 11% under 18, 29% 18 to 20, 12% 21 to 24, 10% 25 to 29, 16% 30 to 39, 10% 40 to 49, 5% 50 to 59, 2% 60 plus, and 5% unknown.

N = 13716

	SENSING		INTUITION	
	THINKING	FEELING	FEELING	THINKING

ISTJ	ISFJ	INFJ	INTJ
N= 900	N= 1548	N= 490	N= 272
%= 6.56	%= 11.29	%= 3.57	%= 1.98
■■■■■■■	■■■■■■■■■■■	■■■■	■■
	■		

ISTP	ISFP	INFP	INTP
N= 329	N= 798	N= 758	N= 276
%= 2.40	%= 5.82	%= 5.53	%= 2.01
■■	■■■■■■	■■■■■■	■■

ESTP	ESFP	ENFP	ENTP
N= 425	N= 1220	N= 1637	N= 467
%= 3.10	%= 8.89	%= 11.93	%= 3.40
■■■	■■■■■■■■■	■■■■■■■■■■■	■■■
		■■	

ESTJ	ESFJ	ENFJ	ENTJ
N= 1178	N= 2133	N= 877	N= 408
%= 8.59	%= 15.55	%= 6.39	%= 2.97
■■■■■■■■	■■■■■■■■■■■	■■■■■■	■■■
	■■■■■■		

JUDGMENT — INTROVERSION — PERCEPTION — PERCEPTION — EXTRAVERSION — JUDGMENT

	N	%
E	8345	60.84
I	5371	39.16
S	8531	62.20
N	5185	37.80
T	4255	31.02
F	9461	68.98
J	7806	56.91
P	5910	43.09
I J	3210	23.40
I P	2161	15.76
E P	3749	27.33
E J	4596	33.51
S T	2832	20.65
S F	5699	41.55
N F	3762	27.43
N T	1423	10.37
S J	5759	41.99
S P	2772	20.21
N P	3138	22.88
N J	2047	14.92
T J	2758	20.11
T P	1497	10.91
F P	4413	32.17
F J	5048	36.80
I N	1796	13.09
E N	3389	24.71
I S	3575	26.06
E S	4956	36.13
E T	2478	18.07
E F	5867	42.77
I F	3594	26.20
I T	1777	12.96
S dom	4093	29.84
N dom	2866	20.90
T dom	2191	15.97
F dom	4566	33.29

Note: ■ = 1% of sample   8631528

This table is one of a series of tables from the CAPT-MBTI Data Bank of MBTI records submitted to CAPT for computer scoring between 1971 and December 1982. This sample was drawn from 55,971 Form F records and 32,671 Form G records. These two data banks were comprised of 56% females and 44% males; education level completed: 6% some grade school, 30% high school diploma, 25% some college, 18% bachelor degrees, 11% masters degrees, 3% doctoral or post doctoral work, and 6% unknown. Age group percentages were: 11% under 18, 29% 18 to 20, 12% 21 to 24, 10% 25 to 29, 16% 30 to 39, 10% 40 to 49, 5% 50 to 59, 2% 60 plus, and 5% unknown.

N = 5738

	SENSING		INTUITION	
	THINKING	FEELING	FEELING	THINKING

ISTJ	ISFJ	INFJ	INTJ
N= 463	N= 653	N= 268	N= 197
%= 8.07	%= 11.38	%= 4.67	%= 3.43
■■■■■■■■	■■■■■■■■■■■ ■	■■■■■	■■■

ISTP	ISFP	INFP	INTP
N= 129	N= 275	N= 360	N= 152
%= 2.25	%= 4.79	%= 6.27	%= 2.65
■■	■■■■■	■■■■■■	■■■

ESTP	ESFP	ENFP	ENTP
N= 134	N= 342	N= 604	N= 238
%= 2.34	%= 5.96	%= 10.53	%= 4.15
■■	■■■■■■	■■■■■■■■■■ ■	■■■■

ESTJ	ESFJ	ENFJ	ENTJ
N= 545	N= 705	N= 396	N= 277
%= 9.50	%= 12.29	%= 6.90	%= 4.83
■■■■■■■■■	■■■■■■■■■■■■ ■■	■■■■■■■	■■■■■

JUDGMENT — INTROVERSION
PERCEPTION

PERCEPTION — EXTRAVERSION
JUDGMENT

	N	%
E	3241	56.48
I	2497	43.52
S	3246	56.57
N	2492	43.43
T	2135	37.21
F	3603	62.79
J	3504	61.07
P	2234	38.93
I J	1581	27.55
I P	916	15.96
E P	1318	22.97
E J	1923	33.51
S T	1271	22.15
S F	1975	34.42
N F	1628	28.37
N T	864	15.06
S J	2366	41.23
S P	880	15.34
N P	1354	23.60
N J	1138	19.83
T J	1482	25.83
T P	653	11.38
F P	1581	27.55
F J	2022	35.24
I N	977	17.03
E N	1515	26.40
I S	1520	26.49
E S	1726	30.08
E T	1194	20.81
E F	2047	35.67
I F	1556	27.12
I T	941	16.40
S dom	1592	27.74
N dom	1307	22.78
T dom	1103	19.22
F dom	1736	30.25

Note: ■ = 1% of sample   8631529

This table is one of a series of tables from the CAPT-MBTI Data Bank of MBTI records submitted to CAPT for computer scoring between 1971 and December 1982. This sample was drawn from 55,971 Form F records and 32,671 Form G records. These two data banks were comprised of 56% females and 44% males; education level completed: 6% some grade school, 30% high school diploma, 25% some college, 18% bachelor degrees, 11% masters degrees, 3% doctoral or post doctoral work, and 6% unknown. Age group percentages were: 11% under 18, 29% 18 to 20, 12% 21 to 24, 10% 25 to 29, 16% 30 to 39, 10% 40 to 49, 5% 50 to 59, 2% 60 plus, and 5% unknown.

N = 5178

	SENSING		INTUITION	
	THINKING	FEELING	FEELING	THINKING

ISTJ	ISFJ	INFJ	INTJ
N= 532	N= 553	N= 286	N= 291
%= 10.27	%= 10.68	%= 5.52	%= 5.62
■■■■■■■■■■	■■■■■■■■■■ ■	■■■■■	■■■■■

ISTP	ISFP	INFP	INTP
N= 134	N= 227	N= 379	N= 184
%= 2.59	%= 4.38	%= 7.32	%= 3.55
■■■	■■■■	■■■■■■■	■■■■

ESTP	ESFP	ENFP	ENTP
N= 104	N= 220	N= 468	N= 241
%= 2.01	%= 4.25	%= 9.04	%= 4.65
■■	■■■■	■■■■■■■■■	■■■■■

ESTJ	ESFJ	ENFJ	ENTJ
N= 455	N= 482	N= 320	N= 302
%= 8.79	%= 9.31	%= 6.18	%= 5.83
■■■■■■■■■	■■■■■■■■■	■■■■■■	■■■■■■

JUDGMENT — INTROVERSION — PERCEPTION — PERCEPTION — EXTRAVERSION — JUDGMENT

	N	%
E	2592	50.06
I	2586	49.94
S	2707	52.28
N	2471	47.72
T	2243	43.32
F	2935	56.68
J	3221	62.21
P	1957	37.79
I J	1662	32.10
I P	924	17.84
E P	1033	19.95
E J	1559	30.11
S T	1225	23.66
S F	1482	28.62
N F	1453	28.06
N T	1018	19.66
S J	2022	39.05
S P	685	13.23
N P	1272	24.57
N J	1199	23.16
T J	1580	30.51
T P	663	12.80
F P	1294	24.99
F J	1641	31.69
I N	1140	22.02
E N	1331	25.70
I S	1446	27.93
E S	1261	24.35
E T	1102	21.28
E F	1490	28.78
I F	1445	27.91
I T	1141	22.04
S dom	1409	27.21
N dom	1286	24.84
T dom	1075	20.76
F dom	1408	27.19

Note: ■ = 1% of sample   8631530

This table is one of a series of tables from the CAPT-MBTI Data Bank of MBTI records submitted to CAPT for computer scoring between 1971 and December 1982. This sample was drawn from 55,971 Form F records and 32,671 Form G records. These two data banks were comprised of 56% females and 44% males; education level completed: 6% some grade school, 30% high school diploma, 25% some college, 18% bachelor degrees, 11% masters degrees, 3% doctoral or post doctoral work, and 6% unknown. Age group percentages were: 11% under 18, 29% 18 to 20, 12% 21 to 24, 10% 25 to 29, 16% 30 to 39, 10% 40 to 49, 5% 50 to 59, 2% 60 plus, and 5% unknown.

Females: Age Group 30 To 39

N = 8711

	SENSING		INTUITION	
	THINKING	FEELING	FEELING	THINKING

ISTJ	ISFJ	INFJ	INTJ
N= 925	N= 985	N= 505	N= 472
%= 10.62	%= 11.31	%= 5.80	%= 5.42
■■■■■■■■■■	■■■■■■■■■■	■■■■■	■■■■■
■	■		

ISTP	ISFP	INFP	INTP
N= 194	N= 379	N= 618	N= 326
%= 2.23	%= 4.35	%= 7.09	%= 3.74
■■	■■■■	■■■■■■■	■■■■

ESTP	ESFP	ENFP	ENTP
N= 147	N= 318	N= 779	N= 350
%= 1.69	%= 3.65	%= 8.94	%= 4.02
■■	■■■■	■■■■■■■■■	■■■■

ESTJ	ESFJ	ENFJ	ENTJ
N= 771	N= 823	N= 572	N= 547
%= 8.85	%= 9.45	%= 6.57	%= 6.28
■■■■■■■■■	■■■■■■■■■	■■■■■■■	■■■■■■

(Column right: JUDGMENT / INTROVERSION / PERCEPTION — PERCEPTION / EXTRAVERSION / JUDGMENT)

	N	%
E	4307	49.44
I	4404	50.56
S	4542	52.14
N	4169	47.86
T	3732	42.84
F	4979	57.16
J	5600	64.29
P	3111	35.71
I J	2887	33.14
I P	1517	17.41
E P	1594	18.30
E J	2713	31.14
S T	2037	23.38
S F	2505	28.76
N F	2474	28.40
N T	1695	19.46
S J	3504	40.23
S P	1038	11.92
N P	2073	23.80
N J	2096	24.06
T J	2715	31.17
T P	1017	11.67
F P	2094	24.04
F J	2885	33.12
I N	1921	22.05
E N	2248	25.81
I S	2483	28.50
E S	2059	23.64
E T	1815	20.84
E F	2492	28.61
I F	2487	28.55
I T	1917	22.01
S dom	2375	27.26
N dom	2106	24.18
T dom	1838	21.10
F dom	2392	27.46

Note: ■ = 1% of sample   8631531

This table is one of a series of tables from the CAPT-MBTI Data Bank of MBTI records submitted to CAPT for computer scoring between 1971 and December 1982. This sample was drawn from 55,971 Form F records and 32,671 Form G records. These two data banks were comprised of 56% females and 44% males; education level completed: 6% some grade school, 30% high school diploma, 25% some college, 18% bachelor degrees, 11% masters degrees, 3% doctoral or post doctoral work, and 6% unknown. Age group percentages were: 11% under 18, 29% 18 to 20, 12% 21 to 24, 10% 25 to 29, 16% 30 to 39, 10% 40 to 49, 5% 50 to 59, 2% 60 plus, and 5% unknown.

Females: Age Group 40 To 49

N = 4811

	SENSING		INTUITION	
	THINKING	FEELING	FEELING	THINKING

ISTJ	ISFJ	INFJ	INTJ
N= 466	N= 568	N= 294	N= 223
%= 9.69	%= 11.81	%= 6.11	%= 4.64

ISTP	ISFP	INFP	INTP
N= 90	N= 198	N= 336	N= 159
%= 1.87	%= 4.12	%= 6.98	%= 3.30

ESTP	ESFP	ENFP	ENTP
N= 69	N= 181	N= 447	N= 154
%= 1.43	%= 3.76	%= 9.29	%= 3.20

ESTJ	ESFJ	ENFJ	ENTJ
N= 458	N= 465	N= 403	N= 300
%= 9.52	%= 9.67	%= 8.38	%= 6.24

	N	%
E	2477	51.49
I	2334	48.51
S	2495	51.86
N	2316	48.14
T	1919	39.89
F	2892	60.11
J	3177	66.04
P	1634	33.96
I J	1551	32.24
I P	783	16.28
E P	851	17.69
E J	1626	33.80
S T	1083	22.51
S F	1412	29.35
N F	1480	30.76
N T	836	17.38
S J	1957	40.68
S P	538	11.18
N P	1096	22.78
N J	1220	25.36
T J	1447	30.08
T P	472	9.81
F P	1162	24.15
F J	1730	35.96
I N	1012	21.04
E N	1304	27.10
I S	1322	27.48
E S	1173	24.38
E T	981	20.39
E F	1496	31.10
I F	1396	29.02
I T	938	19.50
S dom	1284	26.69
N dom	1118	23.24
T dom	1007	20.93
F dom	1402	29.14

Note: ■ = 1% of sample   8631532

This table is one of a series of tables from the CAPT-MBTI Data Bank of MBTI records submitted to CAPT for computer scoring between 1971 and December 1982. This sample was drawn from 55,971 Form F records and 32,671 Form G records. These two data banks were comprised of 56% females and 44% males; education level completed: 6% some grade school, 30% high school diploma, 25% some college, 18% bachelor degrees, 11% masters degrees, 3% doctoral or post doctoral work, and 6% unknown. Age group percentages were: 11% under 18, 29% 18 to 20, 12% 21 to 24, 10% 25 to 29, 16% 30 to 39, 10% 40 to 49, 5% 50 to 59, 2% 60 plus, and 5% unknown.

71

N = 2470

	SENSING		INTUITION	
	THINKING	FEELING	FEELING	THINKING

ISTJ	ISFJ	INFJ	INTJ
N= 258	N= 368	N= 144	N= 93
%= 10.45	%= 14.90	%= 5.83	%= 3.77
■■■■■■■■■■	■■■■■■■■■■■■■■	■■■■■■	■■■■
	■■■■■		

ISTP	ISFP	INFP	INTP
N= 38	N= 97	N= 168	N= 58
%= 1.54	%= 3.93	%= 6.80	%= 2.35
■■	■■■■	■■■■■■■	■■

ESTP	ESFP	ENFP	ENTP
N= 28	N= 97	N= 227	N= 84
%= 1.13	%= 3.93	%= 9.19	%= 3.40
■	■■■■	■■■■■■■■■	■■■

ESTJ	ESFJ	ENFJ	ENTJ
N= 236	N= 259	N= 178	N= 137
%= 9.55	%= 10.49	%= 7.21	%= 5.55
■■■■■■■■■■	■■■■■■■■■■	■■■■■■■	■■■■■■

JUDGMENT — INTROVERSION — PERCEPTION — PERCEPTION — EXTRAVERSION — JUDGMENT

	N	%
E	1246	50.45
I	1224	49.55
S	1381	55.91
N	1089	44.09
T	932	37.73
F	1538	62.27
J	1673	67.73
P	797	32.27
I J	863	34.94
I P	361	14.62
E P	436	17.65
E J	810	32.79
S T	560	22.67
S F	821	33.24
N F	717	29.03
N T	372	15.06
S J	1121	45.38
S P	260	10.53
N P	537	21.74
N J	552	22.35
T J	724	29.31
T P	208	8.42
F P	589	23.85
F J	949	38.42
I N	463	18.74
E N	626	25.34
I S	761	30.81
E S	620	25.10
E T	485	19.64
E F	761	30.81
I F	777	31.46
I T	447	18.10
S dom	751	30.40
N dom	548	22.19
T dom	469	18.99
F dom	702	28.42

Note: ■ = 1% of sample   8631533

This table is one of a series of tables from the CAPT-MBTI Data Bank of MBTI records submitted to CAPT for computer scoring between 1971 and December 1982. This sample was drawn from 55,971 Form F records and 32,671 Form G records. These two data banks were comprised of 56% females and 44% males; education level completed: 6% some grade school, 30% high school diploma, 25% some college, 18% bachelor degrees, 11% masters degrees, 3% doctoral or post doctoral work, and 6% unknown. Age group percentages were: 11% under 18, 29% 18 to 20, 12% 21 to 24, 10% 25 to 29, 16% 30 to 39, 10% 40 to 49, 5% 50 to 59, 2% 60 plus, and 5% unknown.

N = 846

	SENSING		INTUITION			N	%
	THINKING	FEELING	FEELING	THINKING			

ISTJ	ISFJ	INFJ	INTJ
N= 102	N= 154	N= 55	N= 34
%= 12.06	%= 18.20	%= 6.50	%= 4.02
■■■■■■■■■■■■	■■■■■■■■■■■■	■■■■■■■	■■■■
■■	■■■■■■■■		

ISTP	ISFP	INFP	INTP
N= 13	N= 22	N= 49	N= 18
%= 1.54	%= 2.60	%= 5.79	%= 2.13
■■	■■■	■■■■■■	■■

ESTP	ESFP	ENFP	ENTP
N= 8	N= 24	N= 62	N= 12
%= .95	%= 2.84	%= 7.33	%= 1.42
■	■■■	■■■■■■■	■

ESTJ	ESFJ	ENFJ	ENTJ
N= 91	N= 103	N= 70	N= 29
%= 10.76	%= 12.17	%= 8.27	%= 3.43
■■■■■■■■■■■	■■■■■■■■■■■■	■■■■■■■■	■■■
■	■■		

JUDGMENT — INTROVERSION — PERCEPTION
PERCEPTION — EXTRAVERSION — JUDGMENT

	N	%
E	399	47.16
I	447	52.84
S	517	61.11
N	329	38.89
T	307	36.29
F	539	63.71
J	638	75.41
P	208	24.59
I J	345	40.78
I P	102	12.06
E P	106	12.53
E J	293	34.63
S T	214	25.30
S F	303	35.82
N F	236	27.90
N T	93	10.99
S J	450	53.19
S P	67	7.92
N P	141	16.67
N J	188	22.22
T J	256	30.26
T P	51	6.03
F P	157	18.56
F J	382	45.15
I N	156	18.44
E N	173	20.45
I S	291	34.40
E S	226	26.71
E T	140	16.55
E F	259	30.61
I F	280	33.10
I T	167	19.74
S dom	288	34.04
N dom	163	19.27
T dom	151	17.85
F dom	244	28.84

Note: ■ = 1% of sample   8631534

This table is one of a series of tables from the CAPT-MBTI Data Bank of MBTI records submitted to CAPT for computer scoring between 1971 and December 1982. This sample was drawn from 55,971 Form F records and 32,671 Form G records. These two data banks were comprised of 56% females and 44% males; education level completed: 6% some grade school, 30% high school diploma, 25% some college, 18% bachelor degrees, 11% masters degrees, 3% doctoral or post doctoral work, and 6% unknown. Age group percentages were: 11% under 18, 29% 18 to 20, 12% 21 to 24, 10% 25 to 29, 16% 30 to 39, 10% 40 to 49, 5% 50 to 59, 2% 60 plus, and 5% unknown.

N = 3979

	SENSING		INTUITION	
	THINKING	FEELING	FEELING	THINKING

ISTJ	ISFJ	INFJ	INTJ
N= 445	N= 170	N= 96	N= 215
%= 11.18	%= 4.27	%= 2.41	%= 5.40
■■■■■■■■■■■ ■	■■■■	■■	■■■■■

ISTP	ISFP	INFP	INTP
N= 267	N= 194	N= 233	N= 305
%= 6.71	%= 4.88	%= 5.86	%= 7.67
■■■■■■■	■■■■■	■■■■■■	■■■■■■■■

ESTP	ESFP	ENFP	ENTP
N= 302	N= 243	N= 299	N= 319
%= 7.59	%= 6.11	%= 7.51	%= 8.02
■■■■■■■	■■■■■■	■■■■■■■	■■■■■■■■

ESTJ	ESFJ	ENFJ	ENTJ
N= 436	N= 178	N= 98	N= 179
%= 10.96	%= 4.47	%= 2.46	%= 4.50
■■■■■■■■■■ ■	■■■■	■■	■■■■

JUDGMENT — INTROVERSION — PERCEPTION — PERCEPTION — EXTRAVERSION — JUDGMENT

	N	%
E	2054	51.62
I	1925	48.38
S	2235	56.17
N	1744	43.83
T	2468	62.03
F	1511	37.97
J	1817	45.66
P	2162	54.34
I J	926	23.27
I P	999	25.11
E P	1163	29.23
E J	891	22.39
S T	1450	36.44
S F	785	19.73
N F	726	18.25
N T	1018	25.58
S J	1229	30.89
S P	1006	25.28
N P	1156	29.05
N J	588	14.78
T J	1275	32.04
T P	1193	29.98
F P	969	24.35
F J	542	13.62
I N	849	21.34
E N	895	22.49
I S	1076	27.04
E S	1159	29.13
E T	1236	31.06
E F	818	20.56
I F	693	17.42
I T	1232	30.96
S dom	1160	29.15
N dom	929	23.35
T dom	1187	29.83
F dom	703	17.67

Note: ■ = 1% of sample

8631519

This table is one of a series of tables from the CAPT-MBTI Data Bank of MBTI records submitted to CAPT for computer scoring between 1971 and December 1982. This sample was drawn from 55,971 Form F records and 32,671 Form G records. These two data banks were comprised of 56% females and 44% males; education level completed: 6% some grade school, 30% high school diploma, 25% some college, 18% bachelor degrees, 11% masters degrees, 3% doctoral or post doctoral work, and 6% unknown. Age group percentages were: 11% under 18, 29% 18 to 20, 12% 21 to 24, 10% 25 to 29, 16% 30 to 39, 10% 40 to 49, 5% 50 to 59, 2% 60 plus, and 5% unknown.

Males: Age Group 18 To 20

N = 11897

	SENSING		INTUITION	
	THINKING	FEELING	FEELING	THINKING

ISTJ	ISFJ	INFJ	INTJ
N= 1407	N= 643	N= 308	N= 614
%= 11.83	%= 5.40	%= 2.59	%= 5.16
■■■■■■■■■■ ■■	■■■■■	■■■	■■■■■

ISTP	ISFP	INFP	INTP
N= 810	N= 507	N= 651	N= 750
%= 6.81	%= 4.26	%= 5.47	%= 6.30
■■■■■■■	■■■■	■■■■■	■■■■■■

ESTP	ESFP	ENFP	ENTP
N= 880	N= 567	N= 779	N= 792
%= 7.40	%= 4.77	%= 6.55	%= 6.66
■■■■■■■	■■■■■	■■■■■■■	■■■■■■■

ESTJ	ESFJ	ENFJ	ENTJ
N= 1510	N= 679	N= 351	N= 649
%= 12.69	%= 5.71	%= 2.95	%= 5.46
■■■■■■■■■■ ■■■	■■■■■■	■■■	■■■■■

	N	%
E	6207	52.17
I	5690	47.83
S	7003	58.86
N	4894	41.14
T	7412	62.30
F	4485	37.70
J	6161	51.79
P	5736	48.21
I J	2972	24.98
I P	2718	22.85
E P	3018	25.37
E J	3189	26.81
S T	4607	38.72
S F	2396	20.14
N F	2089	17.56
N T	2805	23.58
S J	4239	35.63
S P	2764	23.23
N P	2972	24.98
N J	1922	16.16
T J	4180	35.13
T P	3232	27.17
F P	2504	21.05
F J	1981	16.65
I N	2323	19.53
E N	2571	21.61
I S	3367	28.30
E S	3636	30.56
E T	3831	32.20
E F	2376	19.97
I F	2109	17.73
I T	3581	30.10
S dom	3497	29.39
N dom	2493	20.95
T dom	3719	31.26
F dom	2188	18.39

Note: ■ = 1% of sample   8631520

This table is one of a series of tables from the CAPT-MBTI Data Bank of MBTI records submitted to CAPT for computer scoring between 1971 and December 1982. This sample was drawn from 55,971 Form F records and 32,671 Form G records. These two data banks were comprised of 56% females and 44% males; education level completed: 6% some grade school, 30% high school diploma, 25% some college, 18% bachelor degrees, 11% masters degrees, 3% doctoral or post doctoral work, and 6% unknown. Age group percentages were: 11% under 18, 29% 18 to 20, 12% 21 to 24, 10% 25 to 29, 16% 30 to 39, 10% 40 to 49, 5% 50 to 59, 2% 60 plus, and 5% unknown.

N = 5320

	SENSING		INTUITION	
	THINKING	FEELING	FEELING	THINKING

ISTJ	**ISFJ**	**INFJ**	**INTJ**
N= 697	N= 297	N= 167	N= 350
%= 13.10	%= 5.58	%= 3.14	%= 6.58
■■■■■■■■■■ ■■■	■■■■■■	■■■	■■■■■■■

ISTP	**ISFP**	**INFP**	**INTP**
N= 281	N= 164	N= 293	N= 322
%= 5.28	%= 3.08	%= 5.51	%= 6.05
■■■■■	■■■	■■■■■■	■■■■■■

ESTP	**ESFP**	**ENFP**	**ENTP**
N= 233	N= 158	N= 340	N= 374
%= 4.38	%= 2.97	%= 6.39	%= 7.03
■■■■	■■■	■■■■■■	■■■■■■■

ESTJ	**ESFJ**	**ENFJ**	**ENTJ**
N= 683	N= 313	N= 222	N= 426
%= 12.84	%= 5.88	%= 4.17	%= 8.01
■■■■■■■■■■ ■■■	■■■■■■	■■■■	■■■■■■■■

JUDGMENT — INTROVERSION — PERCEPTION — PERCEPTION — EXTRAVERSION — JUDGMENT

	N	%
E	2749	51.67
I	2571	48.33
S	2826	53.12
N	2494	46.88
T	3366	63.27
F	1954	36.73
J	3155	59.30
P	2165	40.70
I J	1511	28.40
I P	1060	19.92
E P	1105	20.77
E J	1644	30.90
S T	1894	35.60
S F	932	17.52
N F	1022	19.21
N T	1472	27.67
S J	1990	37.41
S P	836	15.71
N P	1329	24.98
N J	1165	21.90
T J	2156	40.53
T P	1210	22.74
F P	955	17.95
F J	999	18.78
I N	1132	21.28
E N	1362	25.60
I S	1439	27.05
E S	1387	26.07
E T	1716	32.26
E F	1033	19.42
I F	921	17.31
I T	1650	31.02
S dom	1385	26.03
N dom	1231	23.14
T dom	1712	32.18
F dom	992	18.65

Note: ■ = 1% of sample

8631521

This table is one of a series of tables from the CAPT-MBTI Data Bank of MBTI records submitted to CAPT for computer scoring between 1971 and December 1982. This sample was drawn from 55,971 Form F records and 32,671 Form G records. These two data banks were comprised of 56% females and 44% males; education level completed: 6% some grade school, 30% high school diploma, 25% some college, 18% bachelor degrees, 11% masters degrees, 3% doctoral or post doctoral work, and 6% unknown. Age group percentages were: 11% under 18, 29% 18 to 20, 12% 21 to 24, 10% 25 to 29, 16% 30 to 39, 10% 40 to 49, 5% 50 to 59, 2% 60 plus, and 5% unknown.

Males: Age Group 25 To 29

N = 3814

	SENSING		INTUITION	
	THINKING	FEELING	FEELING	THINKING

ISTJ	ISFJ	INFJ	INTJ
N= 573	N= 193	N= 139	N= 331
%= 15.02	%= 5.06	%= 3.64	%= 8.68
■■■■■■■■■■■■■■■	■■■■■	■■■■	■■■■■■■■
■■■■■			

ISTP	ISFP	INFP	INTP
N= 182	N= 92	N= 231	N= 298
%= 4.77	%= 2.41	%= 6.06	%= 7.81
■■■■■	■■	■■■■■■	■■■■■■■■

ESTP	ESFP	ENFP	ENTP
N= 116	N= 73	N= 244	N= 237
%= 3.04	%= 1.91	%= 6.40	%= 6.21
■■■	■■	■■■■■■	■■■■■■

ESTJ	ESFJ	ENFJ	ENTJ
N= 482	N= 145	N= 141	N= 337
%= 12.64	%= 3.80	%= 3.70	%= 8.84
■■■■■■■■■■■■	■■■■	■■■■	■■■■■■■■
■■■			

	N	%
E	1775	46.54
I	2039	53.46
S	1856	48.66
N	1958	51.34
T	2556	67.02
F	1258	32.98
J	2341	61.38
P	1473	38.62
I J	1236	32.41
I P	803	21.05
E P	670	17.57
E J	1105	28.97
ST	1353	35.47
SF	503	13.19
NF	755	19.80
NT	1203	31.54
S J	1393	36.52
S P	463	12.14
NP	1010	26.48
NJ	948	24.86
TJ	1723	45.18
TP	833	21.84
FP	640	16.78
FJ	618	16.20
IN	999	26.19
EN	959	25.14
IS	1040	27.27
ES	816	21.39
ET	1172	30.73
EF	603	15.81
IF	655	17.17
IT	1384	36.29
S dom	955	25.04
N dom	951	24.93
T dom	1299	34.06
F dom	609	15.97

Note: ■ = 1% of sample   8631522

This table is one of a series of tables from the CAPT-MBTI Data Bank of MBTI records submitted to CAPT for computer scoring between 1971 and December 1982. This sample was drawn from 55,971 Form F records and 32,671 Form G records. These two data banks were comprised of 56% females and 44% males; education level completed: 6% some grade school, 30% high school diploma, 25% some college, 18% bachelor degrees, 11% masters degrees, 3% doctoral or post doctoral work, and 6% unknown. Age group percentages were: 11% under 18, 29% 18 to 20, 12% 21 to 24, 10% 25 to 29, 16% 30 to 39, 10% 40 to 49, 5% 50 to 59, 2% 60 plus, and 5% unknown.

N = 5601

	SENSING		INTUITION				N	%
	THINKING	FEELING	FEELING	THINKING				

ISTJ	ISFJ	INFJ	INTJ
N= 950	N= 259	N= 204	N= 516
%= 16.96	%= 4.62	%= 3.64	%= 9.21
■■■■■■■■■■■■■■■■■	■■■■■	■■■■	■■■■■■■■■
■■■■■■■			

ISTP	ISFP	INFP	INTP
N= 204	N= 98	N= 274	N= 369
%= 3.64	%= 1.75	%= 4.89	%= 6.59
■■■■	■■	■■■■■	■■■■■■■

ESTP	ESFP	ENFP	ENTP
N= 180	N= 77	N= 286	N= 309
%= 3.21	%= 1.37	%= 5.11	%= 5.52
■■■	■	■■■■■	■■■■■■

ESTJ	ESFJ	ENFJ	ENTJ
N= 910	N= 218	N= 199	N= 548
%= 16.25	%= 3.89	%= 3.55	%= 9.78
■■■■■■■■■■■■■■■■	■■■■	■■■■	■■■■■■■■■■
■■■■■■			

JUDGMENT — INTROVERSION — PERCEPTION
PERCEPTION — EXTRAVERSION — JUDGMENT

	N	%
E	2727	48.69
I	2874	51.31
S	2896	51.71
N	2705	48.29
T	3986	71.17
F	1615	28.83
J	3804	67.92
P	1797	32.08
I J	1929	34.44
I P	945	16.87
E P	852	15.21
E J	1875	33.48
S T	2244	40.06
S F	652	11.64
N F	963	17.19
N T	1742	31.10
S J	2337	41.72
S P	559	9.98
N P	1238	22.10
N J	1467	26.19
T J	2924	52.20
T P	1062	18.96
F P	735	13.12
F J	880	15.71
I N	1363	24.33
E N	1342	23.96
I S	1511	26.98
E S	1385	24.73
E T	1947	34.76
E F	780	13.93
I F	835	14.91
I T	2039	36.40
S dom	1466	26.17
N dom	1315	23.48
T dom	2031	36.26
F dom	789	14.09

Note: ■ = 1% of sample   8631523

This table is one of a series of tables from the CAPT-MBTI Data Bank of MBTI records submitted to CAPT for computer scoring between 1971 and December 1982. This sample was drawn from 55,971 Form F records and 32,671 Form G records. These two data banks were comprised of 56% females and 44% males; education level completed: 6% some grade school, 30% high school diploma, 25% some college, 18% bachelor degrees, 11% masters degrees, 3% doctoral or post doctoral work, and 6% unknown. Age group percentages were: 11% under 18, 29% 18 to 20, 12% 21 to 24, 10% 25 to 29, 16% 30 to 39, 10% 40 to 49, 5% 50 to 59, 2% 60 plus, and 5% unknown.

N = 3812

	SENSING		INTUITION	
	THINKING	FEELING	FEELING	THINKING

ISTJ	ISFJ	INFJ	INTJ
N= 805	N= 167	N= 118	N= 312
%= 21.12	%= 4.38	%= 3.10	%= 8.18
■■■■■■■■■	■■■■	■■■	■■■■■■■■
■■■■■■■■■			
■			

ISTP	ISFP	INFP	INTP
N= 141	N= 59	N= 154	N= 185
%= 3.70	%= 1.55	%= 4.04	%= 4.85
■■■■	■■	■■■■	■■■■■

ESTP	ESFP	ENFP	ENTP
N= 123	N= 65	N= 176	N= 188
%= 3.23	%= 1.71	%= 4.62	%= 4.93
■■■	■■	■■■■■	■■■■■

ESTJ	ESFJ	ENFJ	ENTJ
N= 668	N= 130	N= 140	N= 381
%= 17.52	%= 3.41	%= 3.67	%= 9.99
■■■■■■■■■	■■■	■■■■	■■■■■■■■■
■■■■■■■			

JUDGMENT — INTROVERSION — PERCEPTION — PERCEPTION — EXTRAVERSION — JUDGMENT

	N	%
E	1871	49.08
I	1941	50.92
S	2158	56.61
N	1654	43.39
T	2803	73.53
F	1009	26.47
J	2721	71.38
P	1091	28.62
I J	1402	36.78
I P	539	14.14
E P	552	14.48
E J	1319	34.60
S T	1737	45.57
S F	421	11.04
N F	588	15.42
N T	1066	27.96
S J	1770	46.43
S P	388	10.18
N P	703	18.44
N J	951	24.95
T J	2166	56.82
T P	637	16.71
F P	454	11.91
F J	555	14.56
I N	769	20.17
E N	885	23.22
I S	1172	30.75
E S	986	25.87
E T	1360	35.68
E F	511	13.41
I F	498	13.06
I T	1443	37.85
S dom	1160	30.43
N dom	794	20.83
T dom	1375	36.07
F dom	483	12.67

Note: ■ = 1% of sample   8631524

This table is one of a series of tables from the CAPT-MBTI Data Bank of MBTI records submitted to CAPT for computer scoring between 1971 and December 1982. This sample was drawn from 55,971 Form F records and 32,671 Form G records. These two data banks were comprised of 56% females and 44% males; education level completed: 6% some grade school, 30% high school diploma, 25% some college, 18% bachelor degrees, 11% masters degrees, 3% doctoral or post doctoral work, and 6% unknown. Age group percentages were: 11% under 18, 29% 18 to 20, 12% 21 to 24, 10% 25 to 29, 16% 30 to 39, 10% 40 to 49, 5% 50 to 59, 2% 60 plus, and 5% unknown.

N = 1795

	SENSING		INTUITION	
	THINKING	FEELING	FEELING	THINKING

ISTJ	ISFJ	INFJ	INTJ
N= 376	N= 84	N= 47	N= 138
%= 20.95	%= 4.68	%= 2.62	%= 7.69
■■■■■■■■■	■■■■■	■■■	■■■■■■■■
■■■■■■■■■			
■			

ISTP	ISFP	INFP	INTP
N= 64	N= 42	N= 61	N= 70
%= 3.57	%= 2.34	%= 3.40	%= 3.90
■■■■	■■	■■■	■■■■

ESTP	ESFP	ENFP	ENTP
N= 59	N= 30	N= 85	N= 75
%= 3.29	%= 1.67	%= 4.74	%= 4.18
■■■	■■	■■■■■	■■■■

ESTJ	ESFJ	ENFJ	ENTJ
N= 330	N= 96	N= 68	N= 170
%= 18.38	%= 5.35	%= 3.79	%= 9.47
■■■■■■■■	■■■■■	■■■■	■■■■■■■■
■■■■■■■			

JUDGMENT — INTROVERSION / PERCEPTION — EXTRAVERSION / PERCEPTION / JUDGMENT

	N	%
E	913	50.86
I	882	49.14
S	1081	60.22
N	714	39.78
T	1282	71.42
F	513	28.58
J	1309	72.92
P	486	27.08
I J	645	35.93
I P	237	13.20
E P	249	13.87
E J	664	36.99
S T	829	46.18
S F	252	14.04
N F	261	14.54
N T	453	25.24
S J	886	49.36
S P	195	10.86
N P	291	16.21
N J	423	23.57
T J	1014	56.49
T P	268	14.93
F P	218	12.14
F J	295	16.43
I N	316	17.60
E N	398	22.17
I S	566	31.53
E S	515	28.69
E T	634	35.32
E F	279	15.54
I F	234	13.04
I T	648	36.10
S dom	549	30.58
N dom	345	19.22
T dom	634	35.32
F dom	267	14.87

Note: ■ = 1% of sample   8631525

This table is one of a series of tables from the CAPT-MBTI Data Bank of MBTI records submitted to CAPT for computer scoring between 1971 and December 1982. This sample was drawn from 55,971 Form F records and 32,671 Form G records. These two data banks were comprised of 56% females and 44% males; education level completed: 6% some grade school, 30% high school diploma, 25% some college, 18% bachelor degrees, 11% masters degrees, 3% doctoral or post doctoral work, and 6% unknown. Age group percentages were: 11% under 18, 29% 18 to 20, 12% 21 to 24, 10% 25 to 29, 16% 30 to 39, 10% 40 to 49, 5% 50 to 59, 2% 60 plus, and 5% unknown.

Males: Age Group 60 Plus

N = 495

	SENSING		INTUITION	
	THINKING	FEELING	FEELING	THINKING

ISTJ	ISFJ	INFJ	INTJ
N= 105	N= 32	N= 13	N= 42
%= 21.21	%= 6.46	%= 2.63	%= 8.48

ISTP	ISFP	INFP	INTP
N= 15	N= 22	N= 19	N= 12
%= 3.03	%= 4.44	%= 3.84	%= 2.42

ESTP	ESFP	ENFP	ENTP
N= 10	N= 13	N= 25	N= 9
%= 2.02	%= 2.63	%= 5.05	%= 1.82

ESTJ	ESFJ	ENFJ	ENTJ
N= 103	N= 19	N= 17	N= 39
%= 20.81	%= 3.84	%= 3.43	%= 7.88

JUDGMENT — PERCEPTION — PERCEPTION — JUDGMENT

INTROVERSION — EXTRAVERSION

	N	%
E	235	47.47
I	260	52.53
S	319	64.44
N	176	35.56
T	335	67.68
F	160	32.32
J	370	74.75
P	125	25.25
I J	192	38.79
I P	68	13.74
E P	57	11.52
E J	178	35.96
S T	233	47.07
S F	86	17.37
N F	74	14.95
N T	102	20.61
S J	259	52.32
S P	60	12.12
N P	65	13.13
N J	111	22.42
T J	289	58.38
T P	46	9.29
F P	79	15.96
F J	81	16.36
I N	86	17.37
E N	90	18.18
I S	174	35.15
E S	145	29.29
E T	161	32.53
E F	74	14.95
I F	86	17.37
I T	174	35.15
S dom	160	32.32
N dom	89	17.98
T dom	169	34.14
F dom	77	15.56

Note: ■ = 1% of sample   8631526

This table is one of a series of tables from the CAPT-MBTI Data Bank of MBTI records submitted to CAPT for computer scoring between 1971 and December 1982. This sample was drawn from 55,971 Form F records and 32,671 Form G records. These two data banks were comprised of 56% females and 44% males; education level completed: 6% some grade school, 30% high school diploma, 25% some college, 18% bachelor degrees, 11% masters degrees, 3% doctoral or post doctoral work, and 6% unknown. Age group percentages were: 11% under 18, 29% 18 to 20, 12% 21 to 24, 10% 25 to 29, 16% 30 to 39, 10% 40 to 49, 5% 50 to 59, 2% 60 plus, and 5% unknown.

EXTRAVERT-INTROVERT

E Percent	I	Total Sample Size	Sample Description
68.16	31.84	4387	Females: High School Students from Pennsylvania
66.04	33.96	321	Females: Traditional Age Junior High School Students
64.85	35.15	9320	High School Students from Pennsylvania
61.91	38.09	4933	Males: High School Students from Pennsylvania
61.61	38.39	4973	Females: Age Group 15 To 17
60.84	39.16	13716	Females: Age Group 18 To 20
60.49	39.51	1607	Females: Traditional Age High School Students
59.76	40.24	14519	Females: Traditional Age College Students
57.42	42.58	256	Males: Traditional Age Junior High School Students
56.48	43.52	5738	Females: Age Group 21 To 24
55.71	44.29	32731	Females: Form F Databank
54.69	45.31	16880	Females: Form G Databank
53.22	46.78	232557	CAPT Databank Total Population
52.33	47.67	1204	Males: Traditional Age High School Students
52.17	47.83	11897	Males: Age Group 18 To 20
51.67	48.33	5320	Males: Age Group 21 To 24
51.62	48.38	3979	Males: Age Group 15 To 17
51.49	48.51	4811	Females: Age Group 40 To 49
51.39	48.61	23240	Males: Form F Databank
51.18	48.82	12637	Males: Traditional Age College Students
50.97	49.03	926	Males: Adult High School Graduates Without College
50.86	49.14	1795	Males: Age Group 50 To 59
50.45	49.55	2470	Females: Age Group 50 To 59
50.18	49.82	3551	Females: Non-Traditional Age College Students
50.06	49.94	5178	Females: Age Group 25 To 29
49.48	50.52	7952	Females: Adult College Graduates
49.44	50.56	8711	Females: Age Group 30 To 39
49.33	50.67	15791	Males: Form G Databank
49.08	50.92	3812	Males: Age Group 40 To 49
48.69	51.31	5601	Males: Age Group 30 To 39
48.65	51.35	6814	Males: Adult College Graduates
47.47	52.53	495	Males: Age Group 60 Plus
47.23	52.77	343	Males: Adult High School Dropouts
47.16	52.84	846	Females: Age Group 60 Plus
46.68	53.32	2277	Females: Adult High School Graduates, Without College
46.54	53.46	3814	Males: Age Group 25 To 29
45.60	54.40	636	Females: Adult High School Dropouts
44.24	55.76	1501	Males: Adult Non-Traditional Age College Students
43.25	56.75	659	Females: SRI Sample
40.45	59.55	1105	Total SRI Sample
36.32	63.68	446	Males: SRI Sample

S Percent N	Total Sample Size	Sample Description
81.32 18.68	926	Males: Adult High School Graduates Without College
78.00 22.00	659	Females: SRI Sample
75.93 24.07	1105	Total SRI Sample
74.00 26.00	2277	Females: Adult High School Graduates, Without College
72.87 27.13	446	Males: SRI Sample
72.01 27.99	636	Females: Adult High School Dropouts
70.66 29.34	4387	Females: High School Students from Pennsylvania
69.39 30.61	343	Males: Adult High School Dropouts
68.13 31.87	9320	High School Students from Pennsylvania
65.88 34.12	4933	Males: High School Students from Pennsylvania
64.44 35.56	495	Males: Age Group 60 Plus
62.20 37.80	13716	Females: Age Group 18 To 20
61.40 38.60	14519	Females: Traditional Age College Students
61.39 38.61	3551	Females: Non-Traditional Age College Students
61.11 38.89	846	Females: Age Group 60 Plus
60.22 39.78	1795	Males: Age Group 50 To 59
58.86 41.14	11897	Males: Age Group 18 To 20
58.21 41.79	12637	Males: Traditional Age College Students
57.45 42.55	4973	Females: Age Group 15 To 17
57.16 42.84	1501	Males: Adult Non-Traditional Age College Students
56.61 43.39	3812	Males: Age Group 40 To 49
56.57 43.43	5738	Females: Age Group 21 To 24
56.38 43.62	32731	Females: Form F Databank
56.36 43.64	15791	Males: Form G Databank
56.24 43.76	16880	Females: Form G Databank
56.17 43.83	3979	Males: Age Group 15 To 17
55.91 44.09	2470	Females: Age Group 50 To 59
55.08 44.92	256	Males: Traditional Age Junior High School Students
54.77 45.23	23240	Males: Form F Databank
54.12 45.88	232557	CAPT Databank Total Population
53.58 46.42	321	Females: Traditional Age Junior High School Students
53.12 46.88	5320	Males: Age Group 21 To 24
52.28 47.72	5178	Females: Age Group 25 To 29
52.14 47.86	8711	Females: Age Group 30 To 39
51.86 48.14	4811	Females: Age Group 40 To 49
51.77 48.23	1607	Females: Traditional Age High School Students
51.71 48.29	5601	Males: Age Group 30 To 39
51.41 48.59	1204	Males: Traditional Age High School Students
49.62 50.38	6814	Males: Adult College Graduates
48.66 51.34	3814	Males: Age Group 25 To 29
46.79 53.21	7952	Females: Adult College Graduates

THINKING-FEELING

T Percent F		Total Sample Size	Sample Description
76.13	23.87	926	Males: Adult High School Graduates Without College
74.66	25.34	446	Males: SRI Sample
73.53	26.47	3812	Males: Age Group 40 To 49
71.42	28.58	1795	Males: Age Group 50 To 59
71.17	28.83	5601	Males: Age Group 30 To 39
70.89	29.11	1501	Males: Adult Non-Traditional Age College Students
70.88	29.12	6814	Males: Adult College Graduates
69.68	30.32	343	Males: Adult High School Dropouts
69.56	30.44	15791	Males: Form G Databank
67.68	32.32	495	Males: Age Group 60 Plus
67.02	32.98	3814	Males: Age Group 25 To 29
65.62	34.38	256	Males: Traditional Age Junior High School Students
63.55	36.45	23240	Males: Form F Databank
63.39	36.61	12637	Males: Traditional Age College Students
63.27	36.73	5320	Males: Age Group 21 To 24
62.30	37.70	11897	Males: Age Group 18 To 20
62.03	37.97	3979	Males: Age Group 15 To 17
61.06	38.94	4933	Males: High School Students from Pennsylvania
59.63	40.37	1204	Males: Traditional Age High School Students
50.41	49.59	1105	Total SRI Sample
47.55	52.45	9320	High School Students from Pennsylvania
43.32	56.68	5178	Females: Age Group 25 To 29
42.96	57.04	7952	Females: Adult College Graduates
42.84	57.16	8711	Females: Age Group 30 To 39
42.34	57.66	232557	CAPT Databank Total Population
41.98	58.02	636	Females: Adult High School Dropouts
41.77	58.23	16880	Females: Form G Databank
40.16	59.84	3551	Females: Non-Traditional Age College Students
39.89	60.11	4811	Females: Age Group 40 To 49
38.32	61.68	321	Females: Traditional Age Junior High School Students
37.73	62.27	2470	Females: Age Group 50 To 59
37.21	62.79	5738	Females: Age Group 21 To 24
36.29	63.71	846	Females: Age Group 60 Plus
35.92	64.08	2277	Females: Adult High School Graduates, Without College
34.60	65.40	32731	Females: Form F Databank
33.99	66.01	659	Females: SRI Sample
32.37	67.63	4387	Females: High School Students from Pennsylvania
32.27	67.73	4973	Females: Age Group 15 To 17
31.79	68.21	14519	Females: Traditional Age College Students
31.02	68.98	13716	Females: Age Group 18 To 20
27.50	72.50	1607	Females: Traditional Age High School Students

JUDGMENT-PERCEPTION

J Percent	P	Total Sample Size	Sample Description
75.41	24.59	846	Females: Age Group 60 Plus
74.75	25.25	495	Males: Age Group 60 Plus
72.92	27.08	1795	Males: Age Group 50 To 59
72.25	27.75	926	Males: Adult High School Graduates Without College
71.38	28.62	3812	Males: Age Group 40 To 49
69.73	30.27	446	Males: SRI Sample
68.93	31.07	6814	Males: Adult College Graduates
67.92	32.08	5601	Males: Age Group 30 To 39
67.77	32.23	636	Females: Adult High School Dropouts
67.73	32.27	2470	Females: Age Group 50 To 59
67.64	32.36	343	Males: Adult High School Dropouts
67.54	32.46	7952	Females: Adult College Graduates
66.15	33.85	1105	Total SRI Sample
66.04	33.96	4811	Females: Age Group 40 To 49
65.26	34.74	2277	Females: Adult High School Graduates, Without College
64.29	35.71	8711	Females: Age Group 30 To 39
63.73	36.27	659	Females: SRI Sample
63.50	36.50	3551	Females: Non-Traditional Age College Students
63.42	36.58	1501	Males: Adult Non-Traditional Age College Students
62.21	37.79	5178	Females: Age Group 25 To 29
61.38	38.62	3814	Males: Age Group 25 To 29
61.11	38.89	16880	Females: Form G Databank
61.07	38.93	5738	Females: Age Group 21 To 24
59.47	40.53	32731	Females: Form F Databank
59.32	40.68	23240	Males: Form F Databank
59.30	40.70	5320	Males: Age Group 21 To 24
57.86	42.14	15791	Males: Form G Databank
57.66	42.34	14519	Females: Traditional Age College Students
57.60	42.40	4387	Females: High School Students from Pennsylvania
56.98	43.02	232557	CAPT Databank Total Population
56.91	43.09	13716	Females: Age Group 18 To 20
54.62	45.38	9320	High School Students from Pennsylvania
53.00	47.00	12637	Males: Traditional Age College Students
51.98	48.02	4933	Males: High School Students from Pennsylvania
51.79	48.21	11897	Males: Age Group 18 To 20
48.08	51.92	4973	Females: Age Group 15 To 17
45.66	54.34	3979	Males: Age Group 15 To 17
44.86	55.14	321	Females: Traditional Age Junior High School Students
40.82	59.18	1607	Females: Traditional Age High School Students
39.29	60.71	1204	Males: Traditional Age High School Students
31.25	68.75	256	Males: Traditional Age Junior High School Students

SENSING-THINKING

Percent ST	Total Sample Size	Sample Description
62.85	926	Males: Adult High School Graduates Without College
56.28	446	Males: SRI Sample
49.85	343	Males: Adult High School Dropouts
47.07	495	Males: Age Group 60 Plus
46.18	1795	Males: Age Group 50 To 59
45.57	3812	Males: Age Group 40 To 49
42.44	1501	Males: Adult Non-Traditional Age College Students
41.43	15791	Males: Form G Databank
41.41	256	Males: Traditional Age Junior High School Students
40.85	4933	Males: High School Students from Pennsylvania
40.06	5601	Males: Age Group 30 To 39
39.10	1105	Total SRI Sample
38.81	12637	Males: Traditional Age College Students
38.72	11897	Males: Age Group 18 To 20
38.67	6814	Males: Adult College Graduates
37.50	23240	Males: Form F Databank
36.44	3979	Males: Age Group 15 To 17
35.60	5320	Males: Age Group 21 To 24
35.47	3814	Males: Age Group 25 To 29
32.58	9320	High School Students from Pennsylvania
32.14	1204	Males: Traditional Age High School Students
31.13	636	Females: Adult High School Dropouts
27.54	2277	Females: Adult High School Graduates, Without College
27.47	659	Females: SRI Sample
26.16	3551	Females: Non-Traditional Age College Students
25.30	846	Females: Age Group 60 Plus
25.28	16880	Females: Form G Databank
24.78	232557	CAPT Databank Total Population
23.66	5178	Females: Age Group 25 To 29
23.38	8711	Females: Age Group 30 To 39
23.27	4387	Females: High School Students from Pennsylvania
22.74	321	Females: Traditional Age Junior High School Students
22.67	2470	Females: Age Group 50 To 59
22.51	4811	Females: Age Group 40 To 49
22.15	5738	Females: Age Group 21 To 24
21.98	7952	Females: Adult College Graduates
20.80	14519	Females: Traditional Age College Students
20.65	13716	Females: Age Group 18 To 20
20.23	32731	Females: Form F Databank
19.85	4973	Females: Age Group 15 To 17
15.74	1607	Females: Traditional Age High School Students

SENSING-FEELING

Percent SF	Total Sample Size	Sample Description
50.53	659	Females: SRI Sample
47.39	4387	Females: High School Students from Pennsylvania
46.46	2277	Females: Adult High School Graduates, Without College
41.55	13716	Females: Age Group 18 To 20
40.88	636	Females: Adult High School Dropouts
40.60	14519	Females: Traditional Age College Students
37.60	4973	Females: Age Group 15 To 17
36.83	1105	Total SRI Sample
36.14	32731	Females: Form F Databank
36.03	1607	Females: Traditional Age High School Students
35.82	846	Females: Age Group 60 Plus
35.56	9320	High School Students from Pennsylvania
35.23	3551	Females: Non-Traditional Age College Students
34.42	5738	Females: Age Group 21 To 24
33.24	2470	Females: Age Group 50 To 59
30.96	16880	Females: Form G Databank
30.84	321	Females: Traditional Age Junior High School Students
29.35	4811	Females: Age Group 40 To 49
29.34	232557	CAPT Databank Total Population
28.76	8711	Females: Age Group 30 To 39
28.62	5178	Females: Age Group 25 To 29
25.04	4933	Males: High School Students from Pennsylvania
24.81	7952	Females: Adult College Graduates
20.14	11897	Males: Age Group 18 To 20
19.73	3979	Males: Age Group 15 To 17
19.53	343	Males: Adult High School Dropouts
19.40	12637	Males: Traditional Age College Students
19.27	1204	Males: Traditional Age High School Students
18.47	926	Males: Adult High School Graduates Without College
17.52	5320	Males: Age Group 21 To 24
17.37	495	Males: Age Group 60 Plus
17.27	23240	Males: Form F Databank
16.59	446	Males: SRI Sample
14.93	15791	Males: Form G Databank
14.72	1501	Males: Adult Non-Traditional Age College Students
14.04	1795	Males: Age Group 50 To 59
13.67	256	Males: Traditional Age Junior High School Students
13.19	3814	Males: Age Group 25 To 29
11.64	5601	Males: Age Group 30 To 39
11.04	3812	Males: Age Group 40 To 49
10.95	6814	Males: Adult College Graduates

INTUITION-FEELING

Percent NF	Total Sample Size	Sample Description
36.47	1607	Females: Traditional Age High School Students
32.23	7952	Females: Adult College Graduates
30.84	321	Females: Traditional Age Junior High School Students
30.76	4811	Females: Age Group 40 To 49
30.12	4973	Females: Age Group 15 To 17
29.25	32731	Females: Form F Databank
29.03	2470	Females: Age Group 50 To 59
28.40	8711	Females: Age Group 30 To 39
28.37	5738	Females: Age Group 21 To 24
28.32	232557	CAPT Databank Total Population
28.06	5178	Females: Age Group 25 To 29
27.90	846	Females: Age Group 60 Plus
27.62	14519	Females: Traditional Age College Students
27.43	13716	Females: Age Group 18 To 20
27.27	16880	Females: Form G Databank
24.61	3551	Females: Non-Traditional Age College Students
21.10	1204	Males: Traditional Age High School Students
20.70	256	Males: Traditional Age Junior High School Students
20.24	4387	Females: High School Students from Pennsylvania
19.80	3814	Males: Age Group 25 To 29
19.21	5320	Males: Age Group 21 To 24
19.17	23240	Males: Form F Databank
18.25	3979	Males: Age Group 15 To 17
18.17	6814	Males: Adult College Graduates
17.61	2277	Females: Adult High School Graduates, Without College
17.56	11897	Males: Age Group 18 To 20
17.21	12637	Males: Traditional Age College Students
17.19	5601	Males: Age Group 30 To 39
17.14	636	Females: Adult High School Dropouts
16.89	9320	High School Students from Pennsylvania
15.52	15791	Males: Form G Databank
15.48	659	Females: SRI Sample
15.42	3812	Males: Age Group 40 To 49
14.95	495	Males: Age Group 60 Plus
14.54	1795	Males: Age Group 50 To 59
14.39	1501	Males: Adult Non-Traditional Age College Students
13.91	4933	Males: High School Students from Pennsylvania
12.76	1105	Total SRI Sample
10.79	343	Males: Adult High School Dropouts
8.74	446	Males: SRI Sample
5.40	926	Males: Adult High School Graduates Without College

INTUITION-THINKING

Percent NT	Total Sample Size	Sample Description
32.21	6814	Males: Adult College Graduates
31.54	3814	Males: Age Group 25 To 29
31.10	5601	Males: Age Group 30 To 39
28.45	1501	Males: Adult Non-Traditional Age College Students
28.12	15791	Males: Form G Databank
27.96	3812	Males: Age Group 40 To 49
27.67	5320	Males: Age Group 21 To 24
27.49	1204	Males: Traditional Age High School Students
26.05	23240	Males: Form F Databank
25.58	3979	Males: Age Group 15 To 17
25.24	1795	Males: Age Group 50 To 59
24.58	12637	Males: Traditional Age College Students
24.22	256	Males: Traditional Age Junior High School Students
23.58	11897	Males: Age Group 18 To 20
20.98	7952	Females: Adult College Graduates
20.61	495	Males: Age Group 60 Plus
20.21	4933	Males: High School Students from Pennsylvania
19.83	343	Males: Adult High School Dropouts
19.66	5178	Females: Age Group 25 To 29
19.46	8711	Females: Age Group 30 To 39
18.39	446	Males: SRI Sample
17.56	232557	CAPT Databank Total Population
17.38	4811	Females: Age Group 40 To 49
16.48	16880	Females: Form G Databank
15.58	321	Females: Traditional Age Junior High School Students
15.06	5738	Females: Age Group 21 To 24
15.06	2470	Females: Age Group 50 To 59
14.98	9320	High School Students from Pennsylvania
14.37	32731	Females: Form F Databank
14.00	3551	Females: Non-Traditional Age College Students
13.28	926	Males: Adult High School Graduates Without College
12.43	4973	Females: Age Group 15 To 17
11.76	1607	Females: Traditional Age High School Students
11.31	1105	Total SRI Sample
10.99	14519	Females: Traditional Age College Students
10.99	846	Females: Age Group 60 Plus
10.85	636	Females: Adult High School Dropouts
10.37	13716	Females: Age Group 18 To 20
9.10	4387	Females: High School Students from Pennsylvania
8.39	2277	Females: Adult High School Graduates, Without College
6.53	659	Females: SRI Sample

ART
&
COMMUNICATION

Section II

ART AND COMMUNICATION

Samples in Section II

Name of Sample	Number in Sample
Actors	62
Architects	124
Designers	55
Editors and Reporters	113
Fine Artists	114
Journalists	52
Librarians	267
Library Attendants and Assistants	84
Media Specialists	106
Musicians and Composers	136
Photographers	59
Public Relations Workers and Publicity Writers	89
Writers, Artists, Entertainers, and Agents	208

Composite Samples

ARTISTS AND ENTERTAINERS	378
WRITERS AND JOURNALISTS	530

Comments

The samples of this section tend mainly to be people concerned with the creative arts and communications. Creativity implies the creation of something new which is not in existence. Intuition is the function which is directed more toward new possibilities than to present actualities, more toward the symbolic than to the real, and more toward imagination than to the practical. We would therefore expect intuitive types to outnumber sensing types in these samples. (In the general population, we expect about 75% sensing types.)

The four types combining intuition and feeling are in theory the types most likely to be concerned with communication. Since the arts are a medium of communication, we expect more of the intuitives in this section to prefer feeling than thinking.

While types with intuition are expected to predominate in the samples of this section, the proportion of intuitives is expected to range from a very high percent for the most creative samples to a lower percent for samples where collecting and organizing data is important.

Samples in fields with direct communication with people may have more E's and F's; samples requiring more solitary or analytical work may have more I's and T's.

Summary listings of tables for EI, SN, TF, JP, ST, SF, NF and NT will be found after the last type table.

Actors

N = 62

	SENSING		INTUITION	
	THINKING	FEELING	FEELING	THINKING

ISTJ	ISFJ	INFJ	INTJ
N= 3	N= 1	N= 1	N= 6
%= 4.84	%= 1.61	%= 1.61	%= 9.68
■■■■■	■■	■■	■■■■■■■■■■

ISTP	ISFP	INFP	INTP
N= 0	N= 0	N= 7	N= 5
%= 0.00	%= 0.00	%= 11.29	%= 8.06
		■■■■■■■■■■■	■■■■■■■■
		■	

ESTP	ESFP	ENFP	ENTP
N= 2	N= 3	N= 10	N= 7
%= 3.23	%= 4.84	%= 16.13	%= 11.29
■■■	■■■■■	■■■■■■■■■■■	■■■■■■■■■■■
		■■■■■■	■

ESTJ	ESFJ	ENFJ	ENTJ
N= 3	N= 0	N= 8	N= 6
%= 4.84	%= 0.00	%= 12.90	%= 9.68
■■■■■		■■■■■■■■■■■	■■■■■■■■■■
		■■■	

JUDGMENT — INTROVERSION — PERCEPTION — PERCEPTION — EXTRAVERSION — JUDGMENT

	N	%
E	39	62.90
I	23	37.10
S	12	19.35
N	50	80.65
T	32	51.61
F	30	48.39
J	28	45.16
P	34	54.84
I J	11	17.74
I P	12	19.35
E P	22	35.48
E J	17	27.42
S T	8	12.90
S F	4	6.45
N F	26	41.94
N T	24	38.71
S J	7	11.29
S P	5	8.06
N P	29	46.77
N J	21	33.87
T J	18	29.03
T P	14	22.58
F P	20	32.26
F J	10	16.13
I N	19	30.65
E N	31	50.00
I S	4	6.45
E S	8	12.90
E T	18	29.03
E F	21	33.87
I F	9	14.52
I T	14	22.58
S dom	9	14.52
N dom	24	38.71
T dom	14	22.58
F dom	15	24.19

Note: ■ = 1% of sample   8629400

This table is one of a series of tables from the CAPT-MBTI Data Bank of MBTI records submitted to CAPT for computer scoring between 1971 and June, 1984. This sample was drawn from 59,784 records with usable occupational codes from the total data bank of 232,557. This data bank has 51% Form F cases from 1971 to March, 1978, 35% Form F cases from 1978 to June, 1984 and 14% Form G cases from 1978 to December, 1982. An analysis of Form F and G data banks showed the data banks were comprised of 56% females and 44% males; education level completed: 6% some grade school, 30% high school diploma, 25% some college, 18% bachelor degrees, 11% masters degrees, 3% doctoral or post doctoral work, and 6% unknown. Age group percentages were: 11% under 18, 29% 18 to 20, 12% 21 to 24, 10% 25 to 29, 16% 30 to 39, 10% 40 to 49, 5% 50 to 59, 2% 60 plus, and 5% unknown.

N = 124

| | SENSING | | INTUITION | |
| | THINKING | FEELING | FEELING | THINKING |

ISTJ	ISFJ	INFJ	INTJ			N	%
N= 9	N= 4	N= 12	N= 25		E	37	29.84
%= 7.26	%= 3.23	%= 9.68	%= 20.16		I	87	70.16
■■■■■■■	■■■	■■■■■■■■■■	■■■■■■■■■■		S	22	17.74
			■■■■■■■■■■		N	102	82.26
					T	70	56.45
					F	54	43.55
					J	73	58.87
					P	51	41.13
ISTP	ISFP	INFP	INTP		I J	50	40.32
N= 0	N= 1	N= 21	N= 15		I P	37	29.84
%= 0.00	%= .81	%= 16.94	%= 12.10		E P	14	11.29
	■	■■■■■■■■■■	■■■■■■■■■■		E J	23	18.55
		■■■■■■■	■■		S T	16	12.90
					S F	6	4.84
					N F	48	38.71
					N T	54	43.55
ESTP	ESFP	ENFP	ENTP		S J	21	16.94
N= 0	N= 0	N= 8	N= 6		S P	1	.81
%= 0.00	%= 0.00	%= 6.45	%= 4.84		N P	50	40.32
		■■■■■■	■■■■■		N J	52	41.94
					T J	49	39.52
					T P	21	16.94
					F P	30	24.19
					F J	24	19.35
ESTJ	ESFJ	ENFJ	ENTJ		I N	73	58.87
N= 7	N= 1	N= 7	N= 8		E N	29	23.39
%= 5.65	%= .81	%= 5.65	%= 6.45		I S	14	11.29
■■■■■	■	■■■■■	■■■■■		E S	8	6.45
					E T	21	16.94
					E F	16	12.90
					I F	38	30.65
					I T	49	39.52
					S dom	13	10.48
					N dom	51	41.13
					T dom	30	24.19
					F dom	30	24.19

Note: ■ = 1% of sample   8623101

Data collected by Donald W. MacKinnon at the Institute of Personality Assessment and Research, University of California, Berkeley during 1961. Subjects were males and a composite of three matched groups. The first group were 40 architects rated by a panel of experts as being highly creative. The second group were 43 architects who had at least two years experience and had been associated with one of the highly creative architects. The final group was composed of 41 architects none of whom had ever worked with any of the creative architects. All subjects in groups two and three were selected from the Directory of Architects (1955) and matched to group one with respect to age and geographic location of practice. These data are used with permission and were cited in:

MacKinnon, D. W. (1962). The nature and nurture of creative talent. American Psychologist, 17, 484-495.

Designers

N = 55

		SENSING		INTUITION				N	%

	THINKING	FEELING	FEELING	THINKING

ISTJ	ISFJ	INFJ	INTJ
N= 7	N= 2	N= 3	N= 4
%= 12.73	%= 3.64	%= 5.45	%= 7.27

ISTP	ISFP	INFP	INTP
N= 1	N= 2	N= 5	N= 1
%= 1.82	%= 3.64	%= 9.09	%= 1.82

ESTP	ESFP	ENFP	ENTP
N= 1	N= 5	N= 6	N= 3
%= 1.82	%= 9.09	%= 10.91	%= 5.45

ESTJ	ESFJ	ENFJ	ENTJ
N= 2	N= 3	N= 5	N= 5
%= 3.64	%= 5.45	%= 9.09	%= 9.09

	N	%
E	30	54.55
I	25	45.45
S	23	41.82
N	32	58.18
T	24	43.64
F	31	56.36
J	31	56.36
P	24	43.64
I J	16	29.09
I P	9	16.36
E P	15	27.27
E J	15	27.27
S T	11	20.00
S F	12	21.82
N F	19	34.55
N T	13	23.64
S J	14	25.45
S P	9	16.36
N P	15	27.27
N J	17	30.91
T J	18	32.73
T P	6	10.91
F P	18	32.73
F J	13	23.64
I N	13	23.64
E N	19	34.55
I S	12	21.82
E S	11	20.00
E T	11	20.00
E F	19	34.55
I F	12	21.82
I T	13	23.64
S dom	15	27.27
N dom	16	29.09
T dom	9	16.36
F dom	15	27.27

Note: ■ = 1% of sample   8629401

This table is one of a series of tables from the CAPT-MBTI Data Bank of MBTI records submitted to CAPT for computer scoring between 1971 and June, 1984. This sample was drawn from 59,784 records with usable occupational codes from the total data bank of 232,557. This data bank has 51% Form F cases from 1971 to March, 1978, 35% Form F cases from 1978 to June, 1984 and 14% Form G cases from 1978 to December, 1982. An analysis of Form F and G data banks showed the data banks were comprised of 56% females and 44% males; education level completed: 6% some grade school, 30% high school diploma, 25% some college, 18% bachelor degrees, 11% masters degrees, 3% doctoral or post doctoral work, and 6% unknown. Age group percentages were: 11% under 18, 29% 18 to 20, 12% 21 to 24, 10% 25 to 29, 16% 30 to 39, 10% 40 to 49, 5% 50 to 59, 2% 60 plus, and 5% unknown.

Editors and Reporters

N = 113

	SENSING		INTUITION	
	THINKING	FEELING	FEELING	THINKING

ISTJ	ISFJ	INFJ	INTJ
N= 8	N= 7	N= 5	N= 9
%= 7.08	%= 6.19	%= 4.42	%= 7.96
■■■■■■■	■■■■■■	■■■■	■■■■■■■■

ISTP	ISFP	INFP	INTP
N= 2	N= 3	N= 19	N= 8
%= 1.77	%= 2.65	%= 16.81	%= 7.08
■■	■■■	■■■■■■■■■■ ■■■■■■■	■■■■■■■

ESTP	ESFP	ENFP	ENTP
N= 6	N= 6	N= 14	N= 6
%= 5.31	%= 5.31	%= 12.39	%= 5.31
■■■■■	■■■■■	■■■■■■■■■■ ■■	■■■■■

ESTJ	ESFJ	ENFJ	ENTJ
N= 1	N= 3	N= 8	N= 8
%= .88	%= 2.65	%= 7.08	%= 7.08
■	■■■	■■■■■■■	■■■■■■■

JUDGMENT — INTROVERSION — PERCEPTION — PERCEPTION — EXTRAVERSION — JUDGMENT

	N	%
E	52	46.02
I	61	53.98
S	36	31.86
N	77	68.14
T	48	42.48
F	65	57.52
J	49	43.36
P	64	56.64
I J	29	25.66
I P	32	28.32
E P	32	28.32
E J	20	17.70
S T	17	15.04
S F	19	16.81
N F	46	40.71
N T	31	27.43
S J	19	16.81
S P	17	15.04
N P	47	41.59
N J	30	26.55
T J	26	23.01
T P	22	19.47
F P	42	37.17
F J	23	20.35
I N	41	36.28
E N	36	31.86
I S	20	17.70
E S	16	14.16
E T	21	18.58
E F	31	27.43
I F	34	30.09
I T	27	23.89
S dom	27	23.89
N dom	34	30.09
T dom	19	16.81
F dom	33	29.20

Note: ■ = 1% of sample   8629402

This table is one of a series of tables from the CAPT-MBTI Data Bank of MBTI records submitted to CAPT for computer scoring between 1971 and June, 1984. This sample was drawn from 59,784 records with usable occupational codes from the total data bank of 232,557. This data bank has 51% Form F cases from 1971 to March, 1978, 35% Form F cases from 1978 to June, 1984 and 14% Form G cases from 1978 to December, 1982. An analysis of Form F and G data banks showed the data banks were comprised of 56% females and 44% males; education level completed: 6% some grade school, 30% high school diploma, 25% some college, 18% bachelor degrees, 11% masters degrees, 3% doctoral or post doctoral work, and 6% unknown. Age group percentages were: 11% under 18, 29% 18 to 20, 12% 21 to 24, 10% 25 to 29, 16% 30 to 39, 10% 40 to 49, 5% 50 to 59, 2% 60 plus, and 5% unknown.

Fine Artists

N = 114

	SENSING		INTUITION	
	THINKING	FEELING	FEELING	THINKING

ISTJ	ISFJ	INFJ	INTJ
N= 2	N= 3	N= 19	N= 8
%= 1.75	%= 2.63	%= 16.67	%= 7.02
■■	■■■	■■■■■■■■■■ ■■■■■■■	■■■■■■■

ISTP	ISFP	INFP	INTP
N= 0	N= 1	N= 25	N= 12
%= 0.00	%= .88	%= 21.93	%= 10.53
	■	■■■■■■■■■■ ■■■■■■■■■■ ■■	■■■■■■■■■■ ■

ESTP	ESFP	ENFP	ENTP
N= 1	N= 0	N= 16	N= 0
%= .88	%= 0.00	%= 14.04	%= 0.00
■		■■■■■■■■■■ ■■■■	

ESTJ	ESFJ	ENFJ	ENTJ
N= 1	N= 2	N= 14	N= 10
%= .88	%= 1.75	%= 12.28	%= 8.77
■	■■	■■■■■■■■■■ ■■	■■■■■■■■■■

JUDGMENT — INTROVERSION
PERCEPTION
PERCEPTION — EXTRAVERSION
JUDGMENT

	N	%
E	44	38.60
I	70	61.40
S	10	8.77
N	104	91.23
T	34	29.82
F	80	70.18
J	59	51.75
P	55	48.25
I J	32	28.07
I P	38	33.33
E P	17	14.91
E J	27	23.68
S T	4	3.51
S F	6	5.26
N F	74	64.91
N T	30	26.32
S J	8	7.02
S P	2	1.75
N P	53	46.49
N J	51	44.74
T J	21	18.42
T P	13	11.40
F P	42	36.84
F J	38	33.33
I N	64	56.14
E N	40	35.09
I S	6	5.26
E S	4	3.51
E T	12	10.53
E F	32	28.07
I F	48	42.11
I T	22	19.30
S dom	6	5.26
N dom	43	37.72
T dom	23	20.18
F dom	42	36.84

Note: ■ = 1% of sample   8623100

Data collected by Robert Simon during April 1978. Subjects were 32% male and 68% female volunteers responding to a letter from the researcher soliciting participants. Subjects represented 55% of the membership of a Fine Arts Guild, part of the Fine Arts Society in San Diego, California. Demographic data collected from a subset of 30 subjects showed an average of three years in college with 50% of those being art majors; ages ranged from 30 to 68, with an average age of 55. Approximately 23% depended solely on their artwork for an income. These data are used with permission and were cited in:

Simon, R. S. (1979). Jungian types and creativity of professional fine artists. Unpublished doctoral dissertation, United States International University.

Journalists

N = 52

	SENSING		INTUITION	
	THINKING	FEELING	FEELING	THINKING

ISTJ	ISFJ	INFJ	INTJ
N= 2	N= 2	N= 2	N= 4
%= 3.85	%= 3.85	%= 3.85	%= 7.69
■■■■	■■■■	■■■■	■■■■■■■■

ISTP	ISFP	INFP	INTP
N= 0	N= 2	N= 8	N= 2
%= 0.00	%= 3.85	%= 15.38	%= 3.85
	■■■■	■■■■■■■■■■■■■■■	■■■■

ESTP	ESFP	ENFP	ENTP
N= 2	N= 1	N= 11	N= 6
%= 3.85	%= 1.92	%= 21.15	%= 11.54
■■■■	■■	■■■■■■■■■■■■■■■■■■■■■■	■■■■■■■■■■■

ESTJ	ESFJ	ENFJ	ENTJ
N= 3	N= 3	N= 3	N= 1
%= 5.77	%= 5.77	%= 5.77	%= 1.92
■■■■■■	■■■■■■	■■■■■■	■■

JUDGMENT — INTROVERSION — PERCEPTION — PERCEPTION — EXTRAVERSION — JUDGMENT

	N	%
E	30	57.69
I	22	42.31
S	15	28.85
N	37	71.15
T	20	38.46
F	32	61.54
J	20	38.46
P	32	61.54
I J	10	19.23
I P	12	23.08
E P	20	38.46
E J	10	19.23
S T	7	13.46
S F	8	15.38
N F	24	46.15
N T	13	25.00
S J	10	19.23
S P	5	9.62
N P	27	51.92
N J	10	19.23
T J	10	19.23
T P	10	19.23
F P	22	42.31
F J	10	19.23
I N	16	30.77
E N	21	40.38
I S	6	11.54
E S	9	17.31
E T	12	23.08
E F	18	34.62
I F	14	26.92
I T	8	15.38
S dom	7	13.46
N dom	23	44.23
T dom	6	11.54
F dom	16	30.77

Note: ■ = 1% of sample   8629403

This table is one of a series of tables from the CAPT-MBTI Data Bank of MBTI records submitted to CAPT for computer scoring between 1971 and June, 1984. This sample was drawn from 59,784 records with usable occupational codes from the total data bank of 232,557. This data bank has 51% Form F cases from 1971 to March, 1978, 35% Form F cases from 1978 to June, 1984 and 14% Form G cases from 1978 to December, 1982. An analysis of Form F and G data banks showed the data banks were comprised of 56% females and 44% males; education level completed: 6% some grade school, 30% high school diploma, 25% some college, 18% bachelor degrees, 11% masters degrees, 3% doctoral or post doctoral work, and 6% unknown. Age group percentages were: 11% under 18, 29% 18 to 20, 12% 21 to 24, 10% 25 to 29, 16% 30 to 39, 10% 40 to 49, 5% 50 to 59, 2% 60 plus, and 5% unknown.

Librarians

N = 267

	SENSING		INTUITION			N	%

<table>
<tr><td colspan="2" align="center">SENSING</td><td colspan="2" align="center">INTUITION</td></tr>
<tr><td align="center">THINKING</td><td align="center">FEELING</td><td align="center">FEELING</td><td align="center">THINKING</td></tr>
</table>

ISTJ	ISFJ	INFJ	INTJ
N= 29	N= 51	N= 19	N= 10
%= 10.86	%= 19.10	%= 7.12	%= 3.75
■■■■■■■■■■	■■■■■■■■■■	■■■■■■■	■■■■
■	■■■■■■■■■		

ISTP	ISFP	INFP	INTP
N= 6	N= 11	N= 28	N= 8
%= 2.25	%= 4.12	%= 10.49	%= 3.00
■■	■■■■	■■■■■■■■■■	■■■

ESTP	ESFP	ENFP	ENTP
N= 2	N= 9	N= 20	N= 12
%= .75	%= 3.37	%= 7.49	%= 4.49
■	■■■	■■■■■■■	■■■■

ESTJ	ESFJ	ENFJ	ENTJ
N= 15	N= 20	N= 21	N= 6
%= 5.62	%= 7.49	%= 7.87	%= 2.25
■■■■■■	■■■■■■■	■■■■■■■■	■■

JUDGMENT / INTROVERSION / PERCEPTION / PERCEPTION / EXTRAVERSION / JUDGMENT

	N	%
E	105	39.33
I	162	60.67
S	143	53.56
N	124	46.44
T	88	32.96
F	179	67.04
J	171	64.04
P	96	35.96
I J	109	40.82
I P	53	19.85
E P	43	16.10
E J	62	23.22
S T	52	19.48
S F	91	34.08
N F	88	32.96
N T	36	13.48
S J	115	43.07
S P	28	10.49
N P	68	25.47
N J	56	20.97
T J	60	22.47
T P	28	10.49
F P	68	25.47
F J	111	41.57
I N	65	24.34
E N	59	22.10
I S	97	36.33
E S	46	17.23
E T	35	13.11
E F	70	26.22
I F	109	40.82
I T	53	19.85
S dom	91	34.08
N dom	61	22.85
T dom	35	13.11
F dom	80	29.96

Note: ■ = 1% of sample   8629408

This table is one of a series of tables from the CAPT-MBTI Data Bank of MBTI records submitted to CAPT for computer scoring between 1971 and June, 1984. This sample was drawn from 59,784 records with usable occupational codes from the total data bank of 232,557. This data bank has 51% Form F cases from 1971 to March, 1978, 35% Form F cases from 1978 to June, 1984 and 14% Form G cases from 1978 to December, 1982. An analysis of Form F and G data banks showed the data banks were comprised of 56% females and 44% males; education level completed: 6% some grade school, 30% high school diploma, 25% some college, 18% bachelor degrees, 11% masters degrees, 3% doctoral or post doctoral work, and 6% unknown. Age group percentages were: 11% under 18, 29% 18 to 20, 12% 21 to 24, 10% 25 to 29, 16% 30 to 39, 10% 40 to 49, 5% 50 to 59, 2% 60 plus, and 5% unknown.

Library Attendants and Assistants

N = 84

	SENSING		INTUITION	
	THINKING	FEELING	FEELING	THINKING

ISTJ	ISFJ	INFJ	INTJ
N= 10	N= 13	N= 3	N= 3
%= 11.90	%= 15.48	%= 3.57	%= 3.57
■■■■■■■■■■■■	■■■■■■■■■■■■■■	■■■■	■■■■
■■	■■■■■		

ISTP	ISFP	INFP	INTP
N= 2	N= 5	N= 5	N= 1
%= 2.38	%= 5.95	%= 5.95	%= 1.19
■■	■■■■■■	■■■■■■	■

ESTP	ESFP	ENFP	ENTP
N= 3	N= 8	N= 5	N= 1
%= 3.57	%= 9.52	%= 5.95	%= 1.19
■■■■	■■■■■■■■■■	■■■■■■	■

ESTJ	ESFJ	ENFJ	ENTJ
N= 6	N= 8	N= 8	N= 3
%= 7.14	%= 9.52	%= 9.52	%= 3.57
■■■■■■■■	■■■■■■■■■■■	■■■■■■■■■■	■■■■

JUDGMENT — INTROVERSION — PERCEPTION — PERCEPTION — EXTRAVERSION — JUDGMENT

	N	%
E	42	50.00
I	42	50.00
S	55	65.48
N	29	34.52
T	29	34.52
F	55	65.48
J	54	64.29
P	30	35.71
I J	29	34.52
I P	13	15.48
E P	17	20.24
E J	25	29.76
S T	21	25.00
S F	34	40.48
N F	21	25.00
N T	8	9.52
S J	37	44.05
S P	18	21.43
N P	12	14.29
N J	17	20.24
T J	22	26.19
T P	7	8.33
F P	23	27.38
F J	32	38.10
I N	12	14.29
E N	17	20.24
I S	30	35.71
E S	25	29.76
E T	13	15.48
E F	29	34.52
I F	26	30.95
I T	16	19.05
S dom	34	40.48
N dom	12	14.29
T dom	12	14.29
F dom	26	30.95

Note: ■ = 1% of sample   8629409

This table is one of a series of tables from the CAPT-MBTI Data Bank of MBTI records submitted to CAPT for computer scoring between 1971 and June, 1984. This sample was drawn from 59,784 records with usable occupational codes from the total data bank of 232,557. This data bank has 51% Form F cases from 1971 to March, 1978, 35% Form F cases from 1978 to June, 1984 and 14% Form G cases from 1978 to December, 1982. An analysis of Form F and G data banks showed the data banks were comprised of 56% females and 44% males; education level completed: 6% some grade school, 30% high school diploma, 25% some college, 18% bachelor degrees, 11% masters degrees, 3% doctoral or post doctoral work, and 6% unknown. Age group percentages were: 11% under 18, 29% 18 to 20, 12% 21 to 24, 10% 25 to 29, 16% 30 to 39, 10% 40 to 49, 5% 50 to 59, 2% 60 plus, and 5% unknown.

Media Specialists

	SENSING		INTUITION	
	THINKING	FEELING	FEELING	THINKING

ISTJ	ISFJ	INFJ	INTJ
N= 12	N= 10	N= 10	N= 5
%= 11.32	%= 9.43	%= 9.43	%= 4.72

ISTP	ISFP	INFP	INTP
N= 6	N= 6	N= 12	N= 2
%= 5.66	%= 5.66	%= 11.32	%= 1.89

ESTP	ESFP	ENFP	ENTP
N= 0	N= 2	N= 8	N= 5
%= 0.00	%= 1.89	%= 7.55	%= 4.72

ESTJ	ESFJ	ENFJ	ENTJ
N= 8	N= 9	N= 3	N= 8
%= 7.55	%= 8.49	%= 2.83	%= 7.55

	N	%
E	43	40.57
I	63	59.43
S	53	50.00
N	53	50.00
T	46	43.40
F	60	56.60
J	65	61.32
P	41	38.68
I J	37	34.91
I P	26	24.53
E P	15	14.15
E J	28	26.42
S T	26	24.53
S F	27	25.47
N F	33	31.13
N T	20	18.87
S J	39	36.79
S P	14	13.21
N P	27	25.47
N J	26	24.53
T J	33	31.13
T P	13	12.26
F P	28	26.42
F J	32	30.19
I N	29	27.36
E N	24	22.64
I S	34	32.08
E S	19	17.92
E T	21	19.81
E F	22	20.75
I F	38	35.85
I T	25	23.58
S dom	24	22.64
N dom	28	26.42
T dom	24	22.64
F dom	30	28.30

Note: ■ = 1% of sample   8629413

This table is one of a series of tables from the CAPT-MBTI Data Bank of MBTI records submitted to CAPT for computer scoring between 1971 and June, 1984. This sample was drawn from 59,784 records with usable occupational codes from the total data bank of 232,557. This data bank has 51% Form F cases from 1971 to March, 1978, 35% Form F cases from 1978 to June, 1984 and 14% Form G cases from 1978 to December, 1982. An analysis of Form F and G data banks showed the data banks were comprised of 56% females and 44% males; education level completed: 6% some grade school, 30% high school diploma, 25% some college, 18% bachelor degrees, 11% masters degrees, 3% doctoral or post doctoral work, and 6% unknown. Age group percentages were: 11% under 18, 29% 18 to 20, 12% 21 to 24, 10% 25 to 29, 16% 30 to 39, 10% 40 to 49, 5% 50 to 59, 2% 60 plus, and 5% unknown.

Musicians and Composers

N = 136

	SENSING		INTUITION	
	THINKING	FEELING	FEELING	THINKING

ISTJ N= 4 %= 2.94 ■■■	**ISFJ** N= 7 %= 5.15 ■■■■■	**INFJ** N= 6 %= 4.41 ■■■■	**INTJ** N= 12 %= 8.82 ■■■■■■■■■
ISTP N= 3 %= 2.21 ■■	**ISFP** N= 2 %= 1.47 ■	**INFP** N= 13 %= 9.56 ■■■■■■■■■■	**INTP** N= 7 %= 5.15 ■■■■■
ESTP N= 3 %= 2.21 ■■	**ESFP** N= 6 %= 4.41 ■■■■	**ENFP** N= 23 %= 16.91 ■■■■■■■■■■■ ■■■■■■■	**ENTP** N= 8 %= 5.88 ■■■■■■
ESTJ N= 8 %= 5.88 ■■■■■■	**ESFJ** N= 14 %= 10.29 ■■■■■■■■■■■	**ENFJ** N= 15 %= 11.03 ■■■■■■■■■■■ ■	**ENTJ** N= 5 %= 3.68 ■■■■

Side labels: JUDGMENT / INTROVERSION / PERCEPTION / PERCEPTION / EXTRAVERSION / JUDGMENT

	N	%
E	82	60.29
I	54	39.71
S	47	34.56
N	89	65.44
T	50	36.76
F	86	63.24
J	71	52.21
P	65	47.79
I J	29	21.32
I P	25	18.38
E P	40	29.41
E J	42	30.88
S T	18	13.24
S F	29	21.32
N F	57	41.91
N T	32	23.53
S J	33	24.26
S P	14	10.29
N P	51	37.50
N J	38	27.94
T J	29	21.32
T P	21	15.44
F P	44	32.35
F J	42	30.88
I N	38	27.94
E N	51	37.50
I S	16	11.76
E S	31	22.79
E T	24	17.65
E F	58	42.65
I F	28	20.59
I T	26	19.12
S dom	20	14.71
N dom	49	36.03
T dom	23	16.91
F dom	44	32.35

Note: ■ = 1% of sample   8629404

This table is one of a series of tables from the CAPT-MBTI Data Bank of MBTI records submitted to CAPT for computer scoring between 1971 and June, 1984. This sample was drawn from 59,784 records with usable occupational codes from the total data bank of 232,557. This data bank has 51% Form F cases from 1971 to March, 1978, 35% Form F cases from 1978 to June, 1984 and 14% Form G cases from 1978 to December, 1982. An analysis of Form F and G data banks showed the data banks were comprised of 56% females and 44% males; education level completed: 6% some grade school, 30% high school diploma, 25% some college, 18% bachelor degrees, 11% masters degrees, 3% doctoral or post doctoral work, and 6% unknown. Age group percentages were: 11% under 18, 29% 18 to 20, 12% 21 to 24, 10% 25 to 29, 16% 30 to 39, 10% 40 to 49, 5% 50 to 59, 2% 60 plus, and 5% unknown.

Photographers

N = 59

	SENSING		INTUITION				N	%
	THINKING	FEELING	FEELING	THINKING				

ISTJ	ISFJ	INFJ	INTJ
N= 3	N= 1	N= 2	N= 7
%= 5.08	%= 1.69	%= 3.39	%= 11.86
■■■■■	■■	■■■	■■■■■■■■■■■■ ■■

ISTP	ISFP	INFP	INTP
N= 2	N= 1	N= 4	N= 5
%= 3.39	%= 1.69	%= 6.78	%= 8.47
■■■	■■	■■■■■■■	■■■■■■■■

ESTP	ESFP	ENFP	ENTP
N= 0	N= 1	N= 6	N= 10
%= 0.00	%= 1.69	%= 10.17	%= 16.95
	■■	■■■■■■■■■■	■■■■■■■■■■ ■■■■■■■

ESTJ	ESFJ	ENFJ	ENTJ
N= 5	N= 3	N= 4	N= 5
%= 8.47	%= 5.08	%= 6.78	%= 8.47
■■■■■■■■	■■■■■	■■■■■■■	■■■■■■■■

	N	%
E	34	57.63
I	25	42.37
S	16	27.12
N	43	72.88
T	37	62.71
F	22	37.29
J	30	50.85
P	29	49.15
I J	13	22.03
I P	12	20.34
E P	17	28.81
E J	17	28.81
S T	10	16.95
S F	6	10.17
N F	16	27.12
N T	27	45.76
S J	12	20.34
S P	4	6.78
N P	25	42.37
N J	18	30.51
T J	20	33.90
T P	17	28.81
F P	12	20.34
F J	10	16.95
I N	18	30.51
E N	25	42.37
I S	7	11.86
E S	9	15.25
E T	20	33.90
E F	14	23.73
I F	8	13.56
I T	17	28.81
S dom	5	8.47
N dom	25	42.37
T dom	17	28.81
F dom	12	20.34

Note: ■ = 1% of sample   8629405

This table is one of a series of tables from the CAPT-MBTI Data Bank of MBTI records submitted to CAPT for computer scoring between 1971 and June, 1984. This sample was drawn from 59,784 records with usable occupational codes from the total data bank of 232,557. This data bank has 51% Form F cases from 1971 to March, 1978, 35% Form F cases from 1978 to June, 1984 and 14% Form G cases from 1978 to December, 1982. An analysis of Form F and G data banks showed the data banks were comprised of 56% females and 44% males; education level completed: 6% some grade school, 30% high school diploma, 25% some college, 18% bachelor degrees, 11% masters degrees, 3% doctoral or post doctoral work, and 6% unknown. Age group percentages were: 11% under 18, 29% 18 to 20, 12% 21 to 24, 10% 25 to 29, 16% 30 to 39, 10% 40 to 49, 5% 50 to 59, 2% 60 plus, and 5% unknown.

Public Relations Workers and Publicity Writers

N = 89

	SENSING		INTUITION	
	THINKING	FEELING	FEELING	THINKING

ISTJ	ISFJ	INFJ	INTJ
N= 3	N= 5	N= 6	N= 5
%= 3.37	%= 5.62	%= 6.74	%= 5.62
■■■	■■■■■■	■■■■■■	■■■■■■

ISTP	ISFP	INFP	INTP
N= 1	N= 2	N= 3	N= 5
%= 1.12	%= 2.25	%= 3.37	%= 5.62
■	■■	■■■	■■■■■■

ESTP	ESFP	ENFP	ENTP
N= 3	N= 3	N= 14	N= 8
%= 3.37	%= 3.37	%= 15.73	%= 8.99
■■■	■■■	■■■■■■■■■■ ■■■■■■	■■■■■■■■■

ESTJ	ESFJ	ENFJ	ENTJ
N= 13	N= 6	N= 7	N= 5
%= 14.61	%= 6.74	%= 7.87	%= 5.62
■■■■■■■■■■ ■■■■■	■■■■■■■	■■■■■■■■	■■■■■■

	N	%
E	59	66.29
I	30	33.71
S	36	40.45
N	53	59.55
T	43	48.31
F	46	51.69
J	50	56.18
P	39	43.82
I J	19	21.35
I P	11	12.36
E P	28	31.46
E J	31	34.83
ST	20	22.47
SF	16	17.98
NF	30	33.71
NT	23	25.84
S J	27	30.34
S P	9	10.11
NP	30	33.71
NJ	23	25.84
T J	26	29.21
T P	17	19.10
F P	22	24.72
F J	24	26.97
I N	19	21.35
E N	34	38.20
I S	11	12.36
E S	25	28.09
ET	29	32.58
EF	30	33.71
I F	16	17.98
I T	14	15.73
S dom	14	15.73
N dom	33	37.08
T dom	24	26.97
F dom	18	20.22

Note: ■ = 1% of sample   8629406

This table is one of a series of tables from the CAPT-MBTI Data Bank of MBTI records submitted to CAPT for computer scoring between 1971 and June, 1984. This sample was drawn from 59,784 records with usable occupational codes from the total data bank of 232,557. This data bank has 51% Form F cases from 1971 to March, 1978, 35% Form F cases from 1978 to June, 1984 and 14% Form G cases from 1978 to December, 1982. An analysis of Form F and G data banks showed the data banks were comprised of 56% females and 44% males; education level completed: 6% some grade school, 30% high school diploma, 25% some college, 18% bachelor degrees, 11% masters degrees, 3% doctoral or post doctoral work, and 6% unknown. Age group percentages were: 11% under 18, 29% 18 to 20, 12% 21 to 24, 10% 25 to 29, 16% 30 to 39, 10% 40 to 49, 5% 50 to 59, 2% 60 plus, and 5% unknown.

Writers, Artists, Entertainers, and Agents

N = 208

	SENSING		INTUITION	
	THINKING	FEELING	FEELING	THINKING
	ISTJ N= 5 %= 2.40 ■■	**ISFJ** N= 4 %= 1.92 ■■	**INFJ** N= 9 %= 4.33 ■■■■	**INTJ** N= 20 %= 9.62 ■■■■■■■■■■
	ISTP N= 4 %= 1.92 ■■	**ISFP** N= 3 %= 1.44 ■	**INFP** N= 34 %= 16.35 ■■■■■■■■ ■■■■■■	**INTP** N= 26 %= 12.50 ■■■■■■■■ ■■■
	ESTP N= 0 %= 0.00	**ESFP** N= 4 %= 1.92 ■■	**ENFP** N= 40 %= 19.23 ■■■■■■■■ ■■■■■■■■	**ENTP** N= 16 %= 7.69 ■■■■■■■■
	ESTJ N= 6 %= 2.88 ■■■	**ESFJ** N= 3 %= 1.44 ■	**ENFJ** N= 25 %= 12.02 ■■■■■■■■■■ ■■	**ENTJ** N= 9 %= 4.33 ■■■■

(Right margin labels: JUDGMENT / PERCEPTION — INTROVERSION; PERCEPTION / JUDGMENT — EXTRAVERSION)

	N	%
E	103	49.52
I	105	50.48
S	29	13.94
N	179	86.06
T	86	41.35
F	122	58.65
J	81	38.94
P	127	61.06
I J	38	18.27
I P	67	32.21
E P	60	28.85
E J	43	20.67
S T	15	7.21
S F	14	6.73
N F	108	51.92
N T	71	34.13
S J	18	8.65
S P	11	5.29
N P	116	55.77
N J	63	30.29
T J	40	19.23
T P	46	22.12
F P	81	38.94
F J	41	19.71
I N	89	42.79
E N	90	43.27
I S	16	7.69
E S	13	6.25
E T	31	14.90
E F	72	34.62
I F	50	24.04
I T	55	26.44
S dom	13	6.25
N dom	85	40.87
T dom	45	21.63
F dom	65	31.25

Note: ■ = 1% of sample   8629407

This table is one of a series of tables from the CAPT-MBTI Data Bank of MBTI records submitted to CAPT for computer scoring between 1971 and June, 1984. This sample was drawn from 59,784 records with usable occupational codes from the total data bank of 232,557. This data bank has 51% Form F cases from 1971 to March, 1978, 35% Form F cases from 1978 to June, 1984 and 14% Form G cases from 1978 to December, 1982. An analysis of Form F and G data banks showed the data banks were comprised of 56% females and 44% males; education level completed: 6% some grade school, 30% high school diploma, 25% some college, 18% bachelor degrees, 11% masters degrees, 3% doctoral or post doctoral work, and 6% unknown. Age group percentages were: 11% under 18, 29% 18 to 20, 12% 21 to 24, 10% 25 to 29, 16% 30 to 39, 10% 40 to 49, 5% 50 to 59, 2% 60 plus, and 5% unknown.

ARTISTS AND ENTERTAINERS

N = 378

	SENSING		INTUITION	
	THINKING	FEELING	FEELING	THINKING
JUDGMENT (INTROVERSION)	ISTJ N= 22 %= 5.82 ■■■■■■	ISFJ N= 13 %= 3.44 ■■■	INFJ N= 17 %= 4.50 ■■■■	INTJ N= 35 %= 9.26 ■■■■■■■■■
PERCEPTION	ISTP N= 7 %= 1.85 ■■	ISFP N= 6 %= 1.59 ■■	INFP N= 38 %= 10.05 ■■■■■■■■■■	INTP N= 20 %= 5.29 ■■■■■
PERCEPTION (EXTRAVERSION)	ESTP N= 6 %= 1.59 ■■	ESFP N= 19 %= 5.03 ■■■■■	ENFP N= 57 %= 15.08 ■■■■■■■■■■■ ■■■■■	ENTP N= 33 %= 8.73 ■■■■■■■■■
JUDGMENT	ESTJ N= 21 %= 5.56 ■■■■■■	ESFJ N= 23 %= 6.08 ■■■■■■	ENFJ N= 38 %= 10.05 ■■■■■■■■■■	ENTJ N= 23 %= 6.08 ■■■■■■

	N	%
E	220	58.20
I	158	41.80
S	117	30.95
N	261	69.05
T	167	44.18
F	211	55.82
J	192	50.79
P	186	49.21
I J	87	23.02
I P	71	18.78
E P	115	30.42
E J	105	27.78
S T	56	14.81
S F	61	16.14
N F	150	39.68
N T	111	29.37
S J	79	20.90
S P	38	10.05
N P	148	39.15
N J	113	29.89
T J	101	26.72
T P	66	17.46
F P	120	31.75
F J	91	24.07
I N	110	29.10
E N	151	39.95
I S	48	12.70
E S	69	18.25
E T	83	21.96
E F	137	36.24
I F	74	19.58
I T	84	22.22
S dom	60	15.87
N dom	142	37.57
T dom	71	18.78
F dom	105	27.78

Note: ■ = 1% of sample   8629412

This table is one of a series of tables from the CAPT-MBTI Data Bank of MBTI records submitted to CAPT for computer scoring between 1971 and June, 1984. This sample was drawn from 59,784 records with usable occupational codes from the total data bank of 232,557. This data bank has 51% Form F cases from 1971 to March, 1978, 35% Form F cases from 1978 to June, 1984 and 14% Form G cases from 1978 to December, 1982. An analysis of Form F and G data banks showed the data banks were comprised of 56% females and 44% males; education level completed: 6% some grade school, 30% high school diploma, 25% some college, 18% bachelor degrees, 11% masters degrees, 3% doctoral or post doctoral work, and 6% unknown. Age group percentages were: 11% under 18, 29% 18 to 20, 12% 21 to 24, 10% 25 to 29, 16% 30 to 39, 10% 40 to 49, 5% 50 to 59, 2% 60 plus, and 5% unknown.

WRITERS AND JOURNALISTS

N = 530

	SENSING		INTUITION	
	THINKING	FEELING	FEELING	THINKING

ISTJ	ISFJ	INFJ	INTJ
N= 23	N= 21	N= 23	N= 45
%= 4.34	%= 3.96	%= 4.34	%= 8.49
■■■■	■■■■	■■■■	■■■■■■■■

ISTP	ISFP	INFP	INTP
N= 7	N= 12	N= 72	N= 46
%= 1.32	%= 2.26	%= 13.58	%= 8.68
■	■■	■■■■■■■■■■	■■■■■■■■■
		■■■■	

ESTP	ESFP	ENFP	ENTP
N= 14	N= 19	N= 91	N= 39
%= 2.64	%= 3.58	%= 17.17	%= 7.36
■■■	■■■■	■■■■■■■■■■	■■■■■■■
		■■■■■■■	

ESTJ	ESFJ	ENFJ	ENTJ
N= 26	N= 18	N= 46	N= 28
%= 4.91	%= 3.40	%= 8.68	%= 5.28
■■■■■	■■■	■■■■■■■■■	■■■■■

JUDGMENT — INTROVERSION — PERCEPTION — PERCEPTION — EXTRAVERSION — JUDGMENT

	N	%
E	281	53.02
I	249	46.98
S	140	26.42
N	390	73.58
T	228	43.02
F	302	56.98
J	230	43.40
P	300	56.60
I J	112	21.13
I P	137	25.85
E P	163	30.75
E J	118	22.26
S T	70	13.21
S F	70	13.21
N F	232	43.77
N T	158	29.81
S J	88	16.60
S P	52	9.81
N P	248	46.79
N J	142	26.79
T J	122	23.02
T P	106	20.00
F P	194	36.60
F J	108	20.38
I N	186	35.09
E N	204	38.49
I S	63	11.89
E S	77	14.53
E T	107	20.19
E F	174	32.83
I F	128	24.15
I T	121	22.83
S dom	77	14.53
N dom	198	37.36
T dom	107	20.19
F dom	148	27.92

Note: ■ = 1% of sample   8629410

This table is one of a series of tables from the CAPT-MBTI Data Bank of MBTI records submitted to CAPT for computer scoring between 1971 and June, 1984. This sample was drawn from 59,784 records with usable occupational codes from the total data bank of 232,557. This data bank has 51% Form F cases from 1971 to March, 1978, 35% Form F cases from 1978 to June, 1984 and 14% Form G cases from 1978 to December, 1982. An analysis of Form F and G data banks showed the data banks were comprised of 56% females and 44% males; education level completed: 6% some grade school, 30% high school diploma, 25% some college, 18% bachelor degrees, 11% masters degrees, 3% doctoral or post doctoral work, and 6% unknown. Age group percentages were: 11% under 18, 29% 18 to 20, 12% 21 to 24, 10% 25 to 29, 16% 30 to 39, 10% 40 to 49, 5% 50 to 59, 2% 60 plus, and 5% unknown.

EXTRAVERT-INTROVERT

E Percent	I	Total Sample Size	Sample Description
66.29	33.71	89	Public Relations Workers and Publicity Writers
62.90	37.10	62	Actors
60.29	39.71	136	Musicians and Composers
58.20	41.80	378	ARTISTS AND ENTERTAINERS
57.69	42.31	52	Journalists
57.63	42.37	59	Photographers
54.55	45.45	55	Designers
53.02	46.98	530	WRITERS AND JOURNALISTS
50.00	50.00	84	Library Attendants and Assistants
49.52	50.48	208	Writers, Artists, Entertainers, and Agents
46.02	53.98	113	Editors and Reporters
40.57	59.43	106	Media Specialists
39.33	60.67	267	Librarians
38.60	61.40	114	Fine Artists
29.84	70.16	124	Architects

SENSING-INTUITION

S Percent	N	Total Sample Size	Sample Description
65.48	34.52	84	Library Attendants and Assistants
53.56	46.44	267	Librarians
50.00	50.00	106	Media Specialists
41.82	58.18	55	Designers
40.45	59.55	89	Public Relations Workers and Publicity Writers
34.56	65.44	136	Musicians and Composers
31.86	68.14	113	Editors and Reporters
30.95	69.05	378	ARTISTS AND ENTERTAINERS
28.85	71.15	52	Journalists
27.12	72.88	59	Photographers
26.42	73.58	530	WRITERS AND JOURNALISTS
19.35	80.65	62	Actors
17.74	82.26	124	Architects
13.94	86.06	208	Writers, Artists, Entertainers, and Agents
8.77	91.23	114	Fine Artists

THINKING-FEELING

T Percent	F	Total Sample Size	Sample Description
62.71	37.29	59	Photographers
56.45	43.55	124	Architects
51.61	48.39	62	Actors
48.31	51.69	89	Public Relations Workers and Publicity Writers
44.18	55.82	378	ARTISTS AND ENTERTAINERS
43.64	56.36	55	Designers
43.40	56.60	106	Media Specialists
43.02	56.98	530	WRITERS AND JOURNALISTS
42.48	57.52	113	Editors and Reporters
41.35	58.65	208	Writers, Artists, Entertainers, and Agents
38.46	61.54	52	Journalists
36.76	63.24	136	Musicians and Composers
34.52	65.48	84	Library Attendants and Assistants
32.96	67.04	267	Librarians
29.82	70.18	114	Fine Artists

JUDGMENT-PERCEPTION

J Percent	P	Total Sample Size	Sample Description
64.29	35.71	84	Library Attendants and Assistants
64.04	35.96	267	Librarians
61.32	38.68	106	Media Specialists
58.87	41.13	124	Architects
56.36	43.64	55	Designers
56.18	43.82	89	Public Relations Workers and Publicity Writers
52.21	47.79	136	Musicians and Composers
51.75	48.25	114	Fine Artists
50.85	49.15	59	Photographers
50.79	49.21	378	ARTISTS AND ENTERTAINERS
45.16	54.84	62	Actors
43.40	56.60	530	WRITERS AND JOURNALISTS
43.36	56.64	113	Editors and Reporters
38.94	61.06	208	Writers, Artists, Entertainers, and Agents
38.46	61.54	52	Journalists

Percent ST	Total Sample Size	Sample Description
25.00	84	Library Attendants and Assistants
24.53	106	Media Specialists
22.47	89	Public Relations Workers and Publicity Writers
20.00	55	Designers
19.48	267	Librarians
16.95	59	Photographers
15.04	113	Editors and Reporters
14.81	378	ARTISTS AND ENTERTAINERS
13.46	52	Journalists
13.24	136	Musicians and Composers
13.21	530	WRITERS AND JOURNALISTS
12.90	124	Architects
12.90	62	Actors
7.21	208	Writers, Artists, Entertainers, and Agents
3.51	114	Fine Artists

SENSING-FEELING

Percent SF	Total Sample Size	Sample Description
40.48	84	Library Attendants and Assistants
34.08	267	Librarians
25.47	106	Media Specialists
21.82	55	Designers
21.32	136	Musicians and Composers
17.98	89	Public Relations Workers and Publicity Writers
16.81	113	Editors and Reporters
16.14	378	ARTISTS AND ENTERTAINERS
15.38	52	Journalists
13.21	530	WRITERS AND JOURNALISTS
10.17	59	Photographers
6.73	208	Writers, Artists, Entertainers, and Agents
6.45	62	Actors
5.26	114	Fine Artists
4.84	124	Architects

INTUITION-FEELING

Percent NF	Total Sample Size	Sample Description
64.91	114	Fine Artists
51.92	208	Writers, Artists, Entertainers, and Agents
46.15	52	Journalists
43.77	530	WRITERS AND JOURNALISTS
41.94	62	Actors
41.91	136	Musicians and Composers
40.71	113	Editors and Reporters
39.68	378	ARTISTS AND ENTERTAINERS
38.71	124	Architects
34.55	55	Designers
33.71	89	Public Relations Workers and Publicity Writers
32.96	267	Librarians
31.13	106	Media Specialists
27.12	59	Photographers
25.00	84	Library Attendants and Assistants

INTUITION-THINKING

Percent NT	Total Sample Size	Sample Description
45.76	59	Photographers
43.55	124	Architects
38.71	62	Actors
34.13	208	Writers, Artists, Entertainers, and Agents
29.81	530	WRITERS AND JOURNALISTS
29.37	378	ARTISTS AND ENTERTAINERS
27.43	113	Editors and Reporters
26.32	114	Fine Artists
25.84	89	Public Relations Workers and Publicity Writers
25.00	52	Journalists
23.64	55	Designers
23.53	136	Musicians and Composers
18.87	106	Media Specialists
13.48	267	Librarians
9.52	84	Library Attendants and Assistants

BUSINESS
&
MANAGEMENT

Section III

BUSINESS AND MANAGEMENT

Samples in Section III

Name of Sample	Number in Sample
Accountants	427
Administrators: Managers and Supervisors	3678
Auditors	143
Bank Employees	835
Bank Employees, Exempt	110
Bank Employees, Non-Exempt	222
Bookkeepers	150
Business: General, Self-employed	250
Cashiers	274
Certified Public Accountants	494
Clerical Supervisors	56
Clerks in a Japanese Trading Company	165
Consultants: Canadian	111
Consultants: General	192
Consultants: Management	71
Consultants: Management Analysts	89
Coordinators	172
Credit Investigators and Mortgage Brokers	136
Employment Development Specialists	80
Females in Leadership Development Program	181
Insurance Agents, Brokers, and Underwriters	101
Males in Leadership Development Program	1051
Managers: England	849
Managers: Federal Executives	1394
Managers: Financial and Bank Officers	756
Managers: High Level Corporate Executives	136
Managers: Japanese Chief Executives	118
Managers: Middle Managers in a Japanese Chemical Company	366
Managers: Middle Managers in a Japanese Heavy Industrial	116
Managers: Office	102
Managers: Participants in Women in Management Conference	98
Managers: Regional Telephone Company Low Level Managers	230
Managers: Restaurant, Cafeteria, Bar and Food Service	312
Managers: Retail Stores	316
Managers: Sales	83
Managers: Small Business	150
Managers: Top Managers in Large Japanese Companies	56
Marketing Personnel	83
Members of a Human Resources Planners Association	108
Personnel and Labor Relations Workers	90
Public Accountants	333

Purchasing Agents	80
Real Estate Agents and Brokers	166
Receptionists	100
Sales Agents, Retail Trade	67
Sales Clerks, Retail Trade	108
Sales Representatives	179
Salespeople in a Japanese Trading Company	275
Secretaries: Executive and Administrative Assistants	333
Secretaries: Legal	77
Secretaries: Medical	68
Stock Clerks and Storekeepers	67
Typists	107

Composite Samples

CLERICAL AND KINDRED WORKERS	3339
MANAGERS AND ADMINISTRATORS	7463
OFFICE MACHINE OPERATORS	4905
SALES WORKERS	1750
SECRETARIES	1604

Comments

The samples of this section include white-collar workers from clerical workers to top managers. The tables include people in a number of fields, e.g. banking, accounting, sales. There are also tables of consultants to organizations.

This section has a substantial number of contributed samples and samples from dissertations and other research. These include the data from the Nippon Recruit Center in Tokyo and data from managers in England. Since these data are similar to the tables for United States samples, they are an important contribution to the cross-cultural validity of Jung's theory and the MBTI.

Look for more extraverts in fields where there is constant communication with other people and activity away from the office; look for more introverts in occupations requiring quiet and concentration.

Occupations in business, industry, government and other organizations are expected to have more sensing than intuitive types, as does the general population. However, more intuitive types may be found in occupations where it is important to be good at forecasting the unknown, to deal with complex abstract or theoretical models, or to be good at "reading between the lines."

Expect more thinking types in production and planning management, and in oversight of tasks requiring production or mathematics. Look for more feeling types in occupations where friendly service is important.

Expect samples of managers at all level to have more J's than P's. Most samples of management have substantial numbers of the tough-minded TJ types with operational and production managers more likely to report STJ and long-range planning managers NTJ. Notice the proportion of the tough-minded TJ's as opposed to the friendly, adaptable FP's. You should find more TJ's in managerial jobs and more FP's giving service.

Summary listings of tables for EI, SN, TF, JP, ST, SF, NF and NT will be found after the last type table.

Accountants

	SENSING		INTUITION	
	THINKING	FEELING	FEELING	THINKING

ISTJ	ISFJ	INFJ	INTJ
N= 86	N= 42	N= 15	N= 18
%= 20.14	%= 9.84	%= 3.51	%= 4.22
■■■■■■■■■■ ■■■■■■■■■■	■■■■■■■■■■	■■■■	■■■■

ISTP	ISFP	INFP	INTP
N= 20	N= 17	N= 17	N= 19
%= 4.68	%= 3.98	%= 3.98	%= 4.45
■■■■■	■■■■	■■■■	■■■■

ESTP	ESFP	ENFP	ENTP
N= 9	N= 6	N= 26	N= 17
%= 2.11	%= 1.41	%= 6.09	%= 3.98
■■	■	■■■■■■	■■■■

ESTJ	ESFJ	ENFJ	ENTJ
N= 53	N= 33	N= 18	N= 31
%= 12.41	%= 7.73	%= 4.22	%= 7.26
■■■■■■■■■■ ■■	■■■■■■■■	■■■■	■■■■■■■

JUDGMENT — INTROVERSION — PERCEPTION — PERCEPTION — EXTRAVERSION — JUDGMENT

	N	%
E	193	45.20
I	234	54.80
S	266	62.30
N	161	37.70
T	253	59.25
F	174	40.75
J	296	69.32
P	131	30.68
I J	161	37.70
I P	73	17.10
E P	58	13.58
E J	135	31.62
S T	168	39.34
S F	98	22.95
N F	76	17.80
N T	85	19.91
S J	214	50.12
S P	52	12.18
N P	79	18.50
N J	82	19.20
T J	188	44.03
T P	65	15.22
F P	66	15.46
F J	108	25.29
I N	69	16.16
E N	92	21.55
I S	165	38.64
E S	101	23.65
E T	110	25.76
E F	83	19.44
I F	91	21.31
I T	143	33.49
S dom	143	33.49
N dom	76	17.80
T dom	123	28.81
F dom	85	19.91

Note: ■ = 1% of sample   8629300

This table is one of a series of tables from the CAPT-MBTI Data Bank of MBTI records submitted to CAPT for computer scoring between 1971 and June, 1984. This sample was drawn from 59,784 records with usable occupational codes from the total data bank of 232,557. This data bank has 51% Form F cases from 1971 to March, 1978, 35% Form F cases from 1978 to June, 1984 and 14% Form G cases from 1978 to December, 1982. An analysis of Form F and G data banks showed the data banks were comprised of 56% females and 44% males; education level completed: 6% some grade school, 30% high school diploma, 25% some college, 18% bachelor degrees, 11% masters degrees, 3% doctoral or post doctoral work, and 6% unknown. Age group percentages were: 11% under 18, 29% 18 to 20, 12% 21 to 24, 10% 25 to 29, 16% 30 to 39, 10% 40 to 49, 5% 50 to 59, 2% 60 plus, and 5% unknown.

Administrators: Managers and Supervisors

N = 3678

	SENSING		INTUITION	
	THINKING	FEELING	FEELING	THINKING

ISTJ	ISFJ	INFJ	INTJ
N= 584	N= 225	N= 99	N= 198
%= 15.88	%= 6.12	%= 2.69	%= 5.38
■■■■■■■■■■■■■■■ ■■■■■	■■■■■■	■■■	■■■■■

ISTP	ISFP	INFP	INTP
N= 112	N= 103	N= 158	N= 149
%= 3.05	%= 2.80	%= 4.30	%= 4.05
■■■	■■■	■■■■	■■■■

ESTP	ESFP	ENFP	ENTP
N= 108	N= 113	N= 237	N= 181
%= 2.94	%= 3.07	%= 6.44	%= 4.92
■■■	■■■	■■■■■■	■■■■■

ESTJ	ESFJ	ENFJ	ENTJ
N= 645	N= 242	N= 151	N= 373
%= 17.54	%= 6.58	%= 4.11	%= 10.14
■■■■■■■■■■■■■■■■■	■■■■■■■	■■■■	■■■■■■■■■■

JUDGMENT — INTROVERSION — PERCEPTION — PERCEPTION — EXTRAVERSION — JUDGMENT

	N	%
E	2050	55.74
I	1628	44.26
S	2132	57.97
N	1546	42.03
T	2350	63.89
F	1328	36.11
J	2517	68.43
P	1161	31.57
I J	1106	30.07
I P	522	14.19
E P	639	17.37
E J	1411	38.36
S T	1449	39.40
S F	683	18.57
N F	645	17.54
N T	901	24.50
S J	1696	46.11
S P	436	11.85
N P	725	19.71
N J	821	22.32
T J	1800	48.94
T P	550	14.95
F P	611	16.61
F J	717	19.49
I N	604	16.42
E N	942	25.61
I S	1024	27.84
E S	1108	30.13
E T	1307	35.54
E F	743	20.20
I F	585	15.91
I T	1043	28.36
S dom	1030	28.00
N dom	715	19.44
T dom	1279	34.77
F dom	654	17.78

Note: ■ = 1% of sample   8629313

This table is one of a series of tables from the CAPT-MBTI Data Bank of MBTI records submitted to CAPT for computer scoring between 1971 and June, 1984. This sample was drawn from 59,784 records with usable occupational codes from the total data bank of 232,557. This data bank has 51% Form F cases from 1971 to March, 1978, 35% Form F cases from 1978 to June, 1984 and 14% Form G cases from 1978 to December, 1982. An analysis of Form F and G data banks showed the data banks were comprised of 56% females and 44% males; education level completed: 6% some grade school, 30% high school diploma, 25% some college, 18% bachelor degrees, 11% masters degrees, 3% doctoral or post doctoral work, and 6% unknown. Age group percentages were: 11% under 18, 29% 18 to 20, 12% 21 to 24, 10% 25 to 29, 16% 30 to 39, 10% 40 to 49, 5% 50 to 59, 2% 60 plus, and 5% unknown.

Auditors

N = 143

	SENSING		INTUITION					N	%
	THINKING	FEELING	FEELING	THINKING					

ISTJ N= 29 %= 20.28 ■■■■■■■■■ ■■■■■■■■■	**ISFJ** N= 7 %= 4.90 ■■■■■	**INFJ** N= 4 %= 2.80 ■■■	**INTJ** N= 13 %= 9.09 ■■■■■■■■■	JUDGMENT	INTROVERSION
ISTP N= 5 %= 3.50 ■■■	**ISFP** N= 2 %= 1.40 ■	**INFP** N= 3 %= 2.10 ■■	**INTP** N= 7 %= 4.90 ■■■■■	PERCEPTION	
ESTP N= 10 %= 6.99 ■■■■■■■	**ESFP** N= 2 %= 1.40 ■	**ENFP** N= 9 %= 6.29 ■■■■■■	**ENTP** N= 8 %= 5.59 ■■■■■	PERCEPTION	EXTRAVERSION
ESTJ N= 22 %= 15.38 ■■■■■■■■■■ ■■■■■	**ESFJ** N= 4 %= 2.80 ■■■	**ENFJ** N= 4 %= 2.80 ■■■	**ENTJ** N= 14 %= 9.79 ■■■■■■■■■■	JUDGMENT	

	N	%
E	73	51.05
I	70	48.95
S	81	56.64
N	62	43.36
T	108	75.52
F	35	24.48
J	97	67.83
P	46	32.17
I J	53	37.06
I P	17	11.89
E P	29	20.28
E J	44	30.77
S T	66	46.15
S F	15	10.49
N F	20	13.99
N T	42	29.37
S J	62	43.36
S P	19	13.29
N P	27	18.88
N J	35	24.48
T J	78	54.55
T P	30	20.98
F P	16	11.19
F J	19	13.29
I N	27	18.88
E N	35	24.48
I S	43	30.07
E S	38	26.57
E T	54	37.76
E F	19	13.29
I F	16	11.19
I T	54	37.76
S dom	48	33.57
N dom	34	23.78
T dom	48	33.57
F dom	13	9.09

Note: ■ = 1% of sample   8629303

This table is one of a series of tables from the CAPT-MBTI Data Bank of MBTI records submitted to CAPT for computer scoring between 1971 and June, 1984. This sample was drawn from 59,784 records with usable occupational codes from the total data bank of 232,557. This data bank has 51% Form F cases from 1971 to March, 1978, 35% Form F cases from 1978 to June, 1984 and 14% Form G cases from 1978 to December, 1982. An analysis of Form F and G data banks showed the data banks were comprised of 56% females and 44% males; education level completed: 6% some grade school, 30% high school diploma, 25% some college, 18% bachelor degrees, 11% masters degrees, 3% doctoral or post doctoral work, and 6% unknown. Age group percentages were: 11% under 18, 29% 18 to 20, 12% 21 to 24, 10% 25 to 29, 16% 30 to 39, 10% 40 to 49, 5% 50 to 59, 2% 60 plus, and 5% unknown.

Bank Employees

N = 835

	SENSING		INTUITION	
	THINKING	FEELING	FEELING	THINKING

ISTJ	ISFJ	INFJ	INTJ
N= 127	N= 88	N= 11	N= 27
%= 15.21	%= 10.54	%= 1.32	%= 3.23

ISTP	ISFP	INFP	INTP
N= 29	N= 33	N= 27	N= 25
%= 3.47	%= 3.95	%= 3.23	%= 2.99

ESTP	ESFP	ENFP	ENTP
N= 36	N= 48	N= 33	N= 39
%= 4.31	%= 5.75	%= 3.95	%= 4.67

ESTJ	ESFJ	ENFJ	ENTJ
N= 151	N= 86	N= 25	N= 50
%= 18.08	%= 10.30	%= 2.99	%= 5.99

JUDGMENT — INTROVERSION — PERCEPTION — PERCEPTION — EXTRAVERSION — JUDGMENT

Note: ■ = 1% of sample   8623302

	N	%
E	468	56.05
I	367	43.95
S	598	71.62
N	237	28.38
T	484	57.96
F	351	42.04
J	565	67.66
P	270	32.34
I J	253	30.30
I P	114	13.65
E P	156	18.68
E J	312	37.37
S T	343	41.08
S F	255	30.54
N F	96	11.50
N T	141	16.89
S J	452	54.13
S P	146	17.49
N P	124	14.85
N J	113	13.53
T J	355	42.51
T P	129	15.45
F P	141	16.89
F J	210	25.15
I N	90	10.78
E N	147	17.60
I S	277	33.17
E S	321	38.44
E T	276	33.05
E F	192	22.99
I F	159	19.04
I T	208	24.91
S dom	299	35.81
N dom	110	13.17
T dom	255	30.54
F dom	171	20.48

Data collected by Wayne Mitchell and George West in 1981. Subjects were employees of a large southeastern bank. Personnel from all levels of the company were included. Sample was essentially all employees in the company No gender, race or educational level data were reported. These data are used with permission and have not been published elsewhere to date.

N = 110

	SENSING		INTUITION	
	THINKING	FEELING	FEELING	THINKING

ISTJ	ISFJ	INFJ	INTJ
N= 28	N= 12	N= 0	N= 2
%= 25.45	%= 10.91	%= 0.00	%= 1.82
■■■■■■■■■■ ■■■■■■■■■■ ■■■■■	■■■■■■■■■■ ■		■■

ISTP	ISFP	INFP	INTP
N= 5	N= 4	N= 2	N= 1
%= 4.55	%= 3.64	%= 1.82	%= .91
■■■■■	■■■■	■■	■

ESTP	ESFP	ENFP	ENTP
N= 4	N= 3	N= 3	N= 1
%= 3.64	%= 2.73	%= 2.73	%= .91
■■■■	■■■	■■■	■

ESTJ	ESFJ	ENFJ	ENTJ
N= 28	N= 10	N= 3	N= 4
%= 25.45	%= 9.09	%= 2.73	%= 3.64
■■■■■■■■■■ ■■■■■■■■■■ ■■■■■	■■■■■■■■■■	■■■	■■■■

JUDGMENT — INTROVERSION — PERCEPTION — PERCEPTION — EXTRAVERSION — JUDGMENT

	N	%
E	56	50.91
I	54	49.09
S	94	85.45
N	16	14.55
T	73	66.36
F	37	33.64
J	87	79.09
P	23	20.91
I J	42	38.18
I P	12	10.91
E P	11	10.00
E J	45	40.91
S T	65	59.09
S F	29	26.36
N F	8	7.27
N T	8	7.27
S J	78	70.91
S P	16	14.55
N P	7	6.36
N J	9	8.18
T J	62	56.36
T P	11	10.00
F P	12	10.91
F J	25	22.73
I N	5	4.55
E N	11	10.00
I S	49	44.55
E S	45	40.91
E T	37	33.64
E F	19	17.27
I F	18	16.36
I T	36	32.73
S dom	47	42.73
N dom	6	5.45
T dom	38	34.55
F dom	19	17.27

Note: ■ = 1% of sample   8623121

Data collected by Orville Pierson at Mainstream Access Inc. in October 1984. Subjects were all 55 to 65 years old and employed for 10 to 35 years by a mid-sized New York City bank. All subjects were exempt employees (managerial, professional, etc.) attending a retirement workshop and represented all employees of their age group at the bank. No gender, race or level of education data were reported. These data are used with permission and have not been published elsewhere to date.

Bank Employees, Non-Exempt

N = 222

	SENSING		INTUITION	
	THINKING	FEELING	FEELING	THINKING

ISTJ	ISFJ	INFJ	INTJ
N= 56	N= 39	N= 0	N= 3
%= 25.23	%= 17.57	%= 0.00	%= 1.35
■■■■■■■■■■	■■■■■■■■■■		■
■■■■■■■■■■	■■■■■■■		
■■■■■			

ISTP	ISFP	INFP	INTP
N= 4	N= 10	N= 2	N= 1
%= 1.80	%= 4.50	%= .90	%= .45
■■	■■■■■	■	

ESTP	ESFP	ENFP	ENTP
N= 5	N= 18	N= 1	N= 2
%= 2.25	%= 8.11	%= .45	%= .90
■■	■■■■■■■■		■

ESTJ	ESFJ	ENFJ	ENTJ
N= 38	N= 35	N= 1	N= 7
%= 17.12	%= 15.77	%= .45	%= 3.15
■■■■■■■■■■	■■■■■■■■■■		■■■
■■■■■■■	■■■■■		

(Vertical labels at right of grid: JUDGMENT — INTROVERSION — PERCEPTION; PERCEPTION — EXTRAVERSION — JUDGMENT)

	N	%
E	107	48.20
I	115	51.80
S	205	92.34
N	17	7.66
T	116	52.25
F	106	47.75
J	179	80.63
P	43	19.37
I J	98	44.14
I P	17	7.66
E P	26	11.71
E J	81	36.49
S T	103	46.40
S F	102	45.95
N F	4	1.80
N T	13	5.86
S J	168	75.68
S P	37	16.67
N P	6	2.70
N J	11	4.95
T J	104	46.85
T P	12	5.41
F P	31	13.96
F J	75	33.78
I N	6	2.70
E N	11	4.95
I S	109	49.10
E S	96	43.24
E T	52	23.42
E F	55	24.77
I F	51	22.97
I T	64	28.83
S dom	118	53.15
N dom	6	2.70
T dom	50	22.52
F dom	48	21.62

Note: ■ = 1% of sample

8623120

Data collected by Orville Pierson at Mainstream Access Inc. in October 1984. Subjects were all 55 to 65 years old and employed for 10 to 35 years by a mid-sized New York City bank. All subjects were non-exempt employees (tellers, bookkeepers, etc.) attending a retirement workshop and represented all employees of their age group at the bank. No gender, race or level of education data were reported. These data are used with permission and have not been published elsewhere to date.

Bookkeepers

N = 150

	SENSING		INTUITION	
	THINKING	FEELING	FEELING	THINKING

ISTJ	ISFJ	INFJ	INTJ
N= 15	N= 24	N= 7	N= 2
%= 10.00	%= 16.00	%= 4.67	%= 1.33
■■■■■■■■■■	■■■■■■■■■■■■■■■■	■■■■■	■

ISTP	ISFP	INFP	INTP
N= 5	N= 14	N= 8	N= 2
%= 3.33	%= 9.33	%= 5.33	%= 1.33
■■■	■■■■■■■■■	■■■■■	■

ESTP	ESFP	ENFP	ENTP
N= 2	N= 11	N= 15	N= 6
%= 1.33	%= 7.33	%= 10.00	%= 4.00
■	■■■■■■■	■■■■■■■■■■	■■■■

ESTJ	ESFJ	ENFJ	ENTJ
N= 12	N= 19	N= 7	N= 1
%= 8.00	%= 12.67	%= 4.67	%= .67
■■■■■■■■	■■■■■■■■■■■■■	■■■■■	■

Labels (left to right / top to bottom): JUDGMENT · INTROVERSION · PERCEPTION · PERCEPTION · EXTRAVERSION · JUDGMENT

	N	%
E	73	48.67
I	77	51.33
S	102	68.00
N	48	32.00
T	45	30.00
F	105	70.00
J	87	58.00
P	63	42.00
I J	48	32.00
I P	29	19.33
E P	34	22.67
E J	39	26.00
S T	34	22.67
S F	68	45.33
N F	37	24.67
N T	11	7.33
S J	70	46.67
S P	32	21.33
N P	31	20.67
N J	17	11.33
T J	30	20.00
T P	15	10.00
F P	48	32.00
F J	57	38.00
I N	19	12.67
E N	29	19.33
I S	58	38.67
E S	44	29.33
E T	21	14.00
E F	52	34.67
I F	53	35.33
I T	24	16.00
S dom	52	34.67
N dom	30	20.00
T dom	20	13.33
F dom	48	32.00

Note: ■ = 1% of sample   8629319

This table is one of a series of tables from the CAPT-MBTI Data Bank of MBTI records submitted to CAPT for computer scoring between 1971 and June, 1984. This sample was drawn from 59,784 records with usable occupational codes from the total data bank of 232,557. This data bank has 51% Form F cases from 1971 to March, 1978, 35% Form F cases from 1978 to June, 1984 and 14% Form G cases from 1978 to December, 1982. An analysis of Form F and G data banks showed the data banks were comprised of 56% females and 44% males; education level completed: 6% some grade school, 30% high school diploma, 25% some college, 18% bachelor degrees, 11% masters degrees, 3% doctoral or post doctoral work, and 6% unknown. Age group percentages were: 11% under 18, 29% 18 to 20, 12% 21 to 24, 10% 25 to 29, 16% 30 to 39, 10% 40 to 49, 5% 50 to 59, 2% 60 plus, and 5% unknown.

Business: General, Self-employed

N = 250

	SENSING		INTUITION				N	%
	THINKING	FEELING	FEELING	THINKING				

ISTJ	ISFJ	INFJ	INTJ
N= 34	N= 19	N= 8	N= 7
%= 13.60	%= 7.60	%= 3.20	%= 2.80
∎∎∎∎∎∎∎∎∎∎∎∎∎	∎∎∎∎∎∎∎	∎∎∎	∎∎∎

ISTP	ISFP	INFP	INTP
N= 8	N= 4	N= 11	N= 17
%= 3.20	%= 1.60	%= 4.40	%= 6.80
∎∎∎	∎∎	∎∎∎∎	∎∎∎∎∎∎∎

ESTP	ESFP	ENFP	ENTP
N= 12	N= 12	N= 26	N= 10
%= 4.80	%= 4.80	%= 10.40	%= 4.00
∎∎∎∎∎	∎∎∎∎∎	∎∎∎∎∎∎∎∎∎∎	∎∎∎∎

ESTJ	ESFJ	ENFJ	ENTJ
N= 32	N= 14	N= 10	N= 26
%= 12.80	%= 5.60	%= 4.00	%= 10.40
∎∎∎∎∎∎∎∎∎∎∎∎∎	∎∎∎∎∎∎	∎∎∎∎	∎∎∎∎∎∎∎∎∎∎

JUDGMENT — INTROVERSION
PERCEPTION
PERCEPTION — EXTRAVERSION
JUDGMENT

	N	%
E	142	56.80
I	108	43.20
S	135	54.00
N	115	46.00
T	146	58.40
F	104	41.60
J	150	60.00
P	100	40.00
I J	68	27.20
I P	40	16.00
E P	60	24.00
E J	82	32.80
S T	86	34.40
S F	49	19.60
N F	55	22.00
N T	60	24.00
S J	99	39.60
S P	36	14.40
N P	64	25.60
N J	51	20.40
T J	99	39.60
T P	47	18.80
F P	53	21.20
F J	51	20.40
I N	43	17.20
E N	72	28.80
I S	65	26.00
E S	70	28.00
E T	80	32.00
E F	62	24.80
I F	42	16.80
I T	66	26.40
S dom	77	30.80
N dom	51	20.40
T dom	83	33.20
F dom	39	15.60

Note: ∎ = 1% of sample   8629307

This table is one of a series of tables from the CAPT-MBTI Data Bank of MBTI records submitted to CAPT for computer scoring between 1971 and June, 1984. This sample was drawn from 59,784 records with usable occupational codes from the total data bank of 232,557. This data bank has 51% Form F cases from 1971 to March, 1978, 35% Form F cases from 1978 to June, 1984 and 14% Form G cases from 1978 to December, 1982. An analysis of Form F and G data banks showed the data banks were comprised of 56% females and 44% males; education level completed: 6% some grade school, 30% high school diploma, 25% some college, 18% bachelor degrees, 11% masters degrees, 3% doctoral or post doctoral work, and 6% unknown. Age group percentages were: 11% under 18, 29% 18 to 20, 12% 21 to 24, 10% 25 to 29, 16% 30 to 39, 10% 40 to 49, 5% 50 to 59, 2% 60 plus, and 5% unknown.

Cashiers

						N	%
					E	162	59.12
					I	112	40.88
					S	175	63.87
					N	99	36.13
					T	83	30.29
					F	191	69.71
					J	158	57.66
					P	116	42.34

	SENSING		INTUITION	
	THINKING	FEELING	FEELING	THINKING

ISTJ	ISFJ	INFJ	INTJ
N= 27	N= 37	N= 10	N= 1
%= 9.85	%= 13.50	%= 3.65	%= .36
■■■■■■■■■■	■■■■■■■■■■■■■■ ■■■■	■■■■	

ISTP	ISFP	INFP	INTP
N= 6	N= 12	N= 15	N= 4
%= 2.19	%= 4.38	%= 5.47	%= 1.46
■■	■■■■	■■■■■	■

ESTP	ESFP	ENFP	ENTP
N= 7	N= 26	N= 36	N= 10
%= 2.55	%= 9.49	%= 13.14	%= 3.65
■■■	■■■■■■■■■	■■■■■■■■■■ ■■■	■■■■

ESTJ	ESFJ	ENFJ	ENTJ
N= 24	N= 36	N= 19	N= 4
%= 8.76	%= 13.14	%= 6.93	%= 1.46
■■■■■■■■■	■■■■■■■■■■■■■ ■■■	■■■■■■■	■

JUDGMENT — INTROVERSION — PERCEPTION — EXTRAVERSION — JUDGMENT — PERCEPTION

	N	%
I J	75	27.37
I P	37	13.50
E P	79	28.83
E J	83	30.29
S T	64	23.36
S F	111	40.51
N F	80	29.20
N T	19	6.93
S J	124	45.26
S P	51	18.61
N P	65	23.72
N J	34	12.41
T J	56	20.44
T P	27	9.85
F P	89	32.48
F J	102	37.23
I N	30	10.95
E N	69	25.18
I S	82	29.93
E S	93	33.94
E T	45	16.42
E F	117	42.70
I F	74	27.01
I T	38	13.87
S dom	97	35.40
N dom	57	20.80
T dom	38	13.87
F dom	82	29.93

Note: ■ = 1% of sample   8629320

This table is one of a series of tables from the CAPT-MBTI Data Bank of MBTI records submitted to CAPT for computer scoring between 1971 and June, 1984. This sample was drawn from 59,784 records with usable occupational codes from the total data bank of 232,557. This data bank has 51% Form F cases from 1971 to March, 1978, 35% Form F cases from 1978 to June, 1984 and 14% Form G cases from 1978 to December, 1982. An analysis of Form F and G data banks showed the data banks were comprised of 56% females and 44% males; education level completed: 6% some grade school, 30% high school diploma, 25% some college, 18% bachelor degrees, 11% masters degrees, 3% doctoral or post doctoral work, and 6% unknown. Age group percentages were: 11% under 18, 29% 18 to 20, 12% 21 to 24, 10% 25 to 29, 16% 30 to 39, 10% 40 to 49, 5% 50 to 59, 2% 60 plus, and 5% unknown.

Certified Public Accountants

N = 494

	SENSING		INTUITION	
	THINKING	FEELING	FEELING	THINKING

ISTJ	ISFJ	INFJ	INTJ
N= 132	N= 25	N= 10	N= 28
%= 26.72	%= 5.06	%= 2.02	%= 5.67
■■■■■■■■■■	■■■■■	■■	■■■■■■
■■■■■■■■■■			
■■■■■■■			

ISTP	ISFP	INFP	INTP
N= 23	N= 6	N= 9	N= 24
%= 4.66	%= 1.21	%= 1.82	%= 4.86
■■■■■	■	■■	■■■■■

ESTP	ESFP	ENFP	ENTP
N= 15	N= 5	N= 17	N= 29
%= 3.04	%= 1.01	%= 3.44	%= 5.87
■■■	■	■■■	■■■■■■

ESTJ	ESFJ	ENFJ	ENTJ
N= 95	N= 20	N= 15	N= 41
%= 19.23	%= 4.05	%= 3.04	%= 8.30
■■■■■■■■■■	■■■■	■■■	■■■■■■■■
■■■■■■■■■			

	N	%
E	237	47.98
I	257	52.02
S	321	64.98
N	173	35.02
T	387	78.34
F	107	21.66
J	366	74.09
P	128	25.91
I J	195	39.47
I P	62	12.55
E P	66	13.36
E J	171	34.62
S T	265	53.64
S F	56	11.34
N F	51	10.32
N T	122	24.70
S J	272	55.06
S P	49	9.92
N P	79	15.99
N J	94	19.03
T J	296	59.92
T P	91	18.42
F P	37	7.49
F J	70	14.17
I N	71	14.37
E N	102	20.65
I S	186	37.65
E S	135	27.33
E T	180	36.44
E F	57	11.54
I F	50	10.12
I T	207	41.90
S dom	177	35.83
N dom	84	17.00
T dom	183	37.04
F dom	50	10.12

Note: ■ = 1% of sample   8623117

Data collected by Paul J. Otte from June to July 1983. Sample was 97.3% of original sample of 512 accountants in 24 Michigan firms with 8 to 63 professional staff. It was a subset selected from 31 willing participant firms. The final sample appeared to reasonably approximate the distribution of firm size for each region of the state. Accountants were 20% female and 80% male; 33% partners and 67% nonpartners; 46% accounting/auditing, 31% tax and 23% management advisory service. These data are used with permission and were cited in:

Otte, P. J. (1983). Psychological typology of the local firm Certified Public Accountant. Unpublished doctoral dissertation, Western Michigan University, Kalamazoo, Michigan.

Clerical Supervisors

N = 56

	SENSING		INTUITION	
	THINKING	FEELING	FEELING	THINKING

ISTJ	ISFJ	INFJ	INTJ
N= 2	N= 12	N= 1	N= 1
%= 3.57	%= 21.43	%= 1.79	%= 1.79
■■■■	■■■■■■■■■■	■■	■■
	■■■■■■■■■		
	■		

ISTP	ISFP	INFP	INTP
N= 0	N= 6	N= 3	N= 2
%= 0.00	%= 10.71	%= 5.36	%= 3.57
	■■■■■■■■■■	■■■■■	■■■■
	■		

ESTP	ESFP	ENFP	ENTP
N= 1	N= 5	N= 4	N= 3
%= 1.79	%= 8.93	%= 7.14	%= 5.36
■■	■■■■■■■■■	■■■■■■■	■■■■■

ESTJ	ESFJ	ENFJ	ENTJ
N= 7	N= 5	N= 4	N= 0
%= 12.50	%= 8.93	%= 7.14	%= 0.00
■■■■■■■■■■	■■■■■■■■■	■■■■■■■	
■■■			

JUDGMENT — INTROVERSION — PERCEPTION — PERCEPTION — EXTRAVERSION — JUDGMENT

	N	%
E	29	51.79
I	27	48.21
S	38	67.86
N	18	32.14
T	16	28.57
F	40	71.43
J	32	57.14
P	24	42.86
I J	16	28.57
I P	11	19.64
E P	13	23.21
E J	16	28.57
S T	10	17.86
S F	28	50.00
N F	12	21.43
N T	6	10.71
S J	26	46.43
S P	12	21.43
N P	12	21.43
N J	6	10.71
T J	10	17.86
T P	6	10.71
F P	18	32.14
F J	22	39.29
I N	7	12.50
E N	11	19.64
I S	20	35.71
E S	18	32.14
E T	11	19.64
E F	18	32.14
I F	22	39.29
I T	5	8.93
S dom	20	35.71
N dom	9	16.07
T dom	9	16.07
F dom	18	32.14

Note: ■ = 1% of sample   8629321

This table is one of a series of tables from the CAPT-MBTI Data Bank of MBTI records submitted to CAPT for computer scoring between 1971 and June, 1984. This sample was drawn from 59,784 records with usable occupational codes from the total data bank of 232,557. This data bank has 51% Form F cases from 1971 to March, 1978, 35% Form F cases from 1978 to June, 1984 and 14% Form G cases from 1978 to December, 1982. An analysis of Form F and G data banks showed the data banks were comprised of 56% females and 44% males; education level completed: 6% some grade school, 30% high school diploma, 25% some college, 18% bachelor degrees, 11% masters degrees, 3% doctoral or post doctoral work, and 6% unknown. Age group percentages were: 11% under 18, 29% 18 to 20, 12% 21 to 24, 10% 25 to 29, 16% 30 to 39, 10% 40 to 49, 5% 50 to 59, 2% 60 plus, and 5% unknown.

Clerks in a Japanese Trading Company

N = 165

	SENSING		INTUITION				N	%
	THINKING	FEELING	FEELING	THINKING				

ISTJ	ISFJ	INFJ	INTJ
N= 2	N= 28	N= 7	N= 4
%= 1.21	%= 16.97	%= 4.24	%= 2.42
■	■■■■■■■■■■ ■■■■■■■	■■■■	■■

ISTP	ISFP	INFP	INTP
N= 2	N= 28	N= 11	N= 3
%= 1.21	%= 16.97	%= 6.67	%= 1.82
■	■■■■■■■■■■ ■■■■■■■	■■■■■■■	■■

ESTP	ESFP	ENFP	ENTP
N= 5	N= 26	N= 18	N= 2
%= 3.03	%= 15.76	%= 10.91	%= 1.21
■■■	■■■■■■■■■■ ■■■■■	■■■■■■■■■■ ■	■

ESTJ	ESFJ	ENFJ	ENTJ
N= 5	N= 15	N= 7	N= 2
%= 3.03	%= 9.09	%= 4.24	%= 1.21
■■■	■■■■■■■■■	■■■■	■

	N	%
E	80	48.48
I	85	51.52
S	111	67.27
N	54	32.73
T	25	15.15
F	140	84.85
J	70	42.42
P	95	57.58
I J	41	24.85
I P	44	26.67
E P	51	30.91
E J	29	17.58
S T	14	8.48
S F	97	58.79
N F	43	26.06
N T	11	6.67
S J	50	30.30
S P	61	36.97
N P	34	20.61
N J	20	12.12
T J	13	7.88
T P	12	7.27
F P	83	50.30
F J	57	34.55
I N	25	15.15
E N	29	17.58
I S	60	36.36
E S	51	30.91
E T	14	8.48
E F	66	40.00
I F	74	44.85
I T	11	6.67
S dom	61	36.97
N dom	31	18.79
T dom	12	7.27
F dom	61	36.97

Note: ■ = 1% of sample   8623112

Data collected by Takeshi Ohsawa at the Nippon Recruit Center, Tokyo, Japan from 1964 to 1975. No other demographic data were reported. These data are used with permission and were cited in:

Ohsawa, T. (1975, October). MBTI experiences in Japan: Career choice, selection, placement and counseling for individual development. Paper presented at the First National Conference on the Myers-Briggs Type Indicator, Gainesville, FL.

Consultants: Canadian

N = 111

	SENSING		INTUITION	
	THINKING	FEELING	FEELING	THINKING

ISTJ	ISFJ	INFJ	INTJ
N= 23	N= 0	N= 0	N= 18
%= 20.72	%= 0.00	%= 0.00	%= 16.22
■■■■■■■■■ ■■■■■■■■■ ■			■■■■■■■■■ ■■■■■

ISTP	ISFP	INFP	INTP
N= 5	N= 0	N= 2	N= 17
%= 4.50	%= 0.00	%= 1.80	%= 15.32
■■■■■		■■	■■■■■■■■■ ■■■■■

ESTP	ESFP	ENFP	ENTP
N= 3	N= 1	N= 2	N= 5
%= 2.70	%= .90	%= 1.80	%= 4.50
■■■	■	■■	■■■■■

ESTJ	ESFJ	ENFJ	ENTJ
N= 13	N= 0	N= 0	N= 22
%= 11.71	%= 0.00	%= 0.00	%= 19.82
■■■■■■■■■ ■■			■■■■■■■■■ ■■■■■■■■■

JUDGMENT — INTROVERSION — PERCEPTION — PERCEPTION — EXTRAVERSION — JUDGMENT

	N	%
E	46	41.44
I	65	58.56
S	45	40.54
N	66	59.46
T	106	95.50
F	5	4.50
J	76	68.47
P	35	31.53
I J	41	36.94
I P	24	21.62
E P	11	9.91
E J	35	31.53
S T	44	39.64
S F	1	.90
N F	4	3.60
N T	62	55.86
S J	36	32.43
S P	9	8.11
N P	26	23.42
N J	40	36.04
T J	76	68.47
T P	30	27.03
F P	5	4.50
F J	0	0.00
I N	37	33.33
E N	29	26.13
I S	28	25.23
E S	17	15.32
E T	43	38.74
E F	3	2.70
I F	2	1.80
I T	63	56.76
S dom	27	24.32
N dom	25	22.52
T dom	57	51.35
F dom	2	1.80

Note: ■ = 1% of sample   8623301

Data collected by Peter Wade of Bishop's University, Quebec during May and June 1980 using Form G. Subjects were volunteers from 15 firms out of a pool of 1200 management consultants working for the 18 member firms of the Canadian Association of Management Consultants. Two firms were the source of 42% of the volunteers. The distribution of functional specialties in the sample was representative of the large firms in the total population. Consultants were 15% female and 85% male; the average age was 34 with 46% between 31 and 35, and 14% above 40. These data are used with permission and were cited in:

Wade, P. F. (1981). Some factors affecting problem solving effectiveness in business: A study of management consultants. Unpublished doctoral dissertation, McGill University.

Consultants: General

N = 192

	SENSING		INTUITION	
	THINKING	FEELING	FEELING	THINKING

ISTJ	ISFJ	INFJ	INTJ
N= 18	N= 8	N= 10	N= 12
%= 9.38	%= 4.17	%= 5.21	%= 6.25
■■■■■■■■■	■■■■	■■■■■	■■■■■■

ISTP	ISFP	INFP	INTP
N= 3	N= 3	N= 12	N= 7
%= 1.56	%= 1.56	%= 6.25	%= 3.65
■■	■■	■■■■■■	■■■■

ESTP	ESFP	ENFP	ENTP
N= 7	N= 3	N= 22	N= 16
%= 3.65	%= 1.56	%= 11.46	%= 8.33
■■■■	■■	■■■■■■■■■■■ ■	■■■■■■■■

ESTJ	ESFJ	ENFJ	ENTJ
N= 16	N= 9	N= 22	N= 24
%= 8.33	%= 4.69	%= 11.46	%= 12.50
■■■■■■■■	■■■■■	■■■■■■■■■■■ ■	■■■■■■■■■■■■ ■■■

JUDGMENT — INTROVERSION — PERCEPTION — PERCEPTION — EXTRAVERSION — JUDGMENT

	N	%
E	119	61.98
I	73	38.02
S	67	34.90
N	125	65.10
T	103	53.65
F	89	46.35
J	119	61.98
P	73	38.02
I J	48	25.00
I P	25	13.02
E P	48	25.00
E J	71	36.98
S T	44	22.92
S F	23	11.98
N F	66	34.38
N T	59	30.73
S J	51	26.56
S P	16	8.33
N P	57	29.69
N J	68	35.42
T J	70	36.46
T P	33	17.19
F P	40	20.83
F J	49	25.52
I N	41	21.35
E N	84	43.75
I S	32	16.67
E S	35	18.23
E T	63	32.81
E F	56	29.17
I F	33	17.19
I T	40	20.83
S dom	36	18.75
N dom	60	31.25
T dom	50	26.04
F dom	46	23.96

Note: ■ = 1% of sample   8629302

This table is one of a series of tables from the CAPT-MBTI Data Bank of MBTI records submitted to CAPT for computer scoring between 1971 and June, 1984. This sample was drawn from 59,784 records with usable occupational codes from the total data bank of 232,557. This data bank has 51% Form F cases from 1971 to March, 1978, 35% Form F cases from 1978 to June, 1984 and 14% Form G cases from 1978 to December, 1982. An analysis of Form F and G data banks showed the data banks were comprised of 56% females and 44% males; education level completed: 6% some grade school, 30% high school diploma, 25% some college, 18% bachelor degrees, 11% masters degrees, 3% doctoral or post doctoral work, and 6% unknown. Age group percentages were: 11% under 18, 29% 18 to 20, 12% 21 to 24, 10% 25 to 29, 16% 30 to 39, 10% 40 to 49, 5% 50 to 59, 2% 60 plus, and 5% unknown.

Consultants: Management

N = 71

SENSING	INTUITION
THINKING FEELING	FEELING THINKING

ISTJ	ISFJ	INFJ	INTJ
N= 11	N= 1	N= 1	N= 11
%= 15.49	%= 1.41	%= 1.41	%= 15.49

ISTP	ISFP	INFP	INTP
N= 1	N= 1	N= 0	N= 4
%= 1.41	%= 1.41	%= 0.00	%= 5.63

ESTP	ESFP	ENFP	ENTP
N= 1	N= 0	N= 1	N= 6
%= 1.41	%= 0.00	%= 1.41	%= 8.45

ESTJ	ESFJ	ENFJ	ENTJ
N= 15	N= 0	N= 2	N= 16
%= 21.13	%= 0.00	%= 2.82	%= 22.54

	N	%
E	41	57.75
I	30	42.25
S	30	42.25
N	41	57.75
T	65	91.55
F	6	8.45
J	57	80.28
P	14	19.72
I J	24	33.80
I P	6	8.45
E P	8	11.27
E J	33	46.48
S T	28	39.44
S F	2	2.82
N F	4	5.63
N T	37	52.11
S J	27	38.03
S P	3	4.23
N P	11	15.49
N J	30	42.25
T J	53	74.65
T P	12	16.90
F P	2	2.82
F J	4	5.63
I N	16	22.54
E N	25	35.21
I S	14	19.72
E S	16	22.54
E T	38	53.52
E F	3	4.23
I F	3	4.23
I T	27	38.03
S dom	13	18.31
N dom	19	26.76
T dom	36	50.70
F dom	3	4.23

Note: ■ = 1% of sample   8623300

Data collected by Mary McCaulley in October 1984. Subjects were management consultants who were officers and principals of an international management consulting firm. Data were collected for a session of an officer/principal meeting. Consultants were 1% female and 99% male, education level: 17% had bachelors degrees, 77% had masters degrees and 6% had Ph.D.s, 1% black and 99% white. These data are used with permission and have not been published elsewhere to date.

Consultants: Management Analysts

N = 89

	SENSING		INTUITION	
	THINKING	FEELING	FEELING	THINKING

ISTJ	ISFJ	INFJ	INTJ
N= 12	N= 4	N= 6	N= 7
%= 13.48	%= 4.49	%= 6.74	%= 7.87
■■■■■■■■■■■■■	■■■■	■■■■■■■	■■■■■■■■

ISTP	ISFP	INFP	INTP
N= 3	N= 2	N= 7	N= 2
%= 3.37	%= 2.25	%= 7.87	%= 2.25
■■■	■■	■■■■■■■■	■■

ESTP	ESFP	ENFP	ENTP
N= 0	N= 0	N= 11	N= 7
%= 0.00	%= 0.00	%= 12.36	%= 7.87
		■■■■■■■■■■■■	■■■■■■■■

ESTJ	ESFJ	ENFJ	ENTJ
N= 10	N= 4	N= 6	N= 8
%= 11.24	%= 4.49	%= 6.74	%= 8.99
■■■■■■■■■■■	■■■■	■■■■■■■	■■■■■■■■■

JUDGMENT — INTROVERSION — PERCEPTION — EXTRAVERSION — JUDGMENT

	N	%
E	46	51.69
I	43	48.31
S	35	39.33
N	54	60.67
T	49	55.06
F	40	44.94
J	57	64.04
P	32	35.96
I J	29	32.58
I P	14	15.73
E P	18	20.22
E J	28	31.46
S T	25	28.09
S F	10	11.24
N F	30	33.71
N T	24	26.97
S J	30	33.71
S P	5	5.62
N P	27	30.34
N J	27	30.34
T J	37	41.57
T P	12	13.48
F P	20	22.47
F J	20	22.47
I N	22	24.72
E N	32	35.96
I S	21	23.60
E S	14	15.73
E T	25	28.09
E F	21	23.60
I F	19	21.35
I T	24	26.97
S dom	16	17.98
N dom	31	34.83
T dom	23	25.84
F dom	19	21.35

Note: ■ = 1% of sample

8629312

This table is one of a series of tables from the CAPT-MBTI Data Bank of MBTI records submitted to CAPT for computer scoring between 1971 and June, 1984. This sample was drawn from 59,784 records with usable occupational codes from the total data bank of 232,557. This data bank has 51% Form F cases from 1971 to March, 1978, 35% Form F cases from 1978 to June, 1984 and 14% Form G cases from 1978 to December, 1982. An analysis of Form F and G data banks showed the data banks were comprised of 56% females and 44% males; education level completed: 6% some grade school, 30% high school diploma, 25% some college, 18% bachelor degrees, 11% masters degrees, 3% doctoral or post doctoral work, and 6% unknown. Age group percentages were: 11% under 18, 29% 18 to 20, 12% 21 to 24, 10% 25 to 29, 16% 30 to 39, 10% 40 to 49, 5% 50 to 59, 2% 60 plus, and 5% unknown.

Coordinators

SENSING		INTUITION	
THINKING	FEELING	FEELING	THINKING

ISTJ	ISFJ	INFJ	INTJ
N= 20	N= 12	N= 9	N= 10
%= 11.63	%= 6.98	%= 5.23	%= 5.81
■■■■■■■■■■ ■■	■■■■■■■	■■■■■	■■■■■■

ISTP	ISFP	INFP	INTP
N= 3	N= 6	N= 7	N= 7
%= 1.74	%= 3.49	%= 4.07	%= 4.07
■■	■■■	■■■■	■■■■

ESTP	ESFP	ENFP	ENTP
N= 3	N= 6	N= 20	N= 10
%= 1.74	%= 3.49	%= 11.63	%= 5.81
■■	■■■	■■■■■■■■■■ ■■	■■■■■■

ESTJ	ESFJ	ENFJ	ENTJ
N= 21	N= 14	N= 13	N= 11
%= 12.21	%= 8.14	%= 7.56	%= 6.40
■■■■■■■■■■■■ ■■	■■■■■■■■	■■■■■■■■	■■■■■■

JUDGMENT — INTROVERSION — PERCEPTION — PERCEPTION — EXTRAVERSION — JUDGMENT

	N	%
E	98	56.98
I	74	43.02
S	85	49.42
N	87	50.58
T	85	49.42
F	87	50.58
J	110	63.95
P	62	36.05
I J	51	29.65
I P	23	13.37
E P	39	22.67
E J	59	34.30
S T	47	27.33
S F	38	22.09
N F	49	28.49
N T	38	22.09
S J	67	38.95
S P	18	10.47
N P	44	25.58
N J	43	25.00
T J	62	36.05
T P	23	13.37
F P	39	22.67
F J	48	27.91
I N	33	19.19
E N	54	31.40
I S	41	23.84
E S	44	25.58
E T	45	26.16
E F	53	30.81
I F	34	19.77
I T	40	23.26
S dom	41	23.84
N dom	49	28.49
T dom	42	24.42
F dom	40	23.26

Note: ■ = 1% of sample   8629305

This table is one of a series of tables from the CAPT-MBTI Data Bank of MBTI records submitted to CAPT for computer scoring between 1971 and June, 1984. This sample was drawn from 59,784 records with usable occupational codes from the total data bank of 232,557. This data bank has 51% Form F cases from 1971 to March, 1978, 35% Form F cases from 1978 to June, 1984 and 14% Form G cases from 1978 to December, 1982. An analysis of Form F and G data banks showed the data banks were comprised of 56% females and 44% males; education level completed: 6% some grade school, 30% high school diploma, 25% some college, 18% bachelor degrees, 11% masters degrees, 3% doctoral or post doctoral work, and 6% unknown. Age group percentages were: 11% under 18, 29% 18 to 20, 12% 21 to 24, 10% 25 to 29, 16% 30 to 39, 10% 40 to 49, 5% 50 to 59, 2% 60 plus, and 5% unknown.

Credit Investigators and Mortgage Brokers

N = 136

	SENSING		INTUITION	
	THINKING	FEELING	FEELING	THINKING

ISTJ	ISFJ	INFJ	INTJ
N= 13	N= 6	N= 1	N= 11
%= 9.56	%= 4.41	%= .74	%= 8.09
■■■■■■■■■	■■■■	■	■■■■■■■■

ISTP	ISFP	INFP	INTP
N= 4	N= 0	N= 3	N= 5
%= 2.94	%= 0.00	%= 2.21	%= 3.68
■■■		■■	■■■■

ESTP	ESFP	ENFP	ENTP
N= 6	N= 1	N= 9	N= 14
%= 4.41	%= .74	%= 6.62	%= 10.29
■■■■	■	■■■■■■■	■■■■■■■■■■

ESTJ	ESFJ	ENFJ	ENTJ
N= 25	N= 9	N= 7	N= 22
%= 18.38	%= 6.62	%= 5.15	%= 16.18
■■■■■■■■■■ ■■■■■■■■	■■■■■■■	■■■■■	■■■■■■■■■■■ ■■■■■■

	N	%
E	93	68.38
I	43	31.62
S	64	47.06
N	72	52.94
T	100	73.53
F	36	26.47
J	94	69.12
P	42	30.88
I J	31	22.79
I P	12	8.82
E P	30	22.06
E J	63	46.32
S T	48	35.29
S F	16	11.76
N F	20	14.71
N T	52	38.24
S J	53	38.97
S P	11	8.09
N P	31	22.79
N J	41	30.15
T J	71	52.21
T P	29	21.32
F P	13	9.56
F J	23	16.91
I N	20	14.71
E N	52	38.24
I S	23	16.91
E S	41	30.15
E T	67	49.26
E F	26	19.12
I F	10	7.35
I T	33	24.26
S dom	26	19.12
N dom	35	25.74
T dom	56	41.18
F dom	19	13.97

Note: ■ = 1% of sample

8629308

This table is one of a series of tables from the CAPT-MBTI Data Bank of MBTI records submitted to CAPT for computer scoring between 1971 and June, 1984. This sample was drawn from 59,784 records with usable occupational codes from the total data bank of 232,557. This data bank has 51% Form F cases from 1971 to March, 1978, 35% Form F cases from 1978 to June, 1984 and 14% Form G cases from 1978 to December, 1982. An analysis of Form F and G data banks showed the data banks were comprised of 56% females and 44% males; education level completed: 6% some grade school, 30% high school diploma, 25% some college, 18% bachelor degrees, 11% masters degrees, 3% doctoral or post doctoral work, and 6% unknown. Age group percentages were: 11% under 18, 29% 18 to 20, 12% 21 to 24, 10% 25 to 29, 16% 30 to 39, 10% 40 to 49, 5% 50 to 59, 2% 60 plus, and 5% unknown.

Employment Development Specialists

	SENSING		INTUITION	
	THINKING	FEELING	FEELING	THINKING

ISTJ	ISFJ	INFJ	INTJ
N= 7	N= 6	N= 1	N= 6
%= 8.75	%= 7.50	%= 1.25	%= 7.50
■■■■■■■■	■■■■■■■	■	■■■■■■■

ISTP	ISFP	INFP	INTP
N= 3	N= 2	N= 8	N= 4
%= 3.75	%= 2.50	%= 10.00	%= 5.00
■■■■	■■■	■■■■■■■■■■	■■■■■

ESTP	ESFP	ENFP	ENTP
N= 0	N= 1	N= 9	N= 4
%= 0.00	%= 1.25	%= 11.25	%= 5.00
	■	■■■■■■■■■■■ ■	■■■■■

ESTJ	ESFJ	ENFJ	ENTJ
N= 9	N= 4	N= 6	N= 10
%= 11.25	%= 5.00	%= 7.50	%= 12.50
■■■■■■■■■■■ ■	■■■■■	■■■■■■■■	■■■■■■■■■■■■ ■■■

JUDGMENT — INTROVERSION — PERCEPTION — EXTRAVERSION — PERCEPTION — JUDGMENT

	N	%
E	43	53.75
I	37	46.25
S	32	40.00
N	48	60.00
T	43	53.75
F	37	46.25
J	49	61.25
P	31	38.75
I J	20	25.00
I P	17	21.25
E P	14	17.50
E J	29	36.25
S T	19	23.75
S F	13	16.25
N F	24	30.00
N T	24	30.00
S J	26	32.50
S P	6	7.50
N P	25	31.25
N J	23	28.75
T J	32	40.00
T P	11	13.75
F P	20	25.00
F J	17	21.25
I N	19	23.75
E N	29	36.25
I S	18	22.50
E S	14	17.50
E T	23	28.75
E F	20	25.00
I F	17	21.25
I T	20	25.00
S dom	14	17.50
N dom	20	25.00
T dom	26	32.50
F dom	20	25.00

Note: ■ = 1% of sample

8629334

This table is one of a series of tables from the CAPT-MBTI Data Bank of MBTI records submitted to CAPT for computer scoring between 1971 and June, 1984. This sample was drawn from 59,784 records with usable occupational codes from the total data bank of 232,557. This data bank has 51% Form F cases from 1971 to March, 1978, 35% Form F cases from 1978 to June, 1984 and 14% Form G cases from 1978 to December, 1982. An analysis of Form F and G data banks showed the data banks were comprised of 56% females and 44% males; education level completed: 6% some grade school, 30% high school diploma, 25% some college, 18% bachelor degrees, 11% masters degrees, 3% doctoral or post doctoral work, and 6% unknown. Age group percentages were: 11% under 18, 29% 18 to 20, 12% 21 to 24, 10% 25 to 29, 16% 30 to 39, 10% 40 to 49, 5% 50 to 59, 2% 60 plus, and 5% unknown.

Females in Leadership Development Program

	SENSING		INTUITION	
	THINKING	FEELING	FEELING	THINKING

ISTJ	ISFJ	INFJ	INTJ
N= 13	N= 5	N= 3	N= 17
%= 7.18	%= 2.76	%= 1.66	%= 9.39
■■■■■■■	■■■	■■	■■■■■■■■■

ISTP	ISFP	INFP	INTP
N= 5	N= 2	N= 8	N= 13
%= 2.76	%= 1.10	%= 4.42	%= 7.18
■■■	■	■■■■	■■■■■■■

ESTP	ESFP	ENFP	ENTP
N= 7	N= 0	N= 30	N= 19
%= 3.87	%= 0.00	%= 16.57	%= 10.50
■■■■		■■■■■■■■■■■■■■■■	■■■■■■■■■■■
		■■■■■■■	

ESTJ	ESFJ	ENFJ	ENTJ
N= 15	N= 7	N= 11	N= 26
%= 8.29	%= 3.87	%= 6.08	%= 14.36
■■■■■■■■	■■■■	■■■■■■	■■■■■■■■■■■■■■
			■■■■

JUDGMENT / PERCEPTION — INTROVERSION
PERCEPTION / JUDGMENT — EXTRAVERSION

	N	%
E	115	63.54
I	66	36.46
S	54	29.83
N	127	70.17
T	115	63.54
F	66	36.46
J	97	53.59
P	84	46.41
I J	38	20.99
I P	28	15.47
E P	56	30.94
E J	59	32.60
S T	40	22.10
S F	14	7.73
N F	52	28.73
N T	75	41.44
S J	40	22.10
S P	14	7.73
N P	70	38.67
N J	57	31.49
T J	71	39.23
T P	44	24.31
F P	40	22.10
F J	26	14.36
I N	41	22.65
E N	86	47.51
I S	25	13.81
E S	29	16.02
E T	67	37.02
E F	48	26.52
I F	18	9.94
I T	48	26.52
S dom	25	13.81
N dom	69	38.12
T dom	59	32.60
F dom	28	15.47

Note: ■ = 1% of sample   8630401

Data collected by Ellen Van Velsor and David Campbell of the Center for Creative Leadership from 1979 to 1983. Subjects were females attending the center. The subjects were mostly in middle to lower level management, non-management and professional positions in business and industry. These data are used with permission and were cited in:

Myers, I. B. & McCaulley, M. H. (1985). Manual: A Guide to the Development and Use of the Myers-Briggs Type Indicator. Palo Alto, CA: Consulting Psychologists Press.

Insurance Agents, Brokers, and Underwriters

N = 101

	SENSING		INTUITION	
	THINKING	FEELING	FEELING	THINKING

ISTJ	ISFJ	INFJ	INTJ
N= 7	N= 3	N= 4	N= 4
%= 6.93	%= 2.97	%= 3.96	%= 3.96
∎∎∎∎∎∎∎	∎∎∎	∎∎∎∎	∎∎∎∎

ISTP	ISFP	INFP	INTP
N= 4	N= 2	N= 4	N= 3
%= 3.96	%= 1.98	%= 3.96	%= 2.97
∎∎∎∎	∎∎	∎∎∎∎	∎∎∎

ESTP	ESFP	ENFP	ENTP
N= 4	N= 7	N= 14	N= 6
%= 3.96	%= 6.93	%= 13.86	%= 5.94
∎∎∎∎	∎∎∎∎∎∎∎	∎∎∎∎∎∎∎∎∎∎∎∎∎∎	∎∎∎∎∎∎

ESTJ	ESFJ	ENFJ	ENTJ
N= 22	N= 9	N= 4	N= 4
%= 21.78	%= 8.91	%= 3.96	%= 3.96
∎∎∎∎∎∎∎∎∎∎∎∎∎∎∎∎∎∎∎∎∎∎	∎∎∎∎∎∎∎∎∎	∎∎∎∎	∎∎∎∎

	N	%
E	70	69.31
I	31	30.69
S	58	57.43
N	43	42.57
T	54	53.47
F	47	46.53
J	57	56.44
P	44	43.56
I J	18	17.82
I P	13	12.87
E P	31	30.69
E J	39	38.61
S T	37	36.63
S F	21	20.79
N F	26	25.74
N T	17	16.83
S J	41	40.59
S P	17	16.83
N P	27	26.73
N J	16	15.84
T J	37	36.63
T P	17	16.83
F P	27	26.73
F J	20	19.80
I N	15	14.85
E N	28	27.72
I S	16	15.84
E S	42	41.58
E T	36	35.64
E F	34	33.66
I F	13	12.87
I T	18	17.82
S dom	21	20.79
N dom	28	27.72
T dom	33	32.67
F dom	19	18.81

Note: ∎ = 1% of sample   8629314

This table is one of a series of tables from the CAPT-MBTI Data Bank of MBTI records submitted to CAPT for computer scoring between 1971 and June, 1984. This sample was drawn from 59,784 records with usable occupational codes from the total data bank of 232,557. This data bank has 51% Form F cases from 1971 to March, 1978, 35% Form F cases from 1978 to June, 1984 and 14% Form G cases from 1978 to December, 1982. An analysis of Form F and G data banks showed the data banks were comprised of 56% females and 44% males; education level completed: 6% some grade school, 30% high school diploma, 25% some college, 18% bachelor degrees, 11% masters degrees, 3% doctoral or post doctoral work, and 6% unknown. Age group percentages were: 11% under 18, 29% 18 to 20, 12% 21 to 24, 10% 25 to 29, 16% 30 to 39, 10% 40 to 49, 5% 50 to 59, 2% 60 plus, and 5% unknown.

141

Males in Leadership Development Program

	SENSING		INTUITION	
	THINKING	FEELING	FEELING	THINKING

ISTJ	ISFJ	INFJ	INTJ
N= 249	N= 18	N= 13	N= 122
%= 23.69	%= 1.71	%= 1.24	%= 11.61
■■■■■■■■■■ ■■■■■■■■■■ ■■■■	■■	■	■■■■■■■■■■■ ■■

ISTP	ISFP	INFP	INTP·
N= 45	N= 7	N= 24	N= 56
%= 4.28	%= .67	%= 2.28	%= 5.33
■■■■	■	■■	■■■■■

ESTP	ESFP	ENFP	ENTP
N= 32	N= 10	N= 33	N= 66
%= 3.04	%= .95	%= 3.14	%= 6.28
■■■	■	■■■	■■■■■■

ESTJ	ESFJ	ENFJ	ENTJ
N= 196	N= 32	N= 13	N= 135
%= 18.65	%= 3.04	%= 1.24	%= 12.84
■■■■■■■■■■ ■■■■■■■■■	■■■	■	■■■■■■■■■■■■ ■■■

Judgment — Introversion — Perception — Extraversion — Perception — Judgment

	N	%
E	517	49.19
I	534	50.81
S	589	56.04
N	462	43.96
T	901	85.73
F	150	14.27
J	778	74.02
P	273	25.98
I J	402	38.25
I P	132	12.56
E P	141	13.42
E J	376	35.78
S T	522	49.67
S F	67	6.37
N F	83	7.90
N T	379	36.06
S J	495	47.10
S P	94	8.94
N P	179	17.03
N J	283	26.93
T J	702	66.79
T P	199	18.93
F P	74	7.04
F J	76	7.23
I N	215	20.46
E N	247	23.50
I S	319	30.35
E S	270	25.69
E T	429	40.82
E F	88	8.37
I F	62	5.90
I T	472	44.91
S dom	309	29.40
N dom	234	22.26
T dom	432	41.10
F dom	76	7.23

Note: ■ = 1% of sample   8630400

Data collected by Ellen Van Velsor and David Campbell of the Center for Creative Leadership from 1979 to 1983. Subjects were males attending the center. The subjects were mostly middle to upper middle level managers in business and industry; their ages were predominantly early to mid forties. These data are used with permission and were cited in:

Myers, I. B. & McCaulley, M. H. (1985). Manual: A Guide to the Development and Use of the Myers-Briggs Type Indicator. Palo Alto, CA: Consulting Psychologists Press.

Managers: England

N = 849

		SENSING		INTUITION	
	THINKING	FEELING	FEELING	THINKING	

ISTJ	ISFJ	INFJ	INTJ
N= 202	N= 55	N= 20	N= 55
%= 23.79	%= 6.48	%= 2.36	%= 6.48
■■■■■■■■■■ ■■■■■■■■■■ ■■■■	■■■■■■	■■	■■■■■■

ISTP	ISFP	INFP	INTP
N= 37	N= 10	N= 26	N= 25
%= 4.36	%= 1.18	%= 3.06	%= 2.94
■■■■	■	■■■	■■■

ESTP	ESFP	ENFP	ENTP
N= 33	N= 10	N= 25	N= 36
%= 3.89	%= 1.18	%= 2.94	%= 4.24
■■■■	■	■■■	■■■■

ESTJ	ESFJ	ENFJ	ENTJ
N= 176	N= 50	N= 14	N= 75
%= 20.73	%= 5.89	%= 1.65	%= 8.83
■■■■■■■■■■ ■■■■■■■■■■ ■	■■■■■■	■■	■■■■■■■■■

	N	%
E	419	49.35
I	430	50.65
S	573	67.49
N	276	32.51
T	639	75.27
F	210	24.73
J	647	76.21
P	202	23.79
I J	332	39.10
I P	98	11.54
E P	104	12.25
E J	315	37.10
S T	448	52.77
S F	125	14.72
N F	85	10.01
N T	191	22.50
S J	483	56.89
S P	90	10.60
N P	112	13.19
N J	164	19.32
T J	508	59.84
T P	131	15.43
F P	71	8.36
F J	139	16.37
I N	126	14.84
E N	150	17.67
I S	304	35.81
E S	269	31.68
E T	320	37.69
E F	99	11.66
I F	111	13.07
I T	319	37.57
S dom	300	35.34
N dom	136	16.02
T dom	313	36.87
F dom	100	11.78

Note: ■ = 1% of sample   8623109

Data collected by Charles Margerison and Ralph Lewis at the Cranfield School of Management, England. Subjects were managers attending business school short courses. These data are used with permission and were cited in:

Lewis, R., & Margerison, C. J. (1979). Personal mapping - Understanding personal preferences. Cranfield, Bedford, England: Management and Organization Development Research Centre, Cranfield School of Management.

Managers: Federal Executives

N = 1394

	SENSING		INTUITION			N	%
	THINKING	FEELING	FEELING	THINKING			

ISTJ	ISFJ	INFJ	INTJ
N= 366	N= 38	N= 25	N= 208
%= 26.26	%= 2.73	%= 1.79	%= 14.92
■■■■■■■■■■ ■■■■■■■■■■ ■■■■■■	■■■	■■	■■■■■■■■■■ ■■■■■

ISTP	ISFP	INFP	INTP
N= 75	N= 6	N= 33	N= 127
%= 5.38	%= .43	%= 2.37	%= 9.11
■■■■■		■■	■■■■■■■■■

ESTP	ESFP	ENFP	ENTP
N= 28	N= 8	N= 34	N= 81
%= 2.01	%= .57	%= 2.44	%= 5.81
■■	■	■■	■■■■■■

ESTJ	ESFJ	ENFJ	ENTJ
N= 172	N= 19	N= 26	N= 148
%= 12.34	%= 1.36	%= 1.87	%= 10.62
■■■■■■■■■■■■ ■■	■	■■	■■■■■■■■■■■ ■

Right-side labels: JUDGMENT / INTROVERSION / PERCEPTION / PERCEPTION / EXTRAVERSION / JUDGMENT

	N	%
E	516	37.02
I	878	62.98
S	712	51.08
N	682	48.92
T	1205	86.44
F	189	13.56
J	1002	71.88
P	392	28.12
I J	637	45.70
I P	241	17.29
E P	151	10.83
E J	365	26.18
S T	641	45.98
S F	71	5.09
N F	118	8.46
N T	564	40.46
S J	595	42.68
S P	117	8.39
N P	275	19.73
N J	407	29.20
T J	894	64.13
T P	311	22.31
F P	81	5.81
F J	108	7.75
I N	393	28.19
E N	289	20.73
I S	485	34.79
E S	227	16.28
E T	429	30.77
E F	87	6.24
I F	102	7.32
I T	776	55.67
S dom	440	31.56
N dom	348	24.96
T dom	522	37.45
F dom	84	6.03

Note: ■ = 1% of sample

8623111

Data collected by John W. Pickering from June 1983 to September 1986. Subjects were senior federal government executives. A subset of 671 executives were composed of 90.5% males and 9.5% females; 90% were between 35 and 55 years old; 5% had some college, 34% bachelors degrees, 44% masters or professional degrees, 14% doctorates, 3% post-doctorates; 92% were white; 75% had their professional training in either business, engineering, hard sciences or law; 17% had 11-15 years of federal service, 25% had 16-20, 26% had 21-25, and 18% had 26-30; 37% had 10-15 years as a supervisor; 22% supervised a total of 21-50 employees and 20% supervised 101-500. These data are used with permission and have not been published elsewhere to date.

Managers: Financial and Bank Officers

N = 756

SENSING		INTUITION	
THINKING	FEELING	FEELING	THINKING

ISTJ	ISFJ	INFJ	INTJ
N= 128	N= 29	N= 8	N= 37
%= 16.93	%= 3.84	%= 1.06	%= 4.89
■■■■■■■■■■ ■■■■■■■	■■■■	■	■■■■■

ISTP	ISFP	INFP	INTP
N= 29	N= 16	N= 21	N= 25
%= 3.84	%= 2.12	%= 2.78	%= 3.31
■■■■	■■	■■■	■■■

ESTP	ESFP	ENFP	ENTP
N= 32	N= 15	N= 28	N= 50
%= 4.23	%= 1.98	%= 3.70	%= 6.61
■■■■	■■	■■■■	■■■■■■■

ESTJ	ESFJ	ENFJ	ENTJ
N= 193	N= 50	N= 22	N= 73
%= 25.53	%= 6.61	%= 2.91	%= 9.66
■■■■■■■■■ ■■■■■■■■■ ■■■■■■	■■■■■■■	■■■	■■■■■■■■■■

JUDGMENT — INTROVERSION — PERCEPTION — PERCEPTION — EXTRAVERSION — JUDGMENT

	N	%
E	463	61.24
I	293	38.76
S	492	65.08
N	264	34.92
T	567	75.00
F	189	25.00
J	540	71.43
P	216	28.57
I J	202	26.72
I P	91	12.04
E P	125	16.53
E J	338	44.71
S T	382	50.53
S F	110	14.55
N F	79	10.45
N T	185	24.47
S J	400	52.91
S P	92	12.17
N P	124	16.40
N J	140	18.52
T J	431	57.01
T P	136	17.99
F P	80	10.58
F J	109	14.42
I N	91	12.04
E N	173	22.88
I S	202	26.72
E S	290	38.36
E T	348	46.03
E F	115	15.21
I F	74	9.79
I T	219	28.97
S dom	204	26.98
N dom	123	16.27
T dom	320	42.33
F dom	109	14.42

Note: ■ = 1% of sample   8629304

This table is one of a series of tables from the CAPT-MBTI Data Bank of MBTI records submitted to CAPT for computer scoring between 1971 and June, 1984. This sample was drawn from 59,784 records with usable occupational codes from the total data bank of 232,557. This data bank has 51% Form F cases from 1971 to March, 1978, 35% Form F cases from 1978 to June, 1984 and 14% Form G cases from 1978 to December, 1982. An analysis of Form F and G data banks showed the data banks were comprised of 56% females and 44% males; education level completed: 6% some grade school, 30% high school diploma, 25% some college, 18% bachelor degrees, 11% masters degrees, 3% doctoral or post doctoral work, and 6% unknown. Age group percentages were: 11% under 18, 29% 18 to 20, 12% 21 to 24, 10% 25 to 29, 16% 30 to 39, 10% 40 to 49, 5% 50 to 59, 2% 60 plus, and 5% unknown.

Managers: High Level Corporate Executives

N = 136

	SENSING		INTUITION	
	THINKING	FEELING	FEELING	THINKING

ISTJ	ISFJ	INFJ	INTJ
N= 33	N= 0	N= 1	N= 15
%= 24.26	%= 0.00	%= .74	%= 11.03
■■■■■■■■■		■	■■■■■■■■■■
■■■■■■■■■			■
■■■■			

ISTP	ISFP	INFP	INTP
N= 6	N= 1	N= 3	N= 4
%= 4.41	%= .74	%= 2.21	%= 2.94
■■■■	■	■■	■■■

ESTP	ESFP	ENFP	ENTP
N= 4	N= 4	N= 1	N= 11
%= 2.94	%= 2.94	%= .74	%= 8.09
■■■	■■■	■	■■■■■■■■

ESTJ	ESFJ	ENFJ	ENTJ
N= 27	N= 3	N= 1	N= 22
%= 19.85	%= 2.21	%= .74	%= 16.18
■■■■■■■■■	■■	■	■■■■■■■■■■
■■■■■■■■■			■■■■■■

JUDGMENT · INTROVERSION · PERCEPTION · PERCEPTION · EXTRAVERSION · JUDGMENT

	N	%
E	73	53.68
I	63	46.32
S	78	57.35
N	58	42.65
T	122	89.71
F	14	10.29
J	102	75.00
P	34	25.00
I J	49	36.03
I P	14	10.29
E P	20	14.71
E J	53	38.97
S T	70	51.47
S F	8	5.88
N F	6	4.41
N T	52	38.24
S J	63	46.32
S P	15	11.03
N P	19	13.97
N J	39	28.68
T J	97	71.32
T P	25	18.38
F P	9	6.62
F J	5	3.68
I N	23	16.91
E N	35	25.74
I S	40	29.41
E S	38	27.94
E T	64	47.06
E F	9	6.62
I F	5	3.68
I T	58	42.65
S dom	41	30.15
N dom	28	20.59
T dom	59	43.38
F dom	8	5.88

Note: ■ = 1% of sample   8623114

Data collected by Ellen Van Velsor and David Campbell at the Center for Creative Leadership in Greensboro, North Carolina from January 1979 to October 1983. Subjects were comprised of vice presidents, presidents and chief executive officers in business and industrial organizations of more than 10 employees. Executives were approximately 5% female and 95% male. Subjects were attending a leadership development program at the center during this period. These data are used with permission and have not been published elsewhere to date.

Managers: Japanese Chief Executives

N = 118

<table>
<tr><td colspan="2" align="center">SENSING</td><td colspan="2" align="center">INTUITION</td></tr>
<tr><td>THINKING</td><td>FEELING</td><td>FEELING</td><td>THINKING</td></tr>
<tr>
<td>ISTJ
N= 7
%= 5.93
■■■■■■</td>
<td>ISFJ
N= 5
%= 4.24
■■■■</td>
<td>INFJ
N= 2
%= 1.69
■■</td>
<td>INTJ
N= 19
%= 16.10
■■■■■■■■■
■■■■■■</td>
</tr>
<tr>
<td>ISTP
N= 1
%= .85
■</td>
<td>ISFP
N= 2
%= 1.69
■■</td>
<td>INFP
N= 0
%= 0.00</td>
<td>INTP
N= 3
%= 2.54
■■■</td>
</tr>
<tr>
<td>ESTP
N= 10
%= 8.47
■■■■■■■■</td>
<td>ESFP
N= 7
%= 5.93
■■■■■■</td>
<td>ENFP
N= 5
%= 4.24
■■■■</td>
<td>ENTP
N= 3
%= 2.54
■■■</td>
</tr>
<tr>
<td>ESTJ
N= 25
%= 21.19
■■■■■■■■■■
■■■■■■■■■■
■</td>
<td>ESFJ
N= 6
%= 5.08
■■■■■</td>
<td>ENFJ
N= 4
%= 3.39
■■■</td>
<td>ENTJ
N= 19
%= 16.10
■■■■■■■■■
■■■■■■</td>
</tr>
</table>

	N	%
E	79	66.95
I	39	33.05
S	63	53.39
N	55	46.61
T	87	73.73
F	31	26.27
J	87	73.73
P	31	26.27
I J	33	27.97
I P	6	5.08
E P	25	21.19
E J	54	45.76
S T	43	36.44
S F	20	16.95
N F	11	9.32
N T	44	37.29
S J	43	36.44
S P	20	16.95
N P	11	9.32
N J	44	37.29
T J	70	59.32
T P	17	14.41
F P	14	11.86
F J	17	14.41
I N	24	20.34
E N	31	26.27
I S	15	12.71
E S	48	40.68
E T	57	48.31
E F	22	18.64
I F	9	7.63
I T	30	25.42
S dom	29	24.58
N dom	29	24.58
T dom	48	40.68
F dom	12	10.17

Note: ■ = 1% of sample   8623105

Data collected by Takeshi Ohsawa at the Nippon Recruit Center, Tokyo, Japan from 1964 to 1975. No other demographic data were reported. These data are used with permission and were cited in:

Ohsawa, T. (1975, October). MBTI experiences in Japan: Career choice, selection, placement and counseling for individual development. Paper presented at the First National Conference on the Myers-Briggs Type Indicator, Gainesville, FL.

Managers: Middle Managers in
a Japanese Chemical Company

N = 366

	SENSING		INTUITION	
	THINKING	FEELING	FEELING	THINKING

ISTJ	ISFJ	INFJ	INTJ
N= 48	N= 27	N= 2	N= 12
%= 13.11	%= 7.38	%= .55	%= 3.28
■■■■■■■■■■	■■■■■■■	■	■■■
■■■			

ISTP	ISFP	INFP	INTP
N= 15	N= 19	N= 4	N= 9
%= 4.10	%= 5.19	%= 1.09	%= 2.46
■■■■	■■■■■	■	■■

ESTP	ESFP	ENFP	ENTP
N= 28	N= 24	N= 9	N= 22
%= 7.65	%= 6.56	%= 2.46	%= 6.01
■■■■■■■■	■■■■■■■	■■	■■■■■■

ESTJ	ESFJ	ENFJ	ENTJ
N= 77	N= 29	N= 8	N= 33
%= 21.04	%= 7.92	%= 2.19	%= 9.02
■■■■■■■■■■	■■■■■■■■	■■	■■■■■■■■■
■■■■■■■■■■			
■			

JUDGMENT — INTROVERSION — PERCEPTION — PERCEPTION — EXTRAVERSION — JUDGMENT

	N	%
E	230	62.84
I	136	37.16
S	267	72.95
N	99	27.05
T	244	66.67
F	122	33.33
J	236	64.48
P	130	35.52
I J	89	24.32
I P	47	12.84
E P	83	22.68
E J	147	40.16
S T	168	45.90
S F	99	27.05
N F	23	6.28
N T	76	20.77
S J	181	49.45
S P	86	23.50
N P	44	12.02
N J	55	15.03
T J	170	46.45
T P	74	20.22
F P	56	15.30
F J	66	18.03
I N	27	7.38
E N	72	19.67
I S	109	29.78
E S	158	43.17
E T	160	43.72
E F	70	19.13
I F	52	14.21
I T	84	22.95
S dom	127	34.70
N dom	45	12.30
T dom	134	36.61
F dom	60	16.39

Note: ■ = 1% of sample   8623103

Data collected by Takeshi Ohsawa at the Nippon Recruit Center, Tokyo, Japan from 1964 to 1975. No other demographic data were reported. These data are used with permission and were cited in:

Ohsawa, T. (1975, October). MBTI experiences in Japan: Career choice, selection, placement and counseling for individual development. Paper presented at the First National Conference on the Myers-Briggs Type Indicator, Gainesville, FL.

Managers: Middle Managers in a Japanese Heavy Industrial Company

N = 116

	SENSING		INTUITION	
	THINKING	FEELING	FEELING	THINKING

ISTJ	ISFJ	INFJ	INTJ
N= 22	N= 6	N= 2	N= 14
%= 18.97	%= 5.17	%= 1.72	%= 12.07
■■■■■■■■■■ ■■■■■■■■■	■■■■■	■■	■■■■■■■■■■ ■■

ISTP	ISFP	INFP	INTP
N= 8	N= 6	N= 6	N= 11
%= 6.90	%= 5.17	%= 5.17	%= 9.48
■■■■■■■	■■■■■	■■■■■	■■■■■■■■■

ESTP	ESFP	ENFP	ENTP
N= 2	N= 4	N= 3	N= 11
%= 1.72	%= 3.45	%= 2.59	%= 9.48
■■	■■■	■■■	■■■■■■■■■

ESTJ	ESFJ	ENFJ	ENTJ
N= 13	N= 4	N= 0	N= 4
%= 11.21	%= 3.45	%= 0.00	%= 3.45
■■■■■■■■■■ ■	■■■		■■■

JUDGMENT — INTROVERSION — PERCEPTION — PERCEPTION — EXTRAVERSION — JUDGMENT

	N	%
E	41	35.34
I	75	64.66
S	65	56.03
N	51	43.97
T	85	73.28
F	31	26.72
J	65	56.03
P	51	43.97
I J	44	37.93
I P	31	26.72
E P	20	17.24
E J	21	18.10
S T	45	38.79
S F	20	17.24
N F	11	9.48
N T	40	34.48
S J	45	38.79
S P	20	17.24
N P	31	26.72
N J	20	17.24
T J	53	45.69
T P	32	27.59
F P	19	16.38
F J	12	10.34
I N	33	28.45
E N	18	15.52
I S	42	36.21
E S	23	19.83
E T	30	25.86
E F	11	9.48
I F	20	17.24
I T	55	47.41
S dom	34	29.31
N dom	30	25.86
T dom	36	31.03
F dom	16	13.79

Note: ■ = 1% of sample   8623104

Data collected by Takeshi Ohsawa at the Nippon Recruit Center, Tokyo, Japan from 1964 to 1975. No other demographic data were reported. These data are used with permission and were cited in:

Ohsawa, T. (1975, October). MBTI experiences in Japan: Career choice, selection, placement and counseling for individual development. Paper presented at the First National Conference on the Myers-Briggs Type Indicator, Gainesville, FL.

Managers: Office

N = 102

| | SENSING | | INTUITION | |
| | THINKING | FEELING | FEELING | THINKING |

ISTJ	ISFJ	INFJ	INTJ
N= 8	N= 9	N= 3	N= 3
%= 7.84	%= 8.82	%= 2.94	%= 2.94

ISTP	ISFP	INFP	INTP
N= 3	N= 5	N= 7	N= 2
%= 2.94	%= 4.90	%= 6.86	%= 1.96

ESTP	ESFP	ENFP	ENTP
N= 0	N= 2	N= 14	N= 3
%= 0.00	%= 1.96	%= 13.73	%= 2.94

ESTJ	ESFJ	ENFJ	ENTJ
N= 14	N= 15	N= 7	N= 7
%= 13.73	%= 14.71	%= 6.86	%= 6.86

	N	%
E	62	60.78
I	40	39.22
S	56	54.90
N	46	45.10
T	40	39.22
F	62	60.78
J	66	64.71
P	36	35.29
I J	23	22.55
I P	17	16.67
E P	19	18.63
E J	43	42.16
ST	25	24.51
SF	31	30.39
NF	31	30.39
NT	15	14.71
S J	46	45.10
S P	10	9.80
N P	26	25.49
N J	20	19.61
T J	32	31.37
T P	8	7.84
F P	28	27.45
F J	34	33.33
I N	15	14.71
E N	31	30.39
I S	25	24.51
E S	31	30.39
E T	24	23.53
E F	38	37.25
I F	24	23.53
I T	16	15.69
S dom	19	18.63
N dom	23	22.55
T dom	26	25.49
F dom	34	33.33

Note: ■ = 1% of sample   8629309

This table is one of a series of tables from the CAPT-MBTI Data Bank of MBTI records submitted to CAPT for computer scoring between 1971 and June, 1984. This sample was drawn from 59,784 records with usable occupational codes from the total data bank of 232,557. This data bank has 51% Form F cases from 1971 to March, 1978, 35% Form F cases from 1978 to June, 1984 and 14% Form G cases from 1978 to December, 1982. An analysis of Form F and G data banks showed the data banks were comprised of 56% females and 44% males; education level completed: 6% some grade school, 30% high school diploma, 25% some college, 18% bachelor degrees, 11% masters degrees, 3% doctoral or post doctoral work, and 6% unknown. Age group percentages were: 11% under 18, 29% 18 to 20, 12% 21 to 24, 10% 25 to 29, 16% 30 to 39, 10% 40 to 49, 5% 50 to 59, 2% 60 plus, and 5% unknown.

150

Managers: Participants in Women in Management Conference

N = 98

	SENSING		INTUITION	
	THINKING	FEELING	FEELING	THINKING

ISTJ	ISFJ	INFJ	INTJ
N= 9	N= 7	N= 4	N= 6
%= 9.18	%= 7.14	%= 4.08	%= 6.12
■■■■■■■■■	■■■■■■■	■■■■	■■■■■■

ISTP	ISFP	INFP	INTP
N= 3	N= 5	N= 10	N= 8
%= 3.06	%= 5.10	%= 10.20	%= 8.16
■■■	■■■■■	■■■■■■■■■■	■■■■■■■■

ESTP	ESFP	ENFP	ENTP
N= 3	N= 3	N= 5	N= 7
%= 3.06	%= 3.06	%= 5.10	%= 7.14
■■■	■■■	■■■■■	■■■■■■■

ESTJ	ESFJ	ENFJ	ENTJ
N= 10	N= 7	N= 3	N= 8
%= 10.20	%= 7.14	%= 3.06	%= 8.16
■■■■■■■■■■	■■■■■■■	■■■	■■■■■■■■

	N	%
E	46	46.94
I	52	53.06
S	47	47.96
N	51	52.04
T	54	55.10
F	44	44.90
J	54	55.10
P	44	44.90
I J	26	26.53
I P	26	26.53
E P	18	18.37
E J	28	28.57
S T	25	25.51
S F	22	22.45
N F	22	22.45
N T	29	29.59
S J	33	33.67
S P	14	14.29
N P	30	30.61
N J	21	21.43
T J	33	33.67
T P	21	21.43
F P	23	23.47
F J	21	21.43
I N	28	28.57
E N	23	23.47
I S	24	24.49
E S	23	23.47
E T	28	28.57
E F	18	18.37
I F	26	26.53
I T	26	26.53
S dom	22	22.45
N dom	22	22.45
T dom	29	29.59
F dom	25	25.51

Note: ■ = 1% of sample

8623119

Data collected by Carolyn Griffis from February 20 - 22, 1975. Subjects were female attendees of the Second Annual Women in Management Conference held at the University of Florida who volunteered to answer the MBTI after hearing a presentation about it. No other demographic data were reported. These data are used with permission and have not been published elsewhere to date.

Managers: Regional Telephone Company Low Level Managers

N = 230

	SENSING		INTUITION	
	THINKING	FEELING	FEELING	THINKING

ISTJ	ISFJ	INFJ	INTJ
N= 71	N= 22	N= 5	N= 8
%= 30.87	%= 9.57	%= 2.17	3.48
■■■■■■■■■ ■■■■■■■■■ ■■■■■■■■■ ■	■■■■■■■■■	■■	■■■

ISTP	ISFP	INFP	INTP
N= 12	N= 8	N= 1	N= 9
%= 5.22	%= 3.48	.43	%= 3.91
■■■■■	■■■		■■■■

ESTP	ESFP	ENFP	ENTP
N= 6	N= 4	N= 9	N= 9
%= 2.61	%= 1.74	%= 3.91	%= 3.91
■■■	■■	■■■■	■■■■

ESTJ	ESFJ	ENFJ	ENTJ
N= 43	N= 12	N= 2	N= 9
%= 18.70	%= 5.22	%= .87	%= 3.91
■■■■■■■■■ ■■■■■■■■■	■■■■■	■	■■■■

(Right margin labels: JUDGMENT, PERCEPTION — INTROVERSION; PERCEPTION, JUDGMENT — EXTRAVERSION)

Note: ■ = 1% of sample   8623107

	N	%
E	94	40.87
I	136	59.13
S	178	77.39
N	52	22.61
T	167	72.61
F	63	27.39
J	172	74.78
P	58	25.22
I J	106	46.09
I P	30	13.04
E P	28	12.17
E J	66	28.70
S T	132	57.39
S F	46	20.00
N F	17	7.39
N T	35	15.22
S J	148	64.35
S P	30	13.04
N P	28	12.17
N J	24	10.43
T J	131	56.96
T P	36	15.65
F P	22	9.57
F J	41	17.83
I N	23	10.00
E N	29	12.61
I S	113	49.13
E S	65	28.26
E T	67	29.13
E F	27	11.74
I F	36	15.65
I T	100	43.48
S dom	103	44.78
N dom	31	13.48
T dom	73	31.74
F dom	23	10.00

Data collected by Larrie Loehr from February 1982 to December 1982 using Form G. Subjects were all of the first level managers, which included supervisors and technical specialists, in a 1300 member mid-atlantic states independent telephone company. No gender, race or educational level data were reported. These data are used with permission and have not been published elsewhere to date.

Managers: Restaurant, Cafeteria, Bar and Food Service

N = 312

	SENSING		INTUITION	
	THINKING	FEELING	FEELING	THINKING

ISTJ	ISFJ	INFJ	INTJ
N= 42	N= 28	N= 5	N= 6
%= 13.46	%= 8.97	%= 1.60	%= 1.92
■■■■■■■■■■ ■■■	■■■■■■■■■	■■	■■

ISTP	ISFP	INFP	INTP
N= 5	N= 10	N= 4	N= 4
%= 1.60	%= 3.21	%= 1.28	%= 1.28
■■	■■■	■	■

ESTP	ESFP	ENFP	ENTP
N= 9	N= 13	N= 15	N= 17
%= 2.88	%= 4.17	%= 4.81	%= 5.45
■■■	■■■■	■■■■■	■■■■■

ESTJ	ESFJ	ENFJ	ENTJ
N= 86	N= 30	N= 8	N= 30
%= 27.56	%= 9.62	%= 2.56	%= 9.62
■■■■■■■■■■ ■■■■■■■■■■ ■■■■■■■■	■■■■■■■■■■	■■■	■■■■■■■■■■

JUDGMENT — INTROVERSION — PERCEPTION — EXTRAVERSION — JUDGMENT

	N	%
E	208	66.67
I	104	33.33
S	223	71.47
N	89	28.53
T	199	63.78
F	113	36.22
J	235	75.32
P	77	24.68
I J	81	25.96
I P	23	7.37
E P	54	17.31
E J	154	49.36
S T	142	45.51
S F	81	25.96
N F	32	10.26
N T	57	18.27
S J	186	59.62
S P	37	11.86
N P	40	12.82
N J	49	15.71
T J	164	52.56
T P	35	11.22
F P	42	13.46
F J	71	22.76
I N	19	6.09
E N	70	22.44
I S	85	27.24
E S	138	44.23
E T	142	45.51
E F	66	21.15
I F	47	15.06
I T	57	18.27
S dom	92	29.49
N dom	43	13.78
T dom	125	40.06
F dom	52	16.67

Note: ■ = 1% of sample   8629310

This table is one of a series of tables from the CAPT-MBTI Data Bank of MBTI records submitted to CAPT for computer scoring between 1971 and June, 1984. This sample was drawn from 59,784 records with usable occupational codes from the total data bank of 232,557. This data bank has 51% Form F cases from 1971 to March, 1978, 35% Form F cases from 1978 to June, 1984 and 14% Form G cases from 1978 to December, 1982. An analysis of Form F and G data banks showed the data banks were comprised of 56% females and 44% males; education level completed: 6% some grade school, 30% high school diploma, 25% some college, 18% bachelor degrees, 11% masters degrees, 3% doctoral or post doctoral work, and 6% unknown. Age group percentages were: 11% under 18, 29% 18 to 20, 12% 21 to 24, 10% 25 to 29, 16% 30 to 39, 10% 40 to 49, 5% 50 to 59, 2% 60 plus, and 5% unknown.

Managers: Retail Stores

N = 316

	SENSING		INTUITION				N	%
	THINKING	FEELING	FEELING	THINKING				

<table>
<tr><td colspan="4"></td><td></td><td>E</td><td>205</td><td>64.87</td></tr>
<tr>
<td>ISTJ
N= 83
%= 26.27
■■■■■■■■■
■■■■■■■■■
■■■■■■</td>
<td>ISFJ
N= 7
%= 2.22
■■</td>
<td>INFJ
N= 1
%= .32</td>
<td>INTJ
N= 10
%= 3.16
■■■</td>
<td>JUDGMENT / INTROVERSION</td>
<td>I
S
N
T
F
J
P</td>
<td>111
261
55
294
22
289
27</td>
<td>35.13
82.59
17.41
93.04
6.96
91.46
8.54</td>
</tr>
<tr>
<td>ISTP
N= 4
%= 1.27
■</td>
<td>ISFP
N= 1
%= .32</td>
<td>INFP
N= 0
%= 0.00</td>
<td>INTP
N= 5
%= 1.58
■■</td>
<td>PERCEPTION</td>
<td>I J
I P
E P
E J</td>
<td>101
10
17
188</td>
<td>31.96
3.16
5.38
59.49</td>
</tr>
<tr>
<td>ESTP
N= 8
%= 2.53
■■■</td>
<td>ESFP
N= 3
%= .95
■</td>
<td>ENFP
N= 1
%= .32</td>
<td>ENTP
N= 5
%= 1.58
■■</td>
<td>PERCEPTION / EXTRAVERSION</td>
<td>ST
SF
NF
NT

S J
S P
N P
N J

T J
T P
F P
F J</td>
<td>242
19
3
52

245
16
11
44

272
22
5
17</td>
<td>76.58
6.01
.95
16.46

77.53
5.06
3.48
13.92

86.08
6.96
1.58
5.38</td>
</tr>
<tr>
<td>ESTJ
N= 147
%= 46.52
■■■■■■■■■
■■■■■■■■■
■■■■■■■■■
■■■■■■■■■
■■■■■■■</td>
<td>ESFJ
N= 8
%= 2.53
■■■</td>
<td>ENFJ
N= 1
%= .32</td>
<td>ENTJ
N= 32
%= 10.13
■■■■■■■■■■</td>
<td>JUDGMENT</td>
<td>IN
EN
I S
ES

ET
EF
I F
I T

S dom
N dom
T dom
F dom</td>
<td>16
39
95
166

192
13
9
102

101
17
188
10</td>
<td>5.06
12.34
30.06
52.53

60.76
4.11
2.85
32.28

31.96
5.38
59.49
3.16</td>
</tr>
</table>

Note: ■ = 1% of sample   8623110

Data collected by Walter Gaster in 1982. Subjects were managers of stores with more than 20,000 square feet of selling space that were part of a national mass merchandizer with coast to coast outlets. This sample represents approximately 99% of all managers of this store size in this chain. Managers were 100% male and the average age was 39.7, with a range from 23 to 65. The range of educational level was from 11th grade to above a masters degree, the average being between one and two years of college; 94% were white. These data are used with permission and were cited in:

Gaster, W. D. (1982). A study of personality type as a predictor of success in retail store management (Doctoral dissertation, Louisiana Technical University). Dissertation Abstracts International, 43(12), 4020A.

N = 83

	SENSING		INTUITION	
	THINKING	FEELING	FEELING	THINKING

ISTJ	ISFJ	INFJ	INTJ
N= 12	N= 2	N= 0	N= 8
%= 14.46	%= 2.41	%= 0.00	%= 9.64
■■■■■■■■■■	■■		■■■■■■■■■
■■■■			

ISTP	ISFP	INFP	INTP
N= 3	N= 3	N= 1	N= 1
%= 3.61	%= 3.61	%= 1.20	%= 1.20
■■■■	■■■■	■	■

ESTP	ESFP	ENFP	ENTP
N= 2	N= 3	N= 1	N= 6
%= 2.41	%= 3.61	%= 1.20	%= 7.23
■■	■■■■	■	■■■■■■■

ESTJ	ESFJ	ENFJ	ENTJ
N= 20	N= 4	N= 3	N= 14
%= 24.10	%= 4.82	%= 3.61	%= 16.87
■■■■■■■■■■	■■■■■	■■■■	■■■■■■■■■■
■■■■■■■■■■			■■■■■■■
■■■■			

JUDGMENT — INTROVERSION — PERCEPTION — PERCEPTION — EXTRAVERSION — JUDGMENT

	N	%
E	53	63.86
I	30	36.14
S	49	59.04
N	34	40.96
T	66	79.52
F	17	20.48
J	63	75.90
P	20	24.10
I J	22	26.51
I P	8	9.64
E P	12	14.46
E J	41	49.40
S T	37	44.58
S F	12	14.46
N F	5	6.02
N T	29	34.94
S J	38	45.78
S P	11	13.25
N P	9	10.84
N J	25	30.12
T J	54	65.06
T P	12	14.46
F P	8	9.64
F J	9	10.84
I N	10	12.05
E N	24	28.92
I S	20	24.10
E S	29	34.94
E T	42	50.60
E F	11	13.25
I F	6	7.23
I T	24	28.92
S dom	19	22.89
N dom	15	18.07
T dom	38	45.78
F dom	11	13.25

Note: ■ = 1% of sample   8629311

This table is one of a series of tables from the CAPT-MBTI Data Bank of MBTI records submitted to CAPT for computer scoring between 1971 and June, 1984. This sample was drawn from 59,784 records with usable occupational codes from the total data bank of 232,557. This data bank has 51% Form F cases from 1971 to March, 1978, 35% Form F cases from 1978 to June, 1984 and 14% Form G cases from 1978 to December, 1982. An analysis of Form F and G data banks showed the data banks were comprised of 56% females and 44% males; education level completed: 6% some grade school, 30% high school diploma, 25% some college, 18% bachelor degrees, 11% masters degrees, 3% doctoral or post doctoral work, and 6% unknown. Age group percentages were: 11% under 18, 29% 18 to 20, 12% 21 to 24, 10% 25 to 29, 16% 30 to 39, 10% 40 to 49, 5% 50 to 59, 2% 60 plus, and 5% unknown.

Managers: Small Business

	SENSING		INTUITION	
	THINKING	FEELING	FEELING	THINKING

ISTJ	ISFJ	INFJ	INTJ
N= 43	N= 8	N= 2	N= 4
%= 28.67	%= 5.33	%= 1.33	%= 2.67

ISTP	ISFP	INFP	INTP
N= 10	N= 3	N= 0	N= 1
%= 6.67	%= 2.00	%= 0.00	%= .67

ESTP	ESFP	ENFP	ENTP
N= 11	N= 6	N= 3	N= 3
%= 7.33	%= 4.00	%= 2.00	%= 2.00

ESTJ	ESFJ	ENFJ	ENTJ
N= 42	N= 6	N= 0	N= 8
%= 28.00	%= 4.00	%= 0.00	%= 5.33

	N	%
E	79	52.67
I	71	47.33
S	129	86.00
N	21	14.00
T	122	81.33
F	28	18.67
J	113	75.33
P	37	24.67
I J	57	38.00
I P	14	9.33
E P	23	15.33
E J	56	37.33
S T	106	70.67
S F	23	15.33
N F	5	3.33
N T	16	10.67
S J	99	66.00
S P	30	20.00
N P	7	4.67
N J	14	9.33
T J	97	64.67
T P	25	16.67
F P	12	8.00
F J	16	10.67
I N	7	4.67
E N	14	9.33
I S	64	42.67
E S	65	43.33
E T	64	42.67
E F	15	10.00
I F	13	8.67
I T	58	38.67
S dom	68	45.33
N dom	12	8.00
T dom	61	40.67
F dom	9	6.00

Note: ■ = 1% of sample   8623108

Data collected by Frank Hoy of Small Business Development Center at the University of Georgia in 1978. Subjects were from businesses meeting the criteria: 1) within 150 miles of a mid-sized university city northwest of Houston, Texas, 2) not in metropolitan areas, 3) listed in 1978-79 Directory of Texas Manufacturers, 4) listed with Texas Industrial Commission, 5) firm size not more than 50 nor less than five, and 6) not partnerships or cooperatives. A randomized subset of the 319 eligible businesses, 50% manufacturers and 50% retailers, was made. Subjects' ages ranged from 24 to 74, median 47; educational levels ranged from 5 to 20, median 14; median years of service was 8.5. These data are used with permission and were cited in:

Hoy, F., & Hellriegel, D. (1982). The Kilmann and Herden model of organizational effectiveness criteria for small business managers. Academy of Management Journal, 25(2), 308-322.

Managers: Top Managers in Large Japanese Companies

	SENSING		INTUITION	
	THINKING	FEELING	FEELING	THINKING

ISTJ	ISFJ	INFJ	INTJ
N= 4	N= 4	N= 1	N= 7
%= 7.14	%= 7.14	%= 1.79	%= 12.50
■■■■■■■	■■■■■■■	■■	■■■■■■■■■■■■ ■■■

ISTP	ISFP	INFP	INTP
N= 0	N= 2	N= 0	N= 2
%= 0.00	%= 3.57	%= 0.00	%= 3.57
	■■■■		■■■■

ESTP	ESFP	ENFP	ENTP
N= 6	N= 3	N= 4	N= 2
%= 10.71	%= 5.36	%= 7.14	%= 3.57
■■■■■■■■■■ ■	■■■■■	■■■■■■■	■■■■

ESTJ	ESFJ	ENFJ	ENTJ
N= 11	N= 2	N= 2	N= 6
%= 19.64	%= 3.57	%= 3.57	%= 10.71
■■■■■■■■■■ ■■■■■■■■■■	■■■■	■■■■	■■■■■■■■■■ ■

JUDGMENT · INTROVERSION · PERCEPTION / PERCEPTION · EXTRAVERSION · JUDGMENT

	N	%
E	36	64.29
I	20	35.71
S	32	57.14
N	24	42.86
T	38	67.86
F	18	32.14
J	37	66.07
P	19	33.93
I J	16	28.57
I P	4	7.14
E P	15	26.79
E J	21	37.50
S T	21	37.50
S F	11	19.64
N F	7	12.50
N T	17	30.36
S J	21	37.50
S P	11	19.64
N P	8	14.29
N J	16	28.57
T J	28	50.00
T P	10	17.86
F P	9	16.07
F J	9	16.07
I N	10	17.86
E N	14	25.00
I S	10	17.86
E S	22	39.29
E T	25	44.64
E F	11	19.64
I F	7	12.50
I T	13	23.21
S dom	17	30.36
N dom	14	25.00
T dom	19	33.93
F dom	6	10.71

Note: ■ = 1% of sample   8623102

Data collected by Takeshi Ohsawa at the Nippon Recruit Center, Tokyo, Japan from 1964 to 1975. No other demographic data were reported. These data are used with permission and were cited in:

Ohsawa, T. (1975, October). MBTI experiences in Japan: Career choice, selection, placement and counseling for individual development. Paper presented at the First National Conference on the Myers-Briggs Type Indicator, Gainesville, FL.

Marketing Personnel

N = 83

	SENSING		INTUITION				N	%
	THINKING	FEELING	FEELING	THINKING				

ISTJ	ISFJ	INFJ	INTJ
N= 5	N= 0	N= 6	N= 2
%= 6.02	%= 0.00	%= 7.23	%= 2.41
■■■■■■		■■■■■■■	■■

ISTP	ISFP	INFP	INTP
N= 2	N= 3	N= 2	N= 1
%= 2.41	%= 3.61	%= 2.41	%= 1.20
■■	■■■■	■■	■

ESTP	ESFP	ENFP	ENTP
N= 8	N= 2	N= 8	N= 11
%= 9.64	%= 2.41	%= 9.64	%= 13.25
■■■■■■■■■■	■■	■■■■■■■■■■	■■■■■■■■■■ ■■■

ESTJ	ESFJ	ENFJ	ENTJ
N= 9	N= 4	N= 7	N= 13
%= 10.84	%= 4.82	%= 8.43	%= 15.66
■■■■■■■■■■ ■	■■■■■	■■■■■■■■	■■■■■■■■■■ ■■■■■■

JUDGMENT — INTROVERSION — PERCEPTION — PERCEPTION — EXTRAVERSION — JUDGMENT

	N	%
E	62	74.70
I	21	25.30
S	33	39.76
N	50	60.24
T	51	61.45
F	32	38.55
J	46	55.42
P	37	44.58
I J	13	15.66
I P	8	9.64
E P	29	34.94
E J	33	39.76
S T	24	28.92
S F	9	10.84
N F	23	27.71
N T	27	32.53
S J	18	21.69
S P	15	18.07
N P	22	26.51
N J	28	33.73
T J	29	34.94
T P	22	26.51
F P	15	18.07
F J	17	20.48
I N	11	13.25
E N	39	46.99
I S	10	12.05
E S	23	27.71
E T	41	49.40
E F	21	25.30
I F	11	13.25
I T	10	12.05
S dom	15	18.07
N dom	27	32.53
T dom	25	30.12
F dom	16	19.28

Note: ■ = 1% of sample

8629306

This table is one of a series of tables from the CAPT-MBTI Data Bank of MBTI records submitted to CAPT for computer scoring between 1971 and June, 1984. This sample was drawn from 59,784 records with usable occupational codes from the total data bank of 232,557. This data bank has 51% Form F cases from 1971 to March, 1978, 35% Form F cases from 1978 to June, 1984 and 14% Form G cases from 1978 to December, 1982. An analysis of Form F and G data banks showed the data banks were comprised of 56% females and 44% males; education level completed: 6% some grade school, 30% high school diploma, 25% some college, 18% bachelor degrees, 11% masters degrees, 3% doctoral or post doctoral work, and 6% unknown. Age group percentages were: 11% under 18, 29% 18 to 20, 12% 21 to 24, 10% 25 to 29, 16% 30 to 39, 10% 40 to 49, 5% 50 to 59, 2% 60 plus, and 5% unknown.

Members of a Human Resources Planners Association

N = 108

	SENSING		INTUITION	
	THINKING	FEELING	FEELING	THINKING

ISTJ	ISFJ	INFJ	INTJ
N= 12	N= 1	N= 4	N= 16
%= 11.11	%= .93	%= 3.70	%= 14.81
∎∎∎∎∎∎∎∎∎∎∎ ∎	∎	∎∎∎∎	∎∎∎∎∎∎∎∎∎∎ ∎∎∎∎∎

ISTP	ISFP	INFP	INTP
N= 3	N= 1	N= 1	N= 5
%= 2.78	%= .93	%= .93	%= 4.63
∎∎∎	∎	∎	∎∎∎∎∎

ESTP	ESFP	ENFP	ENTP
N= 2	N= 0	N= 13	N= 7
%= 1.85	%= 0.00	%= 12.04	%= 6.48
∎∎		∎∎∎∎∎∎∎∎∎∎ ∎∎	∎∎∎∎∎∎

ESTJ	ESFJ	ENFJ	ENTJ
N= 5	N= 8	N= 8	N= 22
%= 4.63	%= 7.41	%= 7.41	%= 20.37
∎∎∎∎∎	∎∎∎∎∎∎∎	∎∎∎∎∎∎∎	∎∎∎∎∎∎∎∎∎∎ ∎∎∎∎∎∎∎∎∎∎

JUDGMENT / INTROVERSION / PERCEPTION / PERCEPTION / EXTRAVERSION / JUDGMENT

	N	%
E	65	60.19
I	43	39.81
S	32	29.63
N	76	70.37
T	72	66.67
F	36	33.33
J	76	70.37
P	32	29.63
I J	33	30.56
I P	10	9.26
E P	22	20.37
E J	43	39.81
S T	22	20.37
S F	10	9.26
N F	26	24.07
N T	50	46.30
S J	26	24.07
S P	6	5.56
N P	26	24.07
N J	50	46.30
T J	55	50.93
T P	17	15.74
F P	15	13.89
F J	21	19.44
I N	26	24.07
E N	50	46.30
I S	17	15.74
E S	15	13.89
E T	36	33.33
E F	29	26.85
I F	7	6.48
I T	36	33.33
S dom	15	13.89
N dom	40	37.04
T dom	35	32.41
F dom	18	16.67

Note: ∎ = 1% of sample   8623118

Data collected by Randall E. Ruppart and Nancy Hutchenes during May 1982, using Form G. Subjects were approximately two thirds of the members of the New York Human Resources Planners Association who were administered the MBTI in a double blind procedure for a professional consultation. It was estimated that two thirds or more were male and the modal age range was 35 to 40. All planners had at least a four year college degree and most were employed by large corporations involved in planning. These data are used with permission and have not been published elsewhere to date.

Personnel and Labor Relations Workers

N = 90

	SENSING		INTUITION					N	%
	THINKING	FEELING	FEELING	THINKING					

ISTJ	ISFJ	INFJ	INTJ
N= 14	N= 4	N= 5	N= 4
%= 15.56	%= 4.44	%= 5.56	%= 4.44
■■■■■■■■■■	■■■■	■■■■■■	■■■■
■■■■■■			

ISTP	ISFP	INFP	INTP
N= 3	N= 3	N= 5	N= 3
%= 3.33	%= 3.33	%= 5.56	%= 3.33
■■■	■■■	■■■■■■	■■■

ESTP	ESFP	ENFP	ENTP
N= 4	N= 3	N= 3	N= 6
%= 4.44	%= 3.33	%= 3.33	%= 6.67
■■■■	■■■	■■■	■■■■■■■

ESTJ	ESFJ	ENFJ	ENTJ
N= 12	N= 7	N= 1	N= 13
%= 13.33	%= 7.78	%= 1.11	%= 14.44
■■■■■■■■■■■■	■■■■■■■■	■	■■■■■■■■■■■■
■■■			■■■■

	N	%
E	49	54.44
I	41	45.56
S	50	55.56
N	40	44.44
T	59	65.56
F	31	34.44
J	60	66.67
P	30	33.33
I J	27	30.00
I P	14	15.56
E P	16	17.78
E J	33	36.67
S T	33	36.67
S F	17	18.89
N F	14	15.56
N T	26	28.89
S J	37	41.11
S P	13	14.44
N P	17	18.89
N J	23	25.56
T J	43	47.78
T P	16	17.78
F P	14	15.56
F J	17	18.89
I N	17	18.89
E N	23	25.56
I S	24	26.67
E S	26	28.89
E T	35	38.89
E F	14	15.56
I F	17	18.89
I T	24	26.67
S dom	25	27.78
N dom	18	20.00
T dom	31	34.44
F dom	16	17.78

Note: ■ = 1% of sample

8629301

This table is one of a series of tables from the CAPT-MBTI Data Bank of MBTI records submitted to CAPT for computer scoring between 1971 and June, 1984. This sample was drawn from 59,784 records with usable occupational codes from the total data bank of 232,557. This data bank has 51% Form F cases from 1971 to March, 1978, 35% Form F cases from 1978 to June, 1984 and 14% Form G cases from 1978 to December, 1982. An analysis of Form F and G data banks showed the data banks were comprised of 56% females and 44% males; education level completed: 6% some grade school, 30% high school diploma, 25% some college, 18% bachelor degrees, 11% masters degrees, 3% doctoral or post doctoral work, and 6% unknown. Age group percentages were: 11% under 18, 29% 18 to 20, 12% 21 to 24, 10% 25 to 29, 16% 30 to 39, 10% 40 to 49, 5% 50 to 59, 2% 60 plus, and 5% unknown.

Public Accountants

N = 333

	SENSING		INTUITION	
	THINKING	FEELING	FEELING	THINKING

ISTJ	ISFJ	INFJ	INTJ
N= 66	N= 22	N= 10	N= 41
%= 19.82	%= 6.61	%= 3.00	%= 12.31
■■■■■■■■■■	■■■■■■■	■■■	■■■■■■■■■■
■■■■■■■■■■			■■

ISTP	ISFP	INFP	INTP
N= 7	N= 9	N= 14	N= 9
%= 2.10	%= 2.70	%= 4.20	%= 2.70
■■	■■■	■■■■	■■■

ESTP	ESFP	ENFP	ENTP
N= 5	N= 4	N= 16	N= 20
%= 1.50	%= 1.20	%= 4.80	%= 6.01
■■	■	■■■■■	■■■■■■

ESTJ	ESFJ	ENFJ	ENTJ
N= 46	N= 17	N= 16	N= 31
%= 13.81	%= 5.11	%= 4.80	%= 9.31
■■■■■■■■■■	■■■■■	■■■■■	■■■■■■■■■■
■■■■			

JUDGMENT — INTROVERSION — PERCEPTION — PERCEPTION — EXTRAVERSION — JUDGMENT

	N	%
E	155	46.55
I	178	53.45
S	176	52.85
N	157	47.15
T	225	67.57
F	108	32.43
J	249	74.77
P	84	25.23
I J	139	41.74
I P	39	11.71
E P	45	13.51
E J	110	33.03
S T	124	37.24
S F	52	15.62
N F	56	16.82
N T	101	30.33
S J	151	45.35
S P	25	7.51
N P	59	17.72
N J	98	29.43
T J	184	55.26
T P	41	12.31
F P	43	12.91
F J	65	19.52
I N	74	22.22
E N	83	24.92
I S	104	31.23
E S	72	21.62
E T	102	30.63
E F	53	15.92
I F	55	16.52
I T	123	36.94
S dom	97	29.13
N dom	87	26.13
T dom	93	27.93
F dom	56	16.82

Note: ■ = 1% of sample   8623116

Data collected by Philip F. Jacoby from July to November 1978. Subjects were from three "Big Eight" public accounting firms' Washington, D.C. offices. Of the initial 657 invitations, 51% voluntarily responded. The group was comprised of 50% CPAs and 50% non-CPAs; 14% partners, 24% managers, 32% seniors and 29% juniors; 56% specialized in audits, 11% in tax and 33% in management advisory services. No further demographic data were reported. These data are used with permission and were cited in:

Jacoby, P. F. (1980). An empirical descriptive study of selected personality characteristics of professional accountants based on Jungian typology. Unpublished doctoral dissertation, George Washington University.

Purchasing Agents

N = 80

	SENSING		INTUITION	
	THINKING	FEELING	FEELING	THINKING

ISTJ	ISFJ	INFJ	INTJ
N= 19	N= 6	N= 1	N= 1
%= 23.75	%= 7.50	%= 1.25	%= 1.25
■■■■■■■■■■	■■■■■■■	■	■
■■■■■■■■■■			
■■■■			

ISTP	ISFP	INFP	INTP
N= 2	N= 2	N= 0	N= 4
%= 2.50	%= 2.50	%= 0.00	%= 5.00
■■■	■■■		■■■■■

ESTP	ESFP	ENFP	ENTP
N= 3	N= 3	N= 3	N= 2
%= 3.75	%= 3.75	%= 3.75	%= 2.50
■■■■	■■■■	■■■■	■■■

ESTJ	ESFJ	ENFJ	ENTJ
N= 23	N= 4	N= 1	N= 6
%= 28.75	%= 5.00	%= 1.25	%= 7.50
■■■■■■■■■■	■■■■■	■	■■■■■■■■
■■■■■■■■■■			
■■■■■■■■■			

JUDGMENT — INTROVERSION — PERCEPTION — EXTRAVERSION — JUDGMENT
PERCEPTION

	N	%
E	45	56.25
I	35	43.75
S	62	77.50
N	18	22.50
T	60	75.00
F	20	25.00
J	61	76.25
P	19	23.75
I J	27	33.75
I P	8	10.00
E P	11	13.75
E J	34	42.50
S T	47	58.75
S F	15	18.75
N F	5	6.25
N T	13	16.25
S J	52	65.00
S P	10	12.50
N P	9	11.25
N J	9	11.25
T J	49	61.25
T P	11	13.75
F P	8	10.00
F J	12	15.00
I N	6	7.50
E N	12	15.00
I S	29	36.25
E S	33	41.25
E T	34	42.50
E F	11	13.75
I F	9	11.25
I T	26	32.50
S dom	31	38.75
N dom	7	8.75
T dom	35	43.75
F dom	7	8.75

Note: ■ = 1% of sample   8623115

Data collected by Norman Ellis in 1971 using Form F. Subjects were purchasing agents from local Texas and Oklahoma NAPA groups who volunteered. The group seemed to match the national membership. Ages were 9% under 30, 29% 30 to 39, 45% 40 to 49 and 17% over 50. Degrees were 39% high school or less, 14% technical college, 42% non-technical college and 5% graduate school. 36% had less than 5 years experience, 14% had 6 to 10, and 50% had over 10. 25% were in companies with sales over 100 million, 23% 50 to 100 million, 20% under 10 million and 32% no data. These data are used with permission and are cited in: Ellis, N. D. (1973). The relationship between identifiable attributes and decision-making ability of purchasing personnel as measured by the results of a management game (Doctoral dissertation, North Texas State University, 1973). Dissertation Abstracts International, 34, 1417A-1418A. (University Microfilms No. 73-22, 841)

Real Estate Agents and Brokers

N = 166

	SENSING		INTUITION	
	THINKING	FEELING	FEELING	THINKING

ISTJ	ISFJ	INFJ	INTJ
N= 20	N= 12	N= 2	N= 8
%= 12.05	%= 7.23	%= 1.20	%= 4.82
■■■■■■■■■■	■■■■■■■	■	■■■■■
■■			

ISTP	ISFP	INFP	INTP
N= 4	N= 7	N= 9	N= 7
%= 2.41	%= 4.22	%= 5.42	%= 4.22
■■	■■■■	■■■■■	■■■■

ESTP	ESFP	ENFP	ENTP
N= 6	N= 9	N= 7	N= 10
%= 3.61	%= 5.42	%= 4.22	%= 6.02
■■■■	■■■■■	■■■■	■■■■■■

ESTJ	ESFJ	ENFJ	ENTJ
N= 27	N= 16	N= 9	N= 13
%= 16.27	%= 9.64	%= 5.42	%= 7.83
■■■■■■■■■■	■■■■■■■■■■	■■■■■	■■■■■■■■
■■■■■■			

JUDGMENT · INTROVERSION · PERCEPTION · PERCEPTION · EXTRAVERSION · JUDGMENT

	N	%
E	97	58.43
I	69	41.57
S	101	60.84
N	65	39.16
T	95	57.23
F	71	42.77
J	107	64.46
P	59	35.54
I J	42	25.30
I P	27	16.27
E P	32	19.28
E J	65	39.16
S T	57	34.34
S F	44	26.51
N F	27	16.27
N T	38	22.89
S J	75	45.18
S P	26	15.66
N P	33	19.88
N J	32	19.28
T J	68	40.96
T P	27	16.27
F P	32	19.28
F J	39	23.49
I N	26	15.66
E N	39	23.49
I S	43	25.90
E S	58	34.94
E T	56	33.73
E F	41	24.70
I F	30	18.07
I T	39	23.49
S dom	47	28.31
N dom	27	16.27
T dom	51	30.72
F dom	41	24.70

Note: ■ = 1% of sample   8629315

This table is one of a series of tables from the CAPT-MBTI Data Bank of MBTI records submitted to CAPT for computer scoring between 1971 and June, 1984. This sample was drawn from 59,784 records with usable occupational codes from the total data bank of 232,557. This data bank has 51% Form F cases from 1971 to March, 1978, 35% Form F cases from 1978 to June, 1984 and 14% Form G cases from 1978 to December, 1982. An analysis of Form F and G data banks showed the data banks were comprised of 56% females and 44% males; education level completed: 6% some grade school, 30% high school diploma, 25% some college, 18% bachelor degrees, 11% masters degrees, 3% doctoral or post doctoral work, and 6% unknown. Age group percentages were: 11% under 18, 29% 18 to 20, 12% 21 to 24, 10% 25 to 29, 16% 30 to 39, 10% 40 to 49, 5% 50 to 59, 2% 60 plus, and 5% unknown.

Receptionists

N = 100

	SENSING		INTUITION	
	THINKING	FEELING	FEELING	THINKING

ISTJ	ISFJ	INFJ	INTJ
N= 6	N= 12	N= 5	N= 0
%= 6.00	%= 12.00	%= 5.00	%= 0.00
■■■■■■	■■■■■■■■■■■■	■■■■■	
	■■		

ISTP	ISFP	INFP	INTP
N= 0	N= 4	N= 8	N= 3
%= 0.00	%= 4.00	%= 8.00	%= 3.00
	■■■■	■■■■■■■■	■■■

ESTP	ESFP	ENFP	ENTP
N= 1	N= 11	N= 15	N= 2
%= 1.00	%= 11.00	%= 15.00	%= 2.00
■	■■■■■■■■■■■	■■■■■■■■■■■	■■
	■	■■■■■	

ESTJ	ESFJ	ENFJ	ENTJ
N= 8	N= 18	N= 5	N= 2
%= 8.00	%= 18.00	%= 5.00	%= 2.00
■■■■■■■■	■■■■■■■■■■■■	■■■■■	■■
	■■■■■■■		

(JUDGMENT — INTROVERSION — PERCEPTION — PERCEPTION — EXTRAVERSION — JUDGMENT)

	N	%
E	62	62.00
I	38	38.00
S	60	60.00
N	40	40.00
T	22	22.00
F	78	78.00
J	56	56.00
P	44	44.00
I J	23	23.00
I P	15	15.00
E P	29	29.00
E J	33	33.00
S T	15	15.00
S F	45	45.00
N F	33	33.00
N T	7	7.00
S J	44	44.00
S P	16	16.00
N P	28	28.00
N J	12	12.00
T J	16	16.00
T P	6	6.00
F P	38	38.00
F J	40	40.00
I N	16	16.00
E N	24	24.00
I S	22	22.00
E S	38	38.00
E T	13	13.00
E F	49	49.00
I F	29	29.00
I T	9	9.00
S dom	30	30.00
N dom	22	22.00
T dom	13	13.00
F dom	35	35.00

Note: ■ = 1% of sample   8629322

This table is one of a series of tables from the CAPT-MBTI Data Bank of MBTI records submitted to CAPT for computer scoring between 1971 and June, 1984. This sample was drawn from 59,784 records with usable occupational codes from the total data bank of 232,557. This data bank has 51% Form F cases from 1971 to March, 1978, 35% Form F cases from 1978 to June, 1984 and 14% Form G cases from 1978 to December, 1982. An analysis of Form F and G data banks showed the data banks were comprised of 56% females and 44% males; education level completed: 6% some grade school, 30% high school diploma, 25% some college, 18% bachelor degrees, 11% masters degrees, 3% doctoral or post-doctoral work, and 6% unknown. Age group percentages were: 11% under 18, 29% 18 to 20, 12% 21 to 24, 10% 25 to 29, 16% 30 to 39, 10% 40 to 49, 5% 50 to 59, 2% 60 plus, and 5% unknown.

Sales Agents, Retail Trade

N = 67

	SENSING		INTUITION	
	THINKING	FEELING	FEELING	THINKING

ISTJ	ISFJ	INFJ	INTJ
N= 3	N= 9	N= 0	N= 2
%= 4.48	%= 13.43	%= 0.00	%= 2.99
■■■■	■■■■■■■■■		■■■
	■■■		

ISTP	ISFP	INFP	INTP
N= 3	N= 4	N= 1	N= 6
%= 4.48	%= 5.97	%= 1.49	%= 8.96
■■■■	■■■■■■	■	■■■■■■■■■

ESTP	ESFP	ENFP	ENTP
N= 3	N= 3	N= 1	N= 8
%= 4.48	%= 4.48	%= 1.49	%= 11.94
■■■■	■■■■	■	■■■■■■■■■■■
			■■

ESTJ	ESFJ	ENFJ	ENTJ
N= 10	N= 5	N= 5	N= 4
%= 14.93	%= 7.46	%= 7.46	%= 5.97
■■■■■■■■■■■	■■■■■■■■	■■■■■■■	■■■■■■
■■■■■			

JUDGMENT — INTROVERSION — PERCEPTION — PERCEPTION — EXTRAVERSION — JUDGMENT

	N	%
E	39	58.21
I	28	41.79
S	40	59.70
N	27	40.30
T	39	58.21
F	28	41.79
J	38	56.72
P	29	43.28
I J	14	20.90
I P	14	20.90
E P	15	22.39
E J	24	35.82
S T	19	28.36
S F	21	31.34
N F	7	10.45
N T	20	29.85
S J	27	40.30
S P	13	19.40
N P	16	23.88
N J	11	16.42
T J	19	28.36
T P	20	29.85
F P	9	13.43
F J	19	28.36
I N	9	13.43
E N	18	26.87
I S	19	28.36
E S	21	31.34
E T	25	37.31
E F	14	20.90
I F	14	20.90
I T	14	20.90
S dom	18	26.87
N dom	11	16.42
T dom	23	34.33
F dom	15	22.39

Note: ■ = 1% of sample   8629318

This table is one of a series of tables from the CAPT-MBTI Data Bank of MBTI records submitted to CAPT for computer scoring between 1971 and June, 1984. This sample was drawn from 59,784 records with usable occupational codes from the total data bank of 232,557. This data bank has 51% Form F cases from 1971 to March, 1978, 35% Form F cases from 1978 to June, 1984 and 14% Form G cases from 1978 to December, 1982. An analysis of Form F and G data banks showed the data banks were comprised of 56% females and 44% males; education level completed: 6% some grade school, 30% high school diploma, 25% some college, 18% bachelor degrees, 11% masters degrees, 3% doctoral or post doctoral work, and 6% unknown. Age group percentages were: 11% under 18, 29% 18 to 20, 12% 21 to 24, 10% 25 to 29, 16% 30 to 39, 10% 40 to 49, 5% 50 to 59, 2% 60 plus, and 5% unknown.

Sales Clerks, Retail Trade

N = 108

						N	%
SENSING		**INTUITION**					
THINKING	FEELING	FEELING	THINKING				

ISTJ	ISFJ	INFJ	INTJ		E	73	67.59
N= 11	N= 5	N= 2	N= 1	JUDGMENT	I	35	32.41
%= 10.19	%= 4.63	%= 1.85	%= .93		S	64	59.26
■■■■■■■■■■	■■■■■	■■	■		N	44	40.74
					T	49	45.37
					F	59	54.63
					J	63	58.33
					P	45	41.67
ISTP	ISFP	INFP	INTP	PERCEPTION	I J	19	17.59
N= 2	N= 6	N= 4	N= 4		I P	16	14.81
%= 1.85	%= 5.56	%= 3.70	%= 3.70		E P	29	26.85
■■	■■■■■■	■■■■	■■■■		E J	44	40.74
					ST	31	28.70
					SF	33	30.56
					NF	26	24.07
					NT	18	16.67
ESTP	ESFP	ENFP	ENTP	PERCEPTION	S J	42	38.89
N= 8	N= 6	N= 11	N= 4		S P	22	20.37
%= 7.41	%= 5.56	%= 10.19	%= 3.70		NP	23	21.30
■■■■■■■	■■■■■■	■■■■■■■■■■	■■■■		NJ	21	19.44
					TJ	31	28.70
					TP	18	16.67
					FP	27	25.00
					FJ	32	29.63
ESTJ	ESFJ	ENFJ	ENTJ	JUDGMENT	IN	11	10.19
N= 10	N= 16	N= 9	N= 9		EN	33	30.56
%= 9.26	%= 14.81	%= 8.33	%= 8.33		I S	24	22.22
■■■■■■■■■	■■■■■■■■■■■■■■■	■■■■■■■■	■■■■■■■■		ES	40	37.04
					ET	31	28.70
					EF	42	38.89
					I F	17	15.74
					I T	18	16.67
					S dom	30	27.78
					N dom	18	16.67
					T dom	25	23.15
					F dom	35	32.41

(Vertical labels: JUDGMENT / PERCEPTION under INTROVERSION; PERCEPTION / JUDGMENT under EXTRAVERSION)

Note: ■ = 1% of sample   8629317

This table is one of a series of tables from the CAPT-MBTI Data Bank of MBTI records submitted to CAPT for computer scoring between 1971 and June, 1984. This sample was drawn from 59,784 records with usable occupational codes from the total data bank of 232,557. This data bank has 51% Form F cases from 1971 to March, 1978, 35% Form F cases from 1978 to June, 1984 and 14% Form G cases from 1978 to December, 1982. An analysis of Form F and G data banks showed the data banks were comprised of 56% females and 44% males; education level completed: 6% some grade school, 30% high school diploma, 25% some college, 18% bachelor degrees, 11% masters degrees, 3% doctoral or post doctoral work, and 6% unknown. Age group percentages were: 11% under 18, 29% 18 to 20, 12% 21 to 24, 10% 25 to 29, 16% 30 to 39, 10% 40 to 49, 5% 50 to 59, 2% 60 plus, and 5% unknown.

Sales Representatives

	SENSING		INTUITION	
	THINKING	FEELING	FEELING	THINKING

ISTJ	ISFJ	INFJ	INTJ
N= 13	N= 14	N= 4	N= 6
%= 7.26	%= 7.82	%= 2.23	%= 3.35
■■■■■■■	■■■■■■■■	■■	■■■

ISTP	ISFP	INFP	INTP
N= 7	N= 2	N= 11	N= 2
%= 3.91	%= 1.12	%= 6.15	%= 1.12
■■■■	■	■■■■■■	■

ESTP	ESFP	ENFP	ENTP
N= 9	N= 11	N= 13	N= 10
%= 5.03	%= 6.15	%= 7.26	%= 5.59
■■■■■	■■■■■■	■■■■■■■	■■■■■■

ESTJ	ESFJ	ENFJ	ENTJ
N= 40	N= 15	N= 7	N= 15
%= 22.35	%= 8.38	%= 3.91	%= 8.38
■■■■■■■■■■■■■■■■■■■■■■	■■■■■■■■	■■■■	■■■■■■■■

JUDGMENT — INTROVERSION — PERCEPTION — PERCEPTION — EXTRAVERSION — JUDGMENT

	N	%
E	120	67.04
I	59	32.96
S	111	62.01
N	68	37.99
T	102	56.98
F	77	43.02
J	114	63.69
P	65	36.31
I J	37	20.67
I P	22	12.29
E P	43	24.02
E J	77	43.02
S T	69	38.55
S F	42	23.46
N F	35	19.55
N T	33	18.44
S J	82	45.81
S P	29	16.20
N P	36	20.11
N J	32	17.88
T J	74	41.34
T P	28	15.64
F P	37	20.67
F J	40	22.35
I N	23	12.85
E N	45	25.14
I S	36	20.11
E S	75	41.90
E T	74	41.34
E F	46	25.70
I F	31	17.32
I T	28	15.64
S dom	47	26.26
N dom	33	18.44
T dom	64	35.75
F dom	35	19.55

Note: ■ = 1% of sample   8629316

This table is one of a series of tables from the CAPT-MBTI Data Bank of MBTI records submitted to CAPT for computer scoring between 1971 and June, 1984. This sample was drawn from 59,784 records with usable occupational codes from the total data bank of 232,557. This data bank has 51% Form F cases from 1971 to March, 1978, 35% Form F cases from 1978 to June, 1984 and 14% Form G cases from 1978 to December, 1982. An analysis of Form F and G data banks showed the data banks were comprised of 56% females and 44% males; education level completed: 6% some grade school, 30% high school diploma, 25% some college, 18% bachelor degrees, 11% masters degrees, 3% doctoral or post doctoral work, and 6% unknown. Age group percentages were: 11% under 18, 29% 18 to 20, 12% 21 to 24, 10% 25 to 29, 16% 30 to 39, 10% 40 to 49, 5% 50 to 59, 2% 60 plus, and 5% unknown.

Salespeople in a Japanese Trading Company

N = 275

	SENSING		INTUITION	
	THINKING	FEELING	FEELING	THINKING

ISTJ	ISFJ	INFJ	INTJ
N= 7	N= 8	N= 2	N= 7
%= 2.55	%= 2.91	%= .73	%= 2.55
■■■	■■■	■	■■■

ISTP	ISFP	INFP	INTP
N= 9	N= 29	N= 14	N= 14
%= 3.27	%= 10.55	%= 5.09	%= 5.09
■■■	■■■■■■■■■■ ■	■■■■■	■■■■■

ESTP	ESFP	ENFP	ENTP
N= 22	N= 46	N= 30	N= 24
%= 8.00	%= 16.73	%= 10.91	%= 8.73
■■■■■■■■	■■■■■■■■■■ ■■■■■■■	■■■■■■■■■■ ■	■■■■■■■■■

ESTJ	ESFJ	ENFJ	ENTJ
N= 25	N= 17	N= 4	N= 17
%= 9.09	%= 6.18	%= 1.45	%= 6.18
■■■■■■■■■	■■■■■■	■	■■■■■■

JUDGMENT — INTROVERSION — PERCEPTION — PERCEPTION — EXTRAVERSION — JUDGMENT

	N	%
E	185	67.27
I	90	32.73
S	163	59.27
N	112	40.73
T	125	45.45
F	150	54.55
J	87	31.64
P	188	68.36
I J	24	8.73
I P	66	24.00
E P	122	44.36
E J	63	22.91
S T	63	22.91
S F	100	36.36
N F	50	18.18
N T	62	22.55
S J	57	20.73
S P	106	38.55
N P	82	29.82
N J	30	10.91
T J	56	20.36
T P	69	25.09
F P	119	43.27
F J	31	11.27
I N	37	13.45
E N	75	27.27
I S	53	19.27
E S	110	40.00
E T	88	32.00
E F	97	35.27
I F	53	19.27
I T	37	13.45
S dom	83	30.18
N dom	63	22.91
T dom	65	23.64
F dom	64	23.27

Note: ■ = 1% of sample   8623113

Data collected by Takeshi Ohsawa at the Nippon Recruit Center, Tokyo, Japan from 1964 to 1975. Subjects were sales personnel in a wholesale department of Japanese trading company. No other demographic data were reported. These data are used with permission and were cited in:

Ohsawa, T. (1975, October). MBTI experiences in Japan: Career choice, selection, placement and counseling for individual development. Paper presented at the First National Conference on the Myers-Briggs Type Indicator, Gainesville, FL.

Secretaries: Executive and Administrative Assistants

N = 333

	SENSING		INTUITION	
	THINKING	FEELING	FEELING	THINKING

ISTJ	ISFJ	INFJ	INTJ
N= 43	N= 26	N= 12	N= 16
%= 12.91	%= 7.81	%= 3.60	%= 4.80
■■■■■■■■■■■■ ■■■	■■■■■■■■	■■■■	■■■■■

ISTP	ISFP	INFP	INTP
N= 6	N= 17	N= 31	N= 8
%= 1.80	%= 5.11	%= 9.31	%= 2.40
■■	■■■■■	■■■■■■■■■	■■

ESTP	ESFP	ENFP	ENTP
N= 8	N= 17	N= 30	N= 10
%= 2.40	%= 5.11	%= 9.01	%= 3.00
■■	■■■■■	■■■■■■■■■	■■■

ESTJ	ESFJ	ENFJ	ENTJ
N= 38	N= 30	N= 24	N= 17
%= 11.41	%= 9.01	%= 7.21	%= 5.11
■■■■■■■■■■■ ■	■■■■■■■■■	■■■■■■■	■■■■■

JUDGMENT — INTROVERSION — PERCEPTION — PERCEPTION — EXTRAVERSION — JUDGMENT

	N	%
E	174	52.25
I	159	47.75
S	185	55.56
N	148	44.44
T	146	43.84
F	187	56.16
J	206	61.86
P	127	38.14
I J	97	29.13
I P	62	18.62
E P	65	19.52
E J	109	32.73
S T	95	28.53
S F	90	27.03
N F	97	29.13
N T	51	15.32
S J	137	41.14
S P	48	14.41
N P	79	23.72
N J	69	20.72
T J	114	34.23
T P	32	9.61
F P	95	28.53
F J	92	27.63
I N	67	20.12
E N	81	24.32
I S	92	27.63
E S	93	27.93
E T	73	21.92
E F	101	30.33
I F	86	25.83
I T	73	21.92
S dom	94	28.23
N dom	68	20.42
T dom	69	20.72
F dom	102	30.63

Note: ■ = 1% of sample   8629326

This table is one of a series of tables from the CAPT-MBTI Data Bank of MBTI records submitted to CAPT for computer scoring between 1971 and June, 1984. This sample was drawn from 59,784 records with usable occupational codes from the total data bank of 232,557. This data bank has 51% Form F cases from 1971 to March, 1978, 35% Form F cases from 1978 to June, 1984 and 14% Form G cases from 1978 to December, 1982. An analysis of Form F and G data banks showed the data banks were comprised of 56% females and 44% males; education level completed: 6% some grade school, 30% high school diploma, 25% some college, 18% bachelor degrees, 11% masters degrees, 3% doctoral or post doctoral work, and 6% unknown. Age group percentages were: 11% under 18, 29% 18 to 20, 12% 21 to 24, 10% 25 to 29, 16% 30 to 39, 10% 40 to 49, 5% 50 to 59, 2% 60 plus, and 5% unknown.

Secretaries: Legal

	SENSING		INTUITION	
	THINKING	FEELING	FEELING	THINKING

ISTJ	ISFJ	INFJ	INTJ
N= 10	N= 11	N= 4	N= 3
%= 12.99	%= 14.29	%= 5.19	%= 3.90
■■■■■■■■■■■■	■■■■■■■■■■■■■■	■■■■■	■■■■
■■■	■■■■		

ISTP	ISFP	INFP	INTP
N= 6	N= 6	N= 3	N= 5
%= 7.79	%= 7.79	%= 3.90	%= 6.49
■■■■■■■■	■■■■■■■■	■■■■	■■■■■■

ESTP	ESFP	ENFP	ENTP
N= 2	N= 3	N= 2	N= 2
%= 2.60	%= 3.90	%= 2.60	%= 2.60
■■■	■■■■	■■■	■■■

ESTJ	ESFJ	ENFJ	ENTJ
N= 5	N= 7	N= 4	N= 4
%= 6.49	%= 9.09	%= 5.19	%= 5.19
■■■■■■	■■■■■■■■■	■■■■■	■■■■■

JUDGMENT — INTROVERSION — PERCEPTION — PERCEPTION — EXTRAVERSION — JUDGMENT

	N	%
E	29	37.66
I	48	62.34
S	50	64.94
N	27	35.06
T	37	48.05
F	40	51.95
J	48	62.34
P	29	37.66
I J	28	36.36
I P	20	25.97
E P	9	11.69
E J	20	25.97
S T	23	29.87
S F	27	35.06
N F	13	16.88
N T	14	18.18
S J	33	42.86
S P	17	22.08
N P	12	15.58
N J	15	19.48
T J	22	28.57
T P	15	19.48
F P	14	18.18
F J	26	33.77
I N	15	19.48
E N	12	15.58
I S	33	42.86
E S	17	22.08
E T	13	16.88
E F	16	20.78
I F	24	31.17
I T	24	31.17
S dom	26	33.77
N dom	11	14.29
T dom	20	25.97
F dom	20	25.97

Note: ■ = 1% of sample

8629323

This table is one of a series of tables from the CAPT-MBTI Data Bank of MBTI records submitted to CAPT for computer scoring between 1971 and June, 1984. This sample was drawn from 59,784 records with usable occupational codes from the total data bank of 232,557. This data bank has 51% Form F cases from 1971 to March, 1978, 35% Form F cases from 1978 to June, 1984 and 14% Form G cases from 1978 to December, 1982. An analysis of Form F and G data banks showed the data banks were comprised of 56% females and 44% males; education level completed: 6% some grade school, 30% high school diploma, 25% some college, 18% bachelor degrees, 11% masters degrees, 3% doctoral or post doctoral work, and 6% unknown. Age group percentages were: 11% under 18, 29% 18 to 20, 12% 21 to 24, 10% 25 to 29, 16% 30 to 39, 10% 40 to 49, 5% 50 to 59, 2% 60 plus, and 5% unknown.

Secretaries: Medical

N = 68

	SENSING		INTUITION					
	THINKING	FEELING	FEELING	THINKING			N	%

ISTJ	ISFJ	INFJ	INTJ
N= 7	N= 8	N= 4	N= 2
%= 10.29	%= 11.76	%= 5.88	%= 2.94
■■■■■■■■■■	■■■■■■■■■■ ■■	■■■■■■	■■■

ISTP	ISFP	INFP	INTP
N= 1	N= 3	N= 5	N= 1
%= 1.47	%= 4.41	%= 7.35	%= 1.47
■	■■■■	■■■■■■■	■

ESTP	ESFP	ENFP	ENTP
N= 1	N= 5	N= 5	N= 1
%= 1.47	%= 7.35	%= 7.35	%= 1.47
■	■■■■■■■	■■■■■■■	■

ESTJ	ESFJ	ENFJ	ENTJ
N= 5	N= 14	N= 1	N= 5
%= 7.35	%= 20.59	%= 1.47	%= 7.35
■■■■■■■	■■■■■■■■■■ ■■■■■■■■■■ ■	■	■■■■■■■

JUDGMENT — INTROVERSION — PERCEPTION — PERCEPTION — EXTRAVERSION — JUDGMENT

	N	%
E	37	54.41
I	31	45.59
S	44	64.71
N	24	35.29
T	23	33.82
F	45	66.18
J	46	67.65
P	22	32.35
I J	21	30.88
I P	10	14.71
E P	12	17.65
E J	25	36.76
S T	14	20.59
S F	30	44.12
N F	15	22.06
N T	9	13.24
S J	34	50.00
S P	10	14.71
N P	12	17.65
N J	12	17.65
T J	19	27.94
T P	4	5.88
F P	18	26.47
F J	27	39.71
I N	12	17.65
E N	12	17.65
I S	19	27.94
E S	25	36.76
E T	12	17.65
E F	25	36.76
I F	20	29.41
I T	11	16.18
S dom	21	30.88
N dom	12	17.65
T dom	12	17.65
F dom	23	33.82

Note: ■ = 1% of sample   8629324

This table is one of a series of tables from the CAPT-MBTI Data Bank of MBTI records submitted to CAPT for computer scoring between 1971 and June, 1984. This sample was drawn from 59,784 records with usable occupational codes from the total data bank of 232,557. This data bank has 51% Form F cases from 1971 to March, 1978, 35% Form F cases from 1978 to June, 1984 and 14% Form G cases from 1978 to December, 1982. An analysis of Form F and G data banks showed the data banks were comprised of 56% females and 44% males; education level completed: 6% some grade school, 30% high school diploma, 25% some college, 18% bachelor degrees, 11% masters degrees, 3% doctoral or post doctoral work, and 6% unknown. Age group percentages were: 11% under 18, 29% 18 to 20, 12% 21 to 24, 10% 25 to 29, 16% 30 to 39, 10% 40 to 49, 5% 50 to 59, 2% 60 plus, and 5% unknown.

Stock Clerks and Storekeepers

N = 67

	SENSING		INTUITION	
	THINKING	FEELING	FEELING	THINKING

ISTJ	ISFJ	INFJ	INTJ
N= 8	N= 2	N= 4	N= 0
%= 11.94	%= 2.99	%= 5.97	%= 0.00
■■■■■■■■■■■■	■■■	■■■■■■	
■■			

ISTP	ISFP	INFP	INTP
N= 3	N= 9	N= 1	N= 4
%= 4.48	%= 13.43	%= 1.49	%= 5.97
■■■■	■■■■■■■■■■	■	■■■■■■
	■■■		

ESTP	ESFP	ENFP	ENTP
N= 4	N= 5	N= 6	N= 3
%= 5.97	%= 7.46	%= 8.96	%= 4.48
■■■■■■	■■■■■■■	■■■■■■■■■	■■■■

ESTJ	ESFJ	ENFJ	ENTJ
N= 9	N= 3	N= 2	N= 4
%= 13.43	%= 4.48	%= 2.99	%= 5.97
■■■■■■■■■■	■■■■	■■■	■■■■■■
■■■			

	N	%
E	36	53.73
I	31	46.27
S	43	64.18
N	24	35.82
T	35	52.24
F	32	47.76
J	32	47.76
P	35	52.24
I J	14	20.90
I P	17	25.37
E P	18	26.87
E J	18	26.87
S T	24	35.82
S F	19	28.36
N F	13	19.40
N T	11	16.42
S J	22	32.84
S P	21	31.34
N P	14	20.90
N J	10	14.93
T J	21	31.34
T P	14	20.90
F P	21	31.34
F J	11	16.42
I N	9	13.43
E N	15	22.39
I S	22	32.84
E S	21	31.34
E T	20	29.85
E F	16	23.88
I F	16	23.88
I T	15	22.39
S dom	19	28.36
N dom	13	19.40
T dom	20	29.85
F dom	15	22.39

Note: ■ = 1% of sample

8629327

This table is one of a series of tables from the CAPT-MBTI Data Bank of MBTI records submitted to CAPT for computer scoring between 1971 and June, 1984. This sample was drawn from 59,784 records with usable occupational codes from the total data bank of 232,557. This data bank has 51% Form F cases from 1971 to March, 1978, 35% Form F cases from 1978 to June, 1984 and 14% Form G cases from 1978 to December, 1982. An analysis of Form F and G data banks showed the data banks were comprised of 56% females and 44% males; education level completed: 6% some grade school, 30% high school diploma, 25% some college, 18% bachelor degrees, 11% masters degrees, 3% doctoral or post doctoral work, and 6% unknown. Age group percentages were: 11% under 18, 29% 18 to 20, 12% 21 to 24, 10% 25 to 29, 16% 30 to 39, 10% 40 to 49, 5% 50 to 59, 2% 60 plus, and 5% unknown.

Typists

	SENSING		INTUITION	
	THINKING	FEELING	FEELING	THINKING

ISTJ	ISFJ	INFJ	INTJ
N= 8	N= 18	N= 4	N= 1
%= 7.48	%= 16.82	%= 3.74	%= .93
■■■■■■■	■■■■■■■■■■ ■■■■■■■	■■■■	■

ISTP	ISFP	INFP	INTP
N= 5	N= 8	N= 6	N= 0
%= 4.67	%= 7.48	%= 5.61	%= 0.00
■■■■■	■■■■■■■	■■■■■■	

ESTP	ESFP	ENFP	ENTP
N= 1	N= 9	N= 8	N= 6
%= .93	%= 8.41	%= 7.48	%= 5.61
■	■■■■■■■■	■■■■■■■	■■■■■■

ESTJ	ESFJ	ENFJ	ENTJ
N= 13	N= 15	N= 4	N= 1
%= 12.15	%= 14.02	%= 3.74	%= .93
■■■■■■■■■■ ■■	■■■■■■■■■■ ■■■■	■■■■	■

	N	%
E	57	53.27
I	50	46.73
S	77	71.96
N	30	28.04
T	35	32.71
F	72	67.29
J	64	59.81
P	43	40.19
I J	31	28.97
I P	19	17.76
E P	24	22.43
E J	33	30.84
S T	27	25.23
S F	50	46.73
N F	22	20.56
N T	8	7.48
S J	54	50.47
S P	23	21.50
N P	20	18.69
N J	10	9.35
T J	23	21.50
T P	12	11.21
F P	31	28.97
F J	41	38.32
I N	11	10.28
E N	19	17.76
I S	39	36.45
E S	38	35.51
E T	21	19.63
E F	36	33.64
I F	36	33.64
I T	14	13.08
S dom	36	33.64
N dom	19	17.76
T dom	19	17.76
F dom	33	30.84

Note: ■ = 1% of sample   8629328

This table is one of a series of tables from the CAPT-MBTI Data Bank of MBTI records submitted to CAPT for computer scoring between 1971 and June, 1984. This sample was drawn from 59,784 records with usable occupational codes from the total data bank of 232,557. This data bank has 51% Form F cases from 1971 to March, 1978, 35% Form F cases from 1978 to June, 1984 and 14% Form G cases from 1978 to December, 1982. An analysis of Form F and G data banks showed the data banks were comprised of 56% females and 44% males; education level completed: 6% some grade school, 30% high school diploma, 25% some college, 18% bachelor degrees, 11% masters degrees, 3% doctoral or post doctoral work, and 6% unknown. Age group percentages were: 11% under 18, 29% 18 to 20, 12% 21 to 24, 10% 25 to 29, 16% 30 to 39, 10% 40 to 49, 5% 50 to 59, 2% 60 plus, and 5% unknown.

CLERICAL AND KINDRED WORKERS

N = 3339

	SENSING		INTUITION	
	THINKING	FEELING	FEELING	THINKING

ISTJ	ISFJ	INFJ	INTJ
N= 276	N= 449	N= 142	N= 88
%= 8.27	%= 13.45	%= 4.25	%= 2.64
■■■■■■■■	■■■■■■■■■■■■■ ■■■	■■■■	■■■

ISTP	ISFP	INFP	INTP
N= 83	N= 210	N= 273	N= 88
%= 2.49	%= 6.29	%= 8.18	%= 2.64
■■	■■■■■■	■■■■■■■■	■■■

ESTP	ESFP	ENFP	ENTP
N= 91	N= 233	N= 382	N= 106
%= 2.73	%= 6.98	%= 11.44	%= 3.17
■■■	■■■■■■■	■■■■■■■■■■■ ■	■■■

ESTJ	ESFJ	ENFJ	ENTJ
N= 261	N= 417	N= 161	N= 79
%= 7.82	%= 12.49	%= 4.82	%= 2.37
■■■■■■■■	■■■■■■■■■■■■ ■■	■■■■■	■■

JUDGMENT — INTROVERSION — PERCEPTION
PERCEPTION — EXTRAVERSION — JUDGMENT

	N	%
E	1730	51.81
I	1609	48.19
S	2020	60.50
N	1319	39.50
T	1072	32.11
F	2267	67.89
J	1873	56.09
P	1466	43.91
I J	955	28.60
I P	654	19.59
E P	812	24.32
E J	918	27.49
S T	711	21.29
S F	1309	39.20
N F	958	28.69
N T	361	10.81
S J	1403	42.02
S P	617	18.48
N P	849	25.43
N J	470	14.08
T J	704	21.08
T P	368	11.02
F P	1098	32.88
F J	1169	35.01
I N	591	17.70
E N	728	21.80
I S	1018	30.49
E S	1002	30.01
E T	537	16.08
E F	1193	35.73
I F	1074	32.17
I T	535	16.02
S dom	1049	31.42
N dom	718	21.50
T dom	511	15.30
F dom	1061	31.78

Note: ■ = 1% of sample   8629330

This table is one of a series of tables from the CAPT-MBTI Data Bank of MBTI records submitted to CAPT for computer scoring between 1971 and June, 1984. This sample was drawn from 59,784 records with usable occupational codes from the total data bank of 232,557. This data bank has 51% Form F cases from 1971 to March, 1978, 35% Form F cases from 1978 to June, 1984 and 14% Form G cases from 1978 to December, 1982. An analysis of Form F and G data banks showed the data banks were comprised of 56% females and 44% males; education level completed: 6% some grade school, 30% high school diploma, 25% some college, 18% bachelor degrees, 11% masters degrees, 3% doctoral or post doctoral work, and 6% unknown. Age group percentages were: 11% under 18, 29% 18 to 20, 12% 21 to 24, 10% 25 to 29, 16% 30 to 39, 10% 40 to 49, 5% 50 to 59, 2% 60 plus, and 5% unknown.

MANAGERS AND ADMINISTRATORS

N = 7463

	SENSING		INTUITION			N	%
	THINKING	FEELING	FEELING	THINKING			

ISTJ	ISFJ	INFJ	INTJ			E	4229	56.67

ISTJ
N= 1115
%= 14.94
■■■■■■■■■■
■■■■■

ISFJ
N= 469
%= 6.28
■■■■■■

INFJ
N= 232
%= 3.11
■■■

INTJ
N= 421
%= 5.64
■■■■■■

ISTP
N= 201
%= 2.69
■■■

ISFP
N= 189
%= 2.53
■■■

INFP
N= 340
%= 4.56
■■■■■

INTP
N= 267
%= 3.58
■■■■

ESTP
N= 202
%= 2.71
■■■

ESFP
N= 209
%= 2.80
■■■

ENFP
N= 517
%= 6.93
■■■■■■■

ENTP
N= 365
%= 4.89
■■■■■

ESTJ
N= 1272
%= 17.04
■■■■■■■■■■
■■■■■■■

ESFJ
N= 546
%= 7.32
■■■■■■■

ENFJ
N= 367
%= 4.92
■■■■■

ENTJ
N= 751
%= 10.06
■■■■■■■■■■

	N	%
E	4229	56.67
I	3234	43.33
S	4203	56.32
N	3260	43.68
T	4594	61.56
F	2869	38.44
J	5173	69.32
P	2290	30.68
I J	2237	29.97
I P	997	13.36
E P	1293	17.33
E J	2936	39.34
S T	2790	37.38
S F	1413	18.93
N F	1456	19.51
N T	1804	24.17
S J	3402	45.58
S P	801	10.73
N P	1489	19.95
N J	1771	23.73
T J	3559	47.69
T P	1035	13.87
F P	1255	16.82
F J	1614	21.63
I N	1260	16.88
E N	2000	26.80
I S	1974	26.45
E S	2229	29.87
E T	2590	34.70
E F	1639	21.96
I F	1230	16.48
I T	2004	26.85
S dom	1995	26.73
N dom	1535	20.57
T dom	2491	33.38
F dom	1442	19.32

JUDGMENT INTROVERSION

PERCEPTION

PERCEPTION EXTRAVERSION

JUDGMENT

Note: ■ = 1% of sample   8629331

This table is one of a series of tables from the CAPT-MBTI Data Bank of MBTI records submitted to CAPT for computer scoring between 1971 and June, 1984. This sample was drawn from 59,784 records with usable occupational codes from the total data bank of 232,557. This data bank has 51% Form F cases from 1971 to March, 1978, 35% Form F cases from 1978 to June, 1984 and 14% Form G cases from 1978 to December, 1982. An analysis of Form F and G data banks showed the data banks were comprised of 56% females and 44% males; education level completed: 6% some grade school, 30% high school diploma, 25% some college, 18% bachelor degrees, 11% masters degrees, 3% doctoral or post doctoral work, and 6% unknown. Age group percentages were: 11% under 18, 29% 18 to 20, 12% 21 to 24, 10% 25 to 29, 16% 30 to 39, 10% 40 to 49, 5% 50 to 59, 2% 60 plus, and 5% unknown.

OFFICE MACHINE OPERATORS

N = 4905

	SENSING		INTUITION	
	THINKING	FEELING	FEELING	THINKING

ISTJ	ISFJ	INFJ	INTJ
N= 419	N= 651	N= 212	N= 147
%= 8.54	%= 13.27	%= 4.32	%= 3.00
■■■■■■■■	■■■■■■■■■■ ■■■	■■■■	■■■

ISTP	ISFP	INFP	INTP
N= 136	N= 310	N= 400	N= 124
%= 2.77	%= 6.32	%= 8.15	%= 2.53
■■■	■■■■■■	■■■■■■■■	■■■

ESTP	ESFP	ENFP	ENTP
N= 123	N= 318	N= 556	N= 142
%= 2.51	%= 6.48	%= 11.34	%= 2.90
■■■	■■■■■■	■■■■■■■■■■■ ■	■■■

ESTJ	ESFJ	ENFJ	ENTJ
N= 381	N= 605	N= 231	N= 150
%= 7.77	%= 12.33	%= 4.71	%= 3.06
■■■■■■■■	■■■■■■■■■■■■ ■■	■■■■■	■■■

JUDGMENT — INTROVERSION — PERCEPTION — PERCEPTION — EXTRAVERSION — JUDGMENT

	N	%
E	2506	51.09
I	2399	48.91
S	2943	60.00
N	1962	40.00
T	1622	33.07
F	3283	66.93
J	2796	57.00
P	2109	43.00
I J	1429	29.13
I P	970	19.78
E P	1139	23.22
E J	1367	27.87
S T	1059	21.59
S F	1884	38.41
N F	1399	28.52
N T	563	11.48
S J	2056	41.92
S P	887	18.08
N P	1222	24.91
N J	740	15.09
T J	1097	22.36
T P	525	10.70
F P	1584	32.29
F J	1699	34.64
I N	883	18.00
E N	1079	22.00
I S	1516	30.91
E S	1427	29.09
E T	796	16.23
E F	1710	34.86
I F	1573	32.07
I T	826	16.84
S dom	1511	30.81
N dom	1057	21.55
T dom	791	16.13
F dom	1546	31.52

Note: ■ = 1% of sample   8629332

This table is one of a series of tables from the CAPT-MBTI Data Bank of MBTI records submitted to CAPT for computer scoring between 1971 and June, 1984. This sample was drawn from 59,784 records with usable occupational codes from the total data bank of 232,557. This data bank has 51% Form F cases from 1971 to March, 1978, 35% Form F cases from 1978 to June, 1984 and 14% Form G cases from 1978 to December, 1982. An analysis of Form F and G data banks showed the data banks were comprised of 56% females and 44% males; education level completed: 6% some grade school, 30% high school diploma, 25% some college, 18% bachelor degrees, 11% masters degrees, 3% doctoral or post doctoral work, and 6% unknown. Age group percentages were: 11% under 18, 29% 18 to 20, 12% 21 to 24, 10% 25 to 29, 16% 30 to 39, 10% 40 to 49, 5% 50 to 59, 2% 60 plus, and 5% unknown.

SALES WORKERS

N = 1750

	SENSING		INTUITION	
	THINKING	FEELING	FEELING	THINKING

ISTJ	ISFJ	INFJ	INTJ
N= 129	N= 130	N= 44	N= 57
%= 7.37	%= 7.43	%= 2.51	%= 3.26
■■■■■■■	■■■■■■■	■■■	■■■

ISTP	ISFP	INFP	INTP
N= 57	N= 84	N= 107	N= 60
%= 3.26	%= 4.80	%= 6.11	%= 3.43
■■■	■■■■■	■■■■■■	■■■

ESTP	ESFP	ENFP	ENTP
N= 75	N= 112	N= 193	N= 102
%= 4.29	%= 6.40	%= 11.03	%= 5.83
■■■■	■■■■■■	■■■■■■■■■■ ■	■■■■■■

ESTJ	ESFJ	ENFJ	ENTJ
N= 222	N= 176	N= 95	N= 107
%= 12.69	%= 10.06	%= 5.43	%= 6.11
■■■■■■■■■■■ ■■■	■■■■■■■■■■■	■■■■■	■■■■■■

JUDGMENT — INTROVERSION — PERCEPTION
PERCEPTION — EXTRAVERSION — JUDGMENT

	N	%
E	1082	61.83
I	668	38.17
S	985	56.29
N	765	43.71
T	809	46.23
F	941	53.77
J	960	54.86
P	790	45.14
I J	360	20.57
I P	308	17.60
E P	482	27.54
E J	600	34.29
S T	483	27.60
S F	502	28.69
N F	439	25.09
N T	326	18.63
S J	657	37.54
S P	328	18.74
N P	462	26.40
N J	303	17.31
T J	515	29.43
T P	294	16.80
F P	496	28.34
F J	445	25.43
I N	268	15.31
E N	497	28.40
I S	400	22.86
E S	585	33.43
E T	506	28.91
E F	576	32.91
I F	365	20.86
I T	303	17.31
S dom	446	25.49
N dom	396	22.63
T dom	446	25.49
F dom	462	26.40

Note: ■ = 1% of sample   8629333

This table is one of a series of tables from the CAPT-MBTI Data Bank of MBTI records submitted to CAPT for computer scoring between 1971 and June, 1984. This sample was drawn from 59,784 records with usable occupational codes from the total data bank of 232,557. This data bank has 51% Form F cases from 1971 to March, 1978, 35% Form F cases from 1978 to June, 1984 and 14% Form G cases from 1978 to December, 1982. An analysis of Form F and G data banks showed the data banks were comprised of 56% females and 44% males; education level completed: 6% some grade school, 30% high school diploma, 25% some college, 18% bachelor degrees, 11% masters degrees, 3% doctoral or post doctoral work, and 6% unknown. Age group percentages were: 11% under 18, 29% 18 to 20, 12% 21 to 24, 10% 25 to 29, 16% 30 to 39, 10% 40 to 49, 5% 50 to 59, 2% 60 plus, and 5% unknown.

SECRETARIES

	SENSING		INTUITION	
	THINKING	FEELING	FEELING	THINKING

ISTJ	ISFJ	INFJ	INTJ
N= 152	N= 221	N= 74	N= 54
%= 9.48	%= 13.78	%= 4.61	%= 3.37
■■■■■■■■■	■■■■■■■■■■■■■■	■■■■■	■■■

ISTP	ISFP	INFP	INTP
N= 48	N= 104	N= 128	N= 32
%= 2.99	%= 6.48	%= 7.98	%= 2.00
■■■	■■■■■■	■■■■■■■■	■■

ESTP	ESFP	ENFP	ENTP
N= 38	N= 83	N= 163	N= 33
%= 2.37	%= 5.17	%= 10.16	%= 2.06
■■	■■■■■	■■■■■■■■■■	■■

ESTJ	ESFJ	ENFJ	ENTJ
N= 122	N= 201	N= 88	N= 63
%= 7.61	%= 12.53	%= 5.49	%= 3.93
■■■■■■■■	■■■■■■■■■■■■■	■■■■■	■■■■

JUDGMENT — INTROVERSION — PERCEPTION — PERCEPTION — EXTRAVERSION — JUDGMENT

	N	%
E	791	49.31
I	813	50.69
S	969	60.41
N	635	39.59
T	542	33.79
F	1062	66.21
J	975	60.79
P	629	39.21
I J	501	31.23
I P	312	19.45
E P	317	19.76
E J	474	29.55
S T	360	22.44
S F	609	37.97
N F	453	28.24
N T	182	11.35
S J	696	43.39
S P	273	17.02
N P	356	22.19
N J	279	17.39
T J	391	24.38
T P	151	9.41
F P	478	29.80
F J	584	36.41
I N	288	17.96
E N	347	21.63
I S	525	32.73
E S	444	27.68
E T	256	15.96
E F	535	33.35
I F	527	32.86
I T	286	17.83
S dom	494	30.80
N dom	324	20.20
T dom	265	16.52
F dom	521	32.48

Note: ■ = 1% of sample   8629325

This table is one of a series of tables from the CAPT-MBTI Data Bank of MBTI records submitted to CAPT for computer scoring between 1971 and June, 1984. This sample was drawn from 59,784 records with usable occupational codes from the total data bank of 232,557. This data bank has 51% Form F cases from 1971 to March, 1978, 35% Form F cases from 1978 to June, 1984 and 14% Form G cases from 1978 to December, 1982. An analysis of Form F and G data banks showed the data banks were comprised of 56% females and 44% males; education level completed: 6% some grade school, 30% high school diploma, 25% some college, 18% bachelor degrees, 11% masters degrees, 3% doctoral or post doctoral work, and 6% unknown. Age group percentages were: 11% under 18, 29% 18 to 20, 12% 21 to 24, 10% 25 to 29, 16% 30 to 39, 10% 40 to 49, 5% 50 to 59, 2% 60 plus, and 5% unknown.

E Percent	I	Total Sample Size	Sample Description
74.70	25.30	83	Marketing Personnel
69.31	30.69	101	Insurance Agents, Brokers, and Underwriters
68.38	31.62	136	Credit Investigators and Mortgage Brokers
67.59	32.41	108	Sales Clerks, Retail Trade
67.27	32.73	275	Salespeople in a Japanese Trading Company
67.04	32.96	179	Sales Representatives
66.95	33.05	118	Managers: Japanese Chief Executives
66.67	33.33	312	Managers: Restaurant, Cafeteria, Bar and Food Service
64.87	35.13	316	Managers: Retail Stores
64.29	35.71	56	Managers: Top Managers in Large Japanese Companies
63.86	36.14	83	Managers: Sales
63.54	36.46	181	Females in Leadership Development Program
62.84	37.16	366	Managers: Middle Managers in a Japanese Chemical Company
62.00	38.00	100	Receptionists
61.98	38.02	192	Consultants: General
61.83	38.17	1750	SALES WORKERS
61.24	38.76	756	Managers: Financial and Bank Officers
60.78	39.22	102	Managers: Office
60.19	39.81	108	Members of a Human Resources Planners Association
59.12	40.88	274	Cashiers
58.43	41.57	166	Real Estate Agents and Brokers
58.21	41.79	67	Sales Agents, Retail Trade
57.75	42.25	71	Consultants: Management
56.98	43.02	172	Coordinators
56.80	43.20	250	Business: General, Self-employed
56.67	43.33	7463	MANAGERS AND ADMINISTRATORS
56.25	43.75	80	Purchasing Agents
56.05	43.95	835	Bank Employees
55.74	44.26	3678	Administrators: Managers and Supervisors
54.44	45.56	90	Personnel and Labor Relations Workers
54.41	45.59	68	Secretaries: Medical
53.75	46.25	80	Employment Development Specialists
53.73	46.27	67	Stock Clerks and Storekeepers
53.68	46.32	136	Managers: High Level Corporate Executives
53.27	46.73	107	Typists
52.67	47.33	150	Managers: Small Business
52.25	47.75	333	Secretaries: Executive and Administrative Assistants
51.81	48.19	3339	CLERICAL AND KINDRED WORKERS
51.79	48.21	56	Clerical Supervisors
51.69	48.31	89	Consultants: Management Analysts
51.09	48.91	4905	OFFICE MACHINE OPERATORS
51.05	48.95	143	Auditors
50.91	49.09	110	Bank Employees, Exempt
49.35	50.65	849	Managers: England
49.31	50.69	1604	SECRETARIES
49.19	50.81	1051	Males in Leadership Development Program
48.67	51.33	150	Bookkeepers
48.48	51.52	165	Clerks in a Japanese Trading Company
48.20	51.80	222	Bank Employees, Non-Exempt
47.98	52.02	494	Certified Public Accountants

EXTRAVERT-INTROVERT

E Percent	I	Total Sample Size	Sample Description
46.94	53.06	98	Managers: Participants in Women in Management Conference
46.55	53.45	333	Public Accountants
45.20	54.80	427	Accountants
41.44	58.56	111	Consultants: Canadian
40.87	59.13	230	Managers: Regional Telephone Company Low Level Managers
37.66	62.34	77	Secretaries: Legal
37.02	62.98	1394	Managers: Federal Executives
35.34	64.66	116	Managers: Middle Managers in a Japanese Heavy Industrial Co

S Percent	N	Total Sample Size	Sample Description
92.34	7.66	222	Bank Employees, Non-Exempt
86.00	14.00	150	Managers: Small Business
85.45	14.55	110	Bank Employees, Exempt
82.59	17.41	316	Managers: Retail Stores
77.50	22.50	80	Purchasing Agents
77.39	22.61	230	Managers: Regional Telephone Company Low Level Managers
72.95	27.05	366	Managers: Middle Managers in a Japanese Chemical Company
71.96	28.04	107	Typists
71.62	28.38	835	Bank Employees
71.47	28.53	312	Managers: Restaurant, Cafeteria, Bar and Food Service
68.00	32.00	150	Bookkeepers
67.86	32.14	56	Clerical Supervisors
67.49	32.51	849	Managers: England
67.27	32.73	165	Clerks in a Japanese Trading Company
65.08	34.92	756	Managers: Financial and Bank Officers
64.98	35.02	494	Certified Public Accountants
64.94	35.06	77	Secretaries: Legal
64.71	35.29	68	Secretaries: Medical
64.18	35.82	67	Stock Clerks and Storekeepers
63.87	36.13	274	Cashiers
62.30	37.70	427	Accountants
62.01	37.99	179	Sales Representatives
60.84	39.16	166	Real Estate Agents and Brokers
60.50	39.50	3339	CLERICAL AND KINDRED WORKERS
60.41	39.59	1604	SECRETARIES
60.00	40.00	4905	OFFICE MACHINE OPERATORS
60.00	40.00	100	Receptionists
59.70	40.30	67	Sales Agents, Retail Trade
59.27	40.73	275	Salespeople in a Japanese Trading Company
59.26	40.74	108	Sales Clerks, Retail Trade
59.04	40.96	83	Managers: Sales
57.97	42.03	3678	Administrators: Managers and Supervisors
57.43	42.57	101	Insurance Agents, Brokers, and Underwriters
57.35	42.65	136	Managers: High Level Corporate Executives
57.14	42.86	56	Managers: Top Managers in Large Japanese Companies
56.64	43.36	143	Auditors
56.32	43.68	7463	MANAGERS AND ADMINISTRATORS
56.29	43.71	1750	SALES WORKERS
56.04	43.96	1051	Males in Leadership Development Program
56.03	43.97	116	Managers: Middle Managers in a Japanese Heavy Industrial Co
55.56	44.44	333	Secretaries: Executive and Administrative Assistants
55.56	44.44	90	Personnel and Labor Relations Workers
54.90	45.10	102	Managers: Office
54.00	46.00	250	Business: General, Self-employed
53.39	46.61	118	Managers: Japanese Chief Executives
52.85	47.15	333	Public Accountants
51.08	48.92	1394	Managers: Federal Executives
49.42	50.58	172	Coordinators
47.96	52.04	98	Managers: Participants in Women in Management Conference
47.06	52.94	136	Credit Investigators and Mortgage Brokers

SENSING-INTUITION

S Percent	N	Total Sample Size	Sample Description
42.25	57.75	71	Consultants: Management
40.54	59.46	111	Consultants: Canadian
40.00	60.00	80	Employment Development Specialists
39.76	60.24	83	Marketing Personnel
39.33	60.67	89	Consultants: Management Analysts
34.90	65.10	192	Consultants: General
29.83	70.17	181	Females in Leadership Development Program
29.63	70.37	108	Members of a Human Resources Planners Association

THINKING-FEELING

T Percent	F	Total Sample Size	Sample Description
95.50	4.50	111	Consultants: Canadian
93.04	6.96	316	Managers: Retail Stores
91.55	8.45	71	Consultants: Management
89.71	10.29	136	Managers: High Level Corporate Executives
86.44	13.56	1394	Managers: Federal Executives
85.73	14.27	1051	Males in Leadership Development Program
81.33	18.67	150	Managers: Small Business
79.52	20.48	83	Managers: Sales
78.34	21.66	494	Certified Public Accountants
75.52	24.48	143	Auditors
75.27	24.73	849	Managers: England
75.00	25.00	756	Managers: Financial and Bank Officers
75.00	25.00	80	Purchasing Agents
73.73	26.27	118	Managers: Japanese Chief Executives
73.53	26.47	136	Credit Investigators and Mortgage Brokers
73.28	26.72	116	Managers: Middle Managers in a Japanese Heavy Industrial Co
72.61	27.39	230	Managers: Regional Telephone Company Low Level Managers
67.86	32.14	56	Managers: Top Managers in Large Japanese Companies
67.57	32.43	333	Public Accountants
66.67	33.33	366	Managers: Middle Managers in a Japanese Chemical Company
66.67	33.33	108	Members of a Human Resources Planners Association
66.36	33.64	110	Bank Employees, Exempt
65.56	34.44	90	Personnel and Labor Relations Workers
63.89	36.11	3678	Administrators: Managers and Supervisors
63.78	36.22	312	Managers: Restaurant, Cafeteria, Bar and Food Service
63.54	36.46	181	Females in Leadership Development Program
61.56	38.44	7463	MANAGERS AND ADMINISTRATORS
61.45	38.55	83	Marketing Personnel
59.25	40.75	427	Accountants
58.40	41.60	250	Business: General, Self-employed
58.21	41.79	67	Sales Agents, Retail Trade
57.96	42.04	835	Bank Employees
57.23	42.77	166	Real Estate Agents and Brokers
56.98	43.02	179	Sales Representatives
55.10	44.90	98	Managers: Participants in Women in Management Conference
55.06	44.94	89	Consultants: Management Analysts
53.75	46.25	80	Employment Development Specialists
53.65	46.35	192	Consultants: General
53.47	46.53	101	Insurance Agents, Brokers, and Underwriters
52.25	47.75	222	Bank Employees, Non-Exempt
52.24	47.76	67	Stock Clerks and Storekeepers
49.42	50.58	172	Coordinators
48.05	51.95	77	Secretaries: Legal
46.23	53.77	1750	SALES WORKERS
45.45	54.55	275	Salespeople in a Japanese Trading Company
45.37	54.63	108	Sales Clerks, Retail Trade
43.84	56.16	333	Secretaries: Executive and Administrative Assistants
39.22	60.78	102	Managers: Office
33.82	66.18	68	Secretaries: Medical
33.79	66.21	1604	SECRETARIES

THINKING-FEELING

T Percent	F	Total Sample Size	Sample Description
33.07	66.93	4905	OFFICE MACHINE OPERATORS
32.71	67.29	107	Typists
32.11	67.89	3339	CLERICAL AND KINDRED WORKERS
30.29	69.71	274	Cashiers
30.00	70.00	150	Bookkeepers
28.57	71.43	56	Clerical Supervisors
22.00	78.00	100	Receptionists
15.15	84.85	165	Clerks in a Japanese Trading Company

J Percent	P	Total Sample Size	Sample Description
91.46	8.54	316	Managers: Retail Stores
80.63	19.37	222	Bank Employees, Non-Exempt
80.28	19.72	71	Consultants: Management
79.09	20.91	110	Bank Employees, Exempt
76.25	23.75	80	Purchasing Agents
76.21	23.79	849	Managers: England
75.90	24.10	83	Managers: Sales
75.33	24.67	150	Managers: Small Business
75.32	24.68	312	Managers: Restaurant, Cafeteria, Bar and Food Service
75.00	25.00	136	Managers: High Level Corporate Executives
74.78	25.22	230	Managers: Regional Telephone Company Low Level Managers
74.77	25.23	333	Public Accountants
74.09	25.91	494	Certified Public Accountants
74.02	25.98	1051	Males in Leadership Development Program
73.73	26.27	118	Managers: Japanese Chief Executives
71.88	28.12	1394	Managers: Federal Executives
71.43	28.57	756	Managers: Financial and Bank Officers
70.37	29.63	108	Members of a Human Resources Planners Association
69.32	30.68	7463	MANAGERS AND ADMINISTRATORS
69.32	30.68	427	Accountants
69.12	30.88	136	Credit Investigators and Mortgage Brokers
68.47	31.53	111	Consultants: Canadian
68.43	31.57	3678	Administrators: Managers and Supervisors
67.83	32.17	143	Auditors
67.66	32.34	835	Bank Employees
67.65	32.35	68	Secretaries: Medical
66.67	33.33	90	Personnel and Labor Relations Workers
66.07	33.93	56	Managers: Top Managers in Large Japanese Companies
64.71	35.29	102	Managers: Office
64.48	35.52	366	Managers: Middle Managers in a Japanese Chemical Company
64.46	35.54	166	Real Estate Agents and Brokers
64.04	35.96	89	Consultants: Management Analysts
63.95	36.05	172	Coordinators
63.69	36.31	179	Sales Representatives
62.34	37.66	77	Secretaries: Legal
61.98	38.02	192	Consultants: General
61.86	38.14	333	Secretaries: Executive and Administrative Assistants
61.25	38.75	80	Employment Development Specialists
60.79	39.21	1604	SECRETARIES
60.00	40.00	250	Business: General, Self-employed
59.81	40.19	107	Typists
58.33	41.67	108	Sales Clerks, Retail Trade
58.00	42.00	150	Bookkeepers
57.66	42.34	274	Cashiers
57.14	42.86	56	Clerical Supervisors
57.00	43.00	4905	OFFICE MACHINE OPERATORS
56.72	43.28	67	Sales Agents, Retail Trade
56.44	43.56	101	Insurance Agents, Brokers, and Underwriters
56.09	43.91	3339	CLERICAL AND KINDRED WORKERS
56.03	43.97	116	Managers: Middle Managers in a Japanese Heavy Industrial Co

JUDGMENT-PERCEPTION

J Percent	P	Total Sample Size	Sample Description
56.00	44.00	100	Receptionists
55.42	44.58	83	Marketing Personnel
55.10	44.90	98	Managers: Participants in Women in Management Conference
54.86	45.14	1750	SALES WORKERS
53.59	46.41	181	Females in Leadership Development Program
47.76	52.24	67	Stock Clerks and Storekeepers
42.42	57.58	165	Clerks in a Japanese Trading Company
31.64	68.36	275	Salespeople in a Japanese Trading Company

Percent ST	Total Sample Size	Sample Description
76.58	316	Managers: Retail Stores
70.67	150	Managers: Small Business
59.09	110	Bank Employees, Exempt
58.75	80	Purchasing Agents
57.39	230	Managers: Regional Telephone Company Low Level Managers
53.64	494	Certified Public Accountants
52.77	849	Managers: England
51.47	136	Managers: High Level Corporate Executives
50.53	756	Managers: Financial and Bank Officers
49.67	1051	Males in Leadership Development Program
46.40	222	Bank Employees, Non-Exempt
46.15	143	Auditors
45.98	1394	Managers: Federal Executives
45.90	366	Managers: Middle Managers in a Japanese Chemical Company
45.51	312	Managers: Restaurant, Cafeteria, Bar and Food Service
44.58	83	Managers: Sales
41.08	835	Bank Employees
39.64	111	Consultants: Canadian
39.44	71	Consultants: Management
39.40	3678	Administrators: Managers and Supervisors
39.34	427	Accountants
38.79	116	Managers: Middle Managers in a Japanese Heavy Industrial Company
38.55	179	Sales Representatives
37.50	56	Managers: Top Managers in Large Japanese Companies
37.38	7463	MANAGERS AND ADMINISTRATORS
37.24	333	Public Accountants
36.67	90	Personnel and Labor Relations Workers
36.63	101	Insurance Agents, Brokers, and Underwriters
36.44	118	Managers: Japanese Chief Executives
35.82	67	Stock Clerks and Storekeepers
35.29	136	Credit Investigators and Mortgage Brokers
34.40	250	Business: General, Self-employed
34.34	166	Real Estate Agents and Brokers
29.87	77	Secretaries: Legal
28.92	83	Marketing Personnel
28.70	108	Sales Clerks, Retail Trade
28.53	333	Secretaries: Executive and Administrative Assistants
28.36	67	Sales Agents, Retail Trade
28.09	89	Consultants: Management Analysts
27.60	1750	SALES WORKERS
27.33	172	Coordinators
25.51	98	Managers: Participants in Women in Management Conference
25.23	107	Typists
24.51	102	Managers: Office
23.75	80	Employment Development Specialists
23.36	274	Cashiers
22.92	192	Consultants: General
22.91	275	Salespeople in a Japanese Trading Company
22.67	150	Bookkeepers
22.44	1604	SECRETARIES

SENSING-THINKING

Percent ST	Total Sample Size	Sample Description
22.10	181	Females in Leadership Development Program
21.59	4905	OFFICE MACHINE OPERATORS
21.29	3339	CLERICAL AND KINDRED WORKERS
20.59	68	Secretaries: Medical
20.37	108	Members of a Human Resources Planners Association
17.86	56	Clerical Supervisors
15.00	100	Receptionists
8.48	165	Clerks in a Japanese Trading Company

Percent SF	Total Sample Size	Sample Description
58.79	165	Clerks in a Japanese Trading Company
50.00	56	Clerical Supervisors
46.73	107	Typists
45.95	222	Bank Employees, Non-Exempt
45.33	150	Bookkeepers
45.00	100	Receptionists
44.12	68	Secretaries: Medical
40.51	274	Cashiers
39.20	3339	CLERICAL AND KINDRED WORKERS
38.41	4905	OFFICE MACHINE OPERATORS
37.97	1604	SECRETARIES
36.36	275	Salespeople in a Japanese Trading Company
35.06	77	Secretaries: Legal
31.34	67	Sales Agents, Retail Trade
30.56	108	Sales Clerks, Retail Trade
30.54	835	Bank Employees
30.39	102	Managers: Office
28.69	1750	SALES WORKERS
28.36	67	Stock Clerks and Storekeepers
27.05	366	Managers: Middle Managers in a Japanese Chemical Company
27.03	333	Secretaries: Executive and Administrative Assistants
26.51	166	Real Estate Agents and Brokers
26.36	110	Bank Employees, Exempt
25.96	312	Managers: Restaurant, Cafeteria, Bar and Food Service
23.46	179	Sales Representatives
22.95	427	Accountants
22.45	98	Managers: Participants in Women in Management Conference
22.09	172	Coordinators
20.79	101	Insurance Agents, Brokers, and Underwriters
20.00	230	Managers: Regional Telephone Company Low Level Managers
19.64	56	Managers: Top Managers in Large Japanese Companies
19.60	250	Business: General, Self-employed
18.93	7463	MANAGERS AND ADMINISTRATORS
18.89	90	Personnel and Labor Relations Workers
18.75	80	Purchasing Agents
18.57	3678	Administrators: Managers and Supervisors
17.24	116	Managers: Middle Managers in a Japanese Heavy Industrial Company
16.95	118	Managers: Japanese Chief Executives
16.25	80	Employment Development Specialists
15.62	333	Public Accountants
15.33	150	Managers: Small Business
14.72	849	Managers: England
14.55	756	Managers: Financial and Bank Officers
14.46	83	Managers: Sales
11.98	192	Consultants: General
11.76	136	Credit Investigators and Mortgage Brokers
11.34	494	Certified Public Accountants
11.24	89	Consultants: Management Analysts
10.84	83	Marketing Personnel
10.49	143	Auditors

SENSING-FEELING

Percent SF	Total Sample Size	Sample Description
9.26	108	Members of a Human Resources Planners Association
7.73	181	Females in Leadership Development Program
6.37	1051	Males in Leadership Development Program
6.01	316	Managers: Retail Stores
5.88	136	Managers: High Level Corporate Executives
5.09	1394	Managers: Federal Executives
2.82	71	Consultants: Management
.90	111	Consultants: Canadian

INTUITION-FEELING

Percent NF	Total Sample Size	Sample Description
34.38	192	Consultants: General
33.71	89	Consultants: Management Analysts
33.00	100	Receptionists
30.39	102	Managers: Office
30.00	80	Employment Development Specialists
29.20	274	Cashiers
29.13	333	Secretaries: Executive and Administrative Assistants
28.73	181	Females in Leadership Development Program
28.69	3339	CLERICAL AND KINDRED WORKERS
28.52	4905	OFFICE MACHINE OPERATORS
28.49	172	Coordinators
28.24	1604	SECRETARIES
27.71	83	Marketing Personnel
26.06	165	Clerks in a Japanese Trading Company
25.74	101	Insurance Agents, Brokers, and Underwriters
25.09	1750	SALES WORKERS
24.67	150	Bookkeepers
24.07	108	Sales Clerks, Retail Trade
24.07	108	Members of a Human Resources Planners Association
22.45	98	Managers: Participants in Women in Management Conference
22.06	68	Secretaries: Medical
22.00	250	Business: General, Self-employed
21.43	56	Clerical Supervisors
20.56	107	Typists
19.55	179	Sales Representatives
19.51	7463	MANAGERS AND ADMINISTRATORS
19.40	67	Stock Clerks and Storekeepers
18.18	275	Salespeople in a Japanese Trading Company
17.80	427	Accountants
17.54	3678	Administrators: Managers and Supervisors
16.88	77	Secretaries: Legal
16.82	333	Public Accountants
16.27	166	Real Estate Agents and Brokers
15.56	90	Personnel and Labor Relations Workers
14.71	136	Credit Investigators and Mortgage Brokers
13.99	143	Auditors
12.50	56	Managers: Top Managers in Large Japanese Companies
11.50	835	Bank Employees
10.45	756	Managers: Financial and Bank Officers
10.45	67	Sales Agents, Retail Trade
10.32	494	Certified Public Accountants
10.26	312	Managers: Restaurant, Cafeteria, Bar and Food Service
10.01	849	Managers: England
9.48	116	Managers: Middle Managers in a Japanese Heavy Industrial Company
9.32	118	Managers: Japanese Chief Executives
8.46	1394	Managers: Federal Executives
7.90	1051	Males in Leadership Development Program
7.39	230	Managers: Regional Telephone Company Low Level Managers
7.27	110	Bank Employees, Exempt
6.28	366	Managers: Middle Managers in a Japanese Chemical Company

INTUITION-FEELING

Percent NF	Total Sample Size	Sample Description
6.25	80	Purchasing Agents
6.02	83	Managers: Sales
5.63	71	Consultants: Management
4.41	136	Managers: High Level Corporate Executives
3.60	111	Consultants: Canadian
3.33	150	Managers: Small Business
1.80	222	Bank Employees, Non-Exempt
.95	316	Managers: Retail Stores

Percent NT	Total Sample Size	Sample Description
55.86	111	Consultants: Canadian
52.11	71	Consultants: Management
46.30	108	Members of a Human Resources Planners Association
41.44	181	Females in Leadership Development Program
40.46	1394	Managers: Federal Executives
38.24	136	Managers: High Level Corporate Executives
38.24	136	Credit Investigators and Mortgage Brokers
37.29	118	Managers: Japanese Chief Executives
36.06	1051	Males in Leadership Development Program
34.94	83	Managers: Sales
34.48	116	Managers: Middle Managers in a Japanese Heavy Industrial Company
32.53	83	Marketing Personnel
30.73	192	Consultants: General
30.36	56	Managers: Top Managers in Large Japanese Companies
30.33	333	Public Accountants
30.00	80	Employment Development Specialists
29.85	67	Sales Agents, Retail Trade
29.59	98	Managers: Participants in Women in Management Conference
29.37	143	Auditors
28.89	90	Personnel and Labor Relations Workers
26.97	89	Consultants: Management Analysts
24.70	494	Certified Public Accountants
24.50	3678	Administrators: Managers and Supervisors
24.47	756	Managers: Financial and Bank Officers
24.17	7463	MANAGERS AND ADMINISTRATORS
24.00	250	Business: General, Self-employed
22.89	166	Real Estate Agents and Brokers
22.55	275	Salespeople in a Japanese Trading Company
22.50	849	Managers: England
22.09	172	Coordinators
20.77	366	Managers: Middle Managers in a Japanese Chemical Company
19.91	427	Accountants
18.63	1750	SALES WORKERS
18.44	179	Sales Representatives
18.27	312	Managers: Restaurant, Cafeteria, Bar and Food Service
18.18	77	Secretaries: Legal
16.89	835	Bank Employees
16.83	101	Insurance Agents, Brokers, and Underwriters
16.67	108	Sales Clerks, Retail Trade
16.46	316	Managers: Retail Stores
16.42	67	Stock Clerks and Storekeepers
16.25	80	Purchasing Agents
15.32	333	Secretaries: Executive and Administrative Assistants
15.22	230	Managers: Regional Telephone Company Low Level Managers
14.71	102	Managers: Office
13.24	68	Secretaries: Medical
11.48	4905	OFFICE MACHINE OPERATORS
11.35	1604	SECRETARIES
10.81	3339	CLERICAL AND KINDRED WORKERS
10.71	56	Clerical Supervisors

INTUITION-THINKING

Percent NT	Total Sample Size	Sample Description
10.67	150	Managers: Small Business
7.48	107	Typists
7.33	150	Bookkeepers
7.27	110	Bank Employees, Exempt
7.00	100	Receptionists
6.93	274	Cashiers
6.67	165	Clerks in a Japanese Trading Company
5.86	222	Bank Employees, Non-Exempt

COUNSELING
&
MENTAL HEALTH

Section IV

COUNSELING AND MENTAL HEALTH

Samples in Section IV

Name of Sample	Number in Sample
Certified Psychodramatists	170
College and University Resident Assistants	177
Composite of Practitioners in Social Work	169
Counselors: General	359
Counselors: General	932
Counselors: Rehabilitation	177
Counselors: Runaway Youth	117
Counselors: School	287
Counselors: Suicide and Crisis	262
Counselors: Vocational and Educational	673
Psychologists	289
Social Workers	479

Composite Samples

COUNSELORS	1803
PSYCHOLOGISTS	402
SOCIAL SCIENTISTS	490

Comments

Most of the MBTI Data Bank and contributed samples in this section are concerned with counseling and psychotherapy. Also included are social workers and university residence hall assistants since these often serve as a first line of defense for identifying student mental distress. Some of the data in this section come from summary data from a CAPT state-of-the-art report on medicine and other health professions (McCaulley, 1978). That report discusses issues relating to the selection, teaching, clinical performance, work settings and satisfaction for both students and practitioners. Data selected from the Monograph for inclusion in this edition of the Atlas refer to samples of practitioners, not students.

When you review the tables, look for sizeable numbers of extraverts and introverts; you expect more extraverts to be in samples where treatment is active or time-limited.

The preference most expected in counseling samples is intuition, since this is the function that enables counselors to see patterns, meanings, and relationships of ideas and behavior. For comparison, keep in mind that about 75% of the general population report a preference for sensing. Samples where the major effort is the counseling itself may show more intuitives than samples where considerable paper-work is required to provide services (such as in vocational rehabilitation or social work).

Expect more feeling types, and note especially the proportion of the samples that share NF.

Most health professionals have a majority of J types. Counseling samples typically have fewer J's than other health fields; they often have a majority of P's. A hallmark of counseling is the ability to suspend judgment to be able to listen and understand.

Summary listings of tables for EI, SN, TF, JP, ST, SF, NF and NT will be found after the last type table.

Certified Psychodramatists

N = 170

	SENSING		INTUITION	
	THINKING	FEELING	FEELING	THINKING

ISTJ	ISFJ	INFJ	INTJ
N= 5	N= 4	N= 20	N= 5
%= 2.94	%= 2.35	%= 11.76	%= 2.94
■■■	■■	■■■■■■■■■ ■■	■■■

ISTP	ISFP	INFP	INTP
N= 0	N= 2	N= 16	N= 8
%= 0.00	%= 1.18	%= 9.41	%= 4.71
	■	■■■■■■■■■	■■■■■

ESTP	ESFP	ENFP	ENTP
N= 0	N= 3	N= 50	N= 12
%= 0.00	%= 1.76	%= 29.41	%= 7.06
	■■	■■■■■■■■■ ■■■■■■■■■ ■■■■■■■■■	■■■■■■■

ESTJ	ESFJ	ENFJ	ENTJ
N= 2	N= 6	N= 22	N= 15
%= 1.18	%= 3.53	%= 12.94	%= 8.82
■	■■■■	■■■■■■■■■ ■■■	■■■■■■■■■

Right side labels: JUDGMENT — INTROVERSION — PERCEPTION — PERCEPTION — EXTRAVERSION — JUDGMENT

	N	%
E	110	64.71
I	60	35.29
S	22	12.94
N	148	87.06
T	47	27.65
F	123	72.35
J	79	46.47
P	91	53.53
I J	34	20.00
I P	26	15.29
E P	65	38.24
E J	45	26.47
S T	7	4.12
S F	15	8.82
N F	108	63.53
N T	40	23.53
S J	17	10.00
S P	5	2.94
N P	86	50.59
N J	62	36.47
T J	27	15.88
T P	20	11.76
F P	71	41.76
F J	52	30.59
I N	49	28.82
E N	99	58.24
I S	11	6.47
E S	11	6.47
E T	29	17.06
E F	81	47.65
I F	42	24.71
I T	18	10.59
S dom	12	7.06
N dom	87	51.18
T dom	25	14.71
F dom	46	27.06

Note: ■ = 1% of sample   8623176

Data collected by Dale Richard Buchanan in the Psychodrama Section of Saint Elizabeths Hospital in Washington, D.C. and Jane Taylor of the U.S. Department of the Navy during 1984. Subjects were certified psychodramatists from 234 listed in the directory of the American Board of Examiners in Psychodrama, Sociometry, and Group Psychotherapy who participated in the study. No significant differences were found between the population and the sample based on level of training or sex. The psychodramatists had 3.5% with bachelors degrees, 58.5% masters, 37.5% Ph.D.s and 0.5% M.D.s; 46% were trained in psychology, 29% in social work and 25% in other fields. These data are used with permission and are cited in:

Buchanan, D. R. & Taylor, J. A. (1986). Jungian Typology of Professional Psychodramatists: Myers-Briggs Type Indicator Analysis of Certified Psychodramatists. Psychological Reports, 58, 391-400.

College and University Resident Assistants

	SENSING		INTUITION	
	THINKING	FEELING	FEELING	THINKING

ISTJ	ISFJ	INFJ	INTJ
N= 5	N= 12	N= 8	N= 5
%= 2.82	%= 6.78	%= 4.52	%= 2.82
■■■	■■■■■■■	■■■■■	■■■

ISTP	ISFP	INFP	INTP
N= 3	N= 8	N= 16	N= 6
%= 1.69	%= 4.52	%= 9.04	%= 3.39
■■	■■■■■	■■■■■■■■■	■■■

ESTP	ESFP	ENFP	ENTP
N= 5	N= 4	N= 31	N= 7
%= 2.82	%= 2.26	%= 17.51	%= 3.95
■■■	■■	■■■■■■■■■■ ■■■■■■■	■■■■

ESTJ	ESFJ	ENFJ	ENTJ
N= 14	N= 16	N= 18	N= 19
%= 7.91	%= 9.04	%= 10.17	%= 10.73
■■■■■■■■	■■■■■■■■■	■■■■■■■■■■	■■■■■■■■■■ ■

JUDGMENT — INTROVERSION — PERCEPTION — PERCEPTION — EXTRAVERSION — JUDGMENT

	N	%
E	114	64.41
I	63	35.59
S	67	37.85
N	110	62.15
T	64	36.16
F	113	63.84
J	97	54.80
P	80	45.20
I J	30	16.95
I P	33	18.64
E P	47	26.55
E J	67	37.85
S T	27	15.25
S F	40	22.60
N F	73	41.24
N T	37	20.90
S J	47	26.55
S P	20	11.30
N P	60	33.90
N J	50	28.25
T J	43	24.29
T P	21	11.86
F P	59	33.33
F J	54	30.51
I N	35	19.77
E N	75	42.37
I S	28	15.82
E S	39	22.03
E T	45	25.42
E F	69	38.98
I F	44	24.86
I T	19	10.73
S dom	26	14.69
N dom	51	28.81
T dom	42	23.73
F dom	58	32.77

Note: ■ = 1% of sample   8629453

This table is one of a series of tables from the CAPT-MBTI Data Bank of MBTI records submitted to CAPT for computer scoring between 1971 and June, 1984. This sample was drawn from 59,784 records with usable occupational codes from the total data bank of 232,557. This data bank has 51% Form F cases from 1971 to March, 1978, 35% Form F cases from 1978 to June, 1984 and 14% Form G cases from 1978 to December, 1982. An analysis of Form F and G data banks showed the data banks were comprised of 56% females and 44% males; education level completed: 6% some grade school, 30% high school diploma, 25% some college, 18% bachelor degrees, 11% masters degrees, 3% doctoral or post doctoral work, and 6% unknown. Age group percentages were: 11% under 18, 29% 18 to 20, 12% 21 to 24, 10% 25 to 29, 16% 30 to 39, 10% 40 to 49, 5% 50 to 59, 2% 60 plus, and 5% unknown.

Composite of Practitioners in Social Work

N = 169

	SENSING		INTUITION	
	THINKING	FEELING	FEELING	THINKING

ISTJ	ISFJ	INFJ	INTJ
N= 7	N= 9	N= 17	N= 8
%= 4.14	%= 5.33	%= 10.06	%= 4.73
■■■■	■■■■■	■■■■■■■■■■	■■■■■

ISTP	ISFP	INFP	INTP
N= 1	N= 2	N= 18	N= 3
%= .59	%= 1.18	%= 10.65	%= 1.78
■	■	■■■■■■■■■■ ■	■■

ESTP	ESFP	ENFP	ENTP
N= 2	N= 11	N= 42	N= 11
%= 1.18	%= 6.51	%= 24.85	%= 6.51
■	■■■■■■■	■■■■■■■■■■ ■■■■■■■■■■ ■■■■■	■■■■■■■

ESTJ	ESFJ	ENFJ	ENTJ
N= 14	N= 6	N= 16	N= 2
%= 8.28	%= 3.55	%= 9.47	%= 1.18
■■■■■■■■	■■■■	■■■■■■■■■	■

Left side vertical labels: JUDGMENT / PERCEPTION (INTROVERSION); PERCEPTION / JUDGMENT (EXTRAVERSION)

	N	%
E	104	61.54
I	65	38.46
S	52	30.77
N	117	69.23
T	48	28.40
F	121	71.60
J	79	46.75
P	90	53.25
I J	41	24.26
I P	24	14.20
E P	66	39.05
E J	38	22.49
S T	24	14.20
S F	28	16.57
N F	93	55.03
N T	24	14.20
S J	36	21.30
S P	16	9.47
N P	74	43.79
N J	43	25.44
T J	31	18.34
T P	17	10.06
F P	73	43.20
F J	48	28.40
I N	46	27.22
E N	71	42.01
I S	19	11.24
E S	33	19.53
E T	29	17.16
E F	75	44.38
I F	46	27.22
I T	19	11.24
S dom	29	17.16
N dom	78	46.15
T dom	20	11.83
F dom	42	24.85

Note: ■ = 1% of sample   8623172

Subjects in this sample came from four main sources and were originally compiled especially for publication in:

McCaulley, M. H. (1978). Application of the Myers-Briggs Type Indicator to medicine and other health professions (Monograph I, Contract No. 231-76-0051, Health Resources Administration, DHEW). Gainesville, FL: Center for Applications of Psychological Type.

The four sources used were: 1) the CAPT health databank in 1977, 2) data solicited from medical and health professionals through advertising and personal communication, 3) the Myers Longitudinal Medical Sample initially collected in the 1950s and followed up in the 1970s and 4) data extracted from published research up to that time.

Counselors: General

N = 359

	SENSING		INTUITION	
	THINKING	FEELING	FEELING	THINKING

ISTJ	ISFJ	INFJ	INTJ
N= 21	N= 20	N= 28	N= 11
%= 5.85	%= 5.57	%= 7.80	%= 3.06

ISTP	ISFP	INFP	INTP
N= 4	N= 16	N= 50	N= 9
%= 1.11	%= 4.46	%= 13.93	%= 2.51

ESTP	ESFP	ENFP	ENTP
N= 4	N= 11	N= 84	N= 11
%= 1.11	%= 3.06	%= 23.40	%= 3.06

ESTJ	ESFJ	ENFJ	ENTJ
N= 18	N= 24	N= 41	N= 7
%= 5.01	%= 6.69	%= 11.42	%= 1.95

	N	%
E	200	55.71
I	159	44.29
S	118	32.87
N	241	67.13
T	85	23.68
F	274	76.32
J	170	47.35
P	189	52.65
I J	80	22.28
I P	79	22.01
E P	110	30.64
E J	90	25.07
S T	47	13.09
S F	71	19.78
N F	203	56.55
N T	38	10.58
S J	83	23.12
S P	35	9.75
N P	154	42.90
N J	87	24.23
T J	57	15.88
T P	28	7.80
F P	161	44.85
F J	113	31.48
I N	98	27.30
E N	143	39.83
I S	61	16.99
E S	57	15.88
E T	40	11.14
E F	160	44.57
I F	114	31.75
I T	45	12.53
S dom	56	15.60
N dom	134	37.33
T dom	38	10.58
F dom	131	36.49

Note: ■ = 1% of sample   8623174

Subjects in this sample came from four main sources and were originally compiled especially for publication in:
McCaulley, M. H. (1978). Application of the Myers-Briggs Type Indicator to medicine and other health professions (Monograph I, Contract No. 231-76-0051, Health Resources Administration, DHEW). Gainesville, FL: Center for Applications of Psychological Type.
The four sources used were: 1) the CAPT health databank in 1977, 2) data solicited from medical and health professionals through advertising and personal communication, 3) the Myers Longitudinal Medical Sample initially collected in the 1950s and followed up in the 1970s and 4) data extracted from published research up to that time.

Counselors: General

N = 932

	SENSING		INTUITION	
	THINKING	FEELING	FEELING	THINKING

ISTJ	ISFJ	INFJ	INTJ
N= 60	N= 53	N= 64	N= 38
%= 6.44	%= 5.69	%= 6.87	%= 4.08
■■■■■■	■■■■■	■■■■■■	■■■■

ISTP	ISFP	INFP	INTP
N= 19	N= 29	N= 116	N= 31
%= 2.04	%= 3.11	%= 12.45	%= 3.33
■■	■■■	■■■■■■■■■■ ■■	■■■

ESTP	ESFP	ENFP	ENTP
N= 18	N= 33	N= 167	N= 42
%= 1.93	%= 3.54	%= 17.92	%= 4.51
■■	■■■■	■■■■■■■■■■ ■■■■■■■	■■■■■

ESTJ	ESFJ	ENFJ	ENTJ
N= 57	N= 65	N= 95	N= 45
%= 6.12	%= 6.97	%= 10.19	%= 4.83
■■■■■■	■■■■■■■	■■■■■■■■■■	■■■■■

JUDGMENT — INTROVERSION — PERCEPTION — PERCEPTION — EXTRAVERSION — JUDGMENT

	N	%
E	522	56.01
I	410	43.99
S	334	35.84
N	598	64.16
T	310	33.26
F	622	66.74
J	477	51.18
P	455	48.82
I J	215	23.07
I P	195	20.92
E P	260	27.90
E J	262	28.11
S T	154	16.52
S F	180	19.31
N F	442	47.42
N T	156	16.74
S J	235	25.21
S P	99	10.62
N P	356	38.20
N J	242	25.97
T J	200	21.46
T P	110	11.80
F P	345	37.02
F J	277	29.72
I N	249	26.72
E N	349	37.45
I S	161	17.27
E S	173	18.56
E T	162	17.38
E F	360	38.63
I F	262	28.11
I T	148	15.88
S dom	164	17.60
N dom	311	33.37
T dom	152	16.31
F dom	305	32.73

Note: ■ = 1% of sample

8629452

This table is one of a series of tables from the CAPT-MBTI Data Bank of MBTI records submitted to CAPT for computer scoring between 1971 and June, 1984. This sample was drawn from 59,784 records with usable occupational codes from the total data bank of 232,557. This data bank has 51% Form F cases from 1971 to March, 1978, 35% Form F cases from 1978 to June, 1984 and 14% Form G cases from 1978 to December, 1982. An analysis of Form F and G data banks showed the data banks were comprised of 56% females and 44% males; education level completed: 6% some grade school, 30% high school diploma, 25% some college, 18% bachelor degrees, 11% masters degrees, 3% doctoral or post doctoral work, and 6% unknown. Age group percentages were: 11% under 18, 29% 18 to 20, 12% 21 to 24, 10% 25 to 29, 16% 30 to 39, 10% 40 to 49, 5% 50 to 59, 2% 60 plus, and 5% unknown.

Counselors: Rehabilitation

	SENSING		INTUITION	
	THINKING	FEELING	FEELING	THINKING

ISTJ	ISFJ	INFJ	INTJ
N= 9	N= 13	N= 9	N= 6
%= 5.08	%= 7.34	%= 5.08	%= 3.39
■■■■■	■■■■■■■	■■■■■	■■■

ISTP	ISFP	INFP	INTP
N= 6	N= 8	N= 20	N= 7
%= 3.39	%= 4.52	%= 11.30	%= 3.95
■■■	■■■■■	■■■■■■■■■■ ■	■■■■

ESTP	ESFP	ENFP	ENTP
N= 3	N= 11	N= 36	N= 8
%= 1.69	%= 6.21	%= 20.34	%= 4.52
■■	■■■■■■	■■■■■■■■■■ ■■■■■■■■■■	■■■■■

ESTJ	ESFJ	ENFJ	ENTJ
N= 14	N= 10	N= 11	N= 6
%= 7.91	%= 5.65	%= 6.21	%= 3.39
■■■■■■■■	■■■■■■	■■■■■■	■■■

JUDGMENT / INTROVERSION / PERCEPTION / PERCEPTION / EXTRAVERSION / JUDGMENT

	N	%
E	99	55.93
I	78	44.07
S	74	41.81
N	103	58.19
T	59	33.33
F	118	66.67
J	78	44.07
P	99	55.93
I J	37	20.90
I P	41	23.16
E P	58	32.77
E J	41	23.16
S T	32	18.08
S F	42	23.73
N F	76	42.94
N T	27	15.25
S J	46	25.99
S P	28	15.82
N P	71	40.11
N J	32	18.08
T J	35	19.77
T P	24	13.56
F P	75	42.37
F J	43	24.29
I N	42	23.73
E N	61	34.46
I S	36	20.34
E S	38	21.47
E T	31	17.51
E F	68	38.42
I F	50	28.25
I T	28	15.82
S dom	36	20.34
N dom	59	33.33
T dom	33	18.64
F dom	49	27.68

Note: ■ = 1% of sample   8629451

This table is one of a series of tables from the CAPT-MBTI Data Bank of MBTI records submitted to CAPT for computer scoring between 1971 and June, 1984. This sample was drawn from 59,784 records with usable occupational codes from the total data bank of 232,557. This data bank has 51% Form F cases from 1971 to March, 1978, 35% Form F cases from 1978 to June, 1984 and 14% Form G cases from 1978 to December, 1982. An analysis of Form F and G data banks showed the data banks were comprised of 56% females and 44% males; education level completed: 6% some grade school, 30% high school diploma, 25% some college, 18% bachelor degrees, 11% masters degrees, 3% doctoral or post doctoral work, and 6% unknown. Age group percentages were: 11% under 18, 29% 18 to 20, 12% 21 to 24, 10% 25 to 29, 16% 30 to 39, 10% 40 to 49, 5% 50 to 59, 2% 60 plus, and 5% unknown.

Counselors: Runaway Youth

N = 117

	SENSING		INTUITION	
	THINKING	FEELING	FEELING	THINKING
JUDGMENT (INTROVERSION)	**ISTJ** N= 3 %= 2.56 ■■■	**ISFJ** N= 8 %= 6.84 ■■■■■■■	**INFJ** N= 4 %= 3.42 ■■■	**INTJ** N= 2 %= 1.71 ■■
PERCEPTION (INTROVERSION)	**ISTP** N= 2 %= 1.71 ■■	**ISFP** N= 9 %= 7.69 ■■■■■■■■	**INFP** N= 22 %= 18.80 ■■■■■■■■■■ ■■■■■■■■	**INTP** N= 7 %= 5.98 ■■■■■■
PERCEPTION (EXTRAVERSION)	**ESTP** N= 4 %= 3.42 ■■■	**ESFP** N= 2 %= 1.71 ■■	**ENFP** N= 23 %= 19.66 ■■■■■■■■■■ ■■■■■■■■■	**ENTP** N= 5 %= 4.27 ■■■■
JUDGMENT (EXTRAVERSION)	**ESTJ** N= 3 %= 2.56 ■■■	**ESFJ** N= 4 %= 3.42 ■■■	**ENFJ** N= 14 %= 11.97 ■■■■■■■■■■■ ■■	**ENTJ** N= 5 %= 4.27 ■■■■

	N	%
E	60	51.28
I	57	48.72
S	35	29.91
N	82	70.09
T	31	26.50
F	86	73.50
J	43	36.75
P	74	63.25
I J	17	14.53
I P	40	34.19
E P	34	29.06
E J	26	22.22
S T	12	10.26
S F	23	19.66
N F	63	53.85
N T	19	16.24
S J	18	15.38
S P	17	14.53
N P	57	48.72
N J	25	21.37
T J	13	11.11
T P	18	15.38
F P	56	47.86
F J	30	25.64
I N	35	29.91
E N	47	40.17
I S	22	18.80
E S	13	11.11
E T	17	14.53
E F	43	36.75
I F	43	36.75
I T	14	11.97
S dom	17	14.53
N dom	34	29.06
T dom	17	14.53
F dom	49	41.88

Note: ■ = 1% of sample   8623170

Data collected by Gene Elliott during 1974. The subjects were 49% male and 51% female full time salaried and regular staff members of 38 centers serving runaway youth. The subjects' ages ranged from 20 to 59, mean age 26.5. The education levels were: 40% graduate school study or degree, 38% bachelors degree, 17% some college and 5% high school diploma. Half of the centers were in urban areas, 25% in suburban areas and 25% in small towns and cities. This sample represents about half of all full time runaway counselors in the country during 1974. These data are used with permission and were cited in:

Elliott, G. V. (1975). A descriptive study of characteristics and personality types of counselors of runaway youth (Doctoral dissertation, University of Maryland, 1975). Dissertation Abstracts International, 36, 3119B-3120B. (University Microfilms No. 75-28, 741)

Counselors: School

N = 287

	SENSING		INTUITION	
THINKING	FEELING	FEELING	THINKING

	N	%
E	183	63.76
I	104	36.24
S	111	38.68
N	176	61.32
T	86	29.97
F	201	70.03
J	152	52.96
P	135	47.04
I J	52	18.12
I P	52	18.12
E P	83	28.92
E J	100	34.84
S T	48	16.72
S F	63	21.95
N F	138	48.08
N T	38	13.24
S J	84	29.27
S P	27	9.41
N P	108	37.63
N J	68	23.69
T J	60	20.91
T P	26	9.06
F P	109	37.98
F J	92	32.06
I N	60	20.91
E N	116	40.42
I S	44	15.33
E S	67	23.34
E T	57	19.86
E F	126	43.90
I F	75	26.13
I T	29	10.10
S dom	49	17.07
N dom	86	29.97
T dom	47	16.38
F dom	105	36.59

ISTJ N= 16, %= 5.57
ISFJ N= 17, %= 5.92
INFJ N= 14, %= 4.88
INTJ N= 5, %= 1.74
ISTP N= 4, %= 1.39
ISFP N= 7, %= 2.44
INFP N= 37, %= 12.89
INTP N= 4, %= 1.39
ESTP N= 4, %= 1.39
ESFP N= 12, %= 4.18
ENFP N= 53, %= 18.47
ENTP N= 14, %= 4.88
ESTJ N= 24, %= 8.36
ESFJ N= 27, %= 9.41
ENFJ N= 34, %= 11.85
ENTJ N= 15, %= 5.23

Note: ■ = 1% of sample   8623175

Subjects in this sample came from four main sources and were originally compiled especially for publication in:
McCaulley, M. H. (1978). Application of the Myers-Briggs Type Indicator to medicine and other health professions (Monograph I, Contract No. 231-76-0051, Health Resources Administration, DHEW). Gainesville, FL: Center for Applications of Psychological Type.
The four sources used were: 1) the CAPT health databank in 1977, 2) data solicited from medical and health professionals through advertising and personal communication, 3) the Myers Longitudinal Medical Sample initially collected in the 1950s and followed up in the 1970s and 4) data extracted from published research up to that time.

Counselors: Suicide and Crisis

N = 262

	SENSING		INTUITION	
	THINKING	FEELING	FEELING	THINKING

ISTJ	ISFJ	INFJ	INTJ
N= 9	N= 14	N= 25	N= 7
%= 3.44	%= 5.34	%= 9.54	%= 2.67
■■■	■■■■■	■■■■■■■■■■	■■■

ISTP	ISFP	INFP	INTP
N= 1	N= 2	N= 41	N= 17
%= .38	%= .76	%= 15.65	%= 6.49
	■	■■■■■■■■■■ ■■■■■■	■■■■■■

ESTP	ESFP	ENFP	ENTP
N= 4	N= 6	N= 45	N= 16
%= 1.53	%= 2.29	%= 17.18	%= 6.11
■■	■■	■■■■■■■■■■■ ■■■■■■■	■■■■■■

ESTJ	ESFJ	ENFJ	ENTJ
N= 8	N= 17	N= 33	N= 17
%= 3.05	%= 6.49	%= 12.60	%= 6.49
■■■	■■■■■■	■■■■■■■■■■■■ ■■■	■■■■■■

JUDGMENT / PERCEPTION — INTROVERSION
PERCEPTION / JUDGMENT — EXTRAVERSION

	N	%
E	146	55.73
I	116	44.27
S	61	23.28
N	201	76.72
T	79	30.15
F	183	69.85
J	130	49.62
P	132	50.38
I J	55	20.99
I P	61	23.28
E P	71	27.10
E J	75	28.63
S T	22	8.40
S F	39	14.89
N F	144	54.96
N T	57	21.76
S J	48	18.32
S P	13	4.96
N P	119	45.42
N J	82	31.30
T J	41	15.65
T P	38	14.50
F P	94	35.88
F J	89	33.97
I N	90	34.35
E N	111	42.37
I S	26	9.92
E S	35	13.36
E T	45	17.18
E F	101	38.55
I F	82	31.30
I T	34	12.98
S dom	33	12.60
N dom	93	35.50
T dom	43	16.41
F dom	93	35.50

Note: ■ = 1% of sample   8708301

Data collected by Gerald Macdaid at the Alachua County Crisis Center from January 1984 to April 1987. Subjects were approximately 40% male and 60% female volunteer phone counselors, ranging in age from 18 to 65, with the modal age being 21. This sample was 100% of the volunteers who successfully completed 50 hours of suicide and crisis intervention training and 10 hours of supervised probationary telephone counseling in a county agency crisis center located in a moderately sized university city in north central Florida. These data are used with permission and have not been published elsewhere to date.

Counselors: Vocational and Educational

N = 673

	SENSING		INTUITION	
	THINKING	FEELING	FEELING	THINKING

ISTJ	ISFJ	INFJ	INTJ
N= 50	N= 43	N= 34	N= 21
%= 7.43	%= 6.39	%= 5.05	%= 3.12
■■■■■■■	■■■■■■	■■■■■	■■■

ISTP	ISFP	INFP	INTP
N= 10	N= 15	N= 76	N= 24
%= 1.49	%= 2.23	%= 11.29	%= 3.57
■	■■	■■■■■■■■■■	■■■■
		■	

ESTP	ESFP	ENFP	ENTP
N= 7	N= 26	N= 113	N= 32
%= 1.04	%= 3.86	%= 16.79	%= 4.75
■	■■■■	■■■■■■■■■■	■■■■■
		■■■■■■■	

ESTJ	ESFJ	ENFJ	ENTJ
N= 58	N= 51	N= 73	N= 40
%= 8.62	%= 7.58	%= 10.85	%= 5.94
■■■■■■■■	■■■■■■■■	■■■■■■■■■■	■■■■■■
		■	

JUDGMENT — INTROVERSION — PERCEPTION — PERCEPTION — EXTRAVERSION — JUDGMENT

	N	%
E	400	59.44
I	273	40.56
S	260	38.63
N	413	61.37
T	242	35.96
F	431	64.04
J	370	54.98
P	303	45.02
I J	148	21.99
I P	125	18.57
E P	178	26.45
E J	222	32.99
S T	125	18.57
S F	135	20.06
N F	296	43.98
N T	117	17.38
S J	202	30.01
S P	58	8.62
N P	245	36.40
N J	168	24.96
T J	169	25.11
T P	73	10.85
F P	230	34.18
F J	201	29.87
I N	155	23.03
E N	258	38.34
I S	118	17.53
E S	142	21.10
E T	137	20.36
E F	263	39.08
I F	168	24.96
I T	105	15.60
S dom	126	18.72
N dom	200	29.72
T dom	132	19.61
F dom	215	31.95

Note: ■ = 1% of sample   8629450

This table is one of a series of tables from the CAPT-MBTI Data Bank of MBTI records submitted to CAPT for computer scoring between 1971 and June, 1984. This sample was drawn from 59,784 records with usable occupational codes from the total data bank of 232,557. This data bank has 51% Form F cases from 1971 to March, 1978, 35% Form F cases from 1978 to June, 1984 and 14% Form G cases from 1978 to December, 1982. An analysis of Form F and G data banks showed the data banks were comprised of 56% females and 44% males; education level completed: 6% some grade school, 30% high school diploma, 25% some college, 18% bachelor degrees, 11% masters degrees, 3% doctoral or post doctoral work, and 6% unknown. Age group percentages were: 11% under 18, 29% 18 to 20, 12% 21 to 24, 10% 25 to 29, 16% 30 to 39, 10% 40 to 49, 5% 50 to 59, 2% 60 plus, and 5% unknown.

Psychologists

N = 289

	SENSING		INTUITION			N	%

<table>
<tr><td colspan="2" align="center">SENSING</td><td colspan="2" align="center">INTUITION</td></tr>
<tr><td align="center">THINKING</td><td align="center">FEELING</td><td align="center">FEELING</td><td align="center">THINKING</td></tr>
<tr>
<td>ISTJ
N= 12
%= 4.15
■■■■</td>
<td>ISFJ
N= 10
%= 3.46
■■■</td>
<td>INFJ
N= 20
%= 6.92
■■■■■■■</td>
<td>INTJ
N= 18
%= 6.23
■■■■■■</td>
</tr>
<tr>
<td>ISTP
N= 7
%= 2.42
■■</td>
<td>ISFP
N= 5
%= 1.73
■■</td>
<td>INFP
N= 52
%= 17.99
■■■■■■■■■■
■■■■■■■■</td>
<td>INTP
N= 23
%= 7.96
■■■■■■■■</td>
</tr>
<tr>
<td>ESTP
N= 2
%= .69
■</td>
<td>ESFP
N= 6
%= 2.08
■■</td>
<td>ENFP
N= 44
%= 15.22
■■■■■■■■■■
■■■■■</td>
<td>ENTP
N= 22
%= 7.61
■■■■■■■■</td>
</tr>
<tr>
<td>ESTJ
N= 11
%= 3.81
■■■■</td>
<td>ESFJ
N= 3
%= 1.04
■</td>
<td>ENFJ
N= 28
%= 9.69
■■■■■■■■■</td>
<td>ENTJ
N= 26
%= 9.00
■■■■■■■■■</td>
</tr>
</table>

	N	%
E	142	49.13
I	147	50.87
S	56	19.38
N	233	80.62
T	121	41.87
F	168	58.13
J	128	44.29
P	161	55.71
I J	60	20.76
I P	87	30.10
E P	74	25.61
E J	68	23.53
ST	32	11.07
SF	24	8.30
NF	144	49.83
NT	89	30.80
S J	36	12.46
S P	20	6.92
NP	141	48.79
NJ	92	31.83
T J	67	23.18
T P	54	18.69
F P	107	37.02
F J	61	21.11
IN	113	39.10
EN	120	41.52
I S	34	11.76
ES	22	7.61
ET	61	21.11
EF	81	28.03
I F	87	30.10
I T	60	20.76
S dom	30	10.38
N dom	104	35.99
T dom	67	23.18
F dom	88	30.45

Note: ■ = 1% of sample   8623173

Subjects in this sample came from four main sources and were originally compiled especially for publication in:
McCaulley, M. H. (1978). Application of the Myers-Briggs Type Indicator to medicine and other health professions (Monograph I, Contract No. 231-76-0051, Health Resources Administration, DHEW). Gainesville, FL: Center for Applications of Psychological Type.
The four sources used were: 1) the CAPT health databank in 1977, 2) data solicited from medical and health professionals through advertising and personal communication, 3) the Myers Longitudinal Medical Sample initially collected in the 1950s and followed up in the 1970s and 4) data extracted from published research up to that time.

208

Social Workers

N = 479

	SENSING		INTUITION				N	%
	THINKING	FEELING	FEELING	THINKING				

ISTJ	ISFJ	INFJ	INTJ
N= 41	N= 38	N= 39	N= 21
%= 8.56	%= 7.93	%= 8.14	%= 4.38
■■■■■■■■■	■■■■■■■■	■■■■■■■■	■■■■

ISTP	ISFP	INFP	INTP
N= 5	N= 12	N= 55	N= 24
%= 1.04	%= 2.51	%= 11.48	%= 5.01
■	■■■	■■■■■■■■■■■ ■	■■■■■

ESTP	ESFP	ENFP	ENTP
N= 7	N= 22	N= 73	N= 22
%= 1.46	%= 4.59	%= 15.24	%= 4.59
■	■■■■■	■■■■■■■■■■■ ■■■■■	■■■■■

ESTJ	ESFJ	ENFJ	ENTJ
N= 30	N= 31	N= 37	N= 22
%= 6.26	%= 6.47	%= 7.72	%= 4.59
■■■■■■	■■■■■■	■■■■■■■■	■■■■■

JUDGMENT — INTROVERSION — PERCEPTION — PERCEPTION — EXTRAVERSION — JUDGMENT

	N	%
E	244	50.94
I	235	49.06
S	186	38.83
N	293	61.17
T	172	35.91
F	307	64.09
J	259	54.07
P	220	45.93
I J	139	29.02
I P	96	20.04
E P	124	25.89
E J	120	25.05
S T	83	17.33
S F	103	21.50
N F	204	42.59
N T	89	18.58
S J	140	29.23
S P	46	9.60
N P	174	36.33
N J	119	24.84
T J	114	23.80
T P	58	12.11
F P	162	33.82
F J	145	30.27
I N	139	29.02
E N	154	32.15
I S	96	20.04
E S	90	18.79
E T	81	16.91
E F	163	34.03
I F	144	30.06
I T	91	19.00
S dom	108	22.55
N dom	155	32.36
T dom	81	16.91
F dom	135	28.18

Note: ■ = 1% of sample   8629449

This table is one of a series of tables from the CAPT-MBTI Data Bank of MBTI records submitted to CAPT for computer scoring between 1971 and June, 1984. This sample was drawn from 59,784 records with usable occupational codes from the total data bank of 232,557. This data bank has 51% Form F cases from 1971 to March, 1978, 35% Form F cases from 1978 to June, 1984 and 14% Form G cases from 1978 to December, 1982. An analysis of Form F and G data banks showed the data banks were comprised of 56% females and 44% males; education level completed: 6% some grade school, 30% high school diploma, 25% some college, 18% bachelor degrees, 11% masters degrees, 3% doctoral or post doctoral work, and 6% unknown. Age group percentages were: 11% under 18, 29% 18 to 20, 12% 21 to 24, 10% 25 to 29, 16% 30 to 39, 10% 40 to 49, 5% 50 to 59, 2% 60 plus, and 5% unknown.

COUNSELORS

N = 1803

	SENSING		INTUITION	
	THINKING	FEELING	FEELING	THINKING

ISTJ	ISFJ	INFJ	INTJ
N= 121	N= 111	N= 109	N= 66
%= 6.71	%= 6.16	%= 6.05	%= 3.66
■■■■■■■	■■■■■■	■■■■■■	■■■■

ISTP	ISFP	INFP	INTP
N= 35	N= 52	N= 215	N= 62
%= 1.94	%= 2.88	%= 11.92	%= 3.44
■■	■■■	■■■■■■■■■■ ■■	■■■

ESTP	ESFP	ENFP	ENTP
N= 28	N= 71	N= 319	N= 82
%= 1.55	%= 3.94	%= 17.69	%= 4.55
■■	■■■■	■■■■■■■■■■ ■■■■■■■■	■■■■■

ESTJ	ESFJ	ENFJ	ENTJ
N= 129	N= 127	N= 183	N= 93
%= 7.15	%= 7.04	%= 10.15	%= 5.16
■■■■■■■	■■■■■■■	■■■■■■■■■■	■■■■■

JUDGMENT / PERCEPTION / INTROVERSION

PERCEPTION / JUDGMENT / EXTRAVERSION

	N	%
E	1032	57.24
I	771	42.76
S	674	37.38
N	1129	62.62
T	616	34.17
F	1187	65.83
J	939	52.08
P	864	47.92
I J	407	22.57
I P	364	20.19
E P	500	27.73
E J	532	29.51
S T	313	17.36
S F	361	20.02
N F	826	45.81
N T	303	16.81
S J	488	27.07
S P	186	10.32
N P	678	37.60
N J	451	25.01
T J	409	22.68
T P	207	11.48
F P	657	36.44
F J	530	29.40
I N	452	25.07
E N	677	37.55
I S	319	17.69
E S	355	19.69
E T	332	18.41
E F	700	38.82
I F	487	27.01
I T	284	15.75
S dom	331	18.36
N dom	576	31.95
T dom	319	17.69
F dom	577	32.00

Note: ■ = 1% of sample

8629454

This table is one of a series of tables from the CAPT-MBTI Data Bank of MBTI records submitted to CAPT for computer scoring between 1971 and June, 1984. This sample was drawn from 59,784 records with usable occupational codes from the total data bank of 232,557. This data bank has 51% Form F cases from 1971 to March, 1978, 35% Form F cases from 1978 to June, 1984 and 14% Form G cases from 1978 to December, 1982. An analysis of Form F and G data banks showed the data banks were comprised of 56% females and 44% males; education level completed: 6% some grade school, 30% high school diploma, 25% some college, 18% bachelor degrees, 11% masters degrees, 3% doctoral or post doctoral work, and 6% unknown. Age group percentages were: 11% under 18, 29% 18 to 20, 12% 21 to 24, 10% 25 to 29, 16% 30 to 39, 10% 40 to 49, 5% 50 to 59, 2% 60 plus, and 5% unknown.

PSYCHOLOGISTS

N = 402

	SENSING		INTUITION	
	THINKING	FEELING	FEELING	THINKING

ISTJ	ISFJ	INFJ	INTJ
N= 12	N= 10	N= 28	N= 43
%= 2.99	%= 2.49	%= 6.97	%= 10.70
■■■	■■	■■■■■■■	■■■■■■■■■■■ ■

ISTP	ISFP	INFP	INTP
N= 6	N= 5	N= 59	N= 34
%= 1.49	%= 1.24	%= 14.68	%= 8.46
■	■	■■■■■■■■■ ■■■■■	■■■■■■■■

ESTP	ESFP	ENFP	ENTP
N= 2	N= 5	N= 74	N= 24
%= .50	%= 1.24	%= 18.41	%= 5.97
	■	■■■■■■■■■■ ■■■■■■■■	■■■■■■

ESTJ	ESFJ	ENFJ	ENTJ
N= 11	N= 9	N= 33	N= 47
%= 2.74	%= 2.24	%= 8.21	%= 11.69
■■■	■■	■■■■■■■■	■■■■■■■■■■■ ■■

Right side labels: JUDGMENT / INTROVERSION / PERCEPTION / PERCEPTION / EXTRAVERSION / JUDGMENT

	N	%
E	205	51.00
I	197	49.00
S	60	14.93
N	342	85.07
T	179	44.53
F	223	55.47
J	193	48.01
P	209	51.99
I J	93	23.13
I P	104	25.87
E P	105	26.12
E J	100	24.88
S T	31	7.71
S F	29	7.21
N F	194	48.26
N T	148	36.82
S J	42	10.45
S P	18	4.48
N P	191	47.51
N J	151	37.56
T J	113	28.11
T P	66	16.42
F P	143	35.57
F J	80	19.90
I N	164	40.80
E N	178	44.28
I S	33	8.21
E S	27	6.72
E T	84	20.90
E F	121	30.10
I F	102	25.37
I T	95	23.63
S dom	29	7.21
N dom	169	42.04
T dom	98	24.38
F dom	106	26.37

Note: ■ = 1% of sample   8629455

This table is one of a series of tables from the CAPT-MBTI Data Bank of MBTI records submitted to CAPT for computer scoring between 1971 and June, 1984. This sample was drawn from 59,784 records with usable occupational codes from the total data bank of 232,557. This data bank has 51% Form F cases from 1971 to March, 1978, 35% Form F cases from 1978 to June, 1984 and 14% Form G cases from 1978 to December, 1982. An analysis of Form F and G data banks showed the data banks were comprised of 56% females and 44% males; education level completed: 6% some grade school, 30% high school diploma, 25% some college, 18% bachelor degrees, 11% masters degrees, 3% doctoral or post doctoral work, and 6% unknown. Age group percentages were: 11% under 18, 29% 18 to 20, 12% 21 to 24, 10% 25 to 29, 16% 30 to 39, 10% 40 to 49, 5% 50 to 59, 2% 60 plus, and 5% unknown.

SOCIAL SCIENTISTS

N = 490

	SENSING		INTUITION	
	THINKING	FEELING	FEELING	THINKING

ISTJ	ISFJ	INFJ	INTJ
N= 20	N= 12	N= 35	N= 52
%= 4.08	%= 2.45	%= 7.14	%= 10.61
■■■■	■■	■■■■■■■	■■■■■■■■■■ ■

ISTP	ISFP	INFP	INTP
N= 7	N= 9	N= 68	N= 44
%= 1.43	%= 1.84	%= 13.88	%= 8.98
■	■■	■■■■■■■■■■ ■■■■	■■■■■■■■■

ESTP	ESFP	ENFP	ENTP
N= 3	N= 8	N= 82	N= 27
%= .61	%= 1.63	%= 16.73	%= 5.51
■	■■	■■■■■■■■■■ ■■■■■■■	■■■■■■

ESTJ	ESFJ	ENFJ	ENTJ
N= 14	N= 14	N= 38	N= 57
%= 2.86	%= 2.86	%= 7.76	%= 11.63
■■■	■■■	■■■■■■■■	■■■■■■■■■■ ■■

JUDGMENT — INTROVERSION
PERCEPTION — INTROVERSION
PERCEPTION — EXTRAVERSION
JUDGMENT — EXTRAVERSION

	N	%
E	243	49.59
I	247	50.41
S	87	17.76
N	403	82.24
T	224	45.71
F	266	54.29
J	242	49.39
P	248	50.61
I J	119	24.29
I P	128	26.12
E P	120	24.49
E J	123	25.10
S T	44	8.98
S F	43	8.78
N F	223	45.51
N T	180	36.73
S J	60	12.24
S P	27	5.51
N P	221	45.10
N J	182	37.14
T J	143	29.18
T P	81	16.53
F P	167	34.08
F J	99	20.20
I N	199	40.61
E N	204	41.63
I S	48	9.80
E S	39	7.96
E T	101	20.61
E F	142	28.98
I F	124	25.31
I T	123	25.10
S dom	43	8.78
N dom	196	40.00
T dom	122	24.90
F dom	129	26.33

Note: ■ = 1% of sample   8629456

This table is one of a series of tables from the CAPT-MBTI Data Bank of MBTI records submitted to CAPT for computer scoring between 1971 and June, 1984. This sample was drawn from 59,784 records with usable occupational codes from the total data bank of 232,557. This data bank has 51% Form F cases from 1971 to March, 1978, 35% Form F cases from 1978 to June, 1984 and 14% Form G cases from 1978 to December, 1982. An analysis of Form F and G data banks showed the data banks were comprised of 56% females and 44% males; education level completed: 6% some grade school, 30% high school diploma, 25% some college, 18% bachelor degrees, 11% masters degrees, 3% doctoral or post doctoral work, and 6% unknown. Age group percentages were: 11% under 18, 29% 18 to 20, 12% 21 to 24, 10% 25 to 29, 16% 30 to 39, 10% 40 to 49, 5% 50 to 59, 2% 60 plus, and 5% unknown.

EXTRAVERT-INTROVERT

E Percent	I	Total Sample Size	Sample Description
64.71	35.29	170	Certified Psychodramatists
64.41	35.59	177	College and University Resident Assistants
63.76	36.24	287	Counselors: School
61.54	38.46	169	Composite of Practitioners in Social Work
59.44	40.56	673	Counselors: Vocational and Educational
57.24	42.76	1803	COUNSELORS
56.01	43.99	932	Counselors: General
55.93	44.07	177	Counselors: Rehabilitation
55.73	44.27	262	Counselors: Suicide and Crisis
55.71	44.29	359	Counselors: General
51.28	48.72	117	Counselors: Runaway Youth
51.00	49.00	402	PSYCHOLOGISTS
50.94	49.06	479	Social Workers
49.59	50.41	490	SOCIAL SCIENTISTS
49.13	50.87	289	Psychologists

SENSING-INTUITION

S Percent	N	Total Sample Size	Sample Description
41.81	58.19	177	Counselors: Rehabilitation
38.83	61.17	479	Social Workers
38.68	61.32	287	Counselors: School
38.63	61.37	673	Counselors: Vocational and Educational
37.85	62.15	177	College and University Resident Assistants
37.38	62.62	1803	COUNSELORS
35.84	64.16	932	Counselors: General
32.87	67.13	359	Counselors: General
30.77	69.23	169	Composite of Practitioners in Social Work
29.91	70.09	117	Counselors: Runaway Youth
23.28	76.72	262	Counselors: Suicide and Crisis
19.38	80.62	289	Psychologists
17.76	82.24	490	SOCIAL SCIENTISTS
14.93	85.07	402	PSYCHOLOGISTS
12.94	87.06	170	Certified Psychodramatists

THINKING-FEELING

T Percent	F	Total Sample Size	Sample Description
45.71	54.29	490	SOCIAL SCIENTISTS
44.53	55.47	402	PSYCHOLOGISTS
41.87	58.13	289	Psychologists
36.16	63.84	177	College and University Resident Assistants
35.96	64.04	673	Counselors: Vocational and Educational
35.91	64.09	479	Social Workers
34.17	65.83	1803	COUNSELORS
33.33	66.67	177	Counselors: Rehabilitation
33.26	66.74	932	Counselors: General
30.15	69.85	262	Counselors: Suicide and Crisis
29.97	70.03	287	Counselors: School
28.40	71.60	169	Composite of Practitioners in Social Work
27.65	72.35	170	Certified Psychodramatists
26.50	73.50	117	Counselors: Runaway Youth
23.68	76.32	359	Counselors: General

JUDGMENT-PERCEPTION

J Percent	P	Total Sample Size	Sample Description
54.98	45.02	673	Counselors: Vocational and Educational
54.80	45.20	177	College and University Resident Assistants
54.07	45.93	479	Social Workers
52.96	47.04	287	Counselors: School
52.08	47.92	1803	COUNSELORS
51.18	48.82	932	Counselors: General
49.62	50.38	262	Counselors: Suicide and Crisis
49.39	50.61	490	SOCIAL SCIENTISTS
48.01	51.99	402	PSYCHOLOGISTS
47.35	52.65	359	Counselors: General
46.75	53.25	169	Composite of Practitioners in Social Work
46.47	53.53	170	Certified Psychodramatists
44.29	55.71	289	Psychologists
44.07	55.93	177	Counselors: Rehabilitation
36.75	63.25	117	Counselors: Runaway Youth

SENSING-THINKING

Percent ST	Total Sample Size	Sample Description
18.57	673	Counselors: Vocational and Educational
18.08	177	Counselors: Rehabilitation
17.36	1803	COUNSELORS
17.33	479	Social Workers
16.72	287	Counselors: School
16.52	932	Counselors: General
15.25	177	College and University Resident Assistants
14.20	169	Composite of Practitioners in Social Work
13.09	359	Counselors: General
11.07	289	Psychologists
10.26	117	Counselors: Runaway Youth
8.98	490	SOCIAL SCIENTISTS
8.40	262	Counselors: Suicide and Crisis
7.71	402	PSYCHOLOGISTS
4.12	170	Certified Psychodramatists

SENSING-FEELING

Percent SF	Total Sample Size	Sample Description
23.73	177	Counselors: Rehabilitation
22.60	177	College and University Resident Assistants
21.95	287	Counselors: School
21.50	479	Social Workers
20.06	673	Counselors: Vocational and Educational
20.02	1803	COUNSELORS
19.78	359	Counselors: General
19.66	117	Counselors: Runaway Youth
19.31	932	Counselors: General
16.57	169	Composite of Practitioners in Social Work
14.89	262	Counselors: Suicide and Crisis
8.82	170	Certified Psychodramatists
8.78	490	SOCIAL SCIENTISTS
8.30	289	Psychologists
7.21	402	PSYCHOLOGISTS

INTUITION-FEELING

Percent NF	Total Sample Size	Sample Description
63.53	170	Certified Psychodramatists
56.55	359	Counselors: General
55.03	169	Composite of Practitioners in Social Work
54.96	262	Counselors: Suicide and Crisis
53.85	117	Counselors: Runaway Youth
49.83	289	Psychologists
48.26	402	PSYCHOLOGISTS
48.08	287	Counselors: School
47.42	932	Counselors: General
45.81	1803	COUNSELORS
45.51	490	SOCIAL SCIENTISTS
43.98	673	Counselors: Vocational and Educational
42.94	177	Counselors: Rehabilitation
42.59	479	Social Workers
41.24	177	College and University Resident Assistants

INTUITION-THINKING

Percent NT	Total Sample Size	Sample Description
36.82	402	PSYCHOLOGISTS
36.73	490	SOCIAL SCIENTISTS
30.80	289	Psychologists
23.53	170	Certified Psychodramatists
21.76	262	Counselors: Suicide and Crisis
20.90	177	College and University Resident Assistants
18.58	479	Social Workers
17.38	673	Counselors: Vocational and Educational
16.81	1803	COUNSELORS
16.74	932	Counselors: General
16.24	117	Counselors: Runaway Youth
15.25	177	Counselors: Rehabilitation
14.20	169	Composite of Practitioners in Social Work
13.24	287	Counselors: School
10.58	359	Counselors: General

EDUCATION

Section V

EDUCATION

Samples in Section V

Name of Sample	Number in Sample
Administrators: Canadian Schools	124
Administrators: Colleges and Technical Institutes	341
Administrators: Educationally Related	122
Administrators: Elementary and Secondary School	1024
Administrators: Student Personnel	51
Consultants: Education	54
School Principals	276
Teacher Aides (except school monitors)	432
Teachers: Adult Education	228
Teachers: Art, Drama and Music	213
Teachers: Coaching	164
Teachers: College Faculty Named as Danforth Associates	705
Teachers: Elementary School	200
Teachers: Elementary School	804
Teachers: English	179
Teachers: Foreign Language in Jr and Sr High School	67
Teachers: Grades 1 through 9, Canada	169
Teachers: Health	223
Teachers: High School	649
Teachers: Junior College	561
Teachers: Mathematics	71
Teachers: Mathematics	413
Teachers: Middle and Junior High School	1128
Teachers: Pre-school	100
Teachers: Reading	96
Teachers: School Grades 1 through 12	281
Teachers: Special Education	173
Teachers: Speech Pathology and Therapy	157
Teachers: Supervising Student Teachers	113
Teachers: Trade, Industrial and Technical	119
Teachers: University	2282
Teaching Assistants	172

Composite Samples

ADMINISTRATORS	1857
TEACHERS	16676

Comments

The educators in this section come mainly from the MBTI Data Bank. The samples were divided by the level taught, and by subject matter. Administrators are reported separately from teachers.

You will find that all MBTI types enter teaching, but not in equal numbers. All MBTI types need to learn. We do not yet know when students learn better from a teacher of a similar type, and when students' minds need to be stretched by teachers very different from themselves. It is useful to look at the teacher tables with two different questions in mind:

1. What types are more or less frequent among teachers in this table?

2. What types of students will be more or less likely to find "kindred spirits" among these teachers?

Teaching requires both extraversion to interact with the class, and introversion to convey ideas and concepts. Despite the extraverted bias of our culture, you can expect to find substantial numbers of introverts in teaching samples. Most of the samples show the E's and I's within 5% of a 50-50 division. Keep in mind the fact that S's account for about 75% of the population, but that relatively more intuitives seek higher education. Since teachers have achieved higher degrees, you will not expect many teacher samples to show 75% sensing types. Look also to see if there are more S's teaching at the lower grades and more N's at the higher grades and in college. Look for teachers of applied subjects to have more S's and teachers of more theoretical or abstract subjects to have more N's.

Look for most samples of teachers to have a majority of feeling types, and for most samples of administrators to have a majority of thinking types. Teachers of the lower grades and teachers of fields where communication is important are particularly likely to have high numbers of feeling types. Teachers of mathematics and sciences often have relatively more thinking types; however, consider that in any field heavily weighted with T's, the F's in that field may be more likely to gravitate into teaching with its human relations and communication challenges, and to leave the actual practice of their science to the T's who enjoy the challenge of logical and analytical work.

You will see that both educational administrators and teachers clearly have more J's than P's. The Manual (page 128) reports on students in alternative programs; significant numbers of these students are perceptive types, especially the EP's and SP's. These perceptive students have fewer teachers of like mind

223

than do judging types.

Administrators in Section V can be compared to managers in Section III.

Summary listings of tables for EI, SN, TF, JP, ST, SF, NF and NT will be found after the last type table.

Administrators: Canadian Schools

	SENSING		INTUITION	
	THINKING	FEELING	FEELING	THINKING

ISTJ	ISFJ	INFJ	INTJ
N= 14	N= 12	N= 9	N= 10
%= 11.29	%= 9.68	%= 7.26	%= 8.06
■■■■■■■■■■■	■■■■■■■■■■	■■■■■■■	■■■■■■■■
■			

ISTP	ISFP	INFP	INTP
N= 0	N= 1	N= 3	N= 1
%= 0.00	%= .81	%= 2.42	%= .81
	■	■■	■

ESTP	ESFP	ENFP	ENTP
N= 1	N= 3	N= 6	N= 2
%= .81	%= 2.42	%= 4.84	%= 1.61
■	■■	■■■■■	■■

ESTJ	ESFJ	ENFJ	ENTJ
N= 27	N= 15	N= 7	N= 13
%= 21.77	%= 12.10	%= 5.65	%= 10.48
■■■■■■■■■■	■■■■■■■■■■	■■■■■■	■■■■■■■■■■
■■■■■■■■■	■■		
■■			

JUDGMENT — INTROVERSION — PERCEPTION
PERCEPTION — EXTRAVERSION — JUDGMENT

	N	%
E	74	59.68
I	50	40.32
S	73	58.87
N	51	41.13
T	68	54.84
F	56	45.16
J	107	86.29
P	17	13.71
I J	45	36.29
I P	5	4.03
E P	12	9.68
E J	62	50.00
S T	42	33.87
S F	31	25.00
N F	25	20.16
N T	26	20.97
S J	68	54.84
S P	5	4.03
N P	12	9.68
N J	39	31.45
T J	64	51.61
T P	4	3.23
F P	13	10.48
F J	43	34.68
I N	23	18.55
E N	28	22.58
I S	27	21.77
E S	46	37.10
E T	43	34.68
E F	31	25.00
I F	25	20.16
I T	25	20.16
S dom	30	24.19
N dom	27	21.77
T dom	41	33.06
F dom	26	20.97

Note: ■ = 1% of sample   8623122

Data collected by Erich A. von Fange during May and July of 1960 using Form E. The subjects were males: 58 school principals and 66 superintendents in Canada. The principals were a composite of 44 of a group attending a leadership conference and 12 from other places. Ages ranged from 23 to 64, median age 41.5; 14% had masters degrees, 74% had bachelors degrees, 10% had no formal degree and 2% unknown; median experience was 16 years. The superintendents, attending a short course, were 6.8% of all positions listed at the time. Ages ranged from 28 to 63, median 48; 36% had one or more graduate degrees, 59% one or more bachelors degrees and 3% no formal degree; median experience 26 years. These data are used with permission and were cited in: Von Fange, E. A. (1961). Implications for school administration of the personality structure of educational personnel. Unpublished doctoral dissertation, University of Alberta.

N = 341

	SENSING		INTUITION	
	THINKING	FEELING	FEELING	THINKING

ISTJ	ISFJ	INFJ	INTJ
N= 35	N= 18	N= 24	N= 29
%= 10.26	%= 5.28	%= 7.04	%= 8.50
■■■■■■■■■■	■■■■■	■■■■■■■	■■■■■■■■■

ISTP	ISFP	INFP	INTP
N= 6	N= 2	N= 22	N= 18
%= 1.76	%= .59	%= 6.45	%= 5.28
■■	■	■■■■■■	■■■■■

ESTP	ESFP	ENFP	ENTP
N= 8	N= 8	N= 32	N= 14
%= 2.35	%= 2.35	%= 9.38	%= 4.11
■■	■■	■■■■■■■■■	■■■■

ESTJ	ESFJ	ENFJ	ENTJ
N= 34	N= 18	N= 24	N= 49
%= 9.97	%= 5.28	%= 7.04	%= 14.37
■■■■■■■■■■	■■■■■	■■■■■■■	■■■■■■■■■■■■■■ ■■■■

JUDGMENT / INTROVERSION / PERCEPTION
PERCEPTION / EXTRAVERSION / JUDGMENT

	N	%
E	187	54.84
I	154	45.16
S	129	37.83
N	212	62.17
T	193	56.60
F	148	43.40
J	231	67.74
P	110	32.26
I J	106	31.09
I P	48	14.08
E P	62	18.18
E J	125	36.66
S T	83	24.34
S F	46	13.49
N F	102	29.91
N T	110	32.26
S J	105	30.79
S P	24	7.04
N P	86	25.22
N J	126	36.95
T J	147	43.11
T P	46	13.49
F P	64	18.77
F J	84	24.63
I N	93	27.27
E N	119	34.90
I S	61	17.89
E S	68	19.94
E T	105	30.79
E F	82	24.05
I F	66	19.35
I T	88	25.81
S dom	69	20.23
N dom	99	29.03
T dom	107	31.38
F dom	66	19.35

Note: ■ = 1% of sample   8629436

This table is one of a series of tables from the CAPT-MBTI Data Bank of MBTI records submitted to CAPT for computer scoring between 1971 and June, 1984. This sample was drawn from 59,784 records with usable occupational codes from the total data bank of 232,557. This data bank has 51% Form F cases from 1971 to March, 1978, 35% Form F cases from 1978 to June, 1984 and 14% Form G cases from 1978 to December, 1982. An analysis of Form F and G data banks showed the data banks were comprised of 56% females and 44% males; education level completed: 6% some grade school, 30% high school diploma, 25% some college, 18% bachelor degrees, 11% masters degrees, 3% doctoral or post doctoral work, and 6% unknown. Age group percentages were: 11% under 18, 29% 18 to 20, 12% 21 to 24, 10% 25 to 29, 16% 30 to 39, 10% 40 to 49, 5% 50 to 59, 2% 60 plus, and 5% unknown.

Administrators: Educationally Related

N = 122

	SENSING		INTUITION				N	%
	THINKING	FEELING	FEELING	THINKING				

ISTJ	ISFJ	INFJ	INTJ
N= 20	N= 7	N= 5	N= 8
%= 16.39	%= 5.74	%= 4.10	%= 6.56
■■■■■■■■■■ ■■■■■	■■■■■■	■■■■	■■■■■■■

ISTP	ISFP	INFP	INTP
N= 4	N= 4	N= 10	N= 5
%= 3.28	%= 3.28	%= 8.20	%= 4.10
■■■	■■■	■■■■■■■■	■■■■

ESTP	ESFP	ENFP	ENTP
N= 2	N= 1	N= 10	N= 4
%= 1.64	%= .82	%= 8.20	%= 3.28
■■	■	■■■■■■■■	■■■

ESTJ	ESFJ	ENFJ	ENTJ
N= 13	N= 8	N= 10	N= 11
%= 10.66	%= 6.56	%= 8.20	%= 9.02
■■■■■■■■■■ ■	■■■■■■■	■■■■■■■■	■■■■■■■■■

	N	%
E	59	48.36
I	63	51.64
S	59	48.36
N	63	51.64
T	67	54.92
F	55	45.08
J	82	67.21
P	40	32.79
I J	40	32.79
I P	23	18.85
E P	17	13.93
E J	42	34.43
S T	39	31.97
S F	20	16.39
N F	35	28.69
N T	28	22.95
S J	48	39.34
S P	11	9.02
N P	29	23.77
N J	34	27.87
T J	52	42.62
T P	15	12.30
F P	25	20.49
F J	30	24.59
I N	28	22.95
E N	35	28.69
I S	35	28.69
E S	24	19.67
E T	30	24.59
E F	29	23.77
I F	26	21.31
I T	37	30.33
S dom	30	24.59
N dom	27	22.13
T dom	33	27.05
F dom	32	26.23

Note: ■ = 1% of sample   8629434

This table is one of a series of tables from the CAPT-MBTI Data Bank of MBTI records submitted to CAPT for computer scoring between 1971 and June, 1984. This sample was drawn from 59,784 records with usable occupational codes from the total data bank of 232,557. This data bank has 51% Form F cases from 1971 to March, 1978, 35% Form F cases from 1978 to June, 1984 and 14% Form G cases from 1978 to December, 1982. An analysis of Form F and G data banks showed the data banks were comprised of 56% females and 44% males; education level completed: 6% some grade school, 30% high school diploma, 25% some college, 18% bachelor degrees, 11% masters degrees, 3% doctoral or post doctoral work, and 6% unknown. Age group percentages were: 11% under 18, 29% 18 to 20, 12% 21 to 24, 10% 25 to 29, 16% 30 to 39, 10% 40 to 49, 5% 50 to 59, 2% 60 plus, and 5% unknown.

227

Administrators: Elementary and Secondary School

N = 1024

	SENSING		INTUITION	
	THINKING	FEELING	FEELING	THINKING

ISTJ	ISFJ	INFJ	INTJ
N= 128	N= 76	N= 40	N= 54
%= 12.50	%= 7.42	%= 3.91	%= 5.27
■■■■■■■■■■	■■■■■■■	■■■■	■■■■■
■■■			

ISTP	ISFP	INFP	INTP
N= 15	N= 27	N= 55	N= 26
%= 1.46	%= 2.64	%= 5.37	%= 2.54
■	■■■	■■■■■	■■■

ESTP	ESFP	ENFP	ENTP
N= 25	N= 28	N= 95	N= 38
%= 2.44	%= 2.73	%= 9.28	%= 3.71
■■	■■■	■■■■■■■■■	■■■■

ESTJ	ESFJ	ENFJ	ENTJ
N= 135	N= 108	N= 86	N= 88
%= 13.18	%= 10.55	%= 8.40	%= 8.59
■■■■■■■■■■	■■■■■■■■■■	■■■■■■■■	■■■■■■■■■
■■■	■		

JUDGMENT — INTROVERSION — PERCEPTION — PERCEPTION — EXTRAVERSION — JUDGMENT

	N	%
E	603	58.89
I	421	41.11
S	542	52.93
N	482	47.07
T	509	49.71
F	515	50.29
J	715	69.82
P	309	30.18
I J	298	29.10
I P	123	12.01
E P	186	18.16
E J	417	40.72
S T	303	29.59
S F	239	23.34
N F	276	26.95
N T	206	20.12
S J	447	43.65
S P	95	9.28
N P	214	20.90
N J	268	26.17
T J	405	39.55
T P	104	10.16
F P	205	20.02
F J	310	30.27
I N	175	17.09
E N	307	29.98
I S	246	24.02
E S	296	28.91
E T	286	27.93
E F	317	30.96
I F	198	19.34
I T	223	21.78
S dom	257	25.10
N dom	227	22.17
T dom	264	25.78
F dom	276	26.95

Note: ■ = 1% of sample   8629437

This table is one of a series of tables from the CAPT-MBTI Data Bank of MBTI records submitted to CAPT for computer scoring between 1971 and June, 1984. This sample was drawn from 59,784 records with usable occupational codes from the total data bank of 232,557. This data bank has 51% Form F cases from 1971 to March, 1978, 35% Form F cases from 1978 to June, 1984 and 14% Form G cases from 1978 to December, 1982. An analysis of Form F and G data banks showed the data banks were comprised of 56% females and 44% males; education level completed: 6% some grade school, 30% high school diploma, 25% some college, 18% bachelor degrees, 11% masters degrees, 3% doctoral or post doctoral work, and 6% unknown. Age group percentages were: 11% under 18, 29% 18 to 20, 12% 21 to 24, 10% 25 to 29, 16% 30 to 39, 10% 40 to 49, 5% 50 to 59, 2% 60 plus, and 5% unknown.

Administrators: Student Personnel

N = 51

	SENSING		INTUITION	
	THINKING	FEELING	FEELING	THINKING

ISTJ	ISFJ	INFJ	INTJ
N= 6	N= 3	N= 2	N= 4
%= 11.76	%= 5.88	%= 3.92	%= 7.84
■■■■■■■■■■■■	■■■■■■	■■■■	■■■■■■■■
■■			

ISTP	ISFP	INFP	INTP
N= 0	N= 0	N= 4	N= 1
%= 0.00	%= 0.00	%= 7.84	%= 1.96
		■■■■■■■■	■■

ESTP	ESFP	ENFP	ENTP
N= 0	N= 0	N= 8	N= 3
%= 0.00	%= 0.00	%= 15.69	%= 5.88
		■■■■■■■■■■■■■■■	■■■■■■
		■■■■■■	

ESTJ	ESFJ	ENFJ	ENTJ
N= 2	N= 9	N= 4	N= 5
%= 3.92	%= 17.65	%= 7.84	%= 9.80
■■■■	■■■■■■■■■■■■■	■■■■■■■■	■■■■■■■■■■
	■■■■■■■■		

JUDGMENT — INTROVERSION — PERCEPTION — PERCEPTION — EXTRAVERSION — JUDGMENT

	N	%
E	31	60.78
I	20	39.22
S	20	39.22
N	31	60.78
T	21	41.18
F	30	58.82
J	35	68.63
P	16	31.37
I J	15	29.41
I P	5	9.80
E P	11	21.57
E J	20	39.22
S T	8	15.69
S F	12	23.53
N F	18	35.29
N T	13	25.49
S J	20	39.22
S P	0	0.00
N P	16	31.37
N J	15	29.41
T J	17	33.33
T P	4	7.84
F P	12	23.53
F J	18	35.29
I N	11	21.57
E N	20	39.22
I S	9	17.65
E S	11	21.57
E T	10	19.61
E F	21	41.18
I F	9	17.65
I T	11	21.57
S dom	9	17.65
N dom	17	33.33
T dom	8	15.69
F dom	17	33.33

Note: ■ = 1% of sample   8623125

Data collected by David Robertson at Radford University during February 1983 using Form G. Subjects were 47% female and 53% male student personnel administrators from 22 colleges and universities who were attending a workshop on preparing student leadership development programs, held in western Virginia. All administrators had completed masters or doctoral studies. These data are used with permission and have not been published elsewhere to date.

Consultants: Education

	SENSING		INTUITION	
	THINKING	FEELING	FEELING	THINKING

ISTJ	ISFJ	INFJ	INTJ
N= 7	N= 2	N= 8	N= 4
%= 12.96	%= 3.70	%= 14.81	%= 7.41
■■■■■■■■■■■■ ■■■	■■■■	■■■■■■■■■■■■■■ ■■■■■	■■■■■■■

ISTP	ISFP	INFP	INTP
N= 0	N= 2	N= 7	N= 0
%= 0.00	%= 3.70	%= 12.96	%= 0.00
	■■■■	■■■■■■■■■■■■ ■■■	

ESTP	ESFP	ENFP	ENTP
N= 0	N= 1	N= 8	N= 2
%= 0.00	%= 1.85	%= 14.81	%= 3.70
	■■	■■■■■■■■■■■■■■ ■■■■■	■■■■

ESTJ	ESFJ	ENFJ	ENTJ
N= 1	N= 4	N= 1	N= 7
%= 1.85	%= 7.41	%= 1.85	%= 12.96
■■	■■■■■■■	■■	■■■■■■■■■■■■ ■■■

JUDGMENT — INTROVERSION — PERCEPTION — EXTRAVERSION — JUDGMENT

	N	%
E	24	44.44
I	30	55.56
S	17	31.48
N	37	68.52
T	21	38.89
F	33	61.11
J	34	62.96
P	20	37.04
I J	21	38.89
I P	9	16.67
E P	11	20.37
E J	13	24.07
S T	8	14.81
S F	9	16.67
N F	24	44.44
N T	13	24.07
S J	14	25.93
S P	3	5.56
N P	17	31.48
N J	20	37.04
T J	19	35.19
T P	2	3.70
F P	18	33.33
F J	15	27.78
I N	19	35.19
E N	18	33.33
I S	11	20.37
E S	6	11.11
E T	10	18.52
E F	14	25.93
I F	19	35.19
I T	11	20.37
S dom	10	18.52
N dom	22	40.74
T dom	8	14.81
F dom	14	25.93

Note: ■ = 1% of sample   8629432

This table is one of a series of tables from the CAPT-MBTI Data Bank of MBTI records submitted to CAPT for computer scoring between 1971 and June, 1984. This sample was drawn from 59,784 records with usable occupational codes from the total data bank of 232,557. This data bank has 51% Form F cases from 1971 to March, 1978, 35% Form F cases from 1978 to June, 1984 and 14% Form G cases from 1978 to December, 1982. An analysis of Form F and G data banks showed the data banks were comprised of 56% females and 44% males; education level completed: 6% some grade school, 30% high school diploma, 25% some college, 18% bachelor degrees, 11% masters degrees, 3% doctoral or post doctoral work, and 6% unknown. Age group percentages were: 11% under 18, 29% 18 to 20, 12% 21 to 24, 10% 25 to 29, 16% 30 to 39, 10% 40 to 49, 5% 50 to 59, 2% 60 plus, and 5% unknown.

School Principals

N = 276

	SENSING		INTUITION	
	THINKING	FEELING	FEELING	THINKING

ISTJ	ISFJ	INFJ	INTJ
N= 70	N= 13	N= 6	N= 24
%= 25.36	%= 4.71	%= 2.17	%= 8.70
■■■■■■■■■■	■■■■■	■■	■■■■■■■■■
■■■■■■■■■■			
■■■■■			

ISTP	ISFP	INFP	INTP
N= 7	N= 7	N= 3	N= 3
%= 2.54	%= 2.54	%= 1.09	%= 1.09
■■■	■■■	■	■

ESTP	ESFP	ENFP	ENTP
N= 6	N= 5	N= 6	N= 4
%= 2.17	%= 1.81	%= 2.17	%= 1.45
■■	■■	■■	■

ESTJ	ESFJ	ENFJ	ENTJ
N= 72	N= 15	N= 7	N= 28
%= 26.09	%= 5.43	%= 2.54	%= 10.14
■■■■■■■■■■	■■■■■	■■■	■■■■■■■■■■
■■■■■■■■■■			
■■■■■■			

JUDGMENT — INTROVERSION — PERCEPTION — EXTRAVERSION — JUDGMENT

	N	%
E	143	51.81
I	133	48.19
S	195	70.65
N	81	29.35
T	214	77.54
F	62	22.46
J	235	85.14
P	41	14.86
I J	113	40.94
I P	20	7.25
E P	21	7.61
E J	122	44.20
S T	155	56.16
S F	40	14.49
N F	22	7.97
N T	59	21.38
S J	170	61.59
S P	25	9.06
N P	16	5.80
N J	65	23.55
T J	194	70.29
T P	20	7.25
F P	21	7.61
F J	41	14.86
I N	36	13.04
E N	45	16.30
I S	97	35.14
E S	98	35.51
E T	110	39.86
E F	33	11.96
I F	29	10.51
I T	104	37.68
S dom	94	34.06
N dom	40	14.49
T dom	110	39.86
F dom	32	11.59

Note: ■ = 1% of sample   8623130

Data collected by Ronald G. Lynch of the Institute of Government, University of North Carolina at Chapel Hill from 1984 to 1986 using Form F. Subjects were school principals attending institute programs. The principals were 80% male and 20% female, all were from North Carolina. These data are used with permission and have not been published elsewhere to date.

Teacher Aides (except school monitors)

N = 432

	SENSING		INTUITION				N	%
	THINKING	FEELING	FEELING	THINKING				

ISTJ	ISFJ	INFJ	INTJ
N= 47	N= 84	N= 17	N= 2
%= 10.88	%= 19.44	%= 3.94	%= .46
■■■■■■■■■■	■■■■■■■■■■	■■■■	
■	■■■■■■■■■		

ISTP	ISFP	INFP	INTP
N= 11	N= 26	N= 29	N= 3
%= 2.55	%= 6.02	%= 6.71	%= .69
■■■	■■■■■■	■■■■■■■	■

ESTP	ESFP	ENFP	ENTP
N= 10	N= 21	N= 32	N= 12
%= 2.31	%= 4.86	%= 7.41	%= 2.78
■■	■■■■■	■■■■■■■	■■■

ESTJ	ESFJ	ENFJ	ENTJ
N= 53	N= 60	N= 16	N= 9
%= 12.27	%= 13.89	%= 3.70	%= 2.08
■■■■■■■■■■■■	■■■■■■■■■■■■	■■■■	■■
■■	■■■■		

JUDGMENT — INTROVERSION — PERCEPTION — PERCEPTION — EXTRAVERSION — JUDGMENT

	N	%
E	213	49.31
I	219	50.69
S	312	72.22
N	120	27.78
T	147	34.03
F	285	65.97
J	288	66.67
P	144	33.33
I J	150	34.72
I P	69	15.97
E P	75	17.36
E J	138	31.94
S T	121	28.01
S F	191	44.21
N F	94	21.76
N T	26	6.02
S J	244	56.48
S P	68	15.74
N P	76	17.59
N J	44	10.19
T J	111	25.69
T P	36	8.33
F P	108	25.00
F J	177	40.97
I N	51	11.81
E N	69	15.97
I S	168	38.89
E S	144	33.33
E T	84	19.44
E F	129	29.86
I F	156	36.11
I T	63	14.58
S dom	162	37.50
N dom	63	14.58
T dom	76	17.59
F dom	131	30.32

Note: ■ = 1% of sample   8629433

This table is one of a series of tables from the CAPT-MBTI Data Bank of MBTI records submitted to CAPT for computer scoring between 1971 and June, 1984. This sample was drawn from 59,784 records with usable occupational codes from the total data bank of 232,557. This data bank has 51% Form F cases from 1971 to March, 1978, 35% Form F cases from 1978 to June, 1984 and 14% Form G cases from 1978 to December, 1982. An analysis of Form F and G data banks showed the data banks were comprised of 56% females and 44% males; education level completed: 6% some grade school, 30% high school diploma, 25% some college, 18% bachelor degrees, 11% masters degrees, 3% doctoral or post doctoral work, and 6% unknown. Age group percentages were: 11% under 18, 29% 18 to 20, 12% 21 to 24, 10% 25 to 29, 16% 30 to 39, 10% 40 to 49, 5% 50 to 59, 2% 60 plus, and 5% unknown.

Teachers: Adult Education

N = 228

	SENSING		INTUITION				N	%
	THINKING	FEELING	FEELING	THINKING				

ISTJ	ISFJ	INFJ	INTJ
N= 23	N= 26	N= 7	N= 6
%= 10.09	%= 11.40	%= 3.07	%= 2.63
■■■■■■■■■■	■■■■■■■■■■■	■■■	■■■

ISTP	ISFP	INFP	INTP
N= 10	N= 11	N= 14	N= 4
%= 4.39	%= 4.82	%= 6.14	%= 1.75
■■■■	■■■■■	■■■■■■	■■

ESTP	ESFP	ENFP	ENTP
N= 9	N= 12	N= 19	N= 8
%= 3.95	%= 5.26	%= 8.33	%= 3.51
■■■■	■■■■■	■■■■■■■■	■■■■

ESTJ	ESFJ	ENFJ	ENTJ
N= 26	N= 31	N= 10	N= 12
%= 11.40	%= 13.60	%= 4.39	%= 5.26
■■■■■■■■■■■	■■■■■■■■■■■■■	■■■■	■■■■■

	N	%
E	127	55.70
I	101	44.30
S	148	64.91
N	80	35.09
T	98	42.98
F	130	57.02
J	141	61.84
P	87	38.16
I J	62	27.19
I P	39	17.11
E P	48	21.05
E J	79	34.65
S T	68	29.82
S F	80	35.09
N F	50	21.93
N T	30	13.16
S J	106	46.49
S P	42	18.42
N P	45	19.74
N J	35	15.35
T J	67	29.39
T P	31	13.60
F P	56	24.56
F J	74	32.46
I N	31	13.60
E N	49	21.49
I S	70	30.70
E S	78	34.21
E T	55	24.12
E F	72	31.58
I F	58	25.44
I T	43	18.86
S dom	70	30.70
N dom	40	17.54
T dom	52	22.81
F dom	66	28.95

Note: ■ = 1% of sample   8629414

This table is one of a series of tables from the CAPT-MBTI Data Bank of MBTI records submitted to CAPT for computer scoring between 1971 and June, 1984. This sample was drawn from 59,784 records with usable occupational codes from the total data bank of 232,557. This data bank has 51% Form F cases from 1971 to March, 1978, 35% Form F cases from 1978 to June, 1984 and 14% Form G cases from 1978 to December, 1982. An analysis of Form F and G data banks showed the data banks were comprised of 56% females and 44% males; education level completed: 6% some grade school, 30% high school diploma, 25% some college, 18% bachelor degrees, 11% masters degrees, 3% doctoral or post doctoral work, and 6% unknown. Age group percentages were: 11% under 18, 29% 18 to 20, 12% 21 to 24, 10% 25 to 29, 16% 30 to 39, 10% 40 to 49, 5% 50 to 59, 2% 60 plus, and 5% unknown.

Teachers: Art, Drama and Music

N = 213

	SENSING		INTUITION	
	THINKING	FEELING	FEELING	THINKING

		N	%
E		112	52.58
I		101	47.42
S		62	29.11
N		151	70.89
T		61	28.64
F		152	71.36
J		109	51.17
P		104	48.83
I J		54	25.35
I P		47	22.07
E P		57	26.76
E J		55	25.82
S T		25	11.74
S F		37	17.37
N F		115	53.99
N T		36	16.90
S J		43	20.19
S P		19	8.92
N P		85	39.91
N J		66	30.99
T J		38	17.84
T P		23	10.80
F P		81	38.03
F J		71	33.33
I N		65	30.52
E N		86	40.38
I S		36	16.90
E S		26	12.21
E T		26	12.21
E F		86	40.38
I F		66	30.99
I T		35	16.43
S dom		33	15.49
N dom		78	36.62
T dom		31	14.55
F dom		71	33.33

ISTJ
N= 12
%= 5.63
■■■■■■

ISFJ
N= 13
%= 6.10
■■■■■■

INFJ
N= 20
%= 9.39
■■■■■■■■■

INTJ
N= 9
%= 4.23
■■■■

ISTP
N= 4
%= 1.88
■■

ISFP
N= 7
%= 3.29
■■■

INFP
N= 26
%= 12.21
■■■■■■■■■■
■■

INTP
N= 10
%= 4.69
■■■■■

ESTP
N= 2
%= .94
■

ESFP
N= 6
%= 2.82
■■■

ENFP
N= 42
%= 19.72
■■■■■■■■■■
■■■■■■■■■■

ENTP
N= 7
%= 3.29
■■■

ESTJ
N= 7
%= 3.29
■■■

ESFJ
N= 11
%= 5.16
■■■■■

ENFJ
N= 27
%= 12.68
■■■■■■■■■■
■■■

ENTJ
N= 10
%= 4.69
■■■■■

JUDGMENT — INTROVERSION — PERCEPTION — PERCEPTION — EXTRAVERSION — JUDGMENT

Note: ■ = 1% of sample

8629415

This table is one of a series of tables from the CAPT-MBTI Data Bank of MBTI records submitted to CAPT for computer scoring between 1971 and June, 1984. This sample was drawn from 59,784 records with usable occupational codes from the total data bank of 232,557. This data bank has 51% Form F cases from 1971 to March, 1978, 35% Form F cases from 1978 to June, 1984 and 14% Form G cases from 1978 to December, 1982. An analysis of Form F and G data banks showed the data banks were comprised of 56% females and 44% males; education level completed: 6% some grade school, 30% high school diploma, 25% some college, 18% bachelor degrees, 11% masters degrees, 3% doctoral or post doctoral work, and 6% unknown. Age group percentages were: 11% under 18, 29% 18 to 20, 12% 21 to 24, 10% 25 to 29, 16% 30 to 39, 10% 40 to 49, 5% 50 to 59, 2% 60 plus, and 5% unknown.

N = 164

	SENSING		INTUITION	
	THINKING	FEELING	FEELING	THINKING

ISTJ	ISFJ	INFJ	INTJ
N= 25	N= 17	N= 3	N= 6
%= 15.24	%= 10.37	%= 1.83	%= 3.66
■■■■■■■■■■■■■■■ ■■■■■	■■■■■■■■■■	■■	■■■■

ISTP	ISFP	INFP	INTP
N= 7	N= 6	N= 5	N= 6
%= 4.27	%= 3.66	%= 3.05	%= 3.66
■■■■	■■■■	■■■	■■■■

ESTP	ESFP	ENFP	ENTP
N= 4	N= 13	N= 11	N= 8
%= 2.44	%= 7.93	%= 6.71	%= 4.88
■■	■■■■■■■■	■■■■■■■	■■■■■

ESTJ	ESFJ	ENFJ	ENTJ
N= 25	N= 19	N= 5	N= 4
%= 15.24	%= 11.59	%= 3.05	%= 2.44
■■■■■■■■■■■■■■■ ■■■■■	■■■■■■■■■■■ ■■	■■■	■■

JUDGMENT — INTROVERSION — PERCEPTION
PERCEPTION — EXTRAVERSION — JUDGMENT

	N	%
E	89	54.27
I	75	45.73
S	116	70.73
N	48	29.27
T	85	51.83
F	79	48.17
J	104	63.41
P	60	36.59
I J	51	31.10
I P	24	14.63
E P	36	21.95
E J	53	32.32
S T	61	37.20
S F	55	33.54
N F	24	14.63
N T	24	14.63
S J	86	52.44
S P	30	18.29
N P	30	18.29
N J	18	10.98
T J	60	36.59
T P	25	15.24
F P	35	21.34
F J	44	26.83
I N	20	12.20
E N	28	17.07
I S	55	33.54
E S	61	37.20
E T	41	25.00
E F	48	29.27
I F	31	18.90
I T	44	26.83
S dom	59	35.98
N dom	28	17.07
T dom	42	25.61
F dom	35	21.34

Note: ■ = 1% of sample   8629416

This table is one of a series of tables from the CAPT-MBTI Data Bank of MBTI records submitted to CAPT for computer scoring between 1971 and June, 1984. This sample was drawn from 59,784 records with usable occupational codes from the total data bank of 232,557. This data bank has 51% Form F cases from 1971 to March, 1978, 35% Form F cases from 1978 to June, 1984 and 14% Form G cases from 1978 to December, 1982. An analysis of Form F and G data banks showed the data banks were comprised of 56% females and 44% males; education level completed: 6% some grade school, 30% high school diploma, 25% some college, 18% bachelor degrees, 11% masters degrees, 3% doctoral or post doctoral work, and 6% unknown. Age group percentages were: 11% under 18, 29% 18 to 20, 12% 21 to 24, 10% 25 to 29, 16% 30 to 39, 10% 40 to 49, 5% 50 to 59, 2% 60 plus, and 5% unknown.

Teachers: College Faculty Named as Danforth Associates

N = 705

	SENSING		INTUITION	
	THINKING	FEELING	FEELING	THINKING

ISTJ	ISFJ	INFJ	INTJ
N= 56	N= 30	N= 72	N= 131
%= 7.94	%= 4.26	%= 10.21	%= 18.58
■■■■■■■■	■■■■	■■■■■■■■■■	■■■■■■■■■■■■■■■■■■

ISTP	ISFP	INFP	INTP
N= 9	N= 8	N= 50	N= 43
%= 1.28	%= 1.13	%= 7.09	%= 6.10
■	■	■■■■■■■	■■■■■■

ESTP	ESFP	ENFP	ENTP
N= 3	N= 9	N= 54	N= 36
%= .43	%= 1.28	%= 7.66	%= 5.11
	■	■■■■■■■■	■■■■■

ESTJ	ESFJ	ENFJ	ENTJ
N= 29	N= 28	N= 53	N= 94
%= 4.11	%= 3.97	%= 7.52	%= 13.33
■■■■	■■■■	■■■■■■■■	■■■■■■■■■■■■■

JUDGMENT — INTROVERSION — PERCEPTION — PERCEPTION — EXTRAVERSION — JUDGMENT

	N	%
E	306	43.40
I	399	56.60
S	172	24.40
N	533	75.60
T	401	56.88
F	304	43.12
J	493	69.93
P	212	30.07
I J	289	40.99
I P	110	15.60
E P	102	14.47
E J	204	28.94
S T	97	13.76
S F	75	10.64
N F	229	32.48
N T	304	43.12
S J	143	20.28
S P	29	4.11
N P	183	25.96
N J	350	49.65
T J	310	43.97
T P	91	12.91
F P	121	17.16
F J	183	25.96
I N	296	41.99
E N	237	33.62
I S	103	14.61
E S	69	9.79
E T	162	22.98
E F	144	20.43
I F	160	22.70
I T	239	33.90
S dom	98	13.90
N dom	293	41.56
T dom	175	24.82
F dom	139	19.72

Note: ■ = 1% of sample

8623128

Data collected by Mary McCaulley of CAPT from 1982 to 1985 using Form F. Subjects were university faculty nominated by their peers for teaching excellence to become members of the Danforth Associate Program. Associates were full time undergraduate faculty concerned with scholarship and student development. This sample was composed of associates attending various biennial regional conferences. No gender, race or educational level data were reported. These data are used with permission and have not been published elsewhere to date.

Teachers: Elementary School

	SENSING		INTUITION	
	THINKING	FEELING	FEELING	THINKING

ISTJ	ISFJ	INFJ	INTJ
N= 15	N= 22	N= 15	N= 11
%= 7.50	%= 11.00	%= 7.50	%= 5.50
■■■■■■■	■■■■■■■■■■■ ■	■■■■■■■	■■■■■

ISTP	ISFP	INFP	INTP
N= 5	N= 5	N= 15	N= 4
%= 2.50	%= 2.50	%= 7.50	%= 2.00
■■■	■■■	■■■■■■■	■■

ESTP	ESFP	ENFP	ENTP
N= 0	N= 7	N= 21	N= 8
%= 0.00	%= 3.50	%= 10.50	%= 4.00
	■■■■	■■■■■■■■■■ ■	■■■■

ESTJ	ESFJ	ENFJ	ENTJ
N= 17	N= 24	N= 19	N= 12
%= 8.50	%= 12.00	%= 9.50	%= 6.00
■■■■■■■■	■■■■■■■■■■■ ■■	■■■■■■■■■	■■■■■

JUDGMENT — INTROVERSION — PERCEPTION
PERCEPTION — EXTRAVERSION — JUDGMENT

	N	%
E	108	54.00
I	92	46.00
S	95	47.50
N	105	52.50
T	72	36.00
F	128	64.00
J	135	67.50
P	65	32.50
I J	63	31.50
I P	29	14.50
E P	36	18.00
E J	72	36.00
S T	37	18.50
S F	58	29.00
N F	70	35.00
N T	35	17.50
S J	78	39.00
S P	17	8.50
N P	48	24.00
N J	57	28.50
T J	55	27.50
T P	17	8.50
F P	48	24.00
F J	80	40.00
I N	45	22.50
E N	60	30.00
I S	47	23.50
E S	48	24.00
E T	37	18.50
E F	71	35.50
I F	57	28.50
I T	35	17.50
S dom	44	22.00
N dom	55	27.50
T dom	38	19.00
F dom	63	31.50

Note: ■ = 1% of sample   8623126

Data collected by James A. Collins during 1965 using Form F. The subjects were 200 teachers from a total of 387 in twelve school districts who volunteered to participate. No gender, race or educational level data were reported. The sample was drawn from schools serving areas that were 7% rural, 65% suburban and 28% industrial areas; 15% high, 67% middle and 18% low socio-economic areas. Teachers served grades kindergarten through sixth and participated anonymously. These data are used with permission and were cited in:

Collins, J. A. (1966). Individual personality and organizational climate (Doctoral dissertation, Claremont Graduate School, 1965). Dissertation Abstracts International, 27, 623A. (University Microfilms No. 66-3361)

Teachers: Elementary School

N = 804

<table>
<thead>
<tr><th colspan="2">SENSING</th><th colspan="2">INTUITION</th></tr>
<tr><th>THINKING</th><th>FEELING</th><th>FEELING</th><th>THINKING</th></tr>
</thead>
<tbody>
<tr>
<td>ISTJ
N= 86
%= 10.70
■■■■■■■■■■
■</td>
<td>ISFJ
N= 144
%= 17.91
■■■■■■■■■■
■■■■■■■■</td>
<td>INFJ
N= 41
%= 5.10
■■■■■</td>
<td>INTJ
N= 17
%= 2.11
■■</td>
</tr>
<tr>
<td>ISTP
N= 14
%= 1.74
■■</td>
<td>ISFP
N= 38
%= 4.73
■■■■■</td>
<td>INFP
N= 37
%= 4.60
■■■■■</td>
<td>INTP
N= 12
%= 1.49
■</td>
</tr>
<tr>
<td>ESTP
N= 7
%= .87
■</td>
<td>ESFP
N= 46
%= 5.72
■■■■■■</td>
<td>ENFP
N= 82
%= 10.20
■■■■■■■■■■</td>
<td>ENTP
N= 12
%= 1.49
■</td>
</tr>
<tr>
<td>ESTJ
N= 68
%= 8.46
■■■■■■■■</td>
<td>ESFJ
N= 100
%= 12.44
■■■■■■■■■■
■■</td>
<td>ENFJ
N= 58
%= 7.21
■■■■■■■</td>
<td>ENTJ
N= 42
%= 5.22
■■■■■</td>
</tr>
</tbody>
</table>

JUDGMENT — INTROVERSION — PERCEPTION — PERCEPTION — EXTRAVERSION — JUDGMENT

	N	%
E	415	51.62
I	389	48.38
S	503	62.56
N	301	37.44
T	258	32.09
F	546	67.91
J	556	69.15
P	248	30.85
I J	288	35.82
I P	101	12.56
E P	147	18.28
E J	268	33.33
S T	175	21.77
S F	328	40.80
N F	218	27.11
N T	83	10.32
S J	398	49.50
S P	105	13.06
N P	143	17.79
N J	158	19.65
T J	213	26.49
T P	45	5.60
F P	203	25.25
F J	343	42.66
I N	107	13.31
E N	194	24.13
I S	282	35.07
E S	221	27.49
E T	129	16.04
E F	286	35.57
I F	260	32.34
I T	129	16.04
S dom	283	35.20
N dom	152	18.91
T dom	136	16.92
F dom	233	28.98

Note: ■ = 1% of sample

8629419

This table is one of a series of tables from the CAPT-MBTI Data Bank of MBTI records submitted to CAPT for computer scoring between 1971 and June, 1984. This sample was drawn from 59,784 records with usable occupational codes from the total data bank of 232,557. This data bank has 51% Form F cases from 1971 to March, 1978, 35% Form F cases from 1978 to June, 1984 and 14% Form G cases from 1978 to December, 1982. An analysis of Form F and G data banks showed the data banks were comprised of 56% females and 44% males; education level completed: 6% some grade school, 30% high school diploma, 25% some college, 18% bachelor degrees, 11% masters degrees, 3% doctoral or post doctoral work, and 6% unknown. Age group percentages were: 11% under 18, 29% 18 to 20, 12% 21 to 24, 10% 25 to 29, 16% 30 to 39, 10% 40 to 49, 5% 50 to 59, 2% 60 plus, and 5% unknown.

Teachers: English

N = 179

	SENSING		INTUITION		
	THINKING	FEELING	FEELING	THINKING	

					N	%
ISTJ N= 15 %= 8.38	**ISFJ** N= 18 %= 10.06	**INFJ** N= 18 %= 10.06	**INTJ** N= 10 %= 5.59	JUDGMENT	E 88 49.16	
ISTP N= 4 %= 2.23	**ISFP** N= 2 %= 1.12	**INFP** N= 19 %= 10.61	**INTP** N= 5 %= 2.79	PERCEPTION		
ESTP N= 0 %= 0.00	**ESFP** N= 2 %= 1.12	**ENFP** N= 22 %= 12.29	**ENTP** N= 5 %= 2.79	PERCEPTION		
ESTJ N= 10 %= 5.59	**ESFJ** N= 13 %= 7.26	**ENFJ** N= 21 %= 11.73	**ENTJ** N= 15 %= 8.38	JUDGMENT		

	N	%
E	88	49.16
I	91	50.84
S	64	35.75
N	115	64.25
T	64	35.75
F	115	64.25
J	120	67.04
P	59	32.96
I J	61	34.08
I P	30	16.76
E P	29	16.20
E J	59	32.96
S T	29	16.20
S F	35	19.55
N F	80	44.69
N T	35	19.55
S J	56	31.28
S P	8	4.47
N P	51	28.49
N J	64	35.75
T J	50	27.93
T P	14	7.82
F P	45	25.14
F J	70	39.11
I N	52	29.05
E N	63	35.20
I S	39	21.79
E S	25	13.97
E T	30	16.76
E F	58	32.40
I F	57	31.84
I T	34	18.99
S dom	35	19.55
N dom	55	30.73
T dom	34	18.99
F dom	55	30.73

Note: ■ = 1% of sample   8629417

This table is one of a series of tables from the CAPT-MBTI Data Bank of MBTI records submitted to CAPT for computer scoring between 1971 and June, 1984. This sample was drawn from 59,784 records with usable occupational codes from the total data bank of 232,557. This data bank has 51% Form F cases from 1971 to March, 1978, 35% Form F cases from 1978 to June, 1984 and 14% Form G cases from 1978 to December, 1982. An analysis of Form F and G data banks showed the data banks were comprised of 56% females and 44% males; education level completed: 6% some grade school, 30% high school diploma, 25% some college, 18% bachelor degrees, 11% masters degrees, 3% doctoral or post doctoral work, and 6% unknown. Age group percentages were: 11% under 18, 29% 18 to 20, 12% 21 to 24, 10% 25 to 29, 16% 30 to 39, 10% 40 to 49, 5% 50 to 59, 2% 60 plus, and 5% unknown.

Teachers: Foreign Language in Junior and Senior High School

N = 67

	SENSING		INTUITION				N	%
	THINKING	FEELING	FEELING	THINKING		E	39	58.21

<table>
<tr><th colspan="4">SENSING / INTUITION quadrant</th></tr>
</table>

	SENSING		INTUITION	
	THINKING	FEELING	FEELING	THINKING
JUDGMENT / INTROVERSION	ISTJ N= 6 %= 8.96 ■■■■■■■■■	ISFJ N= 6 %= 8.96 ■■■■■■■■■	INFJ N= 6 %= 8.96 ■■■■■■■■■	INTJ N= 1 %= 1.49 ■
PERCEPTION / INTROVERSION	ISTP N= 1 %= 1.49 ■	ISFP N= 1 %= 1.49 ■	INFP N= 6 %= 8.96 ■■■■■■■■■	INTP N= 1 %= 1.49 ■
PERCEPTION / EXTRAVERSION	ESTP N= 1 %= 1.49 ■	ESFP N= 4 %= 5.97 ■■■■■■	ENFP N= 7 %= 10.45 ■■■■■■■■■■■	ENTP N= 0 %= 0.00
JUDGMENT / EXTRAVERSION	ESTJ N= 7 %= 10.45 ■■■■■■■■■■■	ESFJ N= 10 %= 14.93 ■■■■■■■■■■■ ■■■■■	ENFJ N= 7 %= 10.45 ■■■■■■■■■■■	ENTJ N= 3 %= 4.48 ■■■■

	N	%
E	39	58.21
I	28	41.79
S	36	53.73
N	31	46.27
T	20	29.85
F	47	70.15
J	46	68.66
P	21	31.34
I J	19	28.36
I P	9	13.43
E P	12	17.91
E J	27	40.30
S T	15	22.39
S F	21	31.34
N F	26	38.81
N T	5	7.46
S J	29	43.28
S P	7	10.45
N P	14	20.90
N J	17	25.37
T J	17	25.37
T P	3	4.48
F P	18	26.87
F J	29	43.28
I N	14	20.90
E N	17	25.37
I S	14	20.90
E S	22	32.84
E T	11	16.42
E F	28	41.79
I F	19	28.36
I T	9	13.43
S dom	17	25.37
N dom	14	20.90
T dom	12	17.91
F dom	24	35.82

Note: ■ = 1% of sample   8623123

Data collected by Myrtle Hunt during October 1974 using Form F. Subjects were all the foreign language teachers in a southwestern Florida county school system. All had at least bachelors degree level education and were certified teachers. No gender or race data were reported. These data are used with permission and have not been published elsewhere to date.

Teachers: Grades 1 through 9, Canada

N = 169

	SENSING			INTUITION				N	%
THINKING		FEELING		FEELING		THINKING			

ISTJ N= 24 %= 14.20 ■■■■■■■■■■■■■■ ■■■■	**ISFJ** N= 23 %= 13.61 ■■■■■■■■■■■■■ ■■■■	**INFJ** N= 10 %= 5.92 ■■■■■■	**INTJ** N= 2 %= 1.18 ■
ISTP N= 2 %= 1.18 ■	**ISFP** N= 6 %= 3.55 ■■■■	**INFP** N= 5 %= 2.96 ■■■	**INTP** N= 5 %= 2.96 ■■■
ESTP N= 2 %= 1.18 ■	**ESFP** N= 6 %= 3.55 ■■■■	**ENFP** N= 4 %= 2.37 ■■	**ENTP** N= 2 %= 1.18 ■
ESTJ N= 25 %= 14.79 ■■■■■■■■■■■■■■ ■■■■■	**ESFJ** N= 27 %= 15.98 ■■■■■■■■■■■■■■■ ■■■■■■	**ENFJ** N= 12 %= 7.10 ■■■■■■■	**ENTJ** N= 14 %= 8.28 ■■■■■■■■

	N	%
E	92	54.44
I	77	45.56
S	115	68.05
N	54	31.95
T	76	44.97
F	93	55.03
J	137	81.07
P	32	18.93
I J	59	34.91
I P	18	10.65
E P	14	8.28
E J	78	46.15
S T	53	31.36
S F	62	36.69
N F	31	18.34
N T	23	13.61
S J	99	58.58
S P	16	9.47
N P	16	9.47
N J	38	22.49
T J	65	38.46
T P	11	6.51
F P	21	12.43
F J	72	42.60
I N	22	13.02
E N	32	18.93
I S	55	32.54
E S	60	35.50
E T	43	25.44
E F	49	28.99
I F	44	26.04
I T	33	19.53
S dom	55	32.54
N dom	18	10.65
T dom	46	27.22
F dom	50	29.59

Note: ■ = 1% of sample   8623129

Data collected by Erich A. von Fange during May and July of 1960 using Form E. Subjects were 73% female and 27% male teachers. Teachers ages ranged from 19 to 66 with 24% under 30, 22% 30-39, 28% 40-49, and 24% 50 and over; 18% had 4 years of college, 2% had more than 4 years and 80% had some college; experience ranged from 1 to 37 years with a median of 11 years. Teachers were from twelve elementary and junior high schools in Canada. These data are used with permission and were cited in: Von Fange, E. A. (1961). Implications for school administration of the personality structure of educational personnel.
 Unpublished doctoral dissertation, University of Alberta.

Teachers: Health

	SENSING		INTUITION	
	THINKING	FEELING	FEELING	THINKING

ISTJ	ISFJ	INFJ	INTJ
N= 19	N= 19	N= 13	N= 17
%= 8.52	%= 8.52	%= 5.83	%= 7.62
■■■■■■■■	■■■■■■■■	■■■■■	■■■■■■■■

ISTP	ISFP	INFP	INTP
N= 6	N= 6	N= 13	N= 10
%= 2.69	%= 2.69	%= 5.83	%= 4.48
■■■	■■■	■■■■■■	■■■■

ESTP	ESFP	ENFP	ENTP
N= 2	N= 7	N= 30	N= 9
%= .90	%= 3.14	%= 13.45	%= 4.04
■	■■■	■■■■■■■■■■ ■■■	■■■■

ESTJ	ESFJ	ENFJ	ENTJ
N= 16	N= 13	N= 30	N= 13
%= 7.17	%= 5.83	%= 13.45	%= 5.83
■■■■■■■	■■■■■■	■■■■■■■■■■ ■■■	■■■■■■

JUDGMENT — INTROVERSION — PERCEPTION / PERCEPTION — EXTRAVERSION — JUDGMENT

Note: ■ = 1% of sample

8629418

	N	%
E	120	53.81
I	103	46.19
S	88	39.46
N	135	60.54
T	92	41.26
F	131	58.74
J	140	62.78
P	83	37.22
I J	68	30.49
I P	35	15.70
E P	48	21.52
E J	72	32.29
ST	43	19.28
SF	45	20.18
NF	86	38.57
NT	49	21.97
S J	67	30.04
S P	21	9.42
N P	62	27.80
N J	73	32.74
TJ	65	29.15
TP	27	12.11
FP	56	25.11
FJ	75	33.63
IN	53	23.77
EN	82	36.77
IS	50	22.42
ES	38	17.04
ET	40	17.94
EF	80	35.87
IF	51	22.87
IT	52	23.32
S dom	47	21.08
N dom	69	30.94
T dom	45	20.18
F dom	62	27.80

This table is one of a series of tables from the CAPT-MBTI Data Bank of MBTI records submitted to CAPT for computer scoring between 1971 and June, 1984. This sample was drawn from 59,784 records with usable occupational codes from the total data bank of 232,557. This data bank has 51% Form F cases from 1971 to March, 1978, 35% Form F cases from 1978 to June, 1984 and 14% Form G cases from 1978 to December, 1982. An analysis of Form F and G data banks showed the data banks were comprised of 56% females and 44% males; education level completed: 6% some grade school, 30% high school diploma, 25% some college, 18% bachelor degrees, 11% masters degrees, 3% doctoral or post doctoral work, and 6% unknown. Age group percentages were: 11% under 18, 29% 18 to 20, 12% 21 to 24, 10% 25 to 29, 16% 30 to 39, 10% 40 to 49, 5% 50 to 59, 2% 60 plus, and 5% unknown.

N = 649

	SENSING		INTUITION	
	THINKING	FEELING	FEELING	THINKING

ISTJ	ISFJ	INFJ	INTJ
N= 77	N= 69	N= 50	N= 35
%= 11.86	%= 10.63	%= 7.70	%= 5.39
▪▪▪▪▪▪▪▪▪▪▪▪	▪▪▪▪▪▪▪▪▪▪▪	▪▪▪▪▪▪▪▪	▪▪▪▪▪
▪▪	▪		

ISTP	ISFP	INFP	INTP
N= 10	N= 16	N= 41	N= 19
%= 1.54	%= 2.47	%= 6.32	%= 2.93
▪▪	▪▪	▪▪▪▪▪▪	▪▪▪

ESTP	ESFP	ENFP	ENTP
N= 7	N= 15	N= 74	N= 23
%= 1.08	%= 2.31	%= 11.40	%= 3.54
▪	▪▪	▪▪▪▪▪▪▪▪▪▪	▪▪▪▪
		▪	

ESTJ	ESFJ	ENFJ	ENTJ
N= 73	N= 55	N= 57	N= 28
%= 11.25	%= 8.47	%= 8.78	%= 4.31
▪▪▪▪▪▪▪▪▪▪▪	▪▪▪▪▪▪▪▪	▪▪▪▪▪▪▪▪▪	▪▪▪▪
▪			

JUDGMENT — INTROVERSION — PERCEPTION — PERCEPTION — EXTRAVERSION — JUDGMENT

	N	%
E	332	51.16
I	317	48.84
S	322	49.61
N	327	50.39
T	272	41.91
F	377	58.09
J	444	68.41
P	205	31.59
I J	231	35.59
I P	86	13.25
E P	119	18.34
E J	213	32.82
S T	167	25.73
S F	155	23.88
N F	222	34.21
N T	105	16.18
S J	274	42.22
S P	48	7.40
N P	157	24.19
N J	170	26.19
T J	213	32.82
T P	59	9.09
F P	146	22.50
F J	231	35.59
I N	145	22.34
E N	182	28.04
I S	172	26.50
E S	150	23.11
E T	131	20.18
E F	201	30.97
I F	176	27.12
I T	141	21.73
S dom	168	25.89
N dom	182	28.04
T dom	130	20.03
F dom	169	26.04

Note: ▪ = 1% of sample   8629420

This table is one of a series of tables from the CAPT-MBTI Data Bank of MBTI records submitted to CAPT for computer scoring between 1971 and June, 1984. This sample was drawn from 59,784 records with usable occupational codes from the total data bank of 232,557. This data bank has 51% Form F cases from 1971 to March, 1978, 35% Form F cases from 1978 to June, 1984 and 14% Form G cases from 1978 to December, 1982. An analysis of Form F and G data banks showed the data banks were comprised of 56% females and 44% males; education level completed: 6% some grade school, 30% high school diploma, 25% some college, 18% bachelor degrees, 11% masters degrees, 3% doctoral or post doctoral work, and 6% unknown. Age group percentages were: 11% under 18, 29% 18 to 20, 12% 21 to 24, 10% 25 to 29, 16% 30 to 39, 10% 40 to 49, 5% 50 to 59, 2% 60 plus, and 5% unknown.

Teachers: Junior College

N = 561

	SENSING		INTUITION	
	THINKING	FEELING	FEELING	THINKING

ISTJ	ISFJ	INFJ	INTJ
N= 68	N= 46	N= 28	N= 39
%= 12.12	%= 8.20	%= 4.99	%= 6.95
■■■■■■■■■■■■	■■■■■■■■	■■■■■	■■■■■■■
■■			

JUDGMENT — INTROVERSION

ISTP	ISFP	INFP	INTP
N= 4	N= 12	N= 45	N= 26
%= .71	%= 2.14	%= 8.02	%= 4.63
■	■■	■■■■■■■■	■■■■■

PERCEPTION

ESTP	ESFP	ENFP	ENTP
N= 8	N= 16	N= 76	N= 28
%= 1.43	%= 2.85	%= 13.55	%= 4.99
■	■■■	■■■■■■■■■■	■■■■■
		■■■■	

PERCEPTION — EXTRAVERSION

ESTJ	ESFJ	ENFJ	ENTJ
N= 38	N= 46	N= 44	N= 37
%= 6.77	%= 8.20	%= 7.84	%= 6.60
■■■■■■■	■■■■■■■■	■■■■■■■■	■■■■■■■

JUDGMENT

	N	%
E	293	52.23
I	268	47.77
S	238	42.42
N	323	57.58
T	248	44.21
F	313	55.79
J	346	61.68
P	215	38.32
I J	181	32.26
I P	87	15.51
E P	128	22.82
E J	165	29.41
S T	118	21.03
S F	120	21.39
N F	193	34.40
N T	130	23.17
S J	198	35.29
S P	40	7.13
N P	175	31.19
N J	148	26.38
T J	182	32.44
T P	66	11.76
F P	149	26.56
F J	164	29.23
I N	138	24.60
E N	185	32.98
I S	130	23.17
E S	108	19.25
E T	111	19.79
E F	182	32.44
I F	131	23.35
I T	137	24.42
S dom	138	24.60
N dom	171	30.48
T dom	105	18.72
F dom	147	26.20

Note: ■ = 1% of sample   8629421

This table is one of a series of tables from the CAPT-MBTI Data Bank of MBTI records submitted to CAPT for computer scoring between 1971 and June, 1984. This sample was drawn from 59,784 records with usable occupational codes from the total data bank of 232,557. This data bank has 51% Form F cases from 1971 to March, 1978, 35% Form F cases from 1978 to June, 1984 and 14% Form G cases from 1978 to December, 1982. An analysis of Form F and G data banks showed the data banks were comprised of 56% females and 44% males; education level completed: 6% some grade school, 30% high school diploma, 25% some college, 18% bachelor degrees, 11% masters degrees, 3% doctoral or post doctoral work, and 6% unknown. Age group percentages were: 11% under 18, 29% 18 to 20, 12% 21 to 24, 10% 25 to 29, 16% 30 to 39, 10% 40 to 49, 5% 50 to 59, 2% 60 plus, and 5% unknown.

Teachers: Mathematics

N = 71

	SENSING		INTUITION	
	THINKING	FEELING	FEELING	THINKING

ISTJ	ISFJ	INFJ	INTJ
N= 13	N= 9	N= 1	N= 5
%= 18.31	%= 12.68	%= 1.41	%= 7.04

ISTP	ISFP	INFP	INTP
N= 2	N= 3	N= 2	N= 6
%= 2.82	%= 4.23	%= 2.82	%= 8.45

ESTP	ESFP	ENFP	ENTP
N= 1	N= 2	N= 2	N= 3
%= 1.41	%= 2.82	%= 2.82	%= 4.23

ESTJ	ESFJ	ENFJ	ENTJ
N= 9	N= 6	N= 4	N= 3
%= 12.68	%= 8.45	%= 5.63	%= 4.23

JUDGMENT — INTROVERSION — PERCEPTION
PERCEPTION — EXTRAVERSION — JUDGMENT

	N	%
E	30	42.25
I	41	57.75
S	45	63.38
N	26	36.62
T	42	59.15
F	29	40.85
J	50	70.42
P	21	29.58
I J	28	39.44
I P	13	18.31
E P	8	11.27
E J	22	30.99
S T	25	35.21
S F	20	28.17
N F	9	12.68
N T	17	23.94
S J	37	52.11
S P	8	11.27
N P	13	18.31
N J	13	18.31
T J	30	42.25
T P	12	16.90
F P	9	12.68
F J	20	28.17
I N	14	19.72
E N	12	16.90
I S	27	38.03
E S	18	25.35
E T	16	22.54
E F	14	19.72
I F	15	21.13
I T	26	36.62
S dom	25	35.21
N dom	11	15.49
T dom	20	28.17
F dom	15	21.13

Note: ■ = 1% of sample   8629425

This table is one of a series of tables from the CAPT-MBTI Data Bank of MBTI records submitted to CAPT for computer scoring between 1971 and June, 1984. This sample was drawn from 59,784 records with usable occupational codes from the total data bank of 232,557. This data bank has 51% Form F cases from 1971 to March, 1978, 35% Form F cases from 1978 to June, 1984 and 14% Form G cases from 1978 to December, 1982. An analysis of Form F and G data banks showed the data banks were comprised of 56% females and 44% males; education level completed: 6% some grade school, 30% high school diploma, 25% some college, 18% bachelor degrees, 11% masters degrees, 3% doctoral or post doctoral work, and 6% unknown. Age group percentages were: 11% under 18, 29% 18 to 20, 12% 21 to 24, 10% 25 to 29, 16% 30 to 39, 10% 40 to 49, 5% 50 to 59, 2% 60 plus, and 5% unknown.

Teachers: Mathematics

N = 413

	SENSING		INTUITION	
	THINKING	FEELING	FEELING	THINKING

ISTJ	ISFJ	INFJ	INTJ
N= 77	N= 42	N= 12	N= 17
%= 18.64	%= 10.17	%= 2.91	%= 4.12
■■■■■■■■■■ ■■■■■■■■	■■■■■■■■■■	■■■	■■■■

ISTP	ISFP	INFP	INTP
N= 10	N= 17	N= 24	N= 17
%= 2.42	%= 4.12	%= 5.81	%= 4.12
■■	■■■■	■■■■■■	■■■■

ESTP	ESFP	ENFP	ENTP
N= 8	N= 22	N= 34	N= 10
%= 1.94	%= 5.33	%= 8.23	%= 2.42
■■	■■■■■	■■■■■■■■	■■

ESTJ	ESFJ	ENFJ	ENTJ
N= 48	N= 34	N= 18	N= 23
%= 11.62	%= 8.23	%= 4.36	%= 5.57
■■■■■■■■■■ ■■	■■■■■■■■	■■■■	■■■■■■

JUDGMENT — INTROVERSION
PERCEPTION
PERCEPTION — EXTRAVERSION
JUDGMENT

	N	%
E	197	47.70
I	216	52.30
S	258	62.47
N	155	37.53
T	210	50.85
F	203	49.15
J	271	65.62
P	142	34.38
I J	148	35.84
I P	68	16.46
E P	74	17.92
E J	123	29.78
S T	143	34.62
S F	115	27.85
N F	88	21.31
N T	67	16.22
S J	201	48.67
S P	57	13.80
N P	85	20.58
N J	70	16.95
T J	165	39.95
T P	45	10.90
F P	97	23.49
F J	106	25.67
I N	70	16.95
E N	85	20.58
I S	146	35.35
E S	112	27.12
E T	89	21.55
E F	108	26.15
I F	95	23.00
I T	121	29.30
S dom	149	36.08
N dom	73	17.68
T dom	98	23.73
F dom	93	22.52

Note: ■ = 1% of sample

8623124

Data collected by Garth Story during August 1971 using Form F. The subjects were 56% female and 44% male mathematics teachers. All teachers had at least a bachelors degree and were certified teachers. Teachers taught grades seven through twelve, 75% had taught for more than three years and 71% had prepared specifically to teach in mathematics. The teachers were from urban Jacksonville and surrounding suburban and rural northeast Florida. These data are used with permission and were cited in:

Story, G. (1973). An analysis of the relationships between personality types of mathematics teachers (7-12) as measured by the Myers-Briggs Type Indicator, and selected factors related to teaching (Doctoral dissertation, University of Florida, 1972). Dissertation Abstracts International, 33, 3471A. (University Microfilms No. 73-978)

Teachers: Middle and Junior High School

N = 1128

	SENSING			INTUITION		
	THINKING	FEELING	FEELING	THINKING		

ISTJ	ISFJ	INFJ	INTJ
N= 126	N= 138	N= 56	N= 51
%= 11.17	%= 12.23	%= 4.96	%= 4.52
■■■■■■■■■■■	■■■■■■■■■■■	■■■■■	■■■■■
■	■■		

ISTP	ISFP	INFP	INTP
N= 26	N= 36	N= 67	N= 27
%= 2.30	%= 3.19	%= 5.94	%= 2.39
■■	■■■	■■■■■■	■■

ESTP	ESFP	ENFP	ENTP
N= 20	N= 43	N= 124	N= 44
%= 1.77	%= 3.81	%= 10.99	%= 3.90
■■	■■■■	■■■■■■■■■■	■■■■
		■	

ESTJ	ESFJ	ENFJ	ENTJ
N= 103	N= 130	N= 88	N= 49
%= 9.13	%= 11.52	%= 7.80	%= 4.34
■■■■■■■■■	■■■■■■■■■■■	■■■■■■■■	■■■■
	■■		

JUDGMENT — INTROVERSION — PERCEPTION — PERCEPTION — EXTRAVERSION — JUDGMENT

	N	%
E	601	53.28
I	527	46.72
S	622	55.14
N	506	44.86
T	446	39.54
F	682	60.46
J	741	65.69
P	387	34.31
I J	371	32.89
I P	156	13.83
E P	231	20.48
E J	370	32.80
S T	275	24.38
S F	347	30.76
N F	335	29.70
N T	171	15.16
S J	497	44.06
S P	125	11.08
N P	262	23.23
N J	244	21.63
T J	329	29.17
T P	117	10.37
F P	270	23.94
F J	412	36.52
I N	201	17.82
E N	305	27.04
I S	326	28.90
E S	296	26.24
E T	216	19.15
E F	385	34.13
I F	297	26.33
I T	230	20.39
S dom	327	28.99
N dom	275	24.38
T dom	205	18.17
F dom	321	28.46

Note: ■ = 1% of sample   8629422

This table is one of a series of tables from the CAPT-MBTI Data Bank of MBTI records submitted to CAPT for computer scoring between 1971 and June, 1984. This sample was drawn from 59,784 records with usable occupational codes from the total data bank of 232,557. This data bank has 51% Form F cases from 1971 to March, 1978, 35% Form F cases from 1978 to June, 1984 and 14% Form G cases from 1978 to December, 1982. An analysis of Form F and G data banks showed the data banks were comprised of 56% females and 44% males; education level completed: 6% some grade school, 30% high school diploma, 25% some college, 18% bachelor degrees, 11% masters degrees, 3% doctoral or post doctoral work, and 6% unknown. Age group percentages were: 11% under 18, 29% 18 to 20, 12% 21 to 24, 10% 25 to 29, 16% 30 to 39, 10% 40 to 49, 5% 50 to 59, 2% 60 plus, and 5% unknown.

Teachers: Pre-school

N = 100

	SENSING		INTUITION				N	%
THINKING	FEELING	FEELING	THINKING			E	52	52.00

The type table:

ISTJ
N= 3
%= 3.00
■■■

ISFJ
N= 20
%= 20.00
■■■■■■■■■■
■■■■■■■■■■

INFJ
N= 7
%= 7.00
■■■■■■■

INTJ
N= 4
%= 4.00
■■■■

ISTP
N= 0
%= 0.00

ISFP
N= 4
%= 4.00
■■■■

INFP
N= 8
%= 8.00
■■■■■■■■

INTP
N= 2
%= 2.00
■■

ESTP
N= 0
%= 0.00

ESFP
N= 8
%= 8.00
■■■■■■■■

ENFP
N= 12
%= 12.00
■■■■■■■■■■
■■

ENTP
N= 1
%= 1.00
■

ESTJ
N= 6
%= 6.00
■■■■■■

ESFJ
N= 12
%= 12.00
■■■■■■■■■■
■■

ENFJ
N= 8
%= 8.00
■■■■■■■■

ENTJ
N= 5
%= 5.00
■■■■■

	N	%
E	52	52.00
I	48	48.00
S	53	53.00
N	47	47.00
T	21	21.00
F	79	79.00
J	65	65.00
P	35	35.00
I J	34	34.00
I P	14	14.00
E P	21	21.00
E J	31	31.00
S T	9	9.00
S F	44	44.00
N F	35	35.00
N T	12	12.00
S J	41	41.00
S P	12	12.00
N P	23	23.00
N J	24	24.00
T J	18	18.00
T P	3	3.00
F P	32	32.00
F J	47	47.00
I N	21	21.00
E N	26	26.00
I S	27	27.00
E S	26	26.00
E T	12	12.00
E F	40	40.00
I F	39	39.00
I T	9	9.00
S dom	31	31.00
N dom	24	24.00
T dom	13	13.00
F dom	32	32.00

Note: ■ = 1% of sample   8629423

This table is one of a series of tables from the CAPT-MBTI Data Bank of MBTI records submitted to CAPT for computer scoring between 1971 and June, 1984. This sample was drawn from 59,784 records with usable occupational codes from the total data bank of 232,557. This data bank has 51% Form F cases from 1971 to March, 1978, 35% Form F cases from 1978 to June, 1984 and 14% Form G cases from 1978 to December, 1982. An analysis of Form F and G data banks showed the data banks were comprised of 56% females and 44% males; education level completed: 6% some grade school, 30% high school diploma, 25% some college, 18% bachelor degrees, 11% masters degrees, 3% doctoral or post doctoral work, and 6% unknown. Age group percentages were: 11% under 18, 29% 18 to 20, 12% 21 to 24, 10% 25 to 29, 16% 30 to 39, 10% 40 to 49, 5% 50 to 59, 2% 60 plus, and 5% unknown.

N = 96

	SENSING		INTUITION	
	THINKING	FEELING	FEELING	THINKING

ISTJ	ISFJ	INFJ	INTJ
N= 7	N= 16	N= 3	N= 2
%= 7.29	%= 16.67	%= 3.12	%= 2.08
■■■■■■■	■■■■■■■■■■ ■■■■■■■	■■■	■■

ISTP	ISFP	INFP	INTP
N= 1	N= 4	N= 9	N= 1
%= 1.04	%= 4.17	%= 9.38	%= 1.04
■	■■■■	■■■■■■■■■	■

ESTP	ESFP	ENFP	ENTP
N= 1	N= 4	N= 8	N= 4
%= 1.04	%= 4.17	%= 8.33	%= 4.17
■	■■■■	■■■■■■■■	■■■■

ESTJ	ESFJ	ENFJ	ENTJ
N= 7	N= 14	N= 6	N= 9
%= 7.29	%= 14.58	%= 6.25	%= 9.38
■■■■■■■	■■■■■■■■■■ ■■■■■	■■■■■■	■■■■■■■■■

JUDGMENT — PERCEPTION — PERCEPTION — JUDGMENT

INTROVERSION — EXTRAVERSION

	N	%
E	53	55.21
I	43	44.79
S	54	56.25
N	42	43.75
T	32	33.33
F	64	66.67
J	64	66.67
P	32	33.33
I J	28	29.17
I P	15	15.62
E P	17	17.71
E J	36	37.50
S T	16	16.67
S F	38	39.58
N F	26	27.08
N T	16	16.67
S J	44	45.83
S P	10	10.42
N P	22	22.92
N J	20	20.83
T J	25	26.04
T P	7	7.29
F P	25	26.04
F J	39	40.62
I N	15	15.62
E N	27	28.13
I S	28	29.17
E S	26	27.08
E T	21	21.88
E F	32	33.33
I F	32	33.33
I T	11	11.46
S dom	28	29.17
N dom	17	17.71
T dom	18	18.75
F dom	33	34.38

Note: ■ = 1% of sample   8629426

This table is one of a series of tables from the CAPT-MBTI Data Bank of MBTI records submitted to CAPT for computer scoring between 1971 and June, 1984. This sample was drawn from 59,784 records with usable occupational codes from the total data bank of 232,557. This data bank has 51% Form F cases from 1971 to March, 1978, 35% Form F cases from 1978 to June, 1984 and 14% Form G cases from 1978 to December, 1982. An analysis of Form F and G data banks showed the data banks were comprised of 56% females and 44% males; education level completed: 6% some grade school, 30% high school diploma, 25% some college, 18% bachelor degrees, 11% masters degrees, 3% doctoral or post doctoral work, and 6% unknown. Age group percentages were: 11% under 18, 29% 18 to 20, 12% 21 to 24, 10% 25 to 29, 16% 30 to 39, 10% 40 to 49, 5% 50 to 59, 2% 60 plus, and 5% unknown.

Teachers: School Grades 1 through 12

N = 281

	SENSING		INTUITION	
	THINKING	FEELING	FEELING	THINKING

ISTJ	ISFJ	INFJ	INTJ
N= 37	N= 59	N= 11	N= 8
%= 13.17	%= 21.00	%= 3.91	%= 2.85
■■■■■■■■■■■■■	■■■■■■■■■■■■	■■■■	■■■
■■■	■■■■■■■■■■		
	■		

ISTP	ISFP	INFP	INTP
N= 7	N= 16	N= 5	N= 4
%= 2.49	%= 5.69	%= 1.78	%= 1.42
■■	■■■■■■	■■	■

ESTP	ESFP	ENFP	ENTP
N= 3	N= 16	N= 23	N= 3
%= 1.07	%= 5.69	%= 8.19	%= 1.07
■	■■■■■■	■■■■■■■■	■

ESTJ	ESFJ	ENFJ	ENTJ
N= 17	N= 52	N= 13	N= 7
%= 6.05	%= 18.51	%= 4.63	%= 2.49
■■■■■■	■■■■■■■■■■	■■■■■	■■
	■■■■■■■■■		

JUDGMENT — INTROVERSION — PERCEPTION
PERCEPTION — EXTRAVERSION — JUDGMENT

	N	%
E	134	47.69
I	147	52.31
S	207	73.67
N	74	26.33
T	86	30.60
F	195	69.40
J	204	72.60
P	77	27.40
I J	115	40.93
I P	32	11.39
E P	45	16.01
E J	89	31.67
S T	64	22.78
S F	143	50.89
N F	52	18.51
N T	22	7.83
S J	165	58.72
S P	42	14.95
N P	35	12.46
N J	39	13.88
T J	69	24.56
T P	17	6.05
F P	60	21.35
F J	135	48.04
I N	28	9.96
E N	46	16.37
I S	119	42.35
E S	88	31.32
E T	30	10.68
E F	104	37.01
I F	91	32.38
I T	56	19.93
S dom	115	40.93
N dom	45	16.01
T dom	35	12.46
F dom	86	30.60

Note: ■ = 1% of sample

8623131

Data collected by Ronald G. Lynch of the Institute of Government, University of North Carolina at Chapel Hill from 1984 to 1986 using Form F. Subjects were 94% female and 6% male teachers in school systems where the principals had attended institute programs and invited the institute to provide a program for their teachers. All teachers taught grades one through twelve in North Carolina. These data are used with permission and have not been published elsewhere to date.

Teachers: Special Education

N = 173

	SENSING THINKING	SENSING FEELING	INTUITION FEELING	INTUITION THINKING	
INTROVERSION	**ISTJ** N= 15 %= 8.67	**ISFJ** N= 17 %= 9.83	**INFJ** N= 12 %= 6.94	**INTJ** N= 11 %= 6.36	JUDGMENT
INTROVERSION	**ISTP** N= 1 %= .58	**ISFP** N= 5 %= 2.89	**INFP** N= 11 %= 6.36	**INTP** N= 6 %= 3.47	PERCEPTION
EXTRAVERSION	**ESTP** N= 2 %= 1.16	**ESFP** N= 6 %= 3.47	**ENFP** N= 23 %= 13.29	**ENTP** N= 7 %= 4.05	PERCEPTION
EXTRAVERSION	**ESTJ** N= 14 %= 8.09	**ESFJ** N= 19 %= 10.98	**ENFJ** N= 10 %= 5.78	**ENTJ** N= 14 %= 8.09	JUDGMENT

Note: ■ = 1% of sample

8629427

	N	%
E	95	54.91
I	78	45.09
S	79	45.66
N	94	54.34
T	70	40.46
F	103	59.54
J	112	64.74
P	61	35.26
I J	55	31.79
I P	23	13.29
E P	38	21.97
E J	57	32.95
S T	32	18.50
S F	47	27.17
N F	56	32.37
N T	38	21.97
S J	65	37.57
S P	14	8.09
N P	47	27.17
N J	47	27.17
T J	54	31.21
T P	16	9.25
F P	45	26.01
F J	58	33.53
I N	40	23.12
E N	54	31.21
I S	38	21.97
E S	41	23.70
E T	37	21.39
E F	58	33.53
I F	45	26.01
I T	33	19.08
S dom	40	23.12
N dom	53	30.64
T dom	35	20.23
F dom	45	26.01

This table is one of a series of tables from the CAPT-MBTI Data Bank of MBTI records submitted to CAPT for computer scoring between 1971 and June, 1984. This sample was drawn from 59,784 records with usable occupational codes from the total data bank of 232,557. This data bank has 51% Form F cases from 1971 to March, 1978, 35% Form F cases from 1978 to June, 1984 and 14% Form G cases from 1978 to December, 1982. An analysis of Form F and G data banks showed the data banks were comprised of 56% females and 44% males; education level completed: 6% some grade school, 30% high school diploma, 25% some college, 18% bachelor degrees, 11% masters degrees, 3% doctoral or post doctoral work, and 6% unknown. Age group percentages were: 11% under 18, 29% 18 to 20, 12% 21 to 24, 10% 25 to 29, 16% 30 to 39, 10% 40 to 49, 5% 50 to 59, 2% 60 plus, and 5% unknown.

Teachers: Speech Pathology and Therapy

N = 157

	SENSING		INTUITION	
	THINKING	FEELING	FEELING	THINKING

ISTJ	ISFJ	INFJ	INTJ
N= 10	N= 31	N= 8	N= 2
%= 6.37	%= 19.75	%= 5.10	%= 1.27
■■■■■■	■■■■■■■■■■ ■■■■■■■■■■	■■■■■	■

JUDGMENT — INTROVERSION

ISTP	ISFP	INFP	INTP
N= 3	N= 6	N= 11	N= 5
%= 1.91	%= 3.82	%= 7.01	%= 3.18
■■	■■■■	■■■■■■■	■■■

PERCEPTION

ESTP	ESFP	ENFP	ENTP
N= 1	N= 6	N= 13	N= 4
%= .64	%= 3.82	%= 8.28	%= 2.55
■	■■■■	■■■■■■■■	■■■

PERCEPTION — EXTRAVERSION

ESTJ	ESFJ	ENFJ	ENTJ
N= 13	N= 25	N= 11	N= 8
%= 8.28	%= 15.92	%= 7.01	%= 5.10
■■■■■■■■	■■■■■■■■■■■■■■■■ ■■■■■■	■■■■■■■	■■■■■

JUDGMENT

	N	%
E	81	51.59
I	76	48.41
S	95	60.51
N	62	39.49
T	46	29.30
F	111	70.70
J	108	68.79
P	49	31.21
I J	51	32.48
I P	25	15.92
E P	24	15.29
E J	57	36.31
S T	27	17.20
S F	68	43.31
N F	43	27.39
N T	19	12.10
S J	79	50.32
S P	16	10.19
N P	33	21.02
N J	29	18.47
T J	33	21.02
T P	13	8.28
F P	36	22.93
F J	75	47.77
I N	26	16.56
E N	36	22.93
I S	50	31.85
E S	45	28.66
E T	26	16.56
E F	55	35.03
I F	56	35.67
I T	20	12.74
S dom	48	30.57
N dom	27	17.20
T dom	29	18.47
F dom	53	33.76

Note: ■ = 1% of sample   8629428

This table is one of a series of tables from the CAPT-MBTI Data Bank of MBTI records submitted to CAPT for computer scoring between 1971 and June, 1984. This sample was drawn from 59,784 records with usable occupational codes from the total data bank of 232,557. This data bank has 51% Form F cases from 1971 to March, 1978, 35% Form F cases from 1978 to June, 1984 and 14% Form G cases from 1978 to December, 1982. An analysis of Form F and G data banks showed the data banks were comprised of 56% females and 44% males; education level completed: 6% some grade school, 30% high school diploma, 25% some college, 18% bachelor degrees, 11% masters degrees, 3% doctoral or post doctoral work, and 6% unknown. Age group percentages were: 11% under 18, 29% 18 to 20, 12% 21 to 24, 10% 25 to 29, 16% 30 to 39, 10% 40 to 49, 5% 50 to 59, 2% 60 plus, and 5% unknown.

Teachers: Supervising Student Teachers

N = 113

	SENSING		INTUITION				N	%
	THINKING	FEELING	FEELING	THINKING		E	64	56.64

ISTJ	ISFJ	INFJ	INTJ
N= 16	N= 18	N= 5	N= 4
%= 14.16	%= 15.93	%= 4.42	%= 3.54
■■■■■■■■■■	■■■■■■■■■■	■■■■	■■■■
■■■■	■■■■■		

ISTP	ISFP	INFP	INTP
N= 0	N= 2	N= 2	N= 2
%= 0.00	%= 1.77	%= 1.77	%= 1.77
	■■	■■	■■

ESTP	ESFP	ENFP	ENTP
N= 1	N= 4	N= 6	N= 6
%= .88	%= 3.54	%= 5.31	%= 5.31
■	■■■■	■■■■■	■■■■■

ESTJ	ESFJ	ENFJ	ENTJ
N= 18	N= 17	N= 8	N= 4
%= 15.93	%= 15.04	%= 7.08	%= 3.54
■■■■■■■■■■	■■■■■■■■■■	■■■■■■■	■■■■
■■■■■■	■■■■■		

JUDGMENT — INTROVERSION — PERCEPTION
PERCEPTION — EXTRAVERSION — JUDGMENT

	N	%
E	64	56.64
I	49	43.36
S	76	67.26
N	37	32.74
T	51	45.13
F	62	54.87
J	90	79.65
P	23	20.35
I J	43	38.05
I P	6	5.31
E P	17	15.04
E J	47	41.59
ST	35	30.97
SF	41	36.28
NF	21	18.58
NT	16	14.16
S J	69	61.06
S P	7	6.19
NP	16	14.16
NJ	21	18.58
T J	42	37.17
T P	9	7.96
F P	14	12.39
F J	48	42.48
IN	13	11.50
EN	24	21.24
I S	36	31.86
ES	40	35.40
ET	29	25.66
EF	35	30.97
I F	27	23.89
I T	22	19.47
S dom	39	34.51
N dom	21	18.58
T dom	24	21.24
F dom	29	25.66

Note: ■ = 1% of sample   8623127

Data collected by Jeffery Hoffman during the fall of 1973 using Form F. Subjects were teachers who were responsible for supervising student teachers. The teachers were 28% male and 72% female; their ages ranged from 21 to 62, with 35% age 30 to 40 and 23% age 24 to 30; they had at least three years of experience; 26% taught grades K-5, 74% 6-12. The sample was drawn from 40 different schools in the Florida panhandle area. These data are used with permission and were cited in:

Hoffman, J. L. (1975). Personality relationships between supervising teachers and student teachers as determined by the Myers-Briggs Type Indicator (Doctoral dissertation, University of Florida, 1974). Dissertation Abstracts International, 36(02), 830A-831A. (University Microfilms No. 75-16, 393)

Teachers: Trade, Industrial and Technical

N = 119

	SENSING		INTUITION			N	%
	THINKING	FEELING	FEELING	THINKING			

ISTJ	ISFJ	INFJ	INTJ		E	65	54.62
N= 22	N= 6	N= 5	N= 5		I	54	45.38
%= 18.49	%= 5.04	%= 4.20	%= 4.20		S	77	64.71
					N	42	35.29

JUDGMENT / INTROVERSION

				T	84	70.59
ISTP	ISFP	INFP	INTP	F	35	29.41
N= 3	N= 2	N= 5	N= 6	J	89	74.79
%= 2.52	%= 1.68	%= 4.20	%= 5.04	P	30	25.21

PERCEPTION

				I J	38	31.93
				I P	16	13.45
ESTP	ESFP	ENFP	ENTP	E P	14	11.76
N= 4	N= 2	N= 5	N= 3	E J	51	42.86
%= 3.36	%= 1.68	%= 4.20	%= 2.52			

PERCEPTION / EXTRAVERSION

				ST	62	52.10
ESTJ	ESFJ	ENFJ	ENTJ	SF	15	12.61
N= 33	N= 5	N= 5	N= 8	NF	20	16.81
%= 27.73	%= 4.20	%= 4.20	%= 6.72	NT	22	18.49

JUDGMENT

S J	66	55.46
S P	11	9.24
N P	19	15.97
N J	23	19.33
T J	68	57.14
T P	16	13.45
F P	14	11.76
F J	21	17.65
I N	21	17.65
E N	21	17.65
I S	33	27.73
E S	44	36.97
E T	48	40.34
E F	17	14.29
I F	18	15.13
I T	36	30.25
S dom	34	28.57
N dom	18	15.13
T dom	50	42.02
F dom	17	14.29

Note: ■ = 1% of sample   8629429

This table is one of a series of tables from the CAPT-MBTI Data Bank of MBTI records submitted to CAPT for computer scoring between 1971 and June, 1984. This sample was drawn from 59,784 records with usable occupational codes from the total data bank of 232,557. This data bank has 51% Form F cases from 1971 to March, 1978, 35% Form F cases from 1978 to June, 1984 and 14% Form G cases from 1978 to December, 1982. An analysis of Form F and G data banks showed the data banks were comprised of 56% females and 44% males; education level completed: 6% some grade school, 30% high school diploma, 25% some college, 18% bachelor degrees, 11% masters degrees, 3% doctoral or post doctoral work, and 6% unknown. Age group percentages were: 11% under 18, 29% 18 to 20, 12% 21 to 24, 10% 25 to 29, 16% 30 to 39, 10% 40 to 49, 5% 50 to 59, 2% 60 plus, and 5% unknown.

Teachers: University

	SENSING		INTUITION	
	THINKING	FEELING	FEELING	THINKING

ISTJ	ISFJ	INFJ	INTJ
N= 293	N= 139	N= 172	N= 248
%= 12.84	%= 6.09	%= 7.54	%= 10.87
■■■■■■■■■■■■ ■■■	■■■■■■	■■■■■■■■	■■■■■■■■■■ ■

ISTP	ISFP	INFP	INTP
N= 38	N= 39	N= 185	N= 123
%= 1.67	%= 1.71	%= 8.11	%= 5.39
■■	■■	■■■■■■■■	■■■■■

ESTP	ESFP	ENFP	ENTP
N= 27	N= 38	N= 207	N= 121
%= 1.18	%= 1.67	%= 9.07	%= 5.30
■	■■	■■■■■■■■■	■■■■■

ESTJ	ESFJ	ENFJ	ENTJ
N= 148	N= 101	N= 183	N= 220
%= 6.49	%= 4.43	%= 8.02	%= 9.64
■■■■■■	■■■■	■■■■■■■■	■■■■■■■■■■

JUDGMENT — INTROVERSION — PERCEPTION — PERCEPTION — EXTRAVERSION — JUDGMENT

	N	%
E	1045	45.79
I	1237	54.21
S	823	36.06
N	1459	63.94
T	1218	53.37
F	1064	46.63
J	1504	65.91
P	778	34.09
I J	852	37.34
I P	385	16.87
E P	393	17.22
E J	652	28.57
S T	506	22.17
S F	317	13.89
N F	747	32.73
N T	712	31.20
S J	681	29.84
S P	142	6.22
N P	636	27.87
N J	823	36.06
T J	909	39.83
T P	309	13.54
F P	469	20.55
F J	595	26.07
I N	728	31.90
E N	731	32.03
I S	509	22.30
E S	314	13.76
E T	516	22.61
E F	529	23.18
I F	535	23.44
I T	702	30.76
S dom	497	21.78
N dom	748	32.78
T dom	529	23.18
F dom	508	22.26

Note: ■ = 1% of sample   8629424

This table is one of a series of tables from the CAPT-MBTI Data Bank of MBTI records submitted to CAPT for computer scoring between 1971 and June, 1984. This sample was drawn from 59,784 records with usable occupational codes from the total data bank of 232,557. This data bank has 51% Form F cases from 1971 to March, 1978, 35% Form F cases from 1978 to June, 1984 and 14% Form G cases from 1978 to December, 1982. An analysis of Form F and G data banks showed the data banks were comprised of 56% females and 44% males; education level completed: 6% some grade school, 30% high school diploma, 25% some college, 18% bachelor degrees, 11% masters degrees, 3% doctoral or post doctoral work, and 6% unknown. Age group percentages were: 11% under 18, 29% 18 to 20, 12% 21 to 24, 10% 25 to 29, 16% 30 to 39, 10% 40 to 49, 5% 50 to 59, 2% 60 plus, and 5% unknown.

Teaching Assistants

N = 172

		SENSING			INTUITION		
	THINKING		FEELING		FEELING		THINKING

				N	%

ISTJ	ISFJ	INFJ	INTJ
N= 21	N= 17	N= 8	N= 14
%= 12.21	%= 9.88	%= 4.65	%= 8.14
■■■■■■■■■■■■	■■■■■■■■■■	■■■■■	■■■■■■■■
■■			

ISTP	ISFP	INFP	INTP
N= 5	N= 3	N= 18	N= 6
%= 2.91	%= 1.74	%= 10.47	%= 3.49
■■■	■■	■■■■■■■■■■	■■■

ESTP	ESFP	ENFP	ENTP
N= 1	N= 6	N= 20	N= 6
%= .58	%= 3.49	%= 11.63	%= 3.49
■	■■■	■■■■■■■■■■■	■■■
		■■	

ESTJ	ESFJ	ENFJ	ENTJ
N= 12	N= 18	N= 12	N= 5
%= 6.98	%= 10.47	%= 6.98	%= 2.91
■■■■■■■	■■■■■■■■■■	■■■■■■■	■■■

JUDGMENT — INTROVERSION — PERCEPTION — PERCEPTION — EXTRAVERSION — JUDGMENT

	N	%
E	80	46.51
I	92	53.49
S	83	48.26
N	89	51.74
T	70	40.70
F	102	59.30
J	107	62.21
P	65	37.79
I J	60	34.88
I P	32	18.60
E P	33	19.19
E J	47	27.33
S T	39	22.67
S F	44	25.58
N F	58	33.72
N T	31	18.02
S J	68	39.53
S P	15	8.72
N P	50	29.07
N J	39	22.67
T J	52	30.23
T P	18	10.47
F P	47	27.33
F J	55	31.98
I N	46	26.74
E N	43	25.00
I S	46	26.74
E S	37	21.51
E T	24	13.95
E F	56	32.56
I F	46	26.74
I T	46	26.74
S dom	45	26.16
N dom	48	27.91
T dom	28	16.28
F dom	51	29.65

Note: ■ = 1% of sample   8629431

This table is one of a series of tables from the CAPT-MBTI Data Bank of MBTI records submitted to CAPT for computer scoring between 1971 and June, 1984. This sample was drawn from 59,784 records with usable occupational codes from the total data bank of 232,557. This data bank has 51% Form F cases from 1971 to March, 1978, 35% Form F cases from 1978 to June, 1984 and 14% Form G cases from 1978 to December, 1982. An analysis of Form F and G data banks showed the data banks were comprised of 56% females and 44% males; education level completed: 6% some grade school, 30% high school diploma, 25% some college, 18% bachelor degrees, 11% masters degrees, 3% doctoral or post doctoral work, and 6% unknown. Age group percentages were: 11% under 18, 29% 18 to 20, 12% 21 to 24, 10% 25 to 29, 16% 30 to 39, 10% 40 to 49, 5% 50 to 59, 2% 60 plus, and 5% unknown.

ADMINISTRATORS

N = 1857

	SENSING		INTUITION	
	THINKING	FEELING	FEELING	THINKING

ISTJ	ISFJ	INFJ	INTJ
N= 246	N= 121	N= 82	N= 128
%= 13.25	%= 6.52	%= 4.42	%= 6.89
■■■■■■■■■■■■■ ■■■	■■■■■■■	■■■■	■■■■■■■

ISTP	ISFP	INFP	INTP
N= 32	N= 37	N= 109	N= 61
%= 1.72	%= 1.99	%= 5.87	%= 3.28
■■	■■	■■■■■■	■■■

ESTP	ESFP	ENFP	ENTP
N= 40	N= 49	N= 166	N= 71
%= 2.15	%= 2.64	%= 8.94	%= 3.82
■■	■■■	■■■■■■■■■	■■■■

ESTJ	ESFJ	ENFJ	ENTJ
N= 236	N= 152	N= 138	N= 189
%= 12.71	%= 8.19	%= 7.43	%= 10.18
■■■■■■■■■■■■ ■■■	■■■■■■■■	■■■■■■■	■■■■■■■■■■

JUDGMENT — INTROVERSION — PERCEPTION — PERCEPTION — EXTRAVERSION — JUDGMENT

	N	%
E	1041	56.06
I	816	43.94
S	913	49.17
N	944	50.83
T	1003	54.01
F	854	45.99
J	1292	69.57
P	565	30.43
I J	577	31.07
I P	239	12.87
E P	326	17.56
E J	715	38.50
S T	554	29.83
S F	359	19.33
N F	495	26.66
N T	449	24.18
S J	755	40.66
S P	158	8.51
N P	407	21.92
N J	537	28.92
T J	799	43.03
T P	204	10.99
F P	361	19.44
F J	493	26.55
I N	380	20.46
E N	564	30.37
I S	436	23.48
E S	477	25.69
E T	536	28.86
E F	505	27.19
I F	349	18.79
I T	467	25.15
S dom	456	24.56
N dom	447	24.07
T dom	518	27.89
F dom	436	23.48

Note: ■ = 1% of sample   8629435

This table is one of a series of tables from the CAPT-MBTI Data Bank of MBTI records submitted to CAPT for computer scoring between 1971 and June, 1984. This sample was drawn from 59,784 records with usable occupational codes from the total data bank of 232,557. This data bank has 51% Form F cases from 1971 to March, 1978, 35% Form F cases from 1978 to June, 1984 and 14% Form G cases from 1978 to December, 1982. An analysis of Form F and G data banks showed the data banks were comprised of 56% females and 44% males; education level completed: 6% some grade school, 30% high school diploma, 25% some college, 18% bachelor degrees, 11% masters degrees, 3% doctoral or post doctoral work, and 6% unknown. Age group percentages were: 11% under 18, 29% 18 to 20, 12% 21 to 24, 10% 25 to 29, 16% 30 to 39, 10% 40 to 49, 5% 50 to 59, 2% 60 plus, and 5% unknown.

TEACHERS

N = 16676

	SENSING		INTUITION	
	THINKING	FEELING	FEELING	THINKING

ISTJ	ISFJ	INFJ	INTJ
N= 1877	N= 1851	N= 1023	N= 871
%= 11.26	%= 11.10	%= 6.13	%= 5.22
■■■■■■■■■■■ ■	■■■■■■■■■■■ ■	■■■■■■	■■■■■

ISTP	ISFP	INFP	INTP
N= 335	N= 549	N= 1189	N= 558
%= 2.01	%= 3.29	%= 7.13	%= 3.35
■■	■■■	■■■■■■■	■■■

ESTP	ESFP	ENFP	ENTP
N= 254	N= 567	N= 1669	N= 607
%= 1.52	%= 3.40	%= 10.01	%= 3.64
■■	■■■	■■■■■■■■■■	■■■■

ESTJ	ESFJ	ENFJ	ENTJ
N= 1502	N= 1543	N= 1283	N= 998
%= 9.01	%= 9.25	%= 7.69	%= 5.98
■■■■■■■■■	■■■■■■■■■	■■■■■■■■	■■■■■

(Right margin labels: JUDGMENT — INTROVERSION — PERCEPTION — PERCEPTION — EXTRAVERSION — JUDGMENT)

	N	%
E	8423	50.51
I	8253	49.49
S	8478	50.84
N	8198	49.16
T	7002	41.99
F	9674	58.01
J	10948	65.65
P	5728	34.35
I J	5622	33.71
I P	2631	15.78
E P	3097	18.57
E J	5326	31.94
S T	3968	23.79
S F	4510	27.04
N F	5164	30.97
N T	3034	18.19
S J	6773	40.62
S P	1705	10.22
N P	4023	24.12
N J	4175	25.04
T J	5248	31.47
T P	1754	10.52
F P	3974	23.83
F J	5700	34.18
I N	3641	21.83
E N	4557	27.33
I S	4612	27.66
E S	3866	23.18
E T	3361	20.15
E F	5062	30.36
I F	4612	27.66
I T	3641	21.83
S dom	4549	27.28
N dom	4170	25.01
T dom	3393	20.35
F dom	4564	27.37

Note: ■ = 1% of sample

8629430

This table is one of a series of tables from the CAPT-MBTI Data Bank of MBTI records submitted to CAPT for computer scoring between 1971 and June, 1984. This sample was drawn from 59,784 records with usable occupational codes from the total data bank of 232,557. This data bank has 51% Form F cases from 1971 to March, 1978, 35% Form F cases from 1978 to June, 1984 and 14% Form G cases from 1978 to December, 1982. An analysis of Form F and G data banks showed the data banks were comprised of 56% females and 44% males; education level completed: 6% some grade school, 30% high school diploma, 25% some college, 18% bachelor degrees, 11% masters degrees, 3% doctoral or post doctoral work, and 6% unknown. Age group percentages were: 11% under 18, 29% 18 to 20, 12% 21 to 24, 10% 25 to 29, 16% 30 to 39, 10% 40 to 49, 5% 50 to 59, 2% 60 plus, and 5% unknown.

E Percent	I	Total Sample Size	Sample Description
60.78	39.22	51	Administrators: Student Personnel
59.68	40.32	124	Administrators: Canadian Schools
58.89	41.11	1024	Administrators: Elementary and Secondary School
58.21	41.79	67	Teachers: Foreign Language in Junior and Senior High School
56.64	43.36	113	Teachers: Supervising Student Teachers
56.06	43.94	1857	ADMINISTRATORS
55.70	44.30	228	Teachers: Adult Education
55.21	44.79	96	Teachers: Reading
54.91	45.09	173	Teachers: Special Education
54.84	45.16	341	Administrators: Colleges and Technical Institutes
54.62	45.38	119	Teachers: Trade, Industrial and Technical
54.44	45.56	169	Teachers: Grades 1 through 9, Canada
54.27	45.73	164	Teachers: Coaching
54.00	46.00	200	Teachers: Elementary School
53.81	46.19	223	Teachers: Health
53.28	46.72	1128	Teachers: Middle and Junior High School
52.58	47.42	213	Teachers: Art, Drama and Music
52.23	47.77	561	Teachers: Junior College
52.00	48.00	100	Teachers: Pre-school
51.81	48.19	276	School Principals
51.62	48.38	804	Teachers: Elementary School
51.59	48.41	157	Teachers: Speech Pathology and Therapy
51.16	48.84	649	Teachers: High School
50.51	49.49	16676	TEACHERS
49.31	50.69	432	Teacher Aides (except school monitors)
49.16	50.84	179	Teachers: English
48.36	51.64	122	Administrators: Educationally Related
47.70	52.30	413	Teachers: Mathematics
47.69	52.31	281	Teachers: School Grades 1 through 12
46.51	53.49	172	Teaching Assistants
45.79	54.21	2282	Teachers: University
44.44	55.56	54	Consultants: Education
43.40	56.60	705	Teachers: College Faculty Named as Danforth Associates
42.25	57.75	71	Teachers: Mathematics

SENSING-INTUITION

S Percent	N	Total Sample Size	Sample Description
73.67	26.33	281	Teachers: School Grades 1 through 12
72.22	27.78	432	Teacher Aides (except school monitors)
70.73	29.27	164	Teachers: Coaching
70.65	29.35	276	School Principals
68.05	31.95	169	Teachers: Grades 1 through 9, Canada
67.26	32.74	113	Teachers: Supervising Student Teachers
64.91	35.09	228	Teachers: Adult Education
64.71	35.29	119	Teachers: Trade, Industrial and Technical
63.38	36.62	71	Teachers: Mathematics
62.56	37.44	804	Teachers: Elementary School
62.47	37.53	413	Teachers: Mathematics
60.51	39.49	157	Teachers: Speech Pathology and Therapy
58.87	41.13	124	Administrators: Canadian Schools
56.25	43.75	96	Teachers: Reading
55.14	44.86	1128	Teachers: Middle and Junior High School
53.73	46.27	67	Teachers: Foreign Language in Junior and Senior High School
53.00	47.00	100	Teachers: Pre-school
52.93	47.07	1024	Administrators: Elementary and Secondary School
50.84	49.16	16676	TEACHERS
49.61	50.39	649	Teachers: High School
49.17	50.83	1857	ADMINISTRATORS
48.36	51.64	122	Administrators: Educationally Related
48.26	51.74	172	Teaching Assistants
47.50	52.50	200	Teachers: Elementary School
45.66	54.34	173	Teachers: Special Education
42.42	57.58	561	Teachers: Junior College
39.46	60.54	223	Teachers: Health
39.22	60.78	51	Administrators: Student Personnel
37.83	62.17	341	Administrators: Colleges and Technical Institutes
36.06	63.94	2282	Teachers: University
35.75	64.25	179	Teachers: English
31.48	68.52	54	Consultants: Education
29.11	70.89	213	Teachers: Art, Drama and Music
24.40	75.60	705	Teachers: College Faculty Named as Danforth Associates

THINKING-FEELING

T Percent	F	Total Sample Size	Sample Description
77.54	22.46	276	School Principals
70.59	29.41	119	Teachers: Trade, Industrial and Technical
59.15	40.85	71	Teachers: Mathematics
56.88	43.12	705	Teachers: College Faculty Named as Danforth Associates
56.60	43.40	341	Administrators: Colleges and Technical Institutes
54.92	45.08	122	Administrators: Educationally Related
54.84	45.16	124	Administrators: Canadian Schools
54.01	45.99	1857	ADMINISTRATORS
53.37	46.63	2282	Teachers: University
51.83	48.17	164	Teachers: Coaching
50.85	49.15	413	Teachers: Mathematics
49.71	50.29	1024	Administrators: Elementary and Secondary School
45.13	54.87	113	Teachers: Supervising Student Teachers
44.97	55.03	169	Teachers: Grades 1 through 9, Canada
44.21	55.79	561	Teachers: Junior College
42.98	57.02	228	Teachers: Adult Education
41.99	58.01	16676	TEACHERS
41.91	58.09	649	Teachers: High School
41.26	58.74	223	Teachers: Health
41.18	58.82	51	Administrators: Student Personnel
40.70	59.30	172	Teaching Assistants
40.46	59.54	173	Teachers: Special Education
39.54	60.46	1128	Teachers: Middle and Junior High School
38.89	61.11	54	Consultants: Education
36.00	64.00	200	Teachers: Elementary School
35.75	64.25	179	Teachers: English
34.03	65.97	432	Teacher Aides (except school monitors)
33.33	66.67	96	Teachers: Reading
32.09	67.91	804	Teachers: Elementary School
30.60	69.40	281	Teachers: School Grades 1 through 12
29.85	70.15	67	Teachers: Foreign Language in Junior and Senior High School
29.30	70.70	157	Teachers: Speech Pathology and Therapy
28.64	71.36	213	Teachers: Art, Drama and Music
21.00	79.00	100	Teachers: Pre-school

JUDGMENT-PERCEPTION

J Percent P	Total Sample Size	Sample Description
86.29 13.71	124	Administrators: Canadian Schools
85.14 14.86	276	School Principals
81.07 18.93	169	Teachers: Grades 1 through 9, Canada
79.65 20.35	113	Teachers: Supervising Student Teachers
74.79 25.21	119	Teachers: Trade, Industrial and Technical
72.60 27.40	281	Teachers: School Grades 1 through 12
70.42 29.58	71	Teachers: Mathematics
69.93 30.07	705	Teachers: College Faculty Named as Danforth Associates
69.82 30.18	1024	Administrators: Elementary and Secondary School
69.57 30.43	1857	ADMINISTRATORS
69.15 30.85	804	Teachers: Elementary School
68.79 31.21	157	Teachers: Speech Pathology and Therapy
68.66 31.34	67	Teachers: Foreign Language in Junior and Senior High School
68.63 31.37	51	Administrators: Student Personnel
68.41 31.59	649	Teachers: High School
67.74 32.26	341	Administrators: Colleges and Technical Institutes
67.50 32.50	200	Teachers: Elementary School
67.21 32.79	122	Administrators: Educationally Related
67.04 32.96	179	Teachers: English
66.67 33.33	432	Teacher Aides (except school monitors)
66.67 33.33	96	Teachers: Reading
65.91 34.09	2282	Teachers: University
65.69 34.31	1128	Teachers: Middle and Junior High School
65.65 34.35	16676	TEACHERS
65.62 34.38	413	Teachers: Mathematics
65.00 35.00	100	Teachers: Pre-school
64.74 35.26	173	Teachers: Special Education
63.41 36.59	164	Teachers: Coaching
62.96 37.04	54	Consultants: Education
62.78 37.22	223	Teachers: Health
62.21 37.79	172	Teaching Assistants
61.84 38.16	228	Teachers: Adult Education
61.68 38.32	561	Teachers: Junior College
51.17 48.83	213	Teachers: Art, Drama and Music

SENSING-THINKING

Percent ST	Total Sample Size	Sample Description
56.16	276	School Principals
52.10	119	Teachers: Trade, Industrial and Technical
37.20	164	Teachers: Coaching
35.21	71	Teachers: Mathematics
34.62	413	Teachers: Mathematics
33.87	124	Administrators: Canadian Schools
31.97	122	Administrators: Educationally Related
31.36	169	Teachers: Grades 1 through 9, Canada
30.97	113	Teachers: Supervising Student Teachers
29.83	1857	ADMINISTRATORS
29.82	228	Teachers: Adult Education
29.59	1024	Administrators: Elementary and Secondary School
28.01	432	Teacher Aides (except school monitors)
25.73	649	Teachers: High School
24.38	1128	Teachers: Middle and Junior High School
24.34	341	Administrators: Colleges and Technical Institutes
23.79	16676	TEACHERS
22.78	281	Teachers: School Grades 1 through 12
22.67	172	Teaching Assistants
22.39	67	Teachers: Foreign Language in Junior and Senior High School
22.17	2282	Teachers: University
21.77	804	Teachers: Elementary School
21.03	561	Teachers: Junior College
19.28	223	Teachers: Health
18.50	200	Teachers: Elementary School
18.50	173	Teachers: Special Education
17.20	157	Teachers: Speech Pathology and Therapy
16.67	96	Teachers: Reading
16.20	179	Teachers: English
15.69	51	Administrators: Student Personnel
14.81	54	Consultants: Education
13.76	705	Teachers: College Faculty Named as Danforth Associates
11.74	213	Teachers: Art, Drama and Music
9.00	100	Teachers: Pre-school

SENSING-FEELING

Percent SF	Total Sample Size	Sample Description
50.89	281	Teachers: School Grades 1 through 12
44.21	432	Teacher Aides (except school monitors)
44.00	100	Teachers: Pre-school
43.31	157	Teachers: Speech Pathology and Therapy
40.80	804	Teachers: Elementary School
39.58	96	Teachers: Reading
36.69	169	Teachers: Grades 1 through 9, Canada
36.28	113	Teachers: Supervising Student Teachers
35.09	228	Teachers: Adult Education
33.54	164	Teachers: Coaching
31.34	67	Teachers: Foreign Language in Junior and Senior High School
30.76	1128	Teachers: Middle and Junior High School
29.00	200	Teachers: Elementary School
28.17	71	Teachers: Mathematics
27.85	413	Teachers: Mathematics
27.17	173	Teachers: Special Education
27.04	16676	TEACHERS
25.58	172	Teaching Assistants
25.00	124	Administrators: Canadian Schools
23.88	649	Teachers: High School
23.53	51	Administrators: Student Personnel
23.34	1024	Administrators: Elementary and Secondary School
21.39	561	Teachers: Junior College
20.18	223	Teachers: Health
19.55	179	Teachers: English
19.33	1857	ADMINISTRATORS
17.37	213	Teachers: Art, Drama and Music
16.67	54	Consultants: Education
16.39	122	Administrators: Educationally Related
14.49	276	School Principals
13.89	2282	Teachers: University
13.49	341	Administrators: Colleges and Technical Institutes
12.61	119	Teachers: Trade, Industrial and Technical
10.64	705	Teachers: College Faculty Named as Danforth Associates

INTUITION-FEELING

Percent NF	Total Sample Size	Sample Description
53.99	213	Teachers: Art, Drama and Music
44.69	179	Teachers: English
44.44	54	Consultants: Education
38.81	67	Teachers: Foreign Language in Junior and Senior High School
38.57	223	Teachers: Health
35.29	51	Administrators: Student Personnel
35.00	200	Teachers: Elementary School
35.00	100	Teachers: Pre-school
34.40	561	Teachers: Junior College
34.21	649	Teachers: High School
33.72	172	Teaching Assistants
32.73	2282	Teachers: University
32.48	705	Teachers: College Faculty Named as Danforth Associates
32.37	173	Teachers: Special Education
30.97	16676	TEACHERS
29.91	341	Administrators: Colleges and Technical Institutes
29.70	1128	Teachers: Middle and Junior High School
28.69	122	Administrators: Educationally Related
27.39	157	Teachers: Speech Pathology and Therapy
27.11	804	Teachers: Elementary School
27.08	96	Teachers: Reading
26.95	1024	Administrators: Elementary and Secondary School
26.66	1857	ADMINISTRATORS
21.93	228	Teachers: Adult Education
21.76	432	Teacher Aides (except school monitors)
21.31	413	Teachers: Mathematics
20.16	124	Administrators: Canadian Schools
18.58	113	Teachers: Supervising Student Teachers
18.51	281	Teachers: School Grades 1 through 12
18.34	169	Teachers: Grades 1 through 9, Canada
16.81	119	Teachers: Trade, Industrial and Technical
14.63	164	Teachers: Coaching
12.68	71	Teachers: Mathematics
7.97	276	School Principals

Percent NT	Total Sample Size	Sample Description
43.12	705	Teachers: College Faculty Named as Danforth Associates
32.26	341	Administrators: Colleges and Technical Institutes
31.20	2282	Teachers: University
25.49	51	Administrators: Student Personnel
24.18	1857	ADMINISTRATORS
24.07	54	Consultants: Education
23.94	71	Teachers: Mathematics
23.17	561	Teachers: Junior College
22.95	122	Administrators: Educationally Related
21.97	223	Teachers: Health
21.97	173	Teachers: Special Education
21.38	276	School Principals
20.97	124	Administrators: Canadian Schools
20.12	1024	Administrators: Elementary and Secondary School
19.55	179	Teachers: English
18.49	119	Teachers: Trade, Industrial and Technical
18.19	16676	TEACHERS
18.02	172	Teaching Assistants
17.50	200	Teachers: Elementary School
16.90	213	Teachers: Art, Drama and Music
16.67	96	Teachers: Reading
16.22	413	Teachers: Mathematics
16.18	649	Teachers: High School
15.16	1128	Teachers: Middle and Junior High School
14.63	164	Teachers: Coaching
14.16	113	Teachers: Supervising Student Teachers
13.61	169	Teachers: Grades 1 through 9, Canada
13.16	228	Teachers: Adult Education
12.10	157	Teachers: Speech Pathology and Therapy
12.00	100	Teachers: Pre-school
10.32	804	Teachers: Elementary School
7.83	281	Teachers: School Grades 1 through 12
7.46	67	Teachers: Foreign Language in Junior and Senior High School
6.02	432	Teacher Aides (except school monitors)

ENGINEERING,
SCIENCE,
&
TECHNOLOGY

Section VI

ENGINEERING, SCIENCE, AND TECHNOLOGY

Samples in Section VI

Name of Sample	Number in Sample
Computer Operations, Systems Researchers and Analysts	65
Computer Professionals	1229
Computer Programmers	200
Computer Specialists	52
Computer Systems Analysts and Support Representatives	86
Computer and Peripheral Equipment Operators	297
Engineers: Aeronautical	54
Engineers: Chemical	52
Engineers: Electrical and Electronic	54
Engineers: Mechanical	77
Engineers: Mining	190
Professional, Technical, and Kindred Workers	82
Research Assistants	67
Research Workers	81
Scientists: Biology	57
Scientists: Chemistry	61
Technicians: Electrical and Electronic Engineering	57

Composite Samples

COMPUTER SPECIALISTS	338
ENGINEERING AND SCIENCE TECHNICIANS	175
ENGINEERS	986
SCIENTISTS: LIFE AND PHYSICAL	226

Comments

The samples of this section tend mainly to be people concerned with the science and technology of the inanimate world, either as professionals or as assistants to professionals. They include samples of scientists, engineers, technicians and technologists (except those in health) and computer specialists of various kinds.

The preference most likely to appear in all these samples is thinking. Engineering and the sciences which deal primarily with the properties of inanimate objects use cause-effect relationships extensively; for this reason, one would expect to find more thinking than feeling types. Even female samples where feeling types are usually in the majority are likely to have a majority of thinking types in engineering and science. You might expect the feeling types in science to become more interested in the aspects of science related to human beings rather than the inanimate world. Thus you might look for relatively more F's in the behavioral sciences and in teachers of science.

Look for the fields where thinking is associated with abstraction, theory or creativity to have more NT types. Look for fields where thinking is used in more tangible, hands-on ways to have more ST types. The two types that in theory should have the greatest affinity for science are INTJ and INTP (concepts (I), theory (N) and logical analysis (T). (You will find the classic samples of creative scientists and mathematicians on page 215 of the MBTI _Manual_.)

The second preference found in tables of this section is intuition. In samples of science students, intuitives are in the majority. However, there is a pattern that shows relatively more sensing types in the sciences which depend on careful observation (e. g. botany, physiology, zoology) and relatively more intuitives in the sciences that rely heavily on theory (e.g. chemistry, physics). We do not yet have large enough samples of practicing scientists to see if these trends hold true for them as well.

The more applied the science, engineering or technological activities, the more one expects to find relatively more extraverts and sensing types. For example, even in these small samples, chemical engineers have more E's and S's than scientists in chemistry. Notice also that the technicians tend to prefer sensing, but the research assistants are more likely to prefer intuition.

Data coming in for computer fields are still relatively new. Expect relatively more sensing types among operators, business programmers, and managers of computer operations. Expect more intuitives among scientific programmers and systems analysts. Programming in theory should attract more introverts. As in the other sections you will find considerably larger numbers among the composite groups than among the specialties. For example, many people simply fill in "Engineer" on answer sheets, without specifying their engineering specialties.

As you look at the tables, keep in mind that fields in science and technology have had ups and downs in popularity since Sputnik. Whenever a field is on a popularity peak, especially if salaries are very high, we should expect to see more of the types theoretically mismatched to the job requirements. At other times when the occupation is less visible, we should expect fewer mismatches and more of the types who have a natural interest in the work itself.

Note that many of these samples are small; while trends are mainly in the expected directions, as always, be cautious about generalizing for any individual type.

Summary listings of tables for EI, SN, TF, JP, ST, SF, NF and NT will be found after the last type table.

Computer Operations, Systems Researchers and Analysts

	SENSING		INTUITION	
	THINKING	FEELING	FEELING	THINKING

ISTJ	ISFJ	INFJ	INTJ
N= 11	N= 3	N= 2	N= 6
%= 16.92	%= 4.62	%= 3.08	%= 9.23
■■■■■■■■■	■■■■■	■■■	■■■■■■■■■
■■■■■■■			

ISTP	ISFP	INFP	INTP
N= 3	N= 1	N= 0	N= 5
%= 4.62	%= 1.54	%= 0.00	%= 7.69
■■■■■	■■		■■■■■■■■

ESTP	ESFP	ENFP	ENTP
N= 1	N= 1	N= 4	N= 5
%= 1.54	%= 1.54	%= 6.15	%= 7.69
■■	■■	■■■■■■	■■■■■■■■

ESTJ	ESFJ	ENFJ	ENTJ
N= 7	N= 3	N= 0	N= 13
%= 10.77	%= 4.62	%= 0.00	%= 20.00
■■■■■■■■■■	■■■■■		■■■■■■■■■■
■			■■■■■■■■■

JUDGMENT — INTROVERSION — PERCEPTION — EXTRAVERSION — JUDGMENT

	N	%
E	34	52.31
I	31	47.69
S	30	46.15
N	35	53.85
T	51	78.46
F	14	21.54
J	45	69.23
P	20	30.77
I J	22	33.85
I P	9	13.85
E P	11	16.92
E J	23	35.38
S T	22	33.85
S F	8	12.31
N F	6	9.23
N T	29	44.62
S J	24	36.92
S P	6	9.23
N P	14	21.54
N J	21	32.31
T J	37	56.92
T P	14	21.54
F P	6	9.23
F J	8	12.31
I N	13	20.00
E N	22	33.85
I S	18	27.69
E S	12	18.46
E T	26	40.00
E F	8	12.31
I F	6	9.23
I T	25	38.46
S dom	16	24.62
N dom	17	26.15
T dom	28	43.08
F dom	4	6.15

Note: ■ = 1% of sample   8629467

This table is one of a series of tables from the CAPT-MBTI Data Bank of MBTI records submitted to CAPT for computer scoring between 1971 and June, 1984. This sample was drawn from 59,784 records with usable occupational codes from the total data bank of 232,557. This data bank has 51% Form F cases from 1971 to March, 1978, 35% Form F cases from 1978 to June, 1984 and 14% Form G cases from 1978 to December, 1982. An analysis of Form F and G data banks showed the data banks were comprised of 56% females and 44% males; education level completed: 6% some grade school, 30% high school diploma, 25% some college, 18% bachelor degrees, 11% masters degrees, 3% doctoral or post doctoral work, and 6% unknown. Age group percentages were: 11% under 18, 29% 18 to 20, 12% 21 to 24, 10% 25 to 29, 16% 30 to 39, 10% 40 to 49, 5% 50 to 59, 2% 60 plus, and 5% unknown.

Computer Professionals

N = 1229

	SENSING		INTUITION	
	THINKING	FEELING	FEELING	THINKING
JUDGMENT (INTROVERSION)	**ISTJ** N= 278 %= 22.62 ■■■■■■■■■ ■■■■■■■■■ ■■■	**ISFJ** N= 48 %= 3.91 ■■■■	**INFJ** N= 33 %= 2.69 ■■■	**INTJ** N= 191 %= 15.54 ■■■■■■■■■ ■■■■■■
PERCEPTION	**ISTP** N= 64 %= 5.21 ■■■■■	**ISFP** N= 18 %= 1.46 ■	**INFP** N= 44 %= 3.58 ■■■■	**INTP** N= 149 %= 12.12 ■■■■■■■■■ ■■
PERCEPTION (EXTRAVERSION)	**ESTP** N= 26 %= 2.12 ■■	**ESFP** N= 9 %= .73 ■	**ENFP** N= 42 %= 3.42 ■■■	**ENTP** N= 69 %= 5.61 ■■■■■■
JUDGMENT	**ESTJ** N= 114 %= 9.28 ■■■■■■■■■	**ESFJ** N= 12 %= .98 ■	**ENFJ** N= 29 %= 2.36 ■■	**ENTJ** N= 103 %= 8.38 ■■■■■■■■

	N	%
E	404	32.87
I	825	67.13
S	569	46.30
N	660	53.70
T	994	80.88
F	235	19.12
J	808	65.74
P	421	34.26
I J	550	44.75
I P	275	22.38
E P	146	11.88
E J	258	20.99
S T	482	39.22
S F	87	7.08
N F	148	12.04
N T	512	41.66
S J	452	36.78
S P	117	9.52
N P	304	24.74
N J	356	28.97
T J	686	55.82
T P	308	25.06
F P	113	9.19
F J	122	9.93
I N	417	33.93
E N	243	19.77
I S	408	33.20
E S	161	13.10
E T	312	25.39
E F	92	7.49
I F	143	11.64
I T	682	55.49
S dom	361	29.37
N dom	335	27.26
T dom	430	34.99
F dom	103	8.38

Note: ■ = 1% of sample   8623188

Data collected by Michael Lyons of NT Systems Corporation from 1982 to 1984 using Form G. Subjects were 73% male and 27% female computer professionals employed by over 100 different companies in a variety of fields. The computer professional modal age group was 30 to 34; 9% had no college, 18% some college, 46% a four year degree, 19% a masters degree, and 3% a doctorate; 36% were in programming and/or analyst roles, 14% engineering, 39% management or leadership roles, 11% were in other roles; 8% had worked less than 3 years, 22% 3 to 5 years, 32% 6 to 10 years, 23% 11 to 15 years, 14% more than 15 years and 1% not given; 83% were from the United States and 17% were from the United Kingdom and Australia. These data were used with permission and are cited in:

Lyons, M. L. (1985). The DP Psyche. Datamation, August 15, 103-109.

Computer Programmers

N = 200

	SENSING		INTUITION	
	THINKING	FEELING	FEELING	THINKING

ISTJ	ISFJ	INFJ	INTJ
N= 22	N= 16	N= 8	N= 20
%= 11.00	%= 8.00	%= 4.00	%= 10.00
■■■■■■■■■■■	■■■■■■■■	■■■■	■■■■■■■■■■

ISTP	ISFP	INFP	INTP
N= 12	N= 7	N= 15	N= 20
%= 6.00	%= 3.50	%= 7.50	%= 10.00
■■■■■■	■■■■	■■■■■■■■	■■■■■■■■■■

ESTP	ESFP	ENFP	ENTP
N= 8	N= 4	N= 11	N= 15
%= 4.00	%= 2.00	%= 5.50	%= 7.50
■■■■	■■	■■■■■■	■■■■■■■■

ESTJ	ESFJ	ENFJ	ENTJ
N= 14	N= 6	N= 4	N= 18
%= 7.00	%= 3.00	%= 2.00	%= 9.00
■■■■■■■	■■■	■■	■■■■■■■■■

JUDGMENT — PERCEPTION — PERCEPTION — JUDGMENT
INTROVERSION — EXTRAVERSION

	N	%
E	80	40.00
I	120	60.00
S	89	44.50
N	111	55.50
T	129	64.50
F	71	35.50
J	108	54.00
P	92	46.00
I J	66	33.00
I P	54	27.00
E P	38	19.00
E J	42	21.00
S T	56	28.00
S F	33	16.50
N F	38	19.00
N T	73	36.50
S J	58	29.00
S P	31	15.50
N P	61	30.50
N J	50	25.00
T J	74	37.00
T P	55	27.50
F P	37	18.50
F J	34	17.00
I N	63	31.50
E N	48	24.00
I S	57	28.50
E S	32	16.00
E T	55	27.50
E F	25	12.50
I F	46	23.00
I T	74	37.00
S dom	50	25.00
N dom	54	27.00
T dom	64	32.00
F dom	32	16.00

Note: ■ = 1% of sample   8629457

This table is one of a series of tables from the CAPT-MBTI Data Bank of MBTI records submitted to CAPT for computer scoring between 1971 and June, 1984. This sample was drawn from 59,784 records with usable occupational codes from the total data bank of 232,557. This data bank has 51% Form F cases from 1971 to March, 1978, 35% Form F cases from 1978 to June, 1984 and 14% Form G cases from 1978 to December, 1982. An analysis of Form F and G data banks showed the data banks were comprised of 56% females and 44% males; education level completed: 6% some grade school, 30% high school diploma, 25% some college, 18% bachelor degrees, 11% masters degrees, 3% doctoral or post doctoral work, and 6% unknown. Age group percentages were: 11% under 18, 29% 18 to 20, 12% 21 to 24, 10% 25 to 29, 16% 30 to 39, 10% 40 to 49, 5% 50 to 59, 2% 60 plus, and 5% unknown.

Computer Specialists

N = 52

	SENSING		INTUITION					N	%
	THINKING	FEELING	FEELING	THINKING					

ISTJ	ISFJ	INFJ	INTJ
N= 7	N= 6	N= 2	N= 4
%= 13.46	%= 11.54	%= 3.85	%= 7.69
■■■■■■■■■■	■■■■■■■■■■■	■■■■	■■■■■■■■
■■■	■■		

ISTP	ISFP	INFP	INTP
N= 1	N= 2	N= 3	N= 2
%= 1.92	%= 3.85	%= 5.77	%= 3.85
■■	■■■■	■■■■■■	■■■■

ESTP	ESFP	ENFP	ENTP
N= 3	N= 2	N= 2	N= 2
%= 5.77	%= 3.85	%= 3.85	%= 3.85
■■■■■■	■■■■	■■■■	■■■■

ESTJ	ESFJ	ENFJ	ENTJ
N= 6	N= 2	N= 0	N= 8
%= 11.54	%= 3.85	%= 0.00	%= 15.38
■■■■■■■■■■■	■■■■		■■■■■■■■■■■■
■■			■■■■■

JUDGMENT — INTROVERSION — PERCEPTION — PERCEPTION — EXTRAVERSION — JUDGMENT

	N	%
E	25	48.08
I	27	51.92
S	29	55.77
N	23	44.23
T	33	63.46
F	19	36.54
J	35	67.31
P	17	32.69
I J	19	36.54
I P	8	15.38
E P	9	17.31
E J	16	30.77
S T	17	32.69
S F	12	23.08
N F	7	13.46
N T	16	30.77
S J	21	40.38
S P	8	15.38
N P	9	17.31
N J	14	26.92
T J	25	48.08
T P	8	15.38
F P	9	17.31
F J	10	19.23
I N	11	21.15
E N	12	23.08
I S	16	30.77
E S	13	25.00
E T	19	36.54
E F	6	11.54
I F	13	25.00
I T	14	26.92
S dom	18	34.62
N dom	10	19.23
T dom	17	32.69
F dom	7	13.46

Note: ■ = 1% of sample   8629459

This table is one of a series of tables from the CAPT-MBTI Data Bank of MBTI records submitted to CAPT for computer scoring between 1971 and June, 1984. This sample was drawn from 59,784 records with usable occupational codes from the total data bank of 232,557. This data bank has 51% Form F cases from 1971 to March, 1978, 35% Form F cases from 1978 to June, 1984 and 14% Form G cases from 1978 to December, 1982. An analysis of Form F and G data banks showed the data banks were comprised of 56% females and 44% males; education level completed: 6% some grade school, 30% high school diploma, 25% some college, 18% bachelor degrees, 11% masters degrees, 3% doctoral or post doctoral work, and 6% unknown. Age group percentages were: 11% under 18, 29% 18 to 20, 12% 21 to 24, 10% 25 to 29, 16% 30 to 39, 10% 40 to 49, 5% 50 to 59, 2% 60 plus, and 5% unknown.

Computer Systems Analysts and Support Representatives

N = 86

| | SENSING | | INTUITION | |
| THINKING | FEELING | FEELING | THINKING |

ISTJ N= 12 %= 13.95	**ISFJ** N= 5 %= 5.81	**INFJ** N= 2 %= 2.33	**INTJ** N= 11 %= 12.79
ISTP N= 3 %= 3.49	**ISFP** N= 3 %= 3.49	**INFP** N= 4 %= 4.65	**INTP** N= 8 %= 9.30
ESTP N= 1 %= 1.16	**ESFP** N= 1 %= 1.16	**ENFP** N= 1 %= 1.16	**ENTP** N= 9 %= 10.47
ESTJ N= 14 %= 16.28	**ESFJ** N= 1 %= 1.16	**ENFJ** N= 3 %= 3.49	**ENTJ** N= 8 %= 9.30

	N	%
E	38	44.19
I	48	55.81
S	40	46.51
N	46	53.49
T	66	76.74
F	20	23.26
J	56	65.12
P	30	34.88
I J	30	34.88
I P	18	20.93
E P	12	13.95
E J	26	30.23
S T	30	34.88
S F	10	11.63
N F	10	11.63
N T	36	41.86
S J	32	37.21
S P	8	9.30
N P	22	25.58
N J	24	27.91
T J	45	52.33
T P	21	24.42
F P	9	10.47
F J	11	12.79
I N	25	29.07
E N	21	24.42
I S	23	26.74
E S	17	19.77
E T	32	37.21
E F	6	6.98
I F	14	16.28
I T	34	39.53
S dom	19	22.09
N dom	23	26.74
T dom	33	38.37
F dom	11	12.79

Note: ■ = 1% of sample   8629458

This table is one of a series of tables from the CAPT-MBTI Data Bank of MBTI records submitted to CAPT for computer scoring between 1971 and June, 1984. This sample was drawn from 59,784 records with usable occupational codes from the total data bank of 232,557. This data bank has 51% Form F cases from 1971 to March, 1978, 35% Form F cases from 1978 to June, 1984 and 14% Form G cases from 1978 to December, 1982. An analysis of Form F and G data banks showed the data banks were comprised of 56% females and 44% males; education level completed: 6% some grade school, 30% high school diploma, 25% some college, 18% bachelor degrees, 11% masters degrees, 3% doctoral or post doctoral work, and 6% unknown. Age group percentages were: 11% under 18, 29% 18 to 20, 12% 21 to 24, 10% 25 to 29, 16% 30 to 39, 10% 40 to 49, 5% 50 to 59, 2% 60 plus, and 5% unknown.

Computer and Peripheral Equipment Operators

N = 297

		SENSING		INTUITION					N	%

	THINKING	FEELING	FEELING	THINKING

ISTJ	ISFJ	INFJ	INTJ
N= 26	N= 37	N= 9	N= 14
%= 8.75	%= 12.46	%= 3.03	%= 4.71
■■■■■■■■■	■■■■■■■■■■■■	■■■	■■■■■

ISTP	ISFP	INFP	INTP
N= 12	N= 19	N= 18	N= 8
%= 4.04	%= 6.40	%= 6.06	%= 2.69
■■■■	■■■■■■	■■■■■■	■■■

ESTP	ESFP	ENFP	ENTP
N= 3	N= 20	N= 48	N= 12
%= 1.01	%= 6.73	%= 16.16	%= 4.04
■	■■■■■■■	■■■■■■■■■■■■■■■■■	■■■■

ESTJ	ESFJ	ENFJ	ENTJ
N= 28	N= 26	N= 10	N= 7
%= 9.43	%= 8.75	%= 3.37	%= 2.36
■■■■■■■■■	■■■■■■■■■	■■■	■■

	N	%
E	154	51.85
I	143	48.15
S	171	57.58
N	126	42.42
T	110	37.04
F	187	62.96
J	157	52.86
P	140	47.14
I J	86	28.96
I P	57	19.19
E P	83	27.95
E J	71	23.91
S T	69	23.23
S F	102	34.34
N F	85	28.62
N T	41	13.80
S J	117	39.39
S P	54	18.18
N P	86	28.96
N J	40	13.47
T J	75	25.25
T P	35	11.78
F P	105	35.35
F J	82	27.61
I N	49	16.50
E N	77	25.93
I S	94	31.65
E S	77	25.93
E T	50	16.84
E F	104	35.02
I F	83	27.95
I T	60	20.20
S dom	86	28.96
N dom	83	27.95
T dom	55	18.52
F dom	73	24.58

Note: ■ = 1% of sample   8629472

This table is one of a series of tables from the CAPT-MBTI Data Bank of MBTI records submitted to CAPT for computer scoring between 1971 and June, 1984. This sample was drawn from 59,784 records with usable occupational codes from the total data bank of 232,557. This data bank has 51% Form F cases from 1971 to March, 1978, 35% Form F cases from 1978 to June, 1984 and 14% Form G cases from 1978 to December, 1982. An analysis of Form F and G data banks showed the data banks were comprised of 56% females and 44% males; education level completed: 6% some grade school, 30% high school diploma, 25% some college, 18% bachelor degrees, 11% masters degrees, 3% doctoral or post doctoral work, and 6% unknown. Age group percentages were: 11% under 18, 29% 18 to 20, 12% 21 to 24, 10% 25 to 29, 16% 30 to 39, 10% 40 to 49, 5% 50 to 59, 2% 60 plus, and 5% unknown.

Engineers: Aeronautical

N = 54

	SENSING		INTUITION				N	%
	THINKING	FEELING	FEELING	THINKING				

ISTJ	ISFJ	INFJ	INTJ
N= 5	N= 7	N= 3	N= 4
%= 9.26	%= 12.96	%= 5.56	%= 7.41
■■■■■■■■■	■■■■■■■■■■■■■	■■■■■■	■■■■■■■

ISTP	ISFP	INFP	INTP
N= 0	N= 0	N= 5	N= 3
%= 0.00	%= 0.00	%= 9.26	%= 5.56
		■■■■■■■■■	■■■■■■

ESTP	ESFP	ENFP	ENTP
N= 1	N= 4	N= 8	N= 4
%= 1.85	%= 7.41	%= 14.81	%= 7.41
■■	■■■■■■■	■■■■■■■■■■■■■■	■■■■■■■

ESTJ	ESFJ	ENFJ	ENTJ
N= 3	N= 3	N= 2	N= 2
%= 5.56	%= 5.56	%= 3.70	%= 3.70
■■■■■■	■■■■■■	■■■■	■■■■

	N	%
E	27	50.00
I	27	50.00
S	23	42.59
N	31	57.41
T	22	40.74
F	32	59.26
J	29	53.70
P	25	46.30
I J	19	35.19
I P	8	14.81
E P	17	31.48
E J	10	18.52
S T	9	16.67
S F	14	25.93
N F	18	33.33
N T	13	24.07
S J	18	33.33
S P	5	9.26
N P	20	37.04
N J	11	20.37
T J	14	25.93
T P	8	14.81
F P	17	31.48
F J	15	27.78
I N	15	27.78
E N	16	29.63
I S	12	22.22
E S	11	20.37
E T	10	18.52
E F	17	31.48
I F	15	27.78
I T	12	22.22
S dom	17	31.48
N dom	19	35.19
T dom	8	14.81
F dom	10	18.52

Note: ■ = 1% of sample   8629460

This table is one of a series of tables from the CAPT-MBTI Data Bank of MBTI records submitted to CAPT for computer scoring between 1971 and June, 1984. This sample was drawn from 59,784 records with usable occupational codes from the total data bank of 232,557. This data bank has 51% Form F cases from 1971 to March, 1978, 35% Form F cases from 1978 to June, 1984 and 14% Form G cases from 1978 to December, 1982. An analysis of Form F and G data banks showed the data banks were comprised of 56% females and 44% males; education level completed: 6% some grade school, 30% high school diploma, 25% some college, 18% bachelor degrees, 11% masters degrees, 3% doctoral or post doctoral work, and 6% unknown. Age group percentages were: 11% under 18, 29% 18 to 20, 12% 21 to 24, 10% 25 to 29, 16% 30 to 39, 10% 40 to 49, 5% 50 to 59, 2% 60 plus, and 5% unknown.

277

Engineers: Chemical

N = 52

	SENSING		INTUITION	
	THINKING	FEELING	FEELING	THINKING

ISTJ	ISFJ	INFJ	INTJ
N= 8	N= 5	N= 2	N= 6
%= 15.38	%= 9.62	%= 3.85	%= 11.54
■■■■■■■■■■■■■■■ ■■■■■	■■■■■■■■■	■■■■	■■■■■■■■■■■ ■■

ISTP	ISFP	INFP	INTP
N= 2	N= 0	N= 2	N= 1
%= 3.85	%= 0.00	%= 3.85	%= 1.92
■■■■		■■■■	■■

ESTP	ESFP	ENFP	ENTP
N= 0	N= 0	N= 1	N= 5
%= 0.00	%= 0.00	%= 1.92	%= 9.62
		■■	■■■■■■■■■

ESTJ	ESFJ	ENFJ	ENTJ
N= 9	N= 4	N= 1	N= 6
%= 17.31	%= 7.69	%= 1.92	%= 11.54
■■■■■■■■■■■■■ ■■■■■■■	■■■■■■■■	■■	■■■■■■■■■■■ ■■

JUDGMENT — INTROVERSION — PERCEPTION — PERCEPTION — EXTRAVERSION — JUDGMENT

	N	%
E	26	50.00
I	26	50.00
S	28	53.85
N	24	46.15
T	37	71.15
F	15	28.85
J	41	78.85
P	11	21.15
I J	21	40.38
I P	5	9.62
E P	6	11.54
E J	20	38.46
S T	19	36.54
S F	9	17.31
N F	6	11.54
N T	18	34.62
S J	26	50.00
S P	2	3.85
N P	9	17.31
N J	15	28.85
T J	29	55.77
T P	8	15.38
F P	3	5.77
F J	12	23.08
I N	11	21.15
E N	13	25.00
I S	15	28.85
E S	13	25.00
E T	20	38.46
E F	6	11.54
I F	9	17.31
I T	17	32.69
S dom	13	25.00
N dom	14	26.92
T dom	18	34.62
F dom	7	13.46

Note: ■ = 1% of sample   8629461

This table is one of a series of tables from the CAPT-MBTI Data Bank of MBTI records submitted to CAPT for computer scoring between 1971 and June, 1984. This sample was drawn from 59,784 records with usable occupational codes from the total data bank of 232,557. This data bank has 51% Form F cases from 1971 to March, 1978, 35% Form F cases from 1978 to June, 1984 and 14% Form G cases from 1978 to December, 1982. An analysis of Form F and G data banks showed the data banks were comprised of 56% females and 44% males; education level completed: 6% some grade school, 30% high school diploma, 25% some college, 18% bachelor degrees, 11% masters degrees, 3% doctoral or post doctoral work, and 6% unknown. Age group percentages were: 11% under 18, 29% 18 to 20, 12% 21 to 24, 10% 25 to 29, 16% 30 to 39, 10% 40 to 49, 5% 50 to 59, 2% 60 plus, and 5% unknown.

Engineers: Electrical and Electronic

N = 54

	SENSING		INTUITION	
	THINKING	FEELING	FEELING	THINKING

ISTJ	ISFJ	INFJ	INTJ
N= 9	N= 5	N= 1	N= 7
%= 16.67	%= 9.26	%= 1.85	%= 12.96
■■■■■■■■■■	■■■■■■■■■	■■	■■■■■■■■■■
■■■■■■			■■■

ISTP	ISFP	INFP	INTP
N= 5	N= 1	N= 3	N= 3
%= 9.26	%= 1.85	%= 5.56	%= 5.56
■■■■■■■■■	■■	■■■■■■	■■■■■■

ESTP	ESFP	ENFP	ENTP
N= 0	N= 1	N= 4	N= 3
%= 0.00	%= 1.85	%= 7.41	%= 5.56
	■■	■■■■■■■	■■■■■■

ESTJ	ESFJ	ENFJ	ENTJ
N= 5	N= 2	N= 1	N= 4
%= 9.26	%= 3.70	%= 1.85	%= 7.41
■■■■■■■■■	■■■■	■■	■■■■■■■

JUDGMENT — INTROVERSION — PERCEPTION — PERCEPTION — EXTRAVERSION — JUDGMENT

	N	%
E	20	37.04
I	34	62.96
S	28	51.85
N	26	48.15
T	36	66.67
F	18	33.33
J	34	62.96
P	20	37.04
I J	22	40.74
I P	12	22.22
E P	8	14.81
E J	12	22.22
S T	19	35.19
S F	9	16.67
N F	9	16.67
N T	17	31.48
S J	21	38.89
S P	7	12.96
N P	13	24.07
N J	13	24.07
T J	25	46.30
T P	11	20.37
F P	9	16.67
F J	9	16.67
I N	14	25.93
E N	12	22.22
I S	20	37.04
E S	8	14.81
E T	12	22.22
E F	8	14.81
I F	10	18.52
I T	24	44.44
S dom	15	27.78
N dom	15	27.78
T dom	17	31.48
F dom	7	12.96

Note: ■ = 1% of sample   8629462

This table is one of a series of tables from the CAPT-MBTI Data Bank of MBTI records submitted to CAPT for computer scoring between 1971 and June, 1984. This sample was drawn from 59,784 records with usable occupational codes from the total data bank of 232,557. This data bank has 51% Form F cases from 1971 to March, 1978, 35% Form F cases from 1978 to June, 1984 and 14% Form G cases from 1978 to December, 1982. An analysis of Form F and G data banks showed the data banks were comprised of 56% females and 44% males; education level completed: 6% some grade school, 30% high school diploma, 25% some college, 18% bachelor degrees, 11% masters degrees, 3% doctoral or post doctoral work, and 6% unknown. Age group percentages were: 11% under 18, 29% 18 to 20, 12% 21 to 24, 10% 25 to 29, 16% 30 to 39, 10% 40 to 49, 5% 50 to 59, 2% 60 plus, and 5% unknown.

Engineers: Mechanical

N = 77

		SENSING		INTUITION					N	%

THINKING	FEELING	FEELING	THINKING

ISTJ N= 15 %= 19.48	**ISFJ** N= 2 %= 2.60	**INFJ** N= 3 %= 3.90	**INTJ** N= 5 %= 6.49
ISTP N= 5 %= 6.49	**ISFP** N= 3 %= 3.90	**INFP** N= 5 %= 6.49	**INTP** N= 3 %= 3.90
ESTP N= 3 %= 3.90	**ESFP** N= 0 %= 0.00	**ENFP** N= 3 %= 3.90	**ENTP** N= 7 %= 9.09
ESTJ N= 14 %= 18.18	**ESFJ** N= 3 %= 3.90	**ENFJ** N= 4 %= 5.19	**ENTJ** N= 2 %= 2.60

JUDGMENT — INTROVERSION — PERCEPTION — PERCEPTION — EXTRAVERSION — JUDGMENT

	N	%
E	36	46.75
I	41	53.25
S	45	58.44
N	32	41.56
T	54	70.13
F	23	29.87
J	48	62.34
P	29	37.66
I J	25	32.47
I P	16	20.78
E P	13	16.88
E J	23	29.87
S T	37	48.05
S F	8	10.39
N F	15	19.48
N T	17	22.08
S J	34	44.16
S P	11	14.29
N P	18	23.38
N J	14	18.18
T J	36	46.75
T P	18	23.38
F P	11	14.29
F J	12	15.58
I N	16	20.78
E N	16	20.78
I S	25	32.47
E S	20	25.97
E T	26	33.77
E F	10	12.99
I F	13	16.88
I T	28	36.36
S dom	20	25.97
N dom	18	23.38
T dom	24	31.17
F dom	15	19.48

Note: ■ = 1% of sample   8629463

This table is one of a series of tables from the CAPT-MBTI Data Bank of MBTI records submitted to CAPT for computer scoring between 1971 and June, 1984. This sample was drawn from 59,784 records with usable occupational codes from the total data bank of 232,557. This data bank has 51% Form F cases from 1971 to March, 1978, 35% Form F cases from 1978 to June, 1984 and 14% Form G cases from 1978 to December, 1982. An analysis of Form F and G data banks showed the data banks were comprised of 56% females and 44% males; education level completed: 6% some grade school, 30% high school diploma, 25% some college, 18% bachelor degrees, 11% masters degrees, 3% doctoral or post doctoral work, and 6% unknown. Age group percentages were: 11% under 18, 29% 18 to 20, 12% 21 to 24, 10% 25 to 29, 16% 30 to 39, 10% 40 to 49, 5% 50 to 59, 2% 60 plus, and 5% unknown.

Engineers: Mining

N = 190

	SENSING		INTUITION	
	THINKING	FEELING	FEELING	THINKING
ISTJ N= 10 %= 5.26 ■■■■■	**ISFJ** N= 19 %= 10.00 ■■■■■■■■■■	**INFJ** N= 10 %= 5.26 ■■■■■	**INTJ** N= 3 %= 1.58 ■■	JUDGMENT (INTROVERSION)
ISTP N= 8 %= 4.21 ■■■■	**ISFP** N= 10 %= 5.26 ■■■■■	**INFP** N= 21 %= 11.05 ■■■■■■■■■■■ ■	**INTP** N= 8 %= 4.21 ■■■■	PERCEPTION
ESTP N= 7 %= 3.68 ■■■■	**ESFP** N= 19 %= 10.00 ■■■■■■■■■■	**ENFP** N= 31 %= 16.32 ■■■■■■■■■■■ ■■■■■■	**ENTP** N= 2 %= 1.05 ■	PERCEPTION (EXTRAVERSION)
ESTJ N= 10 %= 5.26 ■■■■■	**ESFJ** N= 20 %= 10.53 ■■■■■■■■■■ ■	**ENFJ** N= 11 %= 5.79 ■■■■■■	**ENTJ** N= 1 %= .53 ■	JUDGMENT

	N	%
E	101	53.16
I	89	46.84
S	103	54.21
N	87	45.79
T	49	25.79
F	141	74.21
J	84	44.21
P	106	55.79
I J	42	22.11
I P	47	24.74
E P	59	31.05
E J	42	22.11
S T	35	18.42
S F	68	35.79
N F	73	38.42
N T	14	7.37
S J	59	31.05
S P	44	23.16
N P	62	32.63
N J	25	13.16
T J	24	12.63
T P	25	13.16
F P	81	42.63
F J	60	31.58
I N	42	22.11
E N	45	23.68
I S	47	24.74
E S	56	29.47
E T	20	10.53
E F	81	42.63
I F	60	31.58
I T	29	15.26
S dom	55	28.95
N dom	46	24.21
T dom	27	14.21
F dom	62	32.63

Note: ■ = 1% of sample   8629464

This table is one of a series of tables from the CAPT-MBTI Data Bank of MBTI records submitted to CAPT for computer scoring between 1971 and June, 1984. This sample was drawn from 59,784 records with usable occupational codes from the total data bank of 232,557. This data bank has 51% Form F cases from 1971 to March, 1978, 35% Form F cases from 1978 to June, 1984 and 14% Form G cases from 1978 to December, 1982. An analysis of Form F and G data banks showed the data banks were comprised of 56% females and 44% males; education level completed: 6% some grade school, 30% high school diploma, 25% some college, 18% bachelor degrees, 11% masters degrees, 3% doctoral or post doctoral work, and 6% unknown. Age group percentages were: 11% under 18, 29% 18 to 20, 12% 21 to 24, 10% 25 to 29, 16% 30 to 39, 10% 40 to 49, 5% 50 to 59, 2% 60 plus, and 5% unknown.

Professional, Technical, and Kindred Workers

N = 82

		SENSING		INTUITION				N	%
		THINKING	FEELING	FEELING	THINKING				

ISTJ	ISFJ	INFJ	INTJ
N= 10	N= 8	N= 4	N= 1
%= 12.20	%= 9.76	%= 4.88	%= 1.22
■■■■■■■■■■	■■■■■■■■■	■■■■■	■
■■			

ISTP	ISFP	INFP	INTP
N= 1	N= 4	N= 5	N= 4
%= 1.22	%= 4.88	%= 6.10	%= 4.88
■	■■■■■	■■■■■■	■■■■■

ESTP	ESFP	ENFP	ENTP
N= 2	N= 4	N= 2	N= 5
%= 2.44	%= 4.88	%= 2.44	%= 6.10
■■	■■■■■	■■	■■■■■■

ESTJ	ESFJ	ENFJ	ENTJ
N= 11	N= 9	N= 1	N= 11
%= 13.41	%= 10.98	%= 1.22	%= 13.41
■■■■■■■■■■	■■■■■■■■■■	■	■■■■■■■■■■
■■■	■		■■■

Note: ■ = 1% of sample

8629471

	N	%
E	45	54.88
I	37	45.12
S	49	59.76
N	33	40.24
T	45	54.88
F	37	45.12
J	55	67.07
P	27	32.93
I J	23	28.05
I P	14	17.07
E P	13	15.85
E J	32	39.02
S T	24	29.27
S F	25	30.49
N F	12	14.63
N T	21	25.61
S J	38	46.34
S P	11	13.41
N P	16	19.51
N J	17	20.73
T J	33	40.24
T P	12	14.63
F P	15	18.29
F J	22	26.83
I N	14	17.07
E N	19	23.17
I S	23	28.05
E S	26	31.71
E T	29	35.37
E F	16	19.51
I F	21	25.61
I T	16	19.51
S dom	24	29.27
N dom	12	14.63
T dom	27	32.93
F dom	19	23.17

This table is one of a series of tables from the CAPT-MBTI Data Bank of MBTI records submitted to CAPT for computer scoring between 1971 and June, 1984. This sample was drawn from 59,784 records with usable occupational codes from the total data bank of 232,557. This data bank has 51% Form F cases from 1971 to March, 1978, 35% Form F cases from 1978 to June, 1984 and 14% Form G cases from 1978 to December, 1982. An analysis of Form F and G data banks showed the data banks were comprised of 56% females and 44% males; education level completed: 6% some grade school, 30% high school diploma, 25% some college, 18% bachelor degrees, 11% masters degrees, 3% doctoral or post doctoral work, and 6% unknown. Age group percentages were: 11% under 18, 29% 18 to 20, 12% 21 to 24, 10% 25 to 29, 16% 30 to 39, 10% 40 to 49, 5% 50 to 59, 2% 60 plus, and 5% unknown.

Research Assistants

	SENSING		INTUITION	
	THINKING	FEELING	FEELING	THINKING

ISTJ	ISFJ	INFJ	INTJ
N= 5	N= 4	N= 5	N= 5
%= 7.46	%= 5.97	%= 7.46	%= 7.46
■■■■■■■	■■■■■■	■■■■■■■	■■■■■■■

ISTP	ISFP	INFP	INTP
N= 0	N= 0	N= 11	N= 8
%= 0.00	%= 0.00	%= 16.42	%= 11.94
		■■■■■■■■■■	■■■■■■■■■
		■■■■■■	■■

ESTP	ESFP	ENFP	ENTP
N= 0	N= 2	N= 13	N= 2
%= 0.00	%= 2.99	%= 19.40	%= 2.99
	■■■	■■■■■■■■■■	■■■
		■■■■■■■■■	

ESTJ	ESFJ	ENFJ	ENTJ
N= 1	N= 1	N= 2	N= 8
%= 1.49	%= 1.49	%= 2.99	%= 11.94
■	■	■■■	■■■■■■■■■
			■■

JUDGMENT — INTROVERSION — PERCEPTION — PERCEPTION — EXTRAVERSION — JUDGMENT

	N	%
E	29	43.28
I	38	56.72
S	13	19.40
N	54	80.60
T	29	43.28
F	38	56.72
J	31	46.27
P	36	53.73
I J	19	28.36
I P	19	28.36
E P	17	25.37
E J	12	17.91
S T	6	8.96
S F	7	10.45
N F	31	46.27
N T	23	34.33
S J	11	16.42
S P	2	2.99
N P	34	50.75
N J	20	29.85
T J	19	28.36
T P	10	14.93
F P	26	38.81
F J	12	17.91
I N	29	43.28
E N	25	37.31
I S	9	13.43
E S	4	5.97
E T	11	16.42
E F	18	26.87
I F	20	29.85
I T	18	26.87
S dom	11	16.42
N dom	25	37.31
T dom	17	25.37
F dom	14	20.90

Note: ■ = 1% of sample   8629473

This table is one of a series of tables from the CAPT-MBTI Data Bank of MBTI records submitted to CAPT for computer scoring between 1971 and June, 1984. This sample was drawn from 59,784 records with usable occupational codes from the total data bank of 232,557. This data bank has 51% Form F cases from 1971 to March, 1978, 35% Form F cases from 1978 to June, 1984 and 14% Form G cases from 1978 to December, 1982. An analysis of Form F and G data banks showed the data banks were comprised of 56% females and 44% males; education level completed: 6% some grade school, 30% high school diploma, 25% some college, 18% bachelor degrees, 11% masters degrees, 3% doctoral or post doctoral work, and 6% unknown. Age group percentages were: 11% under 18, 29% 18 to 20, 12% 21 to 24, 10% 25 to 29, 16% 30 to 39, 10% 40 to 49, 5% 50 to 59, 2% 60 plus, and 5% unknown.

Research Workers

N = 81

	SENSING		INTUITION				N	%
THINKING	FEELING	FEELING	THINKING					

						E	41	50.62

ISTJ N= 4 %= 4.94 ■■■■■

ISFJ N= 4 %= 4.94 ■■■■■

INFJ N= 5 %= 6.17 ■■■■■■

INTJ N= 11 %= 13.58 ■■■■■■■■■ ■■■■

ISTP N= 1 %= 1.23 ■

ISFP N= 3 %= 3.70 ■■■■

INFP N= 9 %= 11.11 ■■■■■■■■■ ■

INTP N= 3 %= 3.70 ■■■■

ESTP N= 1 %= 1.23 ■

ESFP N= 0 %= 0.00

ENFP N= 8 %= 9.88 ■■■■■■■■■

ENTP N= 7 %= 8.64 ■■■■■■■■

ESTJ N= 6 %= 7.41 ■■■■■■■

ESFJ N= 7 %= 8.64 ■■■■■■■■

ENFJ N= 6 %= 7.41 ■■■■■■■

ENTJ N= 6 %= 7.41 ■■■■■■■

JUDGMENT — INTROVERSION — PERCEPTION
PERCEPTION — EXTRAVERSION — JUDGMENT

	N	%
E	41	50.62
I	40	49.38
S	26	32.10
N	55	67.90
T	39	48.15
F	42	51.85
J	49	60.49
P	32	39.51
I J	24	29.63
I P	16	19.75
E P	16	19.75
E J	25	30.86
S T	12	14.81
S F	14	17.28
N F	28	34.57
N T	27	33.33
S J	21	25.93
S P	5	6.17
N P	27	33.33
N J	28	34.57
T J	27	33.33
T P	12	14.81
F P	20	24.69
F J	22	27.16
I N	28	34.57
E N	27	33.33
I S	12	14.81
E S	14	17.28
E T	20	24.69
E F	21	25.93
I F	21	25.93
I T	19	23.46
S dom	9	11.11
N dom	31	38.27
T dom	16	19.75
F dom	25	30.86

Note: ■ = 1% of sample   8629470

This table is one of a series of tables from the CAPT-MBTI Data Bank of MBTI records submitted to CAPT for computer scoring between 1971 and June, 1984. This sample was drawn from 59,784 records with usable occupational codes from the total data bank of 232,557. This data bank has 51% Form F cases from 1971 to March, 1978, 35% Form F cases from 1978 to June, 1984 and 14% Form G cases from 1978 to December, 1982. An analysis of Form F and G data banks showed the data banks were comprised of 56% females and 44% males; education level completed: 6% some grade school, 30% high school diploma, 25% some college, 18% bachelor degrees, 11% masters degrees, 3% doctoral or post doctoral work, and 6% unknown. Age group percentages were: 11% under 18, 29% 18 to 20, 12% 21 to 24, 10% 25 to 29, 16% 30 to 39, 10% 40 to 49, 5% 50 to 59, 2% 60 plus, and 5% unknown.

Scientists: Biology

N = 57

	SENSING		INTUITION	
	THINKING	FEELING	FEELING	THINKING

ISTJ	ISFJ	INFJ	INTJ
N= 7	N= 3	N= 4	N= 5
%= 12.28	%= 5.26	%= 7.02	%= 8.77
■■■■■■■■■■■■	■■■■■	■■■■■■■	■■■■■■■■■
■■			

ISTP	ISFP	INFP	INTP
N= 0	N= 0	N= 6	N= 5
%= 0.00	%= 0.00	%= 10.53	%= 8.77
		■■■■■■■■■■■	■■■■■■■■■
		■	

ESTP	ESFP	ENFP	ENTP
N= 1	N= 2	N= 2	N= 4
%= 1.75	%= 3.51	%= 3.51	%= 7.02
■■	■■■■	■■■■	■■■■■■■

ESTJ	ESFJ	ENFJ	ENTJ
N= 5	N= 3	N= 3	N= 7
%= 8.77	%= 5.26	%= 5.26	%= 12.28
■■■■■■■■■	■■■■■	■■■■■	■■■■■■■■■■■■
			■■

JUDGMENT / INTROVERSION / PERCEPTION / PERCEPTION / EXTRAVERSION / JUDGMENT

	N	%
E	27	47.37
I	30	52.63
S	21	36.84
N	36	63.16
T	34	59.65
F	23	40.35
J	37	64.91
P	20	35.09
I J	19	33.33
I P	11	19.30
E P	9	15.79
E J	18	31.58
S T	13	22.81
S F	8	14.04
N F	15	26.32
N T	21	36.84
S J	18	31.58
S P	3	5.26
N P	17	29.82
N J	19	33.33
T J	24	42.11
T P	10	17.54
F P	10	17.54
F J	13	22.81
I N	20	35.09
E N	16	28.07
I S	10	17.54
E S	11	19.30
E T	17	29.82
E F	10	17.54
I F	13	22.81
I T	17	29.82
S dom	13	22.81
N dom	15	26.32
T dom	17	29.82
F dom	12	21.05

Note: ■ = 1% of sample   8629465

This table is one of a series of tables from the CAPT-MBTI Data Bank of MBTI records submitted to CAPT for computer scoring between 1971 and June, 1984. This sample was drawn from 59,784 records with usable occupational codes from the total data bank of 232,557. This data bank has 51% Form F cases from 1971 to March, 1978, 35% Form F cases from 1978 to June, 1984 and 14% Form G cases from 1978 to December, 1982. An analysis of Form F and G data banks showed the data banks were comprised of 56% females and 44% males; education level completed: 6% some grade school, 30% high school diploma, 25% some college, 18% bachelor degrees, 11% masters degrees, 3% doctoral or post doctoral work, and 6% unknown. Age group percentages were: 11% under 18, 29% 18 to 20, 12% 21 to 24, 10% 25 to 29, 16% 30 to 39, 10% 40 to 49, 5% 50 to 59, 2% 60 plus, and 5% unknown.

Scientists: Chemistry

N = 61

	SENSING THINKING	SENSING FEELING	INTUITION FEELING	INTUITION THINKING	
	ISTJ N= 10 %= 16.39 ■■■■■■■■■■■■■■■■	**ISFJ** N= 2 %= 3.28 ■■■	**INFJ** N= 3 %= 4.92 ■■■■■	**INTJ** N= 9 %= 14.75 ■■■■■■■■■■■■■■■	INTROVERSION JUDGMENT
	ISTP N= 2 %= 3.28 ■■■	**ISFP** N= 2 %= 3.28 ■■■	**INFP** N= 2 %= 3.28 ■■■	**INTP** N= 8 %= 13.11 ■■■■■■■■■■■■■	INTROVERSION PERCEPTION
	ESTP N= 0 %= 0.00	**ESFP** N= 2 %= 3.28 ■■■	**ENFP** N= 0 %= 0.00	**ENTP** N= 3 %= 4.92 ■■■■■	EXTRAVERSION PERCEPTION
	ESTJ N= 6 %= 9.84 ■■■■■■■■■■	**ESFJ** N= 2 %= 3.28 ■■■	**ENFJ** N= 4 %= 6.56 ■■■■■■■	**ENTJ** N= 6 %= 9.84 ■■■■■■■■■■	EXTRAVERSION JUDGMENT

Note: ■ = 1% of sample

8629466

	N	%
E	23	37.70
I	38	62.30
S	26	42.62
N	35	57.38
T	44	72.13
F	17	27.87
J	42	68.85
P	19	31.15
I J	24	39.34
I P	14	22.95
E P	5	8.20
E J	18	29.51
S T	18	29.51
S F	8	13.11
N F	9	14.75
N T	26	42.62
S J	20	32.79
S P	6	9.84
N P	13	21.31
N J	22	36.07
T J	31	50.82
T P	13	21.31
F P	6	9.84
F J	11	18.03
I N	22	36.07
E N	13	21.31
I S	16	26.23
E S	10	16.39
E T	15	24.59
E F	8	13.11
I F	9	14.75
I T	29	47.54
S dom	14	22.95
N dom	15	24.59
T dom	22	36.07
F dom	10	16.39

This table is one of a series of tables from the CAPT-MBTI Data Bank of MBTI records submitted to CAPT for computer scoring between 1971 and June, 1984. This sample was drawn from 59,784 records with usable occupational codes from the total data bank of 232,557. This data bank has 51% Form F cases from 1971 to March, 1978, 35% Form F cases from 1978 to June, 1984 and 14% Form G cases from 1978 to December, 1982. An analysis of Form F and G data banks showed the data banks were comprised of 56% females and 44% males; education level completed: 6% some grade school, 30% high school diploma, 25% some college, 18% bachelor degrees, 11% masters degrees, 3% doctoral or post doctoral work, and 6% unknown. Age group percentages were: 11% under 18, 29% 18 to 20, 12% 21 to 24, 10% 25 to 29, 16% 30 to 39, 10% 40 to 49, 5% 50 to 59, 2% 60 plus, and 5% unknown.

Technicians: Electrical and Electronic Engineering

N = 57

	SENSING		INTUITION	
	THINKING	FEELING	FEELING	THINKING

ISTJ	ISFJ	INFJ	INTJ
N= 11	N= 4	N= 0	N= 6
%= 19.30	%= 7.02	%= 0.00	%= 10.53
■■■■■■■■■■ ■■■■■■■■■	■■■■■■■		■■■■■■■■■■ ■

ISTP	ISFP	INFP	INTP
N= 5	N= 2	N= 2	N= 3
%= 8.77	%= 3.51	%= 3.51	%= 5.26
■■■■■■■■■	■■■■	■■■■	■■■■■

ESTP	ESFP	ENFP	ENTP
N= 0	N= 1	N= 4	N= 4
%= 0.00	%= 1.75	%= 7.02	%= 7.02
	■■	■■■■■■■	■■■■■■■

ESTJ	ESFJ	ENFJ	ENTJ
N= 5	N= 4	N= 1	N= 5
%= 8.77	%= 7.02	%= 1.75	%= 8.77
■■■■■■■■■	■■■■■■■	■■	■■■■■■■■■

JUDGMENT — INTROVERSION — PERCEPTION — PERCEPTION — EXTRAVERSION — JUDGMENT

	N	%
E	24	42.11
I	33	57.89
S	32	56.14
N	25	43.86
T	39	68.42
F	18	31.58
J	36	63.16
P	21	36.84
I J	21	36.84
I P	12	21.05
E P	9	15.79
E J	15	26.32
S T	21	36.84
S F	11	19.30
N F	7	12.28
N T	18	31.58
S J	24	42.11
S P	8	14.04
N P	13	22.81
N J	12	21.05
T J	27	47.37
T P	12	21.05
F P	9	15.79
F J	9	15.79
I N	11	19.30
E N	14	24.56
I S	22	38.60
E S	10	17.54
E T	14	24.56
E F	10	17.54
I F	8	14.04
I T	25	43.86
S dom	16	28.07
N dom	14	24.56
T dom	18	31.58
F dom	9	15.79

Note: ■ = 1% of sample   8629468

This table is one of a series of tables from the CAPT-MBTI Data Bank of MBTI records submitted to CAPT for computer scoring between 1971 and June, 1984. This sample was drawn from 59,784 records with usable occupational codes from the total data bank of 232,557. This data bank has 51% Form F cases from 1971 to March, 1978, 35% Form F cases from 1978 to June, 1984 and 14% Form G cases from 1978 to December, 1982. An analysis of Form F and G data banks showed the data banks were comprised of 56% females and 44% males; education level completed: 6% some grade school, 30% high school diploma, 25% some college, 18% bachelor degrees, 11% masters degrees, 3% doctoral or post doctoral work, and 6% unknown. Age group percentages were: 11% under 18, 29% 18 to 20, 12% 21 to 24, 10% 25 to 29, 16% 30 to 39, 10% 40 to 49, 5% 50 to 59, 2% 60 plus, and 5% unknown.

COMPUTER SPECIALISTS

N = 338

	SENSING		INTUITION	
	THINKING	FEELING	FEELING	THINKING

ISTJ	ISFJ	INFJ	INTJ
N= 41	N= 27	N= 12	N= 35
%= 12.13	%= 7.99	%= 3.55	%= 10.36
■■■■■■■■■■■■	■■■■■■■■	■■■■	■■■■■■■■■■
■■			

ISTP	ISFP	INFP	INTP
N= 16	N= 12	N= 22	N= 30
%= 4.73	%= 3.55	%= 6.51	%= 8.88
■■■■■	■■■■	■■■■■■■	■■■■■■■■

ESTP	ESFP	ENFP	ENTP
N= 12	N= 7	N= 14	N= 26
%= 3.55	%= 2.07	%= 4.14	%= 7.69
■■■■	■■	■■■■	■■■■■■■■

ESTJ	ESFJ	ENFJ	ENTJ
N= 34	N= 9	N= 7	N= 34
%= 10.06	%= 2.66	%= 2.07	%= 10.06
■■■■■■■■■■	■■■	■■	■■■■■■■■■■

JUDGMENT — INTROVERSION
PERCEPTION
PERCEPTION — EXTRAVERSION
JUDGMENT

	N	%
E	143	42.31
I	195	57.69
S	158	46.75
N	180	53.25
T	228	67.46
F	110	32.54
J	199	58.88
P	139	41.12
I J	115	34.02
I P	80	23.67
E P	59	17.46
E J	84	24.85
S T	103	30.47
S F	55	16.27
N F	55	16.27
N T	125	36.98
S J	111	32.84
S P	47	13.91
N P	92	27.22
N J	88	26.04
T J	144	42.60
T P	84	24.85
F P	55	16.27
F J	55	16.27
I N	99	29.29
E N	81	23.96
I S	96	28.40
E S	62	18.34
E T	106	31.36
E F	37	10.95
I F	73	21.60
I T	122	36.09
S dom	87	25.74
N dom	87	25.74
T dom	114	33.73
F dom	50	14.79

Note: ■ = 1% of sample   8629474

This table is one of a series of tables from the CAPT-MBTI Data Bank of MBTI records submitted to CAPT for computer scoring between 1971 and June, 1984. This sample was drawn from 59,784 records with usable occupational codes from the total data bank of 232,557. This data bank has 51% Form F cases from 1971 to March, 1978, 35% Form F cases from 1978 to June, 1984 and 14% Form G cases from 1978 to December, 1982. An analysis of Form F and G data banks showed the data banks were comprised of 56% females and 44% males; education level completed: 6% some grade school, 30% high school diploma, 25% some college, 18% bachelor degrees, 11% masters degrees, 3% doctoral or post doctoral work, and 6% unknown. Age group percentages were: 11% under 18, 29% 18 to 20, 12% 21 to 24, 10% 25 to 29, 16% 30 to 39, 10% 40 to 49, 5% 50 to 59, 2% 60 plus, and 5% unknown.

ENGINEERING AND SCIENCE TECHNICIANS

N = 175

	SENSING		INTUITION	
	THINKING	FEELING	FEELING	THINKING

ISTJ	ISFJ	INFJ	INTJ
N= 26	N= 14	N= 3	N= 8
%= 14.86	%= 8.00	%= 1.71	%= 4.57
■■■■■■■■■■	■■■■■■■■	■■	■■■■■
■■■■■			

ISTP	ISFP	INFP	INTP
N= 10	N= 10	N= 9	N= 11
%= 5.71	%= 5.71	%= 5.14	%= 6.29
■■■■■■	■■■■■■	■■■■■	■■■■■■

ESTP	ESFP	ENFP	ENTP
N= 5	N= 5	N= 16	N= 11
%= 2.86	%= 2.86	%= 9.14	%= 6.29
■■■	■■■	■■■■■■■■■	■■■■■■

ESTJ	ESFJ	ENFJ	ENTJ
N= 15	N= 12	N= 6	N= 14
%= 8.57	%= 6.86	%= 3.43	%= 8.00
■■■■■■■■■	■■■■■■■	■■■	■■■■■■■■

JUDGMENT — INTROVERSION — PERCEPTION — PERCEPTION — EXTRAVERSION — JUDGMENT

	N	%
E	84	48.00
I	91	52.00
S	97	55.43
N	78	44.57
T	100	57.14
F	75	42.86
J	98	56.00
P	77	44.00
I J	51	29.14
I P	40	22.86
E P	37	21.14
E J	47	26.86
S T	56	32.00
S F	41	23.43
N F	34	19.43
N T	44	25.14
S J	67	38.29
S P	30	17.14
N P	47	26.86
N J	31	17.71
T J	63	36.00
T P	37	21.14
F P	40	22.86
F J	35	20.00
I N	31	17.71
E N	47	26.86
I S	60	34.29
E S	37	21.14
E T	45	25.71
E F	39	22.29
I F	36	20.57
I T	55	31.43
S dom	50	28.57
N dom	38	21.71
T dom	50	28.57
F dom	37	21.14

Note: ■ = 1% of sample   8629475

This table is one of a series of tables from the CAPT-MBTI Data Bank of MBTI records submitted to CAPT for computer scoring between 1971 and June, 1984. This sample was drawn from 59,784 records with usable occupational codes from the total data bank of 232,557. This data bank has 51% Form F cases from 1971 to March, 1978, 35% Form F cases from 1978 to June, 1984 and 14% Form G cases from 1978 to December, 1982. An analysis of Form F and G data banks showed the data banks were comprised of 56% females and 44% males; education level completed: 6% some grade school, 30% high school diploma, 25% some college, 18% bachelor degrees, 11% masters degrees, 3% doctoral or post doctoral work, and 6% unknown. Age group percentages were: 11% under 18, 29% 18 to 20, 12% 21 to 24, 10% 25 to 29, 16% 30 to 39, 10% 40 to 49, 5% 50 to 59, 2% 60 plus, and 5% unknown.

N = 986

	SENSING		INTUITION				N	%
	THINKING	FEELING	FEELING	THINKING				

<table>
<tr><td colspan="4"></td><td></td><td>E</td><td>470</td><td>47.67</td></tr>
</table>

SENSING		INTUITION	
THINKING	FEELING	FEELING	THINKING
ISTJ N= 153 %= 15.52 ■■■■■■■■■■ ■■■■■■	**ISFJ** N= 60 %= 6.09 ■■■■■■	**INFJ** N= 31 %= 3.14 ■■■	**INTJ** N= 76 %= 7.71 ■■■■■■■■
ISTP N= 49 %= 4.97 ■■■■■	**ISFP** N= 25 %= 2.54 ■■■	**INFP** N= 61 %= 6.19 ■■■■■■	**INTP** N= 61 %= 6.19 ■■■■■■
ESTP N= 37 %= 3.75 ■■■■	**ESFP** N= 31 %= 3.14 ■■■	**ENFP** N= 67 %= 6.80 ■■■■■■■	**ENTP** N= 59 %= 5.98 ■■■■■■
ESTJ N= 118 %= 11.97 ■■■■■■■■■■ ■■	**ESFJ** N= 46 %= 4.67 ■■■■■	**ENFJ** N= 38 %= 3.85 ■■■■	**ENTJ** N= 74 %= 7.51 ■■■■■■■■

JUDGMENT — INTROVERSION — PERCEPTION — EXTRAVERSION — JUDGMENT

	N	%
E	470	47.67
I	516	52.33
S	519	52.64
N	467	47.36
T	627	63.59
F	359	36.41
J	596	60.45
P	390	39.55
I J	320	32.45
I P	196	19.88
E P	194	19.68
E J	276	27.99
S T	357	36.21
S F	162	16.43
N F	197	19.98
N T	270	27.38
S J	377	38.24
S P	142	14.40
N P	248	25.15
N J	219	22.21
T J	421	42.70
T P	206	20.89
F P	184	18.66
F J	175	17.75
I N	229	23.23
E N	238	24.14
I S	287	29.11
E S	232	23.53
E T	288	29.21
E F	182	18.46
I F	177	17.95
I T	339	34.38
S dom	281	28.50
N dom	233	23.63
T dom	302	30.63
F dom	170	17.24

Note: ■ = 1% of sample   8629476

This table is one of a series of tables from the CAPT-MBTI Data Bank of MBTI records submitted to CAPT for computer scoring between 1971 and June, 1984. This sample was drawn from 59,784 records with usable occupational codes from the total data bank of 232,557. This data bank has 51% Form F cases from 1971 to March, 1978, 35% Form F cases from 1978 to June, 1984 and 14% Form G cases from 1978 to December, 1982. An analysis of Form F and G data banks showed the data banks were comprised of 56% females and 44% males; education level completed: 6% some grade school, 30% high school diploma, 25% some college, 18% bachelor degrees, 11% masters degrees, 3% doctoral or post doctoral work, and 6% unknown. Age group percentages were: 11% under 18, 29% 18 to 20, 12% 21 to 24, 10% 25 to 29, 16% 30 to 39, 10% 40 to 49, 5% 50 to 59, 2% 60 plus, and 5% unknown.

SCIENTISTS: LIFE AND PHYSICAL

N = 226

	SENSING		INTUITION	
	THINKING	FEELING	FEELING	THINKING

ISTJ	ISFJ	INFJ	INTJ
N= 32	N= 13	N= 10	N= 29
%= 14.16	%= 5.75	%= 4.42	%= 12.83
■■■■■■■■■■	■■■■■	■■■■	■■■■■■■■■■
■■■■			■■■

ISTP	ISFP	INFP	INTP
N= 8	N= 2	N= 12	N= 19
%= 3.54	%= .88	%= 5.31	%= 8.41
■■■■	■	■■■■■	■■■■■■■■

ESTP	ESFP	ENFP	ENTP
N= 3	N= 4	N= 13	N= 15
%= 1.33	%= 1.77	%= 5.75	%= 6.64
■	■■	■■■■■■	■■■■■■■

ESTJ	ESFJ	ENFJ	ENTJ
N= 20	N= 15	N= 8	N= 23
%= 8.85	%= 6.64	%= 3.54	%= 10.18
■■■■■■■■■	■■■■■■■	■■■■	■■■■■■■■■■

JUDGMENT — INTROVERSION — PERCEPTION
PERCEPTION — EXTRAVERSION — JUDGMENT

	N	%
E	101	44.69
I	125	55.31
S	97	42.92
N	129	57.08
T	149	65.93
F	77	34.07
J	150	66.37
P	76	33.63
I J	84	37.17
I P	41	18.14
E P	35	15.49
E J	66	29.20
S T	63	27.88
S F	34	15.04
N F	43	19.03
N T	86	38.05
S J	80	35.40
S P	17	7.52
N P	59	26.11
N J	70	30.97
T J	104	46.02
T P	45	19.91
F P	31	13.72
F J	46	20.35
I N	70	30.97
E N	59	26.11
I S	55	24.34
E S	42	18.58
E T	61	26.99
E F	40	17.70
I F	37	16.37
I T	88	38.94
S dom	52	23.01
N dom	67	29.65
T dom	70	30.97
F dom	37	16.37

Note: ■ = 1% of sample   8629477

This table is one of a series of tables from the CAPT-MBTI Data Bank of MBTI records submitted to CAPT for computer scoring between 1971 and June, 1984. This sample was drawn from 59,784 records with usable occupational codes from the total data bank of 232,557. This data bank has 51% Form F cases from 1971 to March, 1978, 35% Form F cases from 1978 to June, 1984 and 14% Form G cases from 1978 to December, 1982. An analysis of Form F and G data banks showed the data banks were comprised of 56% females and 44% males; education level completed: 6% some grade school, 30% high school diploma, 25% some college, 18% bachelor degrees, 11% masters degrees, 3% doctoral or post doctoral work, and 6% unknown. Age group percentages were: 11% under 18, 29% 18 to 20, 12% 21 to 24, 10% 25 to 29, 16% 30 to 39, 10% 40 to 49, 5% 50 to 59, 2% 60 plus, and 5% unknown.

E Percent I	Total Sample Size	Sample Description
54.88 45.12	82	Professional, Technical, and Kindred Workers
53.16 46.84	190	Engineers: Mining
52.31 47.69	65	Computer Operations, Systems Researchers and Analysts
51.85 48.15	297	Computer and Peripheral Equipment Operators
50.62 49.38	81	Research Workers
50.00 50.00	54	Engineers: Aeronautical
50.00 50.00	52	Engineers: Chemical
48.08 51.92	52	Computer Specialists
48.00 52.00	175	ENGINEERING AND SCIENCE TECHNICIANS
47.67 52.33	986	ENGINEERS
47.37 52.63	57	Scientists: Biology
46.75 53.25	77	Engineers: Mechanical
44.69 55.31	226	SCIENTISTS: LIFE AND PHYSICAL
44.19 55.81	86	Computer Systems Analysts and Support Representatives
43.28 56.72	67	Research Assistants
42.31 57.69	338	COMPUTER SPECIALISTS
42.11 57.89	57	Technicians: Electrical and Electronic Engineering
40.00 60.00	200	Computer Programmers
37.70 62.30	61	Scientists: Chemistry
37.04 62.96	54	Engineers: Electrical and Electronic
32.87 67.13	1229	Computer Professionals

SENSING-INTUITION

S Percent	N	Total Sample Size	Sample Description
59.76	40.24	82	Professional, Technical, and Kindred Workers
58.44	41.56	77	Engineers: Mechanical
57.58	42.42	297	Computer and Peripheral Equipment Operators
56.14	43.86	57	Technicians: Electrical and Electronic Engineering
55.77	44.23	52	Computer Specialists
55.43	44.57	175	ENGINEERING AND SCIENCE TECHNICIANS
54.21	45.79	190	Engineers: Mining
53.85	46.15	52	Engineers: Chemical
52.64	47.36	986	ENGINEERS
51.85	48.15	54	Engineers: Electrical and Electronic
46.75	53.25	338	COMPUTER SPECIALISTS
46.51	53.49	86	Computer Systems Analysts and Support Representatives
46.30	53.70	1229	Computer Professionals
46.15	53.85	65	Computer Operations, Systems Researchers and Analysts
44.50	55.50	200	Computer Programmers
42.92	57.08	226	SCIENTISTS: LIFE AND PHYSICAL
42.62	57.38	61	Scientists: Chemistry
42.59	57.41	54	Engineers: Aeronautical
36.84	63.16	57	Scientists: Biology
32.10	67.90	81	Research Workers
19.40	80.60	67	Research Assistants

THINKING-FEELING

T Percent	F	Total Sample Size	Sample Description
80.88	19.12	1229	Computer Professionals
78.46	21.54	65	Computer Operations, Systems Researchers and Analysts
76.74	23.26	86	Computer Systems Analysts and Support Representatives
72.13	27.87	61	Scientists: Chemistry
71.15	28.85	52	Engineers: Chemical
70.13	29.87	77	Engineers: Mechanical
68.42	31.58	57	Technicians: Electrical and Electronic Engineering
67.46	32.54	338	COMPUTER SPECIALISTS
66.67	33.33	54	Engineers: Electrical and Electronic
65.93	34.07	226	SCIENTISTS: LIFE AND PHYSICAL
64.50	35.50	200	Computer Programmers
63.59	36.41	986	ENGINEERS
63.46	36.54	52	Computer Specialists
59.65	40.35	57	Scientists: Biology
57.14	42.86	175	ENGINEERING AND SCIENCE TECHNICIANS
54.88	45.12	82	Professional, Technical, and Kindred Workers
48.15	51.85	81	Research Workers
43.28	56.72	67	Research Assistants
40.74	59.26	54	Engineers: Aeronautical
37.04	62.96	297	Computer and Peripheral Equipment Operators
25.79	74.21	190	Engineers: Mining

JUDGMENT-PERCEPTION

J Percent	P	Total Sample Size	Sample Description
78.85	21.15	52	Engineers: Chemical
69.23	30.77	65	Computer Operations, Systems Researchers and Analysts
68.85	31.15	61	Scientists: Chemistry
67.31	32.69	52	Computer Specialists
67.07	32.93	82	Professional, Technical, and Kindred Workers
66.37	33.63	226	SCIENTISTS: LIFE AND PHYSICAL
65.74	34.26	1229	Computer Professionals
65.12	34.88	86	Computer Systems Analysts and Support Representatives
64.91	35.09	57	Scientists: Biology
63.16	36.84	57	Technicians: Electrical and Electronic Engineering
62.96	37.04	54	Engineers: Electrical and Electronic
62.34	37.66	77	Engineers: Mechanical
60.49	39.51	81	Research Workers
60.45	39.55	986	ENGINEERS
58.88	41.12	338	COMPUTER SPECIALISTS
56.00	44.00	175	ENGINEERING AND SCIENCE TECHNICIANS
54.00	46.00	200	Computer Programmers
53.70	46.30	54	Engineers: Aeronautical
52.86	47.14	297	Computer and Peripheral Equipment Operators
46.27	53.73	67	Research Assistants
44.21	55.79	190	Engineers: Mining

SENSING-THINKING

Percent ST	Total Sample Size	Sample Description
48.05	77	Engineers: Mechanical
39.22	1229	Computer Professionals
36.84	57	Technicians: Electrical and Electronic Engineering
36.54	52	Engineers: Chemical
36.21	986	ENGINEERS
35.19	54	Engineers: Electrical and Electronic
34.88	86	Computer Systems Analysts and Support Representatives
33.85	65	Computer Operations, Systems Researchers and Analysts
32.69	52	Computer Specialists
32.00	175	ENGINEERING AND SCIENCE TECHNICIANS
30.47	338	COMPUTER SPECIALISTS
29.51	61	Scientists: Chemistry
29.27	82	Professional, Technical, and Kindred Workers
28.00	200	Computer Programmers
27.88	226	SCIENTISTS: LIFE AND PHYSICAL
23.23	297	Computer and Peripheral Equipment Operators
22.81	57	Scientists: Biology
18.42	190	Engineers: Mining
16.67	54	Engineers: Aeronautical
14.81	81	Research Workers
8.96	67	Research Assistants

Percent SF	Total Sample Size	Sample Description
35.79	190	Engineers: Mining
34.34	297	Computer and Peripheral Equipment Operators
30.49	82	Professional, Technical, and Kindred Workers
25.93	54	Engineers: Aeronautical
23.43	175	ENGINEERING AND SCIENCE TECHNICIANS
23.08	52	Computer Specialists
19.30	57	Technicians: Electrical and Electronic Engineering
17.31	52	Engineers: Chemical
17.28	81	Research Workers
16.67	54	Engineers: Electrical and Electronic
16.50	200	Computer Programmers
16.43	986	ENGINEERS
16.27	338	COMPUTER SPECIALISTS
15.04	226	SCIENTISTS: LIFE AND PHYSICAL
14.04	57	Scientists: Biology
13.11	61	Scientists: Chemistry
12.31	65	Computer Operations, Systems Researchers and Analysts
11.63	86	Computer Systems Analysts and Support Representatives
10.45	67	Research Assistants
10.39	77	Engineers: Mechanical
7.08	1229	Computer Professionals

INTUITION-FEELING

Percent NF	Total Sample Size	Sample Description
46.27	67	Research Assistants
38.42	190	Engineers: Mining
34.57	81	Research Workers
33.33	54	Engineers: Aeronautical
28.62	297	Computer and Peripheral Equipment Operators
26.32	57	Scientists: Biology
19.98	986	ENGINEERS
19.48	77	Engineers: Mechanical
19.43	175	ENGINEERING AND SCIENCE TECHNICIANS
19.03	226	SCIENTISTS: LIFE AND PHYSICAL
19.00	200	Computer Programmers
16.67	54	Engineers: Electrical and Electronic
16.27	338	COMPUTER SPECIALISTS
14.75	61	Scientists: Chemistry
14.63	82	Professional, Technical, and Kindred Workers
13.46	52	Computer Specialists
12.28	57	Technicians: Electrical and Electronic Engineering
12.04	1229	Computer Professionals
11.63	86	Computer Systems Analysts and Support Representatives
11.54	52	Engineers: Chemical
9.23	65	Computer Operations, Systems Researchers and Analysts

INTUITION-THINKING

Percent NT	Total Sample Size	Sample Description
44.62	65	Computer Operations, Systems Researchers and Analysts
42.62	61	Scientists: Chemistry
41.86	86	Computer Systems Analysts and Support Representatives
41.66	1229	Computer Professionals
38.05	226	SCIENTISTS: LIFE AND PHYSICAL
36.98	338	COMPUTER SPECIALISTS
36.84	57	Scientists: Biology
36.50	200	Computer Programmers
34.62	52	Engineers: Chemical
34.33	67	Research Assistants
33.33	81	Research Workers
31.58	57	Technicians: Electrical and Electronic Engineering
31.48	54	Engineers: Electrical and Electronic
30.77	52	Computer Specialists
27.38	986	ENGINEERS
25.61	82	Professional, Technical, and Kindred Workers
25.14	175	ENGINEERING AND SCIENCE TECHNICIANS
24.07	54	Engineers: Aeronautical
22.08	77	Engineers: Mechanical
13.80	297	Computer and Peripheral Equipment Operators
7.37	190	Engineers: Mining

GOVERNMENT, JUSTICE, & MILITARY

Section VII

GOVERNMENT, JUSTICE AND MILITARY

Samples in Section VII

Name of Sample	Number in Sample
Administrators: Social Services	101
Air Force Personnel	73
Attorneys - Administrators, non-practicing	84
Corrections Officers and Probation Officers	68
Corrections Sergeants	89
Guards and Watch Keepers	86
Judges	128
Law School Graduates	1874
Lawyers	271
Line Corrections Officers	574
Managers: Fire	60
Managers: Middle Level in City, County and State Gov.	290
Managers: Public	523
Managers: Top Level in City, County and State Government	257
Military Personnel at Naval Technical Training Center	4663
Navy Enlisted Personnel in Basic Electronic Training	1009
Police Officers	439
Police Officers: Australian Senior Officers	99
Police Officers: Commanders	57
Police Officers: Detectives in Urban Community	47
Police Officers: Managers	912
Police Officers: Patrolmen in Urban Community	141
Police Officers: Supervisors in Urban Community	92
Police Officers: Urban Community	280
Police Supervisors	105
Police and Detectives	155
Social Services Workers	92

Composite Samples

LAWYERS AND JUDGES	519
MILITARY PERSONNEL	264
PROTECTIVE SERVICE WORKERS	608

Comments

The samples of this section are mainly people concerned with the fields of law and law enforcement. In theory, justice seeks the impersonal principle that is fair to all (T), and enforcement requires judgment and executive action (J). Look, therefore, for preferences for T and J to be important in samples of this section. Most samples contain primarily males. Since most male samples have a majority of thinking types, this fact gives a second reason to expect T's to be in the majority in type tables of this section.

Expect EI and SN to have their usual relationships. Occupations requiring more action and outside activity should attract relatively more extraverts; occupations requiring more attention to concepts, or more quiet and sustained attention should attract more introverts. Activities concerned with day-to-day attention to immediate events should attract more sensing types (keep in mind that sensing types are in the majority in the general population.) Expect to find more intuitive types where "big picture" thinking, abstract concepts or innovation are important.

These samples contain tables on police and corrections personnel; on firemen; on lawyers and judges; and on military enlisted men and officers. More of the tables in this section come from contributed samples than from the MBTI Data Bank.

The data on police show a consistent trend of SJ types in different parts of the United States and in Australia. In studying this section, look for sizeable numbers of both extraverts and introverts in large numbers.

The judges in the sample are mainly county judges; it is possible that there may be a different mix of types in other judges who are required to rule on issues with a broader conceptual requirement (such as constitutional issues); for example, relatively more intuitive types may be found at the federal level.

The MBTI is being used extensively in the education of military officers, with enlisted personnel, and in the chaplain corps. We hope those collecting such data will make them available for the next edition of this Atlas.

Summary listings of tables for EI, SN, TF, JP, ST, SF, NF and NT will be found after the last type table.

Administrators: Social Services

	SENSING		INTUITION	
	THINKING	FEELING	FEELING	THINKING

ISTJ	ISFJ	INFJ	INTJ
N= 17	N= 20	N= 1	N= 2
%= 16.83	%= 19.80	%= .99	%= 1.98

ISTP	ISFP	INFP	INTP
N= 5	N= 3	N= 2	N= 4
%= 4.95	%= 2.97	%= 1.98	%= 3.96

ESTP	ESFP	ENFP	ENTP
N= 3	N= 2	N= 1	N= 2
%= 2.97	%= 1.98	%= .99	%= 1.98

ESTJ	ESFJ	ENFJ	ENTJ
N= 20	N= 11	N= 5	N= 3
%= 19.80	%= 10.89	%= 4.95	%= 2.97

JUDGMENT — PERCEPTION — PERCEPTION — JUDGMENT
INTROVERSION — EXTRAVERSION

	N	%
E	47	46.53
I	54	53.47
S	81	80.20
N	20	19.80
T	56	55.45
F	45	44.55
J	79	78.22
P	22	21.78
I J	40	39.60
I P	14	13.86
E P	8	7.92
E J	39	38.61
S T	45	44.55
S F	36	35.64
N F	9	8.91
N T	11	10.89
S J	68	67.33
S P	13	12.87
N P	9	8.91
N J	11	10.89
T J	42	41.58
T P	14	13.86
F P	8	7.92
F J	37	36.63
I N	9	8.91
E N	11	10.89
I S	45	44.55
E S	36	35.64
E T	28	27.72
E F	19	18.81
I F	26	25.74
I T	28	27.72
S dom	42	41.58
N dom	6	5.94
T dom	32	31.68
F dom	21	20.79

Note: ■ = 1% of sample   8623161

Data collected by Peter J. Frazier-Koontz of Community Mental Health Center of Lancaster County, Nebraska during September 1983 using Form F. Subjects were 21% male and 79% female county administrators, their supervisors and state administrators of the Department of Social Services in Nebraska. No race or educational level data were reported. These data are used with permission and have not been published elsewhere to date.

Air Force Personnel

N = 73

					N	%
SENSING		**INTUITION**				
THINKING	FEELING	FEELING	THINKING			

ISTJ	ISFJ	INFJ	INTJ
N= 13	N= 6	N= 2	N= 5
%= 17.81	%= 8.22	%= 2.74	%= 6.85
■■■■■■■■■ ■■■■■■■■	■■■■■■■■	■■■	■■■■■■■

ISTP	ISFP	INFP	INTP
N= 7	N= 1	N= 5	N= 0
%= 9.59	%= 1.37	%= 6.85	%= 0.00
■■■■■■■■■	■	■■■■■■■	

ESTP	ESFP	ENFP	ENTP
N= 2	N= 3	N= 8	N= 4
%= 2.74	%= 4.11	%= 10.96	%= 5.48
■■■	■■■■	■■■■■■■■■■ ■	■■■■■

ESTJ	ESFJ	ENFJ	ENTJ
N= 9	N= 5	N= 1	N= 2
%= 12.33	%= 6.85	%= 1.37	%= 2.74
■■■■■■■■■ ■■	■■■■■■■	■	■■■

	N	%
E	34	46.58
I	39	53.42
S	46	63.01
N	27	36.99
T	42	57.53
F	31	42.47
J	43	58.90
P	30	41.10
I J	26	35.62
I P	13	17.81
E P	17	23.29
E J	17	23.29
S T	31	42.47
S F	15	20.55
N F	16	21.92
N T	11	15.07
S J	33	45.21
S P	13	17.81
N P	17	23.29
N J	10	13.70
T J	29	39.73
T P	13	17.81
F P	17	23.29
F J	14	19.18
I N	12	16.44
E N	15	20.55
I S	27	36.99
E S	19	26.03
E T	17	23.29
E F	17	23.29
I F	14	19.18
I T	25	34.25
S dom	24	32.88
N dom	19	26.03
T dom	18	24.66
F dom	12	16.44

Note: ■ = 1% of sample   8629446

This table is one of a series of tables from the CAPT-MBTI Data Bank of MBTI records submitted to CAPT for computer scoring between 1971 and June, 1984. This sample was drawn from 59,784 records with usable occupational codes from the total data bank of 232,557. This data bank has 51% Form F cases from 1971 to March, 1978, 35% Form F cases from 1978 to June, 1984 and 14% Form G cases from 1978 to December, 1982. An analysis of Form F and G data banks showed the data banks were comprised of 56% females and 44% males; education level completed: 6% some grade school, 30% high school diploma, 25% some college, 18% bachelor degrees, 11% masters degrees, 3% doctoral or post doctoral work, and 6% unknown. Age group percentages were: 11% under 18, 29% 18 to 20, 12% 21 to 24, 10% 25 to 29, 16% 30 to 39, 10% 40 to 49, 5% 50 to 59, 2% 60 plus, and 5% unknown.

305

Attorneys - Administrators, non-practicing

N = 84

	SENSING		INTUITION	
	THINKING	FEELING	FEELING	THINKING

				N	%
ISTJ N= 10 %= 11.90 ■■■■■■■■■■ ■■	**ISFJ** N= 3 %= 3.57 ■■■■	**INFJ** N= 3 %= 3.57 ■■■■	**INTJ** N= 15 %= 17.86 ■■■■■■■■■■■ ■■■■■■■		
ISTP N= 3 %= 3.57 ■■■■	**ISFP** N= 2 %= 2.38 ■■	**INFP** N= 7 %= 8.33 ■■■■■■■■	**INTP** N= 5 %= 5.95 ■■■■■■		
ESTP N= 1 %= 1.19 ■	**ESFP** N= 0 %= 0.00	**ENFP** N= 3 %= 3.57 ■■■■	**ENTP** N= 5 %= 5.95 ■■■■■■		
ESTJ N= 1 %= 1.19 ■	**ESFJ** N= 3 %= 3.57 ■■■■	**ENFJ** N= 5 %= 5.95 ■■■■■■	**ENTJ** N= 18 %= 21.43 ■■■■■■■■■■■■ ■■■■■■■■■■■ ■		

	N	%
E	36	42.86
I	48	57.14
S	23	27.38
N	61	72.62
T	58	69.05
F	26	30.95
J	58	69.05
P	26	30.95
I J	31	36.90
I P	17	20.24
E P	9	10.71
E J	27	32.14
S T	15	17.86
S F	8	9.52
N F	18	21.43
N T	43	51.19
S J	17	20.24
S P	6	7.14
N P	20	23.81
N J	41	48.81
T J	44	52.38
T P	14	16.67
F P	12	14.29
F J	14	16.67
I N	30	35.71
E N	31	36.90
I S	18	21.43
E S	5	5.95
E T	25	29.76
E F	11	13.10
I F	15	17.86
I T	33	39.29
S dom	14	16.67
N dom	26	30.95
T dom	27	32.14
F dom	17	20.24

JUDGMENT — INTROVERSION — PERCEPTION — PERCEPTION — EXTRAVERSION — JUDGMENT

Note: ■ = 1% of sample

8629440

This table is one of a series of tables from the CAPT-MBTI Data Bank of MBTI records submitted to CAPT for computer scoring between 1971 and June, 1984. This sample was drawn from 59,784 records with usable occupational codes from the total data bank of 232,557. This data bank has 51% Form F cases from 1971 to March, 1978, 35% Form F cases from 1978 to June, 1984 and 14% Form G cases from 1978 to December, 1982. An analysis of Form F and G data banks showed the data banks were comprised of 56% females and 44% males; education level completed: 6% some grade school, 30% high school diploma, 25% some college, 18% bachelor degrees, 11% masters degrees, 3% doctoral or post doctoral work, and 6% unknown. Age group percentages were: 11% under 18, 29% 18 to 20, 12% 21 to 24, 10% 25 to 29, 16% 30 to 39, 10% 40 to 49, 5% 50 to 59, 2% 60 plus, and 5% unknown.

Corrections Officers and Probation Officers

N = 68

	SENSING		INTUITION	
	THINKING	FEELING	FEELING	THINKING

ISTJ	ISFJ	INFJ	INTJ
N= 8	N= 10	N= 0	N= 2
%= 11.76	%= 14.71	%= 0.00	%= 2.94

ISTP	ISFP	INFP	INTP
N= 5	N= 3	N= 4	N= 1
%= 7.35	%= 4.41	%= 5.88	%= 1.47

ESTP	ESFP	ENFP	ENTP
N= 3	N= 2	N= 3	N= 5
%= 4.41	%= 2.94	%= 4.41	%= 7.35

ESTJ	ESFJ	ENFJ	ENTJ
N= 8	N= 6	N= 1	N= 7
%= 11.76	%= 8.82	%= 1.47	%= 10.29

	N	%
E	35	51.47
I	33	48.53
S	45	66.18
N	23	33.82
T	39	57.35
F	29	42.65
J	42	61.76
P	26	38.24
I J	20	29.41
I P	13	19.12
E P	13	19.12
E J	22	32.35
ST	24	35.29
SF	21	30.88
NF	8	11.76
NT	15	22.06
S J	32	47.06
S P	13	19.12
N P	13	19.12
N J	10	14.71
TJ	25	36.76
TP	14	20.59
FP	12	17.65
FJ	17	25.00
IN	7	10.29
EN	16	23.53
IS	26	38.24
ES	19	27.94
ET	23	33.82
EF	12	17.65
IF	17	25.00
IT	16	23.53
S dom	23	33.82
N dom	10	14.71
T dom	21	30.88
F dom	14	20.59

Note: ■ = 1% of sample   8629443

This table is one of a series of tables from the CAPT-MBTI Data Bank of MBTI records submitted to CAPT for computer scoring between 1971 and June, 1984. This sample was drawn from 59,784 records with usable occupational codes from the total data bank of 232,557. This data bank has 51% Form F cases from 1971 to March, 1978, 35% Form F cases from 1978 to June, 1984 and 14% Form G cases from 1978 to December, 1982. An analysis of Form F and G data banks showed the data banks were comprised of 56% females and 44% males; education level completed: 6% some grade school, 30% high school diploma, 25% some college, 18% bachelor degrees, 11% masters degrees, 3% doctoral or post doctoral work, and 6% unknown. Age group percentages were: 11% under 18, 29% 18 to 20, 12% 21 to 24, 10% 25 to 29, 16% 30 to 39, 10% 40 to 49, 5% 50 to 59, 2% 60 plus, and 5% unknown.

307

Corrections Sergeants

N = 89

	SENSING		INTUITION	
	THINKING	FEELING	FEELING	THINKING

ISTJ	ISFJ	INFJ	INTJ
N= 25	N= 16	N= 0	N= 1
%= 28.09	%= 17.98	%= 0.00	%= 1.12

ISTP	ISFP	INFP	INTP
N= 3	N= 2	N= 0	N= 0
%= 3.37	%= 2.25	%= 0.00	%= 0.00

ESTP	ESFP	ENFP	ENTP
N= 4	N= 0	N= 2	N= 0
%= 4.49	%= 0.00	%= 2.25	%= 0.00

ESTJ	ESFJ	ENFJ	ENTJ
N= 21	N= 10	N= 2	N= 3
%= 23.60	%= 11.24	%= 2.25	%= 3.37

Note: ■ = 1% of sample   8623156

	N	%
E	42	47.19
I	47	52.81
S	81	91.01
N	8	8.99
T	57	64.04
F	32	35.96
J	78	87.64
P	11	12.36
I J	42	47.19
I P	5	5.62
E P	6	6.74
E J	36	40.45
ST	53	59.55
SF	28	31.46
NF	4	4.49
NT	4	4.49
S J	72	80.90
S P	9	10.11
NP	2	2.25
NJ	6	6.74
TJ	50	56.18
TP	7	7.87
FP	4	4.49
FJ	28	31.46
IN	1	1.12
EN	7	7.87
I S	46	51.69
ES	35	39.33
ET	28	31.46
EF	14	15.73
IF	18	20.22
IT	29	32.58
S dom	45	50.56
N dom	3	3.37
T dom	27	30.34
F dom	14	15.73

Data collected by Daniel R. Bogart of the Correctional Training Institute, Florida Department of Offender Rehabilitation from September 1973 to September 1975 using Form F. The subjects were correctional officer sergeants attending the institute. Demographic data available for a subset of 44 line officers showed a mean age of 37 years, a modal educational level of high school diploma or equivalent and a range of two weeks to 20 years of service. No gender or race data were reported. These data are used with permission and have not been published elsewhere to date.

Guards and Watch Keepers

N = 86

	SENSING		INTUITION				N	%
	THINKING	FEELING	FEELING	THINKING		E	40	46.51

ISTJ N= 11 %= 12.79 ■■■■■■■■■■■■ ■■■	**ISFJ** N= 15 %= 17.44 ■■■■■■■■■■■ ■■■■■■■	**INFJ** N= 4 %= 4.65 ■■■■■	**INTJ** N= 2 %= 2.33 ■■
ISTP N= 4 %= 4.65 ■■■■■	**ISFP** N= 1 %= 1.16 ■	**INFP** N= 7 %= 8.14 ■■■■■■■■	**INTP** N= 2 %= 2.33 ■■
ESTP N= 5 %= 5.81 ■■■■■■	**ESFP** N= 2 %= 2.33 ■■	**ENFP** N= 2 %= 2.33 ■■	**ENTP** N= 3 %= 3.49 ■■■
ESTJ N= 13 %= 15.12 ■■■■■■■■■■■■ ■■■■■	**ESFJ** N= 10 %= 11.63 ■■■■■■■■■■■ ■■	**ENFJ** N= 5 %= 5.81 ■■■■■■	**ENTJ** N= 0 %= 0.00

	N	%
E	40	46.51
I	46	53.49
S	61	70.93
N	25	29.07
T	40	46.51
F	46	53.49
J	60	69.77
P	26	30.23
I J	32	37.21
I P	14	16.28
E P	12	13.95
E J	28	32.56
S T	33	38.37
S F	28	32.56
N F	18	20.93
N T	7	8.14
S J	49	56.98
S P	12	13.95
N P	14	16.28
N J	11	12.79
T J	26	30.23
T P	14	16.28
F P	12	13.95
F J	34	39.53
I N	15	17.44
E N	10	11.63
I S	31	36.05
E S	30	34.88
E T	21	24.42
E F	19	22.09
I F	27	31.40
I T	19	22.09
S dom	33	38.37
N dom	11	12.79
T dom	19	22.09
F dom	23	26.74

Note: ■ = 1% of sample   8629441

This table is one of a series of tables from the CAPT-MBTI Data Bank of MBTI records submitted to CAPT for computer scoring between 1971 and June, 1984. This sample was drawn from 59,784 records with usable occupational codes from the total data bank of 232,557. This data bank has 51% Form F cases from 1971 to March, 1978, 35% Form F cases from 1978 to June, 1984 and 14% Form G cases from 1978 to December, 1982. An analysis of Form F and G data banks showed the data banks were comprised of 56% females and 44% males; education level completed: 6% some grade school, 30% high school diploma, 25% some college, 18% bachelor degrees, 11% masters degrees, 3% doctoral or post doctoral work, and 6% unknown. Age group percentages were: 11% under 18, 29% 18 to 20, 12% 21 to 24, 10% 25 to 29, 16% 30 to 39, 10% 40 to 49, 5% 50 to 59, 2% 60 plus, and 5% unknown.

Judges

N = 128

	SENSING		INTUITION	
	THINKING	FEELING	FEELING	THINKING

ISTJ	ISFJ	INFJ	INTJ
N= 19	N= 11	N= 6	N= 6
%= 14.84	%= 8.59	%= 4.69	%= 4.69
■■■■■■■■■■■■■■	■■■■■■■■■	■■■■■	■■■■■
■■■■■			

ISTP	ISFP	INFP	INTP
N= 5	N= 0	N= 4	N= 9
%= 3.91	%= 0.00	%= 3.12	%= 7.03
■■■■		■■■	■■■■■■■

ESTP	ESFP	ENFP	ENTP
N= 3	N= 2	N= 5	N= 5
%= 2.34	%= 1.56	%= 3.91	%= 3.91
■■	■■	■■■■	■■■■

ESTJ	ESFJ	ENFJ	ENTJ
N= 27	N= 11	N= 7	N= 8
%= 21.09	%= 8.59	%= 5.47	%= 6.25
■■■■■■■■■■	■■■■■■■■■	■■■■■	■■■■■■
■■■■■■■■■			
■			

Note: ■ = 1% of sample   8629438

JUDGMENT — INTROVERSION
PERCEPTION
PERCEPTION — EXTRAVERSION
JUDGMENT

	N	%
E	68	53.12
I	60	46.87
S	78	60.94
N	50	39.06
T	82	64.06
F	46	35.94
J	95	74.22
P	33	25.78
I J	42	32.81
I P	18	14.06
E P	15	11.72
E J	53	41.41
S T	54	42.19
S F	24	18.75
N F	22	17.19
N T	28	21.88
S J	68	53.12
S P	10	7.81
N P	23	17.97
N J	27	21.09
T J	60	46.87
T P	22	17.19
F P	11	8.59
F J	35	27.34
I N	25	19.53
E N	25	19.53
I S	35	27.34
E S	43	33.59
E T	43	33.59
E F	25	19.53
I F	21	16.41
I T	39	30.47
S dom	35	27.34
N dom	22	17.19
T dom	49	38.28
F dom	22	17.19

This table is one of a series of tables from the CAPT-MBTI Data Bank of MBTI records submitted to CAPT for computer scoring between 1971 and June, 1984. This sample was drawn from 59,784 records with usable occupational codes from the total data bank of 232,557. This data bank has 51% Form F cases from 1971 to March, 1978, 35% Form F cases from 1978 to June, 1984 and 14% Form G cases from 1978 to December, 1982. An analysis of Form F and G data banks showed the data banks were comprised of 56% females and 44% males; education level completed: 6% some grade school, 30% high school diploma, 25% some college, 18% bachelor degrees, 11% masters degrees, 3% doctoral or post doctoral work, and 6% unknown. Age group percentages were: 11% under 18, 29% 18 to 20, 12% 21 to 24, 10% 25 to 29, 16% 30 to 39, 10% 40 to 49, 5% 50 to 59, 2% 60 plus, and 5% unknown.

Law School Graduates

	SENSING		INTUITION	
	THINKING	FEELING	FEELING	THINKING

ISTJ	ISFJ	INFJ	INTJ
N= 208	N= 45	N= 50	N= 172
%= 11.10	%= 2.40	%= 2.67	%= 9.18
■■■■■■■■■■ ■	■■	■■■	■■■■■■■■■

ISTP	ISFP	INFP	INTP
N= 69	N= 26	N= 89	N= 179
%= 3.68	%= 1.39	%= 4.75	%= 9.55
■■■■	■	■■■■■	■■■■■■■■■

ESTP	ESFP	ENFP	ENTP
N= 75	N= 36	N= 100	N= 199
%= 4.00	%= 1.92	%= 5.34	%= 10.62
■■■■	■■	■■■■■	■■■■■■■■■■ ■

ESTJ	ESFJ	ENFJ	ENTJ
N= 251	N= 66	N= 61	N= 248
%= 13.39	%= 3.52	%= 3.26	%= 13.23
■■■■■■■■■■ ■■■	■■■■	■■■	■■■■■■■■■■ ■■■

JUDGMENT — INTROVERSION — PERCEPTION / PERCEPTION — EXTRAVERSION — JUDGMENT

	N	%
E	1036	55.28
I	838	44.72
S	776	41.41
N	1098	58.59
T	1401	74.76
F	473	25.24
J	1101	58.75
P	773	41.25
I J	475	25.35
I P	363	19.37
E P	410	21.88
E J	626	33.40
S T	603	32.18
S F	173	9.23
N F	300	16.01
N T	798	42.58
S J	570	30.42
S P	206	10.99
N P	567	30.26
N J	531	28.34
T J	879	46.91
T P	522	27.85
F P	251	13.39
F J	222	11.85
I N	490	26.15
E N	608	32.44
I S	348	18.57
E S	428	22.84
E T	773	41.25
E F	263	14.03
I F	210	11.21
I T	628	33.51
S dom	364	19.42
N dom	521	27.80
T dom	747	39.86
F dom	242	12.91

Note: ■ = 1% of sample   8623162

Data collected by Paul V. Miller during September 1963 and 1965 using Form F. Subjects were male law students from seven universities who graduated. These graduates represented 83% of the entering freshmen classes. LSAT means from the various institutions ranged from 558.1 to 609.3 and the standard deviations ranged from 51.53 to 84.10. These data are used with permission and were cited in:

Miller, P. V. (1966). The contribution of non-cognitive variables to the prediction of student performance in law school (Doctoral dissertation, University of Pennsylvania, 1965). Dissertation Abstracts International, 27, 1679A. (University Microfilms No. 66-4630)

Lawyers

N = 271

	SENSING		INTUITION				N	%
	THINKING	FEELING	FEELING	THINKING				

<table>
<tr><td colspan="4">

ISTJ
N= 31
%= 11.44
■■■■■■■■■
■

ISFJ
N= 7
%= 2.58
■■■

INFJ
N= 15
%= 5.54
■■■■■■

INTJ
N= 41
%= 15.13
■■■■■■■■■■
■■■■■

</td></tr>
</table>

E	112	41.33
I	159	58.67
S	83	30.63
N	188	69.37
T	176	64.94
F	95	35.06
J	146	53.87
P	125	46.13
I J	94	34.69
I P	65	23.99
E P	60	22.14
E J	52	19.19
S T	65	23.99
S F	18	6.64
N F	77	28.41
N T	111	40.96
S J	58	21.40
S P	25	9.23
N P	100	36.90
N J	88	32.47
T J	109	40.22
T P	67	24.72
F P	58	21.40
F J	37	13.65
I N	101	37.27
E N	87	32.10
I S	58	21.40
E S	25	9.23
E T	61	22.51
E F	51	18.82
I F	44	16.24
I T	115	42.44
S dom	43	15.87
N dom	111	40.96
T dom	80	29.52
F dom	37	13.65

Grid cells:

ISTP	ISFP	INFP	INTP
N= 16 %= 5.90 ■■■■■■	N= 4 %= 1.48 ■	N= 18 %= 6.64 ■■■■■■■	N= 27 %= 9.96 ■■■■■■■■■■

ESTP	ESFP	ENFP	ENTP
N= 1 %= .37	N= 4 %= 1.48 ■	N= 32 %= 11.81 ■■■■■■■■■■■■ ■■	N= 23 %= 8.49 ■■■■■■■■

ESTJ	ESFJ	ENFJ	ENTJ
N= 17 %= 6.27 ■■■■■■	N= 3 %= 1.11 ■	N= 12 %= 4.43 ■■■■	N= 20 %= 7.38 ■■■■■■■

JUDGMENT — INTROVERSION — PERCEPTION — PERCEPTION — EXTRAVERSION — JUDGMENT

Note: ■ = 1% of sample

8629439

This table is one of a series of tables from the CAPT-MBTI Data Bank of MBTI records submitted to CAPT for computer scoring between 1971 and June, 1984. This sample was drawn from 59,784 records with usable occupational codes from the total data bank of 232,557. This data bank has 51% Form F cases from 1971 to March, 1978, 35% Form F cases from 1978 to June, 1984 and 14% Form G cases from 1978 to December, 1982. An analysis of Form F and G data banks showed the data banks were comprised of 56% females and 44% males; education level completed: 6% some grade school, 30% high school diploma, 25% some college, 18% bachelor degrees, 11% masters degrees, 3% doctoral or post doctoral work, and 6% unknown. Age group percentages were: 11% under 18, 29% 18 to 20, 12% 21 to 24, 10% 25 to 29, 16% 30 to 39, 10% 40 to 49, 5% 50 to 59, 2% 60 plus, and 5% unknown.

Line Corrections Officers

N = 574

		SENSING			INTUITION					N	%

	THINKING	FEELING	FEELING	THINKING		N	%

ISTJ	ISFJ	INFJ	INTJ
N= 138	N= 70	N= 4	N= 3
%= 24.04	%= 12.20	%= .70	%= .52

ISTP	ISFP	INFP	INTP
N= 40	N= 37	N= 10	N= 12
%= 6.97	%= 6.45	%= 1.74	%= 2.09

ESTP	ESFP	ENFP	ENTP
N= 21	N= 22	N= 15	N= 8
%= 3.66	%= 3.83	%= 2.61	%= 1.39

ESTJ	ESFJ	ENFJ	ENTJ
N= 122	N= 57	N= 5	N= 10
%= 21.25	%= 9.93	%= .87	%= 1.74

Right-side table:

	N	%
E	260	45.30
I	314	54.70
S	507	88.33
N	67	11.67
T	354	61.67
F	220	38.33
J	409	71.25
P	165	28.75
I J	215	37.46
I P	99	17.25
E P	66	11.50
E J	194	33.80
S T	321	55.92
S F	186	32.40
N F	34	5.92
N T	33	5.75
S J	387	67.42
S P	120	20.91
N P	45	7.84
N J	22	3.83
T J	273	47.56
T P	81	14.11
F P	84	14.63
F J	136	23.69
I N	29	5.05
E N	38	6.62
I S	285	49.65
E S	222	38.68
E T	161	28.05
E F	99	17.25
I F	121	21.08
I T	193	33.62
S dom	251	43.73
N dom	30	5.23
T dom	184	32.06
F dom	109	18.99

Note: ■ = 1% of sample   8623155

Data collected by Daniel R. Bogart of the Correctional Training Institute, Florida Department of Offender Rehabilitation from September 1973 to September 1975 using Form F. The subjects were correctional officers attending the institute. Demographic data available for a subset of 44 showed a mean age of 37 years, a modal educational level of high school diploma or equivalent and a range of two weeks to 20 years of service. No gender or race data were reported. These data are used with permission and have not been published elsewhere to date.

Managers: Fire

	SENSING		INTUITION	
	THINKING	FEELING	FEELING	THINKING

ISTJ	ISFJ	INFJ	INTJ
N= 9	N= 6	N= 0	N= 1
%= 15.00	%= 10.00	%= 0.00	%= 1.67
■■■■■■■■■■	■■■■■■■■■■		■■
■■■■■			

ISTP	ISFP	INFP	INTP
N= 3	N= 4	N= 0	N= 0
%= 5.00	%= 6.67	%= 0.00	%= 0.00
■■■■■	■■■■■■■		

ESTP	ESFP	ENFP	ENTP
N= 4	N= 3	N= 2	N= 3
%= 6.67	%= 5.00	%= 3.33	%= 5.00
■■■■■■■	■■■■■	■■■	■■■■■

ESTJ	ESFJ	ENFJ	ENTJ
N= 22	N= 1	N= 1	N= 1
%= 36.67	%= 1.67	%= 1.67	%= 1.67
■■■■■■■■■■	■■	■■	■■
■■■■■■■■■■			
■■■■■■■■■■			
■■■■■■			

JUDGMENT — INTROVERSION — PERCEPTION — PERCEPTION — EXTRAVERSION — JUDGMENT

	N	%
E	37	61.67
I	23	38.33
S	52	86.67
N	8	13.33
T	43	71.67
F	17	28.33
J	41	68.33
P	19	31.67
I J	16	26.67
I P	7	11.67
E P	12	20.00
E J	25	41.67
S T	38	63.33
S F	14	23.33
N F	3	5.00
N T	5	8.33
S J	38	63.33
S P	14	23.33
N P	5	8.33
N J	3	5.00
T J	33	55.00
T P	10	16.67
F P	9	15.00
F J	8	13.33
I N	1	1.67
E N	7	11.67
I S	22	36.67
E S	30	50.00
E T	30	50.00
E F	7	11.67
I F	10	16.67
I T	13	21.67
S dom	22	36.67
N dom	6	10.00
T dom	26	43.33
F dom	6	10.00

Note: ■ = 1% of sample   8623166

Data collected by Ron Lynch of the Institute of Government, University of North Carolina at Chapel Hill from 1980 to 1986 using Form F. Subjects were fire managers attending the institute from various states in the southeast. Fire managers were 100% male. These data are used with permission and have not been published elsewhere to date.

Managers: Middle Level in City, County and State Government

N = 290

	SENSING		INTUITION				N	%
	THINKING	FEELING	FEELING	THINKING				

<table>
<tr><td colspan="4">
ISTJ
N= 52
%= 17.93
■■■■■■■■■■
■■■■■■■■
</td></tr>
</table>

ISTJ	ISFJ	INFJ	INTJ			E	162	55.86
N= 52	N= 28	N= 2	N= 17			I	128	44.14
%= 17.93	%= 9.66	%= .69	%= 5.86			S	208	71.72
■■■■■■■■■■	■■■■■■■■■■	■	■■■■■■	JUDGMENT		N	82	28.28
■■■■■■■■						T	206	71.03
						F	84	28.97
						J	221	76.21
					INTROVERSION	P	69	23.79
ISTP	ISFP	INFP	INTP			I J	99	34.14
N= 9	N= 9	N= 5	N= 6			I P	29	10.00
%= 3.10	%= 3.10	%= 1.72	%= 2.07			E P	40	13.79
■■■	■■■	■■	■■	PERCEPTION		E J	122	42.07
						ST	147	50.69
						SF	61	21.03
						NF	23	7.93
						NT	59	20.34
ESTP	ESFP	ENFP	ENTP			S J	168	57.93
N= 16	N= 6	N= 7	N= 11			S P	40	13.79
%= 5.52	%= 2.07	%= 2.41	%= 3.79			N P	29	10.00
■■■■■■	■■	■■	■■■■	PERCEPTION	EXTRAVERSION	N J	53	18.28
						T J	164	56.55
						T P	42	14.48
						F P	27	9.31
						F J	57	19.66
ESTJ	ESFJ	ENFJ	ENTJ			I N	30	10.34
N= 70	N= 18	N= 9	N= 25			E N	52	17.93
%= 24.14	%= 6.21	%= 3.10	%= 8.62			I S	98	33.79
■■■■■■■■■■	■■■■■■	■■■	■■■■■■■■■	JUDGMENT		E S	110	37.93
■■■■■■■■■■						E T	122	42.07
■■■■						E F	40	13.79
						I F	44	15.17
						I T	84	28.97
						S dom	102	35.17
						N dom	37	12.76
						T dom	110	37.93
						F dom	41	14.14

Note: ■ = 1% of sample   8623160

Data collected by Ron Lynch of the Institute of Government, University of North Carolina at Chapel Hill from 1980 to 1983 using Form F. Subjects were 43% female and 57% male middle level city, county and state managers attending the institute from across North Carolina. These data are used with permission and have not been published elsewhere to date.

N = 523

	SENSING		INTUITION	
	THINKING	FEELING	FEELING	THINKING

ISTJ	ISFJ	INFJ	INTJ
N= 138	N= 29	N= 8	N= 29
%= 26.39	%= 5.54	%= 1.53	%= 5.54

ISTP	ISFP	INFP	INTP
N= 25	N= 10	N= 8	N= 15
%= 4.78	%= 1.91	%= 1.53	%= 2.87

ESTP	ESFP	ENFP	ENTP
N= 14	N= 10	N= 18	N= 14
%= 2.68	%= 1.91	%= 3.44	%= 2.68

ESTJ	ESFJ	ENFJ	ENTJ
N= 119	N= 37	N= 13	N= 36
%= 22.75	%= 7.07	%= 2.49	%= 6.88

JUDGMENT — INTROVERSION — PERCEPTION — PERCEPTION — EXTRAVERSION — JUDGMENT

	N	%
E	261	49.90
I	262	50.10
S	382	73.04
N	141	26.96
T	390	74.57
F	133	25.43
J	409	78.20
P	114	21.80
I J	204	39.01
I P	58	11.09
E P	56	10.71
E J	205	39.20
S T	296	56.60
S F	86	16.44
N F	47	8.99
N T	94	17.97
S J	323	61.76
S P	59	11.28
N P	55	10.52
N J	86	16.44
T J	322	61.57
T P	68	13.00
F P	46	8.80
F J	87	16.63
I N	60	11.47
E N	81	15.49
I S	202	38.62
E S	180	34.42
E T	183	34.99
E F	78	14.91
I F	55	10.52
I T	207	39.58
S dom	191	36.52
N dom	69	13.19
T dom	195	37.28
F dom	68	13.00

Note: ■ = 1% of sample   8623164

Data collected by Ron Lynch of the Institute of Government, University of North Carolina at Chapel Hill from 1980 to 1986 using Form F. Subjects were public managers attending various institute programs. Public managers were 26% female, 74% male, and from across the southeastern United States with a predominance of managers from North Carolina. These data are used with permission and have not been published elsewhere to date.

Managers: Top Level in City, County and State Government

	SENSING		INTUITION	
	THINKING	FEELING	FEELING	THINKING

ISTJ	ISFJ	INFJ	INTJ
N= 79	N= 16	N= 5	N= 19
%= 30.74	%= 6.23	%= 1.95	%= 7.39
■■■■■■■■■■ ■■■■■■■■■■ ■■■■■■■■■■ ■	■■■■■■	■■	■■■■■■■

ISTP	ISFP	INFP	INTP
N= 12	N= 4	N= 3	N= 10
%= 4.67	%= 1.56	%= 1.17	%= 3.89
■■■■■	■■	■	■■■■

ESTP	ESFP	ENFP	ENTP
N= 4	N= 4	N= 5	N= 4
%= 1.56	%= 1.56	%= 1.95	%= 1.56
■■	■■	■■	■■

ESTJ	ESFJ	ENFJ	ENTJ
N= 57	N= 10	N= 7	N= 18
%= 22.18	%= 3.89	%= 2.72	%= 7.00
■■■■■■■■■■ ■■■■■■■■■■ ■■	■■■■	■■■	■■■■■■■

Right side labels: JUDGMENT / PERCEPTION — INTROVERSION ; PERCEPTION / JUDGMENT — EXTRAVERSION

	N	%
E	109	42.41
I	148	57.59
S	186	72.37
N	71	27.63
T	203	78.99
F	54	21.01
J	211	82.10
P	46	17.90
I J	119	46.30
I P	29	11.28
E P	17	6.61
E J	92	35.80
S T	152	59.14
S F	34	13.23
N F	20	7.78
N T	51	19.84
S J	162	63.04
S P	24	9.34
N P	22	8.56
N J	49	19.07
T J	173	67.32
T P	30	11.67
F P	16	6.23
F J	38	14.79
I N	37	14.40
E N	34	13.23
I S	111	43.19
E S	75	29.18
E T	83	32.30
E F	26	10.12
I F	28	10.89
I T	120	46.69
S dom	103	40.08
N dom	33	12.84
T dom	97	37.74
F dom	24	9.34

Note: ■ = 1% of sample   8623159

Data collected by Ron Lynch of the Institute of Government, University of North Carolina at Chapel Hill from 1980 to 1983 using Form F. Subjects were 20% female and 80% male top level city, county and state managers attending the institute from across North Carolina. These data are used with permission and have not been published elsewhere to date.

Military Personnel at Naval Technical Training Center

N = 4663

	SENSING		INTUITION				N	%
	THINKING	FEELING	FEELING	THINKING				

ISTJ	ISFJ	INFJ	INTJ
N= 883	N= 395	N= 105	N= 233
%= 18.94	%= 8.47	%= 2.25	%= 5.00
■■■■■■■■■ ■■■■■■■■■	■■■■■■■■	■■	■■■■■

ISTP	ISFP	INFP	INTP
N= 289	N= 250	N= 265	N= 177
%= 6.20	%= 5.36	%= 5.68	%= 3.80
■■■■■■	■■■■■	■■■■■■	■■■■

ESTP	ESFP	ENFP	ENTP
N= 200	N= 192	N= 291	N= 235
%= 4.29	%= 4.12	%= 6.24	%= 5.04
■■■■	■■■■	■■■■■■	■■■■■

ESTJ	ESFJ	ENFJ	ENTJ
N= 555	N= 260	N= 129	N= 204
%= 11.90	%= 5.58	%= 2.77	%= 4.37
■■■■■■■■■■■ ■■	■■■■■■	■■■	■■■■

Note: ■ = 1% of sample

8623157

	N	%
E	2066	44.31
I	2597	55.69
S	3024	64.85
N	1639	35.15
T	2776	59.53
F	1887	40.47
J	2764	59.28
P	1899	40.72
I J	1616	34.66
I P	981	21.04
E P	918	19.69
E J	1148	24.62
S T	1927	41.33
S F	1097	23.53
N F	790	16.94
N T	849	18.21
S J	2093	44.89
S P	931	19.97
N P	968	20.76
N J	671	14.39
T J	1875	40.21
T P	901	19.32
F P	998	21.40
F J	889	19.06
I N	780	16.73
E N	859	18.42
I S	1817	38.97
E S	1207	25.88
E T	1194	25.61
E F	872	18.70
I F	1015	21.77
I T	1582	33.93
S dom	1670	35.81
N dom	864	18.53
T dom	1225	26.27
F dom	904	19.39

Data collected by Keith Waters and Bill Holt. Subjects were military enlisted personnel attending a Class A school in cryptology at a southeastern naval technical training center. No gender, race or educational level data were reported. These data are used with permission and have not been published elsewhere to date.

Navy Enlisted Personnel in Basic Electronic Training

N = 1009

	SENSING		INTUITION	
	THINKING	FEELING	FEELING	THINKING

ISTJ	ISFJ	INFJ	INTJ
N= 128	N= 54	N= 34	N= 47
%= 12.69	%= 5.35	%= 3.37	%= 4.66
■■■■■■■■■■ ■■■	■■■■■	■■■	■■■■■

ISTP	ISFP	INFP	INTP
N= 82	N= 61	N= 78	N= 89
%= 8.13	%= 6.05	%= 7.73	%= 8.82
■■■■■■■■	■■■■■■	■■■■■■■■	■■■■■■■■■

ESTP	ESFP	ENFP	ENTP
N= 48	N= 36	N= 83	N= 76
%= 4.76	%= 3.57	%= 8.23	%= 7.53
■■■■■	■■■■	■■■■■■■■	■■■■■■■■

ESTJ	ESFJ	ENFJ	ENTJ
N= 82	N= 40	N= 22	N= 49
%= 8.13	%= 3.96	%= 2.18	%= 4.86
■■■■■■■■	■■■■	■■	■■■■■

JUDGMENT — INTROVERSION — PERCEPTION — PERCEPTION — EXTRAVERSION — JUDGMENT

	N	%
E	436	43.21
I	573	56.79
S	531	52.63
N	478	47.37
T	601	59.56
F	408	40.44
J	456	45.19
P	553	54.81
I J	263	26.07
I P	310	30.72
E P	243	24.08
E J	193	19.13
S T	340	33.70
S F	191	18.93
N F	217	21.51
N T	261	25.87
S J	304	30.13
S P	227	22.50
N P	326	32.31
N J	152	15.06
T J	306	30.33
T P	295	29.24
F P	258	25.57
F J	150	14.87
I N	248	24.58
E N	230	22.79
I S	325	32.21
E S	206	20.42
E T	255	25.27
E F	181	17.94
I F	227	22.50
I T	346	34.29
S dom	266	26.36
N dom	240	23.79
T dom	302	29.93
F dom	201	19.92

Note: ■ = 1% of sample   8623169

Data collected by Lloyd H. Steele from May 1983 to March 1984 using Form G. Subjects were 95% male and 5% female naval enlisted personnel in basic electronic technology training. Typical ages of subjects were 18 to 20. No other demographic data were reported. These data are used with permission and have not been published elsewhere to date.

Police Officers

	SENSING		INTUITION	
	THINKING	FEELING	FEELING	THINKING

ISTJ	ISFJ	INFJ	INTJ
N= 57	N= 39	N= 3	N= 4
%= 12.98	%= 8.88	%= .68	%= .91

ISTP	ISFP	INFP	INTP
N= 39	N= 32	N= 17	N= 13
%= 8.88	%= 7.29	%= 3.87	%= 2.96

ESTP	ESFP	ENFP	ENTP
N= 32	N= 28	N= 15	N= 23
%= 7.29	%= 6.38	%= 3.42	%= 5.24

ESTJ	ESFJ	ENFJ	ENTJ
N= 78	N= 36	N= 5	N= 18
%= 17.77	%= 8.20	%= 1.14	%= 4.10

JUDGMENT — INTROVERSION — PERCEPTION — PERCEPTION — EXTRAVERSION — JUDGMENT

	N	%
E	235	53.53
I	204	46.47
S	341	77.68
N	98	22.32
T	264	60.14
F	175	39.86
J	240	54.67
P	199	45.33
I J	103	23.46
I P	101	23.01
E P	98	22.32
E J	137	31.21
S T	206	46.92
S F	135	30.75
N F	40	9.11
N T	58	13.21
S J	210	47.84
S P	131	29.84
N P	68	15.49
N J	30	6.83
T J	157	35.76
T P	107	24.37
F P	92	20.96
F J	83	18.91
I N	37	8.43
E N	61	13.90
I S	167	38.04
E S	174	39.64
E T	151	34.40
E F	84	19.13
I F	91	20.73
I T	113	25.74
S dom	156	35.54
N dom	45	10.25
T dom	148	33.71
F dom	90	20.50

Note: ■ = 1% of sample   8623146

Data collected by Wayne Hanewicz of College of Interdisciplinary Technology, Eastern Michigan College, during the late 1970's using Form F. The subjects were veteran police officers who were 99% male; ages ranged from 25 to 45; education levels ranged from high school diploma to two year college degrees; the officers were predominantly white. The police officers were from medium and small sized mid-western police departments. These data are used with permission and were cited in:

Hanewicz, W. (1978). Police personality: A Jungian perspective. Crime & Delinquency, 24(2), 152-172.

Police Officers: Australian Senior Officers

N = 99

	SENSING		INTUITION	
	THINKING	FEELING	FEELING	THINKING

ISTJ	ISFJ	INFJ	INTJ
N= 25	N= 15	N= 2	N= 1
%= 25.25	%= 15.15	%= 2.02	%= 1.01

ISTP	ISFP	INFP	INTP
N= 3	N= 2	N= 1	N= 1
%= 3.03	%= 2.02	%= 1.01	%= 1.01

ESTP	ESFP	ENFP	ENTP
N= 2	N= 3	N= 2	N= 0
%= 2.02	%= 3.03	%= 2.02	%= 0.00

ESTJ	ESFJ	ENFJ	ENTJ
N= 25	N= 11	N= 2	N= 4
%= 25.25	%= 11.11	%= 2.02	%= 4.04

JUDGMENT — INTROVERSION — PERCEPTION — PERCEPTION — EXTRAVERSION — JUDGMENT

	N	%
E	49	49.49
I	50	50.51
S	86	86.87
N	13	13.13
T	61	61.62
F	38	38.38
J	85	85.86
P	14	14.14
I J	43	43.43
I P	7	7.07
E P	7	7.07
E J	42	42.42
S T	55	55.56
S F	31	31.31
N F	7	7.07
N T	6	6.06
S J	76	76.77
S P	10	10.10
N P	4	4.04
N J	9	9.09
T J	55	55.56
T P	6	6.06
F P	8	8.08
F J	30	30.30
I N	5	5.05
E N	8	8.08
I S	45	45.45
E S	41	41.41
E T	31	31.31
E F	18	18.18
I F	20	20.20
I T	30	30.30
S dom	45	45.45
N dom	5	5.05
T dom	33	33.33
F dom	16	16.16

Note: ■ = 1% of sample   8623147

Data collected by Ron Cacioppe of Macquairie University, Australia from 1978 to 1980. The subjects were police officers attending senior officers' courses at the Australian Police College. The officers were 98% male and 2% female. No other demographic data were reported. These data are used with permission and have not been published elsewhere to date.

Police Officers: Commanders

N = 57

	SENSING			INTUITION			
THINKING	FEELING	FEELING	THINKING

ISTJ	ISFJ	INFJ	INTJ
N= 20	N= 4	N= 0	N= 3
%= 35.09	%= 7.02	%= 0.00	%= 5.26
■■■■■■■■■■ ■■■■■■■■■■ ■■■■■■■■■■ ■■■■■	■■■■■■■		■■■■■

ISTP	ISFP	INFP	INTP
N= 2	N= 1	N= 0	N= 1
%= 3.51	%= 1.75	%= 0.00	%= 1.75
■■■■	■■		■■

ESTP	ESFP	ENFP	ENTP
N= 1	N= 0	N= 2	N= 2
%= 1.75	%= 0.00	%= 3.51	%= 3.51
■■		■■■■	■■■■

ESTJ	ESFJ	ENFJ	ENTJ
N= 14	N= 1	N= 2	N= 4
%= 24.56	%= 1.75	%= 3.51	%= 7.02
■■■■■■■■■■ ■■■■■■■■■■ ■■■■■	■■	■■■■	■■■■■■■

JUDGMENT · INTROVERSION · PERCEPTION · PERCEPTION · EXTRAVERSION · JUDGMENT

	N	%
E	26	45.61
I	31	54.39
S	43	75.44
N	14	24.56
T	47	82.46
F	10	17.54
J	48	84.21
P	9	15.79
I J	27	47.37
I P	4	7.02
E P	5	8.77
E J	21	36.84
S T	37	64.91
S F	6	10.53
N F	4	7.02
N T	10	17.54
S J	39	68.42
S P	4	7.02
N P	5	8.77
N J	9	15.79
T J	41	71.93
T P	6	10.53
F P	3	5.26
F J	7	12.28
I N	4	7.02
E N	10	17.54
I S	27	47.37
E S	16	28.07
E T	21	36.84
E F	5	8.77
I F	5	8.77
I T	26	45.61
S dom	25	43.86
N dom	7	12.28
T dom	21	36.84
F dom	4	7.02

Note: ■ = 1% of sample

8623154

Data collected by Ron Lynch of the Institute of Government, University of North Carolina at Chapel Hill from 1984 to 1986 using Form F. Subjects were police commanders attending various institute programs. Police commanders were approximately 95% male, 5% female and mostly from the southeastern United States. These data are used with permission and have not been published elsewhere to date.

Police Officers: Detectives in Urban Community

N = 47

	SENSING		INTUITION	
	THINKING	FEELING	FEELING	THINKING

ISTJ	ISFJ	INFJ	INTJ
N= 8	N= 6	N= 1	N= 2
%= 17.02	%= 12.77	%= 2.13	%= 4.26

ISTP	ISFP	INFP	INTP
N= 0	N= 4	N= 0	N= 1
%= 0.00	%= 8.51	%= 0.00	%= 2.13

ESTP	ESFP	ENFP	ENTP
N= 4	N= 1	N= 3	N= 0
%= 8.51	%= 2.13	%= 6.38	%= 0.00

ESTJ	ESFJ	ENFJ	ENTJ
N= 10	N= 5	N= 2	N= 0
%= 21.28	%= 10.64	%= 4.26	%= 0.00

	N	%
E	25	53.19
I	22	46.81
S	38	80.85
N	9	19.15
T	25	53.19
F	22	46.81
J	34	72.34
P	13	27.66
I J	17	36.17
I P	5	10.64
E P	8	17.02
E J	17	36.17
S T	22	46.81
S F	16	34.04
N F	6	12.77
N T	3	6.38
S J	29	61.70
S P	9	19.15
N P	4	8.51
N J	5	10.64
T J	20	42.55
T P	5	10.64
F P	8	17.02
F J	14	29.79
I N	4	8.51
E N	5	10.64
I S	18	38.30
E S	20	42.55
E T	14	29.79
E F	11	23.40
I F	11	23.40
I T	11	23.40
S dom	19	40.43
N dom	6	12.77
T dom	11	23.40
F dom	11	23.40

Note: ■ = 1% of sample   8623151

Data collected by Wayne Hanewicz of College of Interdisciplinary Technology, Eastern Michigan College, during the late 1970's using Form F. The subjects were a subset of 278 male and 2 female veteran police officers. On the average, the officers were 36.5 years old, completed 13.0 years of education, and were 62% white. The reported ranks were 51% patrol officer, 30% sergeant, 13% lieutenant, and 3% captain; the officers had an average of 10.6 years of service. This sample was collected in a large southeastern urban area. These data are used with permission and were cited in:

Hanewicz, W. (1978). Police personality: A Jungian perspective. Crime & Delinquency, 24(2), 152-172.

Police Officers: Managers

N = 912

	SENSING		INTUITION	
	THINKING	FEELING	FEELING	THINKING

ISTJ	ISFJ	INFJ	INTJ
N= 300	N= 40	N= 6	N= 41
%= 32.89	%= 4.39	%= .66	%= 4.50

ISTP	ISFP	INFP	INTP
N= 49	N= 13	N= 5	N= 21
%= 5.37	%= 1.43	%= .55	%= 2.30

ESTP	ESFP	ENFP	ENTP
N= 22	N= 13	N= 25	N= 20
%= 2.41	%= 1.43	%= 2.74	%= 2.19

ESTJ	ESFJ	ENFJ	ENTJ
N= 243	N= 34	N= 15	N= 65
%= 26.64	%= 3.73	%= 1.64	%= 7.13

JUDGMENT · INTROVERSION · PERCEPTION · PERCEPTION · EXTRAVERSION · JUDGMENT

	N	%
E	437	47.92
I	475	52.08
S	714	78.29
N	198	21.71
T	761	83.44
F	151	16.56
J	744	81.58
P	168	18.42
I J	387	42.43
I P	88	9.65
E P	80	8.77
E J	357	39.14
ST	614	67.32
SF	100	10.96
NF	51	5.59
NT	147	16.12
S J	617	67.65
S P	97	10.64
N P	71	7.79
N J	127	13.93
T J	649	71.16
T P	112	12.28
F P	56	6.14
F J	95	10.42
I N	73	8.00
E N	125	13.71
I S	402	44.08
E S	312	34.21
ET	350	38.38
EF	87	9.54
I F	64	7.02
I T	411	45.07
S dom	375	41.12
N dom	92	10.09
T dom	378	41.45
F dom	67	7.35

Note: ■ = 1% of sample

8623163

Data collected by Ron Lynch of the Institute of Government, University of North Carolina at Chapel Hill from 1980 to 1986 using Form F. Subjects were 3% female and 97% male police managers attending the institute from various states in the southeast. These data are used with permission and have not been published elsewhere to date.

Police Officers: Patrolmen in Urban Community

N = 141

	SENSING		INTUITION				N	%
	THINKING	FEELING	FEELING	THINKING				

ISTJ	ISFJ	INFJ	INTJ
N= 18	N= 8	N= 2	N= 4
%= 12.77	%= 5.67	%= 1.42	%= 2.84
∎∎∎∎∎∎∎∎∎∎∎∎	∎∎∎∎∎	∎	∎∎∎
∎∎∎			

ISTP	ISFP	INFP	INTP
N= 15	N= 3	N= 5	N= 4
%= 10.64	%= 2.13	%= 3.55	%= 2.84
∎∎∎∎∎∎∎∎∎∎	∎∎	∎∎∎∎	∎∎∎
∎			

ESTP	ESFP	ENFP	ENTP
N= 11	N= 8	N= 1	N= 4
%= 7.80	%= 5.67	%= .71	%= 2.84
∎∎∎∎∎∎∎∎	∎∎∎∎∎∎	∎	∎∎∎

ESTJ	ESFJ	ENFJ	ENTJ
N= 35	N= 15	N= 2	N= 6
%= 24.82	%= 10.64	%= 1.42	%= 4.26
∎∎∎∎∎∎∎∎∎∎∎∎	∎∎∎∎∎∎∎∎∎∎∎	∎∎∎∎	∎∎∎∎
∎∎∎∎∎∎∎∎∎∎	∎		
∎∎∎∎∎			

JUDGMENT / INTROVERSION / PERCEPTION / PERCEPTION / EXTRAVERSION / JUDGMENT

	N	%
E	82	58.16
I	59	41.84
S	113	80.14
N	28	19.86
T	97	68.79
F	44	31.21
J	90	63.83
P	51	36.17
I J	32	22.70
I P	27	19.15
E P	24	17.02
E J	58	41.13
S T	79	56.03
S F	34	24.11
N F	10	7.09
N T	18	12.77
S J	76	53.90
S P	37	26.24
N P	14	9.93
N J	14	9.93
T J	63	44.68
T P	34	24.11
F P	17	12.06
F J	27	19.15
I N	15	10.64
E N	13	9.22
I S	44	31.21
E S	69	48.94
E T	56	39.72
E F	26	18.44
I F	18	12.77
I T	41	29.08
S dom	45	31.91
N dom	11	7.80
T dom	60	42.55
F dom	25	17.73

Note: ∎ = 1% of sample   8623149

Data collected by Wayne Hanewicz of College of Interdisciplinary Technology, Eastern Michigan College, during the late 1970's using Form F. The subjects were a subset of 278 male and 2 female veteran police officers. On the average, the officers were 36.5 years old, completed 13.0 years of education, and were 62% white. The reported ranks were 51% patrol officer, 30% sergeant, 13% lieutenant, and 3% captain; the officers had an average of 10.6 years of service. This sample was collected in a large southeastern urban area. These data are used with permission and were cited in:

Hanewicz, W. (1978). Police personality: A Jungian perspective. Crime & Delinquency, 24(2), 152-172.

Police Officers: Supervisors in Urban Community

	SENSING		INTUITION	
	THINKING	FEELING	FEELING	THINKING

ISTJ	ISFJ	INFJ	INTJ
N= 13	N= 10	N= 0	N= 3
%= 14.13	%= 10.87	%= 0.00	%= 3.26
■■■■■■■■■■	■■■■■■■■■■		■■■
■■■■	■		

ISTP	ISFP	INFP	INTP
N= 4	N= 3	N= 1	N= 0
%= 4.35	%= 3.26	%= 1.09	%= 0.00
■■■■	■■■	■	

ESTP	ESFP	ENFP	ENTP
N= 7	N= 7	N= 3	N= 5
%= 7.61	%= 7.61	%= 3.26	%= 5.43
■■■■■■■■	■■■■■■■■	■■■	■■■■■

ESTJ	ESFJ	ENFJ	ENTJ
N= 27	N= 1	N= 2	N= 6
%= 29.35	%= 1.09	%= 2.17	%= 6.52
■■■■■■■■■■	■	■■	■■■■■■■
■■■■■■■■■■			
■■■■■■■■			

JUDGMENT — PERCEPTION — PERCEPTION — JUDGMENT
INTROVERSION — EXTRAVERSION

	N	%
E	58	63.04
I	34	36.96
S	72	78.26
N	20	21.74
T	65	70.65
F	27	29.35
J	62	67.39
P	30	32.61
I J	26	28.26
I P	8	8.70
E P	22	23.91
E J	36	39.13
S T	51	55.43
S F	21	22.83
N F	6	6.52
N T	14	15.22
S J	51	55.43
S P	21	22.83
N P	9	9.78
N J	11	11.96
T J	49	53.26
T P	16	17.39
F P	14	15.22
F J	13	14.13
I N	4	4.35
E N	16	17.39
I S	30	32.61
E S	42	45.65
E T	45	48.91
E F	13	14.13
I F	14	15.22
I T	20	21.74
S dom	37	40.22
N dom	11	11.96
T dom	37	40.22
F dom	7	7.61

Note: ■ = 1% of sample   8623150

Data collected by Wayne Hanewicz of College of Interdisciplinary Technology, Eastern Michigan College, during the late 1970's using Form F. The subjects were a subset of 278 male and 2 female veteran police officers. On the average, the officers were 36.5 years old, completed 13.0 years of education, and were 62% white. The reported ranks were 51% patrol officer, 30% sergeant, 13% lieutenant, and 3% captain; the officers had an average of 10.6 years of service. This sample was collected in a large southeastern urban area. These data are used with permission and were cited in:

Hanewicz, W. (1978). Police personality: A Jungian perspective. Crime & Delinquency, 24(2), 152-172.

Police Officers: Urban Community

N = 280

	SENSING		INTUITION	
	THINKING	FEELING	FEELING	THINKING

ISTJ	ISFJ	INFJ	INTJ
N= 39	N= 24	N= 3	N= 9
%= 13.93	%= 8.57	%= 1.07	%= 3.21
■■■■■■■■■■	■■■■■■■■■	■	■■■
■■■■			

ISTP	ISFP	INFP	INTP
N= 19	N= 10	N= 6	N= 5
%= 6.79	%= 3.57	%= 2.14	%= 1.79
■■■■■■■	■■■■	■■	■■

ESTP	ESFP	ENFP	ENTP
N= 22	N= 16	N= 7	N= 9
%= 7.86	%= 5.71	%= 2.50	%= 3.21
■■■■■■■■	■■■■■■	■■■	■■■

ESTJ	ESFJ	ENFJ	ENTJ
N= 72	N= 21	N= 6	N= 12
%= 25.71	%= 7.50	%= 2.14	%= 4.29
■■■■■■■■■■	■■■■■■■■	■■	■■■■
■■■■■■■■■■			
■■■■■■			

	N	%
E	165	58.93
I	115	41.07
S	223	79.64
N	57	20.36
T	187	66.79
F	93	33.21
J	186	66.43
P	94	33.57
I J	75	26.79
I P	40	14.29
E P	54	19.29
E J	111	39.64
S T	152	54.29
S F	71	25.36
N F	22	7.86
N T	35	12.50
S J	156	55.71
S P	67	23.93
N P	27	9.64
N J	30	10.71
T J	132	47.14
T P	55	19.64
F P	39	13.93
F J	54	19.29
I N	23	8.21
E N	34	12.14
I S	92	32.86
E S	131	46.79
E T	115	41.07
E F	50	17.86
I F	43	15.36
I T	72	25.71
S dom	101	36.07
N dom	28	10.00
T dom	108	38.57
F dom	43	15.36

Note: ■ = 1% of sample   8623148

Data collected by Wayne Hanewicz of College of Interdisciplinary Technology, Eastern Michigan College, during the late 1970's using Form F. The subjects were 278 male and 2 female veteran police officers. On the average, the officers were 36.5 years old, completed 13.0 years of education, and were 62% white. The reported ranks were 51% patrol officer, 30% sergeant, 13% lieutenant, and 3% captain; officers had an average of 10.6 years of service This sample was collected in a large southeastern urban area. These data are used with permission and were cited in:

Hanewicz, W. (1978). Police personality: A Jungian perspective. Crime & Delinquency, 24(2), 152-172.

327

Police Supervisors

N = 105

	SENSING		INTUITION	
	THINKING	FEELING	FEELING	THINKING

ISTJ	**ISFJ**	**INFJ**	**INTJ**
N= 23	N= 11	N= 2	N= 3
%= 21.90	%= 10.48	%= 1.90	%= 2.86
■■■■■■■■■■	■■■■■■■■■■	■■	■■■
■■■■■■■■■			
■■			

ISTP	**ISFP**	**INFP**	**INTP**
N= 5	N= 2	N= 7	N= 2
%= 4.76	%= 1.90	%= 6.67	%= 1.90
■■■■■	■■	■■■■■■■	■■

ESTP	**ESFP**	**ENFP**	**ENTP**
N= 6	N= 4	N= 4	N= 2
%= 5.71	%= 3.81	%= 3.81	%= 1.90
■■■■■■	■■■■	■■■■	■■

ESTJ	**ESFJ**	**ENFJ**	**ENTJ**
N= 20	N= 5	N= 3	N= 6
%= 19.05	%= 4.76	%= 2.86	%= 5.71
■■■■■■■■■	■■■■■	■■■	■■■■■■
■■■■■■■■■			

JUDGMENT — INTROVERSION — PERCEPTION — PERCEPTION — EXTRAVERSION — JUDGMENT

	N	%
E	50	47.62
I	55	52.38
S	76	72.38
N	29	27.62
T	67	63.81
F	38	36.19
J	73	69.52
P	32	30.48
I J	39	37.14
I P	16	15.24
E P	16	15.24
E J	34	32.38
S T	54	51.43
S F	22	20.95
N F	16	15.24
N T	13	12.38
S J	59	56.19
S P	17	16.19
N P	15	14.29
N J	14	13.33
T J	52	49.52
T P	15	14.29
F P	17	16.19
F J	21	20.00
I N	14	13.33
E N	15	14.29
I S	41	39.05
E S	35	33.33
E T	34	32.38
E F	16	15.24
I F	22	20.95
I T	33	31.43
S dom	44	41.90
N dom	11	10.48
T dom	33	31.43
F dom	17	16.19

Note: ■ = 1% of sample   8629444

This table is one of a series of tables from the CAPT-MBTI Data Bank of MBTI records submitted to CAPT for computer scoring between 1971 and June, 1984. This sample was drawn from 59,784 records with usable occupational codes from the total data bank of 232,557. This data bank has 51% Form F cases from 1971 to March, 1978, 35% Form F cases from 1978 to June, 1984 and 14% Form G cases from 1978 to December, 1982. An analysis of Form F and G data banks showed the data banks were comprised of 56% females and 44% males; education level completed: 6% some grade school, 30% high school diploma, 25% some college, 18% bachelor degrees, 11% masters degrees, 3% doctoral or post doctoral work, and 6% unknown. Age group percentages were: 11% under 18, 29% 18 to 20, 12% 21 to 24, 10% 25 to 29, 16% 30 to 39, 10% 40 to 49, 5% 50 to 59, 2% 60 plus, and 5% unknown.

Police and Detectives

	SENSING		INTUITION	
	THINKING	FEELING	FEELING	THINKING

ISTJ	ISFJ	INFJ	INTJ
N= 33	N= 16	N= 1	N= 3
%= 21.29	%= 10.32	%= .65	%= 1.94
■■■■■■■■■	■■■■■■■■■	■	■■
■■■■■■■■■			
■			

ISTP	ISFP	INFP	INTP
N= 9	N= 10	N= 1	N= 5
%= 5.81	%= 6.45	%= .65	%= 3.23
■■■■■■	■■■■■■	■	■■■

ESTP	ESFP	ENFP	ENTP
N= 13	N= 5	N= 2	N= 7
%= 8.39	%= 3.23	%= 1.29	%= 4.52
■■■■■■■■	■■■	■	■■■■■

ESTJ	ESFJ	ENFJ	ENTJ
N= 34	N= 12	N= 2	N= 2
%= 21.94	%= 7.74	%= 1.29	%= 1.29
■■■■■■■■■	■■■■■■■■	■	■
■■■■■■■■			
■■			

JUDGMENT — INTROVERSION — PERCEPTION — EXTRAVERSION — JUDGMENT

	N	%
E	77	49.68
I	78	50.32
S	132	85.16
N	23	14.84
T	106	68.39
F	49	31.61
J	103	66.45
P	52	33.55
I J	53	34.19
I P	25	16.13
E P	27	17.42
E J	50	32.26
S T	89	57.42
S F	43	27.74
N F	6	3.87
N T	17	10.97
S J	95	61.29
S P	37	23.87
N P	15	9.68
N J	8	5.16
T J	72	46.45
T P	34	21.94
F P	18	11.61
F J	31	20.00
I N	10	6.45
E N	13	8.39
I S	68	43.87
E S	64	41.29
E T	56	36.13
E F	21	13.55
I F	28	18.06
I T	50	32.26
S dom	67	43.23
N dom	13	8.39
T dom	50	32.26
F dom	25	16.13

Note: ■ = 1% of sample   8629442

This table is one of a series of tables from the CAPT-MBTI Data Bank of MBTI records submitted to CAPT for computer scoring between 1971 and June, 1984. This sample was drawn from 59,784 records with usable occupational codes from the total data bank of 232,557. This data bank has 51% Form F cases from 1971 to March, 1978, 35% Form F cases from 1978 to June, 1984 and 14% Form G cases from 1978 to December, 1982. An analysis of Form F and G data banks showed the data banks were comprised of 56% females and 44% males; education level completed: 6% some grade school, 30% high school diploma, 25% some college, 18% bachelor degrees, 11% masters degrees, 3% doctoral or post doctoral work, and 6% unknown. Age group percentages were: 11% under 18, 29% 18 to 20, 12% 21 to 24, 10% 25 to 29, 16% 30 to 39, 10% 40 to 49, 5% 50 to 59, 2% 60 plus, and 5% unknown.

Social Services Workers

N = 92

	SENSING		INTUITION			N	%
	THINKING	FEELING	FEELING	THINKING			

ISTJ N= 13 %= 14.13 ■■■■■■■■■ ■■■■	**ISFJ** N= 2 %= 2.17 ■■	**INFJ** N= 3 %= 3.26 ■■■	**INTJ** N= 12 %= 13.04 ■■■■■■■■■■ ■■■
ISTP N= 1 %= 1.09 ■	**ISFP** N= 2 %= 2.17 ■■	**INFP** N= 1 %= 1.09 ■	**INTP** N= 2 %= 2.17 ■■
ESTP N= 5 %= 5.43 ■■■■■	**ESFP** N= 5 %= 5.43 ■■■■■	**ENFP** N= 5 %= 5.43 ■■■■■	**ENTP** N= 1 %= 1.09 ■
ESTJ N= 20 %= 21.74 ■■■■■■■■■■ ■■■■■■■■■ ■■	**ESFJ** N= 10 %= 10.87 ■■■■■■■■■■ ■	**ENFJ** N= 0 %= 0.00	**ENTJ** N= 10 %= 10.87 ■■■■■■■■■■ ■

	N	%
E	56	60.87
I	36	39.13
S	58	63.04
N	34	36.96
T	64	69.57
F	28	30.43
J	70	76.09
P	22	23.91
I J	30	32.61
I P	6	6.52
E P	16	17.39
E J	40	43.48
S T	39	42.39
S F	19	20.65
N F	9	9.78
N T	25	27.17
S J	45	48.91
S P	13	14.13
N P	9	9.78
N J	25	27.17
T J	55	59.78
T P	9	9.78
F P	13	14.13
F J	15	16.30
I N	18	19.57
E N	16	17.39
I S	18	19.57
E S	40	43.48
E T	36	39.13
E F	20	21.74
I F	8	8.70
I T	28	30.43
S dom	25	27.17
N dom	21	22.83
T dom	33	35.87
F dom	13	14.13

Note: ■ = 1% of sample   8623167

Data collected by Ron Lynch of the Institute of Government, University of North Carolina at Chapel Hill from 1980 to 1983 using Form F. Subjects were social services workers attending the institute from across North Carolina. Social service workers were 42% female and 58% male. These data are used with permission and have not been published elsewhere to date.

330

LAWYERS AND JUDGES

N = 519

	SENSING		INTUITION	
	THINKING	FEELING	FEELING	THINKING

ISTJ	ISFJ	INFJ	INTJ
N= 64	N= 24	N= 28	N= 64
%= 12.33	%= 4.62	%= 5.39	%= 12.33
■■■■■■■■■■■■	■■■■■	■■■■■	■■■■■■■■■■■■
■■			■■

ISTP	ISFP	INFP	INTP
N= 25	N= 6	N= 32	N= 42
%= 4.82	%= 1.16	%= 6.17	%= 8.09
■■■■■	■	■■■■■■	■■■■■■■■

ESTP	ESFP	ENFP	ENTP
N= 5	N= 8	N= 42	N= 35
%= .96	%= 1.54	%= 8.09	%= 6.74
■	■■	■■■■■■■■	■■■■■■■

ESTJ	ESFJ	ENFJ	ENTJ
N= 51	N= 21	N= 25	N= 47
%= 9.83	%= 4.05	%= 4.82	%= 9.06
■■■■■■■■■	■■■■	■■■■■	■■■■■■■■■

(Right-side margins: JUDGMENT / INTROVERSION / PERCEPTION / PERCEPTION / EXTRAVERSION / JUDGMENT)

	N	%
E	234	45.09
I	285	54.91
S	204	39.31
N	315	60.69
T	333	64.16
F	186	35.84
J	324	62.43
P	195	37.57
I J	180	34.68
I P	105	20.23
E P	90	17.34
E J	144	27.75
S T	145	27.94
S F	59	11.37
N F	127	24.47
N T	188	36.22
S J	160	30.83
S P	44	8.48
N P	151	29.09
N J	164	31.60
T J	226	43.55
T P	107	20.62
F P	88	16.96
F J	98	18.88
I N	166	31.98
E N	149	28.71
I S	119	22.93
E S	85	16.38
E T	138	26.59
E F	96	18.50
I F	90	17.34
I T	195	37.57
S dom	101	19.46
N dom	169	32.56
T dom	165	31.79
F dom	84	16.18

Note: ■ = 1% of sample   8629445

This table is one of a series of tables from the CAPT-MBTI Data Bank of MBTI records submitted to CAPT for computer scoring between 1971 and June, 1984. This sample was drawn from 59,784 records with usable occupational codes from the total data bank of 232,557. This data bank has 51% Form F cases from 1971 to March, 1978, 35% Form F cases from 1978 to June, 1984 and 14% Form G cases from 1978 to December, 1982. An analysis of Form F and G data banks showed the data banks were comprised of 56% females and 44% males; education level completed: 6% some grade school, 30% high school diploma, 25% some college, 18% bachelor degrees, 11% masters degrees, 3% doctoral or post doctoral work, and 6% unknown. Age group percentages were: 11% under 18, 29% 18 to 20, 12% 21 to 24, 10% 25 to 29, 16% 30 to 39, 10% 40 to 49, 5% 50 to 59, 2% 60 plus, and 5% unknown.

MILITARY PERSONNEL

	SENSING		INTUITION			N	%
	THINKING	FEELING	FEELING	THINKING			

ISTJ	ISFJ	INFJ	INTJ
N= 37	N= 25	N= 9	N= 8
%= 14.02	%= 9.47	%= 3.41	%= 3.03

ISTP	ISFP	INFP	INTP
N= 20	N= 4	N= 16	N= 4
%= 7.58	%= 1.52	%= 6.06	%= 1.52

ESTP	ESFP	ENFP	ENTP
N= 8	N= 12	N= 23	N= 14
%= 3.03	%= 4.55	%= 8.71	%= 5.30

ESTJ	ESFJ	ENFJ	ENTJ
N= 47	N= 17	N= 7	N= 13
%= 17.80	%= 6.44	%= 2.65	%= 4.92

	N	%
E	141	53.41
I	123	46.59
S	170	64.39
N	94	35.61
T	151	57.20
F	113	42.80
J	163	61.74
P	101	38.26
I J	79	29.92
I P	44	16.67
E P	57	21.59
E J	84	31.82
S T	112	42.42
S F	58	21.97
N F	55	20.83
N T	39	14.77
S J	126	47.73
S P	44	16.67
N P	57	21.59
N J	37	14.02
T J	105	39.77
T P	46	17.42
F P	55	20.83
F J	58	21.97
I N	37	14.02
E N	57	21.59
I S	86	32.58
E S	84	31.82
E T	82	31.06
E F	59	22.35
I F	54	20.45
I T	69	26.14
S dom	82	31.06
N dom	54	20.45
T dom	84	31.82
F dom	44	16.67

Note: ■ = 1% of sample   8629447

This table is one of a series of tables from the CAPT-MBTI Data Bank of MBTI records submitted to CAPT for computer scoring between 1971 and June, 1984. This sample was drawn from 59,784 records with usable occupational codes from the total data bank of 232,557. This data bank has 51% Form F cases from 1971 to March, 1978, 35% Form F cases from 1978 to June, 1984 and 14% Form G cases from 1978 to December, 1982. An analysis of Form F and G data banks showed the data banks were comprised of 56% females and 44% males; education level completed: 6% some grade school, 30% high school diploma, 25% some college, 18% bachelor degrees, 11% masters degrees, 3% doctoral or post doctoral work, and 6% unknown. Age group percentages were: 11% under 18, 29% 18 to 20, 12% 21 to 24, 10% 25 to 29, 16% 30 to 39, 10% 40 to 49, 5% 50 to 59, 2% 60 plus, and 5% unknown.

PROTECTIVE SERVICE WORKERS

N = 608

	SENSING		INTUITION	
	THINKING	FEELING	FEELING	THINKING

ISTJ	ISFJ	INFJ	INTJ
N= 108	N= 71	N= 11	N= 14
%= 17.76	%= 11.68	%= 1.81	%= 2.30
■■■■■■■■■	■■■■■■■■■	■■	■■
■■■■■■■	■■		

ISTP	ISFP	INFP	INTP
N= 36	N= 20	N= 27	N= 15
%= 5.92	%= 3.29	%= 4.44	%= 2.47
■■■■■■	■■■	■■■■	■■

ESTP	ESFP	ENFP	ENTP
N= 34	N= 19	N= 17	N= 24
%= 5.59	%= 3.12	%= 2.80	%= 3.95
■■■■■■	■■■	■■■	■■■■

ESTJ	ESFJ	ENFJ	ENTJ
N= 117	N= 51	N= 18	N= 26
%= 19.24	%= 8.39	%= 2.96	%= 4.28
■■■■■■■■■	■■■■■■■■	■■■	■■■■
■■■■■■■■			

JUDGMENT — INTROVERSION — PERCEPTION — PERCEPTION — EXTRAVERSION — JUDGMENT

	N	%
E	306	50.33
I	302	49.67
S	456	75.00
N	152	25.00
T	374	61.51
F	234	38.49
J	416	68.42
P	192	31.58
I J	204	33.55
I P	98	16.12
E P	94	15.46
E J	212	34.87
S T	295	48.52
S F	161	26.48
N F	73	12.01
N T	79	12.99
S J	347	57.07
S P	109	17.93
N P	83	13.65
N J	69	11.35
T J	265	43.59
T P	109	17.93
F P	83	13.65
F J	151	24.84
I N	67	11.02
E N	85	13.98
I S	235	38.65
E S	221	36.35
E T	201	33.06
E F	105	17.27
I F	129	21.22
I T	173	28.45
S dom	232	38.16
N dom	66	10.86
T dom	194	31.91
F dom	116	19.08

Note: ■ = 1% of sample   8629448

This table is one of a series of tables from the CAPT-MBTI Data Bank of MBTI records submitted to CAPT for computer scoring between 1971 and June, 1984. This sample was drawn from 59,784 records with usable occupational codes from the total data bank of 232,557. This data bank has 51% Form F cases from 1971 to March, 1978, 35% Form F cases from 1978 to June, 1984 and 14% Form G cases from 1978 to December, 1982. An analysis of Form F and G data banks showed the data banks were comprised of 56% females and 44% males; education level completed: 6% some grade school, 30% high school diploma, 25% some college, 18% bachelor degrees, 11% masters degrees, 3% doctoral or post doctoral work, and 6% unknown. Age group percentages were: 11% under 18, 29% 18 to 20, 12% 21 to 24, 10% 25 to 29, 16% 30 to 39, 10% 40 to 49, 5% 50 to 59, 2% 60 plus, and 5% unknown.

EXTRAVERT-INTROVERT

E Percent	I	Total Sample Size	Sample Description
63.04	36.96	92	Police Officers: Supervisors in Urban Community
61.67	38.33	60	Managers: Fire
60.87	39.13	92	Social Services Workers
58.93	41.07	280	Police Officers: Urban Community
58.16	41.84	141	Police Officers: Patrolmen in Urban Community
55.86	44.14	290	Managers: Middle Level in City, County and State Government
55.28	44.72	1874	Law School Graduates
53.53	46.47	439	Police Officers
53.41	46.59	264	MILITARY PERSONNEL
53.19	46.81	47	Police Officers: Detectives in Urban Community
53.12	46.87	128	Judges
51.47	48.53	68	Corrections Officers and Probation Officers
50.33	49.67	608	PROTECTIVE SERVICE WORKERS
49.90	50.10	523	Managers: Public
49.68	50.32	155	Police and Detectives
49.49	50.51	99	Police Officers: Australian Senior Officers
47.92	52.08	912	Police Officers: Managers
47.62	52.38	105	Police Supervisors
47.19	52.81	89	Corrections Sergeants
46.58	53.42	73	Air Force Personnel
46.53	53.47	101	Administrators: Social Services
46.51	53.49	86	Guards and Watch Keepers
45.61	54.39	57	Police Officers: Commanders
45.30	54.70	574	Line Corrections Officers
45.09	54.91	519	LAWYERS AND JUDGES
44.31	55.69	4663	Military Personnel at Naval Technical Training Center
43.21	56.79	1009	Navy Enlisted Personnel in Basic Electronic Training
42.86	57.14	84	Attorneys - Administrators, non-practicing
42.41	57.59	257	Managers: Top Level in City, County and State Government
41.33	58.67	271	Lawyers

SENSING-INTUITION

S Percent	N	Total Sample Size	Sample Description
91.01	8.99	89	Corrections Sergeants
88.33	11.67	574	Line Corrections Officers
86.87	13.13	99	Police Officers: Australian Senior Officers
86.67	13.33	60	Managers: Fire
85.16	14.84	155	Police and Detectives
80.85	19.15	47	Police Officers: Detectives in Urban Community
80.20	19.80	101	Administrators: Social Services
80.14	19.86	141	Police Officers: Patrolmen in Urban Community
79.64	20.36	280	Police Officers: Urban Community
78.29	21.71	912	Police Officers: Managers
78.26	21.74	92	Police Officers: Supervisors in Urban Community
77.68	22.32	439	Police Officers
75.44	24.56	57	Police Officers: Commanders
75.00	25.00	608	PROTECTIVE SERVICE WORKERS
73.04	26.96	523	Managers: Public
72.38	27.62	105	Police Supervisors
72.37	27.63	257	Managers: Top Level in City, County and State Government
71.72	28.28	290	Managers: Middle Level in City, County and State Government
70.93	29.07	86	Guards and Watch Keepers
66.18	33.82	68	Corrections Officers and Probation Officers
64.85	35.15	4663	Military Personnel at Naval Technical Training Center
64.39	35.61	264	MILITARY PERSONNEL
63.04	36.96	92	Social Services Workers
63.01	36.99	73	Air Force Personnel
60.94	39.06	128	Judges
52.63	47.37	1009	Navy Enlisted Personnel in Basic Electronic Training
41.41	58.59	1874	Law School Graduates
39.31	60.69	519	LAWYERS AND JUDGES
30.63	69.37	271	Lawyers
27.38	72.62	84	Attorneys - Administrators, non-practicing

THINKING-FEELING

T Percent	F	Total Sample Size	Sample Description
83.44	16.56	912	Police Officers: Managers
82.46	17.54	57	Police Officers: Commanders
78.99	21.01	257	Managers: Top Level in City, County and State Government
74.76	25.24	1874	Law School Graduates
74.57	25.43	523	Managers: Public
71.67	28.33	60	Managers: Fire
71.03	28.97	290	Managers: Middle Level in City, County and State Government
70.65	29.35	92	Police Officers: Supervisors in Urban Community
69.57	30.43	92	Social Services Workers
69.05	30.95	84	Attorneys - Administrators, non-practicing
68.79	31.21	141	Police Officers: Patrolmen in Urban Community
68.39	31.61	155	Police and Detectives
66.79	33.21	280	Police Officers: Urban Community
64.94	35.06	271	Lawyers
64.16	35.84	519	LAWYERS AND JUDGES
64.06	35.94	128	Judges
64.04	35.96	89	Corrections Sergeants
63.81	36.19	105	Police Supervisors
61.67	38.33	574	Line Corrections Officers
61.62	38.38	99	Police Officers: Australian Senior Officers
61.51	38.49	608	PROTECTIVE SERVICE WORKERS
60.14	39.86	439	Police Officers
59.56	40.44	1009	Navy Enlisted Personnel in Basic Electronic Training
59.53	40.47	4663	Military Personnel at Naval Technical Training Center
57.53	42.47	73	Air Force Personnel
57.35	42.65	68	Corrections Officers and Probation Officers
57.20	42.80	264	MILITARY PERSONNEL
55.45	44.55	101	Administrators: Social Services
53.19	46.81	47	Police Officers: Detectives in Urban Community
46.51	53.49	86	Guards and Watch Keepers

JUDGMENT-PERCEPTION

J Percent	P	Total Sample Size	Sample Description
87.64	12.36	89	Corrections Sergeants
85.86	14.14	99	Police Officers: Australian Senior Officers
84.21	15.79	57	Police Officers: Commanders
82.10	17.90	257	Managers: Top Level in City, County and State Government
81.58	18.42	912	Police Officers: Managers
78.22	21.78	101	Administrators: Social Services
78.20	21.80	523	Managers: Public
76.21	23.79	290	Managers: Middle Level in City, County and State Government
76.09	23.91	92	Social Services Workers
74.22	25.78	128	Judges
72.34	27.66	47	Police Officers: Detectives in Urban Community
71.25	28.75	574	Line Corrections Officers
69.77	30.23	86	Guards and Watch Keepers
69.52	30.48	105	Police Supervisors
69.05	30.95	84	Attorneys - Administrators, non-practicing
68.42	31.58	608	PROTECTIVE SERVICE WORKERS
68.33	31.67	60	Managers: Fire
67.39	32.61	92	Police Officers: Supervisors in Urban Community
66.45	33.55	155	Police and Detectives
66.43	33.57	280	Police Officers: Urban Community
63.83	36.17	141	Police Officers: Patrolmen in Urban Community
62.43	37.57	519	LAWYERS AND JUDGES
61.76	38.24	68	Corrections Officers and Probation Officers
61.74	38.26	264	MILITARY PERSONNEL
59.28	40.72	4663	Military Personnel at Naval Technical Training Center
58.90	41.10	73	Air Force Personnel
58.75	41.25	1874	Law School Graduates
54.67	45.33	439	Police Officers
53.87	46.13	271	Lawyers
45.19	54.81	1009	Navy Enlisted Personnel in Basic Electronic Training

SENSING-THINKING

Percent ST	Total Sample Size	Sample Description
67.32	912	Police Officers: Managers
64.91	57	Police Officers: Commanders
63.33	60	Managers: Fire
59.55	89	Corrections Sergeants
59.14	257	Managers: Top Level in City, County and State Government
57.42	155	Police and Detectives
56.60	523	Managers: Public
56.03	141	Police Officers: Patrolmen in Urban Community
55.92	574	Line Corrections Officers
55.56	99	Police Officers: Australian Senior Officers
55.43	92	Police Officers: Supervisors in Urban Community
54.29	280	Police Officers: Urban Community
51.43	105	Police Supervisors
50.69	290	Managers: Middle Level in City, County and State Government
48.52	608	PROTECTIVE SERVICE WORKERS
46.92	439	Police Officers
46.81	47	Police Officers: Detectives in Urban Community
44.55	101	Administrators: Social Services
42.47	73	Air Force Personnel
42.42	264	MILITARY PERSONNEL
42.39	92	Social Services Workers
42.19	128	Judges
41.33	4663	Military Personnel at Naval Technical Training Center
38.37	86	Guards and Watch Keepers
35.29	68	Corrections Officers and Probation Officers
33.70	1009	Navy Enlisted Personnel in Basic Electronic Training
32.18	1874	Law School Graduates
27.94	519	LAWYERS AND JUDGES
23.99	271	Lawyers
17.86	84	Attorneys - Administrators, non-practicing

Percent SF	Total Sample Size	Sample Description
35.64	101	Administrators: Social Services
34.04	47	Police Officers: Detectives in Urban Community
32.56	86	Guards and Watch Keepers
32.40	574	Line Corrections Officers
31.46	89	Corrections Sergeants
31.31	99	Police Officers: Australian Senior Officers
30.88	68	Corrections Officers and Probation Officers
30.75	439	Police Officers
27.74	155	Police and Detectives
26.48	608	PROTECTIVE SERVICE WORKERS
25.36	280	Police Officers: Urban Community
24.11	141	Police Officers: Patrolmen in Urban Community
23.53	4663	Military Personnel at Naval Technical Training Center
23.33	60	Managers: Fire
22.83	92	Police Officers: Supervisors in Urban Community
21.97	264	MILITARY PERSONNEL
21.03	290	Managers: Middle Level in City, County and State Government
20.95	105	Police Supervisors
20.65	92	Social Services Workers
20.55	73	Air Force Personnel
18.93	1009	Navy Enlisted Personnel in Basic Electronic Training
18.75	128	Judges
16.44	523	Managers: Public
13.23	257	Managers: Top Level in City, County and State Government
11.37	519	LAWYERS AND JUDGES
10.96	912	Police Officers: Managers
10.53	57	Police Officers: Commanders
9.52	84	Attorneys - Administrators, non-practicing
9.23	1874	Law School Graduates
6.64	271	Lawyers

INTUITION-FEELING

Percent NF	Total Sample Size	Sample Description
28.41	271	Lawyers
24.47	519	LAWYERS AND JUDGES
21.92	73	Air Force Personnel
21.51	1009	Navy Enlisted Personnel in Basic Electronic Training
21.43	84	Attorneys - Administrators, non-practicing
20.93	86	Guards and Watch Keepers
20.83	264	MILITARY PERSONNEL
17.19	128	Judges
16.94	4663	Military Personnel at Naval Technical Training Center
16.01	1874	Law School Graduates
15.24	105	Police Supervisors
12.77	47	Police Officers: Detectives in Urban Community
12.01	608	PROTECTIVE SERVICE WORKERS
11.76	68	Corrections Officers and Probation Officers
9.78	92	Social Services Workers
9.11	439	Police Officers
8.99	523	Managers: Public
8.91	101	Administrators: Social Services
7.93	290	Managers: Middle Level in City, County and State Government
7.86	280	Police Officers: Urban Community
7.78	257	Managers: Top Level in City, County and State Government
7.09	141	Police Officers: Patrolmen in Urban Community
7.07	99	Police Officers: Australian Senior Officers
7.02	57	Police Officers: Commanders
6.52	92	Police Officers: Supervisors in Urban Community
5.92	574	Line Corrections Officers
5.59	912	Police Officers: Managers
5.00	60	Managers: Fire
4.49	89	Corrections Sergeants
3.87	155	Police and Detectives

Percent NT	Total Sample Size	Sample Description
51.19	84	Attorneys - Administrators, non-practicing
42.58	1874	Law School Graduates
40.96	271	Lawyers
36.22	519	LAWYERS AND JUDGES
27.17	92	Social Services Workers
25.87	1009	Navy Enlisted Personnel in Basic Electronic Training
22.06	68	Corrections Officers and Probation Officers
21.88	128	Judges
20.34	290	Managers: Middle Level in City, County and State Government
19.84	257	Managers: Top Level in City, County and State Government
18.21	4663	Military Personnel at Naval Technical Training Center
17.97	523	Managers: Public
17.54	57	Police Officers: Commanders
16.12	912	Police Officers: Managers
15.22	92	Police Officers: Supervisors in Urban Community
15.07	73	Air Force Personnel
14.77	264	MILITARY PERSONNEL
13.21	439	Police Officers
12.99	608	PROTECTIVE SERVICE WORKERS
12.77	141	Police Officers: Patrolmen in Urban Community
12.50	280	Police Officers: Urban Community
12.38	105	Police Supervisors
10.97	155	Police and Detectives
10.89	101	Administrators: Social Services
8.33	60	Managers: Fire
8.14	86	Guards and Watch Keepers
6.38	47	Police Officers: Detectives in Urban Community
6.06	99	Police Officers: Australian Senior Officers
5.75	574	Line Corrections Officers
4.49	89	Corrections Sergeants

HEALTH

Section VIII

HEALTH

Samples in Section VIII

Name of Sample	Number in Sample
Administrators: Health	202
Clinical Laboratory Technologists and Technicians	223
Dental Assistants	72
Dental Hygienists	60
Dentists	52
Dentists	85
Dietitians	243
Dietitians and Nutritionists	323
Doctors of Osteopathy	135
Health Education Practitioners	182
Laboratory Technologists	167
Medical Assistants	79
Medical Technologists	973
Medical Technologists (4 year)	638
Nursing: Administrators	94
Nursing: Aides, Orderlies, and Attendants	314
Nursing: Composite of Critical Care Nurses	155
Nursing: Consultants	146
Nursing: Educators	305
Nursing: Licensed Practical Nurses	260
Nursing: Public Health	83
Nursing: Registered Nurses	2351
Nursing: Registered Nurses, no specialty stated	1880
Optometrists	70
Pharmacists	123
Pharmacists	191
Physicians: Family Practice, General Practice	139
Physicians: Pathology	61
Physicians: Psychiatry	68
Practitioners in Medicine (M.D.s)	1881
Practitioners in Radiologic Technology	53
Practitioners in Speech Pathology	122
Public Service Aides and Community Health Workers	238
Radiologic Technologists and Technicians	126
Speech Pathologists	106
Therapists: Occupational	118
Therapists: Occupational	245
Therapists: Physical	148
Therapists: Physical	155
Therapists: Practitioners in Respiratory Therapy	127
Therapists: Respiratory	195

Composite Samples

ALLIED HEALTH AND HEALTH PRACTIONERS, N.E.C.	469
DOCTORS OF MEDICINE	1603
HEALTH CARE THERAPISTS	765
HEALTH SERVICE WORKERS	900
HEALTH TECHNOLOGISTS AND TECHNICIANS	1291
NURSES	3103

Comments

The samples of this section tend mainly to be people concerned provision of health services at all levels. This section of the Atlas includes summary data from a state-of-the-art report on medicine and other health professions brought together by CAPT in 1978 (McCaulley, 1978). That report discusses issues relating to the selection, teaching, clinical performance, work settings and satisfaction for both students and practitioners. Data selected from the Monograph for inclusion in Atlas tables refer to practitioners, not students. Many MBTI data in health so far are confined to student samples. Data on these can be found in McCaulley (1978).

The earliest data on the health professions were collected in the 1950's by Isabel Myers in her samples of over 5,000 medical students and over 10,000 nursing students. Her medical sample from 45 medical schools was almost evenly balanced between E's and I's, S's and N's, T's and F's, and J's and P's; today's students have considerably more N's, F's and J's. CAPT found 4,953 of these medical students to be in medical practice in the late 1970's. Extensive data on the specialties and methods of practice of the sample are reported in McCaulley (1977). Tables are not included in this Atlas.

The allied health samples were mainly collected in the Southeastern part of the United States. Samples in dentistry and pharmacy are still very small and should be interpreted with special caution.

In looking at the tables in this section, look for more extraverts in fields where immediate, direct action is important, and where many patients are typically seen in any day. Look for introverts in fields where work is relatively solitary (as in laboratories) or where work requires a long attention span. Note especially the large numbers of ISTJ and ISFJ, the most thorough and responsible of the types.

Look for sensing types to be relatively more frequent in the fields providing direct, hands-on patient care. Since intuitive types in general are somewhat more likely to continue on to higher education, expect more sensing types in those fields requiring less education beyond high school, and intuitive types in fields with post-baccalaureate training. Look for intuitive types also in any field requiring subtle communication or imagination.

Health occupations typically require a solid grounding in the sciences and the empathy of patient care; regardless of type preference, the work in health occupations requires daily use of both thinking and feeling. Even so, look for relatively more thinking types in fields requiring constant use of science or technology, and for more feeling types in fields with a large amount of direct patient care, particularly bedside care or patient support.

The health professions place high value on responsibility and dependability. The CAPT monograph in health showed more J's than expected from the general population for most health practitioners except for counselors where the need to stay open for understanding seemed to be associated with relatively more perceptive types. You will see that J's are still in the majority in Atlas samples. You will see relatively more perceptive types in a few fields where flexibility to changing demands is required.

Summary listings of tables for EI, SN, TF, JP, ST, SF, NF and NT will be found after the last type table.

Administrators: Health

N = 202

	SENSING		INTUITION	
	THINKING	FEELING	FEELING	THINKING

ISTJ	ISFJ	INFJ	INTJ
N= 26	N= 24	N= 14	N= 9
%= 12.87	%= 11.88	%= 6.93	%= 4.46
■■■■■■■■■■■■ ■■■	■■■■■■■■■■■ ■■	■■■■■■■	■■■■

JUDGMENT / INTROVERSION

ISTP	ISFP	INFP	INTP
N= 4	N= 0	N= 14	N= 6
%= 1.98	%= 0.00	%= 6.93	%= 2.97
■■		■■■■■■■	■■■

PERCEPTION

ESTP	ESFP	ENFP	ENTP
N= 3	N= 5	N= 12	N= 7
%= 1.49	%= 2.48	%= 5.94	%= 3.47
■	■■	■■■■■■	■■■

PERCEPTION / EXTRAVERSION

ESTJ	ESFJ	ENFJ	ENTJ
N= 22	N= 18	N= 11	N= 27
%= 10.89	%= 8.91	%= 5.45	%= 13.37
■■■■■■■■■■ ■	■■■■■■■■■	■■■■■	■■■■■■■■■■■■■ ■■■

JUDGMENT

	N	%
E	105	51.98
I	97	48.02
S	102	50.50
N	100	49.50
T	104	51.49
F	98	48.51
J	151	74.75
P	51	25.25
I J	73	36.14
I P	24	11.88
E P	27	13.37
E J	78	38.61
S T	55	27.23
S F	47	23.27
N F	51	25.25
N T	49	24.26
S J	90	44.55
S P	12	5.94
N P	39	19.31
N J	61	30.20
T J	84	41.58
T P	20	9.90
F P	31	15.35
F J	67	33.17
I N	43	21.29
E N	57	28.22
I S	54	26.73
E S	48	23.76
E T	59	29.21
E F	46	22.77
I F	52	25.74
I T	45	22.28
S dom	58	28.71
N dom	42	20.79
T dom	59	29.21
F dom	43	21.29

Note: ■ = 1% of sample   8629355

This table is one of a series of tables from the CAPT-MBTI Data Bank of MBTI records submitted to CAPT for computer scoring between 1971 and June, 1984. This sample was drawn from 59,784 records with usable occupational codes from the total data bank of 232,557. This data bank has 51% Form F cases from 1971 to March, 1978, 35% Form F cases from 1978 to June, 1984 and 14% Form G cases from 1978 to December, 1982. An analysis of Form F and G data banks showed the data banks were comprised of 56% females and 44% males; education level completed: 6% some grade school, 30% high school diploma, 25% some college, 18% bachelor degrees, 11% masters degrees, 3% doctoral or post doctoral work, and 6% unknown. Age group percentages were: 11% under 18, 29% 18 to 20, 12% 21 to 24, 10% 25 to 29, 16% 30 to 39, 10% 40 to 49, 5% 50 to 59, 2% 60 plus, and 5% unknown.

Clinical Laboratory Technologists and Technicians

N = 223

	N	%
E	93	41.70
I	130	58.30
S	124	55.61
N	99	44.39
T	101	45.29
F	122	54.71
J	129	57.85
P	94	42.15
I J	74	33.18
I P	56	25.11
E P	38	17.04
E J	55	24.66
S T	63	28.25
S F	61	27.35
N F	61	27.35
N T	38	17.04
S J	91	40.81
S P	33	14.80
N P	61	27.35
N J	38	17.04
T J	72	32.29
T P	29	13.00
F P	65	29.15
F J	57	25.56
I N	61	27.35
E N	38	17.04
I S	69	30.94
E S	55	24.66
E T	44	19.73
E F	49	21.97
I F	73	32.74
I T	57	25.56
S dom	70	31.39
N dom	42	18.83
T dom	47	21.08
F dom	64	28.70

SENSING — THINKING / FEELING; **INTUITION** — FEELING / THINKING

ISTJ	ISFJ	INFJ	INTJ
N= 28	N= 25	N= 8	N= 13
%= 12.56	%= 11.21	%= 3.59	%= 5.83

ISTP	ISFP	INFP	INTP
N= 4	N= 12	N= 28	N= 12
%= 1.79	%= 5.38	%= 12.56	%= 5.38

ESTP	ESFP	ENFP	ENTP
N= 6	N= 11	N= 14	N= 7
%= 2.69	%= 4.93	%= 6.28	%= 3.14

ESTJ	ESFJ	ENFJ	ENTJ
N= 25	N= 13	N= 11	N= 6
%= 11.21	%= 5.83	%= 4.93	%= 2.69

Note: ■ = 1% of sample   8629351

This table is one of a series of tables from the CAPT-MBTI Data Bank of MBTI records submitted to CAPT for computer scoring between 1971 and June, 1984. This sample was drawn from 59,784 records with usable occupational codes from the total data bank of 232,557. This data bank has 51% Form F cases from 1971 to March, 1978, 35% Form F cases from 1978 to June, 1984 and 14% Form G cases from 1978 to December, 1982. An analysis of Form F and G data banks showed the data banks were comprised of 56% females and 44% males; education level completed: 6% some grade school, 30% high school diploma, 25% some college, 18% bachelor degrees, 11% masters degrees, 3% doctoral or post doctoral work, and 6% unknown. Age group percentages were: 11% under 18, 29% 18 to 20, 12% 21 to 24, 10% 25 to 29, 16% 30 to 39, 10% 40 to 49, 5% 50 to 59, 2% 60 plus, and 5% unknown.

Dental Assistants

N = 72

	SENSING		INTUITION	
	THINKING	FEELING	FEELING	THINKING

ISTJ	ISFJ	INFJ	INTJ
N= 5	N= 10	N= 3	N= 2
%= 6.94	%= 13.89	%= 4.17	%= 2.78
■■■■■■■	■■■■■■■■■■	■■■■	■■■
	■■■■		

ISTP	ISFP	INFP	INTP
N= 4	N= 7	N= 3	N= 1
%= 5.56	%= 9.72	%= 4.17	%= 1.39
■■■■■■	■■■■■■■■■■	■■■■	■

ESTP	ESFP	ENFP	ENTP
N= 2	N= 3	N= 7	N= 5
%= 2.78	%= 4.17	%= 9.72	%= 6.94
■■■	■■■■	■■■■■■■■■■	■■■■■■■

ESTJ	ESFJ	ENFJ	ENTJ
N= 5	N= 12	N= 2	N= 1
%= 6.94	%= 16.67	%= 2.78	%= 1.39
■■■■■■■	■■■■■■■■■■	■■■	■
	■■■■■■■		

JUDGMENT · INTROVERSION · PERCEPTION · PERCEPTION · EXTRAVERSION · JUDGMENT

	N	%
E	37	51.39
I	35	48.61
S	48	66.67
N	24	33.33
T	25	34.72
F	47	65.28
J	40	55.56
P	32	44.44
I J	20	27.78
I P	15	20.83
E P	17	23.61
E J	20	27.78
S T	16	22.22
S F	32	44.44
N F	15	20.83
N T	9	12.50
S J	32	44.44
S P	16	22.22
N P	16	22.22
N J	8	11.11
T J	13	18.06
T P	12	16.67
F P	20	27.78
F J	27	37.50
I N	9	12.50
E N	15	20.83
I S	26	36.11
E S	22	30.56
E T	13	18.06
E F	24	33.33
I F	23	31.94
I T	12	16.67
S dom	20	27.78
N dom	17	23.61
T dom	11	15.28
F dom	24	33.33

Note: ■ = 1% of sample   8629356

This table is one of a series of tables from the CAPT-MBTI Data Bank of MBTI records submitted to CAPT for computer scoring between 1971 and June, 1984. This sample was drawn from 59,784 records with usable occupational codes from the total data bank of 232,557. This data bank has 51% Form F cases from 1971 to March, 1978, 35% Form F cases from 1978 to June, 1984 and 14% Form G cases from 1978 to December, 1982. An analysis of Form F and G data banks showed the data banks were comprised of 56% females and 44% males; education level completed: 6% some grade school, 30% high school diploma, 25% some college, 18% bachelor degrees, 11% masters degrees, 3% doctoral or post doctoral work, and 6% unknown. Age group percentages were: 11% under 18, 29% 18 to 20, 12% 21 to 24, 10% 25 to 29, 16% 30 to 39, 10% 40 to 49, 5% 50 to 59, 2% 60 plus, and 5% unknown.

Dental Hygienists

	SENSING	INTUITION	
THINKING	FEELING	FEELING	THINKING

ISTJ	ISFJ	INFJ	INTJ
N= 0	N= 9	N= 4	N= 1
%= 0.00	%= 15.00	%= 6.67	%= 1.67
	■■■■■■■■■ ■■■■■	■■■■■■■	■■

ISTP	ISFP	INFP	INTP
N= 5	N= 0	N= 4	N= 0
%= 8.33	%= 0.00	%= 6.67	%= 0.00
■■■■■■■■		■■■■■■■	

ESTP	ESFP	ENFP	ENTP
N= 0	N= 4	N= 9	N= 3
%= 0.00	%= 6.67	%= 15.00	%= 5.00
	■■■■■■■	■■■■■■■■■ ■■■■■	■■■■■

ESTJ	ESFJ	ENFJ	ENTJ
N= 5	N= 7	N= 6	N= 3
%= 8.33	%= 11.67	%= 10.00	%= 5.00
■■■■■■■■	■■■■■■■■■ ■■	■■■■■■■■■	■■■■■

JUDGMENT — PERCEPTION (INTROVERSION)
PERCEPTION — JUDGMENT (EXTRAVERSION)

	N	%
E	37	61.67
I	23	38.33
S	30	50.00
N	30	50.00
T	17	28.33
F	43	71.67
J	35	58.33
P	25	41.67
I J	14	23.33
I P	9	15.00
E P	16	26.67
E J	21	35.00
S T	10	16.67
S F	20	33.33
N F	23	38.33
N T	7	11.67
S J	21	35.00
S P	9	15.00
N P	16	26.67
N J	14	23.33
T J	9	15.00
T P	8	13.33
F P	17	28.33
F J	26	43.33
I N	9	15.00
E N	21	35.00
I S	14	23.33
E S	16	26.67
E T	11	18.33
E F	26	43.33
I F	17	28.33
I T	6	10.00
S dom	13	21.67
N dom	17	28.33
T dom	13	21.67
F dom	17	28.33

Note: ■ = 1% of sample   8629354

This table is one of a series of tables from the CAPT-MBTI Data Bank of MBTI records submitted to CAPT for computer scoring between 1971 and June, 1984. This sample was drawn from 59,784 records with usable occupational codes from the total data bank of 232,557. This data bank has 51% Form F cases from 1971 to March, 1978, 35% Form F cases from 1978 to June, 1984 and 14% Form G cases from 1978 to December, 1982. An analysis of Form F and G data banks showed the data banks were comprised of 56% females and 44% males; education level completed: 6% some grade school, 30% high school diploma, 25% some college, 18% bachelor degrees, 11% masters degrees, 3% doctoral or post doctoral work, and 6% unknown. Age group percentages were: 11% under 18, 29% 18 to 20, 12% 21 to 24, 10% 25 to 29, 16% 30 to 39, 10% 40 to 49, 5% 50 to 59, 2% 60 plus, and 5% unknown.

Dentists

	SENSING		INTUITION	
	THINKING	FEELING	FEELING	THINKING

ISTJ	ISFJ	INFJ	INTJ
N= 8	N= 7	N= 2	N= 5
%= 15.38	%= 13.46	%= 3.85	%= 9.62
■■■■■■■■■■■■■■■	■■■■■■■■■■■■■	■■■■	■■■■■■■■■■
■■■■■	■■■		

ISTP	ISFP	INFP	INTP
N= 0	N= 1	N= 2	N= 3
%= 0.00	%= 1.92	%= 3.85	%= 5.77
	■■	■■■■	■■■■■■

ESTP	ESFP	ENFP	ENTP
N= 0	N= 1	N= 3	N= 2
%= 0.00	%= 1.92	%= 5.77	%= 3.85
	■■	■■■■■■	■■■■

ESTJ	ESFJ	ENFJ	ENTJ
N= 6	N= 3	N= 3	N= 6
%= 11.54	%= 5.77	%= 5.77	%= 11.54
■■■■■■■■■■■	■■■■■■	■■■■■■	■■■■■■■■■■■
■■		■■	

JUDGMENT — INTROVERSION — PERCEPTION — EXTRAVERSION — JUDGMENT
PERCEPTION

	N	%
E	24	46.15
I	28	53.85
S	26	50.00
N	26	50.00
T	30	57.69
F	22	42.31
J	40	76.92
P	12	23.08
I J	22	42.31
I P	6	11.54
E P	6	11.54
E J	18	34.62
S T	14	26.92
S F	12	23.08
N F	10	19.23
N T	16	30.77
S J	24	46.15
S P	2	3.85
N P	10	19.23
N J	16	30.77
T J	25	48.08
T P	5	9.62
F P	7	13.46
F J	15	28.85
I N	12	23.08
E N	14	26.92
I S	16	30.77
E S	10	19.23
E T	14	26.92
E F	10	19.23
I F	12	23.08
I T	16	30.77
S dom	16	30.77
N dom	12	23.08
T dom	15	28.85
F dom	9	17.31

Note: ■ = 1% of sample   8623136

Subjects in this sample came from four main sources and were originally compiled especially for publication in:
McCaulley, M. H. (1978). Application of the Myers-Briggs Type Indicator to medicine and other health professions (Monograph
I, Contract No. 231-76-0051, Health Resources Administration, DHEW). Gainesville, FL: Center for Applications of
Psychological Type.
The four sources used were: 1) the CAPT health databank in 1977 based on Form F answer sheets scored by 1962 weights, 2)
data solicited from medical and health professionals through advertising and personal communication, 3) the Myers Longitudinal
Medical Sample initially collected in the 1950s and followed up in the 1970s and 4) data extracted from published research up to
that time.

Dentists

N = 85

	SENSING	INTUITION	
THINKING	FEELING	FEELING	THINKING

ISTJ	ISFJ	INFJ	INTJ
N= 19	N= 9	N= 3	N= 6
%= 22.35	%= 10.59	%= 3.53	%= 7.06
■■■■■■■■■■ ■■■■■■■■■ ■■	■■■■■■■■■■ ■	■■■■	■■■■■■■

ISTP	ISFP	INFP	INTP
N= 0	N= 1	N= 2	N= 5
%= 0.00	%= 1.18	%= 2.35	%= 5.88
	■	■■	■■■■■■

ESTP	ESFP	ENFP	ENTP
N= 3	N= 4	N= 6	N= 1
%= 3.53	%= 4.71	%= 7.06	%= 1.18
■■■■	■■■■■	■■■■■■■	■

ESTJ	ESFJ	ENFJ	ENTJ
N= 10	N= 5	N= 3	N= 8
%= 11.76	%= 5.88	%= 3.53	%= 9.41
■■■■■■■■■■ ■■	■■■■■■	■■■■	■■■■■■■■■

JUDGMENT — INTROVERSION — PERCEPTION — PERCEPTION — EXTRAVERSION — JUDGMENT

	N	%
E	40	47.06
I	45	52.94
S	51	60.00
N	34	40.00
T	52	61.18
F	33	38.82
J	63	74.12
P	22	25.88
I J	37	43.53
I P	8	9.41
E P	14	16.47
E J	26	30.59
S T	32	37.65
S F	19	22.35
N F	14	16.47
N T	20	23.53
S J	43	50.59
S P	8	9.41
N P	14	16.47
N J	20	23.53
T J	43	50.59
T P	9	10.59
F P	13	15.29
F J	20	23.53
I N	16	18.82
E N	18	21.18
I S	29	34.12
E S	22	25.88
E T	22	25.88
E F	18	21.18
I F	15	17.65
I T	30	35.29
S dom	35	41.18
N dom	16	18.82
T dom	23	27.06
F dom	11	12.94

Note: ■ = 1% of sample

8629335

This table is one of a series of tables from the CAPT-MBTI Data Bank of MBTI records submitted to CAPT for computer scoring between 1971 and June, 1984. This sample was drawn from 59,784 records with usable occupational codes from the total data bank of 232,557. This data bank has 51% Form F cases from 1971 to March, 1978, 35% Form F cases from 1978 to June, 1984 and 14% Form G cases from 1978 to December, 1982. An analysis of Form F and G data banks showed the data banks were comprised of 56% females and 44% males; education level completed: 6% some grade school, 30% high school diploma, 25% some college, 18% bachelor degrees, 11% masters degrees, 3% doctoral or post doctoral work, and 6% unknown. Age group percentages were: 11% under 18, 29% 18 to 20, 12% 21 to 24, 10% 25 to 29, 16% 30 to 39, 10% 40 to 49, 5% 50 to 59, 2% 60 plus, and 5% unknown.

Dietitians

N = 243

	SENSING		INTUITION	
	THINKING	FEELING	FEELING	THINKING

ISTJ	ISFJ	INFJ	INTJ
N= 29	N= 30	N= 11	N= 9
%= 11.93	%= 12.35	%= 4.53	%= 3.70
■■■■■■■■■■	■■■■■■■■■■	■■■■■	■■■■
■■	■■		

ISTP	ISFP	INFP	INTP
N= 8	N= 7	N= 18	N= 5
%= 3.29	%= 2.88	%= 7.41	%= 2.06
■■■	■■■	■■■■■■■	■■

ESTP	ESFP	ENFP	ENTP
N= 7	N= 11	N= 12	N= 7
%= 2.88	%= 4.53	%= 4.94	%= 2.88
■■■	■■■■■	■■■■■	■■■

ESTJ	ESFJ	ENFJ	ENTJ
N= 30	N= 28	N= 14	N= 17
%= 12.35	%= 11.52	%= 5.76	%= 7.00
■■■■■■■■■■	■■■■■■■■■■	■■■■■■	■■■■■■
■■	■■		

JUDGMENT — INTROVERSION
PERCEPTION
PERCEPTION — EXTRAVERSION
JUDGMENT

	N	%
E	126	51.85
I	117	48.15
S	150	61.73
N	93	38.27
T	112	46.09
F	131	53.91
J	168	69.14
P	75	30.86
I J	79	32.51
I P	38	15.64
E P	37	15.23
E J	89	36.63
S T	74	30.45
S F	76	31.28
N F	55	22.63
N T	38	15.64
S J	117	48.15
S P	33	13.58
N P	42	17.28
N J	51	20.99
T J	85	34.98
T P	27	11.11
F P	48	19.75
F J	83	34.16
I N	43	17.70
E N	50	20.58
I S	74	30.45
E S	76	31.28
E T	61	25.10
E F	65	26.75
I F	66	27.16
I T	51	20.99
S dom	77	31.69
N dom	39	16.05
T dom	60	24.69
F dom	67	27.57

Note: ■ = 1% of sample   8623133

Data collected by Robin Fellers during 1974 using Form F. The subjects were 61% of 400 people randomly selected from 24,075 members listed in the 1973 American Dietetic Association directory. The dietitians were 99% female; ages ranged from 24 to 73 years with a mean of 41.8; years of practice ranged from 0 to 52 with a mean of 10.3; 66% worked for hospitals or extended care facilities, 12% for universities in extension, 8% in public schools, 7% for governmental agencies, and 7% in other settings. These data are used with permission and were cited in:

Fellers, R. B. (1975). Relationships between career satisfaction and personality type for employed dietitians (Doctoral dissertation, University of Florida, 1974). Dissertation Abstracts International, 36(03), 1465A-1466A. (University Microfilms No. 75-19, 331)

Dietitians and Nutritionists

N = 323

	SENSING		INTUITION	
	THINKING	FEELING	FEELING	THINKING

ISTJ	ISFJ	INFJ	INTJ
N= 34	N= 45	N= 17	N= 17
%= 10.53	%= 13.93	%= 5.26	%= 5.26
■■■■■■■■■■	■■■■■■■■■■	■■■■■	■■■■■
■	■■■■		

ISTP	ISFP	INFP	INTP
N= 10	N= 10	N= 26	N= 5
%= 3.10	%= 3.10	%= 8.05	%= 1.55
■■■	■■■	■■■■■■■■	■■

ESTP	ESFP	ENFP	ENTP
N= 9	N= 11	N= 21	N= 7
%= 2.79	%= 3.41	%= 6.50	%= 2.17
■■■	■■■	■■■■■■■	■■

ESTJ	ESFJ	ENFJ	ENTJ
N= 40	N= 28	N= 21	N= 22
%= 12.38	%= 8.67	%= 6.50	%= 6.81
■■■■■■■■■■	■■■■■■■■■	■■■■■■■	■■■■■■■
■■			

JUDGMENT — INTROVERSION — PERCEPTION — PERCEPTION — EXTRAVERSION — JUDGMENT

	N	%
E	159	49.23
I	164	50.77
S	187	57.89
N	136	42.11
T	144	44.58
F	179	55.42
J	224	69.35
P	99	30.65
I J	113	34.98
I P	51	15.79
E P	48	14.86
E J	111	34.37
S T	93	28.79
S F	94	29.10
N F	85	26.32
N T	51	15.79
S J	147	45.51
S P	40	12.38
N P	59	18.27
N J	77	23.84
T J	113	34.98
T P	31	9.60
F P	68	21.05
F J	111	34.37
I N	65	20.12
E N	71	21.98
I S	99	30.65
E S	88	27.24
E T	78	24.15
E F	81	25.08
I F	98	30.34
I T	66	20.43
S dom	99	30.65
N dom	62	19.20
T dom	77	23.84
F dom	85	26.32

Note: ■ = 1% of sample   8629341

This table is one of a series of tables from the CAPT-MBTI Data Bank of MBTI records submitted to CAPT for computer scoring between 1971 and June, 1984. This sample was drawn from 59,784 records with usable occupational codes from the total data bank of 232,557. This data bank has 51% Form F cases from 1971 to March, 1978, 35% Form F cases from 1978 to June, 1984 and 14% Form G cases from 1978 to December, 1982. An analysis of Form F and G data banks showed the data banks were comprised of 56% females and 44% males; education level completed: 6% some grade school, 30% high school diploma, 25% some college, 18% bachelor degrees, 11% masters degrees, 3% doctoral or post doctoral work, and 6% unknown. Age group percentages were: 11% under 18, 29% 18 to 20, 12% 21 to 24, 10% 25 to 29, 16% 30 to 39, 10% 40 to 49, 5% 50 to 59, 2% 60 plus, and 5% unknown.

Doctors of Osteopathy

N = 135

	SENSING		INTUITION	
	THINKING	FEELING	FEELING	THINKING

ISTJ	ISFJ	INFJ	INTJ
N= 12	N= 28	N= 11	N= 8
%= 8.89	%= 20.74	%= 8.15	%= 5.93
■■■■■■■■	■■■■■■■■■	■■■■■■■■	■■■■■■
	■■■■■■■■■		
	■		

ISTP	ISFP	INFP	INTP
N= 3	N= 2	N= 8	N= 3
%= 2.22	%= 1.48	%= 5.93	%= 2.22
■■	■	■■■■■■	■■

ESTP	ESFP	ENFP	ENTP
N= 1	N= 5	N= 10	N= 5
%= .74	%= 3.70	%= 7.41	%= 3.70
■	■■■■	■■■■■■■	■■■■

ESTJ	ESFJ	ENFJ	ENTJ
N= 11	N= 14	N= 8	N= 6
%= 8.15	%= 10.37	%= 5.93	%= 4.44
■■■■■■■■	■■■■■■■■■■	■■■■■■	■■■■

JUDGMENT — INTROVERSION — PERCEPTION — PERCEPTION — EXTRAVERSION — JUDGMENT

	N	%
E	60	44.44
I	75	55.56
S	76	56.30
N	59	43.70
T	49	36.30
F	86	63.70
J	98	72.59
P	37	27.41
I J	59	43.70
I P	16	11.85
E P	21	15.56
E J	39	28.89
S T	27	20.00
S F	49	36.30
N F	37	27.41
N T	22	16.30
S J	65	48.15
S P	11	8.15
N P	26	19.26
N J	33	24.44
T J	37	27.41
T P	12	8.89
F P	25	18.52
F J	61	45.19
I N	30	22.22
E N	29	21.48
I S	45	33.33
E S	31	22.96
E T	23	17.04
E F	37	27.41
I F	49	36.30
I T	26	19.26
S dom	46	34.07
N dom	34	25.19
T dom	23	17.04
F dom	32	23.70

Note: ■ = 1% of sample   8630700

Data collected by Robert Ward of Michigan State University during March and November 1977. Subjects were participants at conferences of the American Academy of Osteopathy and the American Osteopathic Association. No other demographic data were reported. These data are used with permission and have not been published elsewhere to date.

Health Education Practitioners

N = 182

	SENSING		INTUITION	
	THINKING	FEELING	FEELING	THINKING

ISTJ	ISFJ	INFJ	INTJ
N= 15	N= 27	N= 7	N= 9
%= 8.24	%= 14.84	%= 3.85	%= 4.95
■■■■■■■■	■■■■■■■■■■ ■■■■■	■■■■	■■■■■

ISTP	ISFP	INFP	INTP
N= 3	N= 11	N= 9	N= 2
%= 1.65	%= 6.04	%= 4.95	%= 1.10
■■	■■■■■■	■■■■■	■

ESTP	ESFP	ENFP	ENTP
N= 5	N= 4	N= 14	N= 12
%= 2.75	%= 2.20	%= 7.69	%= 6.59
■■■	■■	■■■■■■■■	■■■■■■■

ESTJ	ESFJ	ENFJ	ENTJ
N= 12	N= 27	N= 15	N= 10
%= 6.59	%= 14.84	%= 8.24	%= 5.49
■■■■■■■	■■■■■■■■■■ ■■■■■	■■■■■■■■	■■■■■

JUDGMENT · INTROVERSION · PERCEPTION

PERCEPTION · EXTRAVERSION · JUDGMENT

	N	%
E	99	54.40
I	83	45.60
S	104	57.14
N	78	42.86
T	68	37.36
F	114	62.64
J	122	67.03
P	60	32.97
I J	58	31.87
I P	25	13.74
E P	35	19.23
E J	64	35.16
S T	35	19.23
S F	69	37.91
N F	45	24.73
N T	33	18.13
S J	81	44.51
S P	23	12.64
N P	37	20.33
N J	41	22.53
T J	46	25.27
T P	22	12.09
F P	38	20.88
F J	76	41.76
I N	27	14.84
E N	51	28.02
I S	56	30.77
E S	48	26.37
E T	39	21.43
E F	60	32.97
I F	54	29.67
I T	29	15.93
S dom	51	28.02
N dom	42	23.08
T dom	27	14.84
F dom	62	34.07

Note: ■ = 1% of sample

8623145

Subjects in this sample came from four main sources and were originally compiled especially for publication in:
McCaulley, M. H. (1978). Application of the Myers-Briggs Type Indicator to medicine and other health professions (Monograph I, Contract No. 231-76-0051, Health Resources Administration, DHEW). Gainesville, FL: Center for Applications of Psychological Type.

The four sources used were: 1) the CAPT health databank in 1977 based on Form F answer sheets scored by 1962 weights, 2) data solicited from medical and health professionals through advertising and personal communication, 3) the Myers Longitudinal Medical Sample initially collected in the 1950s and followed up in the 1970s and 4) data extracted from published research up to that time.

Laboratory Technologists

N = 167

	SENSING		INTUITION	
	THINKING	FEELING	FEELING	THINKING

ISTJ	ISFJ	INFJ	INTJ
N= 20	N= 16	N= 5	N= 8
%= 11.98	%= 9.58	%= 2.99	%= 4.79
■■■■■■■■■■■■ ■■	■■■■■■■■■	■■■	■■■■■

ISTP	ISFP	INFP	INTP
N= 2	N= 10	N= 22	N= 6
%= 1.20	%= 5.99	%= 13.17	%= 3.59
■	■■■■■■	■■■■■■■■■■■■■ ■■■	■■■■

ESTP	ESFP	ENFP	ENTP
N= 7	N= 11	N= 9	N= 6
%= 4.19	%= 6.59	%= 5.39	%= 3.59
■■■■	■■■■■■■	■■■■■	■■■■

ESTJ	ESFJ	ENFJ	ENTJ
N= 18	N= 13	N= 9	N= 5
%= 10.78	%= 7.78	%= 5.39	%= 2.99
■■■■■■■■■■ ■	■■■■■■■■	■■■■■	■■■

	N	%
E	78	46.71
I	89	53.29
S	97	58.08
N	70	41.92
T	72	43.11
F	95	56.89
J	94	56.29
P	73	43.71
I J	49	29.34
I P	40	23.95
E P	33	19.76
E J	45	26.95
S T	47	28.14
S F	50	29.94
N F	45	26.95
N T	25	14.97
S J	67	40.12
S P	30	17.96
N P	43	25.75
N J	27	16.17
T J	51	30.54
T P	21	12.57
F P	52	31.14
F J	43	25.75
I N	41	24.55
E N	29	17.37
I S	48	28.74
E S	49	29.34
E T	36	21.56
E F	42	25.15
I F	53	31.74
I T	36	21.56
S dom	54	32.34
N dom	28	16.77
T dom	31	18.56
F dom	54	32.34

Note: ■ = 1% of sample   8623140

Subjects in this sample came from four main sources and were originally compiled especially for publication in:

McCaulley, M. H. (1978). Application of the Myers-Briggs Type Indicator to medicine and other health professions (Monograph I, Contract No. 231-76-0051, Health Resources Administration, DHEW). Gainesville, FL: Center for Applications of Psychological Type.

The four sources used were: 1) the CAPT health databank in 1977 based on Form F answer sheets scored by 1962 weights, 2) data solicited from medical and health professionals through advertising and personal communication, 3) the Myers Longitudinal Medical Sample initially collected in the 1950s and followed up in the 1970s and 4) data extracted from published research up to that time.

Medical Assistants

N = 79

	SENSING		INTUITION			N	%
THINKING	FEELING	FEELING	THINKING				

ISTJ N= 6 %= 7.59 ■■■■■■■	**ISFJ** N= 8 %= 10.13 ■■■■■■■■■■	**INFJ** N= 5 %= 6.33 ■■■■■■	**INTJ** N= 1 %= 1.27 ■
ISTP N= 1 %= 1.27 ■	**ISFP** N= 6 %= 7.59 ■■■■■■■	**INFP** N= 6 %= 7.59 ■■■■■■■	**INTP** N= 3 %= 3.80 ■■■■
ESTP N= 0 %= 0.00	**ESFP** N= 5 %= 6.33 ■■■■■■	**ENFP** N= 10 %= 12.66 ■■■■■■■■■■■■■ ■■■	**ENTP** N= 5 %= 6.33 ■■■■■■
ESTJ N= 10 %= 12.66 ■■■■■■■■■■■■■ ■■■	**ESFJ** N= 8 %= 10.13 ■■■■■■■■■■	**ENFJ** N= 3 %= 3.80 ■■■■	**ENTJ** N= 2 %= 2.53 ■■■

	N	%
E	43	54.43
I	36	45.57
S	44	55.70
N	35	44.30
T	28	35.44
F	51	64.56
J	43	54.43
P	36	45.57
I J	20	25.32
I P	16	20.25
E P	20	25.32
E J	23	29.11
S T	17	21.52
S F	27	34.18
N F	24	30.38
N T	11	13.92
S J	32	40.51
S P	12	15.19
N P	24	30.38
N J	11	13.92
T J	19	24.05
T P	9	11.39
F P	27	34.18
F J	24	30.38
I N	15	18.99
E N	20	25.32
I S	21	26.58
E S	23	29.11
E T	17	21.52
E F	26	32.91
I F	25	31.65
I T	11	13.92
S dom	19	24.05
N dom	21	26.58
T dom	16	20.25
F dom	23	29.11

Note: ■ = 1% of sample   8629359

This table is one of a series of tables from the CAPT-MBTI Data Bank of MBTI records submitted to CAPT for computer scoring between 1971 and June, 1984. This sample was drawn from 59,784 records with usable occupational codes from the total data bank of 232,557. This data bank has 51% Form F cases from 1971 to March, 1978, 35% Form F cases from 1978 to June, 1984 and 14% Form G cases from 1978 to December, 1982. An analysis of Form F and G data banks showed the data banks were comprised of 56% females and 44% males; education level completed: 6% some grade school, 30% high school diploma, 25% some college, 18% bachelor degrees, 11% masters degrees, 3% doctoral or post doctoral work, and 6% unknown. Age group percentages were: 11% under 18, 29% 18 to 20, 12% 21 to 24, 10% 25 to 29, 16% 30 to 39, 10% 40 to 49, 5% 50 to 59, 2% 60 plus, and 5% unknown.

358

Medical Technologists

N = 973

	SENSING		INTUITION	
	THINKING	FEELING	FEELING	THINKING

ISTJ	ISFJ	INFJ	INTJ
N= 129	N= 141	N= 50	N= 41
%= 13.26	%= 14.49	%= 5.14	%= 4.21
■■■■■■■■■■■■■	■■■■■■■■■■■■■■	■■■■■	■■■■
■■■	■■■■		

ISTP	ISFP	INFP	INTP
N= 27	N= 50	N= 71	N= 33
%= 2.77	%= 5.14	%= 7.30	%= 3.39
■■■	■■■■■	■■■■■■■	■■■

ESTP	ESFP	ENFP	ENTP
N= 19	N= 35	N= 64	N= 25
%= 1.95	%= 3.60	%= 6.58	%= 2.57
■■	■■■■	■■■■■■■	■■■

ESTJ	ESFJ	ENFJ	ENTJ
N= 97	N= 97	N= 51	N= 43
%= 9.97	%= 9.97	%= 5.24	%= 4.42
■■■■■■■■■■	■■■■■■■■■■	■■■■■	■■■■

	N	%
E	431	44.30
I	542	55.70
S	595	61.15
N	378	38.85
T	414	42.55
F	559	57.45
J	649	66.70
P	324	33.30
I J	361	37.10
I P	181	18.60
E P	143	14.70
E J	288	29.60
S T	272	27.95
S F	323	33.20
N F	236	24.25
N T	142	14.59
S J	464	47.69
S P	131	13.46
N P	193	19.84
N J	185	19.01
T J	310	31.86
T P	104	10.69
F P	220	22.61
F J	339	34.84
I N	195	20.04
E N	183	18.81
I S	347	35.66
E S	248	25.49
E T	184	18.91
E F	247	25.39
I F	312	32.07
I T	230	23.64
S dom	324	33.30
N dom	180	18.50
T dom	200	20.55
F dom	269	27.65

Note: ■ = 1% of sample   8623139

Subjects in this sample came from four main sources and were originally compiled especially for publication in:
McCaulley, M. H. (1978). Application of the Myers-Briggs Type Indicator to medicine and other health professions (Monograph I, Contract No. 231-76-0051, Health Resources Administration, DHEW). Gainesville, FL: Center for Applications of Psychological Type.
The four sources used were: 1) the CAPT health databank in 1977 based on Form F answer sheets scored by 1962 weights, 2) data solicited from medical and health professionals through advertising and personal communication, 3) the Myers Longitudinal Medical Sample initially collected in the 1950s and followed up in the 1970s and 4) data extracted from published research up to that time.

359

Medical Technologists (4 year)

N = 638

	SENSING		INTUITION	
	THINKING	FEELING	FEELING	THINKING

ISTJ	ISFJ	INFJ	INTJ
N= 84	N= 102	N= 35	N= 29
%= 13.17	%= 15.99	%= 5.49	%= 4.55
■■■■■■■■■■■■■	■■■■■■■■■■■■	■■■■■	■■■■■
■■■	■■■■■■		

ISTP	ISFP	INFP	INTP
N= 13	N= 34	N= 40	N= 25
%= 2.04	%= 5.33	%= 6.27	%= 3.92
■■	■■■■■	■■■■■■	■■■■

ESTP	ESFP	ENFP	ENTP
N= 13	N= 23	N= 37	N= 19
%= 2.04	%= 3.61	%= 5.80	%= 2.98
■■	■■■■	■■■■■■	■■■

ESTJ	ESFJ	ENFJ	ENTJ
N= 60	N= 64	N= 34	N= 26
%= 9.40	%= 10.03	%= 5.33	%= 4.08
■■■■■■■■■	■■■■■■■■■■	■■■■■	■■■■

JUDGMENT — INTROVERSION — PERCEPTION — EXTRAVERSION — JUDGMENT
PERCEPTION

	N	%
E	276	43.26
I	362	56.74
S	393	61.60
N	245	38.40
T	269	42.16
F	369	57.84
J	434	68.03
P	204	31.97
I J	250	39.18
I P	112	17.55
E P	92	14.42
E J	184	28.84
S T	170	26.65
S F	223	34.95
N F	146	22.88
N T	99	15.52
S J	310	48.59
S P	83	13.01
N P	121	18.97
N J	124	19.44
T J	199	31.19
T P	70	10.97
F P	134	21.00
F J	235	36.83
I N	129	20.22
E N	116	18.18
I S	233	36.52
E S	160	25.08
E T	118	18.50
E F	158	24.76
I F	211	33.07
I T	151	23.67
S dom	222	34.80
N dom	120	18.81
T dom	124	19.44
F dom	172	26.96

Note: ■ = 1% of sample

8629353

This table is one of a series of tables from the CAPT-MBTI Data Bank of MBTI records submitted to CAPT for computer scoring between 1971 and June, 1984. This sample was drawn from 59,784 records with usable occupational codes from the total data bank of 232,557. This data bank has 51% Form F cases from 1971 to March, 1978, 35% Form F cases from 1978 to June, 1984 and 14% Form G cases from 1978 to December, 1982. An analysis of Form F and G data banks showed the data banks were comprised of 56% females and 44% males; education level completed: 6% some grade school, 30% high school diploma, 25% some college, 18% bachelor degrees, 11% masters degrees, 3% doctoral or post doctoral work, and 6% unknown. Age group percentages were: 11% under 18, 29% 18 to 20, 12% 21 to 24, 10% 25 to 29, 16% 30 to 39, 10% 40 to 49, 5% 50 to 59, 2% 60 plus, and 5% unknown.

N = 94

	SENSING		INTUITION	
	THINKING	FEELING	FEELING	THINKING

ISTJ	ISFJ	INFJ	INTJ
N= 16	N= 14	N= 4	N= 6
%= 17.02	%= 14.89	%= 4.26	%= 6.38
■■■■■■■■■■■■■■■■■	■■■■■■■■■■■■■■	■■■■	■■■■■■
■■■■■■■	■■■■■		

ISTP	ISFP	INFP	INTP
N= 2	N= 2	N= 3	N= 2
%= 2.13	%= 2.13	%= 3.19	%= 2.13
■■	■■	■■■	■■

ESTP	ESFP	ENFP	ENTP
N= 1	N= 3	N= 5	N= 2
%= 1.06	%= 3.19	%= 5.32	%= 2.13
■	■■■	■■■■■	■■

ESTJ	ESFJ	ENFJ	ENTJ
N= 18	N= 5	N= 7	N= 4
%= 19.15	%= 5.32	%= 7.45	%= 4.26
■■■■■■■■■■■■■■■■■	■■■■■	■■■■■■■	■■■■
■■■■■■■■			

JUDGMENT — INTROVERSION — PERCEPTION — EXTRAVERSION — JUDGMENT

	N	%
E	45	47.87
I	49	52.13
S	61	64.89
N	33	35.11
T	51	54.26
F	43	45.74
J	74	78.72
P	20	21.28
I J	40	42.55
I P	9	9.57
E P	11	11.70
E J	34	36.17
S T	37	39.36
S F	24	25.53
N F	19	20.21
N T	14	14.89
S J	53	56.38
S P	8	8.51
N P	12	12.77
N J	21	22.34
T J	44	46.81
T P	7	7.45
F P	13	13.83
F J	30	31.91
I N	15	15.96
E N	18	19.15
I S	34	36.17
E S	27	28.72
E T	25	26.60
E F	20	21.28
I F	23	24.47
I T	26	27.66
S dom	34	36.17
N dom	17	18.09
T dom	26	27.66
F dom	17	18.09

Note: ■ = 1% of sample   8629346

This table is one of a series of tables from the CAPT-MBTI Data Bank of MBTI records submitted to CAPT for computer scoring between 1971 and June, 1984. This sample was drawn from 59,784 records with usable occupational codes from the total data bank of 232,557. This data bank has 51% Form F cases from 1971 to March, 1978, 35% Form F cases from 1978 to June, 1984 and 14% Form G cases from 1978 to December, 1982. An analysis of Form F and G data banks showed the data banks were comprised of 56% females and 44% males; education level completed: 6% some grade school, 30% high school diploma, 25% some college, 18% bachelor degrees, 11% masters degrees, 3% doctoral or post doctoral work, and 6% unknown. Age group percentages were: 11% under 18, 29% 18 to 20, 12% 21 to 24, 10% 25 to 29, 16% 30 to 39, 10% 40 to 49, 5% 50 to 59, 2% 60 plus, and 5% unknown.

Nursing: Aides, Orderlies, and Attendants

N = 314

<table>
<tr><th colspan="2">SENSING</th><th colspan="2">INTUITION</th></tr>
<tr><th>THINKING</th><th>FEELING</th><th>FEELING</th><th>THINKING</th></tr>
<tr>
<td>ISTJ
N= 23
%= 7.32
■■■■■■■</td>
<td>ISFJ
N= 61
%= 19.43
■■■■■■■■■■
■■■■■■■■■</td>
<td>INFJ
N= 8
%= 2.55
■■■</td>
<td>INTJ
N= 2
%= .64
■</td>
</tr>
<tr>
<td>ISTP
N= 11
%= 3.50
■■■■</td>
<td>ISFP
N= 21
%= 6.69
■■■■■■■</td>
<td>INFP
N= 23
%= 7.32
■■■■■■■</td>
<td>INTP
N= 6
%= 1.91
■■</td>
</tr>
<tr>
<td>ESTP
N= 4
%= 1.27
■</td>
<td>ESFP
N= 21
%= 6.69
■■■■■■■</td>
<td>ENFP
N= 40
%= 12.74
■■■■■■■■■■
■■■</td>
<td>ENTP
N= 3
%= .96
■</td>
</tr>
<tr>
<td>ESTJ
N= 23
%= 7.32
■■■■■■■</td>
<td>ESFJ
N= 40
%= 12.74
■■■■■■■■■■
■■■</td>
<td>ENFJ
N= 13
%= 4.14
■■■■</td>
<td>ENTJ
N= 15
%= 4.78
■■■■■</td>
</tr>
</table>

JUDGMENT — INTROVERSION — PERCEPTION — PERCEPTION — EXTRAVERSION — JUDGMENT

	N	%
E	159	50.64
I	155	49.36
S	204	64.97
N	110	35.03
T	87	27.71
F	227	72.29
J	185	58.92
P	129	41.08
I J	94	29.94
I P	61	19.43
E P	68	21.66
E J	91	28.98
S T	61	19.43
S F	143	45.54
N F	84	26.75
N T	26	8.28
S J	147	46.82
S P	57	18.15
N P	72	22.93
N J	38	12.10
T J	63	20.06
T P	24	7.64
F P	105	33.44
F J	122	38.85
I N	39	12.42
E N	71	22.61
I S	116	36.94
E S	88	28.03
E T	45	14.33
E F	114	36.31
I F	113	35.99
I T	42	13.38
S dom	109	34.71
N dom	53	16.88
T dom	55	17.52
F dom	97	30.89

Note: ■ = 1% of sample   8629357

This table is one of a series of tables from the CAPT-MBTI Data Bank of MBTI records submitted to CAPT for computer scoring between 1971 and June, 1984. This sample was drawn from 59,784 records with usable occupational codes from the total data bank of 232,557. This data bank has 51% Form F cases from 1971 to March, 1978, 35% Form F cases from 1978 to June, 1984 and 14% Form G cases from 1978 to December, 1982. An analysis of Form F and G data banks showed the data banks were comprised of 56% females and 44% males; education level completed: 6% some grade school, 30% high school diploma, 25% some college, 18% bachelor degrees, 11% masters degrees, 3% doctoral or post doctoral work, and 6% unknown. Age group percentages were: 11% under 18, 29% 18 to 20, 12% 21 to 24, 10% 25 to 29, 16% 30 to 39, 10% 40 to 49, 5% 50 to 59, 2% 60 plus, and 5% unknown.

Nursing: Composite of Critical Care Nurses

N = 155

	SENSING		INTUITION			N	%
THINKING	FEELING	FEELING	THINKING				

ISTJ N= 17 %= 10.97 ■■■■■■■■■■ ■	**ISFJ** N= 20 %= 12.90 ■■■■■■■■■■ ■■■	**INFJ** N= 5 %= 3.23 ■■■	**INTJ** N= 5 %= 3.23 ■■■
ISTP N= 4 %= 2.58 ■■■	**ISFP** N= 6 %= 3.87 ■■■■	**INFP** N= 10 %= 6.45 ■■■■■■	**INTP** N= 5 %= 3.23 ■■■
ESTP N= 6 %= 3.87 ■■■■	**ESFP** N= 9 %= 5.81 ■■■■■■	**ENFP** N= 9 %= 5.81 ■■■■■■	**ENTP** N= 9 %= 5.81 ■■■■■■
ESTJ N= 18 %= 11.61 ■■■■■■■■■■ ■■	**ESFJ** N= 14 %= 9.03 ■■■■■■■■■	**ENFJ** N= 11 %= 7.10 ■■■■■■■	**ENTJ** N= 7 %= 4.52 ■■■■■

JUDGMENT — INTROVERSION — PERCEPTION — PERCEPTION — EXTRAVERSION — JUDGMENT

	N	%
E	83	53.55
I	72	46.45
S	94	60.65
N	61	39.35
T	71	45.81
F	84	54.19
J	97	62.58
P	58	37.42
I J	47	30.32
I P	25	16.13
E P	33	21.29
E J	50	32.26
S T	45	29.03
S F	49	31.61
N F	35	22.58
N T	26	16.77
S J	69	44.52
S P	25	16.13
N P	33	21.29
N J	28	18.06
T J	47	30.32
T P	24	15.48
F P	34	21.94
F J	50	32.26
I N	25	16.13
E N	36	23.23
I S	47	30.32
E S	47	30.32
E T	40	25.81
E F	43	27.74
I F	41	26.45
I T	31	20.00
S dom	52	33.55
N dom	28	18.06
T dom	34	21.94
F dom	41	26.45

Note: ■ = 1% of sample

8623132

Data collected by David Williams and Myrna Courage during 1983 using Form F. The subjects were registered nurses in critical care from three north central Florida hospitals who volunteered to participate in a research study of burnout prevention. Half were an experimental group of entering nurses enrolled in a prescribed critical care education program, half were nurses who had 12 to 18 months of critical care experience but less than three months of initial training and had not been enrolled in any designed preparation courses. No gender, race or educational level data were reported. These data are used with permission and have not been published elsewhere to date.

Nursing: Consultants

N = 146

	SENSING			INTUITION				N	%
	THINKING	FEELING	FEELING	THINKING			E	78	53.42

ISTJ	ISFJ	INFJ	INTJ
N= 15	N= 18	N= 6	N= 6
%= 10.27	%= 12.33	%= 4.11	%= 4.11
■■■■■■■■■■	■■■■■■■■■■	■■■■	■■■■
	■■		

ISTP	ISFP	INFP	INTP
N= 4	N= 5	N= 9	N= 5
%= 2.74	%= 3.42	%= 6.16	%= 3.42
■■■	■■■	■■■■■■	■■■

ESTP	ESFP	ENFP	ENTP
N= 1	N= 2	N= 14	N= 3
%= .68	%= 1.37	%= 9.59	%= 2.05
■	■	■■■■■■■■■	■■

ESTJ	ESFJ	ENFJ	ENTJ
N= 18	N= 15	N= 13	N= 12
%= 12.33	%= 10.27	%= 8.90	%= 8.22
■■■■■■■■■■■■	■■■■■■■■■■	■■■■■■■■	■■■■■■■■
■■			

	N	%
E	78	53.42
I	68	46.58
S	78	53.42
N	68	46.58
T	64	43.84
F	82	56.16
J	103	70.55
P	43	29.45
I J	45	30.82
I P	23	15.75
E P	20	13.70
E J	58	39.73
S T	38	26.03
S F	40	27.40
N F	42	28.77
N T	26	17.81
S J	66	45.21
S P	12	8.22
N P	31	21.23
N J	37	25.34
T J	51	34.93
T P	13	8.90
F P	30	20.55
F J	52	35.62
I N	26	17.81
E N	42	28.77
I S	42	28.77
E S	36	24.66
E T	34	23.29
E F	44	30.14
I F	38	26.03
I T	30	20.55
S dom	36	24.66
N dom	29	19.86
T dom	39	26.71
F dom	42	28.77

Note: ■ = 1% of sample   8629343

This table is one of a series of tables from the CAPT-MBTI Data Bank of MBTI records submitted to CAPT for computer scoring between 1971 and June, 1984. This sample was drawn from 59,784 records with usable occupational codes from the total data bank of 232,557. This data bank has 51% Form F cases from 1971 to March, 1978, 35% Form F cases from 1978 to June, 1984 and 14% Form G cases from 1978 to December, 1982. An analysis of Form F and G data banks showed the data banks were comprised of 56% females and 44% males; education level completed: 6% some grade school, 30% high school diploma, 25% some college, 18% bachelor degrees, 11% masters degrees, 3% doctoral or post doctoral work, and 6% unknown. Age group percentages were: 11% under 18, 29% 18 to 20, 12% 21 to 24, 10% 25 to 29, 16% 30 to 39, 10% 40 to 49, 5% 50 to 59, 2% 60 plus, and 5% unknown.

Nursing: Educators

N = 305

	SENSING		INTUITION	
	THINKING	FEELING	FEELING	THINKING

ISTJ	ISFJ	INFJ	INTJ
N= 29	N= 38	N= 18	N= 22
%= 9.51	%= 12.46	%= 5.90	%= 7.21
■■■■■■■■■	■■■■■■■■■■■■	■■■■■■	■■■■■■■
	■■		

ISTP	ISFP	INFP	INTP
N= 7	N= 7	N= 21	N= 14
%= 2.30	%= 2.30	%= 6.89	%= 4.59
■■	■■	■■■■■■■	■■■■■

ESTP	ESFP	ENFP	ENTP
N= 4	N= 10	N= 33	N= 8
%= 1.31	%= 3.28	%= 10.82	%= 2.62
■	■■■	■■■■■■■■■■	■■■
		■	

ESTJ	ESFJ	ENFJ	ENTJ
N= 22	N= 25	N= 26	N= 21
%= 7.21	%= 8.20	%= 8.52	%= 6.89
■■■■■■■	■■■■■■■■	■■■■■■■■	■■■■■■■

JUDGMENT — INTROVERSION — PERCEPTION — EXTRAVERSION — JUDGMENT

	N	%
E	149	48.85
I	156	51.15
S	142	46.56
N	163	53.44
T	127	41.64
F	178	58.36
J	201	65.90
P	104	34.10
I J	107	35.08
I P	49	16.07
E P	55	18.03
E J	94	30.82
S T	62	20.33
S F	80	26.23
N F	98	32.13
N T	65	21.31
S J	114	37.38
S P	28	9.18
N P	76	24.92
N J	87	28.52
T J	94	30.82
T P	33	10.82
F P	71	23.28
F J	107	35.08
I N	75	24.59
E N	88	28.85
I S	81	26.56
E S	61	20.00
E T	55	18.03
E F	94	30.82
I F	84	27.54
I T	72	23.61
S dom	81	26.56
N dom	81	26.56
T dom	64	20.98
F dom	79	25.90

Note: ■ = 1% of sample   8629345

This table is one of a series of tables from the CAPT-MBTI Data Bank of MBTI records submitted to CAPT for computer scoring between 1971 and June, 1984. This sample was drawn from 59,784 records with usable occupational codes from the total data bank of 232,557. This data bank has 51% Form F cases from 1971 to March, 1978, 35% Form F cases from 1978 to June, 1984 and 14% Form G cases from 1978 to December, 1982. An analysis of Form F and G data banks showed the data banks were comprised of 56% females and 44% males; education level completed: 6% some grade school, 30% high school diploma, 25% some college, 18% bachelor degrees, 11% masters degrees, 3% doctoral or post doctoral work, and 6% unknown. Age group percentages were: 11% under 18, 29% 18 to 20, 12% 21 to 24, 10% 25 to 29, 16% 30 to 39, 10% 40 to 49, 5% 50 to 59, 2% 60 plus, and 5% unknown.

Nursing: Licensed Practical Nurses

N = 260

	SENSING		INTUITION	
	THINKING	FEELING	FEELING	THINKING

ISTJ	ISFJ	INFJ	INTJ
N= 24	N= 58	N= 9	N= 4
%= 9.23	%= 22.31	%= 3.46	%= 1.54
■■■■■■■■■	■■■■■■■■■■■	■■■	■■
	■■■■■■■■■■■		
	■■		

ISTP	ISFP	INFP	INTP
N= 9	N= 21	N= 9	N= 4
%= 3.46	%= 8.08	%= 3.46	%= 1.54
■■■	■■■■■■■■	■■■	■■

ESTP	ESFP	ENFP	ENTP
N= 5	N= 10	N= 21	N= 6
%= 1.92	%= 3.85	%= 8.08	%= 2.31
■■	■■■■	■■■■■■■■	■■

ESTJ	ESFJ	ENFJ	ENTJ
N= 26	N= 39	N= 10	N= 5
%= 10.00	%= 15.00	%= 3.85	%= 1.92
■■■■■■■■■■	■■■■■■■■■■■	■■■■	■■
	■■■■■		

JUDGMENT — INTROVERSION — PERCEPTION — PERCEPTION — EXTRAVERSION — JUDGMENT

	N	%
E	122	46.92
I	138	53.08
S	192	73.85
N	68	26.15
T	83	31.92
F	177	68.08
J	175	67.31
P	85	32.69
I J	95	36.54
I P	43	16.54
E P	42	16.15
E J	80	30.77
S T	64	24.62
S F	128	49.23
N F	49	18.85
N T	19	7.31
S J	147	56.54
S P	45	17.31
N P	40	15.38
N J	28	10.77
T J	59	22.69
T P	24	9.23
F P	61	23.46
F J	116	44.62
I N	26	10.00
E N	42	16.15
I S	112	43.08
E S	80	30.77
E T	42	16.15
E F	80	30.77
I F	97	37.31
I T	41	15.77
S dom	97	37.31
N dom	40	15.38
T dom	44	16.92
F dom	79	30.38

Note: ■ = 1% of sample   8629358

This table is one of a series of tables from the CAPT-MBTI Data Bank of MBTI records submitted to CAPT for computer scoring between 1971 and June, 1984. This sample was drawn from 59,784 records with usable occupational codes from the total data bank of 232,557. This data bank has 51% Form F cases from 1971 to March, 1978, 35% Form F cases from 1978 to June, 1984 and 14% Form G cases from 1978 to December, 1982. An analysis of Form F and G data banks showed the data banks were comprised of 56% females and 44% males; education level completed: 6% some grade school, 30% high school diploma, 25% some college, 18% bachelor degrees, 11% masters degrees, 3% doctoral or post doctoral work, and 6% unknown. Age group percentages were: 11% under 18, 29% 18 to 20, 12% 21 to 24, 10% 25 to 29, 16% 30 to 39. 10% 40 to 49. 5% 50 to 59, 2% 60 plus, and 5% unknown.

Nursing: Public Health

N = 83

	SENSING		INTUITION	
	THINKING	FEELING	FEELING	THINKING

ISTJ	ISFJ	INFJ	INTJ
N= 9	N= 15	N= 4	N= 3
%= 10.84	%= 18.07	%= 4.82	%= 3.61

ISTP	ISFP	INFP	INTP
N= 0	N= 5	N= 8	N= 1
%= 0.00	%= 6.02	%= 9.64	%= 1.20

ESTP	ESFP	ENFP	ENTP
N= 0	N= 6	N= 6	N= 2
%= 0.00	%= 7.23	%= 7.23	%= 2.41

ESTJ	ESFJ	ENFJ	ENTJ
N= 5	N= 8	N= 6	N= 5
%= 6.02	%= 9.64	%= 7.23	%= 6.02

	N	%
E	38	45.78
I	45	54.22
S	48	57.83
N	35	42.17
T	25	30.12
F	58	69.88
J	55	66.27
P	28	33.73
I J	31	37.35
I P	14	16.87
E P	14	16.87
E J	24	28.92
ST	14	16.87
SF	34	40.96
NF	24	28.92
NT	11	13.25
S J	37	44.58
S P	11	13.25
N P	17	20.48
N J	18	21.69
T J	22	26.51
T P	3	3.61
F P	25	30.12
F J	33	39.76
IN	16	19.28
EN	19	22.89
I S	29	34.94
ES	19	22.89
ET	12	14.46
EF	26	31.33
I F	32	38.55
I T	13	15.66
S dom	30	36.14
N dom	15	18.07
T dom	11	13.25
F dom	27	32.53

Note: ■ = 1% of sample   8629344

This table is one of a series of tables from the CAPT-MBTI Data Bank of MBTI records submitted to CAPT for computer scoring between 1971 and June, 1984. This sample was drawn from 59,784 records with usable occupational codes from the total data bank of 232,557. This data bank has 51% Form F cases from 1971 to March, 1978, 35% Form F cases from 1978 to June, 1984 and 14% Form G cases from 1978 to December, 1982. An analysis of Form F and G data banks showed the data banks were comprised of 56% females and 44% males; education level completed: 6% some grade school, 30% high school diploma, 25% some college, 18% bachelor degrees, 11% masters degrees, 3% doctoral or post doctoral work, and 6% unknown. Age group percentages were: 11% under 18, 29% 18 to 20, 12% 21 to 24, 10% 25 to 29, 16% 30 to 39, 10% 40 to 49, 5% 50 to 59, 2% 60 plus, and 5% unknown.

Nursing: Registered Nurses

N = 2351

	SENSING		INTUITION	
	THINKING	FEELING	FEELING	THINKING

ISTJ	ISFJ	INFJ	INTJ
N= 215	N= 352	N= 115	N= 81
%= 9.15	%= 14.97	%= 4.89	%= 3.45
■■■■■■■■■	■■■■■■■■■■ ■■■■■	■■■■■	■■■

ISTP	ISFP	INFP	INTP
N= 65	N= 150	N= 190	N= 63
%= 2.76	%= 6.38	%= 8.08	%= 2.68
■■■	■■■■■■	■■■■■■■■	■■■

ESTP	ESFP	ENFP	ENTP
N= 38	N= 92	N= 263	N= 67
%= 1.62	%= 3.91	%= 11.19	%= 2.85
■■	■■■■	■■■■■■■■■■■ ■	■■■

ESTJ	ESFJ	ENFJ	ENTJ
N= 163	N= 262	N= 152	N= 83
%= 6.93	%= 11.14	%= 6.47	%= 3.53
■■■■■■■	■■■■■■■■■■■ ■	■■■■■■	■■■■

JUDGMENT — PERCEPTION — PERCEPTION — JUDGMENT
INTROVERSION — EXTRAVERSION

	N	%
E	1120	47.64
I	1231	52.36
S	1337	56.87
N	1014	43.13
T	775	32.96
F	1576	67.04
J	1423	60.53
P	928	39.47
I J	763	32.45
I P	468	19.91
E P	460	19.57
E J	660	28.07
S T	481	20.46
S F	856	36.41
N F	720	30.63
N T	294	12.51
S J	992	42.19
S P	345	14.67
N P	583	24.80
N J	431	18.33
T J	542	23.05
T P	233	9.91
F P	695	29.56
F J	881	37.47
I N	449	19.10
E N	565	24.03
I S	782	33.26
E S	555	23.61
E T	351	14.93
E F	769	32.71
I F	807	34.33
I T	424	18.03
S dom	697	29.65
N dom	526	22.37
T dom	374	15.91
F dom	754	32.07

Note: ■ = 1% of sample

8623137

Subjects in this sample came from four main sources and were originally compiled especially for publication in:

McCaulley, M. H. (1978). Application of the Myers-Briggs Type Indicator to medicine and other health professions (Monograph I, Contract No. 231-76-0051, Health Resources Administration, DHEW). Gainesville, FL: Center for Applications of Psychological Type.

The four sources used were: 1) the CAPT health databank in 1977 based on Form F answer sheets scored by 1962 weights, 2) data solicited from medical and health professionals through advertising and personal communication, 3) the Myers Longitudinal Medical Sample initially collected in the 1950s and followed up in the 1970s and 4) data extracted from published research up to that time.

Nursing: Registered Nurses, no specialty stated

N = 1880

	SENSING		INTUITION	
	THINKING	FEELING	FEELING	THINKING

ISTJ	ISFJ	INFJ	INTJ
N= 180	N= 296	N= 112	N= 71
%= 9.57	%= 15.74	%= 5.96	%= 3.78
■■■■■■■■■	■■■■■■■■■■	■■■■■■	■■■■
	■■■■■		

ISTP	ISFP	INFP	INTP
N= 46	N= 106	N= 142	N= 55
%= 2.45	%= 5.64	%= 7.55	%= 2.93
■■	■■■■■	■■■■■■■	■■■

ESTP	ESFP	ENFP	ENTP
N= 37	N= 71	N= 177	N= 65
%= 1.97	%= 3.78	%= 9.41	%= 3.46
■■	■■■■	■■■■■■■■	■■■

ESTJ	ESFJ	ENFJ	ENTJ
N= 129	N= 205	N= 115	N= 73
%= 6.86	%= 10.90	%= 6.12	%= 3.88
■■■■■■■	■■■■■■■■■■	■■■■■■	■■■■
	■		

JUDGMENT / PERCEPTION — INTROVERSION
PERCEPTION / JUDGMENT — EXTRAVERSION

	N	%
E	872	46.38
I	1008	53.62
S	1070	56.91
N	810	43.09
T	656	34.89
F	1224	65.11
J	1181	62.82
P	699	37.18
I J	659	35.05
I P	349	18.56
E P	350	18.62
E J	522	27.77
S T	392	20.85
S F	678	36.06
N F	546	29.04
N T	264	14.04
S J	810	43.09
S P	260	13.83
N P	439	23.35
N J	371	19.73
T J	453	24.10
T P	203	10.80
F P	496	26.38
F J	728	38.72
I N	380	20.21
E N	430	22.87
I S	628	33.40
E S	442	23.51
E T	304	16.17
E F	568	30.21
I F	656	34.89
I T	352	18.72
S dom	584	31.06
N dom	425	22.61
T dom	303	16.12
F dom	568	30.21

Note: ■ = 1% of sample   8629342

This table is one of a series of tables from the CAPT-MBTI Data Bank of MBTI records submitted to CAPT for computer scoring between 1971 and June, 1984. This sample was drawn from 59,784 records with usable occupational codes from the total data bank of 232,557. This data bank has 51% Form F cases from 1971 to March, 1978, 35% Form F cases from 1978 to June, 1984 and 14% Form G cases from 1978 to December, 1982. An analysis of Form F and G data banks showed the data banks were comprised of 56% females and 44% males; education level completed: 6% some grade school, 30% high school diploma, 25% some college, 18% bachelor degrees, 11% masters degrees, 3% doctoral or post doctoral work, and 6% unknown. Age group percentages were: 11% under 18, 29% 18 to 20, 12% 21 to 24, 10% 25 to 29, 16% 30 to 39, 10% 40 to 49, 5% 50 to 59, 2% 60 plus, and 5% unknown.

Optometrists

N = 70

	SENSING		INTUITION	
	THINKING	FEELING	FEELING	THINKING

ISTJ	ISFJ	INFJ	INTJ
N= 9	N= 7	N= 2	N= 2
%= 12.86	%= 10.00	%= 2.86	%= 2.86
■■■■■■■■■■■■ ■■■	■■■■■■■■■■	■■■	■■■

ISTP	ISFP	INFP	INTP
N= 4	N= 1	N= 4	N= 1
%= 5.71	%= 1.43	%= 5.71	%= 1.43
■■■■■	■	■■■■■	■

ESTP	ESFP	ENFP	ENTP
N= 3	N= 2	N= 6	N= 1
%= 4.29	%= 2.86	%= 8.57	%= 1.43
■■■■	■■■	■■■■■■■■	■

ESTJ	ESFJ	ENFJ	ENTJ
N= 7	N= 8	N= 8	N= 5
%= 10.00	%= 11.43	%= 11.43	%= 7.14
■■■■■■■■■■	■■■■■■■■■■■ ■	■■■■■■■■■■■ ■	■■■■■■■

JUDGMENT — INTROVERSION — PERCEPTION — PERCEPTION — EXTRAVERSION — JUDGMENT

	N	%
E	40	57.14
I	30	42.86
S	41	58.57
N	29	41.43
T	32	45.71
F	38	54.29
J	48	68.57
P	22	31.43
I J	20	28.57
I P	10	14.29
E P	12	17.14
E J	28	40.00
S T	23	32.86
S F	18	25.71
N F	20	28.57
N T	9	12.86
S J	31	44.29
S P	10	14.29
N P	12	17.14
N J	17	24.29
T J	23	32.86
T P	9	12.86
F P	13	18.57
F J	25	35.71
I N	9	12.86
E N	20	28.57
I S	21	30.00
E S	20	28.57
E T	16	22.86
E F	24	34.29
I F	14	20.00
I T	16	22.86
S dom	21	30.00
N dom	11	15.71
T dom	17	24.29
F dom	21	30.00

Note: ■ = 1% of sample

8629336

This table is one of a series of tables from the CAPT-MBTI Data Bank of MBTI records submitted to CAPT for computer scoring between 1971 and June, 1984. This sample was drawn from 59,784 records with usable occupational codes from the total data bank of 232,557. This data bank has 51% Form F cases from 1971 to March, 1978, 35% Form F cases from 1978 to June 1984 and 14% Form G cases from 1978 to December, 1982. An analysis of Form F and G data banks showed the data banks were comprised of 56% females and 44% males; education level completed: 6% some grade school, 30% high school diploma, 25% some college, 18% bachelor degrees, 11% masters degrees, 3% doctoral or post doctoral work, and 6% unknown. Age group percentages were: 11% under 18, 29% 18 to 20, 12% 21 to 24, 10% 25 to 29, 16% 30 to 39, 10% 40 to 49, 5% 50 to 59, 2% 60 plus, and 5% unknown.

Pharmacists

N = 123

			SENSING		INTUITION	
	THINKING	FEELING		FEELING	THINKING	

	N	%
ISTJ		
N= 13		
%= 10.57		
■■■■■■■■■■		
■		

Type Grid

ISTJ	ISFJ	INFJ	INTJ
N= 13	N= 10	N= 10	N= 7
%= 10.57	%= 8.13	%= 8.13	%= 5.69
■■■■■■■■■■■	■■■■■■■■	■■■■■■■■	■■■■■■

ISTP	ISFP	INFP	INTP
N= 6	N= 3	N= 6	N= 11
%= 4.88	%= 2.44	%= 4.88	%= 8.94
■■■■■	■■	■■■■■	■■■■■■■■■

ESTP	ESFP	ENFP	ENTP
N= 7	N= 2	N= 7	N= 6
%= 5.69	%= 1.63	%= 5.69	%= 4.88
■■■■■■	■■	■■■■■■	■■■■■

ESTJ	ESFJ	ENFJ	ENTJ
N= 10	N= 8	N= 13	N= 4
%= 8.13	%= 6.50	%= 10.57	%= 3.25
■■■■■■■■	■■■■■■■	■■■■■■■■■■■	■■■

Column headings: THINKING / FEELING under SENSING; FEELING / THINKING under INTUITION.
Right-side labels: JUDGMENT, PERCEPTION (INTROVERSION); PERCEPTION, JUDGMENT (EXTRAVERSION).

	N	%
E	57	46.34
I	66	53.66
S	59	47.97
N	64	52.03
T	64	52.03
F	59	47.97
J	75	60.98
P	48	39.02
I J	40	32.52
I P	26	21.14
E P	22	17.89
E J	35	28.46
S T	36	29.27
S F	23	18.70
N F	36	29.27
N T	28	22.76
S J	41	33.33
S P	18	14.63
N P	30	24.39
N J	34	27.64
T J	34	27.64
T P	30	24.39
F P	18	14.63
F J	41	33.33
I N	34	27.64
E N	30	24.39
I S	32	26.02
E S	27	21.95
E T	27	21.95
E F	30	24.39
I F	29	23.58
I T	37	30.08
S dom	32	26.02
N dom	30	24.39
T dom	31	25.20
F dom	30	24.39

Note: ■ = 1% of sample   8623138

Subjects in this sample came from four main sources and were originally compiled especially for publication in:
McCaulley, M. H. (1978). Application of the Myers-Briggs Type Indicator to medicine and other health professions (Monograph I, Contract No. 231-76-0051, Health Resources Administration, DHEW). Gainesville, FL: Center for Applications of Psychological Type.
The four sources used were: 1) the CAPT health databank in 1977 based on Form F answer sheets scored by 1962 weights, 2) data solicited from medical and health professionals through advertising and personal communication, 3) the Myers Longitudinal Medical Sample initially collected in the 1950s and followed up in the 1970s and 4) data extracted from published research up to that time.

Pharmacists

	SENSING		INTUITION	
	THINKING	FEELING	FEELING	THINKING

ISTJ	ISFJ	INFJ	INTJ
N= 22	N= 19	N= 11	N= 10
%= 11.52	%= 9.95	%= 5.76	%= 5.24
■■■■■■■■■■■	■■■■■■■■■■	■■■■■■	■■■■■
■■			

ISTP	ISFP	INFP	INTP
N= 8	N= 7	N= 11	N= 14
%= 4.19	%= 3.66	%= 5.76	%= 7.33
■■■■	■■■■	■■■■■■	■■■■■■■

ESTP	ESFP	ENFP	ENTP
N= 8	N= 4	N= 10	N= 7
%= 4.19	%= 2.09	%= 5.24	%= 3.66
■■■■	■■	■■■■■	■■■■

ESTJ	ESFJ	ENFJ	ENTJ
N= 19	N= 15	N= 16	N= 10
%= 9.95	%= 7.85	%= 8.38	%= 5.24
■■■■■■■■■■	■■■■■■■■	■■■■■■■■	■■■■■

JUDGMENT — INTROVERSION — PERCEPTION — EXTRAVERSION — JUDGMENT

	N	%
E	89	46.60
I	102	53.40
S	102	53.40
N	89	46.60
T	98	51.31
F	93	48.69
J	122	63.87
P	69	36.13
I J	62	32.46
I P	40	20.94
E P	29	15.18
E J	60	31.41
S T	57	29.84
S F	45	23.56
N F	48	25.13
N T	41	21.47
S J	75	39.27
S P	27	14.14
N P	42	21.99
N J	47	24.61
T J	61	31.94
T P	37	19.37
F P	32	16.75
F J	61	31.94
I N	46	24.08
E N	43	22.51
I S	56	29.32
E S	46	24.08
E T	44	23.04
E F	45	23.56
I F	48	25.13
I T	54	28.27
S dom	53	27.75
N dom	38	19.90
T dom	51	26.70
F dom	49	25.65

Note: ■ = 1% of sample   8629337

This table is one of a series of tables from the CAPT-MBTI Data Bank of MBTI records submitted to CAPT for computer scoring between 1971 and June, 1984. This sample was drawn from 59,784 records with usable occupational codes from the total data bank of 232,557. This data bank has 51% Form F cases from 1971 to March, 1978, 35% Form F cases from 1978 to June, 1984 and 14% Form G cases from 1978 to December, 1982. An analysis of Form F and G data banks showed the data banks were comprised of 56% females and 44% males; education level completed: 6% some grade school, 30% high school diploma, 25% some college, 18% bachelor degrees, 11% masters degrees, 3% doctoral or post doctoral work, and 6% unknown. Age group percentages were: 11% under 18, 29% 18 to 20, 12% 21 to 24, 10% 25 to 29, 16% 30 to 39, 10% 40 to 49, 5% 50 to 59, 2% 60 plus, and 5% unknown.

Physicians: Family Practice, General Practice

N = 139

	SENSING		INTUITION	
	THINKING	FEELING	FEELING	THINKING

ISTJ	ISFJ	INFJ	INTJ
N= 7	N= 24	N= 9	N= 5
%= 5.04	%= 17.27	%= 6.47	%= 3.60
■■■■■	■■■■■■■■■■ ■■■■■■■	■■■■■■	■■■■

ISTP	ISFP	INFP	INTP
N= 1	N= 7	N= 9	N= 4
%= .72	%= 5.04	%= 6.47	%= 2.88
■	■■■■■	■■■■■■	■■■

ESTP	ESFP	ENFP	ENTP
N= 5	N= 2	N= 11	N= 2
%= 3.60	%= 1.44	%= 7.91	%= 1.44
■■■■	■	■■■■■■■■	■

ESTJ	ESFJ	ENFJ	ENTJ
N= 15	N= 13	N= 13	N= 12
%= 10.79	%= 9.35	%= 9.35	%= 8.63
■■■■■■■■■■ ■	■■■■■■■■■	■■■■■■■■■	■■■■■■■■■

	N	%
E	73	52.52
I	66	47.48
S	74	53.24
N	65	46.76
T	51	36.69
F	88	63.31
J	98	70.50
P	41	29.50
I J	45	32.37
I P	21	15.11
E P	20	14.39
E J	53	38.13
ST	28	20.14
SF	46	33.09
NF	42	30.22
NT	23	16.55
S J	59	42.45
S P	15	10.79
NP	26	18.71
NJ	39	28.06
TJ	39	28.06
TP	12	8.63
FP	29	20.86
FJ	59	42.45
IN	27	19.42
EN	38	27.34
I S	39	28.06
ES	35	25.18
ET	34	24.46
EF	39	28.06
IF	49	35.25
IT	17	12.23
S dom	38	27.34
N dom	27	19.42
T dom	32	23.02
F dom	42	30.22

Note: ■ = 1% of sample   8629338

This table is one of a series of tables from the CAPT-MBTI Data Bank of MBTI records submitted to CAPT for computer scoring between 1971 and June, 1984. This sample was drawn from 59,784 records with usable occupational codes from the total data bank of 232,557. This data bank has 51% Form F cases from 1971 to March, 1978, 35% Form F cases from 1978 to June, 1984 and 14% Form G cases from 1978 to December, 1982. An analysis of Form F and G data banks showed the data banks were comprised of 56% females and 44% males; education level completed: 6% some grade school, 30% high school diploma, 25% some college, 18% bachelor degrees, 11% masters degrees, 3% doctoral or post doctoral work, and 6% unknown. Age group percentages were: 11% under 18, 29% 18 to 20, 12% 21 to 24, 10% 25 to 29, 16% 30 to 39, 10% 40 to 49, 5% 50 to 59, 2% 60 plus, and 5% unknown.

Physicians: Pathology

N = 61

	SENSING		INTUITION	
	THINKING	FEELING	FEELING	THINKING

ISTJ	ISFJ	INFJ	INTJ
N= 9	N= 2	N= 7	N= 5
%= 14.75	%= 3.28	%= 11.48	%= 8.20
■■■■■■■■■■■■■■	■■■	■■■■■■■■■■■■	■■■■■■■■
■■■■■		■	

ISTP	ISFP	INFP	INTP
N= 4	N= 0	N= 3	N= 4
%= 6.56	%= 0.00	%= 4.92	%= 6.56
■■■■■■■		■■■■■	■■■■■■■

ESTP	ESFP	ENFP	ENTP
N= 2	N= 2	N= 1	N= 2
%= 3.28	%= 3.28	%= 1.64	%= 3.28
■■■	■■■	■■	■■■

ESTJ	ESFJ	ENFJ	ENTJ
N= 11	N= 3	N= 1	N= 5
%= 18.03	%= 4.92	%= 1.64	%= 8.20
■■■■■■■■■■■■■■■■■■	■■■■■	■■	■■■■■■■■
■■■■■■■■			

Right side labels: JUDGMENT — INTROVERSION — PERCEPTION (top block); PERCEPTION — EXTRAVERSION — JUDGMENT (bottom block)

	N	%
E	27	44.26
I	34	55.74
S	33	54.10
N	28	45.90
T	42	68.85
F	19	31.15
J	43	70.49
P	18	29.51
I J	23	37.70
I P	11	18.03
E P	7	11.48
E J	20	32.79
S T	26	42.62
S F	7	11.48
N F	12	19.67
N T	16	26.23
S J	25	40.98
S P	8	13.11
N P	10	16.39
N J	18	29.51
T J	30	49.18
T P	12	19.67
F P	6	9.84
F J	13	21.31
I N	19	31.15
E N	9	14.75
I S	15	24.59
E S	18	29.51
E T	20	32.79
E F	7	11.48
I F	12	19.67
I T	22	36.07
S dom	15	24.59
N dom	15	24.59
T dom	24	39.34
F dom	7	11.48

Note: ■ = 1% of sample

8629339

This table is one of a series of tables from the CAPT-MBTI Data Bank of MBTI records submitted to CAPT for computer scoring between 1971 and June, 1984. This sample was drawn from 59,784 records with usable occupational codes from the total data bank of 232,557. This data bank has 51% Form F cases from 1971 to March, 1978, 35% Form F cases from 1978 to June, 1984 and 14% Form G cases from 1978 to December, 1982. An analysis of Form F and G data banks showed the data banks were comprised of 56% females and 44% males; education level completed: 6% some grade school, 30% high school diploma, 25% some college, 18% bachelor degrees, 11% masters degrees, 3% doctoral or post doctoral work, and 6% unknown. Age group percentages were: 11% under 18, 29% 18 to 20, 12% 21 to 24, 10% 25 to 29, 16% 30 to 39, 10% 40 to 49, 5% 50 to 59, 2% 60 plus, and 5% unknown.

N = 68

	SENSING		INTUITION			N	%
	THINKING	FEELING	FEELING	THINKING			

ISTJ	ISFJ	INFJ	INTJ
N= 5	N= 4	N= 6	N= 4
%= 7.35	%= 5.88	%= 8.82	%= 5.88
■■■■■■■	■■■■■■	■■■■■■■■■	■■■■■■

ISTP	ISFP	INFP	INTP
N= 1	N= 0	N= 14	N= 4
%= 1.47	%= 0.00	%= 20.59	%= 5.88
■		■■■■■■■■■■	■■■■■■
		■■■■■■■■■■	
		■	

ESTP	ESFP	ENFP	ENTP
N= 1	N= 0	N= 7	N= 7
%= 1.47	%= 0.00	%= 10.29	%= 10.29
■		■■■■■■■■■■	■■■■■■■■■■

ESTJ	ESFJ	ENFJ	ENTJ
N= 6	N= 0	N= 6	N= 3
%= 8.82	%= 0.00	%= 8.82	%= 4.41
■■■■■■■■■		■■■■■■■■■	■■■■

JUDGMENT — INTROVERSION — PERCEPTION — PERCEPTION — EXTRAVERSION — JUDGMENT

	N	%
E	30	44.12
I	38	55.88
S	17	25.00
N	51	75.00
T	31	45.59
F	37	54.41
J	34	50.00
P	34	50.00
I J	19	27.94
I P	19	27.94
E P	15	22.06
E J	15	22.06
S T	13	19.12
S F	4	5.88
N F	33	48.53
N T	18	26.47
S J	15	22.06
S P	2	2.94
N P	32	47.06
N J	19	27.94
T J	18	26.47
T P	13	19.12
F P	21	30.88
F J	16	23.53
I N	28	41.18
E N	23	33.82
I S	10	14.71
E S	7	10.29
E T	17	25.00
E F	13	19.12
I F	24	35.29
I T	14	20.59
S dom	10	14.71
N dom	24	35.29
T dom	14	20.59
F dom	20	29.41

Note: ■ = 1% of sample   8629340

This table is one of a series of tables from the CAPT-MBTI Data Bank of MBTI records submitted to CAPT for computer scoring between 1971 and June, 1984. This sample was drawn from 59,784 records with usable occupational codes from the total data bank of 232,557. This data bank has 51% Form F cases from 1971 to March, 1978, 35% Form F cases from 1978 to June, 1984 and 14% Form G cases from 1978 to December, 1982. An analysis of Form F and G data banks showed the data banks were comprised of 56% females and 44% males; education level completed: 6% some grade school, 30% high school diploma, 25% some college, 18% bachelor degrees, 11% masters degrees, 3% doctoral or post doctoral work, and 6% unknown. Age group percentages were: 11% under 18, 29% 18 to 20, 12% 21 to 24, 10% 25 to 29, 16% 30 to 39, 10% 40 to 49, 5% 50 to 59, 2% 60 plus, and 5% unknown.

Composite of Practitioners in Medicine (M.D.s)

N = 1881

	SENSING		INTUITION	
	THINKING	FEELING	FEELING	THINKING

ISTJ	ISFJ	INFJ	INTJ
N= 267	N= 186	N= 152	N= 131
%= 14.19	%= 9.89	%= 8.08	%= 6.96
■■■■■■■■■■■■■■	■■■■■■■■■■	■■■■■■■■	■■■■■■■
■■■■			

JUDGMENT — INTROVERSION

ISTP	ISFP	INFP	INTP
N= 54	N= 45	N= 172	N= 93
%= 2.87	%= 2.39	%= 9.14	%= 4.94
■■■	■■	■■■■■■■■■	■■■■■

PERCEPTION

ESTP	ESFP	ENFP	ENTP
N= 31	N= 35	N= 148	N= 62
%= 1.65	%= 1.86	%= 7.87	%= 3.30
■■	■■	■■■■■■■■	■■■

PERCEPTION — EXTRAVERSION

ESTJ	ESFJ	ENFJ	ENTJ
N= 148	N= 116	N= 119	N= 122
%= 7.87	%= 6.17	%= 6.33	%= 6.49
■■■■■■■■	■■■■■■	■■■■■■	■■■■■■

JUDGMENT

	N	%
E	781	41.52
I	1100	58.48
S	882	46.89
N	999	53.11
T	908	48.27
F	973	51.73
J	1241	65.98
P	640	34.02
I J	736	39.13
I P	364	19.35
E P	276	14.67
E J	505	26.85
S T	500	26.58
S F	382	20.31
N F	591	31.42
N T	408	21.69
S J	717	38.12
S P	165	8.77
N P	475	25.25
N J	524	27.86
T J	668	35.51
T P	240	12.76
F P	400	21.27
F J	573	30.46
I N	548	29.13
E N	451	23.98
I S	552	29.35
E S	330	17.54
E T	363	19.30
E F	418	22.22
I F	555	29.51
I T	545	28.97
S dom	519	27.59
N dom	493	26.21
T dom	417	22.17
F dom	452	24.03

Note: ■ = 1% of sample

8623135

Subjects in this sample came from four main sources and were originally compiled especially for publication in:

McCaulley, M. H. (1978). Application of the Myers-Briggs Type Indicator to medicine and other health professions (Monograph I, Contract No. 231-76-0051, Health Resources Administration, DHEW). Gainesville, FL: Center for Applications of Psychological Type.

The four sources used were: 1) the CAPT health databank in 1977 based on Form F answer sheets scored by 1962 weights, 2) data solicited from medical and health professionals through advertising and personal communication, 3) the Myers Longitudinal Medical Sample initially collected in the 1950s and followed up in the 1970s and 4) data extracted from published research up to that time.

Composite of Practitioners in Radiologic Technology

N = 53

	SENSING		INTUITION	
	THINKING	FEELING	FEELING	THINKING

ISTJ	ISFJ	INFJ	INTJ
N= 4	N= 9	N= 0	N= 2
%= 7.55	%= 16.98	%= 0.00	%= 3.77
■■■■■■■	■■■■■■■■■		■■■■
	■■■■■■		

ISTP	ISFP	INFP	INTP
N= 0	N= 5	N= 1	N= 1
%= 0.00	%= 9.43	%= 1.89	%= 1.89
	■■■■■■■■■	■■	■■

ESTP	ESFP	ENFP	ENTP
N= 5	N= 2	N= 9	N= 3
%= 9.43	%= 3.77	%= 16.98	%= 5.66
■■■■■■■■■	■■■■	■■■■■■■■■	■■■■■■
		■■■■■■	

ESTJ	ESFJ	ENFJ	ENTJ
N= 5	N= 5	N= 1	N= 1
%= 9.43	%= 9.43	%= 1.89	%= 1.89
■■■■■■■■■	■■■■■■■■■	■■	■■

JUDGMENT — INTROVERSION — PERCEPTION — PERCEPTION — EXTRAVERSION — JUDGMENT

	N	%
E	31	58.49
I	22	41.51
S	35	66.04
N	18	33.96
T	21	39.62
F	32	60.38
J	27	50.94
P	26	49.06
I J	15	28.30
I P	7	13.21
E P	19	35.85
E J	12	22.64
S T	14	26.42
S F	21	39.62
N F	11	20.75
N T	7	13.21
S J	23	43.40
S P	12	22.64
N P	14	26.42
N J	4	7.55
T J	12	22.64
T P	9	16.98
F P	17	32.08
F J	15	28.30
I N	4	7.55
E N	14	26.42
I S	18	33.96
E S	17	32.08
E T	14	26.42
E F	17	32.08
I F	15	28.30
I T	7	13.21
S dom	20	37.74
N dom	14	26.42
T dom	7	13.21
F dom	12	22.64

Note: ■ = 1% of sample   8623142

Subjects in this sample came from four main sources and were originally compiled especially for publication in:

McCaulley, M. H. (1978). Application of the Myers-Briggs Type Indicator to medicine and other health professions (Monograph I, Contract No. 231-76-0051, Health Resources Administration, DHEW). Gainesville, FL: Center for Applications of Psychological Type.

The four sources used were: 1) the CAPT health databank in 1977 based on Form F answer sheets scored by 1962 weights, 2) data solicited from medical and health professionals through advertising and personal communication, 3) the Myers Longitudinal Medical Sample initially collected in the 1950s and followed up in the 1970s and 4) data extracted from published research up to that time.

Composite of Practitioners in Speech Pathology

N = 122

	SENSING		INTUITION	
	THINKING	FEELING	FEELING	THINKING

ISTJ	ISFJ	INFJ	INTJ
N= 5	N= 7	N= 8	N= 5
%= 4.10	%= 5.74	%= 6.56	%= 4.10
■■■■	■■■■■■	■■■■■■■	■■■■

ISTP	ISFP	INFP	INTP
N= 3	N= 7	N= 12	N= 4
%= 2.46	%= 5.74	%= 9.84	%= 3.28
■■	■■■■■■	■■■■■■■■■■	■■■

ESTP	ESFP	ENFP	ENTP
N= 1	N= 4	N= 18	N= 10
%= .82	%= 3.28	%= 14.75	%= 8.20
■	■■■	■■■■■■■■■■■■■■ ■■■■■	■■■■■■■■■

ESTJ	ESFJ	ENFJ	ENTJ
N= 8	N= 12	N= 11	N= 7
%= 6.56	%= 9.84	%= 9.02	%= 5.74
■■■■■■■	■■■■■■■■■■	■■■■■■■■■	■■■■■■

JUDGMENT — INTROVERSION — PERCEPTION — PERCEPTION — EXTRAVERSION — JUDGMENT

Note: ■ = 1% of sample

8623144

	N	%
E	71	58.20
I	51	41.80
S	47	38.52
N	75	61.48
T	43	35.25
F	79	64.75
J	63	51.64
P	59	48.36
I J	25	20.49
I P	26	21.31
E P	33	27.05
E J	38	31.15
S T	17	13.93
S F	30	24.59
N F	49	40.16
N T	26	21.31
S J	32	26.23
S P	15	12.30
N P	44	36.07
N J	31	25.41
T J	25	20.49
T P	18	14.75
F P	41	33.61
F J	38	31.15
I N	29	23.77
E N	46	37.70
I S	22	18.03
E S	25	20.49
E T	26	21.31
E F	45	36.89
I F	34	27.87
I T	17	13.93
S dom	17	13.93
N dom	41	33.61
T dom	22	18.03
F dom	42	34.43

Subjects in this sample came from four main sources and were originally compiled especially for publication in:

McCaulley, M. H. (1978). Application of the Myers-Briggs Type Indicator to medicine and other health professions (Monograph I, Contract No. 231-76-0051, Health Resources Administration, DHEW). Gainesville, FL: Center for Applications of Psychological Type.

The four sources used were: 1) the CAPT health databank in 1977 based on Form F answer sheets scored by 1962 weights, 2) data solicited from medical and health professionals through advertising and personal communication, 3) the Myers Longitudinal Medical Sample initially collected in the 1950s and followed up in the 1970s and 4) data extracted from published research up to that time.

Public Service Aides and Community Health Workers

N = 238

<table>
<tr><td colspan="2" align="center">SENSING</td><td colspan="2" align="center">INTUITION</td></tr>
<tr><td align="center">THINKING</td><td align="center">FEELING</td><td align="center">FEELING</td><td align="center">THINKING</td></tr>
</table>

ISTJ	ISFJ	INFJ	INTJ
N= 39	N= 32	N= 5	N= 4
%= 16.39	%= 13.45	%= 2.10	%= 1.68
■■■■■■■■■■ ■■■■■■	■■■■■■■■■■ ■■■	■■	■■

ISTP	ISFP	INFP	INTP
N= 3	N= 11	N= 7	N= 3
%= 1.26	%= 4.62	%= 2.94	%= 1.26
■	■■■■■	■■■	■

ESTP	ESFP	ENFP	ENTP
N= 15	N= 8	N= 9	N= 5
%= 6.30	%= 3.36	%= 3.78	%= 2.10
■■■■■■	■■■	■■■■	■■

ESTJ	ESFJ	ENFJ	ENTJ
N= 55	N= 31	N= 4	N= 7
%= 23.11	%= 13.03	%= 1.68	%= 2.94
■■■■■■■■■■ ■■■■■■■■■■ ■■■	■■■■■■■■■■ ■■■	■■	■■■

Side labels: JUDGMENT — INTROVERSION — PERCEPTION — PERCEPTION — EXTRAVERSION — JUDGMENT

	N	%
E	134	56.30
I	104	43.70
S	194	81.51
N	44	18.49
T	131	55.04
F	107	44.96
J	177	74.37
P	61	25.63
I J	80	33.61
I P	24	10.08
E P	37	15.55
E J	97	40.76
S T	112	47.06
S F	82	34.45
N F	25	10.50
N T	19	7.98
S J	157	65.97
S P	37	15.55
N P	24	10.08
N J	20	8.40
T J	105	44.12
T P	26	10.92
F P	35	14.71
F J	72	30.25
I N	19	7.98
E N	25	10.50
I S	85	35.71
E S	109	45.80
E T	82	34.45
E F	52	21.85
I F	55	23.11
I T	49	20.59
S dom	94	39.50
N dom	23	9.66
T dom	68	28.57
F dom	53	22.27

Note: ■ = 1% of sample   8629365

This table is one of a series of tables from the CAPT-MBTI Data Bank of MBTI records submitted to CAPT for computer scoring between 1971 and June, 1984. This sample was drawn from 59,784 records with usable occupational codes from the total data bank of 232,557. This data bank has 51% Form F cases from 1971 to March, 1978, 35% Form F cases from 1978 to June, 1984 and 14% Form G cases from 1978 to December, 1982. An analysis of Form F and G data banks showed the data banks were comprised of 56% females and 44% males; education level completed: 6% some grade school, 30% high school diploma, 25% some college, 18% bachelor degrees, 11% masters degrees, 3% doctoral or post doctoral work, and 6% unknown. Age group percentages were: 11% under 18, 29% 18 to 20, 12% 21 to 24, 10% 25 to 29, 16% 30 to 39, 10% 40 to 49, 5% 50 to 59, 2% 60 plus, and 5% unknown.

Radiologic Technologists and Technicians

N = 126

	SENSING		INTUITION	
	THINKING	FEELING	FEELING	THINKING

ISTJ	**ISFJ**	**INFJ**	**INTJ**
N= 14	N= 16	N= 3	N= 2
%= 11.11	%= 12.70	%= 2.38	%= 1.59
■■■■■■■■■■■	■■■■■■■■■■■■	■■	■■
■	■■■		

ISTP	**ISFP**	**INFP**	**INTP**
N= 2	N= 10	N= 10	N= 4
%= 1.59	%= 7.94	%= 7.94	%= 3.17
■■	■■■■■■■■	■■■■■■■■	■■■

ESTP	**ESFP**	**ENFP**	**ENTP**
N= 5	N= 7	N= 10	N= 7
%= 3.97	%= 5.56	%= 7.94	%= 5.56
■■■■	■■■■■■	■■■■■■■■	■■■■■■

ESTJ	**ESFJ**	**ENFJ**	**ENTJ**
N= 12	N= 17	N= 3	N= 4
%= 9.52	%= 13.49	%= 2.38	%= 3.17
■■■■■■■■■	■■■■■■■■■■■■	■■	■■■
	■■■		

JUDGMENT — INTROVERSION — PERCEPTION — PERCEPTION — EXTRAVERSION — JUDGMENT

Note: ■ = 1% of sample

8629352

	N	%
E	65	51.59
I	61	48.41
S	83	65.87
N	43	34.13
T	50	39.68
F	76	60.32
J	71	56.35
P	55	43.65
I J	35	27.78
I P	26	20.63
E P	29	23.02
E J	36	28.57
S T	33	26.19
S F	50	39.68
N F	26	20.63
N T	17	13.49
S J	59	46.83
S P	24	19.05
N P	31	24.60
N J	12	9.52
T J	32	25.40
T P	18	14.29
F P	37	29.37
F J	39	30.95
I N	19	15.08
E N	24	19.05
I S	42	33.33
E S	41	32.54
E T	28	22.22
E F	37	29.37
I F	39	30.95
I T	22	17.46
S dom	42	33.33
N dom	22	17.46
T dom	22	17.46
F dom	40	31.75

This table is one of a series of tables from the CAPT-MBTI Data Bank of MBTI records submitted to CAPT for computer scoring between 1971 and June, 1984. This sample was drawn from 59,784 records with usable occupational codes from the total data bank of 232,557. This data bank has 51% Form F cases from 1971 to March, 1978, 35% Form F cases from 1978 to June, 1984 and 14% Form G cases from 1978 to December, 1982. An analysis of Form F and G data banks showed the data banks were comprised of 56% females and 44% males; education level completed: 6% some grade school, 30% high school diploma, 25% some college, 18% bachelor degrees, 11% masters degrees, 3% doctoral or post doctoral work, and 6% unknown. Age group percentages were: 11% under 18, 29% 18 to 20, 12% 21 to 24, 10% 25 to 29, 16% 30 to 39, 10% 40 to 49, 5% 50 to 59, 2% 60 plus, and 5% unknown.

Speech Pathologists

N = 106

	SENSING		INTUITION	
	THINKING	FEELING	FEELING	THINKING

ISTJ	ISFJ	INFJ	INTJ
N= 5	N= 7	N= 7	N= 4
%= 4.72	%= 6.60	%= 6.60	%= 3.77
■■■■■	■■■■■■■	■■■■■■■	■■■■

ISTP	ISFP	INFP	INTP
N= 2	N= 5	N= 11	N= 3
%= 1.89	%= 4.72	%= 10.38	%= 2.83
■■	■■■■■	■■■■■■■■■■■	■■■

ESTP	ESFP	ENFP	ENTP
N= 2	N= 3	N= 15	N= 7
%= 1.89	%= 2.83	%= 14.15	%= 6.60
■■	■■■	■■■■■■■■■■■ ■■■■	■■■■■■■

ESTJ	ESFJ	ENFJ	ENTJ
N= 8	N= 14	N= 8	N= 5
%= 7.55	%= 13.21	%= 7.55	%= 4.72
■■■■■■■■	■■■■■■■■■■■■■ ■■■	■■■■■■■■	■■■■■

JUDGMENT — INTROVERSION — PERCEPTION
PERCEPTION — EXTRAVERSION — JUDGMENT

	N	%
E	62	58.49
I	44	41.51
S	46	43.40
N	60	56.60
T	36	33.96
F	70	66.04
J	58	54.72
P	48	45.28
I J	23	21.70
I P	21	19.81
E P	27	25.47
E J	35	33.02
S T	17	16.04
S F	29	27.36
N F	41	38.68
N T	19	17.92
S J	34	32.08
S P	12	11.32
N P	36	33.96
N J	24	22.64
T J	22	20.75
T P	14	13.21
F P	34	32.08
F J	36	33.96
I N	25	23.58
E N	35	33.02
I S	19	17.92
E S	27	25.47
E T	22	20.75
E F	40	37.74
I F	30	28.30
I T	14	13.21
S dom	17	16.04
N dom	33	31.13
T dom	18	16.98
F dom	38	35.85

Note: ■ = 1% of sample   8629347

This table is one of a series of tables from the CAPT-MBTI Data Bank of MBTI records submitted to CAPT for computer scoring between 1971 and June, 1984. This sample was drawn from 59,784 records with usable occupational codes from the total data bank of 232,557. This data bank has 51% Form F cases from 1971 to March, 1978, 35% Form F cases from 1978 to June, 1984 and 14% Form G cases from 1978 to December, 1982. An analysis of Form F and G data banks showed the data banks were comprised of 56% females and 44% males; education level completed: 6% some grade school, 30% high school diploma, 25% some college, 18% bachelor degrees, 11% masters degrees, 3% doctoral or post doctoral work, and 6% unknown. Age group percentages were: 11% under 18, 29% 18 to 20, 12% 21 to 24, 10% 25 to 29, 16% 30 to 39, 10% 40 to 49, 5% 50 to 59, 2% 60 plus, and 5% unknown.

Therapists: Occupational

N = 245

	SENSING		INTUITION	
	THINKING	FEELING	FEELING	THINKING

ISTJ	ISFJ	INFJ	INTJ
N= 21	N= 22	N= 15	N= 15
%= 8.57	%= 8.98	%= 6.12	%= 6.12
■■■■■■■■	■■■■■■■■■	■■■■■■	■■■■■■

ISTP	ISFP	INFP	INTP
N= 1	N= 11	N= 17	N= 13
%= .41	%= 4.49	%= 6.94	%= 5.31
	■■■■	■■■■■■■	■■■■■

ESTP	ESFP	ENFP	ENTP
N= 8	N= 4	N= 30	N= 8
%= 3.27	%= 1.63	%= 12.24	%= 3.27
■■■	■■	■■■■■■■■■■ ■■	■■■

ESTJ	ESFJ	ENFJ	ENTJ
N= 19	N= 25	N= 17	N= 19
%= 7.76	%= 10.20	%= 6.94	%= 7.76
■■■■■■■■	■■■■■■■■■■	■■■■■■■	■■■■■■■■

JUDGMENT / INTROVERSION / PERCEPTION / PERCEPTION / EXTRAVERSION / JUDGMENT

	N	%
E	130	53.06
I	115	46.94
S	111	45.31
N	134	54.69
T	104	42.45
F	141	57.55
J	153	62.45
P	92	37.55
I J	73	29.80
I P	42	17.14
E P	50	20.41
E J	80	32.65
S T	49	20.00
S F	62	25.31
N F	79	32.24
N T	55	22.45
S J	87	35.51
S P	24	9.80
N P	68	27.76
N J	66	26.94
T J	74	30.20
T P	30	12.24
F P	62	25.31
F J	79	32.24
I N	60	24.49
E N	74	30.20
I S	55	22.45
E S	56	22.86
E T	54	22.04
E F	76	31.02
I F	65	26.53
I T	50	20.41
S dom	55	22.45
N dom	68	27.76
T dom	52	21.22
F dom	70	28.57

Note: ■ = 1% of sample   8629348

This table is one of a series of tables from the CAPT-MBTI Data Bank of MBTI records submitted to CAPT for computer scoring between 1971 and June, 1984. This sample was drawn from 59,784 records with usable occupational codes from the total data bank of 232,557. This data bank has 51% Form F cases from 1971 to March, 1978, 35% Form F cases from 1978 to June, 1984 and 14% Form G cases from 1978 to December, 1982. An analysis of Form F and G data banks showed the data banks were comprised of 56% females and 44% males; education level completed: 6% some grade school, 30% high school diploma, 25% some college, 18% bachelor degrees, 11% masters degrees, 3% doctoral or post doctoral work, and 6% unknown. Age group percentages were: 11% under 18, 29% 18 to 20, 12% 21 to 24, 10% 25 to 29, 16% 30 to 39, 10% 40 to 49, 5% 50 to 59, 2% 60 plus, and 5% unknown.

382

Therapists: Occupational

	SENSING		INTUITION	
	THINKING	FEELING	FEELING	THINKING

ISTJ	ISFJ	INFJ	INTJ
N= 10	N= 18	N= 9	N= 5
%= 8.47	%= 15.25	%= 7.63	%= 4.24
■■■■■■■■	■■■■■■■■■■ ■■■■■	■■■■■■■■	■■■■

JUDGMENT / INTROVERSION

ISTP	ISFP	INFP	INTP
N= 3	N= 4	N= 7	N= 5
%= 2.54	%= 3.39	%= 5.93	%= 4.24
■■■	■■■	■■■■■■	■■■■

PERCEPTION

ESTP	ESFP	ENFP	ENTP
N= 2	N= 2	N= 14	N= 5
%= 1.69	%= 1.69	%= 11.86	%= 4.24
■■	■■	■■■■■■■■■■■■ ■■	■■■■

PERCEPTION / EXTRAVERSION

ESTJ	ESFJ	ENFJ	ENTJ
N= 6	N= 13	N= 4	N= 11
%= 5.08	%= 11.02	%= 3.39	%= 9.32
■■■■■	■■■■■■■■■■■ ■	■■■	■■■■■■■■■

JUDGMENT

	N	%
E	57	48.31
I	61	51.69
S	58	49.15
N	60	50.85
T	47	39.83
F	71	60.17
J	76	64.41
P	42	35.59
I J	42	35.59
I P	19	16.10
E P	23	19.49
E J	34	28.81
S T	21	17.80
S F	37	31.36
N F	34	28.81
N T	26	22.03
S J	47	39.83
S P	11	9.32
N P	31	26.27
N J	29	24.58
T J	32	27.12
T P	15	12.71
F P	27	22.88
F J	44	37.29
I N	26	22.03
E N	34	28.81
I S	35	29.66
E S	23	19.49
E T	24	20.34
E F	33	27.97
I F	38	32.20
I T	23	19.49
S dom	32	27.12
N dom	33	27.97
T dom	25	21.19
F dom	28	23.73

Note: ■ = 1% of sample   8623134

Data collected by Polly U. Brown during January 1973 using Form F. The subjects were 54% of all occupational therapists who were registered and in good standing with the American Occupational Therapy Association and residing in Florida in December 1972. The occupational therapists were 98% female, ages ranged from 22 to 67 with a mean of 36.5; 83% had bachelors degrees, 10% had masters degrees, 7% other. These data are used with permission and were cited in:

Brown, P. U. (1974). Career development and satisfaction of occupational therapists in Florida (Doctoral dissertation, University of Florida, 1973). Dissertation Abstracts International, 34, 6930A. (University Microfilms No. 74-10, 025)

Therapists: Physical

N = 148

	SENSING		INTUITION	
	THINKING	FEELING	FEELING	THINKING

ISTJ	ISFJ	INFJ	INTJ
N= 15	N= 21	N= 5	N= 4
%= 10.14	%= 14.19	%= 3.38	%= 2.70
■■■■■■■■■■	■■■■■■■■■■ ■■■■	■■■	■■■

ISTP	ISFP	INFP	INTP
N= 5	N= 11	N= 13	N= 4
%= 3.38	%= 7.43	%= 8.78	%= 2.70
■■■	■■■■■■■	■■■■■■■■	■■■

ESTP	ESFP	ENFP	ENTP
N= 4	N= 6	N= 17	N= 4
%= 2.70	%= 4.05	%= 11.49	%= 2.70
■■■	■■■■	■■■■■■■■■■ ■	■■■

ESTJ	ESFJ	ENFJ	ENTJ
N= 5	N= 15	N= 15	N= 4
%= 3.38	%= 10.14	%= 10.14	%= 2.70
■■■	■■■■■■■■■■	■■■■■■■■■■	■■■

JUDGMENT — INTROVERSION — PERCEPTION — PERCEPTION — EXTRAVERSION — JUDGMENT

	N	%
E	70	47.30
I	78	52.70
S	82	55.41
N	66	44.59
T	45	30.41
F	103	69.59
J	84	56.76
P	64	43.24
I J	45	30.41
I P	33	22.30
E P	31	20.95
E J	39	26.35
S T	29	19.59
S F	53	35.81
N F	50	33.78
N T	16	10.81
S J	56	37.84
S P	26	17.57
N P	38	25.68
N J	28	18.92
T J	28	18.92
T P	17	11.49
F P	47	31.76
F J	56	37.84
I N	26	17.57
E N	40	27.03
I S	52	35.14
E S	30	20.27
E T	17	11.49
E F	53	35.81
I F	50	33.78
I T	28	18.92
S dom	46	31.08
N dom	30	20.27
T dom	18	12.16
F dom	54	36.49

Note: ■ = 1% of sample   8629349

This table is one of a series of tables from the CAPT-MBTI Data Bank of MBTI records submitted to CAPT for computer scoring between 1971 and June, 1984. This sample was drawn from 59,784 records with usable occupational codes from the total data bank of 232,557. This data bank has 51% Form F cases from 1971 to March, 1978, 35% Form F cases from 1978 to June, 1984 and 14% Form G cases from 1978 to December, 1982. An analysis of Form F and G data banks showed the data banks were comprised of 56% females and 44% males; education level completed: 6% some grade school, 30% high school diploma, 25% some college, 18% bachelor degrees, 11% masters degrees, 3% doctoral or post doctoral work, and 6% unknown. Age group percentages were: 11% under 18, 29% 18 to 20, 12% 21 to 24, 10% 25 to 29, 16% 30 to 39, 10% 40 to 49, 5% 50 to 59, 2% 60 plus, and 5% unknown.

N = 155

	SENSING		INTUITION	
	THINKING	FEELING	FEELING	THINKING

ISTJ	ISFJ	INFJ	INTJ
N= 20	N= 22	N= 6	N= 1
%= 12.90	%= 14.19	%= 3.87	%= .65
■■■■■■■■■■	■■■■■■■■■■	■■■■	■
■■■	■■■■		

ISTP	ISFP	INFP	INTP
N= 8	N= 12	N= 19	N= 3
%= 5.16	%= 7.74	%= 12.26	%= 1.94
■■■■■	■■■■■■■■	■■■■■■■■■■	■■
		■■	

ESTP	ESFP	ENFP	ENTP
N= 3	N= 8	N= 17	N= 5
%= 1.94	%= 5.16	%= 10.97	%= 3.23
■■	■■■■■	■■■■■■■■■■	■■■
		■	

ESTJ	ESFJ	ENFJ	ENTJ
N= 3	N= 14	N= 12	N= 2
%= 1.94	%= 9.03	%= 7.74	%= 1.29
■■	■■■■■■■■■	■■■■■■■■	■

JUDGMENT — INTROVERSION — PERCEPTION — PERCEPTION — EXTRAVERSION — JUDGMENT

	N	%
E	64	41.29
I	91	58.71
S	90	58.06
N	65	41.94
T	45	29.03
F	110	70.97
J	80	51.61
P	75	48.39
I J	49	31.61
I P	42	27.10
E P	33	21.29
E J	31	20.00
S T	34	21.94
S F	56	36.13
N F	54	34.84
N T	11	7.10
S J	59	38.06
S P	31	20.00
N P	44	28.39
N J	21	13.55
T J	26	16.77
T P	19	12.26
F P	56	36.13
F J	54	34.84
I N	29	18.71
E N	36	23.23
I S	62	40.00
E S	28	18.06
E T	13	8.39
E F	51	32.90
I F	59	38.06
I T	32	20.65
S dom	53	34.19
N dom	29	18.71
T dom	16	10.32
F dom	57	36.77

Note: ■ = 1% of sample   8623141

Subjects in this sample came from four main sources and were originally compiled especially for publication in:
McCaulley, M. H. (1978). Application of the Myers-Briggs Type Indicator to medicine and other health professions (Monograph I, Contract No. 231-76-0051, Health Resources Administration, DHEW). Gainesville, FL: Center for Applications of Psychological Type.
The four sources used were: 1) the CAPT health databank in 1977 based on Form F answer sheets scored by 1962 weights, 2) data solicited from medical and health professionals through advertising and personal communication, 3) the Myers Longitudinal Medical Sample initially collected in the 1950s and followed up in the 1970s and 4) data extracted from published research up to that time.

Therapists: Practitioners in Respiratory Therapy

	SENSING		INTUITION	
	THINKING	FEELING	FEELING	THINKING

ISTJ	ISFJ	INFJ	INTJ
N= 14	N= 10	N= 3	N= 5
%= 11.02	%= 7.87	%= 2.36	%= 3.94
■■■■■■■■■■■ ■	■■■■■■■■	■■	■■■■

ISTP	ISFP	INFP	INTP
N= 6	N= 6	N= 9	N= 11
%= 4.72	%= 4.72	%= 7.09	%= 8.66
■■■■■	■■■■■	■■■■■■■	■■■■■■■■■

ESTP	ESFP	ENFP	ENTP
N= 6	N= 13	N= 9	N= 10
%= 4.72	%= 10.24	%= 7.09	%= 7.87
■■■■■	■■■■■■■■■■	■■■■■■■	■■■■■■■■

ESTJ	ESFJ	ENFJ	ENTJ
N= 8	N= 9	N= 4	N= 4
%= 6.30	%= 7.09	%= 3.15	%= 3.15
■■■■■■	■■■■■■■	■■■	■■■

(Right margin labels: JUDGMENT / INTROVERSION / PERCEPTION / PERCEPTION / EXTRAVERSION / JUDGMENT)

	N	%
E	63	49.61
I	64	50.39
S	72	56.69
N	55	43.31
T	64	50.39
F	63	49.61
J	57	44.88
P	70	55.12
I J	32	25.20
I P	32	25.20
E P	38	29.92
E J	25	19.69
S T	34	26.77
S F	38	29.92
N F	25	19.69
N T	30	23.62
S J	41	32.28
S P	31	24.41
N P	39	30.71
N J	16	12.60
T J	31	24.41
T P	33	25.98
F P	37	29.13
F J	26	20.47
I N	28	22.05
E N	27	21.26
I S	36	28.35
E S	36	28.35
E T	28	22.05
E F	35	27.56
I F	28	22.05
I T	36	28.35
S dom	43	33.86
N dom	27	21.26
T dom	29	22.83
F dom	28	22.05

Note: ■ = 1% of sample   8623143

Subjects in this sample came from four main sources and were originally compiled especially for publication in:

McCaulley, M. H. (1978). Application of the Myers-Briggs Type Indicator to medicine and other health professions (Monograph I, Contract No. 231-76-0051, Health Resources Administration, DHEW). Gainesville, FL: Center for Applications of Psychological Type.

The four sources used were: 1) the CAPT health databank in 1977 based on Form F answer sheets scored by 1962 weights, 2) data solicited from medical and health professionals through advertising and personal communication, 3) the Myers Longitudinal Medical Sample initially collected in the 1950s and followed up in the 1970s and 4) data extracted from published research up to that time.

Therapists: Respiratory

N = 195

	SENSING		INTUITION			N	%
THINKING	FEELING	FEELING	THINKING				

<table>
<tr><td colspan="4"></td><td>E</td><td>95</td><td>48.72</td></tr>
</table>

ISTJ	ISFJ	INFJ	INTJ
N= 27	N= 16	N= 6	N= 9
%= 13.85	%= 8.21	%= 3.08	%= 4.62
■■■■■■■■■■■■■	■■■■■■■■	■■■	■■■■■
■■■■			

ISTP	ISFP	INFP	INTP
N= 9	N= 7	N= 12	N= 14
%= 4.62	%= 3.59	%= 6.15	%= 7.18
■■■■■	■■■■	■■■■■■	■■■■■■■

ESTP	ESFP	ENFP	ENTP
N= 8	N= 15	N= 12	N= 12
%= 4.10	%= 7.69	%= 6.15	%= 6.15
■■■■	■■■■■■■■	■■■■■■	■■■■■■

ESTJ	ESFJ	ENFJ	ENTJ
N= 14	N= 17	N= 6	N= 11
%= 7.18	%= 8.72	%= 3.08	%= 5.64
■■■■■■■	■■■■■■■■■	■■■	■■■■■■

Right-side vertical labels: JUDGMENT / PERCEPTION (INTROVERSION); PERCEPTION / JUDGMENT (EXTRAVERSION)

	N	%
E	95	48.72
I	100	51.28
S	113	57.95
N	82	42.05
T	104	53.33
F	91	46.67
J	106	54.36
P	89	45.64
I J	58	29.74
I P	42	21.54
E P	47	24.10
E J	48	24.62
S T	58	29.74
S F	55	28.21
N F	36	18.46
N T	46	23.59
S J	74	37.95
S P	39	20.00
N P	50	25.64
N J	32	16.41
T J	61	31.28
T P	43	22.05
F P	46	23.59
F J	45	23.08
I N	41	21.03
E N	41	21.03
I S	59	30.26
E S	54	27.69
E T	45	23.08
E F	50	25.64
I F	41	21.03
I T	59	30.26
S dom	66	33.85
N dom	39	20.00
T dom	48	24.62
F dom	42	21.54

Note: ■ = 1% of sample   8629350

This table is one of a series of tables from the CAPT-MBTI Data Bank of MBTI records submitted to CAPT for computer scoring between 1971 and June, 1984. This sample was drawn from 59,784 records with usable occupational codes from the total data bank of 232,557. This data bank has 51% Form F cases from 1971 to March, 1978, 35% Form F cases from 1978 to June, 1984 and 14% Form G cases from 1978 to December, 1982. An analysis of Form F and G data banks showed the data banks were comprised of 56% females and 44% males; education level completed: 6% some grade school, 30% high school diploma, 25% some college, 18% bachelor degrees, 11% masters degrees, 3% doctoral or post doctoral work, and 6% unknown. Age group percentages were: 11% under 18, 29% 18 to 20, 12% 21 to 24, 10% 25 to 29, 16% 30 to 39, 10% 40 to 49, 5% 50 to 59, 2% 60 plus, and 5% unknown.

ALLIED HEALTH AND HEALTH
PRACTIONERS, N.E.C.

N = 469

	SENSING		INTUITION	
	THINKING	FEELING	FEELING	THINKING

ISTJ	ISFJ	INFJ	INTJ
N= 60	N= 46	N= 24	N= 30
%= 12.79	%= 9.81	%= 5.12	%= 6.40
■■■■■■■■■■■■	■■■■■■■■■■	■■■■■	■■■■■■
■■■			

ISTP	ISFP	INFP	INTP
N= 13	N= 10	N= 26	N= 28
%= 2.77	%= 2.13	%= 5.54	%= 5.97
■■■	■■	■■■■■■	■■■■■■

ESTP	ESFP	ENFP	ENTP
N= 17	N= 15	N= 36	N= 12
%= 3.62	%= 3.20	%= 7.68	%= 2.56
■■■■	■■■	■■■■■■■■	■■■

ESTJ	ESFJ	ENFJ	ENTJ
N= 51	N= 39	N= 34	N= 28
%= 10.87	%= 8.32	%= 7.25	%= 5.97
■■■■■■■■■■	■■■■■■■■	■■■■■■■	■■■■■■
■			

JUDGMENT — PERCEPTION — PERCEPTION — JUDGMENT
INTROVERSION — EXTRAVERSION

	N	%
E	232	49.47
I	237	50.53
S	251	53.52
N	218	46.48
T	239	50.96
F	230	49.04
J	312	66.52
P	157	33.48
I J	160	34.12
I P	77	16.42
E P	80	17.06
E J	152	32.41
S T	141	30.06
S F	110	23.45
N F	120	25.59
N T	98	20.90
S J	196	41.79
S P	55	11.73
N P	102	21.75
N J	116	24.73
T J	169	36.03
T P	70	14.93
F P	87	18.55
F J	143	30.49
I N	108	23.03
E N	110	23.45
I S	129	27.51
E S	122	26.01
E T	108	23.03
E F	124	26.44
I F	106	22.60
I T	131	27.93
S dom	138	29.42
N dom	102	21.75
T dom	120	25.59
F dom	109	23.24

Note: ■ = 1% of sample   8629411

This table is one of a series of tables from the CAPT-MBTI Data Bank of MBTI records submitted to CAPT for computer scoring between 1971 and June, 1984. This sample was drawn from 59,784 records with usable occupational codes from the total data bank of 232,557. This data bank has 51% Form F cases from 1971 to March, 1978, 35% Form F cases from 1978 to June, 1984 and 14% Form G cases from 1978 to December, 1982. An analysis of Form F and G data banks showed the data banks were comprised of 56% females and 44% males; education level completed: 6% some grade school, 30% high school diploma, 25% some college, 18% bachelor degrees, 11% masters degrees, 3% doctoral or post doctoral work, and 6% unknown. Age group percentages were: 11% under 18, 29% 18 to 20, 12% 21 to 24, 10% 25 to 29, 16% 30 to 39, 10% 40 to 49, 5% 50 to 59, 2% 60 plus, and 5% unknown.

DOCTORS OF MEDICINE

N = 1603

		SENSING			INTUITION		
	THINKING		FEELING		FEELING		THINKING

ISTJ	ISFJ	INFJ	INTJ
N= 210	N= 164	N= 111	N= 120
%= 13.10	%= 10.23	%= 6.92	%= 7.49
■■■■■■■■■■■■■	■■■■■■■■■■	■■■■■■■	■■■■■■■
■■■			

ISTP	ISFP	INFP	INTP
N= 42	N= 51	N= 144	N= 94
%= 2.62	%= 3.18	%= 8.98	%= 5.86
■■■	■■■	■■■■■■■■■	■■■■■■

ESTP	ESFP	ENFP	ENTP
N= 28	N= 31	N= 127	N= 59
%= 1.75	%= 1.93	%= 7.92	%= 3.68
■■	■■	■■■■■■■■	■■■■

ESTJ	ESFJ	ENFJ	ENTJ
N= 133	N= 98	N= 92	N= 99
%= 8.30	%= 6.11	%= 5.74	%= 6.18
■■■■■■■■	■■■■■■	■■■■■■	■■■■■■

JUDGMENT — INTROVERSION — PERCEPTION — PERCEPTION — EXTRAVERSION — JUDGMENT

	N	%
E	667	41.61
I	936	58.39
S	757	47.22
N	846	52.78
T	785	48.97
F	818	51.03
J	1027	64.07
P	576	35.93
I J	605	37.74
I P	331	20.65
E P	245	15.28
E J	422	26.33
S T	413	25.76
S F	344	21.46
N F	474	29.57
N T	372	23.21
S J	605	37.74
S P	152	9.48
N P	424	26.45
N J	422	26.33
T J	562	35.06
T P	223	13.91
F P	353	22.02
F J	465	29.01
I N	469	29.26
E N	377	23.52
I S	467	29.13
E S	290	18.09
E T	319	19.90
E F	348	21.71
I F	470	29.32
I T	466	29.07
S dom	433	27.01
N dom	417	26.01
T dom	368	22.96
F dom	385	24.02

Note: ■ = 1% of sample   8629360

This table is one of a series of tables from the CAPT-MBTI Data Bank of MBTI records submitted to CAPT for computer scoring between 1971 and June, 1984. This sample was drawn from 59,784 records with usable occupational codes from the total data bank of 232,557. This data bank has 51% Form F cases from 1971 to March, 1978, 35% Form F cases from 1978 to June, 1984 and 14% Form G cases from 1978 to December, 1982. An analysis of Form F and G data banks showed the data banks were comprised of 56% females and 44% males; education level completed: 6% some grade school, 30% high school diploma, 25% some college, 18% bachelor degrees, 11% masters degrees, 3% doctoral or post doctoral work, and 6% unknown. Age group percentages were: 11% under 18, 29% 18 to 20, 12% 21 to 24, 10% 25 to 29, 16% 30 to 39, 10% 40 to 49, 5% 50 to 59, 2% 60 plus, and 5% unknown.

HEALTH CARE THERAPISTS

N = 765

	SENSING		INTUITION	
	THINKING	FEELING	FEELING	THINKING

ISTJ	ISFJ	INFJ	INTJ
N= 70	N= 72	N= 37	N= 34
%= 9.15	%= 9.41	%= 4.84	%= 4.44
■■■■■■■■■	■■■■■■■■■	■■■■■	■■■■

ISTP	ISFP	INFP	INTP
N= 20	N= 35	N= 59	N= 37
%= 2.61	%= 4.58	%= 7.71	%= 4.84
■■■	■■■■■	■■■■■■■■	■■■■■

ESTP	ESFP	ENFP	ENTP
N= 22	N= 30	N= 88	N= 40
%= 2.88	%= 3.92	%= 11.50	%= 5.23
■■■	■■■■	■■■■■■■■■■■ ■■	■■■■■

ESTJ	ESFJ	ENFJ	ENTJ
N= 50	N= 77	N= 50	N= 44
%= 6.54	%= 10.07	%= 6.54	%= 5.75
■■■■■■■	■■■■■■■■■■	■■■■■■■	■■■■■■

JUDGMENT — INTROVERSION — PERCEPTION — EXTRAVERSION — JUDGMENT

	N	%
E	401	52.42
I	364	47.58
S	376	49.15
N	389	50.85
T	317	41.44
F	448	58.56
J	434	56.73
P	331	43.27
I J	213	27.84
I P	151	19.74
E P	180	23.53
E J	221	28.89
S T	162	21.18
S F	214	27.97
N F	234	30.59
N T	155	20.26
S J	269	35.16
S P	107	13.99
N P	224	29.28
N J	165	21.57
T J	198	25.88
T P	119	15.56
F P	212	27.71
F J	236	30.85
I N	167	21.83
E N	222	29.02
I S	197	25.75
E S	179	23.40
E T	156	20.39
E F	245	32.03
I F	203	26.54
I T	161	21.05
S dom	194	25.36
N dom	199	26.01
T dom	151	19.74
F dom	221	28.89

Note: ■ = 1% of sample   8629364

This table is one of a series of tables from the CAPT-MBTI Data Bank of MBTI records submitted to CAPT for computer scoring between 1971 and June, 1984. This sample was drawn from 59,784 records with usable occupational codes from the total data bank of 232,557. This data bank has 51% Form F cases from 1971 to March, 1978, 35% Form F cases from 1978 to June, 1984 and 14% Form G cases from 1978 to December, 1982. An analysis of Form F and G data banks showed the data banks were comprised of 56% females and 44% males; education level completed: 6% some grade school, 30% high school diploma, 25% some college, 18% bachelor degrees, 11% masters degrees, 3% doctoral or post doctoral work, and 6% unknown. Age group percentages were: 11% under 18, 29% 18 to 20, 12% 21 to 24, 10% 25 to 29, 16% 30 to 39, 10% 40 to 49, 5% 50 to 59, 2% 60 plus, and 5% unknown.

	SENSING		INTUITION	
	THINKING	FEELING	FEELING	THINKING

ISTJ	ISFJ	INFJ	INTJ
N= 73	N= 154	N= 36	N= 13
%= 8.11	%= 17.11	%= 4.00	%= 1.44
■■■■■■■■	■■■■■■■■■■ ■■■■■■■	■■■■	■

ISTP	ISFP	INFP	INTP
N= 28	N= 62	N= 53	N= 21
%= 3.11	%= 6.89	%= 5.89	%= 2.33
■■■	■■■■■■■	■■■■■■	■■

ESTP	ESFP	ENFP	ENTP
N= 15	N= 47	N= 99	N= 25
%= 1.67	%= 5.22	%= 11.00	%= 2.78
■■	■■■■■	■■■■■■■■■■ ■	■■■

ESTJ	ESFJ	ENFJ	ENTJ
N= 83	N= 122	N= 33	N= 36
%= 9.22	%= 13.56	%= 3.67	%= 4.00
■■■■■■■■■	■■■■■■■■■■ ■■■■	■■■■	■■■■

JUDGMENT — INTROVERSION — PERCEPTION — PERCEPTION — EXTRAVERSION — JUDGMENT

	N	%
E	460	51.11
I	440	48.89
S	584	64.89
N	316	35.11
T	294	32.67
F	606	67.33
J	550	61.11
P	350	38.89
I J	276	30.67
I P	164	18.22
E P	186	20.67
E J	274	30.44
S T	199	22.11
S F	385	42.78
N F	221	24.56
N T	95	10.56
S J	432	48.00
S P	152	16.89
N P	198	22.00
N J	118	13.11
T J	205	22.78
T P	89	9.89
F P	261	29.00
F J	345	38.33
I N	123	13.67
E N	193	21.44
I S	317	35.22
E S	267	29.67
E T	159	17.67
E F	301	33.44
I F	305	33.89
I T	135	15.00
S dom	289	32.11
N dom	173	19.22
T dom	168	18.67
F dom	270	30.00

Note: ■ = 1% of sample   8629361

This table is one of a series of tables from the CAPT-MBTI Data Bank of MBTI records submitted to CAPT for computer scoring between 1971 and June, 1984. This sample was drawn from 59,784 records with usable occupational codes from the total data bank of 232,557. This data bank has 51% Form F cases from 1971 to March, 1978, 35% Form F cases from 1978 to June, 1984 and 14% Form G cases from 1978 to December, 1982. An analysis of Form F and G data banks showed the data banks were comprised of 56% females and 44% males; education level completed: 6% some grade school, 30% high school diploma, 25% some college, 18% bachelor degrees, 11% masters degrees, 3% doctoral or post doctoral work, and 6% unknown. Age group percentages were: 11% under 18, 29% 18 to 20, 12% 21 to 24, 10% 25 to 29, 16% 30 to 39, 10% 40 to 49, 5% 50 to 59, 2% 60 plus, and 5% unknown.

HEALTH TECHNOLOGISTS AND TECHNICIANS

N = 1291

	SENSING		INTUITION	
	THINKING	FEELING	FEELING	THINKING

ISTJ	ISFJ	INFJ	INTJ
N= 150	N= 181	N= 59	N= 58
%= 11.62	%= 14.02	%= 4.57	%= 4.49
■■■■■■■■■■■ ■■	■■■■■■■■■■ ■■■■	■■■■■	■■■■

JUDGMENT — INTROVERSION

ISTP	ISFP	INFP	INTP
N= 27	N= 69	N= 106	N= 47
%= 2.09	%= 5.34	%= 8.21	%= 3.64
■■	■■■■■	■■■■■■■■	■■■■

PERCEPTION

ESTP	ESFP	ENFP	ENTP
N= 32	N= 52	N= 90	N= 47
%= 2.48	%= 4.03	%= 6.97	%= 3.64
■■	■■■■	■■■■■■■	■■■■

PERCEPTION — EXTRAVERSION

ESTJ	ESFJ	ENFJ	ENTJ
N= 136	N= 122	N= 64	N= 51
%= 10.53	%= 9.45	%= 4.96	%= 3.95
■■■■■■■■■■ ■	■■■■■■■■■	■■■■■	■■■■

JUDGMENT

	N	%
E	594	46.01
I	697	53.99
S	769	59.57
N	522	40.43
T	548	42.45
F	743	57.55
J	821	63.59
P	470	36.41
I J	448	34.70
I P	249	19.29
E P	221	17.12
E J	373	28.89
S T	345	26.72
S F	424	32.84
N F	319	24.71
N T	203	15.72
S J	589	45.62
S P	180	13.94
N P	290	22.46
N J	232	17.97
T J	395	30.60
T P	153	11.85
F P	317	24.55
F J	426	33.00
I N	270	20.91
E N	252	19.52
I S	427	33.08
E S	342	26.49
E T	266	20.60
E F	328	25.41
I F	415	32.15
I T	282	21.84
S dom	415	32.15
N dom	254	19.67
T dom	261	20.22
F dom	361	27.96

Note: ■ = 1% of sample

8629362

This table is one of a series of tables from the CAPT-MBTI Data Bank of MBTI records submitted to CAPT for computer scoring between 1971 and June, 1984. This sample was drawn from 59,784 records with usable occupational codes from the total data bank of 232,557. This data bank has 51% Form F cases from 1971 to March, 1978, 35% Form F cases from 1978 to June, 1984 and 14% Form G cases from 1978 to December, 1982. An analysis of Form F and G data banks showed the data banks were comprised of 56% females and 44% males; education level completed: 6% some grade school, 30% high school diploma, 25% some college, 18% bachelor degrees, 11% masters degrees, 3% doctoral or post doctoral work, and 6% unknown. Age group percentages were: 11% under 18, 29% 18 to 20, 12% 21 to 24, 10% 25 to 29, 16% 30 to 39, 10% 40 to 49, 5% 50 to 59, 2% 60 plus, and 5% unknown.

NURSES

N = 3103

	SENSING		INTUITION	
	THINKING	FEELING	FEELING	THINKING

ISTJ	ISFJ	INFJ	INTJ
N= 299	N= 457	N= 162	N= 130
%= 9.64	%= 14.73	%= 5.22	%= 4.19
■■■■■■■■■	■■■■■■■■■■■■■■ ■■■■■	■■■■■	■■■■

ISTP	ISFP	INFP	INTP
N= 75	N= 173	N= 234	N= 97
%= 2.42	%= 5.58	%= 7.54	%= 3.13
■■	■■■■■■	■■■■■■■■	■■■

ESTP	ESFP	ENFP	ENTP
N= 56	N= 117	N= 288	N= 90
%= 1.80	%= 3.77	%= 9.28	%= 2.90
■■	■■■■	■■■■■■■■■	■■■

ESTJ	ESFJ	ENFJ	ENTJ
N= 230	N= 332	N= 216	N= 147
%= 7.41	%= 10.70	%= 6.96	%= 4.74
■■■■■■■	■■■■■■■■■■■ ■	■■■■■■■	■■■■■

JUDGMENT — INTROVERSION — PERCEPTION — PERCEPTION — EXTRAVERSION — JUDGMENT

	N	%
E	1476	47.57
I	1627	52.43
S	1739	56.04
N	1364	43.96
T	1124	36.22
F	1979	63.78
J	1973	63.58
P	1130	36.42
I J	1048	33.77
I P	579	18.66
E P	551	17.76
E J	925	29.81
S T	660	21.27
S F	1079	34.77
N F	900	29.00
N T	464	14.95
S J	1318	42.48
S P	421	13.57
N P	709	22.85
N J	655	21.11
T J	806	25.97
T P	318	10.25
F P	812	26.17
F J	1167	37.61
I N	623	20.08
E N	741	23.88
I S	1004	32.36
E S	735	23.69
E T	523	16.85
E F	953	30.71
I F	1026	33.06
I T	601	19.37
S dom	929	29.94
N dom	670	21.59
T dom	549	17.69
F dom	955	30.78

Note: ■ = 1% of sample   8629363

This table is one of a series of tables from the CAPT-MBTI Data Bank of MBTI records submitted to CAPT for computer scoring between 1971 and June, 1984. This sample was drawn from 59,784 records with usable occupational codes from the total data bank of 232,557. This data bank has 51% Form F cases from 1971 to March, 1978, 35% Form F cases from 1978 to June, 1984 and 14% Form G cases from 1978 to December, 1982. An analysis of Form F and G data banks showed the data banks were comprised of 56% females and 44% males; education level completed: 6% some grade school, 30% high school diploma, 25% some college, 18% bachelor degrees, 11% masters degrees, 3% doctoral or post doctoral work, and 6% unknown. Age group percentages were: 11% under 18, 29% 18 to 20, 12% 21 to 24, 10% 25 to 29, 16% 30 to 39, 10% 40 to 49, 5% 50 to 59, 2% 60 plus, and 5% unknown.

E Percent	I	Total Sample Size	Sample Description
61.67	38.33	60	Dental Hygienists
58.49	41.51	106	Speech Pathologists
58.49	41.51	53	Composite of Practitioners in Radiologic Technology
58.20	41.80	122	Composite of Practitioners in Speech Pathology
57.14	42.86	70	Optometrists
56.30	43.70	238	Public Service Aides and Community Health Workers
54.43	45.57	79	Medical Assistants
54.40	45.60	182	Health Education Practitioners
53.55	46.45	155	Nursing: Composite of Critical Care Nurses
53.42	46.58	146	Nursing: Consultants
53.06	46.94	245	Therapists: Occupational
52.52	47.48	139	Physicians: Family Practice, General Practice
52.42	47.58	765	HEALTH CARE THERAPISTS
51.98	48.02	202	Administrators: Health
51.85	48.15	243	Dietitians
51.59	48.41	126	Radiologic Technologists and Technicians
51.39	48.61	72	Dental Assistants
51.11	48.89	900	HEALTH SERVICE WORKERS
50.64	49.36	314	Nursing: Aides, Orderlies, and Attendants
49.61	50.39	127	Therapists: Practitioners in Respiratory Therapy
49.47	50.53	469	ALLIED HEALTH AND HEALTH PRACTIONERS, N.E.C.
49.23	50.77	323	Dietitians and Nutritionists
48.85	51.15	305	Nursing: Educators
48.72	51.28	195	Therapists: Respiratory
48.31	51.69	118	Therapists: Occupational
47.87	52.13	94	Nursing: Administrators
47.64	52.36	2351	Nursing: Registered Nurses
47.57	52.43	3103	NURSES
47.30	52.70	148	Therapists: Physical
47.06	52.94	85	Dentists
46.92	53.08	260	Nursing: Licensed Practical Nurses
46.71	53.29	167	Laboratory Technologists
46.60	53.40	191	Pharmacists
46.38	53.62	1880	Nursing: Registered Nurses, no specialty stated
46.34	53.66	123	Pharmacists
46.15	53.85	52	Dentists
46.01	53.99	1291	HEALTH TECHNOLOGISTS AND TECHNICIANS
45.78	54.22	83	Nursing: Public Health
44.44	55.56	135	Doctors of Osteopathy
44.30	55.70	973	Medical Technologists
44.26	55.74	61	Physicians: Pathology
44.12	55.88	68	Physicians: Psychiatry
43.26	56.74	638	Medical Technologists (4 year)
41.70	58.30	223	Clinical Laboratory Technologists and Technicians
41.61	58.39	1603	DOCTORS OF MEDICINE
41.52	58.48	1881	Composite of Practitioners in Medicine (M.D.s)
41.29	58.71	155	Therapists: Physical

S Percent	N	Total Sample Size	Sample Description
81.51 18.49	238		Public Service Aides and Community Health Workers
73.85 26.15	260		Nursing: Licensed Practical Nurses
66.67 33.33	72		Dental Assistants
66.04 33.96	53		Composite of Practitioners in Radiologic Technology
65.87 34.13	126		Radiologic Technologists and Technicians
64.97 35.03	314		Nursing: Aides, Orderlies, and Attendants
64.89 35.11	900		HEALTH SERVICE WORKERS
64.89 35.11	94		Nursing: Administrators
61.73 38.27	243		Dietitians
61.60 38.40	638		Medical Technologists (4 year)
61.15 38.85	973		Medical Technologists
60.65 39.35	155		Nursing: Composite of Critical Care Nurses
60.00 40.00	85		Dentists
59.57 40.43	1291		HEALTH TECHNOLOGISTS AND TECHNICIANS
58.57 41.43	70		Optometrists
58.08 41.92	167		Laboratory Technologists
58.06 41.94	155		Therapists: Physical
57.95 42.05	195		Therapists: Respiratory
57.89 42.11	323		Dietitians and Nutritionists
57.83 42.17	83		Nursing: Public Health
57.14 42.86	182		Health Education Practitioners
56.91 43.09	1880		Nursing: Registered Nurses, no specialty stated
56.87 43.13	2351		Nursing: Registered Nurses
56.69 43.31	127		Therapists: Practitioners in Respiratory Therapy
56.30 43.70	135		Doctors of Osteopathy
56.04 43.96	3103		NURSES
55.70 44.30	79		Medical Assistants
55.61 44.39	223		Clinical Laboratory Technologists and Technicians
55.41 44.59	148		Therapists: Physical
54.10 45.90	61		Physicians: Pathology
53.52 46.48	469		ALLIED HEALTH AND HEALTH PRACTIONERS, N.E.C.
53.42 46.58	146		Nursing: Consultants
53.40 46.60	191		Pharmacists
53.24 46.76	139		Physicians: Family Practice, General Practice
50.50 49.50	202		Administrators: Health
50.00 50.00	60		Dental Hygienists
50.00 50.00	52		Dentists
49.15 50.85	765		HEALTH CARE THERAPISTS
49.15 50.85	118		Therapists: Occupational
47.97 52.03	123		Pharmacists
47.22 52.78	1603		DOCTORS OF MEDICINE
46.89 53.11	1881		Composite of Practitioners in Medicine (M.D.s)
46.56 53.44	305		Nursing: Educators
45.31 54.69	245		Therapists: Occupational
43.40 56.60	106		Speech Pathologists
38.52 61.48	122		Composite of Practitioners in Speech Pathology
25.00 75.00	68		Physicians: Psychiatry

THINKING-FEELING

T Percent	F	Total Sample Size	Sample Description
68.85	31.15	61	Physicians: Pathology
61.18	38.82	85	Dentists
57.69	42.31	52	Dentists
55.04	44.96	238	Public Service Aides and Community Health Workers
54.26	45.74	94	Nursing: Administrators
53.33	46.67	195	Therapists: Respiratory
52.03	47.97	123	Pharmacists
51.49	48.51	202	Administrators: Health
51.31	48.69	191	Pharmacists
50.96	49.04	469	ALLIED HEALTH AND HEALTH PRACTIONERS, N.E.C.
50.39	49.61	127	Therapists: Practitioners in Respiratory Therapy
48.97	51.03	1603	DOCTORS OF MEDICINE
48.27	51.73	1881	Composite of Practitioners in Medicine (M.D.s)
46.09	53.91	243	Dietitians
45.81	54.19	155	Nursing: Composite of Critical Care Nurses
45.71	54.29	70	Optometrists
45.59	54.41	68	Physicians: Psychiatry
45.29	54.71	223	Clinical Laboratory Technologists and Technicians
44.58	55.42	323	Dietitians and Nutritionists
43.84	56.16	146	Nursing: Consultants
43.11	56.89	167	Laboratory Technologists
42.55	57.45	973	Medical Technologists
42.45	57.55	1291	HEALTH TECHNOLOGISTS AND TECHNICIANS
42.45	57.55	245	Therapists: Occupational
42.16	57.84	638	Medical Technologists (4 year)
41.64	58.36	305	Nursing: Educators
41.44	58.56	765	HEALTH CARE THERAPISTS
39.83	60.17	118	Therapists: Occupational
39.68	60.32	126	Radiologic Technologists and Technicians
39.62	60.38	53	Composite of Practitioners in Radiologic Technology
37.36	62.64	182	Health Education Practitioners
36.69	63.31	139	Physicians: Family Practice, General Practice
36.30	63.70	135	Doctors of Osteopathy
36.22	63.78	3103	NURSES
35.44	64.56	79	Medical Assistants
35.25	64.75	122	Composite of Practitioners in Speech Pathology
34.89	65.11	1880	Nursing: Registered Nurses, no specialty stated
34.72	65.28	72	Dental Assistants
33.96	66.04	106	Speech Pathologists
32.96	67.04	2351	Nursing: Registered Nurses
32.67	67.33	900	HEALTH SERVICE WORKERS
31.92	68.08	260	Nursing: Licensed Practical Nurses
30.41	69.59	148	Therapists: Physical
30.12	69.88	83	Nursing: Public Health
29.03	70.97	155	Therapists: Physical
28.33	71.67	60	Dental Hygienists
27.71	72.29	314	Nursing: Aides, Orderlies, and Attendants

J Percent	P	Total Sample Size	Sample Description
78.72	21.28	94	Nursing: Administrators
76.92	23.08	52	Dentists
74.75	25.25	202	Administrators: Health
74.37	25.63	238	Public Service Aides and Community Health Workers
74.12	25.88	85	Dentists
72.59	27.41	135	Doctors of Osteopathy
70.55	29.45	146	Nursing: Consultants
70.50	29.50	139	Physicians: Family Practice, General Practice
70.49	29.51	61	Physicians: Pathology
69.35	30.65	323	Dietitians and Nutritionists
69.14	30.86	243	Dietitians
68.57	31.43	70	Optometrists
68.03	31.97	638	Medical Technologists (4 year)
67.31	32.69	260	Nursing: Licensed Practical Nurses
67.03	32.97	182	Health Education Practitioners
66.70	33.30	973	Medical Technologists
66.52	33.48	469	ALLIED HEALTH AND HEALTH PRACTIONERS, N.E.C.
66.27	33.73	83	Nursing: Public Health
65.98	34.02	1881	Composite of Practitioners in Medicine (M.D.s)
65.90	34.10	305	Nursing: Educators
64.41	35.59	118	Therapists: Occupational
64.07	35.93	1603	DOCTORS OF MEDICINE
63.87	36.13	191	Pharmacists
63.59	36.41	1291	HEALTH TECHNOLOGISTS AND TECHNICIANS
63.58	36.42	3103	NURSES
62.82	37.18	1880	Nursing: Registered Nurses, no specialty stated
62.58	37.42	155	Nursing: Composite of Critical Care Nurses
62.45	37.55	245	Therapists: Occupational
61.11	38.89	900	HEALTH SERVICE WORKERS
60.98	39.02	123	Pharmacists
60.53	39.47	2351	Nursing: Registered Nurses
58.92	41.08	314	Nursing: Aides, Orderlies, and Attendants
58.33	41.67	60	Dental Hygienists
57.85	42.15	223	Clinical Laboratory Technologists and Technicians
56.76	43.24	148	Therapists: Physical
56.73	43.27	765	HEALTH CARE THERAPISTS
56.35	43.65	126	Radiologic Technologists and Technicians
56.29	43.71	167	Laboratory Technologists
55.56	44.44	72	Dental Assistants
54.72	45.28	106	Speech Pathologists
54.43	45.57	79	Medical Assistants
54.36	45.64	195	Therapists: Respiratory
51.64	48.36	122	Composite of Practitioners in Speech Pathology
51.61	48.39	155	Therapists: Physical
50.94	49.06	53	Composite of Practitioners in Radiologic Technology
50.00	50.00	68	Physicians: Psychiatry
44.88	55.12	127	Therapists: Practitioners in Respiratory Therapy

Percent ST	Total Sample Size	Sample Description
47.06	238	Public Service Aides and Community Health Workers
42.62	61	Physicians: Pathology
39.36	94	Nursing: Administrators
37.65	85	Dentists
32.86	70	Optometrists
30.45	243	Dietitians
30.06	469	ALLIED HEALTH AND HEALTH PRACTIONERS, N.E.C.
29.84	191	Pharmacists
29.74	195	Therapists: Respiratory
29.27	123	Pharmacists
29.03	155	Nursing: Composite of Critical Care Nurses
28.79	323	Dietitians and Nutritionists
28.25	223	Clinical Laboratory Technologists and Technicians
28.14	167	Laboratory Technologists
27.95	973	Medical Technologists
27.23	202	Administrators: Health
26.92	52	Dentists
26.77	127	Therapists: Practitioners in Respiratory Therapy
26.72	1291	HEALTH TECHNOLOGISTS AND TECHNICIANS
26.65	638	Medical Technologists (4 year)
26.58	1881	Composite of Practitioners in Medicine (M.D.s)
26.42	53	Composite of Practitioners in Radiologic Technology
26.19	126	Radiologic Technologists and Technicians
26.03	146	Nursing: Consultants
25.76	1603	DOCTORS OF MEDICINE
24.62	260	Nursing: Licensed Practical Nurses
22.22	72	Dental Assistants
22.11	900	HEALTH SERVICE WORKERS
21.94	155	Therapists: Physical
21.52	79	Medical Assistants
21.27	3103	NURSES
21.18	765	HEALTH CARE THERAPISTS
20.85	1880	Nursing: Registered Nurses, no specialty stated
20.46	2351	Nursing: Registered Nurses
20.33	305	Nursing: Educators
20.14	139	Physicians: Family Practice, General Practice
20.00	245	Therapists: Occupational
20.00	135	Doctors of Osteopathy
19.59	148	Therapists: Physical
19.43	314	Nursing: Aides, Orderlies, and Attendants
19.23	182	Health Education Practitioners
19.12	68	Physicians: Psychiatry
17.80	118	Therapists: Occupational
16.87	83	Nursing: Public Health
16.67	60	Dental Hygienists
16.04	106	Speech Pathologists
13.93	122	Composite of Practitioners in Speech Pathology

Percent SF	Total Sample Size	Sample Description
49.23	260	Nursing: Licensed Practical Nurses
45.54	314	Nursing: Aides, Orderlies, and Attendants
44.44	72	Dental Assistants
42.78	900	HEALTH SERVICE WORKERS
40.96	83	Nursing: Public Health
39.68	126	Radiologic Technologists and Technicians
39.62	53	Composite of Practitioners in Radiologic Technology
37.91	182	Health Education Practitioners
36.41	2351	Nursing: Registered Nurses
36.30	135	Doctors of Osteopathy
36.13	155	Therapists: Physical
36.06	1880	Nursing: Registered Nurses, no specialty stated
35.81	148	Therapists: Physical
34.95	638	Medical Technologists (4 year)
34.77	3103	NURSES
34.45	238	Public Service Aides and Community Health Workers
34.18	79	Medical Assistants
33.33	60	Dental Hygienists
33.20	973	Medical Technologists
33.09	139	Physicians: Family Practice, General Practice
32.84	1291	HEALTH TECHNOLOGISTS AND TECHNICIANS
31.61	155	Nursing: Composite of Critical Care Nurses
31.36	118	Therapists: Occupational
31.28	243	Dietitians
29.94	167	Laboratory Technologists
29.92	127	Therapists: Practitioners in Respiratory Therapy
29.10	323	Dietitians and Nutritionists
28.21	195	Therapists: Respiratory
27.97	765	HEALTH CARE THERAPISTS
27.40	146	Nursing: Consultants
27.36	106	Speech Pathologists
27.35	223	Clinical Laboratory Technologists and Technicians
26.23	305	Nursing: Educators
25.71	70	Optometrists
25.53	94	Nursing: Administrators
25.31	245	Therapists: Occupational
24.59	122	Composite of Practitioners in Speech Pathology
23.56	191	Pharmacists
23.45	469	ALLIED HEALTH AND HEALTH PRACTIONERS, N.E.C.
23.27	202	Administrators: Health
23.08	52	Dentists
22.35	85	Dentists
21.46	1603	DOCTORS OF MEDICINE
20.31	1881	Composite of Practitioners in Medicine (M.D.s)
18.70	123	Pharmacists
11.48	61	Physicians: Pathology
5.88	68	Physicians: Psychiatry

INTUITION-FEELING

Percent NF	Total Sample Size	Sample Description
48.53	68	Physicians: Psychiatry
40.16	122	Composite of Practitioners in Speech Pathology
38.68	106	Speech Pathologists
38.33	60	Dental Hygienists
34.84	155	Therapists: Physical
33.78	148	Therapists: Physical
32.24	245	Therapists: Occupational
32.13	305	Nursing: Educators
31.42	1881	Composite of Practitioners in Medicine (M.D.s)
30.63	2351	Nursing: Registered Nurses
30.59	765	HEALTH CARE THERAPISTS
30.38	79	Medical Assistants
30.22	139	Physicians: Family Practice, General Practice
29.57	1603	DOCTORS OF MEDICINE
29.27	123	Pharmacists
29.04	1880	Nursing: Registered Nurses, no specialty stated
29.00	3103	NURSES
28.92	83	Nursing: Public Health
28.81	118	Therapists: Occupational
28.77	146	Nursing: Consultants
28.57	70	Optometrists
27.41	135	Doctors of Osteopathy
27.35	223	Clinical Laboratory Technologists and Technicians
26.95	167	Laboratory Technologists
26.75	314	Nursing: Aides, Orderlies, and Attendants
26.32	323	Dietitians and Nutritionists
25.59	469	ALLIED HEALTH AND HEALTH PRACTIONERS, N.E.C.
25.25	202	Administrators: Health
25.13	191	Pharmacists
24.73	182	Health Education Practitioners
24.71	1291	HEALTH TECHNOLOGISTS AND TECHNICIANS
24.56	900	HEALTH SERVICE WORKERS
24.25	973	Medical Technologists
22.88	638	Medical Technologists (4 year)
22.63	243	Dietitians
22.58	155	Nursing: Composite of Critical Care Nurses
20.83	72	Dental Assistants
20.75	53	Composite of Practitioners in Radiologic Technology
20.63	126	Radiologic Technologists and Technicians
20.21	94	Nursing: Administrators
19.69	127	Therapists: Practitioners in Respiratory Therapy
19.67	61	Physicians: Pathology
19.23	52	Dentists
18.85	260	Nursing: Licensed Practical Nurses
18.46	195	Therapists: Respiratory
16.47	85	Dentists
10.50	238	Public Service Aides and Community Health Workers

Percent NT	Total Sample Size	Sample Description
30.77	52	Dentists
26.47	68	Physicians: Psychiatry
26.23	61	Physicians: Pathology
24.26	202	Administrators: Health
23.62	127	Therapists: Practitioners in Respiratory Therapy
23.59	195	Therapists: Respiratory
23.53	85	Dentists
23.21	1603	DOCTORS OF MEDICINE
22.76	123	Pharmacists
22.45	245	Therapists: Occupational
22.03	118	Therapists: Occupational
21.69	1881	Composite of Practitioners in Medicine (M.D.s)
21.47	191	Pharmacists
21.31	305	Nursing: Educators
21.31	122	Composite of Practitioners in Speech Pathology
20.90	469	ALLIED HEALTH AND HEALTH PRACTIONERS, N.E.C.
20.26	765	HEALTH CARE THERAPISTS
18.13	182	Health Education Practitioners
17.92	106	Speech Pathologists
17.81	146	Nursing: Consultants
17.04	223	Clinical Laboratory Technologists and Technicians
16.77	155	Nursing: Composite of Critical Care Nurses
16.55	139	Physicians: Family Practice, General Practice
16.30	135	Doctors of Osteopathy
15.79	323	Dietitians and Nutritionists
15.72	1291	HEALTH TECHNOLOGISTS AND TECHNICIANS
15.64	243	Dietitians
15.52	638	Medical Technologists (4 year)
14.97	167	Laboratory Technologists
14.95	3103	NURSES
14.89	94	Nursing: Administrators
14.59	973	Medical Technologists
14.04	1880	Nursing: Registered Nurses, no specialty stated
13.92	79	Medical Assistants
13.49	126	Radiologic Technologists and Technicians
13.25	83	Nursing: Public Health
13.21	53	Composite of Practitioners in Radiologic Technology
12.86	70	Optometrists
12.51	2351	Nursing: Registered Nurses
12.50	72	Dental Assistants
11.67	60	Dental Hygienists
10.81	148	Therapists: Physical
10.56	900	HEALTH SERVICE WORKERS
8.28	314	Nursing: Aides, Orderlies, and Attendants
7.98	238	Public Service Aides and Community Health Workers
7.31	260	Nursing: Licensed Practical Nurses
7.10	155	Therapists: Physical

INDUSTRY,
SERVICE,
&
TRADE

Section IX

INDUSTRY, SERVICE AND TRADE

Samples in Section IX

Name of Sample	Number in Sample
Carpenters	109
Chain, Rod and Ax Workers; Surveying	54
Child Care Workers (except private household)	55
Construction Laborers (except carpenters helpers)	139
Cooks (except private household)	180
Displaced Coal Miners	196
Displaced Steelworkers	658
Electricians	70
Factory and Site Supervisors	52
Food Counter and Fountain Workers	61
Foremen in Japanese Food Production Company	240
Hairdressers, Cosmetologists and Manicurists	96
Home Management Advisors and Home Economists	58
Lifeguards, Attendants, Recreation and Amusement	211
Operators and Field Technicians Pollution Control	334
Restaurant Workers: Table Setting and Cleaning	51
School Bus Drivers	132
Service Workers (except private household)	169
Steelworkers	105
Waiters and Waitresses	540

Composite Samples

CLEANING SERVICES	67
CRAFT WORKERS	559
FARMERS	72
FOOD SERVICE WORKERS	1082
LABORERS	782
MECHANICS	669
OPERATIVES: NON-SPECIALIZED AND FACTORY WORKERS	97
OPERATIVES: SPECIALIZED	206
OPERATIVES: TRANSPORTATION	144
PERSONAL SERVICE WORKERS	783
PRIVATE HOUSEHOLD WORKERS	3064

Comments

The samples of this section tend mainly to be persons in skilled and unskilled trades, in food services, and in personal services. These are not populations frequently submitted to CAPT for scoring; consequently in many cases the numbers are low. Be very cautious in interpretations from the tables of this section because the persons reported may not be typical of others in these occupations. They may have come into contact with the MBTI because they were more interested in psychology than were others in their field.

In type theory, occupations with more practical hands-on work are expected to attract more sensing types. If the work is with objects and materials, theory predicts it will be more attractive to thinking types; if the work is concerned mainly with people, it should be more attractive to feeling types. Look, therefore, for more ST's among samples in trades and technical fields, and for more SF's in samples concerned with direct services to people.

Look also to see if fields requiring sustained concentration have attracted more introverts and if fields with more outdoor action or more contact with people have attracted more extraverts.

Sensing types more often prefer J than P so the statistical prediction would be that for all samples with S's in the majority you will find more J's. However, look for relatively more J's in fields where system and order are important, and more P's in fields where more flexibility is helpful.

As in all sections in this Atlas, remember the expectations from the general population that the majority are E's, S's and J's, that more males are T's and that more females are F's.

Summary listings of tables for EI, SN, TF, JP, ST, SF, NF and NT will be found after the last type table.

Carpenters

	SENSING		INTUITION	
	THINKING	FEELING	FEELING	THINKING

ISTJ	ISFJ	INFJ	INTJ
N= 10	N= 8	N= 3	N= 2
%= 9.17	%= 7.34	%= 2.75	%= 1.83
■■■■■■■■■	■■■■■■■	■■■	■■

ISTP	ISFP	INFP	INTP
N= 8	N= 9	N= 13	N= 3
%= 7.34	%= 8.26	%= 11.93	%= 2.75
■■■■■■■	■■■■■■■■	■■■■■■■■■■■ ■■	■■■

ESTP	ESFP	ENFP	ENTP
N= 9	N= 7	N= 10	N= 3
%= 8.26	%= 6.42	%= 9.17	%= 2.75
■■■■■■■■	■■■■■■	■■■■■■■■■	■■■

ESTJ	ESFJ	ENFJ	ENTJ
N= 9	N= 7	N= 3	N= 5
%= 8.26	%= 6.42	%= 2.75	%= 4.59
■■■■■■■■	■■■■■■	■■■	■■■■■

	N	%
E	53	48.62
I	56	51.38
S	67	61.47
N	42	38.53
T	49	44.95
F	60	55.05
J	47	43.12
P	62	56.88
I J	23	21.10
I P	33	30.28
E P	29	26.61
E J	24	22.02
S T	36	33.03
S F	31	28.44
N F	29	26.61
N T	13	11.93
S J	34	31.19
S P	33	30.28
N P	29	26.61
N J	13	11.93
T J	26	23.85
T P	23	21.10
F P	39	35.78
F J	21	19.27
I N	21	19.27
E N	21	19.27
I S	35	32.11
E S	32	29.36
E T	26	23.85
E F	27	24.77
I F	33	30.28
I T	23	21.10
S dom	34	31.19
N dom	18	16.51
T dom	25	22.94
F dom	32	29.36

Note: ■ = 1% of sample   8629366

This table is one of a series of tables from the .CAPT-MBTI Data Bank of MBTI records submitted to CAPT for computer scoring between 1971 and June, 1984. This sample was drawn from 59,784 records with usable occupational codes from the total data bank of 232,557. This data bank has 51% Form F cases from 1971 to March, 1978, 35% Form F cases from 1978 to June, 1984 and 14% Form G cases from 1978 to December, 1982. An analysis of Form F and G data banks showed the data banks were comprised of 56% females and 44% males; education level completed: 6% some grade school, 30% high school diploma, 25% some college, 18% bachelor degrees, 11% masters degrees, 3% doctoral or post doctoral work, and 6% unknown. Age group percentages were: 11% under 18, 29% 18 to 20, 12% 21 to 24, 10% 25 to 29, 16% 30 to 39, 10% 40 to 49, 5% 50 to 59, 2% 60 plus, and 5% unknown.

Chain, Rod and Ax Workers; Surveying

	SENSING		INTUITION	
	THINKING	FEELING	FEELING	THINKING

ISTJ	ISFJ	INFJ	INTJ
N= 4	N= 3	N= 0	N= 3
%= 7.41	%= 5.56	%= 0.00	%= 5.56
■■■■■■■	■■■■■■		■■■■■■

ISTP	ISFP	INFP	INTP
N= 4	N= 7	N= 5	N= 5
%= 7.41	%= 12.96	%= 9.26	%= 9.26
■■■■■■■	■■■■■■■■■■■■■ ■■■	■■■■■■■■■	■■■■■■■■■

ESTP	ESFP	ENFP	ENTP
N= 0	N= 2	N= 8	N= 2
%= 0.00	%= 3.70	%= 14.81	%= 3.70
	■■■■	■■■■■■■■■■■■■■ ■■■■■	■■■■

ESTJ	ESFJ	ENFJ	ENTJ
N= 4	N= 2	N= 2	N= 3
%= 7.41	%= 3.70	%= 3.70	%= 5.56
■■■■■■■	■■■■	■■■■	■■■■■■

Column labels (right side): JUDGMENT / PERCEPTION — INTROVERSION; PERCEPTION / JUDGMENT — EXTRAVERSION

	N	%
E	23	42.59
I	31	57.41
S	26	48.15
N	28	51.85
T	25	46.30
F	29	53.70
J	21	38.89
P	33	61.11
I J	10	18.52
I P	21	38.89
E P	12	22.22
E J	11	20.37
S T	12	22.22
S F	14	25.93
N F	15	27.78
N T	13	24.07
S J	13	24.07
S P	13	24.07
N P	20	37.04
N J	8	14.81
T J	14	25.93
T P	11	20.37
F P	22	40.74
F J	7	12.96
I N	13	24.07
E N	15	27.78
I S	18	33.33
E S	8	14.81
E T	9	16.67
E F	14	25.93
I F	15	27.78
I T	16	29.63
S dom	9	16.67
N dom	13	24.07
T dom	16	29.63
F dom	16	29.63

Note: ■ = 1% of sample   8629371

This table is one of a series of tables from the CAPT-MBTI Data Bank of MBTI records submitted to CAPT for computer scoring between 1971 and June, 1984. This sample was drawn from 59,784 records with usable occupational codes from the total data bank of 232,557. This data bank has 51% Form F cases from 1971 to March, 1978, 35% Form F cases from 1978 to June, 1984 and 14% Form G cases from 1978 to December, 1982. An analysis of Form F and G data banks showed the data banks were comprised of 56% females and 44% males; education level completed: 6% some grade school, 30% high school diploma, 25% some college, 18% bachelor degrees, 11% masters degrees, 3% doctoral or post doctoral work, and 6% unknown. Age group percentages were: 11% under 18, 29% 18 to 20, 12% 21 to 24, 10% 25 to 29, 16% 30 to 39, 10% 40 to 49, 5% 50 to 59, 2% 60 plus, and 5% unknown.

Child Care Workers (except private household)

N = 55

	SENSING		INTUITION					N	%
	THINKING	FEELING	FEELING	THINKING			E	32	58.18

	SENSING		INTUITION	
	THINKING	FEELING	FEELING	THINKING

ISTJ	ISFJ	INFJ	INTJ
N= 4	N= 8	N= 0	N= 2
%= 7.27	%= 14.55	%= 0.00	%= 3.64
■■■■■■■	■■■■■■■■■■■■■■		■■■■

ISTP	ISFP	INFP	INTP
N= 1	N= 3	N= 3	N= 2
%= 1.82	%= 5.45	%= 5.45	%= 3.64
■■	■■■■■	■■■■■	■■■■

ESTP	ESFP	ENFP	ENTP
N= 2	N= 8	N= 2	N= 4
%= 3.64	%= 14.55	%= 3.64	%= 7.27
■■■■	■■■■■■■■■■■■■■	■■■■	■■■■■■■

ESTJ	ESFJ	ENFJ	ENTJ
N= 2	N= 8	N= 5	N= 1
%= 3.64	%= 14.55	%= 9.09	%= 1.82
■■■■	■■■■■■■■■■■■■■	■■■■■■■■■	■■

Note: ■ = 1% of sample

8629380

	N	%
E	32	58.18
I	23	41.82
S	36	65.45
N	19	34.55
T	18	32.73
F	37	67.27
J	30	54.55
P	25	45.45
I J	14	25.45
I P	9	16.36
E P	16	29.09
E J	16	29.09
S T	9	16.36
S F	27	49.09
N F	10	18.18
N T	9	16.36
S J	22	40.00
S P	14	25.45
N P	11	20.00
N J	8	14.55
T J	9	16.36
T P	9	16.36
F P	16	29.09
F J	21	38.18
I N	7	12.73
E N	12	21.82
I S	16	29.09
E S	20	36.36
E T	9	16.36
E F	23	41.82
I F	14	25.45
I T	9	16.36
S dom	22	40.00
N dom	8	14.55
T dom	6	10.91
F dom	19	34.55

This table is one of a series of tables from the CAPT-MBTI Data Bank of MBTI records submitted to CAPT for computer scoring between 1971 and June, 1984. This sample was drawn from 59,784 records with usable occupational codes from the total data bank of 232,557. This data bank has 51% Form F cases from 1971 to March, 1978, 35% Form F cases from 1978 to June, 1984 and 14% Form G cases from 1978 to December, 1982. An analysis of Form F and G data banks showed the data banks were comprised of 56% females and 44% males; education level completed: 6% some grade school, 30% high school diploma, 25% some college, 18% bachelor degrees, 11% masters degrees, 3% doctoral or post doctoral work, and 6% unknown. Age group percentages were: 11% under 18, 29% 18 to 20, 12% 21 to 24, 10% 25 to 29, 16% 30 to 39, 10% 40 to 49, 5% 50 to 59, 2% 60 plus, and 5% unknown.

Construction Laborers (except carpenters helpers)

	SENSING		INTUITION	
	THINKING	FEELING	FEELING	THINKING

ISTJ	ISFJ	INFJ	INTJ
N= 12	N= 10	N= 6	N= 2
%= 8.63	%= 7.19	%= 4.32	%= 1.44
■■■■■■■■	■■■■■■■	■■■■	■

ISTP	ISFP	INFP	INTP
N= 10	N= 9	N= 5	N= 2
%= 7.19	%= 6.47	%= 3.60	%= 1.44
■■■■■■■	■■■■■■	■■■■	■

ESTP	ESFP	ENFP	ENTP
N= 9	N= 9	N= 11	N= 13
%= 6.47	%= 6.47	%= 7.91	%= 9.35
■■■■■■	■■■■■■	■■■■■■■■	■■■■■■■■■

ESTJ	ESFJ	ENFJ	ENTJ
N= 17	N= 17	N= 2	N= 5
%= 12.23	%= 12.23	%= 1.44	%= 3.60
■■■■■■■■■■■	■■■■■■■■■■■	■	■■■■
■■	■■		

JUDGMENT — INTROVERSION — PERCEPTION — PERCEPTION — EXTRAVERSION — JUDGMENT

	N	%
E	83	59.71
I	56	40.29
S	93	66.91
N	46	33.09
T	70	50.36
F	69	49.64
J	71	51.08
P	68	48.92
I J	30	21.58
I P	26	18.71
E P	42	30.22
E J	41	29.50
S T	48	34.53
S F	45	32.37
N F	24	17.27
N T	22	15.83
S J	56	40.29
S P	37	26.62
N P	31	22.30
N J	15	10.79
T J	36	25.90
T P	34	24.46
F P	34	24.46
F J	35	25.18
I N	15	10.79
E N	31	22.30
I S	41	29.50
E S	52	37.41
E T	44	31.65
E F	39	28.06
I F	30	21.58
I T	26	18.71
S dom	40	28.78
N dom	32	23.02
T dom	34	24.46
F dom	33	23.74

Note: ■ = 1% of sample   8629372

This table is one of a series of tables from the CAPT-MBTI Data Bank of MBTI records submitted to CAPT for computer scoring between 1971 and June, 1984. This sample was drawn from 59,784 records with usable occupational codes from the total data bank of 232,557. This data bank has 51% Form F cases from 1971 to March, 1978, 35% Form F cases from 1978 to June, 1984 and 14% Form G cases from 1978 to December, 1982. An analysis of Form F and G data banks showed the data banks were comprised of 56% females and 44% males; education level completed: 6% some grade school, 30% high school diploma, 25% some college, 18% bachelor degrees, 11% masters degrees, 3% doctoral or post doctoral work, and 6% unknown. Age group percentages were: 11% under 18, 29% 18 to 20, 12% 21 to 24, 10% 25 to 29, 16% 30 to 39, 10% 40 to 49, 5% 50 to 59, 2% 60 plus, and 5% unknown.

Cooks (except private household)

N = 180

		SENSING			INTUITION		
		THINKING	FEELING	FEELING	THINKING		

ISTJ	ISFJ	INFJ	INTJ
N= 18	N= 9	N= 2	N= 12
%= 10.00	%= 5.00	%= 1.11	%= 6.67
■■■■■■■■■■	■■■■■	■	■■■■■■■

ISTP	ISFP	INFP	INTP
N= 12	N= 14	N= 19	N= 5
%= 6.67	%= 7.78	%= 10.56	%= 2.78
■■■■■■■	■■■■■■■■	■■■■■■■■■■ ■	■■■

ESTP	ESFP	ENFP	ENTP
N= 6	N= 5	N= 20	N= 7
%= 3.33	%= 2.78	%= 11.11	%= 3.89
■■■	■■■	■■■■■■■■■■ ■	■■■■

ESTJ	ESFJ	ENFJ	ENTJ
N= 26	N= 11	N= 11	N= 3
%= 14.44	%= 6.11	%= 6.11	%= 1.67
■■■■■■■■■■ ■■■■	■■■■■■	■■■■■■	■■

JUDGMENT — INTROVERSION — PERCEPTION / PERCEPTION — EXTRAVERSION — JUDGMENT

	N	%
E	89	49.44
I	91	50.56
S	101	56.11
N	79	43.89
T	89	49.44
F	91	50.56
J	92	51.11
P	88	48.89
I J	41	22.78
I P	50	27.78
E P	38	21.11
E J	51	28.33
S T	62	34.44
S F	39	21.67
N F	52	28.89
N T	27	15.00
S J	64	35.56
S P	37	20.56
N P	51	28.33
N J	28	15.56
T J	59	32.78
T P	30	16.67
F P	58	32.22
F J	33	18.33
I N	38	21.11
E N	41	22.78
I S	53	29.44
E S	48	26.67
E T	42	23.33
E F	47	26.11
I F	44	24.44
I T	47	26.11
S dom	38	21.11
N dom	41	22.78
T dom	46	25.56
F dom	55	30.56

Note: ■ = 1% of sample   8629375

This table is one of a series of tables from the CAPT-MBTI Data Bank of MBTI records submitted to CAPT for computer scoring between 1971 and June, 1984. This sample was drawn from 59,784 records with usable occupational codes from the total data bank of 232,557. This data bank has 51% Form F cases from 1971 to March, 1978, 35% Form F cases from 1978 to June, 1984 and 14% Form G cases from 1978 to December, 1982. An analysis of Form F and G data banks showed the data banks were comprised of 56% females and 44% males; education level completed: 6% some grade school, 30% high school diploma, 25% some college, 18% bachelor degrees, 11% masters degrees, 3% doctoral or post doctoral work, and 6% unknown. Age group percentages were: 11% under 18, 29% 18 to 20, 12% 21 to 24, 10% 25 to 29, 16% 30 to 39, 10% 40 to 49, 5% 50 to 59, 2% 60 plus, and 5% unknown.

Displaced Coal Miners

	SENSING		INTUITION	
	THINKING	FEELING	FEELING	THINKING

ISTJ	ISFJ	INFJ	INTJ
N= 42	N= 21	N= 2	N= 10
%= 21.43	%= 10.71	%= 1.02	%= 5.10
■■■■■■■■■■	■■■■■■■■■■	■	■■■■■
■■■■■■■■■■	■		
■			

JUDGMENT — INTROVERSION

ISTP	ISFP	INFP	INTP
N= 17	N= 3	N= 1	N= 4
%= 8.67	%= 1.53	%= .51	%= 2.04
■■■■■■■■■	■■	■	■■

PERCEPTION

ESTP	ESFP	ENFP	ENTP
N= 8	N= 8	N= 3	N= 5
%= 4.08	%= 4.08	%= 1.53	%= 2.55
■■■■	■■■■	■■	■■■

PERCEPTION — EXTRAVERSION

ESTJ	ESFJ	ENFJ	ENTJ
N= 42	N= 17	N= 1	N= 12
%= 21.43	%= 8.67	%= .51	%= 6.12
■■■■■■■■■■	■■■■■■■■■	■	■■■■■■
■■■■■■■■■■			
■			

JUDGMENT

	N	%
E	96	48.98
I	100	51.02
S	158	80.61
N	38	19.39
T	140	71.43
F	56	28.57
J	147	75.00
P	49	25.00
I J	75	38.27
I P	25	12.76
E P	24	12.24
E J	72	36.73
S T	109	55.61
S F	49	25.00
N F	7	3.57
N T	31	15.82
S J	122	62.24
S P	36	18.37
N P	13	6.63
N J	25	12.76
T J	106	54.08
T P	34	17.35
F P	15	7.65
F J	41	20.92
I N	17	8.67
E N	21	10.71
I S	83	42.35
E S	75	38.27
E T	67	34.18
E F	29	14.80
I F	27	13.78
I T	73	37.24
S dom	79	40.31
N dom	20	10.20
T dom	75	38.27
F dom	22	11.22

Note: ■ = 1% of sample

8623192

Data collected by Orville Pierson of Mainstream Access, Inc. from June 1983 to June 1984 using Forms F and G. Subjects were displaced coal miners voluntarily participating in displaced worker programs. All coal miners were residents of a mid-sized mining city in central Pennsylvania or the surrounding counties. No other demographic data were reported. These data are used with permission and have not been published elsewhere to date.

Displaced Steelworkers

N = 658

	SENSING		INTUITION				N	%
	THINKING	FEELING	FEELING	THINKING				

							N	%
ISTJ N= 217 %= 32.98	**ISFJ** N= 67 %= 10.18	**INFJ** N= 3 %= .46	**INTJ** N= 26 %= 3.95	JUDGMENT / INTROVERSION	E	263	39.97
					I	395	60.03
					S	562	85.41
					N	96	14.59
					T	489	74.32
					F	169	25.68
					J	520	79.03
					P	138	20.97
ISTP N= 44 %= 6.69	**ISFP** N= 16 %= 2.43	**INFP** N= 10 %= 1.52	**INTP** N= 12 %= 1.82	PERCEPTION	I J	313	47.57
					I P	82	12.46
					E P	56	8.51
					E J	207	31.46
					S T	416	63.22
					S F	146	22.19
					N F	23	3.50
					N T	73	11.09
ESTP N= 21 %= 3.19	**ESFP** N= 17 %= 2.58	**ENFP** N= 5 %= .76	**ENTP** N= 13 %= 1.98	PERCEPTION / EXTRAVERSION	S J	464	70.52
					S P	98	14.89
					N P	40	6.08
					N J	56	8.51
					T J	399	60.64
					T P	90	13.68
					F P	48	7.29
					F J	121	18.39
ESTJ N= 134 %= 20.36	**ESFJ** N= 46 %= 6.99	**ENFJ** N= 5 %= .76	**ENTJ** N= 22 %= 3.34	JUDGMENT	I N	51	7.75
					E N	45	6.84
					I S	344	52.28
					E S	218	33.13
					E T	190	28.88
					E F	73	11.09
					I F	96	14.59
					I T	299	45.44
					S dom	322	48.94
					N dom	47	7.14
					T dom	212	32.22
					F dom	77	11.70

Note: ■ = 1% of sample

8623191

Data collected by Orville Pierson of Mainstream Access, Inc. from June 1983 to June 1984 using Forms F and G. Subjects were displaced steelworkers voluntarily participating in displaced worker programs. All steelworkers were residents of a mid-sized mining city in central Pennsylvania or the surrounding counties. No other demographic data were reported. These data are used with permission and have not been published elsewhere to date.

Electricians

N = 70

					N	%
SENSING		INTUITION				
THINKING	FEELING	FEELING	THINKING			

ISTJ	ISFJ	INFJ	INTJ
N= 14	N= 9	N= 1	N= 1
%= 20.00	%= 12.86	%= 1.43	%= 1.43
■■■■■■■■■■ ■■■■■■■■■■	■■■■■■■■■■ ■■■	■	■

ISTP	ISFP	INFP	INTP
N= 1	N= 4	N= 5	N= 4
%= 1.43	%= 5.71	%= 7.14	%= 5.71
■	■■■■■■	■■■■■■■	■■■■■■

ESTP	ESFP	ENFP	ENTP
N= 3	N= 5	N= 3	N= 6
%= 4.29	%= 7.14	%= 4.29	%= 8.57
■■■■	■■■■■■■	■■■■	■■■■■■■■■

ESTJ	ESFJ	ENFJ	ENTJ
N= 6	N= 1	N= 2	N= 5
%= 8.57	%= 1.43	%= 2.86	%= 7.14
■■■■■■■■■	■	■■■	■■■■■■■

	N	%
E	31	44.29
I	39	55.71
S	43	61.43
N	27	38.57
T	40	57.14
F	30	42.86
J	39	55.71
P	31	44.29
I J	25	35.71
I P	14	20.00
E P	17	24.29
E J	14	20.00
S T	24	34.29
S F	19	27.14
N F	11	15.71
N T	16	22.86
S J	30	42.86
S P	13	18.57
N P	18	25.71
N J	9	12.86
T J	26	37.14
T P	14	20.00
F P	17	24.29
F J	13	18.57
I N	11	15.71
E N	16	22.86
I S	28	40.00
E S	15	21.43
E T	20	28.57
E F	11	15.71
I F	19	27.14
I T	20	28.57
S dom	31	44.29
N dom	11	15.71
T dom	16	22.86
F dom	12	17.14

Note: ■ = 1% of sample   8629367

This table is one of a series of tables from the CAPT-MBTI Data Bank of MBTI records submitted to CAPT for computer scoring between 1971 and June, 1984. This sample was drawn from 59,784 records with usable occupational codes from the total data bank of 232,557. This data bank has 51% Form F cases from 1971 to March, 1978, 35% Form F cases from 1978 to June, 1984 and 14% Form G cases from 1978 to December, 1982. An analysis of Form F and G data banks showed the data banks were comprised of 56% females and 44% males; education level completed: 6% some grade school, 30% high school diploma, 25% some college, 18% bachelor degrees, 11% masters degrees, 3% doctoral or post doctoral work, and 6% unknown. Age group percentages were: 11% under 18, 29% 18 to 20, 12% 21 to 24, 10% 25 to 29, 16% 30 to 39, 10% 40 to 49, 5% 50 to 59, 2% 60 plus, and 5% unknown.

413

Factory and Site Supervisors

N = 52

	SENSING		INTUITION	
	THINKING	FEELING	FEELING	THINKING

ISTJ	ISFJ	INFJ	INTJ
N= 9	N= 6	N= 0	N= 1
%= 17.31	%= 11.54	%= 0.00	%= 1.92
■■■■■■■■■■■	■■■■■■■■■■■		■■
■■■■■■	■■		

ISTP	ISFP	INFP	INTP
N= 1	N= 2	N= 2	N= 3
%= 1.92	%= 3.85	%= 3.85	%= 5.77
■■	■■■■	■■■■	■■■■■■

ESTP	ESFP	ENFP	ENTP
N= 2	N= 5	N= 2	N= 0
%= 3.85	%= 9.62	%= 3.85	%= 0.00
■■■■	■■■■■■■■■■	■■■■	

ESTJ	ESFJ	ENFJ	ENTJ
N= 13	N= 6	N= 0	N= 0
%= 25.00	%= 11.54	%= 0.00	%= 0.00
■■■■■■■■■■■	■■■■■■■■■■■		
■■■■■■■■■■■	■■		
■■■■■			

JUDGMENT — INTROVERSION — PERCEPTION — PERCEPTION — EXTRAVERSION — JUDGMENT

	N	%
E	28	53.85
I	24	46.15
S	44	84.62
N	8	15.38
T	29	55.77
F	23	44.23
J	35	67.31
P	17	32.69
I J	16	30.77
I P	8	15.38
E P	9	17.31
E J	19	36.54
S T	25	48.08
S F	19	36.54
N F	4	7.69
N T	4	7.69
S J	34	65.38
S P	10	19.23
N P	7	13.46
N J	1	1.92
T J	23	44.23
T P	6	11.54
F P	11	21.15
F J	12	23.08
I N	6	11.54
E N	2	3.85
I S	18	34.62
E S	26	50.00
E T	15	28.85
E F	13	25.00
I F	10	19.23
I T	14	26.92
S dom	22	42.31
N dom	3	5.77
T dom	17	32.69
F dom	10	19.23

Note: ■ = 1% of sample   8629368

This table is one of a series of tables from the CAPT-MBTI Data Bank of MBTI records submitted to CAPT for computer scoring between 1971 and June, 1984. This sample was drawn from 59,784 records with usable occupational codes from the total data bank of 232,557. This data bank has 51% Form F cases from 1971 to March, 1978, 35% Form F cases from 1978 to June, 1984 and 14% Form G cases from 1978 to December, 1982. An analysis of Form F and G data banks showed the data banks were comprised of 56% females and 44% males; education level completed: 6% some grade school, 30% high school diploma, 25% some college, 18% bachelor degrees, 11% masters degrees, 3% doctoral or post doctoral work, and 6% unknown. Age group percentages were: 11% under 18, 29% 18 to 20, 12% 21 to 24, 10% 25 to 29, 16% 30 to 39, 10% 40 to 49, 5% 50 to 59, 2% 60 plus, and 5% unknown.

Food Counter and Fountain Workers

N = 61

	SENSING		INTUITION	
	THINKING	FEELING	FEELING	THINKING

ISTJ	ISFJ	INFJ	INTJ
N= 7	N= 10	N= 1	N= 0
%= 11.48	%= 16.39	%= 1.64	%= 0.00
■■■■■■■■■■■	■■■■■■■■■■	■■	
■	■■■■■■		

ISTP	ISFP	INFP	INTP
N= 1	N= 1	N= 1	N= 6
%= 1.64	%= 1.64	%= 1.64	%= 9.84
■■	■■	■■	■■■■■■■■■■

ESTP	ESFP	ENFP	ENTP
N= 0	N= 4	N= 7	N= 5
%= 0.00	%= 6.56	%= 11.48	%= 8.20
	■■■■■■■	■■■■■■■■■■■	■■■■■■■■
		■	

ESTJ	ESFJ	ENFJ	ENTJ
N= 3	N= 9	N= 5	N= 1
%= 4.92	%= 14.75	%= 8.20	%= 1.64
■■■■■	■■■■■■■■■■■	■■■■■■■■	■■
	■■■■■		

JUDGMENT — INTROVERSION — PERCEPTION — PERCEPTION — EXTRAVERSION — JUDGMENT

	N	%
E	34	55.74
I	27	44.26
S	35	57.38
N	26	42.62
T	23	37.70
F	38	62.30
J	36	59.02
P	25	40.98
I J	18	29.51
I P	9	14.75
E P	16	26.23
E J	18	29.51
S T	11	18.03
S F	24	39.34
N F	14	22.95
N T	12	19.67
S J	29	47.54
S P	6	9.84
N P	19	31.15
N J	7	11.48
T J	11	18.03
T P	12	19.67
F P	13	21.31
F J	25	40.98
I N	8	13.11
E N	18	29.51
I S	19	31.15
E S	16	26.23
E T	9	14.75
E F	25	40.98
I F	13	21.31
I T	14	22.95
S dom	21	34.43
N dom	13	21.31
T dom	11	18.03
F dom	16	26.23

Note: ■ = 1% of sample   8629376

This table is one of a series of tables from the CAPT-MBTI Data Bank of MBTI records submitted to CAPT for computer scoring between 1971 and June, 1984. This sample was drawn from 59,784 records with usable occupational codes from the total data bank of 232,557. This data bank has 51% Form F cases from 1971 to March, 1978, 35% Form F cases from 1978 to June, 1984 and 14% Form G cases from 1978 to December, 1982. An analysis of Form F and G data banks showed the data banks were comprised of 56% females and 44% males; education level completed: 6% some grade school, 30% high school diploma, 25% some college, 18% bachelor degrees, 11% masters degrees, 3% doctoral or post doctoral work, and 6% unknown. Age group percentages were: 11% under 18, 29% 18 to 20, 12% 21 to 24, 10% 25 to 29, 16% 30 to 39, 10% 40 to 49, 5% 50 to 59, 2% 60 plus, and 5% unknown.

Foremen in Japanese Food Production Company

N = 240

	SENSING		INTUITION	
	THINKING	FEELING	FEELING	THINKING

ISTJ	ISFJ	INFJ	INTJ
N= 33	N= 53	N= 8	N= 6
%= 13.75	%= 22.08	%= 3.33	%= 2.50

ISTP	ISFP	INFP	INTP
N= 6	N= 32	N= 5	N= 3
%= 2.50	%= 13.33	%= 2.08	%= 1.25

ESTP	ESFP	ENFP	ENTP
N= 4	N= 14	N= 3	N= 0
%= 1.67	%= 5.83	%= 1.25	%= 0.00

ESTJ	ESFJ	ENFJ	ENTJ
N= 28	N= 27	N= 6	N= 12
%= 11.67	%= 11.25	%= 2.50	%= 5.00

JUDGMENT — INTROVERSION — PERCEPTION — EXTRAVERSION — JUDGMENT

	N	%
E	94	39.17
I	146	60.83
S	197	82.08
N	43	17.92
T	92	38.33
F	148	61.67
J	173	72.08
P	67	27.92
I J	100	41.67
I P	46	19.17
E P	21	8.75
E J	73	30.42
S T	71	29.58
S F	126	52.50
N F	22	9.17
N T	21	8.75
S J	141	58.75
S P	56	23.33
N P	11	4.58
N J	32	13.33
T J	79	32.92
T P	13	5.42
F P	54	22.50
F J	94	39.17
I N	22	9.17
E N	21	8.75
I S	124	51.67
E S	73	30.42
E T	44	18.33
E F	50	20.83
I F	98	40.83
I T	48	20.00
S dom	104	43.33
N dom	17	7.08
T dom	49	20.42
F dom	70	29.17

Note: ■ = 1% of sample

8623189

Data collected by Takeshi Ohsawa at the Nippon Recruit Center, Tokyo, Japan from 1964 to 1975. No other demographic data were reported. These data are used with permission and were cited in:

Ohsawa, T. (1975, October). MBTI experiences in Japan: Career choice, selection, placement and counseling for individual development. Paper presented at the First National Conference on the Myers-Briggs Type Indicator, Gainesville, FL.

Hairdressers, Cosmetologists and Manicurists

N = 96

	SENSING		INTUITION	
	THINKING	FEELING	FEELING	THINKING

ISTJ N= 12 %= 12.50 ■■■■■■■■■■■■ ■■■	**ISFJ** N= 13 %= 13.54 ■■■■■■■■■■■■■ ■■■■	**INFJ** N= 2 %= 2.08 ■■	**INTJ** N= 3 %= 3.12 ■■■	JUDGMENT
ISTP N= 4 %= 4.17 ■■■■	**ISFP** N= 2 %= 2.08 ■■	**INFP** N= 4 %= 4.17 ■■■■	**INTP** N= 1 %= 1.04 ■	PERCEPTION
ESTP N= 2 %= 2.08 ■■	**ESFP** N= 6 %= 6.25 ■■■■■■	**ENFP** N= 7 %= 7.29 ■■■■■■■	**ENTP** N= 5 %= 5.21 ■■■■■	PERCEPTION
ESTJ N= 11 %= 11.46 ■■■■■■■■■■■ ■	**ESFJ** N= 18 %= 18.75 ■■■■■■■■■■■■■ ■■■■■■■■	**ENFJ** N= 5 %= 5.21 ■■■■■	**ENTJ** N= 1 %= 1.04 ■	JUDGMENT

(Side labels: INTROVERSION — PERCEPTION — EXTRAVERSION)

	N	%
E	55	57.29
I	41	42.71
S	68	70.83
N	28	29.17
T	39	40.62
F	57	59.37
J	65	67.71
P	31	32.29
I J	30	31.25
I P	11	11.46
E P	20	20.83
E J	35	36.46
S T	29	30.21
S F	39	40.62
N F	18	18.75
N T	10	10.42
S J	54	56.25
S P	14	14.58
N P	17	17.71
N J	11	11.46
T J	27	28.13
T P	12	12.50
F P	19	19.79
F J	38	39.58
I N	10	10.42
E N	18	18.75
I S	31	32.29
E S	37	38.54
E T	19	19.79
E F	36	37.50
I F	21	21.88
I T	20	20.83
S dom	33	34.38
N dom	17	17.71
T dom	17	17.71
F dom	29	30.21

Note: ■ = 1% of sample   8629381

This table is one of a series of tables from the CAPT-MBTI Data Bank of MBTI records submitted to CAPT for computer scoring between 1971 and June, 1984. This sample was drawn from 59,784 records with usable occupational codes from the total data bank of 232,557. This data bank has 51% Form F cases from 1971 to March, 1978, 35% Form F cases from 1978 to June, 1984 and 14% Form G cases from 1978 to December, 1982. An analysis of Form F and G data banks showed the data banks were comprised of 56% females and 44% males; education level completed: 6% some grade school, 30% high school diploma, 25% some college, 18% bachelor degrees, 11% masters degrees, 3% doctoral or post doctoral work, and 6% unknown. Age group percentages were: 11% under 18, 29% 18 to 20, 12% 21 to 24, 10% 25 to 29, 16% 30 to 39, 10% 40 to 49, 5% 50 to 59, 2% 60 plus, and 5% unknown.

Home Management Advisors and Home Economists

N = 58

	SENSING		INTUITION	
	THINKING	FEELING	FEELING	THINKING

ISTJ	ISFJ	INFJ	INTJ
N= 6	N= 5	N= 4	N= 1
%= 10.34	%= 8.62	%= 6.90	%= 1.72
■■■■■■■■■■	■■■■■■■■■	■■■■■■■	■■

ISTP	ISFP	INFP	INTP
N= 2	N= 2	N= 1	N= 0
%= 3.45	%= 3.45	%= 1.72	%= 0.00
■■■	■■■	■■	

ESTP	ESFP	ENFP	ENTP
N= 1	N= 1	N= 6	N= 0
%= 1.72	%= 1.72	%= 10.34	%= 0.00
■■	■■	■■■■■■■■■■	

ESTJ	ESFJ	ENFJ	ENTJ
N= 6	N= 10	N= 9	N= 4
%= 10.34	%= 17.24	%= 15.52	%= 6.90
■■■■■■■■■■	■■■■■■■■■■	■■■■■■■■■■	■■■■■■■
	■■■■■■■	■■■■■■	

JUDGMENT — INTROVERSION — PERCEPTION — PERCEPTION — EXTRAVERSION — JUDGMENT

	N	%
E	37	63.79
I	21	36.21
S	33	56.90
N	25	43.10
T	20	34.48
F	38	65.52
J	45	77.59
P	13	22.41
I J	16	27.59
I P	5	8.62
E P	8	13.79
E J	29	50.00
S T	15	25.86
S F	18	31.03
N F	20	34.48
N T	5	8.62
S J	27	46.55
S P	6	10.34
N P	7	12.07
N J	18	31.03
T J	17	29.31
T P	3	5.17
F P	10	17.24
F J	28	48.28
I N	6	10.34
E N	19	32.76
I S	15	25.86
E S	18	31.03
E T	11	18.97
E F	26	44.83
I F	12	20.69
I T	9	15.52
S dom	13	22.41
N dom	11	18.97
T dom	12	20.69
F dom	22	37.93

Note: ■ = 1% of sample   8629394

This table is one of a series of tables from the CAPT-MBTI Data Bank of MBTI records submitted to CAPT for computer scoring between 1971 and June, 1984. This sample was drawn from 59,784 records with usable occupational codes from the total data bank of 232,557. This data bank has 51% Form F cases from 1971 to March, 1978, 35% Form F cases from 1978 to June, 1984 and 14% Form G cases from 1978 to December, 1982. An analysis of Form F and G data banks showed the data banks were comprised of 56% females and 44% males; education level completed: 6% some grade school, 30% high school diploma, 25% some college, 18% bachelor degrees, 11% masters degrees, 3% doctoral or post doctoral work, and 6% unknown. Age group percentages were: 11% under 18, 29% 18 to 20, 12% 21 to 24, 10% 25 to 29, 16% 30 to 39, 10% 40 to 49, 5% 50 to 59, 2% 60 plus, and 5% unknown.

Lifeguards, Attendants, Recreation and Amusement

	SENSING		INTUITION	
	THINKING	FEELING	FEELING	THINKING

ISTJ	ISFJ	INFJ	INTJ
N= 23	N= 13	N= 5	N= 5
%= 10.90	%= 6.16	%= 2.37	%= 2.37
■■■■■■■■■■	■■■■■■	■■	■■
■			

ISTP	ISFP	INFP	INTP
N= 6	N= 14	N= 16	N= 8
%= 2.84	%= 6.64	%= 7.58	%= 3.79
■■■	■■■■■■■	■■■■■■■■	■■■■

ESTP	ESFP	ENFP	ENTP
N= 10	N= 17	N= 22	N= 9
%= 4.74	%= 8.06	%= 10.43	%= 4.27
■■■■■	■■■■■■■■	■■■■■■■■■■■	■■■■

ESTJ	ESFJ	ENFJ	ENTJ
N= 26	N= 24	N= 6	N= 7
%= 12.32	%= 11.37	%= 2.84	%= 3.32
■■■■■■■■■■■■	■■■■■■■■■■■	■■■	■■■
■■	■		

JUDGMENT — INTROVERSION — PERCEPTION — PERCEPTION — EXTRAVERSION — JUDGMENT

	N	%
E	121	57.35
I	90	42.65
S	133	63.03
N	78	36.97
T	94	44.55
F	117	55.45
J	109	51.66
P	102	48.34
I J	46	21.80
I P	44	20.85
E P	58	27.49
E J	63	29.86
S T	65	30.81
S F	68	32.23
N F	49	23.22
N T	29	13.74
S J	86	40.76
S P	47	22.27
N P	55	26.07
N J	23	10.90
T J	61	28.91
T P	33	15.64
F P	69	32.70
F J	48	22.75
I N	34	16.11
E N	44	20.85
I S	56	26.54
E S	77	36.49
E T	52	24.64
E F	69	32.70
I F	48	22.75
I T	42	19.91
S dom	63	29.86
N dom	41	19.43
T dom	47	22.27
F dom	60	28.44

Note: ■ = 1% of sample   8629379

This table is one of a series of tables from the CAPT-MBTI Data Bank of MBTI records submitted to CAPT for computer scoring between 1971 and June, 1984. This sample was drawn from 59,784 records with usable occupational codes from the total data bank of 232,557. This data bank has 51% Form F cases from 1971 to March, 1978, 35% Form F cases from 1978 to June, 1984 and 14% Form G cases from 1978 to December, 1982. An analysis of Form F and G data banks showed the data banks were comprised of 56% females and 44% males; education level completed: 6% some grade school, 30% high school diploma, 25% some college, 18% bachelor degrees, 11% masters degrees, 3% doctoral or post doctoral work, and 6% unknown. Age group percentages were: 11% under 18, 29% 18 to 20, 12% 21 to 24, 10% 25 to 29, 16% 30 to 39, 10% 40 to 49, 5% 50 to 59, 2% 60 plus, and 5% unknown.

Operators and Field Technicians in Water Pollution Control

	SENSING		INTUITION				N	%
	THINKING	FEELING	FEELING	THINKING				
	ISTJ N= 129 %= 38.62 ■■■■■■■■■ ■■■■■■■■■ ■■■■■■■■■ ■■■■■■■■	**ISFJ** N= 12 %= 3.59 ■■■■	**INFJ** N= 4 %= 1.20 ■	**INTJ** N= 22 %= 6.59 ■■■■■■■	JUDGMENT	INTROVERSION	E 119 I 215 S 260 N 74 T 291 F 43 J 261 P 73	35.63 64.37 77.84 22.16 87.13 12.87 78.14 21.86
	ISTP N= 19 %= 5.69 ■■■■■■	**ISFP** N= 9 %= 2.69 ■■■	**INFP** N= 2 %= .60 ■	**INTP** N= 18 %= 5.39 ■■■■■	PERCEPTION		I J 167 I P 48 E P 25 E J 94	50.00 14.37 7.49 28.14
	ESTP N= 11 %= 3.29 ■■■	**ESFP** N= 4 %= 1.20 ■	**ENFP** N= 4 %= 1.20 ■	**ENTP** N= 6 %= 1.80 ■■	PERCEPTION	EXTRAVERSION	ST 228 SF 32 NF 11 NT 63	68.26 9.58 3.29 18.86
	ESTJ N= 69 %= 20.66 ■■■■■■■■■ ■■■■■■■■■ ■	**ESFJ** N= 7 %= 2.10 ■■	**ENFJ** N= 1 %= .30	**ENTJ** N= 17 %= 5.09 ■■■■■	JUDGMENT		SJ 217 SP 43 NP 30 NJ 44	64.97 12.87 8.98 13.17

Additional ratios:

	N	%
TJ	237	70.96
TP	54	16.17
FP	19	5.69
FJ	24	7.19
IN	46	13.77
EN	28	8.38
IS	169	50.60
ES	91	27.25
ET	103	30.84
EF	16	4.79
IF	27	8.08
IT	188	56.29
S dom	156	46.71
N dom	36	10.78
T dom	123	36.83
F dom	19	5.69

Note: ■ = 1% of sample

8708302

Data collected by Barbara B. Mitchell of the Center for Training, Research and Education for Environmental Occupations, University of Florida from 1982 through March 1987, using Form G. Subjects were 99% male operators and field technicians in water and wastewater pollution control attending a five day continuing education program at the center. These data are used with permission and have not been published elsewhere to date.

Restaurant Workers: Table Setting and Cleaning

N = 51

	SENSING		INTUITION	
	THINKING	FEELING	FEELING	THINKING

ISTJ	ISFJ	INFJ	INTJ
N= 2	N= 2	N= 1	N= 2
%= 3.92	%= 3.92	%= 1.96	%= 3.92
■■■■	■■■■	■■	■■■■

ISTP	ISFP	INFP	INTP
N= 1	N= 2	N= 6	N= 2
%= 1.96	%= 3.92	%= 11.76	%= 3.92
■■	■■■■	■■■■■■■■■■	■■■■
		■■	

ESTP	ESFP	ENFP	ENTP
N= 3	N= 4	N= 8	N= 4
%= 5.88	%= 7.84	%= 15.69	%= 7.84
■■■■■■	■■■■■■■■	■■■■■■■■■■■■	■■■■■■■■
		■■■■■■	

ESTJ	ESFJ	ENFJ	ENTJ
N= 3	N= 9	N= 0	N= 2
%= 5.88	%= 17.65	%= 0.00	%= 3.92
■■■■■■	■■■■■■■■■■■■		■■■■
	■■■■■■■■		

JUDGMENT — INTROVERSION — PERCEPTION
PERCEPTION — EXTRAVERSION — JUDGMENT

	N	%
E	33	64.71
I	18	35.29
S	26	50.98
N	25	49.02
T	19	37.25
F	32	62.75
J	21	41.18
P	30	58.82
I J	7	13.73
I P	11	21.57
E P	19	37.25
E J	14	27.45
S T	9	17.65
S F	17	33.33
N F	15	29.41
N T	10	19.61
S J	16	31.37
S P	10	19.61
N P	20	39.22
N J	5	9.80
T J	9	17.65
T P	10	19.61
F P	20	39.22
F J	12	23.53
I N	11	21.57
E N	14	27.45
I S	7	13.73
E S	19	37.25
E T	12	23.53
E F	21	41.18
I F	11	21.57
I T	7	13.73
S dom	11	21.57
N dom	15	29.41
T dom	8	15.69
F dom	17	33.33

Note: ■ = 1% of sample   8629374

This table is one of a series of tables from the CAPT-MBTI Data Bank of MBTI records submitted to CAPT for computer scoring between 1971 and June, 1984. This sample was drawn from 59,784 records with usable occupational codes from the total data bank of 232,557. This data bank has 51% Form F cases from 1971 to March, 1978, 35% Form F cases from 1978 to June, 1984 and 14% Form G cases from 1978 to December, 1982. An analysis of Form F and G data banks showed the data banks were comprised of 56% females and 44% males; education level completed: 6% some grade school, 30% high school diploma, 25% some college, 18% bachelor degrees, 11% masters degrees, 3% doctoral or post doctoral work, and 6% unknown. Age group percentages were: 11% under 18, 29% 18 to 20, 12% 21 to 24, 10% 25 to 29, 16% 30 to 39, 10% 40 to 49, 5% 50 to 59, 2% 60 plus, and 5% unknown.

School Bus Drivers

	SENSING	INTUITION	
THINKING	FEELING	FEELING	THINKING

ISTJ	ISFJ	INFJ	INTJ
N= 34	N= 27	N= 1	N= 1
%= 25.76	%= 20.45	%= .76	%= .76

ISTP	ISFP	INFP	INTP
N= 6	N= 9	N= 0	N= 2
%= 4.55	%= 6.82	%= 0.00	%= 1.52

ESTP	ESFP	ENFP	ENTP
N= 4	N= 4	N= 0	N= 0
%= 3.03	%= 3.03	%= 0.00	%= 0.00

ESTJ	ESFJ	ENFJ	ENTJ
N= 29	N= 14	N= 0	N= 1
%= 21.97	%= 10.61	%= 0.00	%= .76

JUDGMENT — INTROVERSION

PERCEPTION

PERCEPTION — EXTRAVERSION

JUDGMENT

	N	%
E	52	39.39
I	80	60.61
S	127	96.21
N	5	3.79
T	77	58.33
F	55	41.67
J	107	81.06
P	25	18.94
I J	63	47.73
I P	17	12.88
E P	8	6.06
E J	44	33.33
S T	73	55.30
S F	54	40.91
N F	1	.76
N T	4	3.03
S J	104	78.79
S P	23	17.42
N P	2	1.52
N J	3	2.27
T J	65	49.24
T P	12	9.09
F P	13	9.85
F J	42	31.82
I N	4	3.03
E N	1	.76
I S	76	57.58
E S	51	38.64
E T	34	25.76
E F	18	13.64
I F	37	28.03
I T	43	32.58
S dom	69	52.27
N dom	2	1.52
T dom	38	28.79
F dom	23	17.42

Note: ■ = 1% of sample

8708303

Data collected by Carolyn Burkett and Gordon Lawerence during June 1986 using Form G. Subjects were 84% female and 16% male school bus drivers attending an inservice training program. Drivers worked for the Volusia County, Florida school system. These data are used with permission and have not been published elsewhere to date.

Service Workers (except private household)

N = 169

	SENSING		INTUITION	
	THINKING	FEELING	FEELING	THINKING

						N	%
ISTJ N= 27 %= 15.98 ■■■■■■■■■■ ■■■■■■	**ISFJ** N= 15 %= 8.88 ■■■■■■■■■	**INFJ** N= 1 %= .59 ■	**INTJ** N= 4 %= 2.37 ■■	JUDGMENT	INTROVERSION	E 87 / I 82 / S 122 / N 47 / T 123 / F 46 / J 97 / P 72	51.48 / 48.52 / 72.19 / 27.81 / 72.78 / 27.22 / 57.40 / 42.60

E	87	51.48
I	82	48.52
S	122	72.19
N	47	27.81
T	123	72.78
F	46	27.22
J	97	57.40
P	72	42.60
I J	47	27.81
I P	35	20.71
E P	37	21.89
E J	50	29.59
S T	93	55.03
S F	29	17.16
N F	17	10.06
N T	30	17.75
S J	86	50.89
S P	36	21.30
N P	36	21.30
N J	11	6.51
T J	72	42.60
T P	51	30.18
F P	21	12.43
F J	25	14.79
I N	23	13.61
E N	24	14.20
I S	59	34.91
E S	63	37.28
E T	69	40.83
E F	18	10.65
I F	28	16.57
I T	54	31.95
S dom	61	36.09
N dom	23	13.61
T dom	64	37.87
F dom	21	12.43

ISTP N= 14 %= 8.28 ■■■■■■■■

ISFP N= 3 %= 1.78 ■■

INFP N= 9 %= 5.33 ■■■■■

INTP N= 9 %= 5.33 ■■■■■

PERCEPTION

ESTP N= 14 %= 8.28 ■■■■■■■■

ESFP N= 5 %= 2.96 ■■■

ENFP N= 4 %= 2.37 ■■

ENTP N= 14 %= 8.28 ■■■■■■■■

PERCEPTION — EXTRAVERSION

ESTJ N= 38 %= 22.49 ■■■■■■■■■■ ■■■■■■■■■■ ■■

ESFJ N= 6 %= 3.55 ■■■■

ENFJ N= 3 %= 1.78 ■■

ENTJ N= 3 %= 1.78 ■■

JUDGMENT

Note: ■ = 1% of sample   8629382

This table is one of a series of tables from the CAPT-MBTI Data Bank of MBTI records submitted to CAPT for computer scoring between 1971 and June, 1984. This sample was drawn from 59,784 records with usable occupational codes from the total data bank of 232,557. This data bank has 51% Form F cases from 1971 to March, 1978, 35% Form F cases from 1978 to June, 1984 and 14% Form G cases from 1978 to December, 1982. An analysis of Form F and G data banks showed the data banks were comprised of 56% females and 44% males; education level completed: 6% some grade school, 30% high school diploma, 25% some college, 18% bachelor degrees, 11% masters degrees, 3% doctoral or post doctoral work, and 6% unknown. Age group percentages were: 11% under 18, 29% 18 to 20, 12% 21 to 24, 10% 25 to 29, 16% 30 to 39, 10% 40 to 49, 5% 50 to 59, 2% 60 plus, and 5% unknown.

Steelworkers

N = 105

	SENSING		INTUITION				N	%
	THINKING	FEELING	FEELING	THINKING				

ISTJ	ISFJ	INFJ	INTJ
N= 33	N= 9	N= 1	N= 2
%= 31.43	%= 8.57	%= .95	%= 1.90

ISTP	ISFP	INFP	INTP
N= 9	N= 3	N= 1	N= 2
%= 8.57	%= 2.86	%= .95	%= 1.90

ESTP	ESFP	ENFP	ENTP
N= 6	N= 2	N= 4	N= 1
%= 5.71	%= 1.90	%= 3.81	%= .95

ESTJ	ESFJ	ENFJ	ENTJ
N= 22	N= 6	N= 1	N= 3
%= 20.95	%= 5.71	%= .95	%= 2.86

	N	%
E	45	42.86
I	60	57.14
S	90	85.71
N	15	14.29
T	78	74.29
F	27	25.71
J	77	73.33
P	28	26.67
I J	45	42.86
I P	15	14.29
E P	13	12.38
E J	32	30.48
S T	70	66.67
S F	20	19.05
N F	7	6.67
N T	8	7.62
S J	70	66.67
S P	20	19.05
N P	8	7.62
N J	7	6.67
T J	60	57.14
T P	18	17.14
F P	10	9.52
F J	17	16.19
I N	6	5.71
E N	9	8.57
I S	54	51.43
E S	36	34.29
E T	32	30.48
E F	13	12.38
I F	14	13.33
I T	46	43.81
S dom	50	47.62
N dom	8	7.62
T dom	36	34.29
F dom	11	10.48

Note: ■ = 1% of sample   8629369

This table is one of a series of tables from the CAPT-MBTI Data Bank of MBTI records submitted to CAPT for computer scoring between 1971 and June, 1984. This sample was drawn from 59,784 records with usable occupational codes from the total data bank of 232,557. This data bank has 51% Form F cases from 1971 to March, 1978, 35% Form F cases from 1978 to June, 1984 and 14% Form G cases from 1978 to December, 1982. An analysis of Form F and G data banks showed the data banks were comprised of 56% females and 44% males; education level completed: 6% some grade school, 30% high school diploma, 25% some college, 18% bachelor degrees, 11% masters degrees, 3% doctoral or post doctoral work, and 6% unknown. Age group percentages were: 11% under 18, 29% 18 to 20, 12% 21 to 24, 10% 25 to 29, 16% 30 to 39, 10% 40 to 49, 5% 50 to 59, 2% 60 plus, and 5% unknown.

Waiters and Waitresses

N = 540

	SENSING		INTUITION	
	THINKING	FEELING	FEELING	THINKING

ISTJ	ISFJ	INFJ	INTJ
N= 36	N= 30	N= 29	N= 19
%= 6.67	%= 5.56	%= 5.37	%= 3.52
■■■■■■■	■■■■■■	■■■■■	■■■■

ISTP	ISFP	INFP	INTP
N= 13	N= 41	N= 48	N= 19
%= 2.41	%= 7.59	%= 8.89	%= 3.52
■■	■■■■■■■■	■■■■■■■■■	■■■■

ESTP	ESFP	ENFP	ENTP
N= 13	N= 56	N= 81	N= 30
%= 2.41	%= 10.37	%= 15.00	%= 5.56
■■	■■■■■■■■■■	■■■■■■■■■■■■■■■ / ■■■■■	■■■■■■

ESTJ	ESFJ	ENFJ	ENTJ
N= 36	N= 48	N= 27	N= 14
%= 6.67	%= 8.89	%= 5.00	%= 2.59
■■■■■■■	■■■■■■■■■	■■■■■	■■■

Right margin labels: JUDGMENT / INTROVERSION / PERCEPTION / PERCEPTION / EXTRAVERSION / JUDGMENT

	N	%
E	305	56.48
I	235	43.52
S	273	50.56
N	267	49.44
T	180	33.33
F	360	66.67
J	239	44.26
P	301	55.74
I J	114	21.11
I P	121	22.41
E P	180	33.33
E J	125	23.15
S T	98	18.15
S F	175	32.41
N F	185	34.26
N T	82	15.19
S J	150	27.78
S P	123	22.78
N P	178	32.96
N J	89	16.48
T J	105	19.44
T P	75	13.89
F P	226	41.85
F J	134	24.81
I N	115	21.30
E N	152	28.15
I S	120	22.22
E S	153	28.33
E T	93	17.22
E F	212	39.26
I F	148	27.41
I T	87	16.11
S dom	135	25.00
N dom	159	29.44
T dom	82	15.19
F dom	164	30.37

Note: ■ = 1% of sample   8629377

This table is one of a series of tables from the CAPT-MBTI Data Bank of MBTI records submitted to CAPT for computer scoring between 1971 and June, 1984. This sample was drawn from 59,784 records with usable occupational codes from the total data bank of 232,557. This data bank has 51% Form F cases from 1971 to March, 1978, 35% Form F cases from 1978 to June, 1984 and 14% Form G cases from 1978 to December, 1982. An analysis of Form F and G data banks showed the data banks were comprised of 56% females and 44% males; education level completed: 6% some grade school, 30% high school diploma, 25% some college, 18% bachelor degrees, 11% masters degrees, 3% doctoral or post doctoral work, and 6% unknown. Age group percentages were: 11% under 18, 29% 18 to 20, 12% 21 to 24, 10% 25 to 29, 16% 30 to 39, 10% 40 to 49, 5% 50 to 59, 2% 60 plus, and 5% unknown.

CLEANING SERVICES

N = 67

	SENSING		INTUITION	
	THINKING	FEELING	FEELING	THINKING

ISTJ	ISFJ	INFJ	INTJ
N= 13	N= 6	N= 2	N= 0
%= 19.40	%= 8.96	%= 2.99	%= 0.00
■■■■■■■■■■ ■■■■■■■■■	■■■■■■■■■	■■■	

ISTP	ISFP	INFP	INTP
N= 5	N= 6	N= 5	N= 0
%= 7.46	%= 8.96	%= 7.46	%= 0.00
■■■■■■■	■■■■■■■■■	■■■■■■■	

ESTP	ESFP	ENFP	ENTP
N= 0	N= 1	N= 2	N= 3
%= 0.00	%= 1.49	%= 2.99	%= 4.48
	■	■■■	■■■■

ESTJ	ESFJ	ENFJ	ENTJ
N= 15	N= 5	N= 4	N= 0
%= 22.39	%= 7.46	%= 5.97	%= 0.00
■■■■■■■■■■ ■■■■■■■■■■ ■■	■■■■■■■	■■■■■■	

JUDGMENT — INTROVERSION — PERCEPTION — EXTRAVERSION — JUDGMENT — PERCEPTION

	N	%
E	30	44.78
I	37	55.22
S	51	76.12
N	16	23.88
T	36	53.73
F	31	46.27
J	45	67.16
P	22	32.84
I J	21	31.34
I P	16	23.88
E P	6	8.96
E J	24	35.82
S T	33	49.25
S F	18	26.87
N F	13	19.40
N T	3	4.48
S J	39	58.21
S P	12	17.91
N P	10	14.93
N J	6	8.96
T J	28	41.79
T P	8	11.94
F P	14	20.90
F J	17	25.37
I N	7	10.45
E N	9	13.43
I S	30	44.78
E S	21	31.34
E T	18	26.87
E F	12	17.91
I F	19	28.36
I T	18	26.87
S dom	20	29.85
N dom	7	10.45
T dom	20	29.85
F dom	20	29.85

Note: ■ = 1% of sample

8629383

This table is one of a series of tables from the CAPT-MBTI Data Bank of MBTI records submitted to CAPT for computer scoring between 1971 and June, 1984. This sample was drawn from 59,784 records with usable occupational codes from the total data bank of 232,557. This data bank has 51% Form F cases from 1971 to March, 1978, 35% Form F cases from 1978 to June, 1984 and 14% Form G cases from 1978 to December, 1982. An analysis of Form F and G data banks showed the data banks were comprised of 56% females and 44% males; education level completed: 6% some grade school, 30% high school diploma, 25% some college, 18% bachelor degrees, 11% masters degrees, 3% doctoral or post doctoral work, and 6% unknown. Age group percentages were: 11% under 18, 29% 18 to 20, 12% 21 to 24, 10% 25 to 29, 16% 30 to 39, 10% 40 to 49, 5% 50 to 59, 2% 60 plus, and 5% unknown.

N = 559

	SENSING		INTUITION	
	THINKING	FEELING	FEELING	THINKING

ISTJ	ISFJ	INFJ	INTJ
N= 94	N= 55	N= 13	N= 14
%= 16.82	%= 9.84	%= 2.33	%= 2.50
■■■■■■■■■■■■	■■■■■■■■■	■■	■■■
■■■■■■■			

ISTP	ISFP	INFP	INTP
N= 36	N= 25	N= 34	N= 24
%= 6.44	%= 4.47	%= 6.08	%= 4.29
■■■■■■	■■■■	■■■■■■	■■■■

ESTP	ESFP	ENFP	ENTP
N= 39	N= 30	N= 32	N= 20
%= 6.98	%= 5.37	%= 5.72	%= 3.58
■■■■■■■	■■■■■	■■■■■■	■■■■

ESTJ	ESFJ	ENFJ	ENTJ
N= 74	N= 36	N= 13	N= 20
%= 13.24	%= 6.44	%= 2.33	%= 3.58
■■■■■■■■■■■	■■■■■■■	■■	■■■■
■■■			

JUDGMENT — INTROVERSION
PERCEPTION
PERCEPTION — EXTRAVERSION
JUDGMENT

	N	%
E	264	47.23
I	295	52.77
S	389	69.59
N	170	30.41
T	321	57.42
F	238	42.58
J	319	57.07
P	240	42.93
I J	176	31.48
I P	119	21.29
E P	121	21.65
E J	143	25.58
S T	243	43.47
S F	146	26.12
N F	92	16.46
N T	78	13.95
S J	259	46.33
S P	130	23.26
N P	110	19.68
N J	60	10.73
T J	202	36.14
T P	119	21.29
F P	121	21.65
F J	117	20.93
I N	85	15.21
E N	85	15.21
I S	210	37.57
E S	179	32.02
E T	153	27.37
E F	111	19.86
I F	127	22.72
I T	168	30.05
S dom	218	39.00
N dom	79	14.13
T dom	154	27.55
F dom	108	19.32

Note: ■ = 1% of sample   8629384

This table is one of a series of tables from the CAPT-MBTI Data Bank of MBTI records submitted to CAPT for computer scoring between 1971 and June, 1984. This sample was drawn from 59,784 records with usable occupational codes from the total data bank of 232,557. This data bank has 51% Form F cases from 1971 to March, 1978, 35% Form F cases from 1978 to June, 1984 and 14% Form G cases from 1978 to December, 1982. An analysis of Form F and G data banks showed the data banks were comprised of 56% females and 44% males; education level completed: 6% some grade school, 30% high school diploma, 25% some college, 18% bachelor degrees, 11% masters degrees, 3% doctoral or post doctoral work, and 6% unknown. Age group percentages were: 11% under 18, 29% 18 to 20, 12% 21 to 24, 10% 25 to 29, 16% 30 to 39, 10% 40 to 49, 5% 50 to 59, 2% 60 plus, and 5% unknown.

FARMERS

N = 72

	SENSING		INTUITION	
	THINKING	FEELING	FEELING	THINKING

ISTJ	ISFJ	INFJ	INTJ
N= 11	N= 6	N= 0	N= 2
%= 15.28	%= 8.33	%= 0.00	%= 2.78
■■■■■■■■■■	■■■■■■■■		■■■
■■■■■			

ISTP	ISFP	INFP	INTP
N= 7	N= 3	N= 3	N= 3
%= 9.72	%= 4.17	%= 4.17	%= 4.17
■■■■■■■■■	■■■■	■■■■	■■■■

ESTP	ESFP	ENFP	ENTP
N= 5	N= 4	N= 0	N= 5
%= 6.94	%= 5.56	%= 0.00	%= 6.94
■■■■■■■	■■■■■■		■■■■■■■

ESTJ	ESFJ	ENFJ	ENTJ
N= 14	N= 5	N= 0	N= 4
%= 19.44	%= 6.94	%= 0.00	%= 5.56
■■■■■■■■■■	■■■■■■■		■■■■■■
■■■■■■■■■			

JUDGMENT — INTROVERSION — PERCEPTION — PERCEPTION — EXTRAVERSION — JUDGMENT

	N	%
E	37	51.39
I	35	48.61
S	55	76.39
N	17	23.61
T	51	70.83
F	21	29.17
J	42	58.33
P	30	41.67
I J	19	26.39
I P	16	22.22
E P	14	19.44
E J	23	31.94
S T	37	51.39
S F	18	25.00
N F	3	4.17
N T	14	19.44
S J	36	50.00
S P	19	26.39
N P	11	15.28
N J	6	8.33
T J	31	43.06
T P	20	27.78
F P	10	13.89
F J	11	15.28
I N	8	11.11
E N	9	12.50
I S	27	37.50
E S	28	38.89
E T	28	38.89
E F	9	12.50
I F	12	16.67
I T	23	31.94
S dom	26	36.11
N dom	7	9.72
T dom	28	38.89
F dom	11	15.28

Note: ■ = 1% of sample

8629385

This table is one of a series of tables from the CAPT-MBTI Data Bank of MBTI records submitted to CAPT for computer scoring between 1971 and June, 1984. This sample was drawn from 59,784 records with usable occupational codes from the total data bank of 232,557. This data bank has 51% Form F cases from 1971 to March, 1978, 35% Form F cases from 1978 to June, 1984 and 14% Form G cases from 1978 to December, 1982. An analysis of Form F and G data banks showed the data banks were comprised of 56% females and 44% males; education level completed: 6% some grade school, 30% high school diploma, 25% some college, 18% bachelor degrees, 11% masters degrees, 3% doctoral or post doctoral work, and 6% unknown. Age group percentages were: 11% under 18, 29% 18 to 20, 12% 21 to 24, 10% 25 to 29, 16% 30 to 39, 10% 40 to 49, 5% 50 to 59, 2% 60 plus, and 5% unknown.

FOOD SERVICE WORKERS

N = 1082

	SENSING		INTUITION	
	THINKING	FEELING	FEELING	THINKING

ISTJ	ISFJ	INFJ	INTJ
N= 88	N= 75	N= 39	N= 39
%= 8.13	%= 6.93	%= 3.60	%= 3.60
■■■■■■■■	■■■■■■■	■■■■	■■■■

ISTP	ISFP	INFP	INTP
N= 35	N= 76	N= 88	N= 45
%= 3.23	%= 7.02	%= 8.13	%= 4.16
■■■	■■■■■■■	■■■■■■■■	■■■■

ESTP	ESFP	ENFP	ENTP
N= 40	N= 85	N= 141	N= 59
%= 3.70	%= 7.86	%= 13.03	%= 5.45
■■■■	■■■■■■■■	■■■■■■■■■■■■■	■■■■■
		■■■	

ESTJ	ESFJ	ENFJ	ENTJ
N= 93	N= 100	N= 55	N= 24
%= 8.60	%= 9.24	%= 5.08	%= 2.22
■■■■■■■■■	■■■■■■■■■	■■■■■	■■

	N	%
E	597	55.18
I	485	44.82
S	592	54.71
N	490	45.29
T	423	39.09
F	659	60.91
J	513	47.41
P	569	52.59
I J	241	22.27
I P	244	22.55
E P	325	30.04
E J	272	25.14
S T	256	23.66
S F	336	31.05
N F	323	29.85
N T	167	15.43
S J	356	32.90
S P	236	21.81
N P	333	30.78
N J	157	14.51
T J	244	22.55
T P	179	16.54
F P	390	36.04
F J	269	24.86
I N	211	19.50
E N	279	25.79
I S	274	25.32
E S	318	29.39
E T	216	19.96
E F	381	35.21
I F	278	25.69
I T	207	19.13
S dom	288	26.62
N dom	278	25.69
T dom	197	18.21
F dom	319	29.48

Note: ■ = 1% of sample   8629386

This table is one of a series of tables from the CAPT-MBTI Data Bank of MBTI records submitted to CAPT for computer scoring between 1971 and June, 1984. This sample was drawn from 59,784 records with usable occupational codes from the total data bank of 232,557. This data bank has 51% Form F cases from 1971 to March, 1978, 35% Form F cases from 1978 to June, 1984 and 14% Form G cases from 1978 to December, 1982. An analysis of Form F and G data banks showed the data banks were comprised of 56% females and 44% males; education level completed: 6% some grade school, 30% high school diploma, 25% some college, 18% bachelor degrees, 11% masters degrees, 3% doctoral or post doctoral work, and 6% unknown. Age group percentages were: 11% under 18, 29% 18 to 20, 12% 21 to 24, 10% 25 to 29, 16% 30 to 39, 10% 40 to 49, 5% 50 to 59, 2% 60 plus, and 5% unknown.

LABORERS

N = 782

		SENSING		INTUITION		
	THINKING	FEELING	FEELING	THINKING		

<table>
<tr>
<td>
ISTJ
N= 75
%= 9.59
■■■■■■■■■■
</td>
<td>
ISFJ
N= 53
%= 6.78
■■■■■■■
</td>
<td>
INFJ
N= 23
%= 2.94
■■■
</td>
<td>
INTJ
N= 17
%= 2.17
■■
</td>
</tr>
<tr>
<td>
ISTP
N= 62
%= 7.93
■■■■■■■■
</td>
<td>
ISFP
N= 45
%= 5.75
■■■■■■
</td>
<td>
INFP
N= 59
%= 7.54
■■■■■■■■
</td>
<td>
INTP
N= 29
%= 3.71
■■■■
</td>
</tr>
<tr>
<td>
ESTP
N= 53
%= 6.78
■■■■■■■
</td>
<td>
ESFP
N= 50
%= 6.39
■■■■■■
</td>
<td>
ENFP
N= 72
%= 9.21
■■■■■■■■■
</td>
<td>
ENTP
N= 44
%= 5.63
■■■■■■
</td>
</tr>
<tr>
<td>
ESTJ
N= 89
%= 11.38
■■■■■■■■■■■
■
</td>
<td>
ESFJ
N= 67
%= 8.57
■■■■■■■■■
</td>
<td>
ENFJ
N= 19
%= 2.43
■■
</td>
<td>
ENTJ
N= 25
%= 3.20
■■■
</td>
</tr>
</table>

JUDGMENT · INTROVERSION · PERCEPTION · PERCEPTION · EXTRAVERSION · JUDGMENT

	N	%
E	419	53.58
I	363	46.42
S	494	63.17
N	288	36.83
T	394	50.38
F	388	49.62
J	368	47.06
P	414	52.94
I J	168	21.48
I P	195	24.94
E P	219	28.01
E J	200	25.58
S T	279	35.68
S F	215	27.49
N F	173	22.12
N T	115	14.71
S J	284	36.32
S P	210	26.85
N P	204	26.09
N J	84	10.74
T J	206	26.34
T P	188	24.04
F P	226	28.90
F J	162	20.72
I N	128	16.37
E N	160	20.46
I S	235	30.05
E S	259	33.12
E T	211	26.98
E F	208	26.60
I F	180	23.02
I T	183	23.40
S dom	231	29.54
N dom	156	19.95
T dom	205	26.21
F dom	190	24.30

Note: ■ = 1% of sample   8629387

This table is one of a series of tables from the CAPT-MBTI Data Bank of MBTI records submitted to CAPT for computer scoring between 1971 and June, 1984. This sample was drawn from 59,784 records with usable occupational codes from the total data bank of 232,557. This data bank has 51% Form F cases from 1971 to March, 1978, 35% Form F cases from 1978 to June, 1984 and 14% Form G cases from 1978 to December, 1982. An analysis of Form F and G data banks showed the data banks were comprised of 56% females and 44% males; education level completed: 6% some grade school, 30% high school diploma, 25% some college, 18% bachelor degrees, 11% masters degrees, 3% doctoral or post doctoral work, and 6% unknown. Age group percentages were: 11% under 18, 29% 18 to 20, 12% 21 to 24, 10% 25 to 29, 16% 30 to 39, 10% 40 to 49, 5% 50 to 59, 2% 60 plus, and 5% unknown.

MECHANICS

N = 669

	SENSING		INTUITION	
	THINKING	FEELING	FEELING	THINKING

ISTJ	ISFJ	INFJ	INTJ
N= 83	N= 63	N= 13	N= 22
%= 12.41	%= 9.42	%= 1.94	%= 3.29
■■■■■■■■■■■■ ■■	■■■■■■■■■	■■	■■■

ISTP	ISFP	INFP	INTP
N= 53	N= 37	N= 45	N= 18
%= 7.92	%= 5.53	%= 6.73	%= 2.69
■■■■■■■■	■■■■■■	■■■■■■■	■■■

ESTP	ESFP	ENFP	ENTP
N= 27	N= 36	N= 55	N= 35
%= 4.04	%= 5.38	%= 8.22	%= 5.23
■■■■	■■■■■	■■■■■■■■	■■■■■

ESTJ	ESFJ	ENFJ	ENTJ
N= 88	N= 50	N= 18	N= 26
%= 13.15	%= 7.47	%= 2.69	%= 3.89
■■■■■■■■■■■■■ ■■■	■■■■■■■■	■■■	■■■■

JUDGMENT — INTROVERSION — PERCEPTION — PERCEPTION — EXTRAVERSION — JUDGMENT

	N	%
E	335	50.07
I	334	49.93
S	437	65.32
N	232	34.68
T	352	52.62
F	317	47.38
J	363	54.26
P	306	45.74
I J	181	27.06
I P	153	22.87
E P	153	22.87
E J	182	27.20
S T	251	37.52
S F	186	27.80
N F	131	19.58
N T	101	15.10
S J	284	42.45
S P	153	22.87
N P	153	22.87
N J	79	11.81
T J	219	32.74
T P	133	19.88
F P	173	25.86
F J	144	21.52
I N	98	14.65
E N	134	20.03
I S	236	35.28
E S	201	30.04
E T	176	26.31
E F	159	23.77
I F	158	23.62
I T	176	26.31
S dom	209	31.24
N dom	125	18.68
T dom	185	27.65
F dom	150	22.42

Note: ■ = 1% of sample   8629388

This table is one of a series of tables from the CAPT-MBTI Data Bank of MBTI records submitted to CAPT for computer scoring between 1971 and June, 1984. This sample was drawn from 59,784 records with usable occupational codes from the total data bank of 232,557. This data bank has 51% Form F cases from 1971 to March, 1978, 35% Form F cases from 1978 to June, 1984 and 14% Form G cases from 1978 to December, 1982. An analysis of Form F and G data banks showed the data banks were comprised of 56% females and 44% males; education level completed: 6% some grade school, 30% high school diploma, 25% some college, 18% bachelor degrees, 11% masters degrees, 3% doctoral or post doctoral work, and 6% unknown. Age group percentages were: 11% under 18, 29% 18 to 20, 12% 21 to 24, 10% 25 to 29, 16% 30 to 39, 10% 40 to 49, 5% 50 to 59, 2% 60 plus, and 5% unknown.

OPERATIVES: NON-SPECIALIZED
AND FACTORY WORKERS

N = 97

	SENSING		INTUITION				N	%
	THINKING	FEELING	FEELING	THINKING				

ISTJ	ISFJ	INFJ	INTJ
N= 16	N= 10	N= 2	N= 3
%= 16.49	%= 10.31	%= 2.06	%= 3.09
■■■■■■■■■■■■■■■■	■■■■■■■■■■	■■	■■■

ISTP	ISFP	INFP	INTP
N= 4	N= 7	N= 4	N= 5
%= 4.12	%= 7.22	%= 4.12	%= 5.15
■■■■	■■■■■■■	■■■■	■■■■■

ESTP	ESFP	ENFP	ENTP
N= 6	N= 6	N= 5	N= 2
%= 6.19	%= 6.19	%= 5.15	%= 2.06
■■■■■■	■■■■■■	■■■■■	■■

ESTJ	ESFJ	ENFJ	ENTJ
N= 9	N= 9	N= 5	N= 4
%= 9.28	%= 9.28	%= 5.15	%= 4.12
■■■■■■■■■	■■■■■■■■■	■■■■■	■■■■

Right side vertical labels: JUDGMENT — INTROVERSION — PERCEPTION — PERCEPTION — EXTRAVERSION — JUDGMENT

	N	%
E	46	47.42
I	51	52.58
S	67	69.07
N	30	30.93
T	49	50.52
F	48	49.48
J	58	59.79
P	39	40.21
I J	31	31.96
I P	20	20.62
E P	19	19.59
E J	27	27.84
ST	35	36.08
SF	32	32.99
NF	16	16.49
NT	14	14.43
S J	44	45.36
S P	23	23.71
N P	16	16.49
N J	14	14.43
T J	32	32.99
T P	17	17.53
F P	22	22.68
F J	26	26.80
I N	14	14.43
E N	16	16.49
I S	37	38.14
E S	30	30.93
E T	21	21.65
E F	25	25.77
I F	23	23.71
I T	28	28.87
S dom	38	39.18
N dom	12	12.37
T dom	22	22.68
F dom	25	25.77

Note: ■ = 1% of sample

8629389

This table is one of a series of tables from the CAPT-MBTI Data Bank of MBTI records submitted to CAPT for computer scoring between 1971 and June, 1984. This sample was drawn from 59,784 records with usable occupational codes from the total data bank of 232,557. This data bank has 51% Form F cases from 1971 to March, 1978, 35% Form F cases from 1978 to June, 1984 and 14% Form G cases from 1978 to December, 1982. An analysis of Form F and G data banks showed the data banks were comprised of 56% females and 44% males; education level completed: 6% some grade school, 30% high school diploma, 25% some college, 18% bachelor degrees, 11% masters degrees, 3% doctoral or post doctoral work, and 6% unknown. Age group percentages were: 11% under 18, 29% 18 to 20, 12% 21 to 24, 10% 25 to 29, 16% 30 to 39, 10% 40 to 49, 5% 50 to 59, 2% 60 plus, and 5% unknown.

N = 206

	SENSING		INTUITION	
	THINKING	FEELING	FEELING	THINKING

ISTJ	ISFJ	INFJ	INTJ
N= 30	N= 17	N= 2	N= 6
%= 14.56	%= 8.25	%= .97	%= 2.91
■■■■■■■■■■■■■■	■■■■■■■■	■	■■■
■■■■■			

ISTP	ISFP	INFP	INTP
N= 11	N= 19	N= 16	N= 11
%= 5.34	%= 9.22	%= 7.77	%= 5.34
■■■■■	■■■■■■■■■	■■■■■■■■	■■■■■

ESTP	ESFP	ENFP	ENTP
N= 4	N= 10	N= 15	N= 6
%= 1.94	%= 4.85	%= 7.28	%= 2.91
■■	■■■■■	■■■■■■■	■■■

ESTJ	ESFJ	ENFJ	ENTJ
N= 22	N= 18	N= 6	N= 13
%= 10.68	%= 8.74	%= 2.91	%= 6.31
■■■■■■■■■■	■■■■■■■■■	■■■	■■■■■■
■			

	N	%
E	94	45.63
I	112	54.37
S	131	63.59
N	75	36.41
T	103	50.00
F	103	50.00
J	114	55.34
P	92	44.66
I J	55	26.70
I P	57	27.67
E P	35	16.99
E J	59	28.64
S T	67	32.52
S F	64	31.07
N F	39	18.93
N T	36	17.48
S J	87	42.23
S P	44	21.36
N P	48	23.30
N J	27	13.11
T J	71	34.47
T P	32	15.53
F P	60	29.13
F J	43	20.87
I N	35	16.99
E N	40	19.42
I S	77	37.38
E S	54	26.21
E T	45	21.84
E F	49	23.79
I F	54	26.21
I T	58	28.16
S dom	61	29.61
N dom	29	14.08
T dom	57	27.67
F dom	59	28.64

Note: ■ = 1% of sample   8629390

This table is one of a series of tables from the CAPT-MBTI Data Bank of MBTI records submitted to CAPT for computer scoring between 1971 and June, 1984. This sample was drawn from 59,784 records with usable occupational codes from the total data bank of 232,557. This data bank has 51% Form F cases from 1971 to March, 1978, 35% Form F cases from 1978 to June, 1984 and 14% Form G cases from 1978 to December, 1982. An analysis of Form F and G data banks showed the data banks were comprised of 56% females and 44% males; education level completed: 6% some grade school, 30% high school diploma, 25% some college, 18% bachelor degrees, 11% masters degrees, 3% doctoral or post doctoral work, and 6% unknown. Age group percentages were: 11% under 18, 29% 18 to 20, 12% 21 to 24, 10% 25 to 29, 16% 30 to 39, 10% 40 to 49, 5% 50 to 59, 2% 60 plus, and 5% unknown.

OPERATIVES: TRANSPORTATION

N = 144

	SENSING		INTUITION	
	THINKING	FEELING	FEELING	THINKING

ISTJ	ISFJ	INFJ	INTJ
N= 20	N= 19	N= 6	N= 4
%= 13.89	%= 13.19	%= 4.17	%= 2.78
██████████	██████████	████	███
████	███		

ISTP	ISFP	INFP	INTP
N= 12	N= 5	N= 7	N= 2
%= 8.33	%= 3.47	%= 4.86	%= 1.39
████████	███	█████	█

ESTP	ESFP	ENFP	ENTP
N= 9	N= 15	N= 3	N= 6
%= 6.25	%= 10.42	%= 2.08	%= 4.17
██████	██████████	██	████

ESTJ	ESFJ	ENFJ	ENTJ
N= 15	N= 11	N= 6	N= 4
%= 10.42	%= 7.64	%= 4.17	%= 2.78
██████████	████████	████	███

JUDGMENT — **INTROVERSION** — **PERCEPTION** — **PERCEPTION** — **EXTRAVERSION** — **JUDGMENT**

	N	%
E	69	47.92
I	75	52.08
S	106	73.61
N	38	26.39
T	72	50.00
F	72	50.00
J	85	59.03
P	59	40.97
I J	49	34.03
I P	26	18.06
E P	33	22.92
E J	36	25.00
S T	56	38.89
S F	50	34.72
N F	22	15.28
N T	16	11.11
S J	65	45.14
S P	41	28.47
N P	18	12.50
N J	20	13.89
T J	43	29.86
T P	29	20.14
F P	30	20.83
F J	42	29.17
I N	19	13.19
E N	19	13.19
I S	56	38.89
E S	50	34.72
E T	34	23.61
E F	35	24.31
I F	37	25.69
I T	38	26.39
S dom	63	43.75
N dom	19	13.19
T dom	33	22.92
F dom	29	20.14

Note: ■ = 1% of sample   8629393

This table is one of a series of tables from the CAPT-MBTI Data Bank of MBTI records submitted to CAPT for computer scoring between 1971 and June, 1984. This sample was drawn from 59,784 records with usable occupational codes from the total data bank of 232,557. This data bank has 51% Form F cases from 1971 to March, 1978, 35% Form F cases from 1978 to June, 1984 and 14% Form G cases from 1978 to December, 1982. An analysis of Form F and G data banks showed the data banks were comprised of 56% females and 44% males; education level completed: 6% some grade school, 30% high school diploma, 25% some college, 18% bachelor degrees, 11% masters degrees, 3% doctoral or post doctoral work, and 6% unknown. Age group percentages were: 11% under 18, 29% 18 to 20, 12% 21 to 24, 10% 25 to 29, 16% 30 to 39, 10% 40 to 49, 5% 50 to 59, 2% 60 plus, and 5% unknown.

PERSONAL SERVICE WORKERS

N = 783

	SENSING			INTUITION					N	%
	THINKING	FEELING		FEELING	THINKING					

<table>
<tr><th colspan="4"></th><th></th><th>N</th><th>%</th></tr>
<tr>
<td>ISTJ
N= 74
%= 9.45
■■■■■■■■■</td>
<td>ISFJ
N= 90
%= 11.49
■■■■■■■■■■
■</td>
<td>INFJ
N= 22
%= 2.81
■■■</td>
<td>INTJ
N= 17
%= 2.17
■■</td>
<td rowspan="2">JUDGMENT
INTROVERSION</td>
<td>E
I
S
N
T
F
J
P</td>
<td>452
331
486
297
330
453
464
319</td>
<td>57.73
42.27
62.07
37.93
42.15
57.85
59.26
40.74</td>
</tr>
<tr>
<td>ISTP
N= 18
%= 2.30
■■</td>
<td>ISFP
N= 39
%= 4.98
■■■■■</td>
<td>INFP
N= 48
%= 6.13
■■■■■■</td>
<td>INTP
N= 23
%= 2.94
■■■</td>
<td>PERCEPTION</td>
<td>I J
I P
E P
E J</td>
<td>203
128
191
261</td>
<td>25.93
16.35
24.39
33.33</td>
</tr>
<tr>
<td rowspan="2"></td><td rowspan="2"></td><td rowspan="2"></td><td rowspan="2"></td><td rowspan="2"></td>
<td>ST
SF
NF
NT</td>
<td>223
263
190
107</td>
<td>28.48
33.59
24.27
13.67</td>
</tr>
<tr>
<td>S J
S P
N P
N J</td>
<td>352
134
185
112</td>
<td>44.96
17.11
23.63
14.30</td>
</tr>
<tr>
<td>ESTP
N= 35
%= 4.47
■■■■</td>
<td>ESFP
N= 42
%= 5.36
■■■■■</td>
<td>ENFP
N= 80
%= 10.22
■■■■■■■■■■</td>
<td>ENTP
N= 34
%= 4.34
■■■■</td>
<td>PERCEPTION
EXTRAVERSION</td>
<td>T J
T P
F P
F J</td>
<td>220
110
209
244</td>
<td>28.10
14.05
26.69
31.16</td>
</tr>
<tr>
<td rowspan="2"></td><td rowspan="2"></td><td rowspan="2"></td><td rowspan="2"></td><td rowspan="2"></td>
<td>IN
EN
IS
ES</td>
<td>110
187
221
265</td>
<td>14.05
23.88
28.22
33.84</td>
</tr>
<tr>
<td>ET
EF
I F
I T</td>
<td>198
254
199
132</td>
<td>25.29
32.44
25.42
16.86</td>
</tr>
<tr>
<td>ESTJ
N= 96
%= 12.26
■■■■■■■■■■■■
■■</td>
<td>ESFJ
N= 92
%= 11.75
■■■■■■■■■■■
■■</td>
<td>ENFJ
N= 40
%= 5.11
■■■■■</td>
<td>ENTJ
N= 33
%= 4.21
■■■■</td>
<td>JUDGMENT</td>
<td>S dom
N dom
T dom
F dom</td>
<td>241
153
170
219</td>
<td>30.78
19.54
21.71
27.97</td>
</tr>
</table>

Note: ■ = 1% of sample   8629391

This table is one of a series of tables from the CAPT-MBTI Data Bank of MBTI records submitted to CAPT for computer scoring between 1971 and June, 1984. This sample was drawn from 59,784 records with usable occupational codes from the total data bank of 232,557. This data bank has 51% Form F cases from 1971 to March, 1978, 35% Form F cases from 1978 to June, 1984 and 14% Form G cases from 1978 to December, 1982. An analysis of Form F and G data banks showed the data banks were comprised of 56% females and 44% males; education level completed: 6% some grade school, 30% high school diploma, 25% some college, 18% bachelor degrees, 11% masters degrees, 3% doctoral or post doctoral work, and 6% unknown. Age group percentages were: 11% under 18, 29% 18 to 20, 12% 21 to 24, 10% 25 to 29, 16% 30 to 39, 10% 40 to 49, 5% 50 to 59, 2% 60 plus, and 5% unknown.

N = 3064

		SENSING			INTUITION					N	%

	THINKING	FEELING	FEELING	THINKING

ISTJ	**ISFJ**	**INFJ**	**INTJ**
N= 197	N= 559	N= 168	N= 69
%= 6.43	%= 18.24	%= 5.48	%= 2.25
■■■■■■	■■■■■■■■■ ■■■■■■■■■	■■■■■	■■

ISTP	**ISFP**	**INFP**	**INTP**
N= 55	N= 207	N= 214	N= 51
%= 1.80	%= 6.76	%= 6.98	%= 1.66
■■	■■■■■■	■■■■■■■	■■

ESTP	**ESFP**	**ENFP**	**ENTP**
N= 52	N= 193	N= 311	N= 67
%= 1.70	%= 6.30	%= 10.15	%= 2.19
■■	■■■■■■	■■■■■■■■■■	■■

ESTJ	**ESFJ**	**ENFJ**	**ENTJ**
N= 216	N= 400	N= 224	N= 81
%= 7.05	%= 13.05	%= 7.31	%= 2.64
■■■■■■■	■■■■■■■■■■■■■ ■■■	■■■■■■■	■■■

JUDGMENT — INTROVERSION — PERCEPTION — PERCEPTION — EXTRAVERSION — JUDGMENT

	N	%
E	1544	50.39
I	1520	49.61
S	1879	61.33
N	1185	38.67
T	788	25.72
F	2276	74.28
J	1914	62.47
P	1150	37.53
I J	993	32.41
I P	527	17.20
E P	623	20.33
E J	921	30.06
S T	520	16.97
S F	1359	44.35
N F	917	29.93
N T	268	8.75
S J	1372	44.78
S P	507	16.55
N P	643	20.99
N J	542	17.69
T J	563	18.37
T P	225	7.34
F P	925	30.19
F J	1351	44.09
I N	502	16.38
E N	683	22.29
I S	1018	33.22
E S	861	28.10
E T	416	13.58
E F	1128	36.81
I F	1148	37.47
I T	372	12.14
S dom	1001	32.67
N dom	615	20.07
T dom	403	13.15
F dom	1045	34.11

Note: ■ = 1% of sample

8629392

This table is one of a series of tables from the CAPT-MBTI Data Bank of MBTI records submitted to CAPT for computer scoring between 1971 and June, 1984. This sample was drawn from 59,784 records with usable occupational codes from the total data bank of 232,557. This data bank has 51% Form F cases from 1971 to March, 1978, 35% Form F cases from 1978 to June, 1984 and 14% Form G cases from 1978 to December, 1982. An analysis of Form F and G data banks showed the data banks were comprised of 56% females and 44% males; education level completed: 6% some grade school, 30% high school diploma, 25% some college, 18% bachelor degrees, 11% masters degrees, 3% doctoral or post doctoral work, and 6% unknown. Age group percentages were: 11% under 18, 29% 18 to 20, 12% 21 to 24, 10% 25 to 29, 16% 30 to 39, 10% 40 to 49, 5% 50 to 59, 2% 60 plus, and 5% unknown.

E Percent	I	Total Sample Size	Sample Description
64.71	35.29	51	Restaurant Workers: Table Setting and Cleaning
63.79	36.21	58	Home Management Advisors and Home Economists
59.71	40.29	139	Construction Laborers (except carpenters helpers)
58.18	41.82	55	Child Care Workers (except private household)
57.73	42.27	783	PERSONAL SERVICE WORKERS
57.35	42.65	211	Lifeguards, Attendants, Recreation and Amusement
57.29	42.71	96	Hairdressers, Cosmetologists and Manicurists
56.48	43.52	540	Waiters and Waitresses
55.74	44.26	61	Food Counter and Fountain Workers
55.18	44.82	1082	FOOD SERVICE WORKERS
53.85	46.15	52	Factory and Site Supervisors
53.58	46.42	782	LABORERS
51.48	48.52	169	Service Workers (except private household)
51.39	48.61	72	FARMERS
50.39	49.61	3064	PRIVATE HOUSEHOLD WORKERS
50.07	49.93	669	MECHANICS
49.44	50.56	180	Cooks (except private household)
48.98	51.02	196	Displaced Coal Miners
48.62	51.38	109	Carpenters
47.92	52.08	144	OPERATIVES: TRANSPORTATION
47.42	52.58	97	OPERATIVES: NON-SPECIALIZED AND FACTORY WORKERS
47.23	52.77	559	CRAFT WORKERS
45.63	54.37	206	OPERATIVES: SPECIALIZED
44.78	55.22	67	CLEANING SERVICES
44.29	55.71	70	Electricians
42.86	57.14	105	Steelworkers
42.59	57.41	54	Chain, Rod and Ax Workers; Surveying
39.97	60.03	658	Displaced Steelworkers
39.39	60.61	132	School Bus Drivers
39.17	60.83	240	Foremen in Japanese Food Production Company
35.63	64.37	334	Operators and Field Technicians in Water Pollution Control

SENSING-INTUITION

S Percent	N	Total Sample Size	Sample Description
96.21	3.79	132	School Bus Drivers
85.71	14.29	105	Steelworkers
85.41	14.59	658	Displaced Steelworkers
84.62	15.38	52	Factory and Site Supervisors
82.08	17.92	240	Foremen in Japanese Food Production Company
80.61	19.39	196	Displaced Coal Miners
77.84	22.16	334	Operators and Field Technicians in Water Pollution Contr
76.39	23.61	72	FARMERS
76.12	23.88	67	CLEANING SERVICES
73.61	26.39	144	OPERATIVES: TRANSPORTATION
72.19	27.81	169	Service Workers (except private household)
70.83	29.17	96	Hairdressers, Cosmetologists and Manicurists
69.59	30.41	559	CRAFT WORKERS
69.07	30.93	97	OPERATIVES: NON-SPECIALIZED AND FACTORY WORKERS
66.91	33.09	139	Construction Laborers (except carpenters helpers)
65.45	34.55	55	Child Care Workers (except private household)
65.32	34.68	669	MECHANICS
63.59	36.41	206	OPERATIVES: SPECIALIZED
63.17	36.83	782	LABORERS
63.03	36.97	211	Lifeguards, Attendants, Recreation and Amusement
62.07	37.93	783	PERSONAL SERVICE WORKERS
61.47	38.53	109	Carpenters
61.43	38.57	70	Electricians
61.33	38.67	3064	PRIVATE HOUSEHOLD WORKERS
57.38	42.62	61	Food Counter and Fountain Workers
56.90	43.10	58	Home Management Advisors and Home Economists
56.11	43.89	180	Cooks (except private household)
54.71	45.29	1082	FOOD SERVICE WORKERS
50.98	49.02	51	Restaurant Workers: Table Setting and Cleaning
50.56	49.44	540	Waiters and Waitresses
48.15	51.85	54	Chain, Rod and Ax Workers; Surveying

T Percent F	Total Sample Size	Sample Description
87.13 12.87	334	Operators and Field Technicians in Water Pollution Control
74.32 25.68	658	Displaced Steelworkers
74.29 25.71	105	Steelworkers
72.78 27.22	169	Service Workers (except private household)
71.43 28.57	196	Displaced Coal Miners
70.83 29.17	72	FARMERS
58.33 41.67	132	School Bus Drivers
57.42 42.58	559	CRAFT WORKERS
57.14 42.86	70	Electricians
55.77 44.23	52	Factory and Site Supervisors
53.73 46.27	67	CLEANING SERVICES
52.62 47.38	669	MECHANICS
50.52 49.48	97	OPERATIVES: NON-SPECIALIZED AND FACTORY WORKERS
50.38 49.62	782	LABORERS
50.36 49.64	139	Construction Laborers (except carpenters helpers)
50.00 50.00	206	OPERATIVES: SPECIALIZED
50.00 50.00	144	OPERATIVES: TRANSPORTATION
49.44 50.56	180	Cooks (except private household)
46.30 53.70	54	Chain, Rod and Ax Workers; Surveying
44.95 55.05	109	Carpenters
44.55 55.45	211	Lifeguards, Attendants, Recreation and Amusement
42.15 57.85	783	PERSONAL SERVICE WORKERS
40.62 59.37	96	Hairdressers, Cosmetologists and Manicurists
39.09 60.91	1082	FOOD SERVICE WORKERS
38.33 61.67	240	Foremen in Japanese Food Production Company
37.70 62.30	61	Food Counter and Fountain Workers
37.25 62.75	51	Restaurant Workers: Table Setting and Cleaning
34.48 65.52	58	Home Management Advisors and Home Economists
33.33 66.67	540	Waiters and Waitresses
32.73 67.27	55	Child Care Workers (except private household)
25.72 74.28	3064	PRIVATE HOUSEHOLD WORKERS

J Percent	P	Total Sample Size	Sample Description
81.06	18.94	132	School Bus Drivers
79.03	20.97	658	Displaced Steelworkers
78.14	21.86	334	Operators and Field Technicians in Water Pollution Contr
77.59	22.41	58	Home Management Advisors and Home Economists
75.00	25.00	196	Displaced Coal Miners
73.33	26.67	105	Steelworkers
72.08	27.92	240	Foremen in Japanese Food Production Company
67.71	32.29	96	Hairdressers, Cosmetologists and Manicurists
67.31	32.69	52	Factory and Site Supervisors
67.16	32.84	67	CLEANING SERVICES
62.47	37.53	3064	PRIVATE HOUSEHOLD WORKERS
59.79	40.21	97	OPERATIVES: NON-SPECIALIZED AND FACTORY WORKERS
59.26	40.74	783	PERSONAL SERVICE WORKERS
59.03	40.97	144	OPERATIVES: TRANSPORTATION
59.02	40.98	61	Food Counter and Fountain Workers
58.33	41.67	72	FARMERS
57.40	42.60	169	Service Workers (except private household)
57.07	42.93	559	CRAFT WORKERS
55.71	44.29	70	Electricians
55.34	44.66	206	OPERATIVES: SPECIALIZED
54.55	45.45	55	Child Care Workers (except private household)
54.26	45.74	669	MECHANICS
51.66	48.34	211	Lifeguards, Attendants, Recreation and Amusement
51.11	48.89	180	Cooks (except private household)
51.08	48.92	139	Construction Laborers (except carpenters helpers)
47.41	52.59	1082	FOOD SERVICE WORKERS
47.06	52.94	782	LABORERS
44.26	55.74	540	Waiters and Waitresses
43.12	56.88	109	Carpenters
41.18	58.82	51	Restaurant Workers: Table Setting and Cleaning
38.89	61.11	54	Chain, Rod and Ax Workers; Surveying

Percent ST	Total Sample Size	Sample Description
68.26	334	Operators and Field Technicians in Water Pollution Control
66.67	105	Steelworkers
63.22	658	Displaced Steelworkers
55.61	196	Displaced Coal Miners
55.30	132	School Bus Drivers
55.03	169	Service Workers (except private household)
51.39	72	FARMERS
49.25	67	CLEANING SERVICES
48.08	52	Factory and Site Supervisors
43.47	559	CRAFT WORKERS
38.89	144	OPERATIVES: TRANSPORTATION
37.52	669	MECHANICS
36.08	97	OPERATIVES: NON-SPECIALIZED AND FACTORY WORKERS
35.68	782	LABORERS
34.53	139	Construction Laborers (except carpenters helpers)
34.44	180	Cooks (except private household)
34.29	70	Electricians
33.03	109	Carpenters
32.52	206	OPERATIVES: SPECIALIZED
30.81	211	Lifeguards, Attendants, Recreation and Amusement
30.21	96	Hairdressers, Cosmetologists and Manicurists
29.58	240	Foremen in Japanese Food Production Company
28.48	783	PERSONAL SERVICE WORKERS
25.86	58	Home Management Advisors and Home Economists
23.66	1082	FOOD SERVICE WORKERS
22.22	54	Chain, Rod and Ax Workers; Surveying
18.15	540	Waiters and Waitresses
18.03	61	Food Counter and Fountain Workers
17.65	51	Restaurant Workers: Table Setting and Cleaning
16.97	3064	PRIVATE HOUSEHOLD WORKERS
16.36	55	Child Care Workers (except private household)

SENSING-FEELING

Percent SF	Total Sample Size	Sample Description
52.50	240	Foremen in Japanese Food Production Company
49.09	55	Child Care Workers (except private household)
44.35	3064	PRIVATE HOUSEHOLD WORKERS
40.91	132	School Bus Drivers
40.62	96	Hairdressers, Cosmetologists and Manicurists
39.34	61	Food Counter and Fountain Workers
36.54	52	Factory and Site Supervisors
34.72	144	OPERATIVES: TRANSPORTATION
33.59	783	PERSONAL SERVICE WORKERS
33.33	51	Restaurant Workers: Table Setting and Cleaning
32.99	97	OPERATIVES: NON-SPECIALIZED AND FACTORY WORKERS
32.41	540	Waiters and Waitresses
32.37	139	Construction Laborers (except carpenters helpers)
32.23	211	Lifeguards, Attendants, Recreation and Amusement
31.07	206	OPERATIVES: SPECIALIZED
31.05	1082	FOOD SERVICE WORKERS
31.03	58	Home Management Advisors and Home Economists
28.44	109	Carpenters
27.80	669	MECHANICS
27.49	782	LABORERS
27.14	70	Electricians
26.87	67	CLEANING SERVICES
26.12	559	CRAFT WORKERS
25.93	54	Chain, Rod and Ax Workers; Surveying
25.00	196	Displaced Coal Miners
25.00	72	FARMERS
22.19	658	Displaced Steelworkers
21.67	180	Cooks (except private household)
19.05	105	Steelworkers
17.16	169	Service Workers (except private household)
9.58	334	Operators and Field Technicians in Water Pollution Control

Percent NF	Total Sample Size	Sample Description
34.48	58	Home Management Advisors and Home Economists
34.26	540	Waiters and Waitresses
29.93	3064	PRIVATE HOUSEHOLD WORKERS
29.85	1082	FOOD SERVICE WORKERS
29.41	51	Restaurant Workers: Table Setting and Cleaning
28.89	180	Cooks (except private household)
27.78	54	Chain, Rod and Ax Workers; Surveying
26.61	109	Carpenters
24.27	783	PERSONAL SERVICE WORKERS
23.22	211	Lifeguards, Attendants, Recreation and Amusement
22.95	61	Food Counter and Fountain Workers
22.12	782	LABORERS
19.58	669	MECHANICS
19.40	67	CLEANING SERVICES
18.93	206	OPERATIVES: SPECIALIZED
18.75	96	Hairdressers, Cosmetologists and Manicurists
18.18	55	Child Care Workers (except private household)
17.27	139	Construction Laborers (except carpenters helpers)
16.49	97	OPERATIVES: NON-SPECIALIZED AND FACTORY WORKERS
16.46	559	CRAFT WORKERS
15.71	70	Electricians
15.28	144	OPERATIVES: TRANSPORTATION
10.06	169	Service Workers (except private household)
9.17	240	Foremen in Japanese Food Production Company
7.69	52	Factory and Site Supervisors
6.67	105	Steelworkers
4.17	72	FARMERS
3.57	196	Displaced Coal Miners
3.50	658	Displaced Steelworkers
3.29	334	Operators and Field Technicians in Water Pollution Control
.76	132	School Bus Drivers

INTUITION-THINKING

Percent NT	Total Sample Size	Sample Description
24.07	54	Chain, Rod and Ax Workers; Surveying
22.86	70	Electricians
19.67	61	Food Counter and Fountain Workers
19.61	51	Restaurant Workers: Table Setting and Cleaning
19.44	72	FARMERS
18.86	334	Operators and Field Technicians in Water Pollution Control
17.75	169	Service Workers (except private household)
17.48	206	OPERATIVES: SPECIALIZED
16.36	55	Child Care Workers (except private household)
15.83	139	Construction Laborers (except carpenters helpers)
15.82	196	Displaced Coal Miners
15.43	1082	FOOD SERVICE WORKERS
15.19	540	Waiters and Waitresses
15.10	669	MECHANICS
15.00	180	Cooks (except private household)
14.71	782	LABORERS
14.43	97	OPERATIVES: NON-SPECIALIZED AND FACTORY WORKERS
13.95	559	CRAFT WORKERS
13.74	211	Lifeguards, Attendants, Recreation and Amusement
13.67	783	PERSONAL SERVICE WORKERS
11.93	109	Carpenters
11.11	144	OPERATIVES: TRANSPORTATION
11.09	658	Displaced Steelworkers
10.42	96	Hairdressers, Cosmetologists and Manicurists
8.75	3064	PRIVATE HOUSEHOLD WORKERS
8.75	240	Foremen in Japanese Food Production Company
8.62	58	Home Management Advisors and Home Economists
7.69	52	Factory and Site Supervisors
7.62	105	Steelworkers
4.48	67	CLEANING SERVICES
3.03	132	School Bus Drivers

RELIGION

Section X

RELIGION

Samples in Section X

Name of Sample	Number in Sample
Brothers in Roman Catholic Religious Orders	114
Candidates for Theology Education	1205
Clergy, all denominations (except priests)	534
Directors of Religious Education	50
Nuns and Other Religious Workers	1147
Ordained Roman Catholic Deacons	102
Priests and Monks	219
Protestant Ministers	1554
Protestant Seminarians	633
Protestants in Specialized Ministries	85
Rabbis	319
Religious Educator, all denominations	79
Roman Catholic Priests	1298
Roman Catholic Seminarians	51
Sisters in Roman Catholic Religious Orders	2002

Composite Samples

RELIGIOUS WORKERS -ALL DENOMINATIONS-	2010

Comments

The samples of this section tend mainly to be people concerned with ministry and religion as a vocation. These include teachers in seminaries, ministers, religious educators and members of religious orders. CAPT owes a special debt to Dr. Randall Ruppart who gave us permission to share the type distributions from the large samples he collected as part of his doctoral dissertation (Ruppart, 1985).

In the very early type tables for samples in ministry, feeling types outnumbered thinking types, a fact that seemed reasonable since feeling is the function concerned with values. In present-day samples feeling types remain in the majority in both males and females. The most striking feature of tables in this section is the substantial proportion of FJ types in almost every table.

Look also for those in active ministry to include relatively more extraverts.

As with all other areas, expect groups with higher education or where innovation seems to be required to have more intuitive types. In other fields of education, higher education faculty often have somewhat more of the rare but academically-oriented IN types.

In the few samples divided into more conservative or liberal in belief, you will find more sensing types among the conservative groups and more intuitives among more liberal denominations. The preferences theoretically associated with conservatism are S (reliance on past experience), F (concern for values which tend to come from the past) and J (consistency in holding positions once they have been decided on). The preferences theoretically associated with liberalism are N (seeing events in terms of new possibilities for the future), T (skepticism) and P (openness to new viewpoints).

Pastors of congregations reported themselves more often to be judging rather than perceptive types. As in other samples, expect groups in managerial positions to include more judging types. This trend may be obscured in the tables in this section since the samples as a whole include a majority of judging types.

These tables raise questions similar to those raised in the education tables: How easy is it for those in ministry to reach persons of different types in their congregations? And how difficult is it for persons in congregations to find ministers who speak their language?. You will see from the tables that the FJ types in congregations should find it easier to find kindred spirits in their pastors than do the TP types.

Summary listings of tables for EI, SN, TF, JP, ST, SF, NF and NT will be found after the last type table.

Brothers in Roman Catholic Religious Orders

N = 114

	SENSING		INTUITION				N	%
	THINKING	FEELING	FEELING	THINKING				

ISTJ	ISFJ	INFJ	INTJ
N= 13	N= 26	N= 4	N= 2
%= 11.40	%= 22.81	%= 3.51	%= 1.75
■■■■■■■■■■ ■	■■■■■■■■■■ ■■■■■■■■■■ ■■■	■■■■	■■

ISTP	ISFP	INFP	INTP
N= 3	N= 6	N= 8	N= 4
%= 2.63	%= 5.26	%= 7.02	%= 3.51
■■■	■■■■■	■■■■■■■	■■■■

ESTP	ESFP	ENFP	ENTP
N= 1	N= 2	N= 15	N= 1
%= .88	%= 1.75	%= 13.16	%= .88
■	■■	■■■■■■■■■■ ■■■	■

ESTJ	ESFJ	ENFJ	ENTJ
N= 3	N= 16	N= 9	N= 1
%= 2.63	%= 14.04	%= 7.89	%= .88
■■■	■■■■■■■■■■ ■■■■	■■■■■■■■■	■

JUDGMENT — INTROVERSION — PERCEPTION — EXTRAVERSION — JUDGMENT
PERCEPTION

	N	%
E	48	42.11
I	66	57.89
S	70	61.40
N	44	38.60
T	28	24.56
F	86	75.44
J	74	64.91
P	40	35.09
I J	45	39.47
I P	21	18.42
E P	19	16.67
E J	29	25.44
S T	20	17.54
S F	50	43.86
N F	36	31.58
N T	8	7.02
S J	58	50.88
S P	12	10.53
N P	28	24.56
N J	16	14.04
T J	19	16.67
T P	9	7.89
F P	31	27.19
F J	55	48.25
I N	18	15.79
E N	26	22.81
I S	48	42.11
E S	22	19.30
E T	6	5.26
E F	42	36.84
I F	44	38.60
I T	22	19.30
S dom	42	36.84
N dom	22	19.30
T dom	11	9.65
F dom	39	34.21

Note: ■ = 1% of sample   8623186

Data collected by Randall E. Ruppart during 1985. Subjects were 100% male brothers in Roman Catholic religious orders. No other demographic data were reported. Data were collected from three main sources: 1) field research by author 2) field research by others contributed to author and 3) published research. These data are used with permission and were cited in:

Ruppart, R. E. (1985). Psychological Types and Occupational Preferences Among Religious Professionals: A Psycho-Social, Historical Perspective. Unpublished doctoral dissertation, New York University.

Candidates for Theology Education

N = 1205

	SENSING		INTUITION	
	THINKING	FEELING	FEELING	THINKING

ISTJ	ISFJ	INFJ	INTJ
N= 26	N= 95	N= 117	N= 49
%= 2.16	%= 7.88	%= 9.71	%= 4.07
■■	■■■■■■■■	■■■■■■■■■■	■■■■

ISTP	ISFP	INFP	INTP
N= 4	N= 45	N= 106	N= 13
%= .33	%= 3.73	%= 8.80	%= 1.08
	■■■■	■■■■■■■■■	■

ESTP	ESFP	ENFP	ENTP
N= 6	N= 61	N= 188	N= 18
%= .50	%= 5.06	%= 15.60	%= 1.49
	■■■■■	■■■■■■■■■■■	■
		■■■■■■	

ESTJ	ESFJ	ENFJ	ENTJ
N= 46	N= 160	N= 217	N= 54
%= 3.82	%= 13.28	%= 18.01	%= 4.48
■■■■	■■■■■■■■■■■■■	■■■■■■■■■■■■	■■■■
	■■■	■■■■■■■■	

JUDGMENT — INTROVERSION / PERCEPTION — PERCEPTION — EXTRAVERSION / JUDGMENT

	N	%
E	750	62.24
I	455	37.76
S	443	36.76
N	762	63.24
T	216	17.93
F	989	82.07
J	764	63.40
P	441	36.60
I J	287	23.82
I P	168	13.94
E P	273	22.66
E J	477	39.59
S T	82	6.80
S F	361	29.96
N F	628	52.12
N T	134	11.12
S J	327	27.14
S P	116	9.63
N P	325	26.97
N J	437	36.27
T J	175	14.52
T P	41	3.40
F P	400	33.20
F J	589	48.88
I N	285	23.65
E N	477	39.59
I S	170	14.11
E S	273	22.66
E T	124	10.29
E F	626	51.95
I F	363	30.12
I T	92	7.63
S dom	188	15.60
N dom	372	30.87
T dom	117	9.71
F dom	528	43.82

Note: ■ = 1% of sample   8623181

Data collected by Randall E. Ruppart during 1985. Subjects were 31% female and 69% male candidates for theological education (both Protestant and Roman Catholic). No other demographic data were reported. Data were collected from three main sources: 1) field research by author 2) field research by others contributed to author and 3) published research. These data are used with permission and were cited in:

Ruppart, R. E. (1985). Psychological Types and Occupational Preferences Among Religious Professionals: A Psycho-Social, Historical Perspective. Unpublished doctoral dissertation, New York University.

Clergy, all denominations (except priests)

N = 534

	SENSING		INTUITION	
	THINKING	FEELING	FEELING	THINKING

ISTJ	ISFJ	INFJ	INTJ
N= 15	N= 43	N= 62	N= 23
%= 2.81	%= 8.05	%= 11.61	%= 4.31
■■■	■■■■■■■■	■■■■■■■■■■■■ ■■	■■■■

ISTP	ISFP	INFP	INTP
N= 4	N= 22	N= 45	N= 12
%= .75	%= 4.12	%= 8.43	%= 2.25
■	■■■■	■■■■■■■■	■■

ESTP	ESFP	ENFP	ENTP
N= 1	N= 13	N= 92	N= 9
%= .19	%= 2.43	%= 17.23	%= 1.69
	■■	■■■■■■■■■■■■ ■■■■■■■	■■

ESTJ	ESFJ	ENFJ	ENTJ
N= 18	N= 48	N= 95	N= 32
%= 3.37	%= 8.99	%= 17.79	%= 5.99
■■■	■■■■■■■■■	■■■■■■■■■■■■ ■■■■■■■■	■■■■■■

JUDGMENT — INTROVERSION — PERCEPTION — PERCEPTION — EXTRAVERSION — JUDGMENT

	N	%
E	308	57.68
I	226	42.32
S	164	30.71
N	370	69.29
T	114	21.35
F	420	78.65
J	336	62.92
P	198	37.08
I J	143	26.78
I P	83	15.54
E P	115	21.54
E J	193	36.14
S T	38	7.12
S F	126	23.60
N F	294	55.06
N T	76	14.23
S J	124	23.22
S P	40	7.49
N P	158	29.59
N J	212	39.70
T J	88	16.48
T P	26	4.87
F P	172	32.21
F J	248	46.44
I N	142	26.59
E N	228	42.70
I S	84	15.73
E S	80	14.98
E T	60	11.24
E F	248	46.44
I F	172	32.21
I T	54	10.11
S dom	72	13.48
N dom	186	34.83
T dom	66	12.36
F dom	210	39.33

Note: ■ = 1% of sample   8629395

This table is one of a series of tables from the CAPT-MBTI Data Bank of MBTI records submitted to CAPT for computer scoring between 1971 and June, 1984. This sample was drawn from 59,784 records with usable occupational codes from the total data bank of 232,557. This data bank has 51% Form F cases from 1971 to March, 1978, 35% Form F cases from 1978 to June, 1984 and 14% Form G cases from 1978 to December, 1982. An analysis of Form F and G data banks showed the data banks were comprised of 56% females and 44% males; education level completed: 6% some grade school, 30% high school diploma, 25% some college, 18% bachelor degrees, 11% masters degrees, 3% doctoral or post doctoral work, and 6% unknown. Age group percentages were: 11% under 18, 29% 18 to 20, 12% 21 to 24, 10% 25 to 29, 16% 30 to 39, 10% 40 to 49, 5% 50 to 59, 2% 60 plus, and 5% unknown.

Directors of Religious Education

N = 50

	SENSING		INTUITION	
	THINKING	FEELING	FEELING	THINKING

ISTJ	ISFJ	INFJ	INTJ
N= 3	N= 4	N= 9	N= 1
%= 6.00	%= 8.00	%= 18.00	%= 2.00
■■■■■■	■■■■■■■■	■■■■■■■■■■ ■■■■■■■■	■■

ISTP	ISFP	INFP	INTP
N= 0	N= 3	N= 2	N= 0
%= 0.00	%= 6.00	%= 4.00	%= 0.00
	■■■■■■	■■■■	

ESTP	ESFP	ENFP	ENTP
N= 0	N= 0	N= 9	N= 1
%= 0.00	%= 0.00	%= 18.00	%= 2.00
		■■■■■■■■■■ ■■■■■■■■	■■

ESTJ	ESFJ	ENFJ	ENTJ
N= 1	N= 6	N= 11	N= 0
%= 2.00	%= 12.00	%= 22.00	%= 0.00
■■	■■■■■■■■■■ ■■	■■■■■■■■■■ ■■■■■■■■■■ ■■	

JUDGMENT — INTROVERSION — PERCEPTION — PERCEPTION — EXTRAVERSION — JUDGMENT

	N	%
E	28	56.00
I	22	44.00
S	17	34.00
N	33	66.00
T	6	12.00
F	44	88.00
J	35	70.00
P	15	30.00
I J	17	34.00
I P	5	10.00
E P	10	20.00
E J	18	36.00
S T	4	8.00
S F	13	26.00
N F	31	62.00
N T	2	4.00
S J	14	28.00
S P	3	6.00
N P	12	24.00
N J	21	42.00
T J	5	10.00
T P	1	2.00
F P	14	28.00
F J	30	60.00
I N	12	24.00
E N	21	42.00
I S	10	20.00
E S	7	14.00
E T	2	4.00
E F	26	52.00
I F	18	36.00
I T	4	8.00
S dom	7	14.00
N dom	20	40.00
T dom	1	2.00
F dom	22	44.00

Note: ■ = 1% of sample

8623183

Data collected by Randall E. Ruppart during 1985. Subjects were 100% female directors of religious education. No other demographic data were reported. Data were collected from three main sources: 1) field research by author 2) field research by others contributed to author and 3) published research. These data are used with permission and were cited in:

Ruppart, R. E. (1985). Psychological Types and Occupational Preferences Among Religious Professionals: A Psycho-Social, Historical Perspective. Unpublished doctoral dissertation, New York University.

Nuns and Other Religious Workers

N = 1147

	SENSING		INTUITION				
	THINKING	FEELING	FEELING	THINKING			

ISTJ	ISFJ	INFJ	INTJ
N= 107	N= 116	N= 48	N= 43
%= 9.33	%= 10.11	%= 4.18	%= 3.75
■■■■■■■■■	■■■■■■■■■■	■■■■	■■■■

ISTP	ISFP	INFP	INTP
N= 22	N= 45	N= 54	N= 27
%= 1.92	%= 3.92	%= 4.71	%= 2.35
■■	■■■■	■■■■■	■■

ESTP	ESFP	ENFP	ENTP
N= 32	N= 70	N= 89	N= 46
%= 2.79	%= 6.10	%= 7.76	%= 4.01
■■■	■■■■■■	■■■■■■■■	■■■■

ESTJ	ESFJ	ENFJ	ENTJ
N= 143	N= 160	N= 68	N= 77
%= 12.47	%= 13.95	%= 5.93	%= 6.71
■■■■■■■■■■■■	■■■■■■■■■■■■■	■■■■■■	■■■■■■■
■■	■■■■		

JUDGMENT — INTROVERSION — PERCEPTION
PERCEPTION — EXTRAVERSION — JUDGMENT

	N	%
E	685	59.72
I	462	40.28
S	695	60.59
N	452	39.41
T	497	43.33
F	650	56.67
J	762	66.43
P	385	33.57
I J	314	27.38
I P	148	12.90
E P	237	20.66
E J	448	39.06
S T	304	26.50
S F	391	34.09
N F	259	22.58
N T	193	16.83
S J	526	45.86
S P	169	14.73
N P	216	18.83
N J	236	20.58
T J	370	32.26
T P	127	11.07
F P	258	22.49
F J	392	34.18
I N	172	15.00
E N	280	24.41
I S	290	25.28
E S	405	35.31
E T	298	25.98
E F	387	33.74
I F	263	22.93
I T	199	17.35
S dom	325	28.33
N dom	226	19.70
T dom	269	23.45
F dom	327	28.51

Note: ■ = 1% of sample

8629398

This table is one of a series of tables from the CAPT-MBTI Data Bank of MBTI records submitted to CAPT for computer scoring between 1971 and June, 1984. This sample was drawn from 59,784 records with usable occupational codes from the total data bank of 232,557. This data bank has 51% Form F cases from 1971 to March, 1978, 35% Form F cases from 1978 to June, 1984 and 14% Form G cases from 1978 to December, 1982. An analysis of Form F and G data banks showed the data banks were comprised of 56% females and 44% males; education level completed: 6% some grade school, 30% high school diploma, 25% some college, 18% bachelor degrees, 11% masters degrees, 3% doctoral or post doctoral work, and 6% unknown. Age group percentages were: 11% under 18, 29% 18 to 20, 12% 21 to 24, 10% 25 to 29, 16% 30 to 39, 10% 40 to 49, 5% 50 to 59, 2% 60 plus, and 5% unknown.

Ordained Roman Catholic Deacons

	SENSING		INTUITION	
	THINKING	FEELING	FEELING	THINKING

ISTJ	ISFJ	INFJ	INTJ
N= 8	N= 13	N= 4	N= 3
%= 7.84	%= 12.75	%= 3.92	%= 2.94
■■■■■■■■	■■■■■■■■■■ ■■■	■■■■	■■■

ISTP	ISFP	INFP	INTP
N= 1	N= 2	N= 2	N= 0
%= .98	%= 1.96	%= 1.96	%= 0.00
■	■■	■■	

ESTP	ESFP	ENFP	ENTP
N= 2	N= 0	N= 5	N= 3
%= 1.96	%= 0.00	%= 4.90	%= 2.94
■■		■■■■■	■■■

ESTJ	ESFJ	ENFJ	ENTJ
N= 14	N= 23	N= 19	N= 3
%= 13.73	%= 22.55	%= 18.63	%= 2.94
■■■■■■■■■■ ■■■■	■■■■■■■■■■■ ■■■■■■■■■■■ ■■■	■■■■■■■■■■ ■■■■■■■■■	■■■

JUDGMENT — INTROVERSION — PERCEPTION — EXTRAVERSION — JUDGMENT
PERCEPTION

	N	%
E	69	67.65
I	33	32.35
S	63	61.76
N	39	38.24
T	34	33.33
F	68	66.67
J	87	85.29
P	15	14.71
I J	28	27.45
I P	5	4.90
E P	10	9.80
E J	59	57.84
S T	25	24.51
S F	38	37.25
N F	30	29.41
N T	9	8.82
S J	58	56.86
S P	5	4.90
N P	10	9.80
N J	29	28.43
T J	28	27.45
T P	6	5.88
F P	9	8.82
F J	59	57.84
I N	9	8.82
E N	30	29.41
I S	24	23.53
E S	39	38.24
E T	22	21.57
E F	47	46.08
I F	21	20.59
I T	12	11.76
S dom	23	22.55
N dom	15	14.71
T dom	18	17.65
F dom	46	45.10

Note: ■ = 1% of sample   8623185

Data collected by Randall E. Ruppart during 1985. Subjects were 100% male ordained Roman Catholic deacons. No other demographic data were reported. Data were collected from three main sources: 1) field research by author 2) field research by others contributed to author and 3) published research. These data are used with permission and were cited in:

Ruppart, R. E. (1985). Psychological Types and Occupational Preferences Among Religious Professionals: A Psycho-Social, Historical Perspective. Unpublished doctoral dissertation, New York University.

Priests and Monks

N = 219

	SENSING		INTUITION	
	THINKING	FEELING	FEELING	THINKING

ISTJ	ISFJ	INFJ	INTJ
N= 20	N= 21	N= 34	N= 7
%= 9.13	%= 9.59	%= 15.53	%= 3.20
■■■■■■■■■	■■■■■■■■■■	■■■■■■■■■■■■■■■	■■■
		■■■■■■	

ISTP	ISFP	INFP	INTP
N= 1	N= 11	N= 18	N= 7
%= .46	%= 5.02	%= 8.22	%= 3.20
	■■■■■	■■■■■■■■	■■■

ESTP	ESFP	ENFP	ENTP
N= 1	N= 2	N= 28	N= 6
%= .46	%= .91	%= 12.79	%= 2.74
	■	■■■■■■■■■■■■	■■■
		■■■	

ESTJ	ESFJ	ENFJ	ENTJ
N= 8	N= 20	N= 30	N= 5
%= 3.65	%= 9.13	%= 13.70	%= 2.28
■■■■	■■■■■■■■■	■■■■■■■■■■■■■	■■
		■■■■	

JUDGMENT — INTROVERSION — PERCEPTION

PERCEPTION — EXTRAVERSION — JUDGMENT

	N	%
E	100	45.66
I	119	54.34
S	84	38.36
N	135	61.64
T	55	25.11
F	164	74.89
J	145	66.21
P	74	33.79
I J	82	37.44
I P	37	16.89
E P	37	16.89
E J	63	28.77
S T	30	13.70
S F	54	24.66
N F	110	50.23
N T	25	11.42
S J	69	31.51
S P	15	6.85
N P	59	26.94
N J	76	34.70
T J	40	18.26
T P	15	6.85
F P	59	26.94
F J	105	47.95
I N	66	30.14
E N	69	31.51
I S	53	24.20
E S	31	14.16
E T	20	9.13
E F	80	36.53
I F	84	38.36
I T	35	15.98
S dom	44	20.09
N dom	75	34.25
T dom	21	9.59
F dom	79	36.07

Note: ■ = 1% of sample   8629396

This table is one of a series of tables from the CAPT-MBTI Data Bank of MBTI records submitted to CAPT for computer scoring between 1971 and June, 1984. This sample was drawn from 59,784 records with usable occupational codes from the total data bank of 232,557. This data bank has 51% Form F cases from 1971 to March, 1978, 35% Form F cases from 1978 to June, 1984 and 14% Form G cases from 1978 to December, 1982. An analysis of Form F and G data banks showed the data banks were comprised of 56% females and 44% males; education level completed: 6% some grade school, 30% high school diploma, 25% some college, 18% bachelor degrees, 11% masters degrees, 3% doctoral or post doctoral work, and 6% unknown. Age group percentages were: 11% under 18, 29% 18 to 20, 12% 21 to 24, 10% 25 to 29, 16% 30 to 39, 10% 40 to 49, 5% 50 to 59, 2% 60 plus, and 5% unknown.

Protestant Ministers

N = 1554

	SENSING		INTUITION	
	THINKING	FEELING	FEELING	THINKING

ISTJ	ISFJ	INFJ	INTJ
N= 65	N= 160	N= 161	N= 63
%= 4.18	%= 10.30	%= 10.36	%= 4.05
■■■■	■■■■■■■■■■	■■■■■■■■■■	■■■■

ISTP	ISFP	INFP	INTP
N= 9	N= 35	N= 137	N= 25
%= .58	%= 2.25	%= 8.82	%= 1.61
■	■■	■■■■■■■■■	■■

ESTP	ESFP	ENFP	ENTP
N= 7	N= 42	N= 211	N= 34
%= .45	%= 2.70	%= 13.58	%= 2.19
	■■■	■■■■■■■■■■	■■
		■■■■	

ESTJ	ESFJ	ENFJ	ENTJ
N= 68	N= 199	N= 255	N= 83
%= 4.38	%= 12.81	%= 16.41	%= 5.34
■■■■	■■■■■■■■■■	■■■■■■■■■■	■■■■■
	■■■	■■■■■■	

Right side vertical labels: JUDGMENT — INTROVERSION — PERCEPTION — PERCEPTION — EXTRAVERSION — JUDGMENT

	N	%
E	899	57.85
I	655	42.15
S	585	37.64
N	969	62.36
T	354	22.78
F	1200	77.22
J	1054	67.82
P	500	32.18
I J	449	28.89
I P	206	13.26
E P	294	18.92
E J	605	38.93
S T	149	9.59
S F	436	28.06
N F	764	49.16
N T	205	13.19
S J	492	31.66
S P	93	5.98
N P	407	26.19
N J	562	36.16
T J	279	17.95
T P	75	4.83
F P	425	27.35
F J	775	49.87
I N	386	24.84
E N	583	37.52
I S	269	17.31
E S	316	20.33
E T	192	12.36
E F	707	45.50
I F	493	31.72
I T	162	10.42
S dom	274	17.63
N dom	469	30.18
T dom	185	11.90
F dom	626	40.28

Note: ■ = 1% of sample   8623178

Data collected by Randall E. Ruppart during 1985. Subjects were 6% female and 94% male Protestant ministers. No other demographic data were reported. Data were collected from three main sources: 1) field research by author 2) field research by others contributed to author and 3) published research. These data are used with permission and were cited in:

Ruppart, R. E. (1985). Psychological Types and Occupational Preferences Among Religious Professionals: A Psycho-Social, Historical Perspective. Unpublished doctoral dissertation, New York University.

Protestant Seminarians

N = 633

	SENSING		INTUITION	
	THINKING	FEELING	FEELING	THINKING

ISTJ	ISFJ	INFJ	INTJ
N= 18	N= 63	N= 55	N= 26
%= 2.84	%= 9.95	%= 8.69	%= 4.11
■■■	■■■■■■■■■■	■■■■■■■■■	■■■■

ISTP	ISFP	INFP	INTP
N= 4	N= 20	N= 55	N= 15
%= .63	%= 3.16	%= 8.69	%= 2.37
■	■■■	■■■■■■■■■	■■

ESTP	ESFP	ENFP	ENTP
N= 7	N= 46	N= 75	N= 10
%= 1.11	%= 7.27	%= 11.85	%= 1.58
■	■■■■■■■	■■■■■■■■■■ ■■	■■

ESTJ	ESFJ	ENFJ	ENTJ
N= 24	N= 104	N= 89	N= 22
%= 3.79	%= 16.43	%= 14.06	%= 3.48
■■■■	■■■■■■■■■■■■ ■■■■■■	■■■■■■■■■■■ ■■■	■■■

JUDGMENT — INTROVERSION — PERCEPTION — PERCEPTION — EXTRAVERSION — JUDGMENT

	N	%
E	377	59.56
I	256	40.44
S	286	45.18
N	347	54.82
T	126	19.91
F	507	80.09
J	401	63.35
P	232	36.65
I J	162	25.59
I P	94	14.85
E P	138	21.80
E J	239	37.76
S T	53	8.37
S F	233	36.81
N F	274	43.29
N T	73	11.53
S J	209	33.02
S P	77	12.16
N P	155	24.49
N J	192	30.33
T J	90	14.22
T P	36	5.69
F P	196	30.96
F J	311	49.13
I N	151	23.85
E N	196	30.96
I S	105	16.59
E S	181	28.59
E T	63	9.95
E F	314	49.61
I F	193	30.49
I T	63	9.95
S dom	134	21.17
N dom	166	26.22
T dom	65	10.27
F dom	268	42.34

Note: ■ = 1% of sample   8623180

Data collected by Randall E. Ruppart during 1985. Subjects were 14% female and 86% male Protestant seminarians. No other demographic data were reported. Data were collected from three main sources: 1) field research by author 2) field research by others contributed to author and 3) published research. These data are used with permission and were cited in:

Ruppart, R. E. (1985). Psychological Types and Occupational Preferences Among Religious Professionals: A Psycho-Social, Historical Perspective. Unpublished doctoral dissertation, New York University.

Protestants in Specialized Ministries

N = 85

	SENSING		INTUITION	
THINKING	FEELING	FEELING	THINKING	

ISTJ	ISFJ	INFJ	INTJ
N= 5	N= 13	N= 10	N= 4
%= 5.88	%= 15.29	%= 11.76	%= 4.71
■■■■■■	■■■■■■■■■■■■■■ ■■■■■	■■■■■■■■■■■■ ■■	■■■■■

ISTP	ISFP	INFP	INTP
N= 1	N= 0	N= 6	N= 2
%= 1.18	%= 0.00	%= 7.06	%= 2.35
■		■■■■■■■	■■

ESTP	ESFP	ENFP	ENTP
N= 1	N= 1	N= 11	N= 5
%= 1.18	%= 1.18	%= 12.94	%= 5.88
■	■	■■■■■■■■■■ ■■■	■■■■■■

ESTJ	ESFJ	ENFJ	ENTJ
N= 1	N= 5	N= 18	N= 2
%= 1.18	%= 5.88	%= 21.18	%= 2.35
■	■■■■■■	■■■■■■■■■■ ■■■■■■■■■■ ■	■■

JUDGMENT / PERCEPTION (INTROVERSION) — PERCEPTION / JUDGMENT (EXTRAVERSION)

	N	%
E	44	51.76
I	41	48.24
S	27	31.76
N	58	68.24
T	21	24.71
F	64	75.29
J	58	68.24
P	27	31.76
I J	32	37.65
I P	9	10.59
E P	18	21.18
E J	26	30.59
S T	8	9.41
S F	19	22.35
N F	45	52.94
N T	13	15.29
S J	24	28.24
S P	3	3.53
N P	24	28.24
N J	34	40.00
T J	12	14.12
T P	9	10.59
F P	18	21.18
F J	46	54.12
I N	22	25.88
E N	36	42.35
I S	19	22.35
E S	8	9.41
E T	9	10.59
E F	35	41.18
I F	29	34.12
I T	12	14.12
S dom	20	23.53
N dom	30	35.29
T dom	6	7.06
F dom	29	34.12

Note: ■ = 1% of sample   8623179

Data collected by Randall E. Ruppart during 1985. Subjects were female and male Protestants in specialized ministries. No other demographic data were reported. Data were collected from three main sources: 1) field research by author 2) field research by others contributed to author and 3) published research. These data are used with permission and were cited in:

Ruppart, R. E. (1985). Psychological Types and Occupational Preferences Among Religious Professionals: A Psycho-Social, Historical Perspective. Unpublished doctoral dissertation, New York University.

457

Rabbis

N = 319

	SENSING		INTUITION	
	THINKING	FEELING	FEELING	THINKING

ISTJ	ISFJ	INFJ	INTJ
N= 26	N= 27	N= 33	N= 22
%= 8.15	%= 8.46	%= 10.34	%= 6.90
■■■■■■■■	■■■■■■■■	■■■■■■■■■■	■■■■■■■

ISTP	ISFP	INFP	INTP
N= 5	N= 10	N= 21	N= 6
%= 1.57	%= 3.13	%= 6.58	%= 1.88
■■	■■■	■■■■■■■	■■

ESTP	ESFP	ENFP	ENTP
N= 3	N= 6	N= 28	N= 6
%= .94	%= 1.88	%= 8.78	%= 1.88
■	■■	■■■■■■■■■	■■

ESTJ	ESFJ	ENFJ	ENTJ
N= 13	N= 44	N= 48	N= 21
%= 4.08	%= 13.79	%= 15.05	%= 6.58
■■■■	■■■■■■■■■■ ■■■■	■■■■■■■■■■ ■■■■■	■■■■■■■

JUDGMENT / INTROVERSION / PERCEPTION / PERCEPTION / EXTRAVERSION / JUDGMENT

	N	%
E	169	52.98
I	150	47.02
S	134	42.01
N	185	57.99
T	102	31.97
F	217	68.03
J	234	73.35
P	85	26.65
I J	108	33.86
I P	42	13.17
E P	43	13.48
E J	126	39.50
S T	47	14.73
S F	87	27.27
N F	130	40.75
N T	55	17.24
S J	110	34.48
S P	24	7.52
N P	61	19.12
N J	124	38.87
T J	82	25.71
T P	20	6.27
F P	65	20.38
F J	152	47.65
I N	82	25.71
E N	103	32.29
I S	68	21.32
E S	66	20.69
E T	43	13.48
E F	126	39.50
I F	91	28.53
I T	59	18.50
S dom	62	19.44
N dom	89	27.90
T dom	45	14.11
F dom	123	38.56

Note: ■ = 1% of sample   8623177

Data collected by Murray Greenfield from April to August 1967 using Form E and more recently re-reported by Randall E. Ruppart in 1985. Subjects were male volunteers, 36% of the membership role of the Rabbinic Alumni of Yeshiva University. The rabbis' ages ranged from 25 to 64 with the modal age group being 35 to 39. All rabbis were college graduates, a large number also had graduate degrees in secular studies. These data are used with permission and were cited in:

Greenfield, M. (1969). The typologies of pulpit and nonpulpit rabbis (Doctoral dissertation, Rutgers State University, 1968). Dissertation Abstracts International, 29, 2114A. (University Microfilms No. 69-1044)

Ruppart, R. E. (1985). Psychological Types and Occupational Preferences Among Religious Professionals: A Psycho-Social, Historical Perspective. Unpublished doctoral dissertation, New York University.

Religious Educator, all denominations

N = 79

	SENSING		INTUITION			N	%
	THINKING	FEELING	FEELING	THINKING			

<table>
<tr><td colspan="4">

ISTJ
N= 3
%= 3.80
■■■■

ISFJ
N= 9
%= 11.39
■■■■■■■■■■■
■

INFJ
N= 7
%= 8.86
■■■■■■■■■

INTJ
N= 5
%= 6.33
■■■■■■

</td></tr>
</table>

	N	%
E	43	54.43
I	36	45.57
S	37	46.84
N	42	53.16
T	18	22.78
F	61	77.22
J	49	62.03
P	30	37.97
I J	24	30.38
I P	12	15.19
E P	18	22.78
E J	25	31.65
S T	10	12.66
S F	27	34.18
N F	34	43.04
N T	8	10.13
S J	29	36.71
S P	8	10.13
N P	22	27.85
N J	20	25.32
T J	15	18.99
T P	3	3.80
F P	27	34.18
F J	34	43.04
I N	23	29.11
E N	19	24.05
I S	13	16.46
E S	24	30.38
E T	9	11.39
E F	34	43.04
I F	27	34.18
I T	9	11.39
S dom	19	24.05
N dom	23	29.11
T dom	8	10.13
F dom	29	36.71

ISTP
N= 1
%= 1.27
■

ISFP
N= 0
%= 0.00

INFP
N= 11
%= 13.92
■■■■■■■■■■
■■■■

INTP
N= 0
%= 0.00

ESTP
N= 1
%= 1.27
■

ESFP
N= 6
%= 7.59
■■■■■■■■

ENFP
N= 10
%= 12.66
■■■■■■■■■■
■■■

ENTP
N= 1
%= 1.27
■

ESTJ
N= 5
%= 6.33
■■■■■■

ESFJ
N= 12
%= 15.19
■■■■■■■■■■■■
■■■■■

ENFJ
N= 6
%= 7.59
■■■■■■■■

ENTJ
N= 2
%= 2.53
■■■

JUDGMENT — INTROVERSION — PERCEPTION — PERCEPTION — EXTRAVERSION — JUDGMENT

Note: ■ = 1% of sample   8629397

This table is one of a series of tables from the CAPT-MBTI Data Bank of MBTI records submitted to CAPT for computer scoring between 1971 and June, 1984. This sample was drawn from 59,784 records with usable occupational codes from the total data bank of 232,557. This data bank has 51% Form F cases from 1971 to March, 1978, 35% Form F cases from 1978 to June, 1984 and 14% Form G cases from 1978 to December, 1982. An analysis of Form F and G data banks showed the data banks were comprised of 56% females and 44% males; education level completed: 6% some grade school, 30% high school diploma, 25% some college, 18% bachelor degrees, 11% masters degrees, 3% doctoral or post doctoral work, and 6% unknown. Age group percentages were: 11% under 18, 29% 18 to 20, 12% 21 to 24, 10% 25 to 29, 16% 30 to 39, 10% 40 to 49, 5% 50 to 59, 2% 60 plus, and 5% unknown.

Roman Catholic Priests

N = 1298

	SENSING		INTUITION				N	%
	THINKING	FEELING	FEELING	THINKING				

<table>
<tr><td colspan="2">

ISTJ

N= 101
%= 7.78

■■■■■■■

</td><td colspan="2">

ISFJ

N= 239
%= 18.41

■■■■■■■■■■
■■■■■■■

</td><td colspan="2">

INFJ

N= 125
%= 9.63

■■■■■■■■■

</td><td colspan="2">

INTJ

N= 26
%= 2.00

■■

</td></tr>
</table>

	N	%
E	628	48.38
I	670	51.62
S	707	54.47
N	591	45.53
T	260	20.03
F	1038	79.97
J	916	70.57
P	382	29.43
I J	491	37.83
I P	179	13.79
E P	203	15.64
E J	425	32.74
S T	193	14.87
S F	514	39.60
N F	524	40.37
N T	67	5.16
S J	602	46.38
S P	105	8.09
N P	277	21.34
N J	314	24.19
T J	224	17.26
T P	36	2.77
F P	346	26.66
F J	692	53.31
I N	269	20.72
E N	322	24.81
I S	401	30.89
E S	306	23.57
E T	114	8.78
E F	514	39.60
I F	524	40.37
I T	146	11.25
S dom	384	29.58
N dom	310	23.88
T dom	116	8.94
F dom	488	37.60

ISTP
N= 8
%= .62
■

ISFP
N= 53
%= 4.08
■■■■

INFP
N= 107
%= 8.24
■■■■■■■■

INTP
N= 11
%= .85
■

ESTP
N= 7
%= .54
■

ESFP
N= 37
%= 2.85
■■■

ENFP
N= 149
%= 11.48
■■■■■■■■■■■
■

ENTP
N= 10
%= .77
■

ESTJ
N= 77
%= 5.93
■■■■■■

ESFJ
N= 185
%= 14.25
■■■■■■■■■■
■■■■

ENFJ
N= 143
%= 11.02
■■■■■■■■■■
■

ENTJ
N= 20
%= 1.54
■■

JUDGMENT — INTROVERSION — PERCEPTION — PERCEPTION — EXTRAVERSION — JUDGMENT

Note: ■ = 1% of sample   8623184

Data collected by Randall E. Ruppart during 1985. Subjects were 100% male Roman Catholic priests. No other demographic data were reported. Data were collected from three main sources: 1) field research by author 2) field research by others contributed to author and 3) published research. These data are used with permission and were cited in:

Ruppart, R. E. (1985). Psychological Types and Occupational Preferences Among Religious Professionals: A Psycho-Social, Historical Perspective. Unpublished doctoral dissertation, New York University.

Roman Catholic Seminarians

N = 51

	SENSING		INTUITION	
	THINKING	FEELING	FEELING	THINKING

ISTJ	ISFJ	INFJ	INTJ
N= 6	N= 4	N= 12	N= 2
%= 11.76	%= 7.84	%= 23.53	%= 3.92
■■■■■■■■■■■■	■■■■■■■■	■■■■■■■■■■■■ ■■■■■■■■■■■■ ■■■■	■■■■

ISTP	ISFP	INFP	INTP
N= 1	N= 0	N= 5	N= 1
%= 1.96	%= 0.00	%= 9.80	%= 1.96
■■		■■■■■■■■■■	■■

ESTP	ESFP	ENFP	ENTP
N= 0	N= 2	N= 5	N= 0
%= 0.00	%= 3.92	%= 9.80	%= 0.00
	■■■■	■■■■■■■■■■	

ESTJ	ESFJ	ENFJ	ENTJ
N= 2	N= 4	N= 5	N= 2
%= 3.92	%= 7.84	%= 9.80	%= 3.92
■■■■	■■■■■■■■	■■■■■■■■■■	■■■■

JUDGMENT — INTROVERSION — PERCEPTION — PERCEPTION — EXTRAVERSION — JUDGMENT

	N	%
E	20	39.22
I	31	60.78
S	19	37.25
N	32	62.75
T	14	27.45
F	37	72.55
J	37	72.55
P	14	27.45
I J	24	47.06
I P	7	13.73
E P	7	13.73
E J	13	25.49
S T	9	17.65
S F	10	19.61
N F	27	52.94
N T	5	9.80
S J	16	31.37
S P	3	5.88
N P	11	21.57
N J	21	41.18
T J	12	23.53
T P	2	3.92
F P	12	23.53
F J	25	49.02
I N	20	39.22
E N	12	23.53
I S	11	21.57
E S	8	15.69
E T	4	7.84
E F	16	31.37
I F	21	41.18
I T	10	19.61
S dom	12	23.53
N dom	19	37.25
T dom	6	11.76
F dom	14	27.45

Note: ■ = 1% of sample   8623187

Data collected by Randall E. Ruppart during 1985. Subjects were 100% male Roman Catholic seminarians. No other demographic data were reported. Data were collected from three main sources: 1) field research by author 2) field research by others contributed to author and 3) published research. These data are used with permission and were cited in:

Ruppart, R. E. (1985). Psychological Types and Occupational Preferences Among Religious Professionals: A Psycho-Social, Historical Perspective. Unpublished doctoral dissertation, New York University.

Sisters in Roman Catholic Religious Orders

N = 2002

	SENSING		INTUITION	
	THINKING	FEELING	FEELING	THINKING

ISTJ	ISFJ	INFJ	INTJ
N= 111	N= 549	N= 184	N= 54
%= 5.54	%= 27.42	%= 9.19	%= 2.70
■■■■■■	■■■■■■■■■■ ■■■■■■■■■■ ■■■■■■■	■■■■■■■■■	■■■

ISTP	ISFP	INFP	INTP
N= 9	N= 75	N= 162	N= 28
%= .45	%= 3.75	%= 8.09	%= 1.40
	■■■■	■■■■■■■■	■

ESTP	ESFP	ENFP	ENTP
N= 17	N= 53	N= 152	N= 28
%= .85	%= 2.65	%= 7.59	%= 1.40
■	■■■	■■■■■■■■	■

ESTJ	ESFJ	ENFJ	ENTJ
N= 76	N= 313	N= 160	N= 31
%= 3.80	%= 15.63	%= 7.99	%= 1.55
■■■■	■■■■■■■■■■ ■■■■■■	■■■■■■■■	■■

JUDGMENT — INTROVERSION — PERCEPTION — PERCEPTION — EXTRAVERSION — JUDGMENT

	N	%
E	830	41.46
I	1172	58.54
S	1203	60.09
N	799	39.91
T	354	17.68
F	1648	82.32
J	1478	73.83
P	524	26.17
I J	898	44.86
I P	274	13.69
E P	250	12.49
E J	580	28.97
S T	213	10.64
S F	990	49.45
N F	658	32.87
N T	141	7.04
S J	1049	52.40
S P	154	7.69
N P	370	18.48
N J	429	21.43
T J	272	13.59
T P	82	4.10
F P	442	22.08
F J	1206	60.24
I N	428	21.38
E N	371	18.53
I S	744	37.16
E S	459	22.93
E T	152	7.59
E F	678	33.87
I F	970	48.45
I T	202	10.09
S dom	730	36.46
N dom	418	20.88
T dom	144	7.19
F dom	710	35.46

Note: ■ = 1% of sample

8623182

Data collected by Randall E. Ruppart during 1985. Subjects were 100% female sisters in Roman Catholic orders. No other demographic data were reported. Data were collected from three main sources: 1) field research by author 2) field research by others contributed to author and 3) published research. These data are used with permission and were cited in:

Ruppart, R. E. (1985). Psychological Types and Occupational Preferences Among Religious Professionals: A Psycho-Social, Historical Perspective. Unpublished doctoral dissertation, New York University.

RELIGIOUS WORKERS -ALL DENOMINATIONS-

N = 2010

	SENSING		INTUITION				N	%
	THINKING	FEELING	FEELING	THINKING				

ISTJ	ISFJ	INFJ	INTJ		E	1157	57.56
N= 145	N= 191	N= 152	N= 79		I	853	42.44
%= 7.21	%= 9.50	%= 7.56	%= 3.93		S	991	49.30
■■■■■■■	■■■■■■■■■	■■■■■■■■	■■■■		N	1019	50.70
					T	694	34.53
					F	1316	65.47
					J	1309	65.12
					P	701	34.88

(JUDGMENT — INTROVERSION)

ISTP	ISFP	INFP	INTP		I J	567	28.21
N= 28	N= 79	N= 133	N= 46		I P	286	14.23
%= 1.39	%= 3.93	%= 6.62	%= 2.29		E P	415	20.65
■	■■■■	■■■■■■	■■		E J	742	36.92

(PERCEPTION)

					ST	385	19.15
					SF	606	30.15
					NF	710	35.32
					NT	309	15.37

ESTP	ESFP	ENFP	ENTP		S J	756	37.61
N= 36	N= 92	N= 224	N= 63		S P	235	11.69
%= 1.79	%= 4.58	%= 11.14	%= 3.13		N P	466	23.18
■■	■■■■■	■■■■■■■■■■ ■	■■■		N J	553	27.51

(PERCEPTION — EXTRAVERSION)

					T J	521	25.92
					T P	173	8.61
					F P	528	26.27
					F J	788	39.20

ESTJ	ESFJ	ENFJ	ENTJ		I N	410	20.40
N= 176	N= 244	N= 201	N= 121		E N	609	30.30
%= 8.76	%= 12.14	%= 10.00	%= 6.02		I S	443	22.04
■■■■■■■■	■■■■■■■■■■■ ■■	■■■■■■■■■■	■■■■■■		E S	548	27.26

(JUDGMENT)

ET	396	19.70
EF	761	37.86
I F	555	27.61
I T	298	14.83

S dom	464	23.08
N dom	518	25.77
T dom	371	18.46
F dom	657	32.69

Note: ■ = 1% of sample   8629399

This table is one of a series of tables from the CAPT-MBTI Data Bank of MBTI records submitted to CAPT for computer scoring between 1971 and June, 1984. This sample was drawn from 59,784 records with usable occupational codes from the total data bank of 232,557. This data bank has 51% Form F cases from 1971 to March, 1978, 35% Form F cases from 1978 to June, 1984 and 14% Form G cases from 1978 to December, 1982. An analysis of Form F and G data banks showed the data banks were comprised of 56% females and 44% males; education level completed: 6% some grade school, 30% high school diploma, 25% some college, 18% bachelor degrees, 11% masters degrees, 3% doctoral or post doctoral work, and 6% unknown. Age group percentages were: 11% under 18, 29% 18 to 20, 12% 21 to 24, 10% 25 to 29, 16% 30 to 39, 10% 40 to 49, 5% 50 to 59, 2% 60 plus, and 5% unknown.

E Percent	I	Total Sample Size	Sample Description
67.65	32.35	102	Ordained Roman Catholic Deacons
62.24	37.76	1205	Candidates for Theology Education
59.72	40.28	1147	Nuns and Other Religious Workers
59.56	40.44	633	Protestant Seminarians
57.85	42.15	1554	Protestant Ministers
57.68	42.32	534	Clergy, all denominations (except priests)
57.56	42.44	2010	RELIGIOUS WORKERS -ALL DENOMINATIONS-
56.00	44.00	50	Directors of Religious Education
54.43	45.57	79	Religious Educator, all denominations
52.98	47.02	319	Rabbis
51.76	48.24	85	Protestants in Specialized Ministries
48.38	51.62	1298	Roman Catholic Priests
45.66	54.34	219	Priests and Monks
42.11	57.89	114	Brothers in Roman Catholic Religious Orders
41.46	58.54	2002	Sisters in Roman Catholic Religious Orders
39.22	60.78	51	Roman Catholic Seminarians

SENSING-INTUITION

S Percent	N	Total Sample Size	Sample Description
61.76	38.24	102	Ordained Roman Catholic Deacons
61.40	38.60	114	Brothers in Roman Catholic Religious Orders
60.59	39.41	1147	Nuns and Other Religious Workers
60.09	39.91	2002	Sisters in Roman Catholic Religious Orders
54.47	45.53	1298	Roman Catholic Priests
49.30	50.70	2010	RELIGIOUS WORKERS -ALL DENOMINATIONS-
46.84	53.16	79	Religious Educator, all denominations
45.18	54.82	633	Protestant Seminarians
42.01	57.99	319	Rabbis
38.36	61.64	219	Priests and Monks
37.64	62.36	1554	Protestant Ministers
37.25	62.75	51	Roman Catholic Seminarians
36.76	63.24	1205	Candidates for Theology Education
34.00	66.00	50	Directors of Religious Education
31.76	68.24	85	Protestants in Specialized Ministries
30.71	69.29	534	Clergy, all denominations (except priests)

THINKING-FEELING

T Percent	F	Total Sample Size	Sample Description
43.33	56.67	1147	Nuns and Other Religious Workers
34.53	65.47	2010	RELIGIOUS WORKERS -ALL DENOMINATIONS-
33.33	66.67	102	Ordained Roman Catholic Deacons
31.97	68.03	319	Rabbis
27.45	72.55	51	Roman Catholic Seminarians
25.11	74.89	219	Priests and Monks
24.71	75.29	85	Protestants in Specialized Ministries
24.56	75.44	114	Brothers in Roman Catholic Religious Orders
22.78	77.22	1554	Protestant Ministers
22.78	77.22	79	Religious Educator, all denominations
21.35	78.65	534	Clergy, all denominations (except priests)
20.03	79.97	1298	Roman Catholic Priests
19.91	80.09	633	Protestant Seminarians
17.93	82.07	1205	Candidates for Theology Education
17.68	82.32	2002	Sisters in Roman Catholic Religious Orders
12.00	88.00	50	Directors of Religious Education

JUDGMENT-PERCEPTION

J Percent	P	Total Sample Size	Sample Description
85.29	14.71	102	Ordained Roman Catholic Deacons
73.83	26.17	2002	Sisters in Roman Catholic Religious Orders
73.35	26.65	319	Rabbis
72.55	27.45	51	Roman Catholic Seminarians
70.57	29.43	1298	Roman Catholic Priests
70.00	30.00	50	Directors of Religious Education
68.24	31.76	85	Protestants in Specialized Ministries
67.82	32.18	1554	Protestant Ministers
66.43	33.57	1147	Nuns and Other Religious Workers
66.21	33.79	219	Priests and Monks
65.12	34.88	2010	RELIGIOUS WORKERS -ALL DENOMINATIONS-
64.91	35.09	114	Brothers in Roman Catholic Religious Orders
63.40	36.60	1205	Candidates for Theology Education
63.35	36.65	633	Protestant Seminarians
62.92	37.08	534	Clergy, all denominations (except priests)
62.03	37.97	79	Religious Educator, all denominations

SENSING-THINKING

Percent ST	Total Sample Size	Sample Description
26.50	1147	Nuns and Other Religious Workers
24.51	102	Ordained Roman Catholic Deacons
19.15	2010	RELIGIOUS WORKERS -ALL DENOMINATIONS-
17.65	51	Roman Catholic Seminarians
17.54	114	Brothers in Roman Catholic Religious Orders
14.87	1298	Roman Catholic Priests
14.73	319	Rabbis
13.70	219	Priests and Monks
12.66	79	Religious Educator, all denominations
10.64	2002	Sisters in Roman Catholic Religious Orders
9.59	1554	Protestant Ministers
9.41	85	Protestants in Specialized Ministries
8.37	633	Protestant Seminarians
8.00	50	Directors of Religious Education
7.12	534	Clergy, all denominations (except priests)
6.80	1205	Candidates for Theology Education

SENSING-FEELING

Percent SF	Total Sample Size	Sample Description
49.45	2002	Sisters in Roman Catholic Religious Orders
43.86	114	Brothers in Roman Catholic Religious Orders
39.60	1298	Roman Catholic Priests
37.25	102	Ordained Roman Catholic Deacons
36.81	633	Protestant Seminarians
34.18	79	Religious Educator, all denominations
34.09	1147	Nuns and Other Religious Workers
30.15	2010	RELIGIOUS WORKERS -ALL DENOMINATIONS-
29.96	1205	Candidates for Theology Education
28.06	1554	Protestant Ministers
27.27	319	Rabbis
26.00	50	Directors of Religious Education
24.66	219	Priests and Monks
23.60	534	Clergy, all denominations (except priests)
22.35	85	Protestants in Specialized Ministries
19.61	51	Roman Catholic Seminarians

INTUITION-FEELING

Percent NF	Total Sample Size	Sample Description
62.00	50	Directors of Religious Education
55.06	534	Clergy, all denominations (except priests)
52.94	85	Protestants in Specialized Ministries
52.94	51	Roman Catholic Seminarians
52.12	1205	Candidates for Theology Education
50.23	219	Priests and Monks
49.16	1554	Protestant Ministers
43.29	633	Protestant Seminarians
43.04	79	Religious Educator, all denominations
40.75	319	Rabbis
40.37	1298	Roman Catholic Priests
35.32	2010	RELIGIOUS WORKERS -ALL DENOMINATIONS-
32.87	2002	Sisters in Roman Catholic Religious Orders
31.58	114	Brothers in Roman Catholic Religious Orders
29.41	102	Ordained Roman Catholic Deacons
22.58	1147	Nuns and Other Religious Workers

INTUITION-THINKING

Percent NT	Total Sample Size	Sample Description
17.24	319	Rabbis
16.83	1147	Nuns and Other Religious Workers
15.37	2010	RELIGIOUS WORKERS -ALL DENOMINATIONS-
15.29	85	Protestants in Specialized Ministries
14.23	534	Clergy, all denominations (except priests)
13.19	1554	Protestant Ministers
11.53	633	Protestant Seminarians
11.42	219	Priests and Monks
11.12	1205	Candidates for Theology Education
10.13	79	Religious Educator, all denominations
9.80	51	Roman Catholic Seminarians
8.82	102	Ordained Roman Catholic Deacons
7.04	2002	Sisters in Roman Catholic Religious Orders
7.02	114	Brothers in Roman Catholic Religious Orders
5.16	1298	Roman Catholic Priests
4.00	50	Directors of Religious Education

STUDENTS

Section XI

STUDENT POPULATIONS

Samples in Section XI

Name of Sample	Number in Sample
College Student Leaders	55
College Students in Student Government	50
Gifted High School Seniors	164
High School Student Leaders	122
High School Students in Australia	3373
High School Students in Florida Future Scientist Program	793
Leaders in Student Government Activities	225
National Merit Scholarship Finalists	1001
Phi Beta Kappa	75
Rhodes Scholars	71
Adrian College - Freshmen	197
Auburn University - Freshmen	10342
Berkshire Christian College - Freshmen and Transfers	403
Concordia College - Freshmen	3149
Franklin and Marshall College - Freshmen	1760
Hope College - Freshmen	1505
Mercer University - Freshmen	1506
Nicholls State University - Freshmen	4150
Parks College - Freshmen and Transfers	405
Rollins College - Freshmen	395
Rosemont College - Freshmen	228
St. Clair College	1973
St. Louis University - Freshmen	550
University of Florida - Freshmen	2514
University of Maine - Freshmen	4035
University of North Carolina at Greensboro - Freshmen	2492
University of Wisconsin at Stevens Point - Freshmen	1169

Comments

The samples of Student Populations are by no means designed to be representative of the large numbers of student populations in the MBTI Data Bank. They supplement the samples of students at various levels which you will find in the first section of Normative Samples.

The first section gives the type tables for the schools named in Table 8.22 on page 137 of the Manual. The purpose of this table was to make clear that each school has a characteristic distribution of types, and that this distribution has implications for faculty and administrators. The type table of a college or university student population gives information about the probable learning styles of most students, the homogeneity or heterogeneity of interests of the student body, the types which will more or less easily find kindred spirits, the fields of study most likely to be popular, and the probable balance of student interest in the more academic versus more applied fields.

The more the focus on liberal arts, the more I and N students are expected. Technical and applied schools are expected to have more sensing types. Schools with a religious orientation are expected to attract more feeling types.

The second group of tables are students with special academic achievements-- Merit Finalists, Phi Beta Kappa and Rhodes Scholars. Here the samples are noteworthy for the proportion of intuitive types.

Summary listings of tables for EI, SN, TF, JP, ST, SF, NF and NT will be found after the last type table.

College Student Leaders

	SENSING		INTUITION	
	THINKING	FEELING	FEELING	THINKING

ISTJ	ISFJ	INFJ	INTJ
N= 2	N= 0	N= 1	N= 3
%= 3.64	%= 0.00	%= 1.82	%= 5.45
■■■■		■■	■■■■■

ISTP	ISFP	INFP	INTP
N= 0	N= 0	N= 1	N= 2
%= 0.00	%= 0.00	%= 1.82	%= 3.64
		■■	■■■■

ESTP	ESFP	ENFP	ENTP
N= 3	N= 0	N= 3	N= 4
%= 5.45	%= 0.00	%= 5.45	%= 7.27
■■■■■		■■■■■	■■■■■■■

ESTJ	ESFJ	ENFJ	ENTJ
N= 15	N= 5	N= 6	N= 10
%= 27.27	%= 9.09	%= 10.91	%= 18.18
■■■■■■■■■■	■■■■■■■■	■■■■■■■■■■	■■■■■■■■■■
■■■■■■■■■■	■		■■■■■■■■
■■■■■■■■			

JUDGMENT — PERCEPTION (INTROVERSION)

PERCEPTION — JUDGMENT (EXTRAVERSION)

	N	%
E	46	83.64
I	9	16.36
S	25	45.45
N	30	54.55
T	39	70.91
F	16	29.09
J	42	76.36
P	13	23.64
I J	6	10.91
I P	3	5.45
E P	10	18.18
E J	36	65.45
S T	20	36.36
S F	5	9.09
N F	11	20.00
N T	19	34.55
S J	22	40.00
S P	3	5.45
N P	10	18.18
N J	20	36.36
T J	30	54.55
T P	9	16.36
F P	4	7.27
F J	12	21.82
I N	7	12.73
E N	23	41.82
I S	2	3.64
E S	23	41.82
E T	32	58.18
E F	14	25.45
I F	2	3.64
I T	7	12.73
S dom	5	9.09
N dom	11	20.00
T dom	27	49.09
F dom	12	21.82

Note: ■ = 1% of sample   8630600

Data collected by Charlotte Jacobsen of Rosemont College on January 21, 1984 using Form G. Subjects were 55% female and 45% male college students attending a leadership conference. Students were a mixture of traditional and non-traditional ages, academic backgrounds and ethnic backgrounds. All students held leadership positions on their campuses and represented institutions from southeastern Pennsylvania. These data are used with permission and have not been published elsewhere to date.

College Students in Student Government

	SENSING		INTUITION	
	THINKING	FEELING	FEELING	THINKING

ISTJ	ISFJ	INFJ	INTJ
N= 0	N= 3	N= 0	N= 1
%= 0.00	%= 6.00	%= 0.00	%= 2.00
	■■■■■■		■■

ISTP	ISFP	INFP	INTP
N= 1	N= 1	N= 2	N= 1
%= 2.00	%= 2.00	%= 4.00	%= 2.00
■■	■■	■■■■	■■

ESTP	ESFP	ENFP	ENTP
N= 2	N= 2	N= 6	N= 3
%= 4.00	%= 4.00	%= 12.00	%= 6.00
■■■■	■■■■	■■■■■■■■■■ ■■	■■■■■■

ESTJ	ESFJ	ENFJ	ENTJ
N= 7	N= 7	N= 9	N= 5
%= 14.00	%= 14.00	%= 18.00	%= 10.00
■■■■■■■■■■ ■■■■	■■■■■■■■■■ ■■■■	■■■■■■■■■■ ■■■■■■■■	■■■■■■■■■■

JUDGMENT — INTROVERSION — PERCEPTION — PERCEPTION — EXTRAVERSION — JUDGMENT

	N	%
E	41	82.00
I	9	18.00
S	23	46.00
N	27	54.00
T	20	40.00
F	30	60.00
J	32	64.00
P	18	36.00
I J	4	8.00
I P	5	10.00
E P	13	26.00
E J	28	56.00
S T	10	20.00
S F	13	26.00
N F	17	34.00
N T	10	20.00
S J	17	34.00
S P	6	12.00
N P	12	24.00
N J	15	30.00
T J	13	26.00
T P	7	14.00
F P	11	22.00
F J	19	38.00
I N	4	8.00
E N	23	46.00
I S	5	10.00
E S	18	36.00
E T	17	34.00
E F	24	48.00
I F	6	12.00
I T	3	6.00
S dom	7	14.00
N dom	10	20.00
T dom	14	28.00
F dom	19	38.00

Note: ■ = 1% of sample   8630602

Data collected by Charlotte Jacobsen of Rosemont College in September 1982 and 1983 using Form G. Subjects were 100% female college students elected to leadership positions in student government. Students were from 17 to 21 years old, all white, mostly Catholic and from the eastern United States. Students were enrolled full time in a moderately selective, Catholic women's college in southeastern Pennsylvania. These data are used with permission and have not been published elsewhere to date.

Gifted High School Seniors

N = 164

	SENSING		INTUITION				N	%
	THINKING	FEELING	FEELING	THINKING				

ISTJ	ISFJ	INFJ	INTJ
N= 13	N= 7	N= 3	N= 9
%= 7.93	%= 4.27	%= 1.83	%= 5.49
■■■■■■■■	■■■■	■■	■■■■■

ISTP	ISFP	INFP	INTP
N= 4	N= 7	N= 11	N= 25
%= 2.44	%= 4.27	%= 6.71	%= 15.24
■■	■■■■	■■■■■■■	■■■■■■■■■■ ■■■■■

ESTP	ESFP	ENFP	ENTP
N= 2	N= 7	N= 27	N= 16
%= 1.22	%= 4.27	%= 16.46	%= 9.76
■	■■■■	■■■■■■■■■■■ ■■■■■■	■■■■■■■■■■

ESTJ	ESFJ	ENFJ	ENTJ
N= 5	N= 9	N= 9	N= 10
%= 3.05	%= 5.49	%= 5.49	%= 6.10
■■■	■■■■■	■■■■■	■■■■■■

JUDGMENT — INTROVERSION — PERCEPTION — PERCEPTION — EXTRAVERSION — JUDGMENT

	N	%
E	85	51.83
I	79	48.17
S	54	32.93
N	110	67.07
T	84	51.22
F	80	48.78
J	65	39.63
P	99	60.37
I J	32	19.51
I P	47	28.66
E P	52	31.71
E J	33	20.12
S T	24	14.63
S F	30	18.29
N F	50	30.49
N T	60	36.59
S J	34	20.73
S P	20	12.20
N P	79	48.17
N J	31	18.90
T J	37	22.56
T P	47	28.66
F P	52	31.71
F J	28	17.07
I N	48	29.27
E N	62	37.80
I S	31	18.90
E S	23	14.02
E T	33	20.12
E F	52	31.71
I F	28	17.07
I T	51	31.10
S dom	29	17.68
N dom	55	33.54
T dom	44	26.83
F dom	36	21.95

Note: ■ = 1% of sample   8628020

Data collected by Carol Clark and Barbara Cloud of the Alachua County Florida School System and Jerry Macdaid of CAPT from 1981 through 1986 using Form F. Subjects were students identified as gifted who chose to participate in an internship in community leadership and development seminars for credit. The criteria used for giftedness were twofold: 1) a score two standard deviations above the mean on an approved individual I.Q. measure, 2) a classroom teacher observing in the student 50% or more of the items on a gifted characteristics checklist. Students were 52% female and 48% male; the modal age was 17, and the students were predominantly white. These data are used with permission and have not been published elsewhere to date.

High School Student Leaders

N = 122

	SENSING		INTUITION	
	THINKING	FEELING	FEELING	THINKING

ISTJ	ISFJ	INFJ	INTJ
N= 12	N= 6	N= 4	N= 5
%= 9.84	%= 4.92	%= 3.28	%= 4.10
■■■■■■■■■	■■■■■	■■■	■■■■

ISTP	ISFP	INFP	INTP
N= 5	N= 4	N= 10	N= 1
%= 4.10	%= 3.28	%= 8.20	%= .82
■■■■	■■■	■■■■■■■■	■

ESTP	ESFP	ENFP	ENTP
N= 3	N= 7	N= 16	N= 9
%= 2.46	%= 5.74	%= 13.11	%= 7.38
■■	■■■■■■	■■■■■■■■■■■■■ ■■■	■■■■■■■

ESTJ	ESFJ	ENFJ	ENTJ
N= 19	N= 6	N= 13	N= 2
%= 15.57	%= 4.92	%= 10.66	%= 1.64
■■■■■■■■■■■■■ ■■■■■■	■■■■■	■■■■■■■■■■■■ ■	■■

JUDGMENT — INTROVERSION

PERCEPTION — INTROVERSION

PERCEPTION — EXTRAVERSION

JUDGMENT — EXTRAVERSION

	N	%
E	75	61.48
I	47	38.52
S	62	50.82
N	60	49.18
T	56	45.90
F	66	54.10
J	67	54.92
P	55	45.08
I J	27	22.13
I P	20	16.39
E P	35	28.69
E J	40	32.79
S T	39	31.97
S F	23	18.85
N F	43	35.25
N T	17	13.93
S J	43	35.25
S P	19	15.57
N P	36	29.51
N J	24	19.67
T J	38	31.15
T P	18	14.75
F P	37	30.33
F J	29	23.77
I N	20	16.39
E N	40	32.79
I S	27	22.13
E S	35	28.69
E T	33	27.05
E F	42	34.43
I F	24	19.67
I T	23	18.85
S dom	28	22.95
N dom	34	27.87
T dom	27	22.13
F dom	33	27.05

Note: ■ = 1% of sample   8630603

Data collected by Charlotte Jacobsen of Rosemont College in January 1982 and August 1983 using Form G. Subjects were 70% female and 30% male high school students attending a leadership development conference. No other demographic data were reported. All students held leadership positions in Red Cross activities and organizations in Pennsylvania, New York and Maryland. These data are used with permission and have not been published elsewhere to date.

High School Students in Australia

N = 3373

	SENSING		INTUITION	
	THINKING	FEELING	FEELING	THINKING

ISTJ	ISFJ	INFJ	INTJ
N= 272	N= 130	N= 43	N= 69
%= 8.06	%= 3.85	%= 1.27	%= 2.05
■■■■■■■■	■■■■	■	■■

ISTP	ISFP	INFP	INTP
N= 174	N= 124	N= 109	N= 129
%= 5.16	%= 3.68	%= 3.23	%= 3.82
■■■■■	■■■■	■■■	■■■■

ESTP	ESFP	ENFP	ENTP
N= 288	N= 305	N= 341	N= 227
%= 8.54	%= 9.04	%= 10.11	%= 6.73
■■■■■■■■	■■■■■■■■■	■■■■■■■■■■	■■■■■■■

ESTJ	ESFJ	ENFJ	ENTJ
N= 582	N= 341	N= 109	N= 130
%= 17.25	%= 10.11	%= 3.23	%= 3.85
■■■■■■■■■■■■■■■■■	■■■■■■■■■■	■■■	■■■■

JUDGMENT — INTROVERSION — PERCEPTION — PERCEPTION — EXTRAVERSION — JUDGMENT

	N	%
E	2323	68.87
I	1050	31.13
S	2216	65.70
N	1157	34.30
T	1871	55.47
F	1502	44.53
J	1676	49.69
P	1697	50.31
I J	514	15.24
I P	536	15.89
E P	1161	34.42
E J	1162	34.45
S T	1316	39.02
S F	900	26.68
N F	602	17.85
N T	555	16.45
S J	1325	39.28
S P	891	26.42
N P	806	23.90
N J	351	10.41
T J	1053	31.22
T P	818	24.25
F P	879	26.06
F J	623	18.47
I N	350	10.38
E N	807	23.93
I S	700	20.75
E S	1516	44.95
E T	1227	36.38
E F	1096	32.49
I F	406	12.04
I T	644	19.09
S dom	995	29.50
N dom	680	20.16
T dom	1015	30.09
F dom	683	20.25

Note: ■ = 1% of sample

8631200

Data collected by Judy Denham of the Western Australian College of Advanced Education during 1980 using Form G. Subjects were students attending high school grades 10, 11 and 12. Students were ages 15 through 17 and attending school in Western Australia. The 10th grade was the last compulsory year of schooling, the 11th and 12th grade students were studying an academic rather than vocational curriculum. These data are used with permission and have not been published elsewhere to date.

High School Students in Florida Future Scientist Program

N = 793

	SENSING		INTUITION	
	THINKING	FEELING	FEELING	THINKING

ISTJ	ISFJ	INFJ	INTJ
N= 40	N= 29	N= 53	N= 92
%= 5.04	%= 3.66	%= 6.68	%= 11.60
■■■■■	■■■■	■■■■■■■	■■■■■■■■■■ ■■

ISTP	ISFP	INFP	INTP
N= 15	N= 13	N= 69	N= 78
%= 1.89	%= 1.64	%= 8.70	%= 9.84
■■	■■	■■■■■■■■■	■■■■■■■■■

ESTP	ESFP	ENFP	ENTP
N= 22	N= 15	N= 122	N= 73
%= 2.77	%= 1.89	%= 15.38	%= 9.21
■■■	■■	■■■■■■■■■■ ■■■■■	■■■■■■■■■

ESTJ	ESFJ	ENFJ	ENTJ
N= 33	N= 23	N= 60	N= 56
%= 4.16	%= 2.90	%= 7.57	%= 7.06
■■■■	■■■	■■■■■■■■	■■■■■■■

JUDGMENT — INTROVERSION — PERCEPTION — PERCEPTION — EXTRAVERSION — JUDGMENT

	N	%
E	404	50.95
I	389	49.05
S	190	23.96
N	603	76.04
T	409	51.58
F	384	48.42
J	386	48.68
P	407	51.32
I J	214	26.99
I P	175	22.07
E P	232	29.26
E J	172	21.69
S T	110	13.87
S F	80	10.09
N F	304	38.34
N T	299	37.70
S J	125	15.76
S P	65	8.20
N P	342	43.13
N J	261	32.91
T J	221	27.87
T P	188	23.71
F P	219	27.62
F J	165	20.81
I N	292	36.82
E N	311	39.22
I S	97	12.23
E S	93	11.73
E T	184	23.20
E F	220	27.74
I F	164	20.68
I T	225	28.37
S dom	106	13.37
N dom	340	42.88
T dom	182	22.95
F dom	165	20.81

Note: ■ = 1% of sample   8628000

Data collected by Elizabeth Abbott of the University of Florida and Mary McCaulley of CAPT from 1974 to 1982 using Form F. The subjects were high school students recommended by their schools to attend summer programs for scientifically gifted students to work with University of Florida faculty. Students were 46% female and 54% male; the modal age was 17; it is estimated that 85% were white and 95% were from the state of Florida. These data are used with permission and have not been published elsewhere to date.

Leaders in Student Government Activities

N = 225

	SENSING		INTUITION	
	THINKING	FEELING	FEELING	THINKING

ISTJ	ISFJ	INFJ	INTJ
N= 11	N= 6	N= 9	N= 2
%= 4.89	%= 2.67	%= 4.00	%= .89
■■■■■	■■■	■■■■	■

ISTP	ISFP	INFP	INTP
N= 8	N= 3	N= 8	N= 6
%= 3.56	%= 1.33	%= 3.56	%= 2.67
■■■■	■	■■■■	■■■

ESTP	ESFP	ENFP	ENTP
N= 8	N= 13	N= 27	N= 18
%= 3.56	%= 5.78	%= 12.00	%= 8.00
■■■■	■■■■■■	■■■■■■■■■■ ■■	■■■■■■■■

ESTJ	ESFJ	ENFJ	ENTJ
N= 47	N= 16	N= 8	N= 35
%= 20.89	%= 7.11	%= 3.56	%= 15.56
■■■■■■■■■■ ■■■■■■■■■■ ■	■■■■■■■	■■■■	■■■■■■■■■■ ■■■■■■

JUDGMENT — INTROVERSION — PERCEPTION
PERCEPTION — EXTRAVERSION — JUDGMENT

	N	%
E	172	76.44
I	53	23.56
S	112	49.78
N	113	50.22
T	135	60.00
F	90	40.00
J	134	59.56
P	91	40.44
I J	28	12.44
I P	25	11.11
E P	66	29.33
E J	106	47.11
S T	74	32.89
S F	38	16.89
N F	52	23.11
N T	61	27.11
S J	80	35.56
S P	32	14.22
N P	59	26.22
N J	54	24.00
T J	95	42.22
T P	40	17.78
F P	51	22.67
F J	39	17.33
I N	25	11.11
E N	88	39.11
I S	28	12.44
E S	84	37.33
E T	108	48.00
E F	64	28.44
I F	26	11.56
I T	27	12.00
S dom	38	16.89
N dom	56	24.89
T dom	96	42.67
F dom	35	15.56

Note: ■ = 1% of sample   8628019

Data collected by Alice Hadwin of Florida Community College at Jacksonville during October 1983. Subjects were student government, activities leaders and sponsors from community colleges in Florida. Students were 44% male and 54% female. No other demographic data were reported. These data are used with permission and have not been published elsewhere to date.

National Merit Scholarship Finalists

N = 1001

	SENSING		INTUITION	
	THINKING	FEELING	FEELING	THINKING

ISTJ	ISFJ	INFJ	INTJ
N= 46	N= 24	N= 67	N= 139
%= 4.60	%= 2.40	%= 6.69	%= 13.89
■■■■■	■■	■■■■■■■	■■■■■■■■■■■■■ ■■■■

ISTP	ISFP	INFP	INTP
N= 25	N= 11	N= 119	N= 140
%= 2.50	%= 1.10	%= 11.89	%= 13.99
■■	■	■■■■■■■■■■ ■■	■■■■■■■■■■ ■■■■

ESTP	ESFP	ENFP	ENTP
N= 7	N= 20	N= 123	N= 110
%= .70	%= 2.00	%= 12.29	%= 10.99
■	■■	■■■■■■■■■■■■ ■■	■■■■■■■■■■■ ■

ESTJ	ESFJ	ENFJ	ENTJ
N= 30	N= 13	N= 54	N= 73
%= 3.00	%= 1.30	%= 5.39	%= 7.29
■■■	■	■■■■■	■■■■■■■

JUDGMENT — INTROVERSION — PERCEPTION — PERCEPTION — EXTRAVERSION — JUDGMENT

	N	%
E	430	42.96
I	571	57.04
S	176	17.58
N	825	82.42
T	570	56.94
F	431	43.06
J	446	44.56
P	555	55.44
I J	276	27.57
I P	295	29.47
E P	260	25.97
E J	170	16.98
S T	108	10.79
S F	68	6.79
N F	363	36.26
N T	462	46.15
S J	113	11.29
S P	63	6.29
N P	492	49.15
N J	333	33.27
T J	288	28.77
T P	282	28.17
F P	273	27.27
F J	158	15.78
I N	465	46.45
E N	360	35.96
I S	106	10.59
E S	70	6.99
E T	220	21.98
E F	210	20.98
I F	221	22.08
I T	350	34.97
S dom	97	9.69
N dom	439	43.86
T dom	268	26.77
F dom	197	19.68

Note: ■ = 1% of sample   8628001

Data collected by John Holland using Form F. Subjects represented a 73% return rate of a one-sixth random sample of approximately 10,000 high school seniors who were National Merit Scholarship Finalists (students scoring the highest, by state, from over 550,000 students who took the qualifying test in March 1959) and graduated from high school in 1960. Students were 33% female and 67% male and mostly high socioeconomic status. These data are used with permission and were cited in:

Myers, I. B. with Myers, P. B. (1980). Gifts Differing. Palo Alto, CA: Consulting Psychologists Press.

Nichols, R. C. & Holland, J. L. (1963). Prediction of the first year college performance of high aptitude students. Psychological Monographs: General and Applied, 77(1, Whole No. 570).

Phi Beta Kappa

N = 75

	SENSING		INTUITION	
	THINKING	FEELING	FEELING	THINKING

ISTJ	ISFJ	INFJ	INTJ
N= 6	N= 3	N= 8	N= 10
%= 8.00	%= 4.00	%= 10.67	%= 13.33
■■■■■■■■	■■■■	■■■■■■■■■■ ■	■■■■■■■■■■■■■ ■■■

ISTP	ISFP	INFP	INTP
N= 2	N= 2	N= 10	N= 8
%= 2.67	%= 2.67	%= 13.33	%= 10.67
■■■	■■■	■■■■■■■■■■■ ■■■	■■■■■■■■■■ ■

ESTP	ESFP	ENFP	ENTP
N= 1	N= 2	N= 8	N= 2
%= 1.33	%= 2.67	%= 10.67	%= 2.67
■	■■■	■■■■■■■■■■ ■	■■■

ESTJ	ESFJ	ENFJ	ENTJ
N= 1	N= 1	N= 5	N= 6
%= 1.33	%= 1.33	%= 6.67	%= 8.00
■	■	■■■■■■■	■■■■■■■■

JUDGMENT — INTROVERSION — PERCEPTION — EXTRAVERSION — JUDGMENT
PERCEPTION

	N	%
E	26	34.67
I	49	65.33
S	18	24.00
N	57	76.00
T	36	48.00
F	39	52.00
J	40	53.33
P	35	46.67
I J	27	36.00
I P	22	29.33
E P	13	17.33
E J	13	17.33
S T	10	13.33
S F	8	10.67
N F	31	41.33
N T	26	34.67
S J	11	14.67
S P	7	9.33
N P	28	37.33
N J	29	38.67
T J	23	30.67
T P	13	17.33
F P	22	29.33
F J	17	22.67
I N	36	48.00
E N	21	28.00
I S	13	17.33
E S	5	6.67
E T	10	13.33
E F	16	21.33
I F	23	30.67
I T	26	34.67
S dom	12	16.00
N dom	28	37.33
T dom	17	22.67
F dom	18	24.00

Note: ■ = 1% of sample   8628002

Data collected by Gerald Macdaid, Mary McCaulley and Richard Kainz of CAPT during 1972, and followed up in 1982, using Form F. Subjects were a subset of over 2500 students who had been entering students at the University of Florida in 1972. Students were graduates nominated to the Phi Beta Kappa honor society for their academic achievement. The sample was comprised of 56% females and 44% males. These data are used with permission and have not been published elsewhere to date.

Rhodes Scholars

N = 71

	SENSING		INTUITION			N	%

THINKING	FEELING	FEELING	THINKING

ISTJ	ISFJ	INFJ	INTJ
N= 0	N= 1	N= 5	N= 8
%= 0.00	%= 1.41	%= 7.04	%= 11.27

ISTP	ISFP	INFP	INTP
N= 1	N= 1	N= 15	N= 10
%= 1.41	%= 1.41	%= 21.13	%= 14.08

ESTP	ESFP	ENFP	ENTP
N= 0	N= 1	N= 9	N= 8
%= 0.00	%= 1.41	%= 12.68	%= 11.27

ESTJ	ESFJ	ENFJ	ENTJ
N= 0	N= 1	N= 6	N= 5
%= 0.00	%= 1.41	%= 8.45	%= 7.04

	N	%
E	30	42.25
I	41	57.75
S	5	7.04
N	66	92.96
T	32	45.07
F	39	54.93
J	26	36.62
P	45	63.38
I J	14	19.72
I P	27	38.03
E P	18	25.35
E J	12	16.90
S T	1	1.41
S F	4	5.63
N F	35	49.30
N T	31	43.66
S J	2	2.82
S P	3	4.23
N P	42	59.15
N J	24	33.80
T J	13	18.31
T P	19	26.76
F P	26	36.62
F J	13	18.31
I N	38	53.52
E N	28	39.44
I S	3	4.23
E S	2	2.82
E T	13	18.31
E F	17	23.94
I F	22	30.99
I T	19	26.76
S dom	2	2.82
N dom	30	42.25
T dom	16	22.54
F dom	23	32.39

Note: ■ = 1% of sample   8628021

Data collected by Peter Myers during the fall of 1947 and 1948. Subjects were beginning Rhodes Scholars. Scholars were all white male students selected from finalists from each of the continental U.S. states, Hawaii, and Alaska. Most scholars' ages ranged from 19 to 22, however a small percentage were as old as 33 since the age eligibility range was extended for this post war group. These data are used with permission and were cited in:

Myers, I. B. with Myers, P. B. (1980). Gifts Differing. Palo Alto, CA: Consulting Psychologists Press.

485

Adrian College – Freshmen

N = 197

	SENSING		INTUITION			N	%
THINKING	FEELING	FEELING	THINKING				

<table>
<tr>
<td colspan="4">

ISTJ	ISFJ	INFJ	INTJ
N= 8	N= 29	N= 9	N= 3
%= 4.06	%= 14.72	%= 4.57	%= 1.52
■■■■	■■■■■■■■■■■■■■	■■■■■	■■
	■■■■■		

</td>
</tr>
</table>

						N	%
					E	113	57.36
					I	84	42.64
					S	126	63.96
					N	71	36.04
					T	40	20.30
					F	157	79.70
					J	105	53.30
					P	92	46.70
					I J	49	24.87
					I P	35	17.77
					E P	57	28.93
					E J	56	28.43
					ST	28	14.21
					SF	98	49.75
					NF	59	29.95
					NT	12	6.09
					S J	75	38.07
					S P	51	25.89
					N P	41	20.81
					N J	30	15.23
					T J	21	10.66
					T P	19	9.64
					F P	73	37.06
					F J	84	42.64
					IN	24	12.18
					EN	47	23.86
					I S	60	30.46
					ES	66	33.50
					ET	22	11.17
					EF	91	46.19
					I F	66	33.50
					I T	18	9.14
					S dom	65	32.99
					N dom	41	20.81
					T dom	17	8.63
					F dom	74	37.56

The following type-table cells appear in the grid:

ISTP — N= 5, %= 2.54 — ■■■
ISFP — N= 18, %= 9.14 — ■■■■■■■■■
INFP — N= 10, %= 5.08 — ■■■■■
INTP — N= 2, %= 1.02 — ■

ESTP — N= 8, %= 4.06 — ■■■■
ESFP — N= 20, %= 10.15 — ■■■■■■■■■■
ENFP — N= 25, %= 12.69 — ■■■■■■■■■■ ■■■
ENTP — N= 4, %= 2.03 — ■■

ESTJ — N= 7, %= 3.55 — ■■■■
ESFJ — N= 31, %= 15.74 — ■■■■■■■■■■■ ■■■■■■
ENFJ — N= 15, %= 7.61 — ■■■■■■■■
ENTJ — N= 3, %= 1.52 — ■■

Side labels: JUDGMENT / PERCEPTION (INTROVERSION); PERCEPTION / JUDGMENT (EXTRAVERSION)

Note: ■ = 1% of sample   8628011

Data collected by R. Garret Demarest of Adrian College during 1978 using Form G. Adrian is a small, church affiliated liberal arts college in Michigan, with a student body of 1000. Subjects were 52% male and 48% female incoming freshmen at the college. Students were mostly from Michigan with some from Ohio. No other demographic data were reported. These data are used with permission and were cited in:

Myers, I. B. & McCaulley, M. H. (1985). Manual: A Guide to the Development and Use of the Myers-Briggs Type Indicator. Palo Alto, CA: Consulting Psychologists Press.

Auburn University – Freshmen

N = 10342

	SENSING		INTUITION				N	%
	THINKING	FEELING	FEELING	THINKING				

ISTJ	ISFJ	INFJ	INTJ
N= 538	N= 872	N= 374	N= 233
%= 5.20	%= 8.43	%= 3.62	%= 2.25
■■■■■	■■■■■■■■	■■■■	■■

ISTP	ISFP	INFP	INTP
N= 336	N= 784	N= 916	N= 353
%= 3.25	%= 7.58	%= 8.86	%= 3.41
■■■	■■■■■■■■	■■■■■■■■■	■■■

ESTP	ESFP	ENFP	ENTP
N= 410	N= 1063	N= 1327	N= 418
%= 3.96	%= 10.28	%= 12.83	%= 4.04
■■■■	■■■■■■■■■■	■■■■■■■■■■ ■■■	■■■■

ESTJ	ESFJ	ENFJ	ENTJ
N= 650	N= 1237	N= 533	N= 298
%= 6.29	%= 11.96	%= 5.15	%= 2.88
■■■■■■	■■■■■■■■■■■ ■■	■■■■■	■■■

JUDGMENT — INTROVERSION — PERCEPTION
PERCEPTION — EXTRAVERSION — JUDGMENT

	N	%
E	5936	57.40
I	4406	42.60
S	5890	56.95
N	4452	43.05
T	3236	31.29
F	7106	68.71
J	4735	45.78
P	5607	54.22
I J	2017	19.50
I P	2389	23.10
E P	3218	31.12
E J	2718	26.28
S T	1934	18.70
S F	3956	38.25
N F	3150	30.46
N T	1302	12.59
S J	3297	31.88
S P	2593	25.07
N P	3014	29.14
N J	1438	13.90
T J	1719	16.62
T P	1517	14.67
F P	4090	39.55
F J	3016	29.16
I N	1876	18.14
E N	2576	24.91
I S	2530	24.46
E S	3360	32.49
E T	1776	17.17
E F	4160	40.22
I F	2946	28.49
I T	1460	14.12
S dom	2883	27.88
N dom	2352	22.74
T dom	1637	15.83
F dom	3470	33.55

Note: ■ = 1% of sample   8628004

Data collected by Harold Grant of Auburn University from 1970 through 1975 using Form F. Subjects were students entering the university, most of whom were tested in the summer before classes started. These data are used with permission and were cited in:

Myers, I. B. & McCaulley, M. H. (1985). Manual: A Guide to the Development and Use of the Myers-Briggs Type Indicator. Palo Alto, CA: Consulting Psychologists Press.

Berkshire Christian College – Freshmen and Transfers

N = 403

	SENSING		INTUITION	
	THINKING	FEELING	FEELING	THINKING

<table>
<tr>
<td>
ISTJ
N= 17
%= 4.22
■■■■
</td>
<td>
ISFJ
N= 68
%= 16.87
■■■■■■■■■■■■■■■■■
</td>
<td>
INFJ
N= 18
%= 4.47
■■■■
</td>
<td>
INTJ
N= 4
%= .99
■
</td>
</tr>
<tr>
<td>
ISTP
N= 13
%= 3.23
■■■
</td>
<td>
ISFP
N= 50
%= 12.41
■■■■■■■■■■■■
</td>
<td>
INFP
N= 42
%= 10.42
■■■■■■■■■■
</td>
<td>
INTP
N= 3
%= .74
■
</td>
</tr>
<tr>
<td>
ESTP
N= 6
%= 1.49
■
</td>
<td>
ESFP
N= 36
%= 8.93
■■■■■■■■■
</td>
<td>
ENFP
N= 41
%= 10.17
■■■■■■■■■■
</td>
<td>
ENTP
N= 3
%= .74
■
</td>
</tr>
<tr>
<td>
ESTJ
N= 9
%= 2.23
■■
</td>
<td>
ESFJ
N= 70
%= 17.37
■■■■■■■■■■■■■■■■■
</td>
<td>
ENFJ
N= 21
%= 5.21
■■■■■
</td>
<td>
ENTJ
N= 2
%= .50
</td>
</tr>
</table>

	N	%
E	188	46.65
I	215	53.35
S	269	66.75
N	134	33.25
T	57	14.14
F	346	85.86
J	209	51.86
P	194	48.14
I J	107	26.55
I P	108	26.80
E P	86	21.34
E J	102	25.31
S T	45	11.17
S F	224	55.58
N F	122	30.27
N T	12	2.98
S J	164	40.69
S P	105	26.05
N P	89	22.08
N J	45	11.17
T J	32	7.94
T P	25	6.20
F P	169	41.94
F J	177	43.92
I N	67	16.63
E N	67	16.63
I S	148	36.72
E S	121	30.02
E T	20	4.96
E F	168	41.69
I F	178	44.17
I T	37	9.18
S dom	127	31.51
N dom	66	16.38
T dom	27	6.70
F dom	183	45.41

Note: ■ = 1% of sample   8628013

Data collected by Garth Story of Berkshire Christian College from 1974 through 1982 using Form F. Subjects were all students entering the college as freshmen or transfers. The college describes itself as a conservative private college with a yearly enrollment of 150 students. All students were pursuing studies directly or indirectly related to christian vocations. Students were approximately 50% male and 50% female; modal age was 18; about 50% were from conservative rural backgrounds. These data are used with permission and were cited in:

Myers, I. B. & McCaulley, M. H. (1985). Manual: A Guide to the Development and Use of the Myers-Briggs Type Indicator.
    Palo Alto, CA: Consulting Psychologists Press.

Concordia College – Freshmen

N = 3149

	SENSING		INTUITION	
	THINKING	FEELING	FEELING	THINKING

ISTJ	ISFJ	INFJ	INTJ
N= 151	N= 445	N= 219	N= 73
%= 4.80	%= 14.13	%= 6.95	%= 2.32

ISTP	ISFP	INFP	INTP
N= 96	N= 278	N= 353	N= 83
%= 3.05	%= 8.83	%= 11.21	%= 2.64

ESTP	ESFP	ENFP	ENTP
N= 52	N= 233	N= 398	N= 58
%= 1.65	%= 7.40	%= 12.64	%= 1.84

ESTJ	ESFJ	ENFJ	ENTJ
N= 123	N= 310	N= 199	N= 78
%= 3.91	%= 9.84	%= 6.32	%= 2.48

JUDGMENT — INTROVERSION — PERCEPTION — EXTRAVERSION — PERCEPTION — JUDGMENT

	N	%
E	1451	46.08
I	1698	53.92
S	1688	53.60
N	1461	46.40
T	714	22.67
F	2435	77.33
J	1598	50.75
P	1551	49.25
I J	888	28.20
I P	810	25.72
E P	741	23.53
E J	710	22.55
S T	422	13.40
S F	1266	40.20
N F	1169	37.12
N T	292	9.27
S J	1029	32.68
S P	659	20.93
N P	892	28.33
N J	569	18.07
T J	425	13.50
T P	289	9.18
F P	1262	40.08
F J	1173	37.25
I N	728	23.12
E N	733	23.28
I S	970	30.80
E S	718	22.80
E T	311	9.88
E F	1140	36.20
I F	1295	41.12
I T	403	12.80
S dom	881	27.98
N dom	748	23.75
T dom	380	12.07
F dom	1140	36.20

Note: ■ = 1% of sample   8628010

Data collected by Erich A. von Fange of Concordia College between 1975 and 1985 using Form F. The subjects were incoming students at Concordia Lutheran College in Ann Arbor, Michigan. Sixty eight percent of these students were planning church-related vocations. Students were 51% female and 49% male. These data are used with permission and were cited in: Myers, I. B. & McCaulley, M. H. (1985). Manual: A Guide to the Development and Use of the Myers-Briggs Type Indicator. Palo Alto, CA: Consulting Psychologists Press.

Franklin and Marshall College – Freshmen

N = 1760

	SENSING		INTUITION	
	THINKING	FEELING	FEELING	THINKING

ISTJ	ISFJ	INFJ	INTJ
N= 160	N= 125	N= 107	N= 90
%= 9.09	%= 7.10	%= 6.08	%= 5.11
■■■■■■■■■	■■■■■■■	■■■■■■	■■■■■

ISTP	ISFP	INFP	INTP
N= 82	N= 87	N= 127	N= 102
%= 4.66	%= 4.94	%= 7.22	%= 5.80
■■■■■	■■■■■	■■■■■■■	■■■■■■

ESTP	ESFP	ENFP	ENTP
N= 77	N= 100	N= 178	N= 104
%= 4.37	%= 5.68	%= 10.11	%= 5.91
■■■■	■■■■■■	■■■■■■■■■■	■■■■■■

ESTJ	ESFJ	ENFJ	ENTJ
N= 130	N= 120	N= 100	N= 71
%= 7.39	%= 6.82	%= 5.68	%= 4.03
■■■■■■■	■■■■■■■	■■■■■■	■■■■

JUDGMENT · INTROVERSION · PERCEPTION · PERCEPTION · EXTRAVERSION · JUDGMENT

	N	%
E	880	50.00
I	880	50.00
S	881	50.06
N	879	49.94
T	816	46.36
F	944	53.64
J	903	51.31
P	857	48.69
I J	482	27.39
I P	398	22.61
E P	459	26.08
E J	421	23.92
S T	449	25.51
S F	432	24.55
N F	512	29.09
N T	367	20.85
S J	535	30.40
S P	346	19.66
N P	511	29.03
N J	368	20.91
T J	451	25.62
T P	365	20.74
F P	492	27.95
F J	452	25.68
I N	426	24.20
E N	453	25.74
I S	454	25.80
E S	427	24.26
E T	382	21.70
E F	498	28.30
I F	446	25.34
I T	434	24.66
S dom	462	26.25
N dom	479	27.22
T dom	385	21.88
F dom	434	24.66

Note: ■ = 1% of sample   8628018

Data collected by O. W. Lacy of Franklin and Marshall College from 1980 through 1983 using Form F. Subjects were students entering the college. Students were 52% male and 48% female; and approximately 98% white. These data are used with permission and were cited in:

Myers, I. B. & McCaulley, M. H. (1985). Manual: A Guide to the Development and Use of the Myers-Briggs Type Indicator. Palo Alto, CA: Consulting Psychologists Press.

Hope College - Freshmen

N = 1505

	SENSING		INTUITION	
	THINKING	FEELING	FEELING	THINKING

ISTJ	ISFJ	INFJ	INTJ
N= 69	N= 136	N= 100	N= 49
%= 4.58	%= 9.04	%= 6.64	%= 3.26
■■■■■	■■■■■■■■■	■■■■■■■	■■■

ISTP	ISFP	INFP	INTP
N= 33	N= 103	N= 164	N= 48
%= 2.19	%= 6.84	%= 10.90	%= 3.19
■■	■■■■■■■	■■■■■■■■■■ ■	■■■

ESTP	ESFP	ENFP	ENTP
N= 38	N= 116	N= 243	N= 48
%= 2.52	%= 7.71	%= 16.15	%= 3.19
■■■	■■■■■■■■	■■■■■■■■■■ ■■■■■■	■■■

ESTJ	ESFJ	ENFJ	ENTJ
N= 66	N= 141	N= 111	N= 40
%= 4.39	%= 9.37	%= 7.38	%= 2.66
■■■■	■■■■■■■■■	■■■■■■■	■■■

JUDGMENT — INTROVERSION — PERCEPTION — PERCEPTION — EXTRAVERSION — JUDGMENT

	N	%
E	803	53.36
I	702	46.64
S	702	46.64
N	803	53.36
T	391	25.98
F	1114	74.02
J	712	47.31
P	793	52.69
I J	354	23.52
I P	348	23.12
E P	445	29.57
E J	358	23.79
S T	206	13.69
S F	496	32.96
N F	618	41.06
N T	185	12.29
S J	412	27.38
S P	290	19.27
N P	503	33.42
N J	300	19.93
T J	224	14.88
T P	167	11.10
F P	626	41.59
F J	488	32.43
I N	361	23.99
E N	442	29.37
I S	341	22.66
E S	361	23.99
E T	192	12.76
E F	611	40.60
I F	503	33.42
I T	199	13.22
S dom	359	23.85
N dom	440	29.24
T dom	187	12.43
F dom	519	34.49

Note: ■ = 1% of sample   8628005

Data collected by R. Garret Demarest of Hope College from 1973 through 1975 using Form F. Subjects were incoming freshmen at the college. Hope College is a small private, church affiliated liberal arts college in Michigan. The student body was approximately 2100 and primarily in residence at the college. Students came mostly from Michigan, with some from the eastern and mid-western states. These data are used with permission and were cited in:

Myers, I. B. & McCaulley, M. H. (1985). Manual: A Guide to the Development and Use of the Myers-Briggs Type Indicator.
  Palo Alto, CA: Consulting Psychologists Press.

Mercer University – Freshmen

N = 1506

	SENSING		INTUITION	
	THINKING	FEELING	FEELING	THINKING

ISTJ	ISFJ	INFJ	INTJ
N= 134	N= 119	N= 44	N= 56
%= 8.90	%= 7.90	%= 2.92	%= 3.72
■■■■■■■■■	■■■■■■■■	■■■	■■■■

ISTP	ISFP	INFP	INTP
N= 40	N= 87	N= 81	N= 58
%= 2.66	%= 5.78	%= 5.38	%= 3.85
■■■	■■■■■■	■■■■■	■■■■

ESTP	ESFP	ENFP	ENTP
N= 58	N= 144	N= 175	N= 53
%= 3.85	%= 9.56	%= 11.62	%= 3.52
■■■■	■■■■■■■■■■	■■■■■■■■■■■ ■■	■■■■

ESTJ	ESFJ	ENFJ	ENTJ
N= 124	N= 177	N= 103	N= 53
%= 8.23	%= 11.75	%= 6.84	%= 3.52
■■■■■■■■	■■■■■■■■■■■ ■■	■■■■■■■	■■■■

JUDGMENT — INTROVERSION — PERCEPTION — PERCEPTION — EXTRAVERSION — JUDGMENT

	N	%
E	887	58.90
I	619	41.10
S	883	58.63
N	623	41.37
T	576	38.25
F	930	61.75
J	810	53.78
P	696	46.22
I J	353	23.44
I P	266	17.66
E P	430	28.55
E J	457	30.35
ST	356	23.64
SF	527	34.99
NF	403	26.76
NT	220	14.61
S J	554	36.79
S P	329	21.85
NP	367	24.37
NJ	256	17.00
TJ	367	24.37
TP	209	13.88
FP	487	32.34
FJ	443	29.42
IN	239	15.87
EN	384	25.50
IS	380	25.23
ES	503	33.40
ET	288	19.12
EF	599	39.77
IF	331	21.98
IT	288	19.12
S dom	455	30.21
N dom	328	21.78
T dom	275	18.26
F dom	448	29.75

Note: ■ = 1% of sample   8628007

Data collected by Charles Schroeder and Barry Jenkins of Mercer University from 1978 through 1981. Subjects were incoming freshmen at the university. Mercer is a private, liberal arts university in central Georgia. Students were approximately 50% female and 50% male; the modal age was 18; 13% black and 87% white; the majority of students were from Georgia with 35% from Florida. These data are used with permission and were cited in:

Myers, I. B. & McCaulley, M. H. (1985). <u>Manual: A Guide to the Development and Use of the Myers-Briggs Type Indicator</u>. Palo Alto, CA: Consulting Psychologists Press.

Nicholls State University – Freshmen

N = 4150

	SENSING		INTUITION				N	%
	THINKING	FEELING	FEELING	THINKING				

ISTJ N= 374 %= 9.01 ■■■■■■■■■	**ISFJ** N= 408 %= 9.83 ■■■■■■■■■	**INFJ** N= 93 %= 2.24 ■■	**INTJ** N= 71 %= 1.71 ■■
ISTP N= 219 %= 5.28 ■■■■■	**ISFP** N= 280 %= 6.75 ■■■■■■■	**INFP** N= 186 %= 4.48 ■■■■	**INTP** N= 101 %= 2.43 ■■
ESTP N= 253 %= 6.10 ■■■■■■	**ESFP** N= 392 %= 9.45 ■■■■■■■■■	**ENFP** N= 337 %= 8.12 ■■■■■■■■	**ENTP** N= 147 %= 3.54 ■■■■
ESTJ N= 503 %= 12.12 ■■■■■■■■■■■■ ■■	**ESFJ** N= 555 %= 13.37 ■■■■■■■■■■■■■ ■■■	**ENFJ** N= 129 %= 3.11 ■■■	**ENTJ** N= 102 %= 2.46 ■■

JUDGMENT · INTROVERSION · PERCEPTION · PERCEPTION · EXTRAVERSION · JUDGMENT

	N	%
E	2418	58.27
I	1732	41.73
S	2984	71.90
N	1166	28.10
T	1770	42.65
F	2380	57.35
J	2235	53.86
P	1915	46.14
I J	946	22.80
I P	786	18.94
E P	1129	27.20
E J	1289	31.06
S T	1349	32.51
S F	1635	39.40
N F	745	17.95
N T	421	10.14
S J	1840	44.34
S P	1144	27.57
N P	771	18.58
N J	395	9.52
T J	1050	25.30
T P	720	17.35
F P	1195	28.80
F J	1185	28.55
I N	451	10.87
E N	715	17.23
I S	1281	30.87
E S	1703	41.04
E T	1005	24.22
E F	1413	34.05
I F	967	23.30
I T	765	18.43
S dom	1427	34.39
N dom	648	15.61
T dom	925	22.29
F dom	1150	27.71

Note: ■ = 1% of sample   8628008

Data collected by Bonnie Bourg of Nicholls State University from 1979 through 1982 using Form G. Subjects were incoming freshmen at Nicholls State, a regional university in Louisiana. Most students planned a major in business, 45% lived at home and commuted. Subjects were 51% female and 49% male, had a modal age of 18 with a high percent of older students; most were from a 12 parish area of Louisiana; 13% black, 81% white, 1% hispanic, 1% oriental-pacific and 3% no data. These data are used with permission and were cited in:

Myers, I. B. & McCaulley, M. H. (1985). Manual: A Guide to the Development and Use of the Myers-Briggs Type Indicator.

    Palo Alto, CA: Consulting Psychologists Press.

Parks College – Freshmen and Transfers

N = 405

	SENSING		INTUITION	
	THINKING	FEELING	FEELING	THINKING

ISTJ	ISFJ	INFJ	INTJ
N= 57	N= 26	N= 7	N= 19
%= 14.07	%= 6.42	%= 1.73	%= 4.69
■■■■■■■■■■■■■■	■■■■■■	■■	■■■■■
■■■■			

ISTP	ISFP	INFP	INTP
N= 33	N= 15	N= 26	N= 21
%= 8.15	%= 3.70	%= 6.42	%= 5.19
■■■■■■■■	■■■■	■■■■■■	■■■■■

ESTP	ESFP	ENFP	ENTP
N= 18	N= 22	N= 32	N= 24
%= 4.44	%= 5.43	%= 7.90	%= 5.93
■■■■	■■■■■	■■■■■■■■	■■■■■■

ESTJ	ESFJ	ENFJ	ENTJ
N= 49	N= 20	N= 18	N= 18
%= 12.10	%= 4.94	%= 4.44	%= 4.44
■■■■■■■■■■■■	■■■■■	■■■■	■■■■
■■			

JUDGMENT — INTROVERSION — PERCEPTION — PERCEPTION — EXTRAVERSION — JUDGMENT

	N	%
E	201	49.63
I	204	50.37
S	240	59.26
N	165	40.74
T	239	59.01
F	166	40.99
J	214	52.84
P	191	47.16
I J	109	26.91
I P	95	23.46
E P	96	23.70
E J	105	25.93
S T	157	38.77
S F	83	20.49
N F	83	20.49
N T	82	20.25
S J	152	37.53
S P	88	21.73
N P	103	25.43
N J	62	15.31
T J	143	35.31
T P	96	23.70
F P	95	23.46
F J	71	17.53
I N	73	18.02
E N	92	22.72
I S	131	32.35
E S	109	26.91
E T	109	26.91
E F	92	22.72
I F	74	18.27
I T	130	32.10
S dom	123	30.37
N dom	82	20.25
T dom	121	29.88
F dom	79	19.51

Note: ■ = 1% of sample

8628009

Data collected by Lois Erickson of Parks College of Saint Louis University during 1982 using Form F. Subjects were incoming freshmen and transfer students at the college. All college programs have a special emphasis on aerospace and aeronautical support occupations. Students were 7% female and 93% male; ranged in age from 18 to 30, with the median at about 24; about 10% were international students, 18% were from St. Louis and 72% from across the U.S. These data are used with permission and were cited in:

Myers, I. B. & McCaulley, M. H. (1985). Manual: A Guide to the Development and Use of the Myers-Briggs Type Indicator. Palo Alto, CA: Consulting Psychologists Press.

Rollins College – Freshmen

N = 395

	SENSING		INTUITION					N	%
	THINKING	FEELING	FEELING	THINKING					

<table>
<tr><td colspan="2">

ISTJ

N= 20
%= 5.06

■■■■■
</td><td colspan="2">

ISFJ

N= 35
%= 8.86

■■■■■■■■■
</td><td colspan="2">

INFJ

N= 29
%= 7.34

■■■■■■■
</td><td colspan="2">

INTJ

N= 12
%= 3.04

■■■
</td></tr>
</table>

Note: ■ = 1% of sample   8628014

	N	%
E	215	54.43
I	180	45.57
S	191	48.35
N	204	51.65
T	145	36.71
F	250	63.29
J	192	48.61
P	203	51.39
I J	96	24.30
I P	84	21.27
E P	119	30.13
E J	96	24.30
S T	78	19.75
S F	113	28.61
N F	137	34.68
N T	67	16.96
S J	113	28.61
S P	78	19.75
N P	125	31.65
N J	79	20.00
T J	71	17.97
T P	74	18.73
F P	129	32.66
F J	121	30.63
I N	90	22.78
E N	114	28.86
I S	90	22.78
E S	101	25.57
E T	86	21.77
E F	129	32.66
I F	121	30.63
I T	59	14.94
S dom	98	24.81
N dom	117	29.62
T dom	66	16.71
F dom	114	28.86

ISTJ N= 20 %= 5.06

ISFJ N= 35 %= 8.86

INFJ N= 29 %= 7.34

INTJ N= 12 %= 3.04

ISTP N= 15 %= 3.80

ISFP N= 20 %= 5.06

INFP N= 37 %= 9.37

INTP N= 12 %= 3.04

ESTP N= 18 %= 4.56

ESFP N= 25 %= 6.33

ENFP N= 47 %= 11.90

ENTP N= 29 %= 7.34

ESTJ N= 25 %= 6.33

ESFJ N= 33 %= 8.35

ENFJ N= 24 %= 6.08

ENTJ N= 14 %= 3.54

JUDGMENT — INTROVERSION — PERCEPTION — PERCEPTION — EXTRAVERSION — JUDGMENT

Data collected by Judith Provost of Rollins College during the Fall of 1984 using Form F. Subjects were approximately 100% of all incoming freshmen at Rollins College. Rollins is a small private four year liberal arts college in Central Florida. The students were 44% female and 56% male, traditional aged college students. Minorities represented less than 10% of the student body. The students were primarily in residence at the college; 50% were from Florida and 50% were from out of state, with most coming from the New England states. These data are used with permission and were cited in:

Myers, I. B. & McCaulley, M. H. (1985). Manual: A Guide to the Development and Use of the Myers-Briggs Type Indicator. Palo Alto, CA: Consulting Psychologists Press.

Rosemont College – Freshmen

	SENSING		INTUITION	
	THINKING	FEELING	FEELING	THINKING

ISTJ	ISFJ	INFJ	INTJ
N= 1	N= 22	N= 8	N= 3
%= .44	%= 9.65	%= 3.51	%= 1.32
	■■■■■■■■■	■■■■	■

ISTP	ISFP	INFP	INTP
N= 1	N= 12	N= 16	N= 4
%= .44	%= 5.26	%= 7.02	%= 1.75
	■■■■■	■■■■■■■	■■

ESTP	ESFP	ENFP	ENTP
N= 17	N= 31	N= 42	N= 14
%= 7.46	%= 13.60	%= 18.42	%= 6.14
■■■■■■■	■■■■■■■■■■■■■ ■■■■	■■■■■■■■■■■■■■ ■■■■■■■■	■■■■■

ESTJ	ESFJ	ENFJ	ENTJ
N= 19	N= 20	N= 14	N= 4
%= 8.33	%= 8.77	%= 6.14	%= 1.75
■■■■■■■■	■■■■■■■■■	■■■■■■	■■

JUDGMENT — INTROVERSION — PERCEPTION — PERCEPTION — EXTRAVERSION — JUDGMENT

	N	%
E	161	70.61
I	67	29.39
S	123	53.95
N	105	46.05
T	63	27.63
F	165	72.37
J	91	39.91
P	137	60.09
I J	34	14.91
I P	33	14.47
E P	104	45.61
E J	57	25.00
S T	38	16.67
S F	85	37.28
N F	80	35.09
N T	25	10.96
S J	62	27.19
S P	61	26.75
N P	76	33.33
N J	29	12.72
T J	27	11.84
T P	36	15.79
F P	101	44.30
F J	64	28.07
I N	31	13.60
E N	74	32.46
I S	36	15.79
E S	87	38.16
E T	54	23.68
E F	107	46.93
I F	58	25.44
I T	9	3.95
S dom	71	31.14
N dom	67	29.39
T dom	28	12.28
F dom	62	27.19

Note: ■ = 1% of sample

8630601

Data collected by Charlotte Jacobsen of Rosemont College in September 1982 and 1983 using Form G. Subjects were 100% freshmen females entering liberal arts and business majors in a moderately selective, Catholic women's college in southeastern Pennsylvania. Students were from middle to upper middle class backgrounds, primarily white, with a few minorities, from the eastern United States. These data are used with permission and have not been published elsewhere to date.

St. Clair College

N = 1973

	SENSING		INTUITION	
	THINKING	FEELING	FEELING	THINKING

ISTJ	ISFJ	INFJ	INTJ
N= 161	N= 201	N= 41	N=. 32
%= 8.16	%= 10.19	%= 2.08	%= 1.62
■■■■■■■■	■■■■■■■■■■	■■	■■

ISTP	ISFP	INFP	INTP
N= 106	N= 197	N= 116	N= 56
%= 5.37	%= 9.98	%= 5.88	%= 2.84
■■■■■	■■■■■■■■■■	■■■■■■	■■■

ESTP	ESFP	ENFP	ENTP
N= 119	N= 191	N= 211	N= 80
%= 6.03	%= 9.68	%= 10.69	%= 4.05
■■■■■■	■■■■■■■■■	■■■■■■■■■■ ■	■■■■

ESTJ	ESFJ	ENFJ	ENTJ
N= 163	N= 208	N= 51	N= 40
%= 8.26	%= 10.54	%= 2.58	%= 2.03
■■■■■■■■	■■■■■■■■■■ ■	■■■	■■

JUDGMENT — INTROVERSION — PERCEPTION — PERCEPTION — EXTRAVERSION — JUDGMENT

	N	%
E	1063	53.88
I	910	46.12
S	1346	68.22
N	627	31.78
T	757	38.37
F	1216	61.63
J	897	45.46
P	1076	54.54
I J	435	22.05
I P	475	24.08
E P	601	30.46
E J	462	23.42
S T	549	27.83
S F	797	40.40
N F	419	21.24
N T	208	10.54
S J	733	37.15
S P	613	31.07
N P	463	23.47
N J	164	8.31
T J	396	20.07
T P	361	18.30
F P	715	36.24
F J	501	25.39
I N	245	12.42
E N	382	19.36
I S	665	33.71
E S	681	34.52
E T	402	20.38
E F	661	33.50
I F	555	28.13
I T	355	17.99
S dom	672	34.06
N dom	364	18.45
T dom	365	18.50
F dom	572	28.99

Note: ■ = 1% of sample   8628003

Data collected by Brian Desbiens, Linda Peters, and Martha Wigle of St. Clair College during 1977 using Form F. Subjects were 76% of 2602 students at St. Clair College of Applied Arts and Technology, a community college in Windsor, Ontario offering terminal diplomas in technical training. Students were approximately 58% female and 42% male; mostly white; predominantly 20 to 21 years old and from a two county area in southwestern Ontario, Canada. These data are used with permission and were cited in:

Myers, I. B. & McCaulley, M. H. (1985). Manual: A Guide to the Development and Use of the Myers-Briggs Type Indicator.
    Palo Alto, CA: Consulting Psychologists Press.

St. Louis University – Freshmen

N = 550

	SENSING		INTUITION	
	THINKING	FEELING	FEELING	THINKING

ISTJ	ISFJ	INFJ	INTJ
N= 30	N= 31	N= 29	N= 14
%= 5.45	%= 5.64	%= 5.27	%= 2.55
■■■■■	■■■■■■	■■■■■	■■■

ISTP	ISFP	INFP	INTP
N= 18	N= 25	N= 36	N= 26
%= 3.27	%= 4.55	%= 6.55	%= 4.73
■■■	■■■■■	■■■■■■■	■■■■■

ESTP	ESFP	ENFP	ENTP
N= 17	N= 44	N= 83	N= 33
%= 3.09	%= 8.00	%= 15.09	%= 6.00
■■■	■■■■■■■■	■■■■■■■■■■ ■■■■■	■■■■■■

ESTJ	ESFJ	ENFJ	ENTJ
N= 40	N= 59	N= 38	N= 27
%= 7.27	%= 10.73	%= 6.91	%= 4.91
■■■■■■■	■■■■■■■■■■ ■	■■■■■■■	■■■■■

JUDGMENT — INTROVERSION — PERCEPTION

PERCEPTION — EXTRAVERSION — JUDGMENT

	N	%
E	341	62.00
I	209	38.00
S	264	48.00
N	286	52.00
T	205	37.27
F	345	62.73
J	268	48.73
P	282	51.27
I J	104	18.91
I P	105	19.09
E P	177	32.18
E J	164	29.82
S T	105	19.09
S F	159	28.91
N F	186	33.82
N T	100	18.18
S J	160	29.09
S P	104	18.91
N P	178	32.36
N J	108	19.64
T J	111	20.18
T P	94	17.09
F P	188	34.18
F J	157	28.55
I N	105	19.09
E N	181	32.91
I S	104	18.91
E S	160	29.09
E T	117	21.27
E F	224	40.73
I F	121	22.00
I T	88	16.00
S dom	122	22.18
N dom	159	28.91
T dom	111	20.18
F dom	158	28.73

Note: ■ = 1% of sample   8628015

Data collected by Charles Schroeder of St. Louis University during 1984 using Form G. Subjects were incoming freshmen at the university. Students were 54% female and 46% male; it is estimated that 90% were white and the predominant ages were 18 and 19. These data are used with permission and were cited in:

Myers, I. B. & McCaulley, M. H. (1985). Manual: A Guide to the Development and Use of the Myers-Briggs Type Indicator. Palo Alto, CA: Consulting Psychologists Press.

University of Florida - Freshmen

N = 2514

	SENSING		INTUITION	
	THINKING	FEELING	FEELING	THINKING

ISTJ	ISFJ	INFJ	INTJ
N= 160	N= 168	N= 113	N= 103
%= 6.36	%= 6.68	%= 4.49	%= 4.10
■■■■■■	■■■■■■■	■■■■	■■■■

ISTP	ISFP	INFP	INTP
N= 80	N= 133	N= 279	N= 127
%= 3.18	%= 5.29	%= 11.10	%= 5.05
■■■	■■■■■	■■■■■■■■■■ ■	■■■■■

ESTP	ESFP	ENFP	ENTP
N= 56	N= 145	N= 353	N= 123
%= 2.23	%= 5.77	%= 14.04	%= 4.89
■■	■■■■■■	■■■■■■■■■■ ■■■■	■■■■■

ESTJ	ESFJ	ENFJ	ENTJ
N= 190	N= 210	N= 165	N= 109
%= 7.56	%= 8.35	%= 6.56	%= 4.34
■■■■■■■■	■■■■■■■■	■■■■■■■	■■■■

JUDGMENT — INTROVERSION
PERCEPTION
PERCEPTION — EXTRAVERSION
JUDGMENT

	N	%
E	1351	53.74
I	1163	46.26
S	1142	45.43
N	1372	54.57
T	948	37.71
F	1566	62.29
J	1218	48.45
P	1296	51.55
I J	544	21.64
I P	619	24.62
E P	677	26.93
E J	674	26.81
S T	486	19.33
S F	656	26.09
N F	910	36.20
N T	462	18.38
S J	728	28.96
S P	414	16.47
N P	882	35.08
N J	490	19.49
T J	562	22.35
T P	386	15.35
F P	910	36.20
F J	656	26.09
I N	622	24.74
E N	750	29.83
I S	541	21.52
E S	601	23.91
E T	478	19.01
E F	873	34.73
I F	693	27.57
I T	470	18.70
S dom	529	21.04
N dom	692	27.53
T dom	506	20.13
F dom	787	31.30

Note: ■ = 1% of sample   8628016

Data collected by Mary McCaulley and Richard Kainz of CAPT during 1972 using Form F. Subjects were entering freshmen at the University of Florida in 1972. Students were 57% male and 43% female; 44% were 18 and 24% were 17 years old; 91% were white and 9% were of other races. These data are used with permission and were cited in:

McCaulley, M. H. (1973). Myers-Briggs Type Indicator applications (Report of Committee #13, University of Florida counseling study). Gainesville: University of Florida, Department of Clinical Psychology.

University of Maine – Freshmen

N = 4035

	SENSING		INTUITION	
	THINKING	FEELING	FEELING	THINKING

ISTJ	ISFJ	INFJ	INTJ
N= 226	N= 288	N= 126	N= 94
%= 5.60	%= 7.14	%= 3.12	%= 2.33
■■■■■■	■■■■■■■	■■■	■■

ISTP	ISFP	INFP	INTP
N= 160	N= 293	N= 331	N= 130
%= 3.97	%= 7.26	%= 8.20	%= 3.22
■■■■	■■■■■■■	■■■■■■■■	■■■

ESTP	ESFP	ENFP	ENTP
N= 199	N= 489	N= 601	N= 198
%= 4.93	%= 12.12	%= 14.89	%= 4.91
■■■■■	■■■■■■■■■■■■	■■■■■■■■■■■■■■	■■■■■
	■■	■■■■	

ESTJ	ESFJ	ENFJ	ENTJ
N= 214	N= 366	N= 213	N= 107
%= 5.30	%= 9.07	%= 5.28	%= 2.65
■■■■■	■■■■■■■■■	■■■■■	■■■

JUDGMENT — INTROVERSION — PERCEPTION — PERCEPTION — EXTRAVERSION — JUDGMENT

	N	%
E	2387	59.16
I	1648	40.84
S	2235	55.39
N	1800	44.61
T	1328	32.91
F	2707	67.09
J	1634	40.50
P	2401	59.50
I J	734	18.19
I P	914	22.65
E P	1487	36.85
E J	900	22.30
S T	799	19.80
S F	1436	35.59
N F	1271	31.50
N T	529	13.11
S J	1094	27.11
S P	1141	28.28
N P	1260	31.23
N J	540	13.38
T J	641	15.89
T P	687	17.03
F P	1714	42.48
F J	993	24.61
I N	681	16.88
E N	1119	27.73
I S	967	23.97
E S	1268	31.43
E T	718	17.79
E F	1669	41.36
I F	1038	25.72
I T	610	15.12
S dom	1202	29.79
N dom	1019	25.25
T dom	611	15.14
F dom	1203	29.81

Note: ■ = 1% of sample   8628006

Data collected by Scott Anchors of the University of Maine at Orono during 1981 and 1982 using Form F. Subjects were approximately 90% of the students entering the university who were tested by mail or during summer orientation programs. The university is a traditional land grant college. Students were approximately 45% female and 55% male; 98% were between the ages of 17 and 19; over 99% were white; 75% were originally from Maine, with the remainder primarily from the New England area. These data are used with permission and were cited in:

Myers, I. B. & McCaulley, M. H. (1985). Manual: A Guide to the Development and Use of the Myers-Briggs Type Indicator. Palo Alto, CA: Consulting Psychologists Press.

University of North Carolina at Greensboro – Freshmen

N = 2492

	SENSING		INTUITION				N	%
	THINKING	FEELING	FEELING	THINKING				

ISTJ	ISFJ	INFJ	INTJ
N= 117	N= 366	N= 90	N= 92
%= 4.70	%= 14.69	%= 3.61	%= 3.69
▪▪▪▪▪	▪▪▪▪▪▪▪▪▪▪▪▪▪▪	▪▪▪▪	▪▪▪▪
	▪▪▪▪▪		

ISTP	ISFP	INFP	INTP
N= 40	N= 171	N= 88	N= 168
%= 1.61	%= 6.86	%= 3.53	%= 6.74
▪▪	▪▪▪▪▪▪▪	▪▪▪▪	▪▪▪▪▪▪▪

ESTP	ESFP	ENFP	ENTP
N= 31	N= 181	N= 99	N= 211
%= 1.24	%= 7.26	%= 3.97	%= 8.47
▪	▪▪▪▪▪▪▪	▪▪▪▪	▪▪▪▪▪▪▪▪

ESTJ	ESFJ	ENFJ	ENTJ
N= 140	N= 372	N= 155	N= 171
%= 5.62	%= 14.93	%= 6.22	%= 6.86
▪▪▪▪▪▪	▪▪▪▪▪▪▪▪▪▪▪▪▪	▪▪▪▪▪▪	▪▪▪▪▪▪▪
	▪▪▪▪▪		

	N	%
E	1360	54.57
I	1132	45.43
S	1418	56.90
N	1074	43.10
T	970	38.92
F	1522	61.08
J	1503	60.31
P	989	39.69
I J	665	26.69
I P	467	18.74
E P	522	20.95
E J	838	33.63
ST	328	13.16
SF	1090	43.74
NF	432	17.34
NT	642	25.76
S J	995	39.93
S P	423	16.97
N P	566	22.71
N J	508	20.39
T J	520	20.87
T P	450	18.06
F P	539	21.63
F J	983	39.45
I N	438	17.58
EN	636	25.52
I S	694	27.85
ES	724	29.05
ET	553	22.19
EF	807	32.38
I F	715	28.69
I T	417	16.73
S dom	695	27.89
N dom	492	19.74
T dom	519	20.83
F dom	786	31.54

JUDGMENT — INTROVERSION — PERCEPTION — PERCEPTION — EXTRAVERSION — JUDGMENT

Note: ▪ = 1% of sample   8628017

Data collected by Donald Reichard and Norman Uhl of the University of North Carolina at Greensboro from 1976 through 1979 using Form F. Subjects were approximately 55% of the incoming freshmen at the university. The university is one of three doctoral granting universities in a 16 campus state university system. Students were approximately 75% female and 25% male; 95% were 18 years old; about 88% were white and 12% were black; and 88% were from in state. These data are used with permission and were cited in:

Myers, I. B. & McCaulley, M. H. (1985). <u>Manual: A Guide to the Development and Use of the Myers-Briggs Type Indicator</u>.

   Palo Alto, CA: Consulting Psychologists Press.

University of Wisconsin at Stevens Point – Freshmen

N = 1169

	SENSING		INTUITION	
	THINKING	FEELING	FEELING	THINKING

ISTJ	ISFJ	INFJ	INTJ
N= 87	N= 79	N= 43	N= 19
%= 7.44	%= 6.76	%= 3.68	%= 1.63
■■■■■■■	■■■■■■■	■■■■	■■

ISTP	ISFP	INFP	INTP
N= 59	N= 58	N= 81	N= 37
%= 5.05	%= 4.96	%= 6.93	%= 3.17
■■■■■	■■■■■	■■■■■■■	■■■

ESTP	ESFP	ENFP	ENTP
N= 57	N= 98	N= 161	N= 53
%= 4.88	%= 8.38	%= 13.77	%= 4.53
■■■■■	■■■■■■■■	■■■■■■■■■■■■■	■■■■■
		■■■■	

ESTJ	ESFJ	ENFJ	ENTJ
N= 100	N= 135	N= 58	N= 44
%= 8.55	%= 11.55	%= 4.96	%= 3.76
■■■■■■■■	■■■■■■■■■■■	■■■■■	■■■■
	■■		

JUDGMENT · PERCEPTION · PERCEPTION · JUDGMENT
INTROVERSION · EXTRAVERSION

	N	%
E	706	60.39
I	463	39.61
S	673	57.57
N	496	42.43
T	456	39.01
F	713	60.99
J	565	48.33
P	604	51.67
I J	228	19.50
I P	235	20.10
E P	369	31.57
E J	337	28.83
S T	303	25.92
S F	370	31.65
N F	343	29.34
N T	153	13.09
S J	401	34.30
S P	272	23.27
N P	332	28.40
N J	164	14.03
T J	250	21.39
T P	206	17.62
F P	398	34.05
F J	315	26.95
I N	180	15.40
E N	316	27.03
I S	283	24.21
E S	390	33.36
E T	254	21.73
E F	452	38.67
I F	261	22.33
I T	202	17.28
S dom	321	27.46
N dom	276	23.61
T dom	240	20.53
F dom	332	28.40

Note: ■ = 1% of sample   8628012

Data collected by Fred Leafgren and Dale Kolstad of the University of Wisconsin at Stevens Point during 1983. Subjects were students entering the university in 1983. Students' majors were largely natural resources programs, with others in liberal arts and sciences. Students were 37% male and 64% female, the modal age was 18 and 85% were from the state of Wisconsin. These data are used with permission and were cited in:

Myers, I. B. & McCaulley, M. H. (1985). Manual: A Guide to the Development and Use of the Myers-Briggs Type Indicator. Palo Alto, CA: Consulting Psychologists Press.

E Percent	I	Total Sample Size	Sample Description
83.64	16.36	55	College Student Leaders
82.00	18.00	50	College Students in Student Government
76.44	23.56	225	Leaders in Student Government Activities
70.61	29.39	228	Rosemont College - Freshmen
68.87	31.13	3373	High School Students in Australia
62.00	38.00	550	St. Louis University - Freshmen
61.48	38.52	122	High School Student Leaders
60.39	39.61	1169	University of Wisconsin at Stevens Point - Freshmen
59.16	40.84	4035	University of Maine - Freshmen
58.90	41.10	1506	Mercer University - Freshmen
58.27	41.73	4150	Nicholls State University - Freshmen
57.40	42.60	10342	Auburn University - Freshmen
57.36	42.64	197	Adrian College - Freshmen
54.57	45.43	2492	University of North Carolina at Greensboro - Freshmen
54.43	45.57	395	Rollins College - Freshmen
53.88	46.12	1973	St. Clair College
53.74	46.26	2514	University of Florida - Freshmen
53.36	46.64	1505	Hope College - Freshmen
51.83	48.17	164	Gifted High School Seniors
50.95	49.05	793	High School Students in Florida Future Scientist Program
50.00	50.00	1760	Franklin and Marshall College - Freshmen
49.63	50.37	405	Parks College - Freshmen and Transfers
46.65	53.35	403	Berkshire Christian College - Freshmen and Transfers
46.08	53.92	3149	Concordia College - Freshmen
42.96	57.04	1001	National Merit Scholarship Finalists
42.25	57.75	71	Rhodes Scholars
34.67	65.33	75	Phi Beta Kappa

S Percent	N	Total Sample Size	Sample Description
71.90	28.10	4150	Nicholls State University - Freshmen
68.22	31.78	1973	St. Clair College
66.75	33.25	403	Berkshire Christian College - Freshmen and Transfers
65.70	34.30	3373	High School Students in Australia
63.96	36.04	197	Adrian College - Freshmen
59.26	40.74	405	Parks College - Freshmen and Transfers
58.63	41.37	1506	Mercer University - Freshmen
57.57	42.43	1169	University of Wisconsin at Stevens Point - Freshmen
56.95	43.05	10342	Auburn University - Freshmen
56.90	43.10	2492	University of North Carolina at Greensboro - Freshmen
55.39	44.61	4035	University of Maine - Freshmen
53.95	46.05	228	Rosemont College - Freshmen
53.60	46.40	3149	Concordia College - Freshmen
50.82	49.18	122	High School Student Leaders
50.06	49.94	1760	Franklin and Marshall College - Freshmen
49.78	50.22	225	Leaders in Student Government Activities
48.35	51.65	395	Rollins College - Freshmen
48.00	52.00	550	St. Louis University - Freshmen
46.64	53.36	1505	Hope College - Freshmen
46.00	54.00	50	College Students in Student Government
45.45	54.55	55	College Student Leaders
45.43	54.57	2514	University of Florida - Freshmen
32.93	67.07	164	Gifted High School Seniors
24.00	76.00	75	Phi Beta Kappa
23.96	76.04	793	High School Students in Florida Future Scientist Program
17.58	82.42	1001	National Merit Scholarship Finalists
7.04	92.96	71	Rhodes Scholars

THINKING-FEELING

T Percent F	Total Sample Size	Sample Description
70.91	29.09	55	College Student Leaders
60.00	40.00	225	Leaders in Student Government Activities
59.01	40.99	405	Parks College - Freshmen and Transfers
56.94	43.06	1001	National Merit Scholarship Finalists
55.47	44.53	3373	High School Students in Australia
51.58	48.42	793	High School Students in Florida Future Scientist Program
51.22	48.78	164	Gifted High School Seniors
48.00	52.00	75	Phi Beta Kappa
46.36	53.64	1760	Franklin and Marshall College - Freshmen
45.90	54.10	122	High School Student Leaders
45.07	54.93	71	Rhodes Scholars
42.65	57.35	4150	Nicholls State University - Freshmen
40.00	60.00	50	College Students in Student Government
39.01	60.99	1169	University of Wisconsin at Stevens Point - Freshmen
38.92	61.08	2492	University of North Carolina at Greensboro - Freshmen
38.37	61.63	1973	St. Clair College
38.25	61.75	1506	Mercer University - Freshmen
37.71	62.29	2514	University of Florida - Freshmen
37.27	62.73	550	St. Louis University - Freshmen
36.71	63.29	395	Rollins College - Freshmen
32.91	67.09	4035	University of Maine - Freshmen
31.29	68.71	10342	Auburn University - Freshmen
27.63	72.37	228	Rosemont College - Freshmen
25.98	74.02	1505	Hope College - Freshmen
22.67	77.33	3149	Concordia College - Freshmen
20.30	79.70	197	Adrian College - Freshmen
14.14	85.86	403	Berkshire Christian College - Freshmen and Transfers

JUDGMENT-PERCEPTION

J Percent	P	Total Sample Size	Sample Description
76.36	23.64	55	College Student Leaders
64.00	36.00	50	College Students in Student Government
60.31	39.69	2492	University of North Carolina at Greensboro - Freshmen
59.56	40.44	225	Leaders in Student Government Activities
54.92	45.08	122	High School Student Leaders
53.86	46.14	4150	Nicholls State University - Freshmen
53.78	46.22	1506	Mercer University - Freshmen
53.33	46.67	75	Phi Beta Kappa
53.30	46.70	197	Adrian College - Freshmen
52.84	47.16	405	Parks College - Freshmen and Transfers
51.86	48.14	403	Berkshire Christian College - Freshmen and Transfers
51.31	48.69	1760	Franklin and Marshall College - Freshmen
50.75	49.25	3149	Concordia College - Freshmen
49.69	50.31	3373	High School Students in Australia
48.73	51.27	550	St. Louis University - Freshmen
48.68	51.32	793	High School Students in Florida Future Scientist Program
48.61	51.39	395	Rollins College - Freshmen
48.45	51.55	2514	University of Florida - Freshmen
48.33	51.67	1169	University of Wisconsin at Stevens Point - Freshmen
47.31	52.69	1505	Hope College - Freshmen
45.78	54.22	10342	Auburn University - Freshmen
45.46	54.54	1973	St. Clair College
44.56	55.44	1001	National Merit Scholarship Finalists
40.50	59.50	4035	University of Maine - Freshmen
39.91	60.09	228	Rosemont College - Freshmen
39.63	60.37	164	Gifted High School Seniors
36.62	63.38	71	Rhodes Scholars

Percent ST	Total Sample Size	Sample Description
39.02	3373	High School Students in Australia
38.77	405	Parks College - Freshmen and Transfers
36.36	55	College Student Leaders
32.89	225	Leaders in Student Government Activities
32.51	4150	Nicholls State University - Freshmen
31.97	122	High School Student Leaders
27.83	1973	St. Clair College
25.92	1169	University of Wisconsin at Stevens Point - Freshmen
25.51	1760	Franklin and Marshall College - Freshmen
23.64	1506	Mercer University - Freshmen
20.00	50	College Students in Student Government
19.80	4035	University of Maine - Freshmen
19.75	395	Rollins College - Freshmen
19.33	2514	University of Florida - Freshmen
19.09	550	St. Louis University - Freshmen
18.70	10342	Auburn University - Freshmen
16.67	228	Rosemont College - Freshmen
14.63	164	Gifted High School Seniors
14.21	197	Adrian College - Freshmen
13.87	793	High School Students in Florida Future Scientist Program
13.69	1505	Hope College - Freshmen
13.40	3149	Concordia College - Freshmen
13.33	75	Phi Beta Kappa
13.16	2492	University of North Carolina at Greensboro - Freshmen
11.17	403	Berkshire Christian College - Freshmen and Transfers
10.79	1001	National Merit Scholarship Finalists
1.41	71	Rhodes Scholars

SENSING-FEELING

Percent SF	Total Sample Size	Sample Description
55.58	403	Berkshire Christian College - Freshmen and Transfers
49.75	197	Adrian College - Freshmen
43.74	2492	University of North Carolina at Greensboro - Freshmen
40.40	1973	St. Clair College
40.20	3149	Concordia College - Freshmen
39.40	4150	Nicholls State University - Freshmen
38.25	10342	Auburn University - Freshmen
37.28	228	Rosemont College - Freshmen
35.59	4035	University of Maine - Freshmen
34.99	1506	Mercer University - Freshmen
32.96	1505	Hope College - Freshmen
31.65	1169	University of Wisconsin at Stevens Point - Freshmen
28.91	550	St. Louis University - Freshmen
28.61	395	Rollins College - Freshmen
26.68	3373	High School Students in Australia
26.09	2514	University of Florida - Freshmen
26.00	50	College Students in Student Government
24.55	1760	Franklin and Marshall College - Freshmen
20.49	405	Parks College - Freshmen and Transfers
18.85	122	High School Student Leaders
18.29	164	Gifted High School Seniors
16.89	225	Leaders in Student Government Activities
10.67	75	Phi Beta Kappa
10.09	793	High School Students in Florida Future Scientist Program
9.09	55	College Student Leaders
6.79	1001	National Merit Scholarship Finalists
5.63	71	Rhodes Scholars

Percent NF	Total Sample Size	Sample Description
49.30	71	Rhodes Scholars
41.33	75	Phi Beta Kappa
41.06	1505	Hope College - Freshmen
38.34	793	High School Students in Florida Future Scientist Program
37.12	3149	Concordia College - Freshmen
36.26	1001	National Merit Scholarship Finalists
36.20	2514	University of Florida - Freshmen
35.25	122	High School Student Leaders
35.09	228	Rosemont College - Freshmen
34.68	395	Rollins College - Freshmen
34.00	50	College Students in Student Government
33.82	550	St. Louis University - Freshmen
31.50	4035	University of Maine - Freshmen
30.49	164	Gifted High School Seniors
30.46	10342	Auburn University - Freshmen
30.27	403	Berkshire Christian College - Freshmen and Transfers
29.95	197	Adrian College - Freshmen
29.34	1169	University of Wisconsin at Stevens Point - Freshmen
29.09	1760	Franklin and Marshall College - Freshmen
26.76	1506	Mercer University - Freshmen
23.11	225	Leaders in Student Government Activities
21.24	1973	St. Clair College
20.49	405	Parks College - Freshmen and Transfers
20.00	55	College Student Leaders
17.95	4150	Nicholls State University - Freshmen
17.85	3373	High School Students in Australia
17.34	2492	University of North Carolina at Greensboro - Freshmen

Percent NT	Total Sample Size	Sample Description
46.15	1001	National Merit Scholarship Finalists
43.66	71	Rhodes Scholars
37.70	793	High School Students in Florida Future Scientist Program
36.59	164	Gifted High School Seniors
34.67	75	Phi Beta Kappa
34.55	55	College Student Leaders
27.11	225	Leaders in Student Government Activities
25.76	2492	University of North Carolina at Greensboro - Freshmen
20.85	1760	Franklin and Marshall College - Freshmen
20.25	405	Parks College - Freshmen and Transfers
20.00	50	College Students in Student Government
18.38	2514	University of Florida - Freshmen
18.18	550	St. Louis University - Freshmen
16.96	395	Rollins College - Freshmen
16.45	3373	High School Students in Australia
14.61	1506	Mercer University - Freshmen
13.93	122	High School Student Leaders
13.11	4035	University of Maine - Freshmen
13.09	1169	University of Wisconsin at Stevens Point - Freshmen
12.59	10342	Auburn University - Freshmen
12.29	1505	Hope College - Freshmen
10.96	228	Rosemont College - Freshmen
10.54	1973	St. Clair College
10.14	4150	Nicholls State University - Freshmen
9.27	3149	Concordia College - Freshmen
6.09	197	Adrian College - Freshmen
2.98	403	Berkshire Christian College - Freshmen and Transfers

SUMMARY TABLES

EXTRAVERT-INTROVERT

E Percent	I	Total Sample Size	Sample Description
83.64	16.36	55	College Student Leaders
82.00	18.00	50	College Students in Student Government
76.44	23.56	225	Leaders in Student Government Activities
74.70	25.30	83	Marketing Personnel
70.61	29.39	228	Rosemont College - Freshmen
69.31	30.69	101	Insurance Agents, Brokers, and Underwriters
68.87	31.13	3373	High School Students in Australia
68.38	31.62	136	Credit Investigators and Mortgage Brokers
68.16	31.84	4387	Females: High School Students from Pennsylvania
67.65	32.35	102	Ordained Roman Catholic Deacons
67.59	32.41	108	Sales Clerks, Retail Trade
67.27	32.73	275	Salespeople in a Japanese Trading Company
67.04	32.96	179	Sales Representatives
66.95	33.05	118	Managers: Japanese Chief Executives
66.67	33.33	312	Managers: Restaurant, Cafeteria, Bar and Food Service
66.29	33.71	89	Public Relations Workers and Publicity Writers
66.04	33.96	321	Females: Traditional Age Junior High School Students
64.87	35.13	316	Managers: Retail Stores
64.85	35.15	9320	High School Students from Pennsylvania
64.71	35.29	170	Certified Psychodramatists
64.71	35.29	51	Restaurant Workers: Table Setting and Cleaning
64.41	35.59	177	College and University Resident Assistants
64.29	35.71	56	Managers: Top Managers in Large Japanese Companies
63.86	36.14	83	Managers: Sales
63.79	36.21	58	Home Management Advisors and Home Economists
63.76	36.24	287	Counselors: School
63.54	36.46	181	Females in Leadership Development Program
63.04	36.96	92	Police Officers: Supervisors in Urban Community
62.90	37.10	62	Actors
62.84	37.16	366	Managers: Middle Managers in a Japanese Chemical Company
62.24	37.76	1205	Candidates for Theology Education
62.00	38.00	550	St. Louis University - Freshmen
62.00	38.00	100	Receptionists
61.98	38.02	192	Consultants: General
61.91	38.09	4933	Males: High School Students from Pennsylvania
61.83	38.17	1750	SALES WORKERS
61.67	38.33	60	Managers: Fire
61.67	38.33	60	Dental Hygienists
61.61	38.39	4973	Females: Age Group 15 To 17
61.54	38.46	169	Composite of Practitioners in Social Work
61.48	38.52	122	High School Student Leaders
61.24	38.76	756	Managers: Financial and Bank Officers
60.87	39.13	92	Social Services Workers
60.84	39.16	13716	Females: Age Group 18 To 20
60.78	39.22	102	Managers: Office
60.78	39.22	51	Administrators: Student Personnel
60.49	39.51	1607	Females: Traditional Age High School Students
60.39	39.61	1169	University of Wisconsin at Stevens Point - Freshmen
60.29	39.71	136	Musicians and Composers
60.19	39.81	108	Members of a Human Resources Planners Association

E Percent	I	Total Sample Size	Sample Description
59.76	40.24	14519	Females: Traditional Age College Students
59.72	40.28	1147	Nuns and Other Religious Workers
59.71	40.29	139	Construction Laborers (except carpenters helpers)
59.68	40.32	124	Administrators: Canadian Schools
59.56	40.44	633	Protestant Seminarians
59.44	40.56	673	Counselors: Vocational and Educational
59.16	40.84	4035	University of Maine - Freshmen
59.12	40.88	274	Cashiers
58.93	41.07	280	Police Officers: Urban Community
58.90	41.10	1506	Mercer University - Freshmen
58.89	41.11	1024	Administrators: Elementary and Secondary School
58.49	41.51	106	Speech Pathologists
58.49	41.51	53	Composite of Practitioners in Radiologic Technology
58.43	41.57	166	Real Estate Agents and Brokers
58.27	41.73	4150	Nicholls State University - Freshmen
58.21	41.79	67	Teachers: Foreign Language in Junior and Senior High School
58.21	41.79	67	Sales Agents, Retail Trade
58.20	41.80	378	ARTISTS AND ENTERTAINERS
58.20	41.80	122	Composite of Practitioners in Speech Pathology
58.18	41.82	55	Child Care Workers (except private household)
58.16	41.84	141	Police Officers: Patrolmen in Urban Community
57.85	42.15	1554	Protestant Ministers
57.75	42.25	71	Consultants: Management
57.73	42.27	783	PERSONAL SERVICE WORKERS
57.69	42.31	52	Journalists
57.68	42.32	534	Clergy, all denominations (except priests)
57.63	42.37	59	Photographers
57.56	42.44	2010	RELIGIOUS WORKERS -ALL DENOMINATIONS-
57.42	42.58	256	Males: Traditional Age Junior High School Students
57.40	42.60	10342	Auburn University - Freshmen
57.36	42.64	197	Adrian College - Freshmen
57.35	42.65	211	Lifeguards, Attendants, Recreation and Amusement
57.29	42.71	96	Hairdressers, Cosmetologists and Manicurists
57.24	42.76	1803	COUNSELORS
57.14	42.86	70	Optometrists
56.98	43.02	172	Coordinators
56.80	43.20	250	Business: General, Self-employed
56.67	43.33	7463	MANAGERS AND ADMINISTRATORS
56.64	43.36	113	Teachers: Supervising Student Teachers
56.48	43.52	5738	Females: Age Group 21 To 24
56.48	43.52	540	Waiters and Waitresses
56.30	43.70	238	Public Service Aides and Community Health Workers
56.25	43.75	80	Purchasing Agents
56.06	43.94	1857	ADMINISTRATORS
56.05	43.95	835	Bank Employees
56.01	43.99	932	Counselors: General
56.00	44.00	50	Directors of Religious Education
55.93	44.07	177	Counselors: Rehabilitation
55.86	44.14	290	Managers: Middle Level in City, County and State Government
55.74	44.26	3678	Administrators: Managers and Supervisors

E Percent	I	Total Sample Size	Sample Description
55.74	44.26	61	Food Counter and Fountain Workers
55.73	44.27	262	Counselors: Suicide and Crisis
55.71	44.29	32731	Females: Form F Databank
55.71	44.29	359	Counselors: General
55.70	44.30	228	Teachers: Adult Education
55.28	44.72	1874	Law School Graduates
55.21	44.79	96	Teachers: Reading
55.18	44.82	1082	FOOD SERVICE WORKERS
54.91	45.09	173	Teachers: Special Education
54.88	45.12	82	Professional, Technical, and Kindred Workers
54.84	45.16	341	Administrators: Colleges and Technical Institutes
54.69	45.31	16880	Females: Form G Databank
54.62	45.38	119	Teachers: Trade, Industrial and Technical
54.57	45.43	2492	University of North Carolina at Greensboro - Freshmen
54.55	45.45	55	Designers
54.44	45.56	169	Teachers: Grades 1 through 9, Canada
54.44	45.56	90	Personnel and Labor Relations Workers
54.43	45.57	395	Rollins College - Freshmen
54.43	45.57	79	Religious Educator, all denominations
54.43	45.57	79	Medical Assistants
54.41	45.59	68	Secretaries: Medical
54.40	45.60	182	Health Education Practitioners
54.27	45.73	164	Teachers: Coaching
54.00	46.00	200	Teachers: Elementary School
53.88	46.12	1973	St. Clair College
53.85	46.15	52	Factory and Site Supervisors
53.81	46.19	223	Teachers: Health
53.75	46.25	80	Employment Development Specialists
53.74	46.26	2514	University of Florida - Freshmen
53.73	46.27	67	Stock Clerks and Storekeepers
53.68	46.32	136	Managers: High Level Corporate Executives
53.58	46.42	782	LABORERS
53.55	46.45	155	Nursing: Composite of Critical Care Nurses
53.53	46.47	439	Police Officers
53.42	46.58	146	Nursing: Consultants
53.41	46.59	264	MILITARY PERSONNEL
53.36	46.64	1505	Hope College - Freshmen
53.28	46.72	1128	Teachers: Middle and Junior High School
53.27	46.73	107	Typists
53.22	46.78	232557	CAPT Databank Total Population
53.19	46.81	47	Police Officers: Detectives in Urban Community
53.16	46.84	190	Engineers: Mining
53.12	46.87	128	Judges
53.06	46.94	245	Therapists: Occupational
53.02	46.98	530	WRITERS AND JOURNALISTS
52.98	47.02	319	Rabbis
52.67	47.33	150	Managers: Small Business
52.58	47.42	213	Teachers: Art, Drama and Music
52.52	47.48	139	Physicians: Family Practice, General Practice
52.42	47.58	765	HEALTH CARE THERAPISTS

E Percent	I	Total Sample Size	Sample Description
52.33	47.67	1204	Males: Traditional Age High School Students
52.31	47.69	65	Computer Operations, Systems Researchers and Analysts
52.25	47.75	333	Secretaries: Executive and Administrative Assistants
52.23	47.77	561	Teachers: Junior College
52.17	47.83	11897	Males: Age Group 18 To 20
52.00	48.00	100	Teachers: Pre-school
51.98	48.02	202	Administrators: Health
51.85	48.15	297	Computer and Peripheral Equipment Operators
51.85	48.15	243	Dietitians
51.83	48.17	164	Gifted High School Seniors
51.81	48.19	3339	CLERICAL AND KINDRED WORKERS
51.81	48.19	276	School Principals
51.79	48.21	56	Clerical Supervisors
51.76	48.24	85	Protestants in Specialized Ministries
51.69	48.31	89	Consultants: Management Analysts
51.67	48.33	5320	Males: Age Group 21 To 24
51.62	48.38	3979	Males: Age Group 15 To 17
51.62	48.38	804	Teachers: Elementary School
51.59	48.41	157	Teachers: Speech Pathology and Therapy
51.59	48.41	126	Radiologic Technologists and Technicians
51.49	48.51	4811	Females: Age Group 40 To 49
51.48	48.52	169	Service Workers (except private household)
51.47	48.53	68	Corrections Officers and Probation Officers
51.39	48.61	23240	Males: Form F Databank
51.39	48.61	72	FARMERS
51.39	48.61	72	Dental Assistants
51.28	48.72	117	Counselors: Runaway Youth
51.18	48.82	12637	Males: Traditional Age College Students
51.16	48.84	649	Teachers: High School
51.11	48.89	900	HEALTH SERVICE WORKERS
51.09	48.91	4905	OFFICE MACHINE OPERATORS
51.05	48.95	143	Auditors
51.00	49.00	402	PSYCHOLOGISTS
50.97	49.03	926	Males: Adult High School Graduates Without College
50.95	49.05	793	High School Students in Florida Future Scientist Program
50.94	49.06	479	Social Workers
50.91	49.09	110	Bank Employees, Exempt
50.86	49.14	1795	Males: Age Group 50 To 59
50.64	49.36	314	Nursing: Aides, Orderlies, and Attendants
50.62	49.38	81	Research Workers
50.51	49.49	16676	TEACHERS
50.45	49.55	2470	Females: Age Group 50 To 59
50.39	49.61	3064	PRIVATE HOUSEHOLD WORKERS
50.33	49.67	608	PROTECTIVE SERVICE WORKERS
50.18	49.82	3551	Females: Non-Traditional Age College Students
50.07	49.93	669	MECHANICS
50.06	49.94	5178	Females: Age Group 25 To 29
50.00	50.00	1760	Franklin and Marshall College - Freshmen
50.00	50.00	84	Library Attendants and Assistants
50.00	50.00	54	Engineers: Aeronautical

EXTRAVERT-INTROVERT

E Percent	I	Total Sample Size	Sample Description
50.00	50.00	52	Engineers: Chemical
49.90	50.10	523	Managers: Public
49.68	50.32	155	Police and Detectives
49.63	50.37	405	Parks College - Freshmen and Transfers
49.61	50.39	127	Therapists: Practitioners in Respiratory Therapy
49.59	50.41	490	SOCIAL SCIENTISTS
49.52	50.48	208	Writers, Artists, Entertainers, and Agents
49.49	50.51	99	Police Officers: Australian Senior Officers
49.48	50.52	7952	Females: Adult College Graduates
49.47	50.53	469	ALLIED HEALTH AND HEALTH PRACTIONERS, N.E.C.
49.44	50.56	8711	Females: Age Group 30 To 39
49.44	50.56	180	Cooks (except private household)
49.35	50.65	849	Managers: England
49.33	50.67	15791	Males: Form G Databank
49.31	50.69	1604	SECRETARIES
49.31	50.69	432	Teacher Aides (except school monitors)
49.23	50.77	323	Dietitians and Nutritionists
49.19	50.81	1051	Males in Leadership Development Program
49.16	50.84	179	Teachers: English
49.13	50.87	289	Psychologists
49.08	50.92	3812	Males: Age Group 40 To 49
48.98	51.02	196	Displaced Coal Miners
48.85	51.15	305	Nursing: Educators
48.72	51.28	195	Therapists: Respiratory
48.69	51.31	5601	Males: Age Group 30 To 39
48.67	51.33	150	Bookkeepers
48.65	51.35	6814	Males: Adult College Graduates
48.62	51.38	109	Carpenters
48.48	51.52	165	Clerks in a Japanese Trading Company
48.38	51.62	1298	Roman Catholic Priests
48.36	51.64	122	Administrators: Educationally Related
48.31	51.69	118	Therapists: Occupational
48.20	51.80	222	Bank Employees, Non-Exempt
48.08	51.92	52	Computer Specialists
48.00	52.00	175	ENGINEERING AND SCIENCE TECHNICIANS
47.98	52.02	494	Certified Public Accountants
47.92	52.08	912	Police Officers: Managers
47.92	52.08	144	OPERATIVES: TRANSPORTATION
47.87	52.13	94	Nursing: Administrators
47.70	52.30	413	Teachers: Mathematics
47.69	52.31	281	Teachers: School Grades 1 through 12
47.67	52.33	986	ENGINEERS
47.64	52.36	2351	Nursing: Registered Nurses
47.62	52.38	105	Police Supervisors
47.57	52.43	3103	NURSES
47.47	52.53	495	Males: Age Group 60 Plus
47.42	52.58	97	OPERATIVES: NON-SPECIALIZED AND FACTORY WORKERS
47.37	52.63	57	Scientists: Biology
47.30	52.70	148	Therapists: Physical
47.23	52.77	559	CRAFT WORKERS

EXTRAVERT-INTROVERT

E Percent	I	Total Sample Size	Sample Description
47.23	52.77	343	Males: Adult High School Dropouts
47.19	52.81	89	Corrections Sergeants
47.16	52.84	846	Females: Age Group 60 Plus
47.06	52.94	85	Dentists
46.94	53.06	98	Managers: Participants in Women in Management Conference
46.92	53.08	260	Nursing: Licensed Practical Nurses
46.75	53.25	77	Engineers: Mechanical
46.71	53.29	167	Laboratory Technologists
46.68	53.32	2277	Females: Adult High School Graduates, Without College
46.65	53.35	403	Berkshire Christian College - Freshmen and Transfers
46.60	53.40	191	Pharmacists
46.58	53.42	73	Air Force Personnel
46.55	53.45	333	Public Accountants
46.54	53.46	3814	Males: Age Group 25 To 29
46.53	53.47	101	Administrators: Social Services
46.51	53.49	172	Teaching Assistants
46.51	53.49	86	Guards and Watch Keepers
46.38	53.62	1880	Nursing: Registered Nurses, no specialty stated
46.34	53.66	123	Pharmacists
46.15	53.85	52	Dentists
46.08	53.92	3149	Concordia College - Freshmen
46.02	53.98	113	Editors and Reporters
46.01	53.99	1291	HEALTH TECHNOLOGISTS AND TECHNICIANS
45.79	54.21	2282	Teachers: University
45.78	54.22	83	Nursing: Public Health
45.66	54.34	219	Priests and Monks
45.63	54.37	206	OPERATIVES: SPECIALIZED
45.61	54.39	57	Police Officers: Commanders
45.60	54.40	636	Females: Adult High School Dropouts
45.30	54.70	574	Line Corrections Officers
45.20	54.80	427	Accountants
45.09	54.91	519	LAWYERS AND JUDGES
44.78	55.22	67	CLEANING SERVICES
44.69	55.31	226	SCIENTISTS: LIFE AND PHYSICAL
44.44	55.56	135	Doctors of Osteopathy
44.44	55.56	54	Consultants: Education
44.31	55.69	4663	Military Personnel at Naval Technical Training Center
44.30	55.70	973	Medical Technologists
44.29	55.71	70	Electricians
44.26	55.74	61	Physicians: Pathology
44.24	55.76	1501	Males: Adult Non-Traditional Age College Students
44.19	55.81	86	Computer Systems Analysts and Support Representatives
44.12	55.88	68	Physicians: Psychiatry
43.40	56.60	705	Teachers: College Faculty Named as Danforth Associates
43.28	56.72	67	Research Assistants
43.26	56.74	638	Medical Technologists (4 year)
43.25	56.75	659	Females: SRI Sample
43.21	56.79	1009	Navy Enlisted Personnel in Basic Electronic Training
42.96	57.04	1001	National Merit Scholarship Finalists
42.86	57.14	105	Steelworkers

E Percent	I	Total Sample Size	Sample Description
42.86	57.14	84	Attorneys - Administrators, non-practicing
42.59	57.41	54	Chain, Rod and Ax Workers; Surveying
42.41	57.59	257	Managers: Top Level in City, County and State Government
42.31	57.69	338	COMPUTER SPECIALISTS
42.25	57.75	71	Teachers: Mathematics
42.25	57.75	71	Rhodes Scholars
42.11	57.89	114	Brothers in Roman Catholic Religious Orders
42.11	57.89	57	Technicians: Electrical and Electronic Engineering
41.70	58.30	223	Clinical Laboratory Technologists and Technicians
41.61	58.39	1603	DOCTORS OF MEDICINE
41.52	58.48	1881	Composite of Practitioners in Medicine (M.D.s)
41.46	58.54	2002	Sisters in Roman Catholic Religious Orders
41.44	58.56	111	Consultants: Canadian
41.33	58.67	271	Lawyers
41.29	58.71	155	Therapists: Physical
40.87	59.13	230	Managers: Regional Telephone Company Low Level Managers
40.57	59.43	106	Media Specialists
40.45	59.55	1105	Total SRI Sample
40.00	60.00	200	Computer Programmers
39.97	60.03	658	Displaced Steelworkers
39.39	60.61	132	School Bus Drivers
39.33	60.67	267	Librarians
39.22	60.78	51	Roman Catholic Seminarians
39.17	60.83	240	Foremen in Japanese Food Production Company
38.60	61.40	114	Fine Artists
37.70	62.30	61	Scientists: Chemistry
37.66	62.34	77	Secretaries: Legal
37.04	62.96	54	Engineers: Electrical and Electronic
37.02	62.98	1394	Managers: Federal Executives
36.32	63.68	446	Males: SRI Sample
35.63	64.37	334	Operators and Field Technicians in Water Pollution Control
35.34	64.66	116	Managers: Middle Managers in a Japanese Heavy Industrial Co
34.67	65.33	75	Phi Beta Kappa
32.87	67.13	1229	Computer Professionals
29.84	70.16	124	Architects

S Percent	N	Total Sample Size	Sample Description
96.21	3.79	132	School Bus Drivers
92.34	7.66	222	Bank Employees, Non-Exempt
91.01	8.99	89	Corrections Sergeants
88.33	11.67	574	Line Corrections Officers
86.87	13.13	99	Police Officers: Australian Senior Officers
86.67	13.33	60	Managers: Fire
86.00	14.00	150	Managers: Small Business
85.71	14.29	105	Steelworkers
85.45	14.55	110	Bank Employees, Exempt
85.41	14.59	658	Displaced Steelworkers
85.16	14.84	155	Police and Detectives
84.62	15.38	52	Factory and Site Supervisors
82.59	17.41	316	Managers: Retail Stores
82.08	17.92	240	Foremen in Japanese Food Production Company
81.51	18.49	238	Public Service Aides and Community Health Workers
81.32	18.68	926	Males: Adult High School Graduates Without College
80.85	19.15	47	Police Officers: Detectives in Urban Community
80.61	19.39	196	Displaced Coal Miners
80.20	19.80	101	Administrators: Social Services
80.14	19.86	141	Police Officers: Patrolmen in Urban Community
79.64	20.36	280	Police Officers: Urban Community
78.29	21.71	912	Police Officers: Managers
78.26	21.74	92	Police Officers: Supervisors in Urban Community
78.00	22.00	659	Females: SRI Sample
77.84	22.16	334	Operators and Field Technicians in Water Pollution Control
77.68	22.32	439	Police Officers
77.50	22.50	80	Purchasing Agents
77.39	22.61	230	Managers: Regional Telephone Company Low Level Managers
76.39	23.61	72	FARMERS
76.12	23.88	67	CLEANING SERVICES
75.93	24.07	1105	Total SRI Sample
75.44	24.56	57	Police Officers: Commanders
75.00	25.00	608	PROTECTIVE SERVICE WORKERS
74.00	26.00	2277	Females: Adult High School Graduates, Without College
73.85	26.15	260	Nursing: Licensed Practical Nurses
73.67	26.33	281	Teachers: School Grades 1 through 12
73.61	26.39	144	OPERATIVES: TRANSPORTATION
73.04	26.96	523	Managers: Public
72.95	27.05	366	Managers: Middle Managers in a Japanese Chemical Company
72.87	27.13	446	Males: SRI Sample
72.38	27.62	105	Police Supervisors
72.37	27.63	257	Managers: Top Level in City, County and State Government
72.22	27.78	432	Teacher Aides (except school monitors)
72.19	27.81	169	Service Workers (except private household)
72.01	27.99	636	Females: Adult High School Dropouts
71.96	28.04	107	Typists
71.90	28.10	4150	Nicholls State University - Freshmen
71.72	28.28	290	Managers: Middle Level in City, County and State Government
71.62	28.38	835	Bank Employees
71.47	28.53	312	Managers: Restaurant, Cafeteria, Bar and Food Service

S Percent	N	Total Sample Size	Sample Description
70.93	29.07	86	Guards and Watch Keepers
70.83	29.17	96	Hairdressers, Cosmetologists and Manicurists
70.73	29.27	164	Teachers: Coaching
70.66	29.34	4387	Females: High School Students from Pennsylvania
70.65	29.35	276	School Principals
69.59	30.41	559	CRAFT WORKERS
69.39	30.61	343	Males: Adult High School Dropouts
69.07	30.93	97	OPERATIVES: NON-SPECIALIZED AND FACTORY WORKERS
68.22	31.78	1973	St. Clair College
68.13	31.87	9320	High School Students from Pennsylvania
68.05	31.95	169	Teachers: Grades 1 through 9, Canada
68.00	32.00	150	Bookkeepers
67.86	32.14	56	Clerical Supervisors
67.49	32.51	849	Managers: England
67.27	32.73	165	Clerks in a Japanese Trading Company
67.26	32.74	113	Teachers: Supervising Student Teachers
66.91	33.09	139	Construction Laborers (except carpenters helpers)
66.75	33.25	403	Berkshire Christian College - Freshmen and Transfers
66.67	33.33	72	Dental Assistants
66.18	33.82	68	Corrections Officers and Probation Officers
66.04	33.96	53	Composite of Practitioners in Radiologic Technology
65.88	34.12	4933	Males: High School Students from Pennsylvania
65.87	34.13	126	Radiologic Technologists and Technicians
65.70	34.30	3373	High School Students in Australia
65.48	34.52	84	Library Attendants and Assistants
65.45	34.55	55	Child Care Workers (except private household)
65.32	34.68	669	MECHANICS
65.08	34.92	756	Managers: Financial and Bank Officers
64.98	35.02	494	Certified Public Accountants
64.97	35.03	314	Nursing: Aides, Orderlies, and Attendants
64.94	35.06	77	Secretaries: Legal
64.91	35.09	228	Teachers: Adult Education
64.89	35.11	900	HEALTH SERVICE WORKERS
64.89	35.11	94	Nursing: Administrators
64.85	35.15	4663	Military Personnel at Naval Technical Training Center
64.71	35.29	119	Teachers: Trade, Industrial and Technical
64.71	35.29	68	Secretaries: Medical
64.44	35.56	495	Males: Age Group 60 Plus
64.39	35.61	264	MILITARY PERSONNEL
64.18	35.82	67	Stock Clerks and Storekeepers
63.96	36.04	197	Adrian College - Freshmen
63.87	36.13	274	Cashiers
63.59	36.41	206	OPERATIVES: SPECIALIZED
63.38	36.62	71	Teachers: Mathematics
63.17	36.83	782	LABORERS
63.04	36.96	92	Social Services Workers
63.03	36.97	211	Lifeguards, Attendants, Recreation and Amusement
63.01	36.99	73	Air Force Personnel
62.56	37.44	804	Teachers: Elementary School
62.47	37.53	413	Teachers: Mathematics

S Percent	N	Total Sample Size	Sample Description
62.30 37.70		427	Accountants
62.20 37.80		13716	Females: Age Group 18 To 20
62.07 37.93		783	PERSONAL SERVICE WORKERS
62.01 37.99		179	Sales Representatives
61.76 38.24		102	Ordained Roman Catholic Deacons
61.73 38.27		243	Dietitians
61.60 38.40		638	Medical Technologists (4 year)
61.47 38.53		109	Carpenters
61.43 38.57		70	Electricians
61.40 38.60		14519	Females: Traditional Age College Students
61.40 38.60		114	Brothers in Roman Catholic Religious Orders
61.39 38.61		3551	Females: Non-Traditional Age College Students
61.33 38.67		3064	PRIVATE HOUSEHOLD WORKERS
61.15 38.85		973	Medical Technologists
61.11 38.89		846	Females: Age Group 60 Plus
60.94 39.06		128	Judges
60.84 39.16		166	Real Estate Agents and Brokers
60.65 39.35		155	Nursing: Composite of Critical Care Nurses
60.59 39.41		1147	Nuns and Other Religious Workers
60.51 39.49		157	Teachers: Speech Pathology and Therapy
60.50 39.50		3339	CLERICAL AND KINDRED WORKERS
60.41 39.59		1604	SECRETARIES
60.22 39.78		1795	Males: Age Group 50 To 59
60.09 39.91		2002	Sisters in Roman Catholic Religious Orders
60.00 40.00		4905	OFFICE MACHINE OPERATORS
60.00 40.00		100	Receptionists
60.00 40.00		85	Dentists
59.76 40.24		82	Professional, Technical, and Kindred Workers
59.70 40.30		67	Sales Agents, Retail Trade
59.57 40.43		1291	HEALTH TECHNOLOGISTS AND TECHNICIANS
59.27 40.73		275	Salespeople in a Japanese Trading Company
59.26 40.74		405	Parks College - Freshmen and Transfers
59.26 40.74		108	Sales Clerks, Retail Trade
59.04 40.96		83	Managers: Sales
58.87 41.13		124	Administrators: Canadian Schools
58.86 41.14		11897	Males: Age Group 18 To 20
58.63 41.37		1506	Mercer University - Freshmen
58.57 41.43		70	Optometrists
58.44 41.56		77	Engineers: Mechanical
58.21 41.79		12637	Males: Traditional Age College Students
58.08 41.92		167	Laboratory Technologists
58.06 41.94		155	Therapists: Physical
57.97 42.03		3678	Administrators: Managers and Supervisors
57.95 42.05		195	Therapists: Respiratory
57.89 42.11		323	Dietitians and Nutritionists
57.83 42.17		83	Nursing: Public Health
57.58 42.42		297	Computer and Peripheral Equipment Operators
57.57 42.43		1169	University of Wisconsin at Stevens Point - Freshmen
57.45 42.55		4973	Females: Age Group 15 To 17
57.43 42.57		101	Insurance Agents, Brokers, and Underwriters

S Percent	N	Total Sample Size	Sample Description
57.38	42.62	61	Food Counter and Fountain Workers
57.35	42.65	136	Managers: High Level Corporate Executives
57.16	42.84	1501	Males: Adult Non-Traditional Age College Students
57.14	42.86	182	Health Education Practitioners
57.14	42.86	56	Managers: Top Managers in Large Japanese Companies
56.95	43.05	10342	Auburn University - Freshmen
56.91	43.09	1880	Nursing: Registered Nurses, no specialty stated
56.90	43.10	2492	University of North Carolina at Greensboro - Freshmen
56.90	43.10	58	Home Management Advisors and Home Economists
56.87	43.13	2351	Nursing: Registered Nurses
56.69	43.31	127	Therapists: Practitioners in Respiratory Therapy
56.64	43.36	143	Auditors
56.61	43.39	3812	Males: Age Group 40 To 49
56.57	43.43	5738	Females: Age Group 21 To 24
56.38	43.62	32731	Females: Form F Databank
56.36	43.64	15791	Males: Form G Databank
56.32	43.68	7463	MANAGERS AND ADMINISTRATORS
56.30	43.70	135	Doctors of Osteopathy
56.29	43.71	1750	SALES WORKERS
56.25	43.75	96	Teachers: Reading
56.24	43.76	16880	Females: Form G Databank
56.17	43.83	3979	Males: Age Group 15 To 17
56.14	43.86	57	Technicians: Electrical and Electronic Engineering
56.11	43.89	180	Cooks (except private household)
56.04	43.96	3103	NURSES
56.04	43.96	1051	Males in Leadership Development Program
56.03	43.97	116	Managers: Middle Managers in a Japanese Heavy Industrial Co
55.91	44.09	2470	Females: Age Group 50 To 59
55.77	44.23	52	Computer Specialists
55.70	44.30	79	Medical Assistants
55.61	44.39	223	Clinical Laboratory Technologists and Technicians
55.56	44.44	333	Secretaries: Executive and Administrative Assistants
55.56	44.44	90	Personnel and Labor Relations Workers
55.43	44.57	175	ENGINEERING AND SCIENCE TECHNICIANS
55.41	44.59	148	Therapists: Physical
55.39	44.61	4035	University of Maine - Freshmen
55.14	44.86	1128	Teachers: Middle and Junior High School
55.08	44.92	256	Males: Traditional Age Junior High School Students
54.90	45.10	102	Managers: Office
54.77	45.23	23240	Males: Form F Databank
54.71	45.29	1082	FOOD SERVICE WORKERS
54.47	45.53	1298	Roman Catholic Priests
54.21	45.79	190	Engineers: Mining
54.12	45.88	232557	CAPT Databank Total Population
54.10	45.90	61	Physicians: Pathology
54.00	46.00	250	Business: General, Self-employed
53.95	46.05	228	Rosemont College - Freshmen
53.85	46.15	52	Engineers: Chemical
53.73	46.27	67	Teachers: Foreign Language in Junior and Senior High School
53.60	46.40	3149	Concordia College - Freshmen

SENSING-INTUITION

S Percent	N	Total Sample Size	Sample Description
53.58	46.42	321	Females: Traditional Age Junior High School Students
53.56	46.44	267	Librarians
53.52	46.48	469	ALLIED HEALTH AND HEALTH PRACTIONERS, N.E.C.
53.42	46.58	146	Nursing: Consultants
53.40	46.60	191	Pharmacists
53.39	46.61	118	Managers: Japanese Chief Executives
53.24	46.76	139	Physicians: Family Practice, General Practice
53.12	46.88	5320	Males: Age Group 21 To 24
53.00	47.00	100	Teachers: Pre-school
52.93	47.07	1024	Administrators: Elementary and Secondary School
52.85	47.15	333	Public Accountants
52.64	47.36	986	ENGINEERS
52.63	47.37	1009	Navy Enlisted Personnel in Basic Electronic Training
52.28	47.72	5178	Females: Age Group 25 To 29
52.14	47.86	8711	Females: Age Group 30 To 39
51.86	48.14	4811	Females: Age Group 40 To 49
51.85	48.15	54	Engineers: Electrical and Electronic
51.77	48.23	1607	Females: Traditional Age High School Students
51.71	48.29	5601	Males: Age Group 30 To 39
51.41	48.59	1204	Males: Traditional Age High School Students
51.08	48.92	1394	Managers: Federal Executives
50.98	49.02	51	Restaurant Workers: Table Setting and Cleaning
50.84	49.16	16676	TEACHERS
50.82	49.18	122	High School Student Leaders
50.56	49.44	540	Waiters and Waitresses
50.50	49.50	202	Administrators: Health
50.06	49.94	1760	Franklin and Marshall College - Freshmen
50.00	50.00	106	Media Specialists
50.00	50.00	60	Dental Hygienists
50.00	50.00	52	Dentists
49.78	50.22	225	Leaders in Student Government Activities
49.62	50.38	6814	Males: Adult College Graduates
49.61	50.39	649	Teachers: High School
49.42	50.58	172	Coordinators
49.30	50.70	2010	RELIGIOUS WORKERS -ALL DENOMINATIONS-
49.17	50.83	1857	ADMINISTRATORS
49.15	50.85	765	HEALTH CARE THERAPISTS
49.15	50.85	118	Therapists: Occupational
48.66	51.34	3814	Males: Age Group 25 To 29
48.36	51.64	122	Administrators: Educationally Related
48.35	51.65	395	Rollins College - Freshmen
48.26	51.74	172	Teaching Assistants
48.15	51.85	54	Chain, Rod and Ax Workers; Surveying
48.00	52.00	550	St. Louis University - Freshmen
47.97	52.03	123	Pharmacists
47.96	52.04	98	Managers: Participants in Women in Management Conference
47.50	52.50	200	Teachers: Elementary School
47.22	52.78	1603	DOCTORS OF MEDICINE
47.06	52.94	136	Credit Investigators and Mortgage Brokers
46.89	53.11	1881	Composite of Practitioners in Medicine (M.D.s)

S Percent	N	Total Sample Size	Sample Description
46.84	53.16	79	Religious Educator, all denominations
46.79	53.21	7952	Females: Adult College Graduates
46.75	53.25	338	COMPUTER SPECIALISTS
46.64	53.36	1505	Hope College - Freshmen
46.56	53.44	305	Nursing: Educators
46.51	53.49	86	Computer Systems Analysts and Support Representative
46.30	53.70	1229	Computer Professionals
46.15	53.85	65	Computer Operations, Systems Researchers and Analyst
46.00	54.00	50	College Students in Student Government
45.66	54.34	173	Teachers: Special Education
45.45	54.55	55	College Student Leaders
45.43	54.57	2514	University of Florida - Freshmen
45.31	54.69	245	Therapists: Occupational
45.18	54.82	633	Protestant Seminarians
44.50	55.50	200	Computer Programmers
43.40	56.60	106	Speech Pathologists
42.92	57.08	226	SCIENTISTS: LIFE AND PHYSICAL
42.62	57.38	61	Scientists: Chemistry
42.59	57.41	54	Engineers: Aeronautical
42.42	57.58	561	Teachers: Junior College
42.25	57.75	71	Consultants: Management
42.01	57.99	319	Rabbis
41.82	58.18	55	Designers
41.81	58.19	177	Counselors: Rehabilitation
41.41	58.59	1874	Law School Graduates
40.54	59.46	111	Consultants: Canadian
40.45	59.55	89	Public Relations Workers and Publicity Writers
40.00	60.00	80	Employment Development Specialists
39.76	60.24	83	Marketing Personnel
39.46	60.54	223	Teachers: Health
39.33	60.67	89	Consultants: Management Analysts
39.31	60.69	519	LAWYERS AND JUDGES
39.22	60.78	51	Administrators: Student Personnel
38.83	61.17	479	Social Workers
38.68	61.32	287	Counselors: School
38.63	61.37	673	Counselors: Vocational and Educational
38.52	61.48	122	Composite of Practitioners in Speech Pathology
38.36	61.64	219	Priests and Monks
37.85	62.15	177	College and University Resident Assistants
37.83	62.17	341	Administrators: Colleges and Technical Institutes
37.64	62.36	1554	Protestant Ministers
37.38	62.62	1803	COUNSELORS
37.25	62.75	51	Roman Catholic Seminarians
36.84	63.16	57	Scientists: Biology
36.76	63.24	1205	Candidates for Theology Education
36.06	63.94	2282	Teachers: University
35.84	64.16	932	Counselors: General
35.75	64.25	179	Teachers: English
34.90	65.10	192	Consultants: General
34.56	65.44	136	Musicians and Composers

S Percent	N	Total Sample Size	Sample Description
34.00	66.00	50	Directors of Religious Education
32.93	67.07	164	Gifted High School Seniors
32.87	67.13	359	Counselors: General
32.10	67.90	81	Research Workers
31.86	68.14	113	Editors and Reporters
31.76	68.24	85	Protestants in Specialized Ministries
31.48	68.52	54	Consultants: Education
30.95	69.05	378	ARTISTS AND ENTERTAINERS
30.77	69.23	169	Composite of Practitioners in Social Work
30.71	69.29	534	Clergy, all denominations (except priests)
30.63	69.37	271	Lawyers
29.91	70.09	117	Counselors: Runaway Youth
29.83	70.17	181	Females in Leadership Development Program
29.63	70.37	108	Members of a Human Resources Planners Association
29.11	70.89	213	Teachers: Art, Drama and Music
28.85	71.15	52	Journalists
27.38	72.62	84	Attorneys - Administrators, non-practicing
27.12	72.88	59	Photographers
26.42	73.58	530	WRITERS AND JOURNALISTS
25.00	75.00	68	Physicians: Psychiatry
24.40	75.60	705	Teachers: College Faculty Named as Danforth Associates
24.00	76.00	75	Phi Beta Kappa
23.96	76.04	793	High School Students in Florida Future Scientist Program
23.28	76.72	262	Counselors: Suicide and Crisis
19.40	80.60	67	Research Assistants
19.38	80.62	289	Psychologists
19.35	80.65	62	Actors
17.76	82.24	490	SOCIAL SCIENTISTS
17.74	82.26	124	Architects
17.58	82.42	1001	National Merit Scholarship Finalists
14.93	85.07	402	PSYCHOLOGISTS
13.94	86.06	208	Writers, Artists, Entertainers, and Agents
12.94	87.06	170	Certified Psychodramatists
8.77	91.23	114	Fine Artists
7.04	92.96	71	Rhodes Scholars

T Percent	F	Total Sample Size	Sample Description
95.50	4.50	111	Consultants: Canadian
93.04	6.96	316	Managers: Retail Stores
91.55	8.45	71	Consultants: Management
89.71	10.29	136	Managers: High Level Corporate Executives
87.13	12.87	334	Operators and Field Technicians in Water Pollution Control
86.44	13.56	1394	Managers: Federal Executives
85.73	14.27	1051	Males in Leadership Development Program
83.44	16.56	912	Police Officers: Managers
82.46	17.54	57	Police Officers: Commanders
81.33	18.67	150	Managers: Small Business
80.88	19.12	1229	Computer Professionals
79.52	20.48	83	Managers: Sales
78.99	21.01	257	Managers: Top Level in City, County and State Government
78.46	21.54	65	Computer Operations, Systems Researchers and Analysts
78.34	21.66	494	Certified Public Accountants
77.54	22.46	276	School Principals
76.74	23.26	86	Computer Systems Analysts and Support Representatives
76.13	23.87	926	Males: Adult High School Graduates Without College
75.52	24.48	143	Auditors
75.27	24.73	849	Managers: England
75.00	25.00	756	Managers: Financial and Bank Officers
75.00	25.00	80	Purchasing Agents
74.76	25.24	1874	Law School Graduates
74.66	25.34	446	Males: SRI Sample
74.57	25.43	523	Managers: Public
74.32	25.68	658	Displaced Steelworkers
74.29	25.71	105	Steelworkers
73.73	26.27	118	Managers: Japanese Chief Executives
73.53	26.47	3812	Males: Age Group 40 To 49
73.53	26.47	136	Credit Investigators and Mortgage Brokers
73.28	26.72	116	Managers: Middle Managers in a Japanese Heavy Industrial Co
72.78	27.22	169	Service Workers (except private household)
72.61	27.39	230	Managers: Regional Telephone Company Low Level Managers
72.13	27.87	61	Scientists: Chemistry
71.67	28.33	60	Managers: Fire
71.43	28.57	196	Displaced Coal Miners
71.42	28.58	1795	Males: Age Group 50 To 59
71.17	28.83	5601	Males: Age Group 30 To 39
71.15	28.85	52	Engineers: Chemical
71.03	28.97	290	Managers: Middle Level in City, County and State Government
70.91	29.09	55	College Student Leaders
70.89	29.11	1501	Males: Adult Non-Traditional Age College Students
70.88	29.12	6814	Males: Adult College Graduates
70.83	29.17	72	FARMERS
70.65	29.35	92	Police Officers: Supervisors in Urban Community
70.59	29.41	119	Teachers: Trade, Industrial and Technical
70.13	29.87	77	Engineers: Mechanical
69.68	30.32	343	Males: Adult High School Dropouts
69.57	30.43	92	Social Services Workers
69.56	30.44	15791	Males: Form G Databank

T Percent	F	Total Sample Size	Sample Description
69.05	30.95	84	Attorneys - Administrators, non-practicing
68.85	31.15	61	Physicians: Pathology
68.79	31.21	141	Police Officers: Patrolmen in Urban Community
68.42	31.58	57	Technicians: Electrical and Electronic Engineering
68.39	31.61	155	Police and Detectives
67.86	32.14	56	Managers: Top Managers in Large Japanese Companies
67.68	32.32	495	Males: Age Group 60 Plus
67.57	32.43	333	Public Accountants
67.46	32.54	338	COMPUTER SPECIALISTS
67.02	32.98	3814	Males: Age Group 25 To 29
66.79	33.21	280	Police Officers: Urban Community
66.67	33.33	366	Managers: Middle Managers in a Japanese Chemical Company
66.67	33.33	108	Members of a Human Resources Planners Association
66.67	33.33	54	Engineers: Electrical and Electronic
66.36	33.64	110	Bank Employees, Exempt
65.93	34.07	226	SCIENTISTS: LIFE AND PHYSICAL
65.62	34.38	256	Males: Traditional Age Junior High School Students
65.56	34.44	90	Personnel and Labor Relations Workers
64.94	35.06	271	Lawyers
64.50	35.50	200	Computer Programmers
64.16	35.84	519	LAWYERS AND JUDGES
64.06	35.94	128	Judges
64.04	35.96	89	Corrections Sergeants
63.89	36.11	3678	Administrators: Managers and Supervisors
63.81	36.19	105	Police Supervisors
63.78	36.22	312	Managers: Restaurant, Cafeteria, Bar and Food Service
63.59	36.41	986	ENGINEERS
63.55	36.45	23240	Males: Form F Databank
63.54	36.46	181	Females in Leadership Development Program
63.46	36.54	52	Computer Specialists
63.39	36.61	12637	Males: Traditional Age College Students
63.27	36.73	5320	Males: Age Group 21 To 24
62.71	37.29	59	Photographers
62.30	37.70	11897	Males: Age Group 18 To 20
62.03	37.97	3979	Males: Age Group 15 To 17
61.67	38.33	574	Line Corrections Officers
61.62	38.38	99	Police Officers: Australian Senior Officers
61.56	38.44	7463	MANAGERS AND ADMINISTRATORS
61.51	38.49	608	PROTECTIVE SERVICE WORKERS
61.45	38.55	83	Marketing Personnel
61.18	38.82	85	Dentists
61.06	38.94	4933	Males: High School Students from Pennsylvania
60.14	39.86	439	Police Officers
60.00	40.00	225	Leaders in Student Government Activities
59.65	40.35	57	Scientists: Biology
59.63	40.37	1204	Males: Traditional Age High School Students
59.56	40.44	1009	Navy Enlisted Personnel in Basic Electronic Training
59.53	40.47	4663	Military Personnel at Naval Technical Training Center
59.25	40.75	427	Accountants
59.15	40.85	71	Teachers: Mathematics

T Percent	F	Total Sample Size	Sample Description
59.01	40.99	405	Parks College - Freshmen and Transfers
58.40	41.60	250	Business: General, Self-employed
58.33	41.67	132	School Bus Drivers
58.21	41.79	67	Sales Agents, Retail Trade
57.96	42.04	835	Bank Employees
57.69	42.31	52	Dentists
57.53	42.47	73	Air Force Personnel
57.42	42.58	559	CRAFT WORKERS
57.35	42.65	68	Corrections Officers and Probation Officers
57.23	42.77	166	Real Estate Agents and Brokers
57.20	42.80	264	MILITARY PERSONNEL
57.14	42.86	175	ENGINEERING AND SCIENCE TECHNICIANS
57.14	42.86	70	Electricians
56.98	43.02	179	Sales Representatives
56.94	43.06	1001	National Merit Scholarship Finalists
56.88	43.12	705	Teachers: College Faculty Named as Danforth Associates
56.60	43.40	341	Administrators: Colleges and Technical Institutes
56.45	43.55	124	Architects
55.77	44.23	52	Factory and Site Supervisors
55.47	44.53	3373	High School Students in Australia
55.45	44.55	101	Administrators: Social Services
55.10	44.90	98	Managers: Participants in Women in Management Conference
55.06	44.94	89	Consultants: Management Analysts
55.04	44.96	238	Public Service Aides and Community Health Workers
54.92	45.08	122	Administrators: Educationally Related
54.88	45.12	82	Professional, Technical, and Kindred Workers
54.84	45.16	124	Administrators: Canadian Schools
54.26	45.74	94	Nursing: Administrators
54.01	45.99	1857	ADMINISTRATORS
53.75	46.25	80	Employment Development Specialists
53.73	46.27	67	CLEANING SERVICES
53.65	46.35	192	Consultants: General
53.47	46.53	101	Insurance Agents, Brokers, and Underwriters
53.37	46.63	2282	Teachers: University
53.33	46.67	195	Therapists: Respiratory
53.19	46.81	47	Police Officers: Detectives in Urban Community
52.62	47.38	669	MECHANICS
52.25	47.75	222	Bank Employees, Non-Exempt
52.24	47.76	67	Stock Clerks and Storekeepers
52.03	47.97	123	Pharmacists
51.83	48.17	164	Teachers: Coaching
51.61	48.39	62	Actors
51.58	48.42	793	High School Students in Florida Future Scientist Program
51.49	48.51	202	Administrators: Health
51.31	48.69	191	Pharmacists
51.22	48.78	164	Gifted High School Seniors
50.96	49.04	469	ALLIED HEALTH AND HEALTH PRACTIONERS, N.E.C.
50.85	49.15	413	Teachers: Mathematics
50.52	49.48	97	OPERATIVES: NON-SPECIALIZED AND FACTORY WORKERS
50.41	49.59	1105	Total SRI Sample

THINKING-FEELING

T Percent	F	Total Sample Size	Sample Description
50.39	49.61	127	Therapists: Practitioners in Respiratory Therapy
50.38	49.62	782	LABORERS
50.36	49.64	139	Construction Laborers (except carpenters helpers)
50.00	50.00	206	OPERATIVES: SPECIALIZED
50.00	50.00	144	OPERATIVES: TRANSPORTATION
49.71	50.29	1024	Administrators: Elementary and Secondary School
49.44	50.56	180	Cooks (except private household)
49.42	50.58	172	Coordinators
48.97	51.03	1603	DOCTORS OF MEDICINE
48.31	51.69	89	Public Relations Workers and Publicity Writers
48.27	51.73	1881	Composite of Practitioners in Medicine (M.D.s)
48.15	51.85	81	Research Workers
48.05	51.95	77	Secretaries: Legal
48.00	52.00	75	Phi Beta Kappa
47.55	52.45	9320	High School Students from Pennsylvania
46.51	53.49	86	Guards and Watch Keepers
46.36	53.64	1760	Franklin and Marshall College - Freshmen
46.30	53.70	54	Chain, Rod and Ax Workers; Surveying
46.23	53.77	1750	SALES WORKERS
46.09	53.91	243	Dietitians
45.90	54.10	122	High School Student Leaders
45.81	54.19	155	Nursing: Composite of Critical Care Nurses
45.71	54.29	490	SOCIAL SCIENTISTS
45.71	54.29	70	Optometrists
45.59	54.41	68	Physicians: Psychiatry
45.45	54.55	275	Salespeople in a Japanese Trading Company
45.37	54.63	108	Sales Clerks, Retail Trade
45.29	54.71	223	Clinical Laboratory Technologists and Technicians
45.13	54.87	113	Teachers: Supervising Student Teachers
45.07	54.93	71	Rhodes Scholars
44.97	55.03	169	Teachers: Grades 1 through 9, Canada
44.95	55.05	109	Carpenters
44.58	55.42	323	Dietitians and Nutritionists
44.55	55.45	211	Lifeguards, Attendants, Recreation and Amusement
44.53	55.47	402	PSYCHOLOGISTS
44.21	55.79	561	Teachers: Junior College
44.18	55.82	378	ARTISTS AND ENTERTAINERS
43.84	56.16	333	Secretaries: Executive and Administrative Assistants
43.84	56.16	146	Nursing: Consultants
43.64	56.36	55	Designers
43.40	56.60	106	Media Specialists
43.33	56.67	1147	Nuns and Other Religious Workers
43.32	56.68	5178	Females: Age Group 25 To 29
43.28	56.72	67	Research Assistants
43.11	56.89	167	Laboratory Technologists
43.02	56.98	530	WRITERS AND JOURNALISTS
42.98	57.02	228	Teachers: Adult Education
42.96	57.04	7952	Females: Adult College Graduates
42.84	57.16	8711	Females: Age Group 30 To 39
42.65	57.35	4150	Nicholls State University - Freshmen

T Percent	F	Total Sample Size	Sample Description
42.55	57.45	973	Medical Technologists
42.48	57.52	113	Editors and Reporters
42.45	57.55	1291	HEALTH TECHNOLOGISTS AND TECHNICIANS
42.45	57.55	245	Therapists: Occupational
42.34	57.66	232557	CAPT Databank Total Population
42.16	57.84	638	Medical Technologists (4 year)
42.15	57.85	783	PERSONAL SERVICE WORKERS
41.99	58.01	16676	TEACHERS
41.98	58.02	636	Females: Adult High School Dropouts
41.91	58.09	649	Teachers: High School
41.87	58.13	289	Psychologists
41.77	58.23	16880	Females: Form G Databank
41.64	58.36	305	Nursing: Educators
41.44	58.56	765	HEALTH CARE THERAPISTS
41.35	58.65	208	Writers, Artists, Entertainers, and Agents
41.26	58.74	223	Teachers: Health
41.18	58.82	51	Administrators: Student Personnel
40.74	59.26	54	Engineers: Aeronautical
40.70	59.30	172	Teaching Assistants
40.62	59.37	96	Hairdressers, Cosmetologists and Manicurists
40.46	59.54	173	Teachers: Special Education
40.16	59.84	3551	Females: Non-Traditional Age College Students
40.00	60.00	50	College Students in Student Government
39.89	60.11	4811	Females: Age Group 40 To 49
39.83	60.17	118	Therapists: Occupational
39.68	60.32	126	Radiologic Technologists and Technicians
39.62	60.38	53	Composite of Practitioners in Radiologic Technology
39.54	60.46	1128	Teachers: Middle and Junior High School
39.22	60.78	102	Managers: Office
39.09	60.91	1082	FOOD SERVICE WORKERS
39.01	60.99	1169	University of Wisconsin at Stevens Point - Freshmen
38.92	61.08	2492	University of North Carolina at Greensboro - Freshmen
38.89	61.11	54	Consultants: Education
38.46	61.54	52	Journalists
38.37	61.63	1973	St. Clair College
38.33	61.67	240	Foremen in Japanese Food Production Company
38.32	61.68	321	Females: Traditional Age Junior High School Students
38.25	61.75	1506	Mercer University - Freshmen
37.73	62.27	2470	Females: Age Group 50 To 59
37.71	62.29	2514	University of Florida - Freshmen
37.70	62.30	61	Food Counter and Fountain Workers
37.36	62.64	182	Health Education Practitioners
37.27	62.73	550	St. Louis University - Freshmen
37.25	62.75	51	Restaurant Workers: Table Setting and Cleaning
37.21	62.79	5738	Females: Age Group 21 To 24
37.04	62.96	297	Computer and Peripheral Equipment Operators
36.76	63.24	136	Musicians and Composers
36.71	63.29	395	Rollins College - Freshmen
36.69	63.31	139	Physicians: Family Practice, General Practice
36.30	63.70	135	Doctors of Osteopathy

T Percent	F	Total Sample Size	Sample Description
36.29	63.71	846	Females: Age Group 60 Plus
36.22	63.78	3103	NURSES
36.16	63.84	177	College and University Resident Assistants
36.00	64.00	200	Teachers: Elementary School
35.96	64.04	673	Counselors: Vocational and Educational
35.92	64.08	2277	Females: Adult High School Graduates, Without College
35.91	64.09	479	Social Workers
35.75	64.25	179	Teachers: English
35.44	64.56	79	Medical Assistants
35.25	64.75	122	Composite of Practitioners in Speech Pathology
34.89	65.11	1880	Nursing: Registered Nurses, no specialty stated
34.72	65.28	72	Dental Assistants
34.60	65.40	32731	Females: Form F Databank
34.53	65.47	2010	RELIGIOUS WORKERS -ALL DENOMINATIONS-
34.52	65.48	84	Library Attendants and Assistants
34.48	65.52	58	Home Management Advisors and Home Economists
34.17	65.83	1803	COUNSELORS
34.03	65.97	432	Teacher Aides (except school monitors)
33.99	66.01	659	Females: SRI Sample
33.96	66.04	106	Speech Pathologists
33.82	66.18	68	Secretaries: Medical
33.79	66.21	1604	SECRETARIES
33.33	66.67	540	Waiters and Waitresses
33.33	66.67	177	Counselors: Rehabilitation
33.33	66.67	102	Ordained Roman Catholic Deacons
33.33	66.67	96	Teachers: Reading
33.26	66.74	932	Counselors: General
33.07	66.93	4905	OFFICE MACHINE OPERATORS
32.96	67.04	2351	Nursing: Registered Nurses
32.96	67.04	267	Librarians
32.91	67.09	4035	University of Maine - Freshmen
32.73	67.27	55	Child Care Workers (except private household)
32.71	67.29	107	Typists
32.67	67.33	900	HEALTH SERVICE WORKERS
32.37	67.63	4387	Females: High School Students from Pennsylvania
32.27	67.73	4973	Females: Age Group 15 To 17
32.11	67.89	3339	CLERICAL AND KINDRED WORKERS
32.09	67.91	804	Teachers: Elementary School
31.97	68.03	319	Rabbis
31.92	68.08	260	Nursing: Licensed Practical Nurses
31.79	68.21	14519	Females: Traditional Age College Students
31.29	68.71	10342	Auburn University - Freshmen
31.02	68.98	13716	Females: Age Group 18 To 20
30.60	69.40	281	Teachers: School Grades 1 through 12
30.41	69.59	148	Therapists: Physical
30.29	69.71	274	Cashiers
30.15	69.85	262	Counselors: Suicide and Crisis
30.12	69.88	83	Nursing: Public Health
30.00	70.00	150	Bookkeepers
29.97	70.03	287	Counselors: School

T Percent	F	Total Sample Size	Sample Description
29.85	70.15	67	Teachers: Foreign Language in Junior and Senior High Schoo
29.82	70.18	114	Fine Artists
29.30	70.70	157	Teachers: Speech Pathology and Therapy
29.03	70.97	155	Therapists: Physical
28.64	71.36	213	Teachers: Art, Drama and Music
28.57	71.43	56	Clerical Supervisors
28.40	71.60	169	Composite of Practitioners in Social Work
28.33	71.67	60	Dental Hygienists
27.71	72.29	314	Nursing: Aides, Orderlies, and Attendants
27.65	72.35	170	Certified Psychodramatists
27.63	72.37	228	Rosemont College - Freshmen
27.50	72.50	1607	Females: Traditional Age High School Students
27.45	72.55	51	Roman Catholic Seminarians
26.50	73.50	117	Counselors: Runaway Youth
25.98	74.02	1505	Hope College - Freshmen
25.79	74.21	190	Engineers: Mining
25.72	74.28	3064	PRIVATE HOUSEHOLD WORKERS
25.11	74.89	219	Priests and Monks
24.71	75.29	85	Protestants in Specialized Ministries
24.56	75.44	114	Brothers in Roman Catholic Religious Orders
23.68	76.32	359	Counselors: General
22.78	77.22	1554	Protestant Ministers
22.78	77.22	79	Religious Educator, all denominations
22.67	77.33	3149	Concordia College - Freshmen
22.00	78.00	100	Receptionists
21.35	78.65	534	Clergy, all denominations (except priests)
21.00	79.00	100	Teachers: Pre-school
20.30	79.70	197	Adrian College - Freshmen
20.03	79.97	1298	Roman Catholic Priests
19.91	80.09	633	Protestant Seminarians
17.93	82.07	1205	Candidates for Theology Education
17.68	82.32	2002	Sisters in Roman Catholic Religious Orders
15.15	84.85	165	Clerks in a Japanese Trading Company
14.14	85.86	403	Berkshire Christian College - Freshmen and Transfers
12.00	88.00	50	Directors of Religious Education

J Percent	P	Total Sample Size	Sample Description
91.46	8.54	316	Managers: Retail Stores
87.64	12.36	89	Corrections Sergeants
86.29	13.71	124	Administrators: Canadian Schools
85.86	14.14	99	Police Officers: Australian Senior Officers
85.29	14.71	102	Ordained Roman Catholic Deacons
85.14	14.86	276	School Principals
84.21	15.79	57	Police Officers: Commanders
82.10	17.90	257	Managers: Top Level in City, County and State Government
81.58	18.42	912	Police Officers: Managers
81.07	18.93	169	Teachers: Grades 1 through 9, Canada
81.06	18.94	132	School Bus Drivers
80.63	19.37	222	Bank Employees, Non-Exempt
80.28	19.72	71	Consultants: Management
79.65	20.35	113	Teachers: Supervising Student Teachers
79.09	20.91	110	Bank Employees, Exempt
79.03	20.97	658	Displaced Steelworkers
78.85	21.15	52	Engineers: Chemical
78.72	21.28	94	Nursing: Administrators
78.22	21.78	101	Administrators: Social Services
78.20	21.80	523	Managers: Public
78.14	21.86	334	Operators and Field Technicians in Water Pollution Control
77.59	22.41	58	Home Management Advisors and Home Economists
76.92	23.08	52	Dentists
76.36	23.64	55	College Student Leaders
76.25	23.75	80	Purchasing Agents
76.21	23.79	849	Managers: England
76.21	23.79	290	Managers: Middle Level in City, County and State Government
76.09	23.91	92	Social Services Workers
75.90	24.10	83	Managers: Sales
75.41	24.59	846	Females: Age Group 60 Plus
75.33	24.67	150	Managers: Small Business
75.32	24.68	312	Managers: Restaurant, Cafeteria, Bar and Food Service
75.00	25.00	196	Displaced Coal Miners
75.00	25.00	136	Managers: High Level Corporate Executives
74.79	25.21	119	Teachers: Trade, Industrial and Technical
74.78	25.22	230	Managers: Regional Telephone Company Low Level Managers
74.77	25.23	333	Public Accountants
74.75	25.25	495	Males: Age Group 60 Plus
74.75	25.25	202	Administrators: Health
74.37	25.63	238	Public Service Aides and Community Health Workers
74.22	25.78	128	Judges
74.12	25.88	85	Dentists
74.09	25.91	494	Certified Public Accountants
74.02	25.98	1051	Males in Leadership Development Program
73.83	26.17	2002	Sisters in Roman Catholic Religious Orders
73.73	26.27	118	Managers: Japanese Chief Executives
73.35	26.65	319	Rabbis
73.33	26.67	105	Steelworkers
72.92	27.08	1795	Males: Age Group 50 To 59
72.60	27.40	281	Teachers: School Grades 1 through 12

J Percent	P	Total Sample Size	Sample Description
72.59	27.41	135	Doctors of Osteopathy
72.55	27.45	51	Roman Catholic Seminarians
72.34	27.66	47	Police Officers: Detectives in Urban Community
72.25	27.75	926	Males: Adult High School Graduates Without College
72.08	27.92	240	Foremen in Japanese Food Production Company
71.88	28.12	1394	Managers: Federal Executives
71.43	28.57	756	Managers: Financial and Bank Officers
71.38	28.62	3812	Males: Age Group 40 To 49
71.25	28.75	574	Line Corrections Officers
70.57	29.43	1298	Roman Catholic Priests
70.55	29.45	146	Nursing: Consultants
70.50	29.50	139	Physicians: Family Practice, General Practice
70.49	29.51	61	Physicians: Pathology
70.42	29.58	71	Teachers: Mathematics
70.37	29.63	108	Members of a Human Resources Planners Association
70.00	30.00	50	Directors of Religious Education
69.93	30.07	705	Teachers: College Faculty Named as Danforth Associates
69.82	30.18	1024	Administrators: Elementary and Secondary School
69.77	30.23	86	Guards and Watch Keepers
69.73	30.27	446	Males: SRI Sample
69.57	30.43	1857	ADMINISTRATORS
69.52	30.48	105	Police Supervisors
69.35	30.65	323	Dietitians and Nutritionists
69.32	30.68	7463	MANAGERS AND ADMINISTRATORS
69.32	30.68	427	Accountants
69.23	30.77	65	Computer Operations, Systems Researchers and Analysts
69.15	30.85	804	Teachers: Elementary School
69.14	30.86	243	Dietitians
69.12	30.88	136	Credit Investigators and Mortgage Brokers
69.05	30.95	84	Attorneys - Administrators, non-practicing
68.93	31.07	6814	Males: Adult College Graduates
68.85	31.15	61	Scientists: Chemistry
68.79	31.21	157	Teachers: Speech Pathology and Therapy
68.66	31.34	67	Teachers: Foreign Language in Junior and Senior High Schoo
68.63	31.37	51	Administrators: Student Personnel
68.57	31.43	70	Optometrists
68.47	31.53	111	Consultants: Canadian
68.43	31.57	3678	Administrators: Managers and Supervisors
68.42	31.58	608	PROTECTIVE SERVICE WORKERS
68.41	31.59	649	Teachers: High School
68.33	31.67	60	Managers: Fire
68.24	31.76	85	Protestants in Specialized Ministries
68.03	31.97	638	Medical Technologists (4 year)
67.92	32.08	5601	Males: Age Group 30 To 39
67.83	32.17	143	Auditors
67.82	32.18	1554	Protestant Ministers
67.77	32.23	636	Females: Adult High School Dropouts
67.74	32.26	341	Administrators: Colleges and Technical Institutes
67.73	32.27	2470	Females: Age Group 50 To 59
67.71	32.29	96	Hairdressers, Cosmetologists and Manicurists

JUDGMENT-PERCEPTION

J Percent	P	Total Sample Size	Sample Description
67.66	32.34	835	Bank Employees
67.65	32.35	68	Secretaries: Medical
67.64	32.36	343	Males: Adult High School Dropouts
67.54	32.46	7952	Females: Adult College Graduates
67.50	32.50	200	Teachers: Elementary School
67.39	32.61	92	Police Officers: Supervisors in Urban Community
67.31	32.69	260	Nursing: Licensed Practical Nurses
67.31	32.69	52	Factory and Site Supervisors
67.31	32.69	52	Computer Specialists
67.21	32.79	122	Administrators: Educationally Related
67.16	32.84	67	CLEANING SERVICES
67.07	32.93	82	Professional, Technical, and Kindred Workers
67.04	32.96	179	Teachers: English
67.03	32.97	182	Health Education Practitioners
66.70	33.30	973	Medical Technologists
66.67	33.33	432	Teacher Aides (except school monitors)
66.67	33.33	96	Teachers: Reading
66.67	33.33	90	Personnel and Labor Relations Workers
66.52	33.48	469	ALLIED HEALTH AND HEALTH PRACTIONERS, N.E.C.
66.45	33.55	155	Police and Detectives
66.43	33.57	1147	Nuns and Other Religious Workers
66.43	33.57	280	Police Officers: Urban Community
66.37	33.63	226	SCIENTISTS: LIFE AND PHYSICAL
66.27	33.73	83	Nursing: Public Health
66.21	33.79	219	Priests and Monks
66.15	33.85	1105	Total SRI Sample
66.07	33.93	56	Managers: Top Managers in Large Japanese Companies
66.04	33.96	4811	Females: Age Group 40 To 49
65.98	34.02	1881	Composite of Practitioners in Medicine (M.D.s)
65.91	34.09	2282	Teachers: University
65.90	34.10	305	Nursing: Educators
65.74	34.26	1229	Computer Professionals
65.69	34.31	1128	Teachers: Middle and Junior High School
65.65	34.35	16676	TEACHERS
65.62	34.38	413	Teachers: Mathematics
65.26	34.74	2277	Females: Adult High School Graduates, Without College
65.12	34.88	2010	RELIGIOUS WORKERS -ALL DENOMINATIONS-
65.12	34.88	86	Computer Systems Analysts and Support Representatives
65.00	35.00	100	Teachers: Pre-school
64.91	35.09	114	Brothers in Roman Catholic Religious Orders
64.91	35.09	57	Scientists: Biology
64.74	35.26	173	Teachers: Special Education
64.71	35.29	102	Managers: Office
64.48	35.52	366	Managers: Middle Managers in a Japanese Chemical Company
64.46	35.54	166	Real Estate Agents and Brokers
64.41	35.59	118	Therapists: Occupational
64.29	35.71	8711	Females: Age Group 30 To 39
64.29	35.71	84	Library Attendants and Assistants
64.07	35.93	1603	DOCTORS OF MEDICINE
64.04	35.96	267	Librarians

JUDGMENT-PERCEPTION

J Percent	P	Total Sample Size	Sample Description
64.04	35.96	89	Consultants: Management Analysts
64.00	36.00	50	College Students in Student Government
63.95	36.05	172	Coordinators
63.87	36.13	191	Pharmacists
63.83	36.17	141	Police Officers: Patrolmen in Urban Community
63.73	36.27	659	Females: SRI Sample
63.69	36.31	179	Sales Representatives
63.59	36.41	1291	HEALTH TECHNOLOGISTS AND TECHNICIANS
63.58	36.42	3103	NURSES
63.50	36.50	3551	Females: Non-Traditional Age College Students
63.42	36.58	1501	Males: Adult Non-Traditional Age College Students
63.41	36.59	164	Teachers: Coaching
63.40	36.60	1205	Candidates for Theology Education
63.35	36.65	633	Protestant Seminarians
63.16	36.84	57	Technicians: Electrical and Electronic Engineering
62.96	37.04	54	Engineers: Electrical and Electronic
62.96	37.04	54	Consultants: Education
62.92	37.08	534	Clergy, all denominations (except priests)
62.82	37.18	1880	Nursing: Registered Nurses, no specialty stated
62.78	37.22	223	Teachers: Health
62.58	37.42	155	Nursing: Composite of Critical Care Nurses
62.47	37.53	3064	PRIVATE HOUSEHOLD WORKERS
62.45	37.55	245	Therapists: Occupational
62.43	37.57	519	LAWYERS AND JUDGES
62.34	37.66	77	Secretaries: Legal
62.34	37.66	77	Engineers: Mechanical
62.21	37.79	5178	Females: Age Group 25 To 29
62.21	37.79	172	Teaching Assistants
62.03	37.97	79	Religious Educator, all denominations
61.98	38.02	192	Consultants: General
61.86	38.14	333	Secretaries: Executive and Administrative Assistants
61.84	38.16	228	Teachers: Adult Education
61.76	38.24	68	Corrections Officers and Probation Officers
61.74	38.26	264	MILITARY PERSONNEL
61.68	38.32	561	Teachers: Junior College
61.38	38.62	3814	Males: Age Group 25 To 29
61.32	38.68	106	Media Specialists
61.25	38.75	80	Employment Development Specialists
61.11	38.89	16880	Females: Form G Databank
61.11	38.89	900	HEALTH SERVICE WORKERS
61.07	38.93	5738	Females: Age Group 21 To 24
60.98	39.02	123	Pharmacists
60.79	39.21	1604	SECRETARIES
60.53	39.47	2351	Nursing: Registered Nurses
60.49	39.51	81	Research Workers
60.45	39.55	986	ENGINEERS
60.31	39.69	2492	University of North Carolina at Greensboro - Freshmen
60.00	40.00	250	Business: General, Self-employed
59.81	40.19	107	Typists
59.79	40.21	97	OPERATIVES: NON-SPECIALIZED AND FACTORY WORKERS

J Percent	P	Total Sample Size	Sample Description
59.56	40.44	225	Leaders in Student Government Activities
59.47	40.53	32731	Females: Form F Databank
59.32	40.68	23240	Males: Form F Databank
59.30	40.70	5320	Males: Age Group 21 To 24
59.28	40.72	4663	Military Personnel at Naval Technical Training Center
59.26	40.74	783	PERSONAL SERVICE WORKERS
59.03	40.97	144	OPERATIVES: TRANSPORTATION
59.02	40.98	61	Food Counter and Fountain Workers
58.92	41.08	314	Nursing: Aides, Orderlies, and Attendants
58.90	41.10	73	Air Force Personnel
58.88	41.12	338	COMPUTER SPECIALISTS
58.87	41.13	124	Architects
58.75	41.25	1874	Law School Graduates
58.33	41.67	108	Sales Clerks, Retail Trade
58.33	41.67	72	FARMERS
58.33	41.67	60	Dental Hygienists
58.00	42.00	150	Bookkeepers
57.86	42.14	15791	Males: Form G Databank
57.85	42.15	223	Clinical Laboratory Technologists and Technicians
57.66	42.34	14519	Females: Traditional Age College Students
57.66	42.34	274	Cashiers
57.60	42.40	4387	Females: High School Students from Pennsylvania
57.40	42.60	169	Service Workers (except private household)
57.14	42.86	56	Clerical Supervisors
57.07	42.93	559	CRAFT WORKERS
57.00	43.00	4905	OFFICE MACHINE OPERATORS
56.98	43.02	232557	CAPT Databank Total Population
56.91	43.09	13716	Females: Age Group 18 To 20
56.76	43.24	148	Therapists: Physical
56.73	43.27	765	HEALTH CARE THERAPISTS
56.72	43.28	67	Sales Agents, Retail Trade
56.44	43.56	101	Insurance Agents, Brokers, and Underwriters
56.36	43.64	55	Designers
56.35	43.65	126	Radiologic Technologists and Technicians
56.29	43.71	167	Laboratory Technologists
56.18	43.82	89	Public Relations Workers and Publicity Writers
56.09	43.91	3339	CLERICAL AND KINDRED WORKERS
56.03	43.97	116	Managers: Middle Managers in a Japanese Heavy Industrial Co
56.00	44.00	175	ENGINEERING AND SCIENCE TECHNICIANS
56.00	44.00	100	Receptionists
55.71	44.29	70	Electricians
55.56	44.44	72	Dental Assistants
55.42	44.58	83	Marketing Personnel
55.34	44.66	206	OPERATIVES: SPECIALIZED
55.10	44.90	98	Managers: Participants in Women in Management Conference
54.98	45.02	673	Counselors: Vocational and Educational
54.92	45.08	122	High School Student Leaders
54.86	45.14	1750	SALES WORKERS
54.80	45.20	177	College and University Resident Assistants
54.72	45.28	106	Speech Pathologists

JUDGMENT-PERCEPTION

J Percent	P	Total Sample Size	Sample Description
54.67	45.33	439	Police Officers
54.62	45.38	9320	High School Students from Pennsylvania
54.55	45.45	55	Child Care Workers (except private household)
54.43	45.57	79	Medical Assistants
54.36	45.64	195	Therapists: Respiratory
54.26	45.74	669	MECHANICS
54.07	45.93	479	Social Workers
54.00	46.00	200	Computer Programmers
53.87	46.13	271	Lawyers
53.86	46.14	4150	Nicholls State University - Freshmen
53.78	46.22	1506	Mercer University - Freshmen
53.70	46.30	54	Engineers: Aeronautical
53.59	46.41	181	Females in Leadership Development Program
53.33	46.67	75	Phi Beta Kappa
53.30	46.70	197	Adrian College - Freshmen
53.00	47.00	12637	Males: Traditional Age College Students
52.96	47.04	287	Counselors: School
52.86	47.14	297	Computer and Peripheral Equipment Operators
52.84	47.16	405	Parks College - Freshmen and Transfers
52.21	47.79	136	Musicians and Composers
52.08	47.92	1803	COUNSELORS
51.98	48.02	4933	Males: High School Students from Pennsylvania
51.86	48.14	403	Berkshire Christian College - Freshmen and Transfers
51.79	48.21	11897	Males: Age Group 18 To 20
51.75	48.25	114	Fine Artists
51.66	48.34	211	Lifeguards, Attendants, Recreation and Amusement
51.64	48.36	122	Composite of Practitioners in Speech Pathology
51.61	48.39	155	Therapists: Physical
51.31	48.69	1760	Franklin and Marshall College - Freshmen
51.18	48.82	932	Counselors: General
51.17	48.83	213	Teachers: Art, Drama and Music
51.11	48.89	180	Cooks (except private household)
51.08	48.92	139	Construction Laborers (except carpenters helpers)
50.94	49.06	53	Composite of Practitioners in Radiologic Technology
50.85	49.15	59	Photographers
50.79	49.21	378	ARTISTS AND ENTERTAINERS
50.75	49.25	3149	Concordia College - Freshmen
50.00	50.00	68	Physicians: Psychiatry
49.69	50.31	3373	High School Students in Australia
49.62	50.38	262	Counselors: Suicide and Crisis
49.39	50.61	490	SOCIAL SCIENTISTS
48.73	51.27	550	St. Louis University - Freshmen
48.68	51.32	793	High School Students in Florida Future Scientist Program
48.61	51.39	395	Rollins College - Freshmen
48.45	51.55	2514	University of Florida - Freshmen
48.33	51.67	1169	University of Wisconsin at Stevens Point - Freshmen
48.08	51.92	4973	Females: Age Group 15 To 17
48.01	51.99	402	PSYCHOLOGISTS
47.76	52.24	67	Stock Clerks and Storekeepers
47.41	52.59	1082	FOOD SERVICE WORKERS

JUDGMENT-PERCEPTION

J Percent	P	Total Sample Size	Sample Description
47.35	52.65	359	Counselors: General
47.31	52.69	1505	Hope College - Freshmen
47.06	52.94	782	LABORERS
46.75	53.25	169	Composite of Practitioners in Social Work
46.47	53.53	170	Certified Psychodramatists
46.27	53.73	67	Research Assistants
45.78	54.22	10342	Auburn University - Freshmen
45.66	54.34	3979	Males: Age Group 15 To 17
45.46	54.54	1973	St. Clair College
45.19	54.81	1009	Navy Enlisted Personnel in Basic Electronic Training
45.16	54.84	62	Actors
44.88	55.12	127	Therapists: Practitioners in Respiratory Therapy
44.86	55.14	321	Females: Traditional Age Junior High School Students
44.56	55.44	1001	National Merit Scholarship Finalists
44.29	55.71	289	Psychologists
44.26	55.74	540	Waiters and Waitresses
44.21	55.79	190	Engineers: Mining
44.07	55.93	177	Counselors: Rehabilitation
43.40	56.60	530	WRITERS AND JOURNALISTS
43.36	56.64	113	Editors and Reporters
43.12	56.88	109	Carpenters
42.42	57.58	165	Clerks in a Japanese Trading Company
41.18	58.82	51	Restaurant Workers: Table Setting and Cleaning
40.82	59.18	1607	Females: Traditional Age High School Students
40.50	59.50	4035	University of Maine - Freshmen
39.91	60.09	228	Rosemont College - Freshmen
39.63	60.37	164	Gifted High School Seniors
39.29	60.71	1204	Males: Traditional Age High School Students
38.94	61.06	208	Writers, Artists, Entertainers, and Agents
38.89	61.11	54	Chain, Rod and Ax Workers; Surveying
38.46	61.54	52	Journalists
36.75	63.25	117	Counselors: Runaway Youth
36.62	63.38	71	Rhodes Scholars
31.64	68.36	275	Salespeople in a Japanese Trading Company
31.25	68.75	256	Males: Traditional Age Junior High School Students

Percent ST	Total Sample Size	Sample Description
76.58	316	Managers: Retail Stores
70.67	150	Managers: Small Business
68.26	334	Operators and Field Technicians in Water Pollution Control
67.32	912	Police Officers: Managers
66.67	105	Steelworkers
64.91	57	Police Officers: Commanders
63.33	60	Managers: Fire
63.22	658	Displaced Steelworkers
62.85	926	Males: Adult High School Graduates Without College
59.55	89	Corrections Sergeants
59.14	257	Managers: Top Level in City, County and State Government
59.09	110	Bank Employees, Exempt
58.75	80	Purchasing Agents
57.42	155	Police and Detectives
57.39	230	Managers: Regional Telephone Company Low Level Managers
56.60	523	Managers: Public
56.28	446	Males: SRI Sample
56.16	276	School Principals
56.03	141	Police Officers: Patrolmen in Urban Community
55.92	574	Line Corrections Officers
55.61	196	Displaced Coal Miners
55.56	99	Police Officers: Australian Senior Officers
55.43	92	Police Officers: Supervisors in Urban Community
55.30	132	School Bus Drivers
55.03	169	Service Workers (except private household)
54.29	280	Police Officers: Urban Community
53.64	494	Certified Public Accountants
52.77	849	Managers: England
52.10	119	Teachers: Trade, Industrial and Technical
51.47	136	Managers: High Level Corporate Executives
51.43	105	Police Supervisors
51.39	72	FARMERS
50.69	290	Managers: Middle Level in City, County and State Government
50.53	756	Managers: Financial and Bank Officers
49.85	343	Males: Adult High School Dropouts
49.67	1051	Males in Leadership Development Program
49.25	67	CLEANING SERVICES
48.52	608	PROTECTIVE SERVICE WORKERS
48.08	52	Factory and Site Supervisors
48.05	77	Engineers: Mechanical
47.07	495	Males: Age Group 60 Plus
47.06	238	Public Service Aides and Community Health Workers
46.92	439	Police Officers
46.81	47	Police Officers: Detectives in Urban Community
46.40	222	Bank Employees, Non-Exempt
46.18	1795	Males: Age Group 50 To 59
46.15	143	Auditors
45.98	1394	Managers: Federal Executives
45.90	366	Managers: Middle Managers in a Japanese Chemical Company
45.57	3812	Males: Age Group 40 To 49

Percent ST	Total Sample Size	Sample Description
45.51	312	Managers: Restaurant, Cafeteria, Bar and Food Service
44.58	83	Managers: Sales
44.55	101	Administrators: Social Services
43.47	559	CRAFT WORKERS
42.62	61	Physicians: Pathology
42.47	73	Air Force Personnel
42.44	1501	Males: Adult Non-Traditional Age College Students
42.42	264	MILITARY PERSONNEL
42.39	92	Social Services Workers
42.19	128	Judges
41.43	15791	Males: Form G Databank
41.41	256	Males: Traditional Age Junior High School Students
41.33	4663	Military Personnel at Naval Technical Training Center
41.08	835	Bank Employees
40.85	4933	Males: High School Students from Pennsylvania
40.06	5601	Males: Age Group 30 To 39
39.64	111	Consultants: Canadian
39.44	71	Consultants: Management
39.40	3678	Administrators: Managers and Supervisors
39.36	94	Nursing: Administrators
39.34	427	Accountants
39.22	1229	Computer Professionals
39.10	1105	Total SRI Sample
39.02	3373	High School Students in Australia
38.89	144	OPERATIVES: TRANSPORTATION
38.81	12637	Males: Traditional Age College Students
38.79	116	Managers: Middle Managers in a Japanese Heavy Industrial Company
38.77	405	Parks College - Freshmen and Transfers
38.72	11897	Males: Age Group 18 To 20
38.67	6814	Males: Adult College Graduates
38.55	179	Sales Representatives
38.37	86	Guards and Watch Keepers
37.65	85	Dentists
37.52	669	MECHANICS
37.50	23240	Males: Form F Databank
37.50	56	Managers: Top Managers in Large Japanese Companies
37.38	7463	MANAGERS AND ADMINISTRATORS
37.24	333	Public Accountants
37.20	164	Teachers: Coaching
36.84	57	Technicians: Electrical and Electronic Engineering
36.67	90	Personnel and Labor Relations Workers
36.63	101	Insurance Agents, Brokers, and Underwriters
36.54	52	Engineers: Chemical
36.44	3979	Males: Age Group 15 To 17
36.44	118	Managers: Japanese Chief Executives
36.36	55	College Student Leaders
36.21	986	ENGINEERS
36.08	97	OPERATIVES: NON-SPECIALIZED AND FACTORY WORKERS
35.82	67	Stock Clerks and Storekeepers
35.68	782	LABORERS

SENSING-THINKING

Percent ST	Total Sample Size	Sample Description
35.60	5320	Males: Age Group 21 To 24
35.47	3814	Males: Age Group 25 To 29
35.29	136	Credit Investigators and Mortgage Brokers
35.29	68	Corrections Officers and Probation Officers
35.21	71	Teachers: Mathematics
35.19	54	Engineers: Electrical and Electronic
34.88	86	Computer Systems Analysts and Support Representatives
34.62	413	Teachers: Mathematics
34.53	139	Construction Laborers (except carpenters helpers)
34.44	180	Cooks (except private household)
34.40	250	Business: General, Self-employed
34.34	166	Real Estate Agents and Brokers
34.29	70	Electricians
33.87	124	Administrators: Canadian Schools
33.85	65	Computer Operations, Systems Researchers and Analysts
33.70	1009	Navy Enlisted Personnel in Basic Electronic Training
33.03	109	Carpenters
32.89	225	Leaders in Student Government Activities
32.86	70	Optometrists
32.69	52	Computer Specialists
32.58	9320	High School Students from Pennsylvania
32.52	206	OPERATIVES: SPECIALIZED
32.51	4150	Nicholls State University - Freshmen
32.18	1874	Law School Graduates
32.14	1204	Males: Traditional Age High School Students
32.00	175	ENGINEERING AND SCIENCE TECHNICIANS
31.97	122	High School Student Leaders
31.97	122	Administrators: Educationally Related
31.36	169	Teachers: Grades 1 through 9, Canada
31.13	636	Females: Adult High School Dropouts
30.97	113	Teachers: Supervising Student Teachers
30.81	211	Lifeguards, Attendants, Recreation and Amusement
30.47	338	COMPUTER SPECIALISTS
30.45	243	Dietitians
30.21	96	Hairdressers, Cosmetologists and Manicurists
30.06	469	ALLIED HEALTH AND HEALTH PRACTIONERS, N.E.C.
29.87	77	Secretaries: Legal
29.84	191	Pharmacists
29.83	1857	ADMINISTRATORS
29.82	228	Teachers: Adult Education
29.74	195	Therapists: Respiratory
29.59	1024	Administrators: Elementary and Secondary School
29.58	240	Foremen in Japanese Food Production Company
29.51	61	Scientists: Chemistry
29.27	123	Pharmacists
29.27	82	Professional, Technical, and Kindred Workers
29.03	155	Nursing: Composite of Critical Care Nurses
28.92	83	Marketing Personnel
28.79	323	Dietitians and Nutritionists
28.70	108	Sales Clerks, Retail Trade

Percent ST	Total Sample Size	Sample Description
28.53	333	Secretaries: Executive and Administrative Assistants
28.48	783	PERSONAL SERVICE WORKERS
28.36	67	Sales Agents, Retail Trade
28.25	223	Clinical Laboratory Technologists and Technicians
28.14	167	Laboratory Technologists
28.09	89	Consultants: Management Analysts
28.01	432	Teacher Aides (except school monitors)
28.00	200	Computer Programmers
27.95	973	Medical Technologists
27.94	519	LAWYERS AND JUDGES
27.88	226	SCIENTISTS: LIFE AND PHYSICAL
27.83	1973	St. Clair College
27.60	1750	SALES WORKERS
27.54	2277	Females: Adult High School Graduates, Without College
27.47	659	Females: SRI Sample
27.33	172	Coordinators
27.23	202	Administrators: Health
26.92	52	Dentists
26.77	127	Therapists: Practitioners in Respiratory Therapy
26.72	1291	HEALTH TECHNOLOGISTS AND TECHNICIANS
26.65	638	Medical Technologists (4 year)
26.58	1881	Composite of Practitioners in Medicine (M.D.s)
26.50	1147	Nuns and Other Religious Workers
26.42	53	Composite of Practitioners in Radiologic Technology
26.19	126	Radiologic Technologists and Technicians
26.16	3551	Females: Non-Traditional Age College Students
26.03	146	Nursing: Consultants
25.92	1169	University of Wisconsin at Stevens Point - Freshmen
25.86	58	Home Management Advisors and Home Economists
25.76	1603	DOCTORS OF MEDICINE
25.73	649	Teachers: High School
25.51	1760	Franklin and Marshall College - Freshmen
25.51	98	Managers: Participants in Women in Management Conference
25.30	846	Females: Age Group 60 Plus
25.28	16880	Females: Form G Databank
25.23	107	Typists
25.00	84	Library Attendants and Assistants
24.78	232557	CAPT Databank Total Population
24.62	260	Nursing: Licensed Practical Nurses
24.53	106	Media Specialists
24.51	102	Ordained Roman Catholic Deacons
24.51	102	Managers: Office
24.38	1128	Teachers: Middle and Junior High School
24.34	341	Administrators: Colleges and Technical Institutes
23.99	271	Lawyers
23.79	16676	TEACHERS
23.75	80	Employment Development Specialists
23.66	5178	Females: Age Group 25 To 29
23.66	1082	FOOD SERVICE WORKERS
23.64	1506	Mercer University - Freshmen

Percent ST	Total Sample Size	Sample Description
23.38	8711	Females: Age Group 30 To 39
23.36	274	Cashiers
23.27	4387	Females: High School Students from Pennsylvania
23.23	297	Computer and Peripheral Equipment Operators
22.92	192	Consultants: General
22.91	275	Salespeople in a Japanese Trading Company
22.81	57	Scientists: Biology
22.78	281	Teachers: School Grades 1 through 12
22.74	321	Females: Traditional Age Junior High School Students
22.67	2470	Females: Age Group 50 To 59
22.67	172	Teaching Assistants
22.67	150	Bookkeepers
22.51	4811	Females: Age Group 40 To 49
22.47	89	Public Relations Workers and Publicity Writers
22.44	1604	SECRETARIES
22.39	67	Teachers: Foreign Language in Junior and Senior High School
22.22	72	Dental Assistants
22.22	54	Chain, Rod and Ax Workers; Surveying
22.17	2282	Teachers: University
22.15	5738	Females: Age Group 21 To 24
22.11	900	HEALTH SERVICE WORKERS
22.10	181	Females in Leadership Development Program
21.98	7952	Females: Adult College Graduates
21.94	155	Therapists: Physical
21.77	804	Teachers: Elementary School
21.59	4905	OFFICE MACHINE OPERATORS
21.52	79	Medical Assistants
21.29	3339	CLERICAL AND KINDRED WORKERS
21.27	3103	NURSES
21.18	765	HEALTH CARE THERAPISTS
21.03	561	Teachers: Junior College
20.85	1880	Nursing: Registered Nurses, no specialty stated
20.80	14519	Females: Traditional Age College Students
20.65	13716	Females: Age Group 18 To 20
20.59	68	Secretaries: Medical
20.46	2351	Nursing: Registered Nurses
20.37	108	Members of a Human Resources Planners Association
20.33	305	Nursing: Educators
20.23	32731	Females: Form F Databank
20.14	139	Physicians: Family Practice, General Practice
20.00	245	Therapists: Occupational
20.00	135	Doctors of Osteopathy
20.00	55	Designers
20.00	50	College Students in Student Government
19.85	4973	Females: Age Group 15 To 17
19.80	4035	University of Maine - Freshmen
19.75	395	Rollins College - Freshmen
19.59	148	Therapists: Physical
19.48	267	Librarians
19.43	314	Nursing: Aides, Orderlies, and Attendants

Percent ST	Total Sample Size	Sample Description
19.33	2514	University of Florida - Freshmen
19.28	223	Teachers: Health
19.23	182	Health Education Practitioners
19.15	2010	RELIGIOUS WORKERS -ALL DENOMINATIONS-
19.12	68	Physicians: Psychiatry
19.09	550	St. Louis University - Freshmen
18.70	10342	Auburn University - Freshmen
18.57	673	Counselors: Vocational and Educational
18.50	200	Teachers: Elementary School
18.50	173	Teachers: Special Education
18.42	190	Engineers: Mining
18.15	540	Waiters and Waitresses
18.08	177	Counselors: Rehabilitation
18.03	61	Food Counter and Fountain Workers
17.86	84	Attorneys - Administrators, non-practicing
17.86	56	Clerical Supervisors
17.80	118	Therapists: Occupational
17.65	51	Roman Catholic Seminarians
17.65	51	Restaurant Workers: Table Setting and Cleaning
17.54	114	Brothers in Roman Catholic Religious Orders
17.36	1803	COUNSELORS
17.33	479	Social Workers
17.20	157	Teachers: Speech Pathology and Therapy
16.97	3064	PRIVATE HOUSEHOLD WORKERS
16.95	59	Photographers
16.87	83	Nursing: Public Health
16.72	287	Counselors: School
16.67	228	Rosemont College - Freshmen
16.67	96	Teachers: Reading
16.67	60	Dental Hygienists
16.67	54	Engineers: Aeronautical
16.52	932	Counselors: General
16.36	55	Child Care Workers (except private household)
16.20	179	Teachers: English
16.04	106	Speech Pathologists
15.74	1607	Females: Traditional Age High School Students
15.69	51	Administrators: Student Personnel
15.25	177	College and University Resident Assistants
15.04	113	Editors and Reporters
15.00	100	Receptionists
14.87	1298	Roman Catholic Priests
14.81	378	ARTISTS AND ENTERTAINERS
14.81	81	Research Workers
14.81	54	Consultants: Education
14.73	319	Rabbis
14.63	164	Gifted High School Seniors
14.21	197	Adrian College - Freshmen
14.20	169	Composite of Practitioners in Social Work
13.93	122	Composite of Practitioners in Speech Pathology
13.87	793	High School Students in Florida Future Scientist Program

Percent ST	Total Sample Size	Sample Description
13.76	705	Teachers: College Faculty Named as Danforth Associates
13.70	219	Priests and Monks
13.69	1505	Hope College - Freshmen
13.46	52	Journalists
13.40	3149	Concordia College - Freshmen
13.33	75	Phi Beta Kappa
13.24	136	Musicians and Composers
13.21	530	WRITERS AND JOURNALISTS
13.16	2492	University of North Carolina at Greensboro - Freshmen
13.09	359	Counselors: General
12.90	124	Architects
12.90	62	Actors
12.66	79	Religious Educator, all denominations
11.74	213	Teachers: Art, Drama and Music
11.17	403	Berkshire Christian College - Freshmen and Transfers
11.07	289	Psychologists
10.79	1001	National Merit Scholarship Finalists
10.64	2002	Sisters in Roman Catholic Religious Orders
10.26	117	Counselors: Runaway Youth
9.59	1554	Protestant Ministers
9.41	85	Protestants in Specialized Ministries
9.00	100	Teachers: Pre-school
8.98	490	SOCIAL SCIENTISTS
8.96	67	Research Assistants
8.48	165	Clerks in a Japanese Trading Company
8.40	262	Counselors: Suicide and Crisis
8.37	633	Protestant Seminarians
8.00	50	Directors of Religious Education
7.71	402	PSYCHOLOGISTS
7.21	208	Writers, Artists, Entertainers, and Agents
7.12	534	Clergy, all denominations (except priests)
6.80	1205	Candidates for Theology Education
4.12	170	Certified Psychodramatists
3.51	114	Fine Artists
1.41	71	Rhodes Scholars

Percent SF	Total Sample Size	Sample Description
58.79	165	Clerks in a Japanese Trading Company
55.58	403	Berkshire Christian College - Freshmen and Transfers
52.50	240	Foremen in Japanese Food Production Company
50.89	281	Teachers: School Grades 1 through 12
50.53	659	Females: SRI Sample
50.00	56	Clerical Supervisors
49.75	197	Adrian College - Freshmen
49.45	2002	Sisters in Roman Catholic Religious Orders
49.23	260	Nursing: Licensed Practical Nurses
49.09	55	Child Care Workers (except private household)
47.39	4387	Females: High School Students from Pennsylvania
46.73	107	Typists
46.46	2277	Females: Adult High School Graduates, Without College
45.95	222	Bank Employees, Non-Exempt
45.54	314	Nursing: Aides, Orderlies, and Attendants
45.33	150	Bookkeepers
45.00	100	Receptionists
44.44	72	Dental Assistants
44.35	3064	PRIVATE HOUSEHOLD WORKERS
44.21	432	Teacher Aides (except school monitors)
44.12	68	Secretaries: Medical
44.00	100	Teachers: Pre-school
43.86	114	Brothers in Roman Catholic Religious Orders
43.74	2492	University of North Carolina at Greensboro - Freshmen
43.31	157	Teachers: Speech Pathology and Therapy
42.78	900	HEALTH SERVICE WORKERS
41.55	13716	Females: Age Group 18 To 20
40.96	83	Nursing: Public Health
40.91	132	School Bus Drivers
40.88	636	Females: Adult High School Dropouts
40.80	804	Teachers: Elementary School
40.62	96	Hairdressers, Cosmetologists and Manicurists
40.60	14519	Females: Traditional Age College Students
40.51	274	Cashiers
40.48	84	Library Attendants and Assistants
40.40	1973	St. Clair College
40.20	3149	Concordia College - Freshmen
39.68	126	Radiologic Technologists and Technicians
39.62	53	Composite of Practitioners in Radiologic Technology
39.60	1298	Roman Catholic Priests
39.58	96	Teachers: Reading
39.40	4150	Nicholls State University - Freshmen
39.34	61	Food Counter and Fountain Workers
39.20	3339	CLERICAL AND KINDRED WORKERS
38.41	4905	OFFICE MACHINE OPERATORS
38.25	10342	Auburn University - Freshmen
37.97	1604	SECRETARIES
37.91	182	Health Education Practitioners
37.60	4973	Females: Age Group 15 To 17
37.28	228	Rosemont College - Freshmen

Percent SF	Total Sample Size	Sample Description
37.25	102	Ordained Roman Catholic Deacons
36.83	1105	Total SRI Sample
36.81	633	Protestant Seminarians
36.69	169	Teachers: Grades 1 through 9, Canada
36.54	52	Factory and Site Supervisors
36.41	2351	Nursing: Registered Nurses
36.36	275	Salespeople in a Japanese Trading Company
36.30	135	Doctors of Osteopathy
36.28	113	Teachers: Supervising Student Teachers
36.14	32731	Females: Form F Databank
36.13	155	Therapists: Physical
36.06	1880	Nursing: Registered Nurses, no specialty stated
36.03	1607	Females: Traditional Age High School Students
35.82	846	Females: Age Group 60 Plus
35.81	148	Therapists: Physical
35.79	190	Engineers: Mining
35.64	101	Administrators: Social Services
35.59	4035	University of Maine - Freshmen
35.56	9320	High School Students from Pennsylvania
35.23	3551	Females: Non-Traditional Age College Students
35.09	228	Teachers: Adult Education
35.06	77	Secretaries: Legal
34.99	1506	Mercer University - Freshmen
34.95	638	Medical Technologists (4 year)
34.77	3103	NURSES
34.72	144	OPERATIVES: TRANSPORTATION
34.45	238	Public Service Aides and Community Health Workers
34.42	5738	Females: Age Group 21 To 24
34.34	297	Computer and Peripheral Equipment Operators
34.18	79	Religious Educator, all denominations
34.18	79	Medical Assistants
34.09	1147	Nuns and Other Religious Workers
34.08	267	Librarians
34.04	47	Police Officers: Detectives in Urban Community
33.59	783	PERSONAL SERVICE WORKERS
33.54	164	Teachers: Coaching
33.33	60	Dental Hygienists
33.33	51	Restaurant Workers: Table Setting and Cleaning
33.24	2470	Females: Age Group 50 To 59
33.20	973	Medical Technologists
33.09	139	Physicians: Family Practice, General Practice
32.99	97	OPERATIVES: NON-SPECIALIZED AND FACTORY WORKERS
32.96	1505	Hope College - Freshmen
32.84	1291	HEALTH TECHNOLOGISTS AND TECHNICIANS
32.56	86	Guards and Watch Keepers
32.41	540	Waiters and Waitresses
32.40	574	Line Corrections Officers
32.37	139	Construction Laborers (except carpenters helpers)
32.23	211	Lifeguards, Attendants, Recreation and Amusement
31.65	1169	University of Wisconsin at Stevens Point - Freshmen

Percent SF	Total Sample Size	Sample Description
31.61	155	Nursing: Composite of Critical Care Nurses
31.46	89	Corrections Sergeants
31.36	118	Therapists: Occupational
31.34	67	Teachers: Foreign Language in Junior and Senior High School
31.34	67	Sales Agents, Retail Trade
31.31	99	Police Officers: Australian Senior Officers
31.28	243	Dietitians
31.07	206	OPERATIVES: SPECIALIZED
31.05	1082	FOOD SERVICE WORKERS
31.03	58	Home Management Advisors and Home Economists
30.96	16880	Females: Form G Databank
30.88	68	Corrections Officers and Probation Officers
30.84	321	Females: Traditional Age Junior High School Students
30.76	1128	Teachers: Middle and Junior High School
30.75	439	Police Officers
30.56	108	Sales Clerks, Retail Trade
30.54	835	Bank Employees
30.49	82	Professional, Technical, and Kindred Workers
30.39	102	Managers: Office
30.15	2010	RELIGIOUS WORKERS -ALL DENOMINATIONS-
29.96	1205	Candidates for Theology Education
29.94	167	Laboratory Technologists
29.92	127	Therapists: Practitioners in Respiratory Therapy
29.35	4811	Females: Age Group 40 To 49
29.34	232557	CAPT Databank Total Population
29.10	323	Dietitians and Nutritionists
29.00	200	Teachers: Elementary School
28.91	550	St. Louis University - Freshmen
28.76	8711	Females: Age Group 30 To 39
28.69	1750	SALES WORKERS
28.62	5178	Females: Age Group 25 To 29
28.61	395	Rollins College - Freshmen
28.44	109	Carpenters
28.36	67	Stock Clerks and Storekeepers
28.21	195	Therapists: Respiratory
28.17	71	Teachers: Mathematics
28.06	1554	Protestant Ministers
27.97	765	HEALTH CARE THERAPISTS
27.85	413	Teachers: Mathematics
27.80	669	MECHANICS
27.74	155	Police and Detectives
27.49	782	LABORERS
27.40	146	Nursing: Consultants
27.36	106	Speech Pathologists
27.35	223	Clinical Laboratory Technologists and Technicians
27.27	319	Rabbis
27.17	173	Teachers: Special Education
27.14	70	Electricians
27.05	366	Managers: Middle Managers in a Japanese Chemical Company
27.04	16676	TEACHERS

SENSING-FEELING

Percent SF	Total Sample Size	Sample Description
27.03	333	Secretaries: Executive and Administrative Assistants
26.87	67	CLEANING SERVICES
26.68	3373	High School Students in Australia
26.51	166	Real Estate Agents and Brokers
26.48	608	PROTECTIVE SERVICE WORKERS
26.36	110	Bank Employees, Exempt
26.23	305	Nursing: Educators
26.12	559	CRAFT WORKERS
26.09	2514	University of Florida - Freshmen
26.00	50	Directors of Religious Education
26.00	50	College Students in Student Government
25.96	312	Managers: Restaurant, Cafeteria, Bar and Food Service
25.93	54	Engineers: Aeronautical
25.93	54	Chain, Rod and Ax Workers; Surveying
25.71	70	Optometrists
25.58	172	Teaching Assistants
25.53	94	Nursing: Administrators
25.47	106	Media Specialists
25.36	280	Police Officers: Urban Community
25.31	245	Therapists: Occupational
25.04	4933	Males: High School Students from Pennsylvania
25.00	196	Displaced Coal Miners
25.00	124	Administrators: Canadian Schools
25.00	72	FARMERS
24.81	7952	Females: Adult College Graduates
24.66	219	Priests and Monks
24.59	122	Composite of Practitioners in Speech Pathology
24.55	1760	Franklin and Marshall College - Freshmen
24.11	141	Police Officers: Patrolmen in Urban Community
23.88	649	Teachers: High School
23.73	177	Counselors: Rehabilitation
23.60	534	Clergy, all denominations (except priests)
23.56	191	Pharmacists
23.53	4663	Military Personnel at Naval Technical Training Center
23.53	51	Administrators: Student Personnel
23.46	179	Sales Representatives
23.45	469	ALLIED HEALTH AND HEALTH PRACTIONERS, N.E.C.
23.43	175	ENGINEERING AND SCIENCE TECHNICIANS
23.34	1024	Administrators: Elementary and Secondary School
23.33	60	Managers: Fire
23.27	202	Administrators: Health
23.08	52	Dentists
23.08	52	Computer Specialists
22.95	427	Accountants
22.83	92	Police Officers: Supervisors in Urban Community
22.60	177	College and University Resident Assistants
22.45	98	Managers: Participants in Women in Management Conference
22.35	85	Protestants in Specialized Ministries
22.35	85	Dentists
22.19	658	Displaced Steelworkers

Percent SF	Total Sample Size	Sample Description
22.09	172	Coordinators
21.97	264	MILITARY PERSONNEL
21.95	287	Counselors: School
21.82	55	Designers
21.67	180	Cooks (except private household)
21.50	479	Social Workers
21.46	1603	DOCTORS OF MEDICINE
21.39	561	Teachers: Junior College
21.32	136	Musicians and Composers
21.03	290	Managers: Middle Level in City, County and State Government
20.95	105	Police Supervisors
20.79	101	Insurance Agents, Brokers, and Underwriters
20.65	92	Social Services Workers
20.55	73	Air Force Personnel
20.49	405	Parks College - Freshmen and Transfers
20.31	1881	Composite of Practitioners in Medicine (M.D.s)
20.18	223	Teachers: Health
20.14	11897	Males: Age Group 18 To 20
20.06	673	Counselors: Vocational and Educational
20.02	1803	COUNSELORS
20.00	230	Managers: Regional Telephone Company Low Level Managers
19.78	359	Counselors: General
19.73	3979	Males: Age Group 15 To 17
19.66	117	Counselors: Runaway Youth
19.64	56	Managers: Top Managers in Large Japanese Companies
19.61	51	Roman Catholic Seminarians
19.60	250	Business: General, Self-employed
19.55	179	Teachers: English
19.53	343	Males: Adult High School Dropouts
19.40	12637	Males: Traditional Age College Students
19.33	1857	ADMINISTRATORS
19.31	932	Counselors: General
19.30	57	Technicians: Electrical and Electronic Engineering
19.27	1204	Males: Traditional Age High School Students
19.05	105	Steelworkers
18.93	7463	MANAGERS AND ADMINISTRATORS
18.93	1009	Navy Enlisted Personnel in Basic Electronic Training
18.89	90	Personnel and Labor Relations Workers
18.85	122	High School Student Leaders
18.75	128	Judges
18.75	80	Purchasing Agents
18.70	123	Pharmacists
18.57	3678	Administrators: Managers and Supervisors
18.47	926	Males: Adult High School Graduates Without College
18.29	164	Gifted High School Seniors
17.98	89	Public Relations Workers and Publicity Writers
17.52	5320	Males: Age Group 21 To 24
17.37	495	Males: Age Group 60 Plus
17.37	213	Teachers: Art, Drama and Music
17.31	52	Engineers: Chemical

Percent SF	Total Sample Size	Sample Description
17.28	81	Research Workers
17.27	23240	Males: Form F Databank
17.24	116	Managers: Middle Managers in a Japanese Heavy Industrial Company
17.16	169	Service Workers (except private household)
16.95	118	Managers: Japanese Chief Executives
16.89	225	Leaders in Student Government Activities
16.81	113	Editors and Reporters
16.67	54	Engineers: Electrical and Electronic
16.67	54	Consultants: Education
16.59	446	Males: SRI Sample
16.57	169	Composite of Practitioners in Social Work
16.50	200	Computer Programmers
16.44	523	Managers: Public
16.43	986	ENGINEERS
16.39	122	Administrators: Educationally Related
16.27	338	COMPUTER SPECIALISTS
16.25	80	Employment Development Specialists
16.14	378	ARTISTS AND ENTERTAINERS
15.62	333	Public Accountants
15.38	52	Journalists
15.33	150	Managers: Small Business
15.04	226	SCIENTISTS: LIFE AND PHYSICAL
14.93	15791	Males: Form G Databank
14.89	262	Counselors: Suicide and Crisis
14.72	1501	Males: Adult Non-Traditional Age College Students
14.72	849	Managers: England
14.55	756	Managers: Financial and Bank Officers
14.49	276	School Principals
14.46	83	Managers: Sales
14.04	1795	Males: Age Group 50 To 59
14.04	57	Scientists: Biology
13.89	2282	Teachers: University
13.67	256	Males: Traditional Age Junior High School Students
13.49	341	Administrators: Colleges and Technical Institutes
13.23	257	Managers: Top Level in City, County and State Government
13.21	530	WRITERS AND JOURNALISTS
13.19	3814	Males: Age Group 25 To 29
13.11	61	Scientists: Chemistry
12.61	119	Teachers: Trade, Industrial and Technical
12.31	65	Computer Operations, Systems Researchers and Analysts
11.98	192	Consultants: General
11.76	136	Credit Investigators and Mortgage Brokers
11.64	5601	Males: Age Group 30 To 39
11.63	86	Computer Systems Analysts and Support Representatives
11.48	61	Physicians: Pathology
11.37	519	LAWYERS AND JUDGES
11.34	494	Certified Public Accountants
11.24	89	Consultants: Management Analysts
11.04	3812	Males: Age Group 40 To 49
10.96	912	Police Officers: Managers

Percent SF	Total Sample Size	Sample Description
10.95	6814	Males: Adult College Graduates
10.84	83	Marketing Personnel
10.67	75	Phi Beta Kappa
10.64	705	Teachers: College Faculty Named as Danforth Associates
10.53	57	Police Officers: Commanders
10.49	143	Auditors
10.45	67	Research Assistants
10.39	77	Engineers: Mechanical
10.17	59	Photographers
10.09	793	High School Students in Florida Future Scientist Program
9.58	334	Operators and Field Technicians in Water Pollution Control
9.52	84	Attorneys - Administrators, non-practicing
9.26	108	Members of a Human Resources Planners Association
9.23	1874	Law School Graduates
9.09	55	College Student Leaders
8.82	170	Certified Psychodramatists
8.78	490	SOCIAL SCIENTISTS
8.30	289	Psychologists
7.73	181	Females in Leadership Development Program
7.21	402	PSYCHOLOGISTS
7.08	1229	Computer Professionals
6.79	1001	National Merit Scholarship Finalists
6.73	208	Writers, Artists, Entertainers, and Agents
6.64	271	Lawyers
6.45	62	Actors
6.37	1051	Males in Leadership Development Program
6.01	316	Managers: Retail Stores
5.88	136	Managers: High Level Corporate Executives
5.88	68	Physicians: Psychiatry
5.63	71	Rhodes Scholars
5.26	114	Fine Artists
5.09	1394	Managers: Federal Executives
4.84	124	Architects
2.82	71	Consultants: Management
.90	111	Consultants: Canadian

Percent NF	Total Sample Size	Sample Description
64.91	114	Fine Artists
63.53	170	Certified Psychodramatists
62.00	50	Directors of Religious Education
56.55	359	Counselors: General
55.06	534	Clergy, all denominations (except priests)
55.03	169	Composite of Practitioners in Social Work
54.96	262	Counselors: Suicide and Crisis
53.99	213	Teachers: Art, Drama and Music
53.85	117	Counselors: Runaway Youth
52.94	85	Protestants in Specialized Ministries
52.94	51	Roman Catholic Seminarians
52.12	1205	Candidates for Theology Education
51.92	208	Writers, Artists, Entertainers, and Agents
50.23	219	Priests and Monks
49.83	289	Psychologists
49.30	71	Rhodes Scholars
49.16	1554	Protestant Ministers
48.53	68	Physicians: Psychiatry
48.26	402	PSYCHOLOGISTS
48.08	287	Counselors: School
47.42	932	Counselors: General
46.27	67	Research Assistants
46.15	52	Journalists
45.81	1803	COUNSELORS
45.51	490	SOCIAL SCIENTISTS
44.69	179	Teachers: English
44.44	54	Consultants: Education
43.98	673	Counselors: Vocational and Educational
43.77	530	WRITERS AND JOURNALISTS
43.29	633	Protestant Seminarians
43.04	79	Religious Educator, all denominations
42.94	177	Counselors: Rehabilitation
42.59	479	Social Workers
41.94	62	Actors
41.91	136	Musicians and Composers
41.33	75	Phi Beta Kappa
41.24	177	College and University Resident Assistants
41.06	1505	Hope College - Freshmen
40.75	319	Rabbis
40.71	113	Editors and Reporters
40.37	1298	Roman Catholic Priests
40.16	122	Composite of Practitioners in Speech Pathology
39.68	378	ARTISTS AND ENTERTAINERS
38.81	67	Teachers: Foreign Language in Junior and Senior High School
38.71	124	Architects
38.68	106	Speech Pathologists
38.57	223	Teachers: Health
38.42	190	Engineers: Mining
38.34	793	High School Students in Florida Future Scientist Program
38.33	60	Dental Hygienists

INTUITION-FEELING

Percent NF	Total Sample Size	Sample Description
37.12	3149	Concordia College - Freshmen
36.47	1607	Females: Traditional Age High School Students
36.26	1001	National Merit Scholarship Finalists
36.20	2514	University of Florida - Freshmen
35.32	2010	RELIGIOUS WORKERS -ALL DENOMINATIONS-
35.29	51	Administrators: Student Personnel
35.25	122	High School Student Leaders
35.09	228	Rosemont College - Freshmen
35.00	200	Teachers: Elementary School
35.00	100	Teachers: Pre-school
34.84	155	Therapists: Physical
34.68	395	Rollins College - Freshmen
34.57	81	Research Workers
34.55	55	Designers
34.48	58	Home Management Advisors and Home Economists
34.40	561	Teachers: Junior College
34.38	192	Consultants: General
34.26	540	Waiters and Waitresses
34.21	649	Teachers: High School
34.00	50	College Students in Student Government
33.82	550	St. Louis University - Freshmen
33.78	148	Therapists: Physical
33.72	172	Teaching Assistants
33.71	89	Public Relations Workers and Publicity Writers
33.71	89	Consultants: Management Analysts
33.33	54	Engineers: Aeronautical
33.00	100	Receptionists
32.96	267	Librarians
32.87	2002	Sisters in Roman Catholic Religious Orders
32.73	2282	Teachers: University
32.48	705	Teachers: College Faculty Named as Danforth Associates
32.37	173	Teachers: Special Education
32.24	245	Therapists: Occupational
32.23	7952	Females: Adult College Graduates
32.13	305	Nursing: Educators
31.58	114	Brothers in Roman Catholic Religious Orders
31.50	4035	University of Maine - Freshmen
31.42	1881	Composite of Practitioners in Medicine (M.D.s)
31.13	106	Media Specialists
30.97	16676	TEACHERS
30.84	321	Females: Traditional Age Junior High School Students
30.76	4811	Females: Age Group 40 To 49
30.63	2351	Nursing: Registered Nurses
30.59	765	HEALTH CARE THERAPISTS
30.49	164	Gifted High School Seniors
30.46	10342	Auburn University - Freshmen
30.39	102	Managers: Office
30.38	79	Medical Assistants
30.27	403	Berkshire Christian College - Freshmen and Transfers
30.22	139	Physicians: Family Practice, General Practice

Percent NF	Total Sample Size	Sample Description
30.12	4973	Females: Age Group 15 To 17
30.00	80	Employment Development Specialists
29.95	197	Adrian College - Freshmen
29.93	3064	PRIVATE HOUSEHOLD WORKERS
29.91	341	Administrators: Colleges and Technical Institutes
29.85	1082	FOOD SERVICE WORKERS
29.70	1128	Teachers: Middle and Junior High School
29.57	1603	DOCTORS OF MEDICINE
29.41	102	Ordained Roman Catholic Deacons
29.41	51	Restaurant Workers: Table Setting and Cleaning
29.34	1169	University of Wisconsin at Stevens Point - Freshmen
29.27	123	Pharmacists
29.25	32731	Females: Form F Databank
29.20	274	Cashiers
29.13	333	Secretaries: Executive and Administrative Assistants
29.09	1760	Franklin and Marshall College - Freshmen
29.04	1880	Nursing: Registered Nurses, no specialty stated
29.03	2470	Females: Age Group 50 To 59
29.00	3103	NURSES
28.92	83	Nursing: Public Health
28.89	180	Cooks (except private household)
28.81	118	Therapists: Occupational
28.77	146	Nursing: Consultants
28.73	181	Females in Leadership Development Program
28.69	3339	CLERICAL AND KINDRED WORKERS
28.69	122	Administrators: Educationally Related
28.62	297	Computer and Peripheral Equipment Operators
28.57	70	Optometrists
28.52	4905	OFFICE MACHINE OPERATORS
28.49	172	Coordinators
28.41	271	Lawyers
28.40	8711	Females: Age Group 30 To 39
28.37	5738	Females: Age Group 21 To 24
28.32	232557	CAPT Databank Total Population
28.24	1604	SECRETARIES
28.06	5178	Females: Age Group 25 To 29
27.90	846	Females: Age Group 60 Plus
27.78	54	Chain, Rod and Ax Workers; Surveying
27.71	83	Marketing Personnel
27.62	14519	Females: Traditional Age College Students
27.43	13716	Females: Age Group 18 To 20
27.41	135	Doctors of Osteopathy
27.39	157	Teachers: Speech Pathology and Therapy
27.35	223	Clinical Laboratory Technologists and Technicians
27.27	16880	Females: Form G Databank
27.12	59	Photographers
27.11	804	Teachers: Elementary School
27.08	96	Teachers: Reading
26.95	1024	Administrators: Elementary and Secondary School
26.95	167	Laboratory Technologists

Percent NF	Total Sample Size	Sample Description
26.76	1506	Mercer University - Freshmen
26.75	314	Nursing: Aides, Orderlies, and Attendants
26.66	1857	ADMINISTRATORS
26.61	109	Carpenters
26.32	323	Dietitians and Nutritionists
26.32	57	Scientists: Biology
26.06	165	Clerks in a Japanese Trading Company
25.74	101	Insurance Agents, Brokers, and Underwriters
25.59	469	ALLIED HEALTH AND HEALTH PRACTIONERS, N.E.C.
25.25	202	Administrators: Health
25.13	191	Pharmacists
25.09	1750	SALES WORKERS
25.00	84	Library Attendants and Assistants
24.73	182	Health Education Practitioners
24.71	1291	HEALTH TECHNOLOGISTS AND TECHNICIANS
24.67	150	Bookkeepers
24.61	3551	Females: Non-Traditional Age College Students
24.56	900	HEALTH SERVICE WORKERS
24.47	519	LAWYERS AND JUDGES
24.27	783	PERSONAL SERVICE WORKERS
24.25	973	Medical Technologists
24.07	108	Sales Clerks, Retail Trade
24.07	108	Members of a Human Resources Planners Association
23.22	211	Lifeguards, Attendants, Recreation and Amusement
23.11	225	Leaders in Student Government Activities
22.95	61	Food Counter and Fountain Workers
22.88	638	Medical Technologists (4 year)
22.63	243	Dietitians
22.58	1147	Nuns and Other Religious Workers
22.58	155	Nursing: Composite of Critical Care Nurses
22.45	98	Managers: Participants in Women in Management Conference
22.12	782	LABORERS
22.06	68	Secretaries: Medical
22.00	250	Business: General, Self-employed
21.93	228	Teachers: Adult Education
21.92	73	Air Force Personnel
21.76	432	Teacher Aides (except school monitors)
21.51	1009	Navy Enlisted Personnel in Basic Electronic Training
21.43	84	Attorneys - Administrators, non-practicing
21.43	56	Clerical Supervisors
21.31	413	Teachers: Mathematics
21.24	1973	St. Clair College
21.10	1204	Males: Traditional Age High School Students
20.93	86	Guards and Watch Keepers
20.83	264	MILITARY PERSONNEL
20.83	72	Dental Assistants
20.75	53	Composite of Practitioners in Radiologic Technology
20.70	256	Males: Traditional Age Junior High School Students
20.63	126	Radiologic Technologists and Technicians
20.56	107	Typists

INTUITION-FEELING

Percent NF	Total Sample Size	Sample Description
20.49	405	Parks College - Freshmen and Transfers
20.24	4387	Females: High School Students from Pennsylvania
20.21	94	Nursing: Administrators
20.16	124	Administrators: Canadian Schools
20.00	55	College Student Leaders
19.98	986	ENGINEERS
19.80	3814	Males: Age Group 25 To 29
19.69	127	Therapists: Practitioners in Respiratory Therapy
19.67	61	Physicians: Pathology
19.58	669	MECHANICS
19.55	179	Sales Representatives
19.51	7463	MANAGERS AND ADMINISTRATORS
19.48	77	Engineers: Mechanical
19.43	175	ENGINEERING AND SCIENCE TECHNICIANS
19.40	67	Stock Clerks and Storekeepers
19.40	67	CLEANING SERVICES
19.23	52	Dentists
19.21	5320	Males: Age Group 21 To 24
19.17	23240	Males: Form F Databank
19.03	226	SCIENTISTS: LIFE AND PHYSICAL
19.00	200	Computer Programmers
18.93	206	OPERATIVES: SPECIALIZED
18.85	260	Nursing: Licensed Practical Nurses
18.75	96	Hairdressers, Cosmetologists and Manicurists
18.58	113	Teachers: Supervising Student Teachers
18.51	281	Teachers: School Grades 1 through 12
18.46	195	Therapists: Respiratory
18.34	169	Teachers: Grades 1 through 9, Canada
18.25	3979	Males: Age Group 15 To 17
18.18	275	Salespeople in a Japanese Trading Company
18.18	55	Child Care Workers (except private household)
18.17	6814	Males: Adult College Graduates
17.95	4150	Nicholls State University - Freshmen
17.85	3373	High School Students in Australia
17.80	427	Accountants
17.61	2277	Females: Adult High School Graduates, Without College
17.56	11897	Males: Age Group 18 To 20
17.54	3678	Administrators: Managers and Supervisors
17.34	2492	University of North Carolina at Greensboro - Freshmen
17.27	139	Construction Laborers (except carpenters helpers)
17.21	12637	Males: Traditional Age College Students
17.19	5601	Males: Age Group 30 To 39
17.19	128	Judges
17.14	636	Females: Adult High School Dropouts
16.94	4663	Military Personnel at Naval Technical Training Center
16.89	9320	High School Students from Pennsylvania
16.88	77	Secretaries: Legal
16.82	333	Public Accountants
16.81	119	Teachers: Trade, Industrial and Technical
16.67	54	Engineers: Electrical and Electronic

Percent NF	Total Sample Size	Sample Description
16.49	97	OPERATIVES: NON-SPECIALIZED AND FACTORY WORKERS
16.47	85	Dentists
16.46	559	CRAFT WORKERS
16.27	338	COMPUTER SPECIALISTS
16.27	166	Real Estate Agents and Brokers
16.01	1874	Law School Graduates
15.71	70	Electricians
15.56	90	Personnel and Labor Relations Workers
15.52	15791	Males: Form G Databank
15.48	659	Females: SRI Sample
15.42	3812	Males: Age Group 40 To 49
15.28	144	OPERATIVES: TRANSPORTATION
15.24	105	Police Supervisors
14.95	495	Males: Age Group 60 Plus
14.75	61	Scientists: Chemistry
14.71	136	Credit Investigators and Mortgage Brokers
14.63	164	Teachers: Coaching
14.63	82	Professional, Technical, and Kindred Workers
14.54	1795	Males: Age Group 50 To 59
14.39	1501	Males: Adult Non-Traditional Age College Students
13.99	143	Auditors
13.91	4933	Males: High School Students from Pennsylvania
13.46	52	Computer Specialists
12.77	47	Police Officers: Detectives in Urban Community
12.76	1105	Total SRI Sample
12.68	71	Teachers: Mathematics
12.50	56	Managers: Top Managers in Large Japanese Companies
12.28	57	Technicians: Electrical and Electronic Engineering
12.04	1229	Computer Professionals
12.01	608	PROTECTIVE SERVICE WORKERS
11.76	68	Corrections Officers and Probation Officers
11.63	86	Computer Systems Analysts and Support Representatives
11.54	52	Engineers: Chemical
11.50	835	Bank Employees
10.79	343	Males: Adult High School Dropouts
10.50	238	Public Service Aides and Community Health Workers
10.45	756	Managers: Financial and Bank Officers
10.45	67	Sales Agents, Retail Trade
10.32	494	Certified Public Accountants
10.26	312	Managers: Restaurant, Cafeteria, Bar and Food Service
10.06	169	Service Workers (except private household)
10.01	849	Managers: England
9.78	92	Social Services Workers
9.48	116	Managers: Middle Managers in a Japanese Heavy Industrial Company
9.32	118	Managers: Japanese Chief Executives
9.23	65	Computer Operations, Systems Researchers and Analysts
9.17	240	Foremen in Japanese Food Production Company
9.11	439	Police Officers
8.99	523	Managers: Public
8.91	101	Administrators: Social Services

Percent NF	Total Sample Size	Sample Description
8.74	446	Males: SRI Sample
8.46	1394	Managers: Federal Executives
7.97	276	School Principals
7.93	290	Managers: Middle Level in City, County and State Government
7.90	1051	Males in Leadership Development Program
7.86	280	Police Officers: Urban Community
7.78	257	Managers: Top Level in City, County and State Government
7.69	52	Factory and Site Supervisors
7.39	230	Managers: Regional Telephone Company Low Level Managers
7.27	110	Bank Employees, Exempt
7.09	141	Police Officers: Patrolmen in Urban Community
7.07	99	Police Officers: Australian Senior Officers
7.02	57	Police Officers: Commanders
6.67	105	Steelworkers
6.52	92	Police Officers: Supervisors in Urban Community
6.28	366	Managers: Middle Managers in a Japanese Chemical Company
6.25	80	Purchasing Agents
6.02	83	Managers: Sales
5.92	574	Line Corrections Officers
5.63	71	Consultants: Management
5.59	912	Police Officers: Managers
5.40	926	Males: Adult High School Graduates Without College
5.00	60	Managers: Fire
4.49	89	Corrections Sergeants
4.41	136	Managers: High Level Corporate Executives
4.17	72	FARMERS
3.87	155	Police and Detectives
3.60	111	Consultants: Canadian
3.57	196	Displaced Coal Miners
3.50	658	Displaced Steelworkers
3.33	150	Managers: Small Business
3.29	334	Operators and Field Technicians in Water Pollution Control
1.80	222	Bank Employees, Non-Exempt
.95	316	Managers: Retail Stores
.76	132	School Bus Drivers

Percent NT	Total Sample Size	Sample Description
55.86	111	Consultants: Canadian
52.11	71	Consultants: Management
51.19	84	Attorneys - Administrators, non-practicing
46.30	108	Members of a Human Resources Planners Association
46.15	1001	National Merit Scholarship Finalists
45.76	59	Photographers
44.62	65	Computer Operations, Systems Researchers and Analysts
43.66	71	Rhodes Scholars
43.55	124	Architects
43.12	705	Teachers: College Faculty Named as Danforth Associates
42.62	61	Scientists: Chemistry
42.58	1874	Law School Graduates
41.86	86	Computer Systems Analysts and Support Representatives
41.66	1229	Computer Professionals
41.44	181	Females in Leadership Development Program
40.96	271	Lawyers
40.46	1394	Managers: Federal Executives
38.71	62	Actors
38.24	136	Managers: High Level Corporate Executives
38.24	136	Credit Investigators and Mortgage Brokers
38.05	226	SCIENTISTS: LIFE AND PHYSICAL
37.70	793	High School Students in Florida Future Scientist Program
37.29	118	Managers: Japanese Chief Executives
36.98	338	COMPUTER SPECIALISTS
36.84	57	Scientists: Biology
36.82	402	PSYCHOLOGISTS
36.73	490	SOCIAL SCIENTISTS
36.59	164	Gifted High School Seniors
36.50	200	Computer Programmers
36.22	519	LAWYERS AND JUDGES
36.06	1051	Males in Leadership Development Program
34.94	83	Managers: Sales
34.67	75	Phi Beta Kappa
34.62	52	Engineers: Chemical
34.55	55	College Student Leaders
34.48	116	Managers: Middle Managers in a Japanese Heavy Industrial Company
34.33	67	Research Assistants
34.13	208	Writers, Artists, Entertainers, and Agents
33.33	81	Research Workers
32.53	83	Marketing Personnel
32.26	341	Administrators: Colleges and Technical Institutes
32.21	6814	Males: Adult College Graduates
31.58	57	Technicians: Electrical and Electronic Engineering
31.54	3814	Males: Age Group 25 To 29
31.48	54	Engineers: Electrical and Electronic
31.20	2282	Teachers: University
31.10	5601	Males: Age Group 30 To 39
30.80	289	Psychologists
30.77	52	Dentists
30.77	52	Computer Specialists

Percent NT	Total Sample Size	Sample Description
30.73	192	Consultants: General
30.36	56	Managers: Top Managers in Large Japanese Companies
30.33	333	Public Accountants
30.00	80	Employment Development Specialists
29.85	67	Sales Agents, Retail Trade
29.81	530	WRITERS AND JOURNALISTS
29.59	98	Managers: Participants in Women in Management Conference
29.37	378	ARTISTS AND ENTERTAINERS
29.37	143	Auditors
28.89	90	Personnel and Labor Relations Workers
28.45	1501	Males: Adult Non-Traditional Age College Students
28.12	15791	Males: Form G Databank
27.96	3812	Males: Age Group 40 To 49
27.67	5320	Males: Age Group 21 To 24
27.49	1204	Males: Traditional Age High School Students
27.43	113	Editors and Reporters
27.38	986	ENGINEERS
27.17	92	Social Services Workers
27.11	225	Leaders in Student Government Activities
26.97	89	Consultants: Management Analysts
26.47	68	Physicians: Psychiatry
26.32	114	Fine Artists
26.23	61	Physicians: Pathology
26.05	23240	Males: Form F Databank
25.87	1009	Navy Enlisted Personnel in Basic Electronic Training
25.84	89	Public Relations Workers and Publicity Writers
25.76	2492	University of North Carolina at Greensboro - Freshmen
25.61	82	Professional, Technical, and Kindred Workers
25.58	3979	Males: Age Group 15 To 17
25.49	51	Administrators: Student Personnel
25.24	1795	Males: Age Group 50 To 59
25.14	175	ENGINEERING AND SCIENCE TECHNICIANS
25.00	52	Journalists
24.70	494	Certified Public Accountants
24.58	12637	Males: Traditional Age College Students
24.50	3678	Administrators: Managers and Supervisors
24.47	756	Managers: Financial and Bank Officers
24.26	202	Administrators: Health
24.22	256	Males: Traditional Age Junior High School Students
24.18	1857	ADMINISTRATORS
24.17	7463	MANAGERS AND ADMINISTRATORS
24.07	54	Engineers: Aeronautical
24.07	54	Consultants: Education
24.07	54	Chain, Rod and Ax Workers; Surveying
24.00	250	Business: General, Self-employed
23.94	71	Teachers: Mathematics
23.64	55	Designers
23.62	127	Therapists: Practitioners in Respiratory Therapy
23.59	195	Therapists: Respiratory
23.58	11897	Males: Age Group 18 To 20

562

Percent NT	Total Sample Size	Sample Description
23.53	170	Certified Psychodramatists
23.53	136	Musicians and Composers
23.53	85	Dentists
23.21	1603	DOCTORS OF MEDICINE
23.17	561	Teachers: Junior College
22.95	122	Administrators: Educationally Related
22.89	166	Real Estate Agents and Brokers
22.86	70	Electricians
22.76	123	Pharmacists
22.55	275	Salespeople in a Japanese Trading Company
22.50	849	Managers: England
22.45	245	Therapists: Occupational
22.09	172	Coordinators
22.08	77	Engineers: Mechanical
22.06	68	Corrections Officers and Probation Officers
22.03	118	Therapists: Occupational
21.97	223	Teachers: Health
21.97	173	Teachers: Special Education
21.88	128	Judges
21.76	262	Counselors: Suicide and Crisis
21.69	1881	Composite of Practitioners in Medicine (M.D.s)
21.47	191	Pharmacists
21.38	276	School Principals
21.31	305	Nursing: Educators
21.31	122	Composite of Practitioners in Speech Pathology
20.98	7952	Females: Adult College Graduates
20.97	124	Administrators: Canadian Schools
20.90	469	ALLIED HEALTH AND HEALTH PRACTIONERS, N.E.C.
20.90	177	College and University Resident Assistants
20.85	1760	Franklin and Marshall College - Freshmen
20.77	366	Managers: Middle Managers in a Japanese Chemical Company
20.61	495	Males: Age Group 60 Plus
20.34	290	Managers: Middle Level in City, County and State Government
20.26	765	HEALTH CARE THERAPISTS
20.25	405	Parks College - Freshmen and Transfers
20.21	4933	Males: High School Students from Pennsylvania
20.12	1024	Administrators: Elementary and Secondary School
20.00	50	College Students in Student Government
19.91	427	Accountants
19.84	257	Managers: Top Level in City, County and State Government
19.83	343	Males: Adult High School Dropouts
19.67	61	Food Counter and Fountain Workers
19.66	5178	Females: Age Group 25 To 29
19.61	51	Restaurant Workers: Table Setting and Cleaning
19.55	179	Teachers: English
19.46	8711	Females: Age Group 30 To 39
19.44	72	FARMERS
18.87	106	Media Specialists
18.86	334	Operators and Field Technicians in Water Pollution Control
18.63	1750	SALES WORKERS

Percent NT	Total Sample Size	Sample Description
18.58	479	Social Workers
18.49	119	Teachers: Trade, Industrial and Technical
18.44	179	Sales Representatives
18.39	446	Males: SRI Sample
18.38	2514	University of Florida - Freshmen
18.27	312	Managers: Restaurant, Cafeteria, Bar and Food Service
18.21	4663	Military Personnel at Naval Technical Training Center
18.19	16676	TEACHERS
18.18	550	St. Louis University - Freshmen
18.18	77	Secretaries: Legal
18.13	182	Health Education Practitioners
18.02	172	Teaching Assistants
17.97	523	Managers: Public
17.92	106	Speech Pathologists
17.81	146	Nursing: Consultants
17.75	169	Service Workers (except private household)
17.56	232557	CAPT Databank Total Population
17.54	57	Police Officers: Commanders
17.50	200	Teachers: Elementary School
17.48	206	OPERATIVES: SPECIALIZED
17.38	4811	Females: Age Group 40 To 49
17.38	673	Counselors: Vocational and Educational
17.24	319	Rabbis
17.04	223	Clinical Laboratory Technologists and Technicians
16.96	395	Rollins College - Freshmen
16.90	213	Teachers: Art, Drama and Music
16.89	835	Bank Employees
16.83	1147	Nuns and Other Religious Workers
16.83	101	Insurance Agents, Brokers, and Underwriters
16.81	1803	COUNSELORS
16.77	155	Nursing: Composite of Critical Care Nurses
16.74	932	Counselors: General
16.67	108	Sales Clerks, Retail Trade
16.67	96	Teachers: Reading
16.55	139	Physicians: Family Practice, General Practice
16.48	16880	Females: Form G Databank
16.46	316	Managers: Retail Stores
16.45	3373	High School Students in Australia
16.42	67	Stock Clerks and Storekeepers
16.36	55	Child Care Workers (except private household)
16.30	135	Doctors of Osteopathy
16.25	80	Purchasing Agents
16.24	117	Counselors: Runaway Youth
16.22	413	Teachers: Mathematics
16.18	649	Teachers: High School
16.12	912	Police Officers: Managers
15.83	139	Construction Laborers (except carpenters helpers)
15.82	196	Displaced Coal Miners
15.79	323	Dietitians and Nutritionists
15.72	1291	HEALTH TECHNOLOGISTS AND TECHNICIANS

Percent NT	Total Sample Size	Sample Description
15.64	243	Dietitians
15.58	321	Females: Traditional Age Junior High School Students
15.52	638	Medical Technologists (4 year)
15.43	1082	FOOD SERVICE WORKERS
15.37	2010	RELIGIOUS WORKERS -ALL DENOMINATIONS-
15.32	333	Secretaries: Executive and Administrative Assistants
15.29	85	Protestants in Specialized Ministries
15.25	177	Counselors: Rehabilitation
15.22	230	Managers: Regional Telephone Company Low Level Managers
15.22	92	Police Officers: Supervisors in Urban Community
15.19	540	Waiters and Waitresses
15.16	1128	Teachers: Middle and Junior High School
15.10	669	MECHANICS
15.07	73	Air Force Personnel
15.06	5738	Females: Age Group 21 To 24
15.06	2470	Females: Age Group 50 To 59
15.00	180	Cooks (except private household)
14.98	9320	High School Students from Pennsylvania
14.97	167	Laboratory Technologists
14.95	3103	NURSES
14.89	94	Nursing: Administrators
14.77	264	MILITARY PERSONNEL
14.71	782	LABORERS
14.71	102	Managers: Office
14.63	164	Teachers: Coaching
14.61	1506	Mercer University - Freshmen
14.59	973	Medical Technologists
14.43	97	OPERATIVES: NON-SPECIALIZED AND FACTORY WORKERS
14.37	32731	Females: Form F Databank
14.23	534	Clergy, all denominations (except priests)
14.20	169	Composite of Practitioners in Social Work
14.16	113	Teachers: Supervising Student Teachers
14.04	1880	Nursing: Registered Nurses, no specialty stated
14.00	3551	Females: Non-Traditional Age College Students
13.95	559	CRAFT WORKERS
13.93	122	High School Student Leaders
13.92	79	Medical Assistants
13.80	297	Computer and Peripheral Equipment Operators
13.74	211	Lifeguards, Attendants, Recreation and Amusement
13.67	783	PERSONAL SERVICE WORKERS
13.61	169	Teachers: Grades 1 through 9, Canada
13.49	126	Radiologic Technologists and Technicians
13.48	267	Librarians
13.28	926	Males: Adult High School Graduates Without College
13.25	83	Nursing: Public Health
13.24	287	Counselors: School
13.24	68	Secretaries: Medical
13.21	439	Police Officers
13.21	53	Composite of Practitioners in Radiologic Technology
13.19	1554	Protestant Ministers

INTUITION-THINKING

Percent NT	Total Sample Size	Sample Description
13.16	228	Teachers: Adult Education
13.11	4035	University of Maine - Freshmen
13.09	1169	University of Wisconsin at Stevens Point - Freshmen
12.99	608	PROTECTIVE SERVICE WORKERS
12.86	70	Optometrists
12.77	141	Police Officers: Patrolmen in Urban Community
12.59	10342	Auburn University - Freshmen
12.51	2351	Nursing: Registered Nurses
12.50	280	Police Officers: Urban Community
12.50	72	Dental Assistants
12.43	4973	Females: Age Group 15 To 17
12.38	105	Police Supervisors
12.29	1505	Hope College - Freshmen
12.10	157	Teachers: Speech Pathology and Therapy
12.00	100	Teachers: Pre-school
11.93	109	Carpenters
11.76	1607	Females: Traditional Age High School Students
11.67	60	Dental Hygienists
11.53	633	Protestant Seminarians
11.48	4905	OFFICE MACHINE OPERATORS
11.42	219	Priests and Monks
11.35	1604	SECRETARIES
11.31	1105	Total SRI Sample
11.12	1205	Candidates for Theology Education
11.11	144	OPERATIVES: TRANSPORTATION
11.09	658	Displaced Steelworkers
10.99	14519	Females: Traditional Age College Students
10.99	846	Females: Age Group 60 Plus
10.97	155	Police and Detectives
10.96	228	Rosemont College - Freshmen
10.89	101	Administrators: Social Services
10.85	636	Females: Adult High School Dropouts
10.81	3339	CLERICAL AND KINDRED WORKERS
10.81	148	Therapists: Physical
10.71	56	Clerical Supervisors
10.67	150	Managers: Small Business
10.58	359	Counselors: General
10.56	900	HEALTH SERVICE WORKERS
10.54	1973	St. Clair College
10.42	96	Hairdressers, Cosmetologists and Manicurists
10.37	13716	Females: Age Group 18 To 20
10.32	804	Teachers: Elementary School
10.14	4150	Nicholls State University - Freshmen
10.13	79	Religious Educator, all denominations
9.80	51	Roman Catholic Seminarians
9.52	84	Library Attendants and Assistants
9.27	3149	Concordia College - Freshmen
9.10	4387	Females: High School Students from Pennsylvania
8.82	102	Ordained Roman Catholic Deacons
8.75	3064	PRIVATE HOUSEHOLD WORKERS

Percent NT	Total Sample Size	Sample Description
8.75	240	Foremen in Japanese Food Production Company
8.62	58	Home Management Advisors and Home Economists
8.39	2277	Females: Adult High School Graduates, Without College
8.33	60	Managers: Fire
8.28	314	Nursing: Aides, Orderlies, and Attendants
8.14	86	Guards and Watch Keepers
7.98	238	Public Service Aides and Community Health Workers
7.83	281	Teachers: School Grades 1 through 12
7.69	52	Factory and Site Supervisors
7.62	105	Steelworkers
7.48	107	Typists
7.46	67	Teachers: Foreign Language in Junior and Senior High School
7.37	190	Engineers: Mining
7.33	150	Bookkeepers
7.31	260	Nursing: Licensed Practical Nurses
7.27	110	Bank Employees, Exempt
7.10	155	Therapists: Physical
7.04	2002	Sisters in Roman Catholic Religious Orders
7.02	114	Brothers in Roman Catholic Religious Orders
7.00	100	Receptionists
6.93	274	Cashiers
6.67	165	Clerks in a Japanese Trading Company
6.53	659	Females: SRI Sample
6.38	47	Police Officers: Detectives in Urban Community
6.09	197	Adrian College - Freshmen
6.06	99	Police Officers: Australian Senior Officers
6.02	432	Teacher Aides (except school monitors)
5.86	222	Bank Employees, Non-Exempt
5.75	574	Line Corrections Officers
5.16	1298	Roman Catholic Priests
4.49	89	Corrections Sergeants
4.48	67	CLEANING SERVICES
4.00	50	Directors of Religious Education
3.03	132	School Bus Drivers
2.98	403	Berkshire Christian College - Freshmen and Transfers

Percent SJ	Total Sample Size	Sample Description
80.90	89	Corrections Sergeants
78.79	132	School Bus Drivers
77.53	316	Managers: Retail Stores
76.77	99	Police Officers: Australian Senior Officers
75.68	222	Bank Employees, Non-Exempt
70.91	110	Bank Employees, Exempt
70.52	658	Displaced Steelworkers
68.42	57	Police Officers: Commanders
67.65	912	Police Officers: Managers
67.42	574	Line Corrections Officers
67.33	101	Administrators: Social Services
66.67	105	Steelworkers
66.00	150	Managers: Small Business
65.97	238	Public Service Aides and Community Health Workers
65.38	52	Factory and Site Supervisors
65.00	80	Purchasing Agents
64.97	334	Operators and Field Technicians in Water Pollution Control
64.35	230	Managers: Regional Telephone Company Low Level Managers
63.71	926	Males: Adult High School Graduates Without College
63.33	60	Managers: Fire
63.04	257	Managers: Top Level in City, County and State Government
62.24	196	Displaced Coal Miners
61.76	523	Managers: Public
61.70	47	Police Officers: Detectives in Urban Community
61.59	276	School Principals
61.29	155	Police and Detectives
61.06	113	Teachers: Supervising Student Teachers
59.62	312	Managers: Restaurant, Cafeteria, Bar and Food Service
58.75	240	Foremen in Japanese Food Production Company
58.72	281	Teachers: School Grades 1 through 12
58.58	169	Teachers: Grades 1 through 9, Canada
58.21	67	CLEANING SERVICES
57.93	290	Managers: Middle Level in City, County and State Government
57.07	608	PROTECTIVE SERVICE WORKERS
56.98	86	Guards and Watch Keepers
56.89	849	Managers: England
56.86	102	Ordained Roman Catholic Deacons
56.54	260	Nursing: Licensed Practical Nurses
56.48	432	Teacher Aides (except school monitors)
56.38	94	Nursing: Administrators
56.25	96	Hairdressers, Cosmetologists and Manicurists
56.19	105	Police Supervisors
55.71	280	Police Officers: Urban Community
55.46	119	Teachers: Trade, Industrial and Technical
55.43	92	Police Officers: Supervisors in Urban Community
55.06	494	Certified Public Accountants
54.93	446	Males: SRI Sample
54.84	124	Administrators: Canadian Schools
54.13	835	Bank Employees
53.93	636	Females: Adult High School Dropouts

Percent SJ	Total Sample Size	Sample Description
53.90	141	Police Officers: Patrolmen in Urban Community
53.76	1105	Total SRI Sample
53.40	2277	Females: Adult High School Graduates, Without College
53.19	846	Females: Age Group 60 Plus
53.12	128	Judges
52.96	659	Females: SRI Sample
52.91	756	Managers: Financial and Bank Officers
52.44	164	Teachers: Coaching
52.40	2002	Sisters in Roman Catholic Religious Orders
52.32	495	Males: Age Group 60 Plus
52.11	71	Teachers: Mathematics
50.89	169	Service Workers (except private household)
50.88	114	Brothers in Roman Catholic Religious Orders
50.59	85	Dentists
50.47	107	Typists
50.32	157	Teachers: Speech Pathology and Therapy
50.12	427	Accountants
50.00	72	FARMERS
50.00	68	Secretaries: Medical
50.00	52	Engineers: Chemical
49.50	804	Teachers: Elementary School
49.45	366	Managers: Middle Managers in a Japanese Chemical Company
49.36	1795	Males: Age Group 50 To 59
48.98	343	Males: Adult High School Dropouts
48.91	92	Social Services Workers
48.67	413	Teachers: Mathematics
48.59	638	Medical Technologists (4 year)
48.15	243	Dietitians
48.15	135	Doctors of Osteopathy
48.00	900	HEALTH SERVICE WORKERS
47.84	439	Police Officers
47.73	264	MILITARY PERSONNEL
47.69	973	Medical Technologists
47.54	61	Food Counter and Fountain Workers
47.37	4387	Females: High School Students from Pennsylvania
47.10	1051	Males in Leadership Development Program
47.06	68	Corrections Officers and Probation Officers
46.83	126	Radiologic Technologists and Technicians
46.82	314	Nursing: Aides, Orderlies, and Attendants
46.67	150	Bookkeepers
46.55	58	Home Management Advisors and Home Economists
46.49	228	Teachers: Adult Education
46.43	3812	Males: Age Group 40 To 49
46.43	56	Clerical Supervisors
46.38	1298	Roman Catholic Priests
46.34	82	Professional, Technical, and Kindred Workers
46.33	559	CRAFT WORKERS
46.32	136	Managers: High Level Corporate Executives
46.15	52	Dentists
46.11	3678	Administrators: Managers and Supervisors

Percent SJ	Total Sample Size	Sample Description
45.86	1147	Nuns and Other Religious Workers
45.83	96	Teachers: Reading
45.81	179	Sales Representatives
45.78	83	Managers: Sales
45.62	1291	HEALTH TECHNOLOGISTS AND TECHNICIANS
45.58	7463	MANAGERS AND ADMINISTRATORS
45.51	323	Dietitians and Nutritionists
45.42	3551	Females: Non-Traditional Age College Students
45.38	2470	Females: Age Group 50 To 59
45.36	97	OPERATIVES: NON-SPECIALIZED AND FACTORY WORKERS
45.35	333	Public Accountants
45.26	274	Cashiers
45.21	146	Nursing: Consultants
45.21	73	Air Force Personnel
45.18	166	Real Estate Agents and Brokers
45.14	144	OPERATIVES: TRANSPORTATION
45.10	102	Managers: Office
44.96	783	PERSONAL SERVICE WORKERS
44.89	4663	Military Personnel at Naval Technical Training Center
44.78	3064	PRIVATE HOUSEHOLD WORKERS
44.58	83	Nursing: Public Health
44.55	202	Administrators: Health
44.52	155	Nursing: Composite of Critical Care Nurses
44.51	182	Health Education Practitioners
44.44	72	Dental Assistants
44.34	4150	Nicholls State University - Freshmen
44.29	70	Optometrists
44.16	77	Engineers: Mechanical
44.06	1128	Teachers: Middle and Junior High School
44.05	84	Library Attendants and Assistants
44.00	100	Receptionists
43.65	1024	Administrators: Elementary and Secondary School
43.40	53	Composite of Practitioners in Radiologic Technology
43.39	1604	SECRETARIES
43.36	143	Auditors
43.28	67	Teachers: Foreign Language in Junior and Senior High School
43.09	1880	Nursing: Registered Nurses, no specialty stated
43.07	267	Librarians
42.90	1501	Males: Adult Non-Traditional Age College Students
42.86	77	Secretaries: Legal
42.86	70	Electricians
42.68	9320	High School Students from Pennsylvania
42.68	1394	Managers: Federal Executives
42.48	3103	NURSES
42.45	669	MECHANICS
42.45	139	Physicians: Family Practice, General Practice
42.23	206	OPERATIVES: SPECIALIZED
42.22	649	Teachers: High School
42.19	2351	Nursing: Registered Nurses
42.11	57	Technicians: Electrical and Electronic Engineering

Percent SJ	Total Sample Size	Sample Description
42.06	14519	Females: Traditional Age College Students
42.02	3339	CLERICAL AND KINDRED WORKERS
41.99	13716	Females: Age Group 18 To 20
41.92	4905	OFFICE MACHINE OPERATORS
41.79	469	ALLIED HEALTH AND HEALTH PRACTIONERS, N.E.C.
41.72	5601	Males: Age Group 30 To 39
41.23	5738	Females: Age Group 21 To 24
41.14	333	Secretaries: Executive and Administrative Assistants
41.11	90	Personnel and Labor Relations Workers
41.00	100	Teachers: Pre-school
40.98	61	Physicians: Pathology
40.81	223	Clinical Laboratory Technologists and Technicians
40.79	16880	Females: Form G Databank
40.76	211	Lifeguards, Attendants, Recreation and Amusement
40.69	403	Berkshire Christian College - Freshmen and Transfers
40.68	4811	Females: Age Group 40 To 49
40.66	1857	ADMINISTRATORS
40.62	16676	TEACHERS
40.61	6814	Males: Adult College Graduates
40.59	101	Insurance Agents, Brokers, and Underwriters
40.51	79	Medical Assistants
40.38	52	Computer Specialists
40.30	67	Sales Agents, Retail Trade
40.29	139	Construction Laborers (except carpenters helpers)
40.23	8711	Females: Age Group 30 To 39
40.12	167	Laboratory Technologists
40.11	32731	Females: Form F Databank
40.00	55	College Student Leaders
40.00	55	Child Care Workers (except private household)
39.93	2492	University of North Carolina at Greensboro - Freshmen
39.83	118	Therapists: Occupational
39.60	250	Business: General, Self-employed
39.53	172	Teaching Assistants
39.39	297	Computer and Peripheral Equipment Operators
39.34	122	Administrators: Educationally Related
39.28	3373	High School Students in Australia
39.27	191	Pharmacists
39.22	51	Administrators: Student Personnel
39.05	5178	Females: Age Group 25 To 29
39.00	200	Teachers: Elementary School
38.97	136	Credit Investigators and Mortgage Brokers
38.95	172	Coordinators
38.89	108	Sales Clerks, Retail Trade
38.89	54	Engineers: Electrical and Electronic
38.82	7952	Females: Adult College Graduates
38.79	116	Managers: Middle Managers in a Japanese Heavy Industrial Company
38.52	4933	Males: High School Students from Pennsylvania
38.29	175	ENGINEERING AND SCIENCE TECHNICIANS
38.27	15791	Males: Form G Databank
38.24	986	ENGINEERS

Percent SJ	Total Sample Size	Sample Description
38.13	23240	Males: Form F Databank
38.12	1881	Composite of Practitioners in Medicine (M.D.s)
38.07	197	Adrian College - Freshmen
38.06	155	Therapists: Physical
38.03	71	Consultants: Management
37.95	195	Therapists: Respiratory
37.84	148	Therapists: Physical
37.74	1603	DOCTORS OF MEDICINE
37.61	2010	RELIGIOUS WORKERS -ALL DENOMINATIONS-
37.57	173	Teachers: Special Education
37.54	232557	CAPT Databank Total Population
37.54	1750	SALES WORKERS
37.53	405	Parks College - Freshmen and Transfers
37.50	56	Managers: Top Managers in Large Japanese Companies
37.41	5320	Males: Age Group 21 To 24
37.38	305	Nursing: Educators
37.21	86	Computer Systems Analysts and Support Representatives
37.15	1973	St. Clair College
36.92	65	Computer Operations, Systems Researchers and Analysts
36.79	1506	Mercer University - Freshmen
36.79	106	Media Specialists
36.78	1229	Computer Professionals
36.71	79	Religious Educator, all denominations
36.52	3814	Males: Age Group 25 To 29
36.44	118	Managers: Japanese Chief Executives
36.32	782	LABORERS
36.19	12637	Males: Traditional Age College Students
35.63	11897	Males: Age Group 18 To 20
35.56	225	Leaders in Student Government Activities
35.56	180	Cooks (except private household)
35.51	245	Therapists: Occupational
35.40	226	SCIENTISTS: LIFE AND PHYSICAL
35.29	561	Teachers: Junior College
35.25	122	High School Student Leaders
35.16	765	HEALTH CARE THERAPISTS
35.00	60	Dental Hygienists
34.48	319	Rabbis
34.45	4973	Females: Age Group 15 To 17
34.30	1169	University of Wisconsin at Stevens Point - Freshmen
34.00	50	College Students in Student Government
33.71	89	Consultants: Management Analysts
33.67	98	Managers: Participants in Women in Management Conference
33.33	123	Pharmacists
33.33	54	Engineers: Aeronautical
33.02	633	Protestant Seminarians
32.90	1082	FOOD SERVICE WORKERS
32.84	338	COMPUTER SPECIALISTS
32.84	67	Stock Clerks and Storekeepers
32.79	61	Scientists: Chemistry
32.68	3149	Concordia College - Freshmen

Percent SJ	Total Sample Size	Sample Description
32.50	80	Employment Development Specialists
32.43	111	Consultants: Canadian
32.28	127	Therapists: Practitioners in Respiratory Therapy
32.08	106	Speech Pathologists
31.88	10342	Auburn University - Freshmen
31.66	1554	Protestant Ministers
31.58	57	Scientists: Biology
31.51	219	Priests and Monks
31.37	51	Roman Catholic Seminarians
31.37	51	Restaurant Workers: Table Setting and Cleaning
31.28	179	Teachers: English
31.19	109	Carpenters
31.05	190	Engineers: Mining
30.89	3979	Males: Age Group 15 To 17
30.83	519	LAWYERS AND JUDGES
30.79	341	Administrators: Colleges and Technical Institutes
30.42	1874	Law School Graduates
30.40	1760	Franklin and Marshall College - Freshmen
30.34	89	Public Relations Workers and Publicity Writers
30.30	165	Clerks in a Japanese Trading Company
30.13	1009	Navy Enlisted Personnel in Basic Electronic Training
30.04	223	Teachers: Health
30.01	673	Counselors: Vocational and Educational
29.84	2282	Teachers: University
29.27	287	Counselors: School
29.23	479	Social Workers
29.09	550	St. Louis University - Freshmen
29.00	200	Computer Programmers
28.96	2514	University of Florida - Freshmen
28.69	1607	Females: Traditional Age High School Students
28.66	321	Females: Traditional Age Junior High School Students
28.61	395	Rollins College - Freshmen
28.24	85	Protestants in Specialized Ministries
28.00	50	Directors of Religious Education
27.78	540	Waiters and Waitresses
27.38	1505	Hope College - Freshmen
27.19	228	Rosemont College - Freshmen
27.14	1205	Candidates for Theology Education
27.11	4035	University of Maine - Freshmen
27.07	1803	COUNSELORS
26.56	192	Consultants: General
26.55	177	College and University Resident Assistants
26.23	122	Composite of Practitioners in Speech Pathology
25.99	177	Counselors: Rehabilitation
25.93	81	Research Workers
25.93	54	Consultants: Education
25.45	55	Designers
25.42	1204	Males: Traditional Age High School Students
25.21	932	Counselors: General
24.26	136	Musicians and Composers

SENSING-JUDGMENT

Percent SJ	Total Sample Size	Sample Description
24.07	108	Members of a Human Resources Planners Association
24.07	54	Chain, Rod and Ax Workers; Surveying
23.22	534	Clergy, all denominations (except priests)
23.12	359	Counselors: General
22.10	181	Females in Leadership Development Program
22.06	68	Physicians: Psychiatry
21.69	83	Marketing Personnel
21.48	256	Males: Traditional Age Junior High School Students
21.40	271	Lawyers
21.30	169	Composite of Practitioners in Social Work
20.90	378	ARTISTS AND ENTERTAINERS
20.73	275	Salespeople in a Japanese Trading Company
20.73	164	Gifted High School Seniors
20.34	59	Photographers
20.28	705	Teachers: College Faculty Named as Danforth Associates
20.24	84	Attorneys - Administrators, non-practicing
20.19	213	Teachers: Art, Drama and Music
19.23	52	Journalists
18.32	262	Counselors: Suicide and Crisis
16.94	124	Architects
16.81	113	Editors and Reporters
16.60	530	WRITERS AND JOURNALISTS
16.42	67	Research Assistants
15.76	793	High School Students in Florida Future Scientist Program
15.38	117	Counselors: Runaway Youth
14.67	75	Phi Beta Kappa
12.46	289	Psychologists
12.24	490	SOCIAL SCIENTISTS
11.29	1001	National Merit Scholarship Finalists
11.29	62	Actors
10.45	402	PSYCHOLOGISTS
10.00	170	Certified Psychodramatists
8.65	208	Writers, Artists, Entertainers, and Agents
7.02	114	Fine Artists
2.82	71	Rhodes Scholars

Percent SP	Total Sample Size	Sample Description
38.55	275	Salespeople in a Japanese Trading Company
36.97	165	Clerks in a Japanese Trading Company
33.59	256	Males: Traditional Age Junior High School Students
31.34	67	Stock Clerks and Storekeepers
31.07	1973	St. Clair College
30.28	109	Carpenters
29.84	439	Police Officers
28.47	144	OPERATIVES: TRANSPORTATION
28.28	4035	University of Maine - Freshmen
27.57	4150	Nicholls State University - Freshmen
27.37	4933	Males: High School Students from Pennsylvania
26.85	782	LABORERS
26.75	228	Rosemont College - Freshmen
26.62	139	Construction Laborers (except carpenters helpers)
26.42	3373	High School Students in Australia
26.39	72	FARMERS
26.24	141	Police Officers: Patrolmen in Urban Community
26.05	403	Berkshire Christian College - Freshmen and Transfers
26.00	1204	Males: Traditional Age High School Students
25.89	197	Adrian College - Freshmen
25.45	9320	High School Students from Pennsylvania
25.45	55	Child Care Workers (except private household)
25.28	3979	Males: Age Group 15 To 17
25.07	10342	Auburn University - Freshmen
25.04	659	Females: SRI Sample
24.92	321	Females: Traditional Age Junior High School Students
24.41	127	Therapists: Practitioners in Respiratory Therapy
24.07	54	Chain, Rod and Ax Workers; Surveying
23.93	280	Police Officers: Urban Community
23.87	155	Police and Detectives
23.71	97	OPERATIVES: NON-SPECIALIZED AND FACTORY WORKERS
23.50	366	Managers: Middle Managers in a Japanese Chemical Company
23.33	240	Foremen in Japanese Food Production Company
23.33	60	Managers: Fire
23.30	4387	Females: High School Students from Pennsylvania
23.27	1169	University of Wisconsin at Stevens Point - Freshmen
23.26	559	CRAFT WORKERS
23.23	11897	Males: Age Group 18 To 20
23.16	190	Engineers: Mining
23.09	1607	Females: Traditional Age High School Students
23.00	4973	Females: Age Group 15 To 17
22.87	669	MECHANICS
22.83	92	Police Officers: Supervisors in Urban Community
22.78	540	Waiters and Waitresses
22.64	53	Composite of Practitioners in Radiologic Technology
22.50	1009	Navy Enlisted Personnel in Basic Electronic Training
22.27	211	Lifeguards, Attendants, Recreation and Amusement
22.22	72	Dental Assistants
22.17	1105	Total SRI Sample
22.08	77	Secretaries: Legal

Percent SP	Total Sample Size	Sample Description
22.02	12637	Males: Traditional Age College Students
21.85	1506	Mercer University - Freshmen
21.81	1082	FOOD SERVICE WORKERS
21.73	405	Parks College - Freshmen and Transfers
21.50	107	Typists
21.43	84	Library Attendants and Assistants
21.43	56	Clerical Supervisors
21.36	206	OPERATIVES: SPECIALIZED
21.33	150	Bookkeepers
21.30	169	Service Workers (except private household)
20.93	3149	Concordia College - Freshmen
20.91	574	Line Corrections Officers
20.60	2277	Females: Adult High School Graduates, Without College
20.56	180	Cooks (except private household)
20.41	343	Males: Adult High School Dropouts
20.37	108	Sales Clerks, Retail Trade
20.21	13716	Females: Age Group 18 To 20
20.00	195	Therapists: Respiratory
20.00	155	Therapists: Physical
20.00	150	Managers: Small Business
19.97	4663	Military Personnel at Naval Technical Training Center
19.75	395	Rollins College - Freshmen
19.66	1760	Franklin and Marshall College - Freshmen
19.64	56	Managers: Top Managers in Large Japanese Companies
19.61	51	Restaurant Workers: Table Setting and Cleaning
19.40	67	Sales Agents, Retail Trade
19.34	14519	Females: Traditional Age College Students
19.27	1505	Hope College - Freshmen
19.23	52	Factory and Site Supervisors
19.15	47	Police Officers: Detectives in Urban Community
19.12	68	Corrections Officers and Probation Officers
19.05	126	Radiologic Technologists and Technicians
19.05	105	Steelworkers
18.91	550	St. Louis University - Freshmen
18.74	1750	SALES WORKERS
18.61	274	Cashiers
18.57	70	Electricians
18.48	3339	CLERICAL AND KINDRED WORKERS
18.42	228	Teachers: Adult Education
18.37	196	Displaced Coal Miners
18.29	164	Teachers: Coaching
18.18	297	Computer and Peripheral Equipment Operators
18.15	314	Nursing: Aides, Orderlies, and Attendants
18.09	15791	Males: Form G Databank
18.08	4905	OFFICE MACHINE OPERATORS
18.08	636	Females: Adult High School Dropouts
18.07	83	Marketing Personnel
17.96	167	Laboratory Technologists
17.94	446	Males: SRI Sample
17.93	608	PROTECTIVE SERVICE WORKERS

Percent SP	Total Sample Size	Sample Description
17.91	67	CLEANING SERVICES
17.81	73	Air Force Personnel
17.60	926	Males: Adult High School Graduates Without College
17.57	148	Therapists: Physical
17.49	835	Bank Employees
17.42	132	School Bus Drivers
17.31	260	Nursing: Licensed Practical Nurses
17.24	116	Managers: Middle Managers in a Japanese Heavy Industrial Company
17.14	175	ENGINEERING AND SCIENCE TECHNICIANS
17.11	783	PERSONAL SERVICE WORKERS
17.02	1604	SECRETARIES
16.97	2492	University of North Carolina at Greensboro - Freshmen
16.95	118	Managers: Japanese Chief Executives
16.89	900	HEALTH SERVICE WORKERS
16.83	101	Insurance Agents, Brokers, and Underwriters
16.67	264	MILITARY PERSONNEL
16.67	222	Bank Employees, Non-Exempt
16.64	23240	Males: Form F Databank
16.58	232557	CAPT Databank Total Population
16.55	3064	PRIVATE HOUSEHOLD WORKERS
16.47	2514	University of Florida - Freshmen
16.36	55	Designers
16.26	32731	Females: Form F Databank
16.20	179	Sales Representatives
16.19	105	Police Supervisors
16.13	155	Nursing: Composite of Critical Care Nurses
16.00	100	Receptionists
15.97	3551	Females: Non-Traditional Age College Students
15.82	177	Counselors: Rehabilitation
15.74	432	Teacher Aides (except school monitors)
15.71	5320	Males: Age Group 21 To 24
15.66	166	Real Estate Agents and Brokers
15.57	122	High School Student Leaders
15.55	238	Public Service Aides and Community Health Workers
15.50	200	Computer Programmers
15.45	16880	Females: Form G Databank
15.38	52	Computer Specialists
15.34	5738	Females: Age Group 21 To 24
15.19	79	Medical Assistants
15.04	113	Editors and Reporters
15.00	60	Dental Hygienists
14.95	281	Teachers: School Grades 1 through 12
14.89	658	Displaced Steelworkers
14.80	223	Clinical Laboratory Technologists and Technicians
14.73	1147	Nuns and Other Religious Workers
14.71	68	Secretaries: Medical
14.67	2351	Nursing: Registered Nurses
14.63	123	Pharmacists
14.58	96	Hairdressers, Cosmetologists and Manicurists
14.55	110	Bank Employees, Exempt

SENSING-PERCEPTION

Percent SP	Total Sample Size	Sample Description
14.53	117	Counselors: Runaway Youth
14.44	90	Personnel and Labor Relations Workers
14.41	333	Secretaries: Executive and Administrative Assistants
14.40	986	ENGINEERS
14.40	250	Business: General, Self-employed
14.29	98	Managers: Participants in Women in Management Conference
14.29	77	Engineers: Mechanical
14.29	70	Optometrists
14.26	1501	Males: Adult Non-Traditional Age College Students
14.22	225	Leaders in Student Government Activities
14.14	191	Pharmacists
14.13	92	Social Services Workers
14.04	57	Technicians: Electrical and Electronic Engineering
13.99	765	HEALTH CARE THERAPISTS
13.95	86	Guards and Watch Keepers
13.94	1291	HEALTH TECHNOLOGISTS AND TECHNICIANS
13.91	338	COMPUTER SPECIALISTS
13.83	1880	Nursing: Registered Nurses, no specialty stated
13.80	413	Teachers: Mathematics
13.79	290	Managers: Middle Level in City, County and State Government
13.58	243	Dietitians
13.57	3103	NURSES
13.46	973	Medical Technologists
13.41	82	Professional, Technical, and Kindred Workers
13.29	143	Auditors
13.25	83	Nursing: Public Health
13.25	83	Managers: Sales
13.23	5178	Females: Age Group 25 To 29
13.21	106	Media Specialists
13.11	61	Physicians: Pathology
13.06	804	Teachers: Elementary School
13.04	230	Managers: Regional Telephone Company Low Level Managers
13.01	638	Medical Technologists (4 year)
12.96	54	Engineers: Electrical and Electronic
12.87	334	Operators and Field Technicians in Water Pollution Control
12.87	101	Administrators: Social Services
12.64	182	Health Education Practitioners
12.50	80	Purchasing Agents
12.38	323	Dietitians and Nutritionists
12.30	122	Composite of Practitioners in Speech Pathology
12.20	164	Gifted High School Seniors
12.18	427	Accountants
12.17	756	Managers: Financial and Bank Officers
12.16	633	Protestant Seminarians
12.14	3814	Males: Age Group 25 To 29
12.12	495	Males: Age Group 60 Plus
12.00	100	Teachers: Pre-school
12.00	50	College Students in Student Government
11.92	8711	Females: Age Group 30 To 39
11.86	312	Managers: Restaurant, Cafeteria, Bar and Food Service

Percent SP	Total Sample Size	Sample Description
11.85	3678	Administrators: Managers and Supervisors
11.73	469	ALLIED HEALTH AND HEALTH PRACTIONERS, N.E.C.
11.69	2010	RELIGIOUS WORKERS -ALL DENOMINATIONS-
11.32	106	Speech Pathologists
11.30	177	College and University Resident Assistants
11.28	523	Managers: Public
11.27	71	Teachers: Mathematics
11.18	4811	Females: Age Group 40 To 49
11.08	1128	Teachers: Middle and Junior High School
11.03	136	Managers: High Level Corporate Executives
10.99	1874	Law School Graduates
10.86	1795	Males: Age Group 50 To 59
10.79	139	Physicians: Family Practice, General Practice
10.73	7463	MANAGERS AND ADMINISTRATORS
10.64	912	Police Officers: Managers
10.62	932	Counselors: General
10.60	849	Managers: England
10.53	2470	Females: Age Group 50 To 59
10.53	114	Brothers in Roman Catholic Religious Orders
10.49	267	Librarians
10.47	172	Coordinators
10.45	67	Teachers: Foreign Language in Junior and Senior High School
10.42	96	Teachers: Reading
10.34	58	Home Management Advisors and Home Economists
10.32	1803	COUNSELORS
10.29	136	Musicians and Composers
10.22	16676	TEACHERS
10.19	157	Teachers: Speech Pathology and Therapy
10.18	3812	Males: Age Group 40 To 49
10.13	79	Religious Educator, all denominations
10.11	89	Public Relations Workers and Publicity Writers
10.11	89	Corrections Sergeants
10.10	99	Police Officers: Australian Senior Officers
10.05	378	ARTISTS AND ENTERTAINERS
9.98	5601	Males: Age Group 30 To 39
9.92	494	Certified Public Accountants
9.84	61	Scientists: Chemistry
9.84	61	Food Counter and Fountain Workers
9.81	530	WRITERS AND JOURNALISTS
9.80	245	Therapists: Occupational
9.80	102	Managers: Office
9.75	359	Counselors: General
9.63	1205	Candidates for Theology Education
9.62	52	Journalists
9.60	479	Social Workers
9.52	1229	Computer Professionals
9.48	1603	DOCTORS OF MEDICINE
9.47	169	Teachers: Grades 1 through 9, Canada
9.47	169	Composite of Practitioners in Social Work
9.42	223	Teachers: Health

Percent SP	Total Sample Size	Sample Description
9.41	287	Counselors: School
9.41	85	Dentists
9.34	257	Managers: Top Level in City, County and State Government
9.33	75	Phi Beta Kappa
9.32	118	Therapists: Occupational
9.30	86	Computer Systems Analysts and Support Representatives
9.28	1024	Administrators: Elementary and Secondary School
9.26	54	Engineers: Aeronautical
9.24	119	Teachers: Trade, Industrial and Technical
9.23	271	Lawyers
9.23	65	Computer Operations, Systems Researchers and Analysts
9.18	305	Nursing: Educators
9.06	276	School Principals
9.02	122	Administrators: Educationally Related
9.01	6814	Males: Adult College Graduates
8.94	1051	Males in Leadership Development Program
8.92	213	Teachers: Art, Drama and Music
8.77	1881	Composite of Practitioners in Medicine (M.D.s)
8.72	172	Teaching Assistants
8.62	673	Counselors: Vocational and Educational
8.51	1857	ADMINISTRATORS
8.51	94	Nursing: Administrators
8.50	200	Teachers: Elementary School
8.48	519	LAWYERS AND JUDGES
8.39	1394	Managers: Federal Executives
8.33	192	Consultants: General
8.22	146	Nursing: Consultants
8.20	793	High School Students in Florida Future Scientist Program
8.15	135	Doctors of Osteopathy
8.11	111	Consultants: Canadian
8.09	1298	Roman Catholic Priests
8.09	173	Teachers: Special Education
8.09	136	Credit Investigators and Mortgage Brokers
8.06	62	Actors
7.97	7952	Females: Adult College Graduates
7.92	846	Females: Age Group 60 Plus
7.81	128	Judges
7.73	181	Females in Leadership Development Program
7.69	2002	Sisters in Roman Catholic Religious Orders
7.52	319	Rabbis
7.52	226	SCIENTISTS: LIFE AND PHYSICAL
7.51	333	Public Accountants
7.50	80	Employment Development Specialists
7.49	534	Clergy, all denominations (except priests)
7.40	649	Teachers: High School
7.14	84	Attorneys - Administrators, non-practicing
7.13	561	Teachers: Junior College
7.04	341	Administrators: Colleges and Technical Institutes
7.02	57	Police Officers: Commanders
6.92	289	Psychologists

SENSING-PERCEPTION

Percent SP	Total Sample Size	Sample Description
6.85	219	Priests and Monks
6.78	59	Photographers
6.29	1001	National Merit Scholarship Finalists
6.22	2282	Teachers: University
6.19	113	Teachers: Supervising Student Teachers
6.17	81	Research Workers
6.00	50	Directors of Religious Education
5.98	1554	Protestant Ministers
5.94	202	Administrators: Health
5.88	51	Roman Catholic Seminarians
5.62	89	Consultants: Management Analysts
5.56	108	Members of a Human Resources Planners Association
5.56	54	Consultants: Education
5.51	490	SOCIAL SCIENTISTS
5.45	55	College Student Leaders
5.29	208	Writers, Artists, Entertainers, and Agents
5.26	57	Scientists: Biology
5.06	316	Managers: Retail Stores
4.96	262	Counselors: Suicide and Crisis
4.90	102	Ordained Roman Catholic Deacons
4.48	402	PSYCHOLOGISTS
4.47	179	Teachers: English
4.23	71	Rhodes Scholars
4.23	71	Consultants: Management
4.11	705	Teachers: College Faculty Named as Danforth Associates
4.03	124	Administrators: Canadian Schools
3.85	52	Engineers: Chemical
3.85	52	Dentists
3.53	85	Protestants in Specialized Ministries
2.99	67	Research Assistants
2.94	170	Certified Psychodramatists
2.94	68	Physicians: Psychiatry
1.75	114	Fine Artists
.81	124	Architects
0	51	Administrators: Student Personnel

Percent NP	Total Sample Size	Sample Description
59.15	71	Rhodes Scholars
55.77	208	Writers, Artists, Entertainers, and Agents
51.92	52	Journalists
50.75	67	Research Assistants
50.59	170	Certified Psychodramatists
49.15	1001	National Merit Scholarship Finalists
48.79	289	Psychologists
48.72	117	Counselors: Runaway Youth
48.17	164	Gifted High School Seniors
47.51	402	PSYCHOLOGISTS
47.06	68	Physicians: Psychiatry
46.79	530	WRITERS AND JOURNALISTS
46.77	62	Actors
46.49	114	Fine Artists
45.42	262	Counselors: Suicide and Crisis
45.10	490	SOCIAL SCIENTISTS
43.79	169	Composite of Practitioners in Social Work
43.13	793	High School Students in Florida Future Scientist Program
42.90	359	Counselors: General
42.37	59	Photographers
41.59	113	Editors and Reporters
40.32	124	Architects
40.11	177	Counselors: Rehabilitation
39.91	213	Teachers: Art, Drama and Music
39.22	51	Restaurant Workers: Table Setting and Cleaning
39.15	378	ARTISTS AND ENTERTAINERS
38.67	181	Females in Leadership Development Program
38.20	932	Counselors: General
37.63	287	Counselors: School
37.60	1803	COUNSELORS
37.50	136	Musicians and Composers
37.33	75	Phi Beta Kappa
37.04	54	Engineers: Aeronautical
37.04	54	Chain, Rod and Ax Workers; Surveying
36.90	271	Lawyers
36.40	673	Counselors: Vocational and Educational
36.33	479	Social Workers
36.09	1607	Females: Traditional Age High School Students
36.07	122	Composite of Practitioners in Speech Pathology
35.16	256	Males: Traditional Age Junior High School Students
35.08	2514	University of Florida - Freshmen
34.72	1204	Males: Traditional Age High School Students
33.96	106	Speech Pathologists
33.90	177	College and University Resident Assistants
33.71	89	Public Relations Workers and Publicity Writers
33.42	1505	Hope College - Freshmen
33.33	228	Rosemont College - Freshmen
33.33	81	Research Workers
32.96	540	Waiters and Waitresses
32.63	190	Engineers: Mining

Percent NP	Total Sample Size	Sample Description
32.36	550	St. Louis University - Freshmen
32.31	1009	Navy Enlisted Personnel in Basic Electronic Training
31.65	395	Rollins College - Freshmen
31.48	54	Consultants: Education
31.37	51	Administrators: Student Personnel
31.25	80	Employment Development Specialists
31.23	4035	University of Maine - Freshmen
31.19	561	Teachers: Junior College
31.15	61	Food Counter and Fountain Workers
30.78	1082	FOOD SERVICE WORKERS
30.71	127	Therapists: Practitioners in Respiratory Therapy
30.61	98	Managers: Participants in Women in Management Conference
30.50	200	Computer Programmers
30.38	79	Medical Assistants
30.34	89	Consultants: Management Analysts
30.26	1874	Law School Graduates
30.22	321	Females: Traditional Age Junior High School Students
29.82	275	Salespeople in a Japanese Trading Company
29.82	57	Scientists: Biology
29.69	192	Consultants: General
29.59	534	Clergy, all denominations (except priests)
29.51	122	High School Student Leaders
29.28	765	HEALTH CARE THERAPISTS
29.14	10342	Auburn University - Freshmen
29.09	519	LAWYERS AND JUDGES
29.07	172	Teaching Assistants
29.05	3979	Males: Age Group 15 To 17
29.03	1760	Franklin and Marshall College - Freshmen
28.96	297	Computer and Peripheral Equipment Operators
28.92	4973	Females: Age Group 15 To 17
28.49	179	Teachers: English
28.40	1169	University of Wisconsin at Stevens Point - Freshmen
28.39	155	Therapists: Physical
28.33	3149	Concordia College - Freshmen
28.33	180	Cooks (except private household)
28.24	85	Protestants in Specialized Ministries
28.00	100	Receptionists
27.87	2282	Teachers: University
27.85	79	Religious Educator, all denominations
27.80	223	Teachers: Health
27.76	245	Therapists: Occupational
27.35	223	Clinical Laboratory Technologists and Technicians
27.27	55	Designers
27.22	338	COMPUTER SPECIALISTS
27.17	173	Teachers: Special Education
26.97	1205	Candidates for Theology Education
26.94	219	Priests and Monks
26.86	175	ENGINEERING AND SCIENCE TECHNICIANS
26.73	101	Insurance Agents, Brokers, and Underwriters
26.72	116	Managers: Middle Managers in a Japanese Heavy Industrial Company

Percent NP	Total Sample Size	Sample Description
26.67	60	Dental Hygienists
26.61	109	Carpenters
26.51	83	Marketing Personnel
26.48	3814	Males: Age Group 25 To 29
26.45	1603	DOCTORS OF MEDICINE
26.44	232557	CAPT Databank Total Population
26.42	53	Composite of Practitioners in Radiologic Technology
26.40	1750	SALES WORKERS
26.27	118	Therapists: Occupational
26.22	225	Leaders in Student Government Activities
26.19	1554	Protestant Ministers
26.11	226	SCIENTISTS: LIFE AND PHYSICAL
26.09	782	LABORERS
26.07	211	Lifeguards, Attendants, Recreation and Amusement
25.96	705	Teachers: College Faculty Named as Danforth Associates
25.75	167	Laboratory Technologists
25.71	70	Electricians
25.68	148	Therapists: Physical
25.64	195	Therapists: Respiratory
25.60	250	Business: General, Self-employed
25.58	172	Coordinators
25.58	86	Computer Systems Analysts and Support Representatives
25.49	102	Managers: Office
25.47	267	Librarians
25.47	106	Media Specialists
25.43	3339	CLERICAL AND KINDRED WORKERS
25.43	405	Parks College - Freshmen and Transfers
25.25	1881	Composite of Practitioners in Medicine (M.D.s)
25.22	341	Administrators: Colleges and Technical Institutes
25.15	986	ENGINEERS
24.98	11897	Males: Age Group 18 To 20
24.98	5320	Males: Age Group 21 To 24
24.97	12637	Males: Traditional Age College Students
24.92	305	Nursing: Educators
24.91	4905	OFFICE MACHINE OPERATORS
24.80	2351	Nursing: Registered Nurses
24.74	1229	Computer Professionals
24.60	126	Radiologic Technologists and Technicians
24.57	5178	Females: Age Group 25 To 29
24.56	114	Brothers in Roman Catholic Religious Orders
24.49	633	Protestant Seminarians
24.48	7952	Females: Adult College Graduates
24.39	123	Pharmacists
24.37	1506	Mercer University - Freshmen
24.27	32731	Females: Form F Databank
24.19	649	Teachers: High School
24.12	16676	TEACHERS
24.07	108	Members of a Human Resources Planners Association
24.07	54	Engineers: Electrical and Electronic
24.06	15791	Males: Form G Databank

Percent NP	Total Sample Size	Sample Description
24.04	23240	Males: Form F Databank
24.00	200	Teachers: Elementary School
24.00	50	Directors of Religious Education
24.00	50	College Students in Student Government
23.90	3373	High School Students in Australia
23.88	67	Sales Agents, Retail Trade
23.81	84	Attorneys - Administrators, non-practicing
23.80	8711	Females: Age Group 30 To 39
23.77	122	Administrators: Educationally Related
23.72	333	Secretaries: Executive and Administrative Assistants
23.72	274	Cashiers
23.63	783	PERSONAL SERVICE WORKERS
23.60	5738	Females: Age Group 21 To 24
23.47	1973	St. Clair College
23.44	16880	Females: Form G Databank
23.42	111	Consultants: Canadian
23.38	77	Engineers: Mechanical
23.35	1880	Nursing: Registered Nurses, no specialty stated
23.30	206	OPERATIVES: SPECIALIZED
23.29	73	Air Force Personnel
23.23	1128	Teachers: Middle and Junior High School
23.18	2010	RELIGIOUS WORKERS -ALL DENOMINATIONS-
23.00	14519	Females: Traditional Age College Students
23.00	100	Teachers: Pre-school
22.93	314	Nursing: Aides, Orderlies, and Attendants
22.92	96	Teachers: Reading
22.88	13716	Females: Age Group 18 To 20
22.87	669	MECHANICS
22.85	3103	NURSES
22.81	57	Technicians: Electrical and Electronic Engineering
22.79	136	Credit Investigators and Mortgage Brokers
22.78	4811	Females: Age Group 40 To 49
22.71	2492	University of North Carolina at Greensboro - Freshmen
22.46	1291	HEALTH TECHNOLOGISTS AND TECHNICIANS
22.32	1501	Males: Adult Non-Traditional Age College Students
22.30	139	Construction Laborers (except carpenters helpers)
22.22	72	Dental Assistants
22.19	1604	SECRETARIES
22.10	5601	Males: Age Group 30 To 39
22.08	403	Berkshire Christian College - Freshmen and Transfers
22.06	6814	Males: Adult College Graduates
22.00	900	HEALTH SERVICE WORKERS
21.99	191	Pharmacists
21.92	1857	ADMINISTRATORS
21.75	469	ALLIED HEALTH AND HEALTH PRACTITIONERS, N.E.C.
21.74	2470	Females: Age Group 50 To 59
21.59	264	MILITARY PERSONNEL
21.57	51	Roman Catholic Seminarians
21.54	65	Computer Operations, Systems Researchers and Analysts
21.43	56	Clerical Supervisors

585

Percent NP	Total Sample Size	Sample Description
21.34	1298	Roman Catholic Priests
21.31	61	Scientists: Chemistry
21.30	169	Service Workers (except private household)
21.30	108	Sales Clerks, Retail Trade
21.29	155	Nursing: Composite of Critical Care Nurses
21.23	146	Nursing: Consultants
21.02	157	Teachers: Speech Pathology and Therapy
20.99	3064	PRIVATE HOUSEHOLD WORKERS
20.90	1024	Administrators: Elementary and Secondary School
20.90	67	Teachers: Foreign Language in Junior and Senior High School
20.90	67	Stock Clerks and Storekeepers
20.81	197	Adrian College - Freshmen
20.76	4663	Military Personnel at Naval Technical Training Center
20.67	150	Bookkeepers
20.66	4933	Males: High School Students from Pennsylvania
20.61	165	Clerks in a Japanese Trading Company
20.58	413	Teachers: Mathematics
20.53	3551	Females: Non-Traditional Age College Students
20.48	83	Nursing: Public Health
20.33	182	Health Education Practitioners
20.11	179	Sales Representatives
20.00	55	Child Care Workers (except private household)
19.95	7463	MANAGERS AND ADMINISTRATORS
19.92	9320	High School Students from Pennsylvania
19.88	166	Real Estate Agents and Brokers
19.84	973	Medical Technologists
19.74	228	Teachers: Adult Education
19.73	1394	Managers: Federal Executives
19.71	3678	Administrators: Managers and Supervisors
19.68	559	CRAFT WORKERS
19.51	82	Professional, Technical, and Kindred Workers
19.31	202	Administrators: Health
19.26	135	Doctors of Osteopathy
19.23	52	Dentists
19.12	319	Rabbis
19.12	68	Corrections Officers and Probation Officers
19.10	4387	Females: High School Students from Pennsylvania
18.97	638	Medical Technologists (4 year)
18.89	90	Personnel and Labor Relations Workers
18.88	143	Auditors
18.83	1147	Nuns and Other Religious Workers
18.71	139	Physicians: Family Practice, General Practice
18.69	107	Typists
18.58	4150	Nicholls State University - Freshmen
18.50	427	Accountants
18.48	2002	Sisters in Roman Catholic Religious Orders
18.44	3812	Males: Age Group 40 To 49
18.31	71	Teachers: Mathematics
18.29	164	Teachers: Coaching
18.27	323	Dietitians and Nutritionists

Percent NP	Total Sample Size	Sample Description
18.18	55	College Student Leaders
17.97	128	Judges
17.79	804	Teachers: Elementary School
17.72	333	Public Accountants
17.71	96	Hairdressers, Cosmetologists and Manicurists
17.65	68	Secretaries: Medical
17.59	432	Teacher Aides (except school monitors)
17.31	52	Engineers: Chemical
17.31	52	Computer Specialists
17.28	243	Dietitians
17.14	70	Optometrists
17.03	1051	Males in Leadership Development Program
16.67	846	Females: Age Group 60 Plus
16.49	97	OPERATIVES: NON-SPECIALIZED AND FACTORY WORKERS
16.47	85	Dentists
16.40	756	Managers: Financial and Bank Officers
16.39	61	Physicians: Pathology
16.28	86	Guards and Watch Keepers
16.21	1795	Males: Age Group 50 To 59
15.99	494	Certified Public Accountants
15.97	119	Teachers: Trade, Industrial and Technical
15.58	77	Secretaries: Legal
15.49	439	Police Officers
15.49	71	Consultants: Management
15.38	260	Nursing: Licensed Practical Nurses
15.28	72	FARMERS
14.93	67	CLEANING SERVICES
14.85	835	Bank Employees
14.29	105	Police Supervisors
14.29	84	Library Attendants and Assistants
14.29	56	Managers: Top Managers in Large Japanese Companies
14.16	113	Teachers: Supervising Student Teachers
14.15	636	Females: Adult High School Dropouts
14.14	2277	Females: Adult High School Graduates, Without College
13.97	136	Managers: High Level Corporate Executives
13.65	608	PROTECTIVE SERVICE WORKERS
13.46	52	Factory and Site Supervisors
13.19	849	Managers: England
13.13	495	Males: Age Group 60 Plus
12.82	312	Managers: Restaurant, Cafeteria, Bar and Food Service
12.77	94	Nursing: Administrators
12.50	144	OPERATIVES: TRANSPORTATION
12.46	281	Teachers: School Grades 1 through 12
12.33	446	Males: SRI Sample
12.17	230	Managers: Regional Telephone Company Low Level Managers
12.07	58	Home Management Advisors and Home Economists
12.02	366	Managers: Middle Managers in a Japanese Chemical Company
11.95	343	Males: Adult High School Dropouts
11.67	1105	Total SRI Sample
11.25	80	Purchasing Agents

INTUITION-PERCEPTION

Percent NP	Total Sample Size	Sample Description
11.23	659	Females: SRI Sample
10.84	83	Managers: Sales
10.52	523	Managers: Public
10.15	926	Males: Adult High School Graduates Without College
10.08	238	Public Service Aides and Community Health Workers
10.00	290	Managers: Middle Level in City, County and State Government
9.93	141	Police Officers: Patrolmen in Urban Community
9.80	102	Ordained Roman Catholic Deacons
9.78	92	Social Services Workers
9.78	92	Police Officers: Supervisors in Urban Community
9.68	155	Police and Detectives
9.68	124	Administrators: Canadian Schools
9.64	280	Police Officers: Urban Community
9.47	169	Teachers: Grades 1 through 9, Canada
9.32	118	Managers: Japanese Chief Executives
8.98	334	Operators and Field Technicians in Water Pollution Control
8.91	101	Administrators: Social Services
8.77	57	Police Officers: Commanders
8.56	257	Managers: Top Level in City, County and State Government
8.51	47	Police Officers: Detectives in Urban Community
8.33	60	Managers: Fire
7.84	574	Line Corrections Officers
7.79	912	Police Officers: Managers
7.62	105	Steelworkers
6.63	196	Displaced Coal Miners
6.36	110	Bank Employees, Exempt
6.08	658	Displaced Steelworkers
5.80	276	School Principals
4.67	150	Managers: Small Business
4.58	240	Foremen in Japanese Food Production Company
4.04	99	Police Officers: Australian Senior Officers
3.48	316	Managers: Retail Stores
2.70	222	Bank Employees, Non-Exempt
2.25	89	Corrections Sergeants
1.52	132	School Bus Drivers

Percent NJ	Total Sample Size	Sample Description
49.65	705	Teachers: College Faculty Named as Danforth Associates
48.81	84	Attorneys - Administrators, non-practicing
46.30	108	Members of a Human Resources Planners Association
44.74	114	Fine Artists
42.25	71	Consultants: Management
42.00	50	Directors of Religious Education
41.94	124	Architects
41.18	51	Roman Catholic Seminarians
40.00	85	Protestants in Specialized Ministries
39.70	534	Clergy, all denominations (except priests)
38.87	319	Rabbis
38.67	75	Phi Beta Kappa
37.56	402	PSYCHOLOGISTS
37.29	118	Managers: Japanese Chief Executives
37.14	490	SOCIAL SCIENTISTS
37.04	54	Consultants: Education
36.95	341	Administrators: Colleges and Technical Institutes
36.47	170	Certified Psychodramatists
36.36	55	College Student Leaders
36.27	1205	Candidates for Theology Education
36.16	1554	Protestant Ministers
36.07	61	Scientists: Chemistry
36.06	2282	Teachers: University
36.04	111	Consultants: Canadian
35.75	179	Teachers: English
35.42	192	Consultants: General
34.70	219	Priests and Monks
34.57	81	Research Workers
33.87	62	Actors
33.80	71	Rhodes Scholars
33.73	83	Marketing Personnel
33.33	57	Scientists: Biology
33.27	1001	National Merit Scholarship Finalists
32.91	793	High School Students in Florida Future Scientist Program
32.74	223	Teachers: Health
32.47	271	Lawyers
32.31	65	Computer Operations, Systems Researchers and Analysts
31.83	289	Psychologists
31.60	519	LAWYERS AND JUDGES
31.49	181	Females in Leadership Development Program
31.45	124	Administrators: Canadian Schools
31.30	262	Counselors: Suicide and Crisis
31.03	58	Home Management Advisors and Home Economists
30.99	213	Teachers: Art, Drama and Music
30.97	226	SCIENTISTS: LIFE AND PHYSICAL
30.91	55	Designers
30.77	52	Dentists
30.51	59	Photographers
30.34	89	Consultants: Management Analysts
30.33	633	Protestant Seminarians

Percent NJ	Total Sample Size	Sample Description
30.29	208	Writers, Artists, Entertainers, and Agents
30.20	202	Administrators: Health
30.15	136	Credit Investigators and Mortgage Brokers
30.12	83	Managers: Sales
30.00	50	College Students in Student Government
29.89	378	ARTISTS AND ENTERTAINERS
29.85	67	Research Assistants
29.51	61	Physicians: Pathology
29.43	333	Public Accountants
29.41	51	Administrators: Student Personnel
29.20	1394	Managers: Federal Executives
28.97	1229	Computer Professionals
28.92	1857	ADMINISTRATORS
28.85	52	Engineers: Chemical
28.75	80	Employment Development Specialists
28.72	7952	Females: Adult College Graduates
28.68	136	Managers: High Level Corporate Executives
28.57	56	Managers: Top Managers in Large Japanese Companies
28.52	305	Nursing: Educators
28.50	200	Teachers: Elementary School
28.43	102	Ordained Roman Catholic Deacons
28.34	1874	Law School Graduates
28.32	6814	Males: Adult College Graduates
28.25	177	College and University Resident Assistants
28.06	139	Physicians: Family Practice, General Practice
27.94	136	Musicians and Composers
27.94	68	Physicians: Psychiatry
27.91	86	Computer Systems Analysts and Support Representatives
27.87	122	Administrators: Educationally Related
27.86	1881	Composite of Practitioners in Medicine (M.D.s)
27.64	123	Pharmacists
27.51	2010	RELIGIOUS WORKERS -ALL DENOMINATIONS-
27.17	173	Teachers: Special Education
27.17	92	Social Services Workers
26.94	245	Therapists: Occupational
26.93	1051	Males in Leadership Development Program
26.92	52	Computer Specialists
26.79	530	WRITERS AND JOURNALISTS
26.55	113	Editors and Reporters
26.38	561	Teachers: Junior College
26.33	1603	DOCTORS OF MEDICINE
26.19	5601	Males: Age Group 30 To 39
26.19	649	Teachers: High School
26.17	1024	Administrators: Elementary and Secondary School
26.04	338	COMPUTER SPECIALISTS
25.97	932	Counselors: General
25.84	89	Public Relations Workers and Publicity Writers
25.56	90	Personnel and Labor Relations Workers
25.44	169	Composite of Practitioners in Social Work
25.41	122	Composite of Practitioners in Speech Pathology

Percent NJ	Total Sample Size	Sample Description
25.37	67	Teachers: Foreign Language in Junior and Senior High School
25.36	4811	Females: Age Group 40 To 49
25.34	146	Nursing: Consultants
25.32	79	Religious Educator, all denominations
25.04	16676	TEACHERS
25.01	1803	COUNSELORS
25.00	200	Computer Programmers
25.00	172	Coordinators
24.96	673	Counselors: Vocational and Educational
24.95	3812	Males: Age Group 40 To 49
24.86	3814	Males: Age Group 25 To 29
24.84	479	Social Workers
24.73	469	ALLIED HEALTH AND HEALTH PRACTITIONERS, N.E.C.
24.61	191	Pharmacists
24.58	118	Therapists: Occupational
24.53	106	Media Specialists
24.48	143	Auditors
24.44	135	Doctors of Osteopathy
24.29	70	Optometrists
24.23	359	Counselors: General
24.19	1298	Roman Catholic Priests
24.07	54	Engineers: Electrical and Electronic
24.Co	8711	Females: Age Group 30 To 39
24.00	225	Leaders in Student Government Activities
24.00	100	Teachers: Pre-school
23.84	323	Dietitians and Nutritionists
23.73	7463	MANAGERS AND ADMINISTRATORS
23.69	287	Counselors: School
23.57	1795	Males: Age Group 50 To 59
23.55	276	School Principals
23.53	85	Dentists
23.33	60	Dental Hygienists
23.16	5178	Females: Age Group 25 To 29
22.67	172	Teaching Assistants
22.64	106	Speech Pathologists
22.53	182	Health Education Practitioners
22.49	169	Teachers: Grades 1 through 9, Canada
22.42	495	Males: Age Group 60 Plus
22.35	2470	Females: Age Group 50 To 59
22.34	94	Nursing: Administrators
22.32	3678	Administrators: Managers and Supervisors
22.22	846	Females: Age Group 60 Plus
22.21	986	ENGINEERS
21.90	5320	Males: Age Group 21 To 24
21.69	83	Nursing: Public Health
21.63	1128	Teachers: Middle and Junior High School
21.57	765	HEALTH CARE THERAPISTS
21.43	2002	Sisters in Roman Catholic Religious Orders
21.43	98	Managers: Participants in Women in Management Conference
21.37	117	Counselors: Runaway Youth

Percent NJ	Total Sample Size	Sample Description
21.19	23240	Males: Form F Databank
21.11	3103	NURSES
21.09	128	Judges
21.05	57	Technicians: Electrical and Electronic Engineering
20.99	243	Dietitians
20.97	267	Librarians
20.91	1760	Franklin and Marshall College - Freshmen
20.83	96	Teachers: Reading
20.73	82	Professional, Technical, and Kindred Workers
20.72	333	Secretaries: Executive and Administrative Assistants
20.58	1147	Nuns and Other Religious Workers
20.52	1501	Males: Adult Non-Traditional Age College Students
20.40	250	Business: General, Self-employed
20.39	2492	University of North Carolina at Greensboro - Freshmen
20.37	54	Engineers: Aeronautical
20.32	16880	Females: Form G Databank
20.24	84	Library Attendants and Assistants
20.00	395	Rollins College - Freshmen
19.93	1505	Hope College - Freshmen
19.83	5738	Females: Age Group 21 To 24
19.73	1880	Nursing: Registered Nurses, no specialty stated
19.67	122	High School Student Leaders
19.65	804	Teachers: Elementary School
19.64	550	St. Louis University - Freshmen
19.61	102	Managers: Office
19.58	15791	Males: Form G Databank
19.49	2514	University of Florida - Freshmen
19.48	77	Secretaries: Legal
19.44	232557	CAPT Databank Total Population
19.44	638	Medical Technologists (4 year)
19.44	108	Sales Clerks, Retail Trade
19.35	32731	Females: Form F Databank
19.33	119	Teachers: Trade, Industrial and Technical
19.32	849	Managers: England
19.28	166	Real Estate Agents and Brokers
19.23	52	Journalists
19.20	427	Accountants
19.07	257	Managers: Top Level in City, County and State Government
19.03	494	Certified Public Accountants
19.01	973	Medical Technologists
18.92	148	Therapists: Physical
18.90	164	Gifted High School Seniors
18.66	343	Males: Adult High School Dropouts
18.58	113	Teachers: Supervising Student Teachers
18.52	756	Managers: Financial and Bank Officers
18.47	157	Teachers: Speech Pathology and Therapy
18.33	2351	Nursing: Registered Nurses
18.31	71	Teachers: Mathematics
18.28	290	Managers: Middle Level in City, County and State Government
18.18	77	Engineers: Mechanical

Percent NJ	Total Sample Size	Sample Description
18.08	3551	Females: Non-Traditional Age College Students
18.08	177	Counselors: Rehabilitation
18.07	3149	Concordia College - Freshmen
18.06	155	Nursing: Composite of Critical Care Nurses
17.97	1291	HEALTH TECHNOLOGISTS AND TECHNICIANS
17.88	179	Sales Representatives
17.71	175	ENGINEERING AND SCIENCE TECHNICIANS
17.69	3064	PRIVATE HOUSEHOLD WORKERS
17.65	68	Secretaries: Medical
17.39	1604	SECRETARIES
17.31	1750	SALES WORKERS
17.24	116	Managers: Middle Managers in a Japanese Heavy Industrial Company
17.04	223	Clinical Laboratory Technologists and Technicians
17.00	1506	Mercer University - Freshmen
16.95	413	Teachers: Mathematics
16.82	12637	Males: Traditional Age College Students
16.48	540	Waiters and Waitresses
16.44	523	Managers: Public
16.42	67	Sales Agents, Retail Trade
16.41	195	Therapists: Respiratory
16.20	321	Females: Traditional Age Junior High School Students
16.17	167	Laboratory Technologists
16.16	11897	Males: Age Group 18 To 20
15.84	101	Insurance Agents, Brokers, and Underwriters
15.79	57	Police Officers: Commanders
15.71	312	Managers: Restaurant, Cafeteria, Bar and Food Service
15.60	14519	Females: Traditional Age College Students
15.56	180	Cooks (except private household)
15.35	228	Teachers: Adult Education
15.31	405	Parks College - Freshmen and Transfers
15.23	197	Adrian College - Freshmen
15.09	4905	OFFICE MACHINE OPERATORS
15.06	1009	Navy Enlisted Personnel in Basic Electronic Training
15.03	366	Managers: Middle Managers in a Japanese Chemical Company
14.93	67	Stock Clerks and Storekeepers
14.92	13716	Females: Age Group 18 To 20
14.81	54	Chain, Rod and Ax Workers; Surveying
14.80	446	Males: SRI Sample
14.78	3979	Males: Age Group 15 To 17
14.71	68	Corrections Officers and Probation Officers
14.55	55	Child Care Workers (except private household)
14.51	1082	FOOD SERVICE WORKERS
14.43	97	OPERATIVES: NON-SPECIALIZED AND FACTORY WORKERS
14.39	4663	Military Personnel at Naval Technical Training Center
14.30	783	PERSONAL SERVICE WORKERS
14.08	3339	CLERICAL AND KINDRED WORKERS
14.04	114	Brothers in Roman Catholic Religious Orders
14.03	1169	University of Wisconsin at Stevens Point - Freshmen
14.02	264	MILITARY PERSONNEL
13.93	912	Police Officers: Managers

INTUITION-JUDGMENT

Percent NJ	Total Sample Size	Sample Description
13.92	316	Managers: Retail Stores
13.92	79	Medical Assistants
13.90	10342	Auburn University - Freshmen
13.89	144	OPERATIVES: TRANSPORTATION
13.88	281	Teachers: School Grades 1 through 12
13.87	1204	Males: Traditional Age High School Students
13.84	636	Females: Adult High School Dropouts
13.70	73	Air Force Personnel
13.63	4973	Females: Age Group 15 To 17
13.55	155	Therapists: Physical
13.53	835	Bank Employees
13.47	297	Computer and Peripheral Equipment Operators
13.46	4933	Males: High School Students from Pennsylvania
13.38	4035	University of Maine - Freshmen
13.33	240	Foremen in Japanese Food Production Company
13.33	105	Police Supervisors
13.17	334	Operators and Field Technicians in Water Pollution Control
13.16	190	Engineers: Mining
13.11	900	HEALTH SERVICE WORKERS
13.11	206	OPERATIVES: SPECIALIZED
12.86	70	Electricians
12.79	86	Guards and Watch Keepers
12.76	196	Displaced Coal Miners
12.72	228	Rosemont College - Freshmen
12.60	127	Therapists: Practitioners in Respiratory Therapy
12.41	274	Cashiers
12.40	1105	Total SRI Sample
12.13	1607	Females: Traditional Age High School Students
12.12	165	Clerks in a Japanese Trading Company
12.10	314	Nursing: Aides, Orderlies, and Attendants
12.00	100	Receptionists
11.96	92	Police Officers: Supervisors in Urban Community
11.94	9320	High School Students from Pennsylvania
11.93	109	Carpenters
11.86	2277	Females: Adult High School Graduates, Without College
11.81	669	MECHANICS
11.48	61	Food Counter and Fountain Workers
11.46	96	Hairdressers, Cosmetologists and Manicurists
11.35	608	PROTECTIVE SERVICE WORKERS
11.33	150	Bookkeepers
11.25	80	Purchasing Agents
11.17	403	Berkshire Christian College - Freshmen and Transfers
11.11	72	Dental Assistants
10.98	164	Teachers: Coaching
10.91	275	Salespeople in a Japanese Trading Company
10.90	211	Lifeguards, Attendants, Recreation and Amusement
10.89	101	Administrators: Social Services
10.79	139	Construction Laborers (except carpenters helpers)
10.77	659	Females: SRI Sample
10.77	260	Nursing: Licensed Practical Nurses

Percent NJ	Total Sample Size	Sample Description
10.74	782	LABORERS
10.73	559	CRAFT WORKERS
10.71	280	Police Officers: Urban Community
10.71	56	Clerical Supervisors
10.64	47	Police Officers: Detectives in Urban Community
10.43	230	Managers: Regional Telephone Company Low Level Managers
10.41	3373	High School Students in Australia
10.23	4387	Females: High School Students from Pennsylvania
10.19	432	Teacher Aides (except school monitors)
9.93	141	Police Officers: Patrolmen in Urban Community
9.80	51	Restaurant Workers: Table Setting and Cleaning
9.77	256	Males: Traditional Age Junior High School Students
9.52	4150	Nicholls State University - Freshmen
9.52	126	Radiologic Technologists and Technicians
9.35	107	Typists
9.33	150	Managers: Small Business
9.09	99	Police Officers: Australian Senior Officers
8.96	67	CLEANING SERVICES
8.53	926	Males: Adult High School Graduates Without College
8.51	658	Displaced Steelworkers
8.40	238	Public Service Aides and Community Health Workers
8.33	72	FARMERS
8.31	1973	St. Clair College
8.18	110	Bank Employees, Exempt
7.55	53	Composite of Practitioners in Radiologic Technology
6.83	439	Police Officers
6.74	89	Corrections Sergeants
6.67	105	Steelworkers
6.51	169	Service Workers (except private household)
5.16	155	Police and Detectives
5.00	60	Managers: Fire
4.95	222	Bank Employees, Non-Exempt
3.83	574	Line Corrections Officers
2.27	132	School Bus Drivers
1.92	52	Factory and Site Supervisors